Blankets

a graphic novel by
CRAIG THOMPSON

DRAWN & QUARTERLY
Montreal

This graphic novel is based on personal experiences, though the names have been changed,
and certain characters, places, and incidents have been modified in the service of the story.
Lyrics/title "Just Like Heaven" by Robert Smith © copyright 1987 APB Music.

drawnandquarterly.com   craigthompsonbooks.com

First edition: 2003
First Drawn & Quarterly hardcover & paperback editions: September 2015
Second Drawn & Quarterly hardcover & paperback editions: November 2016
Printed in China
10 9 8 7 6 5 4 3 2

Library and Archives Canada Cataloguing in Publication
Thompson, Craig, 1975– , author, illustrator
Blankets / Craig Thompson.
ISBN 978-1-77046-220-5 (bound).–ISBN 978-1-77046-218-2 (pbk.)
                                        I. Graphic novels.   I. Title.
PN6727.T48B58 2015   741.5'973   C2015-902369-6

Published in the USA by Drawn & Quarterly, a client publisher of
Farrar, Straus and Giroux
Orders: 888.330.8477

Published in Canada by Drawn & Quarterly, a client publisher of
Raincoast Books
Orders: 800.663.5714

Praise for Craig Thompson's *Blankets*

"BLANKETS has the thematic sophistication, emotional sweep and beauty of (visual) language that mark the best novels... Part teen romance novel, part coming-of-age novel, part faith-in-crisis novel and all comix, BLANKETS is a great American novel."
~Time

"One page after the next opens to wondrous images, and the feelings behind them are sincere and overpowering. I would be unlikely to share BLANKETS with someone who told me they wanted to understand comix. Instead, I would give it to anyone who told me they wanted to read a book that made them feel transcendent, sad, generous, hopeful — but above all, to truly feel something." **~Powells.com**

"This is [Thompson's] tale of growing up, falling in love (and realizing the physical and moral complications that can imply), discovering the texture and limits of his faith and arriving at a point from which he can look back at those experiences... A big graphic novel, in concept and successful execution." **~School Library Journal**

"[A] bittersweet tale of childhood psyche bruising, junior Christian angst and adolescent first love with a lyricism so engaging, the pages fly right by... It's virtual poetry." **~Entertainment Weekly**

"An impressively concrete portrait of emotional ephemera, captured with talent, disarming humor, and a gentle sincerity that glows through on every remarkable page." **~ The AV Club**

"Craig Thompson's BLANKETS is a human story told with beautiful, flowing line-work and is usually the first graphic novel that I'll give to someone new." **~ The Atlantic**

"Recreates the confusion, emotional pain and isolation of the author's rigidly fundamentalist Christian upbringing, along with trepidation of growing into maturity, with a rare combination of sincerity, pictorial lyricism and taste." **~Publishers Weekly**

"BLANKETS is a rare achievement, a work of art that redefines the parameters of its designated medium. No other graphic novel of this kind has been published... Virtually impossible not to read in one sitting." **~Portland Mercury**

"[A] lovely memoir of childhood and first love." **~Washington Post**

"In Thompson's 600-page semi-autobiographical tome, a young man gripped in the often-painful process of discovering his adult self attempts to forge a spiritual and artistic identity even as he falls helplessly in love with a girl who represents everything his life has been missing. Thompson deftly married spare text to often lyrical imagery to create in the reader the same exhilarating tension of first love that seizes his hero." **~ NPR**

"This book is a masterpiece... It's the first truly great graphic novel of the 21st century..." ~**Aintitcool**

"The Cadillac Escalade of graphic novels." ~**MSNBC**

"[Craig Thompson] has produced the most poetic evocation of life in the Upper Midwest since the early novels and stories of F. Scott Fitzgerald." ~**ICV2**

"Reading BLANKETS is like reliving your youth as you wander through the artist's personal trials of fundamentalist religion and teenage heart-break in small-town America. The story has been told many times, but Craig Thompson's version is one of the most honest, warm and compelling renditions. It's like going home with a close friend and discovering how similar your journeys truly are." ~**Paste**

"[A] genuine graphic novel, with a universal appeal that suits it for any collection." ~ **Booklist**, *Starred Review*

"Breaks your heart with the illustrated story of Craig's lonely, isolated childhood in rural Wisconsin..." ~ **Oprah.com**, *The 22 Greatest Love Stories of All Time*

"Drawn in a sweeping, inviting style, its sheer loveliness attracted readers from beyond comics' traditional audience, while the universality of its subject matter and the specificity of Thompson's experience of it kept them turning the pages." ~ **Comic Book Resources**

"Craig Thompson's autobiographical coming-of-age story is sweet and dreamy, covering the profoundly intense experience of falling in love for the first time, questioning your faith and negotiating your relationship with your siblings." ~ **Flavorwire**

"BLANKETS deftly explores with subtle nuance those universal themes that ballast the best coming-of-age tales: Familial ties, sex, spirituality...BLANKETS represents the full potential of the comic-book medium." ~ **Willamette Week**

"A treasure trove of newly constructed or reconstituted techniques for portraying things that comics rarely even attempt to portray." ~**Scott McCloud**, *Esquire*

"BLANKETS officially confirms Craig Thompson's place in the world of graphic novels as one of the true greats." ~ **Brian Michael Bendis**, *Powers*

"In this book, Craig Thompson emerges as a young comics master. In the purest narrative form he tells a highly charged personal story, crammed with pain, discovery, hijinks, penance, religious conviction and its loss...and along comes self-loathing. In this story of family and first love, that which goes awry in life, goes well as art. Mr. Thompson is slyly self-effacing as he bowls us over with his mix of skills. His expert blending of words and pictures and resonant silences makes for a transcendent kind of storytelling that grabs you as you read it and stays with you after you put it down. I'd call that literature." ~ **Jules Feiffer**, *Pulitzer Prize-winner*

Contents:

I *Cubby Hole* 8

II *Stirring Furnace* 66

III *Blank Sheet* 130

IV *Static* 226

V *I Don't Wanna Grow Up* 262

VI *Teen Spirit* 322

VII *Just Like Heaven* 376

VIII *Vanishing Cave* 448

IX *Foot Notes* 544

*For my
family,
with love*

I

Cubby
Hole

When we were young, my little brother
Phil and I shared the same bed.

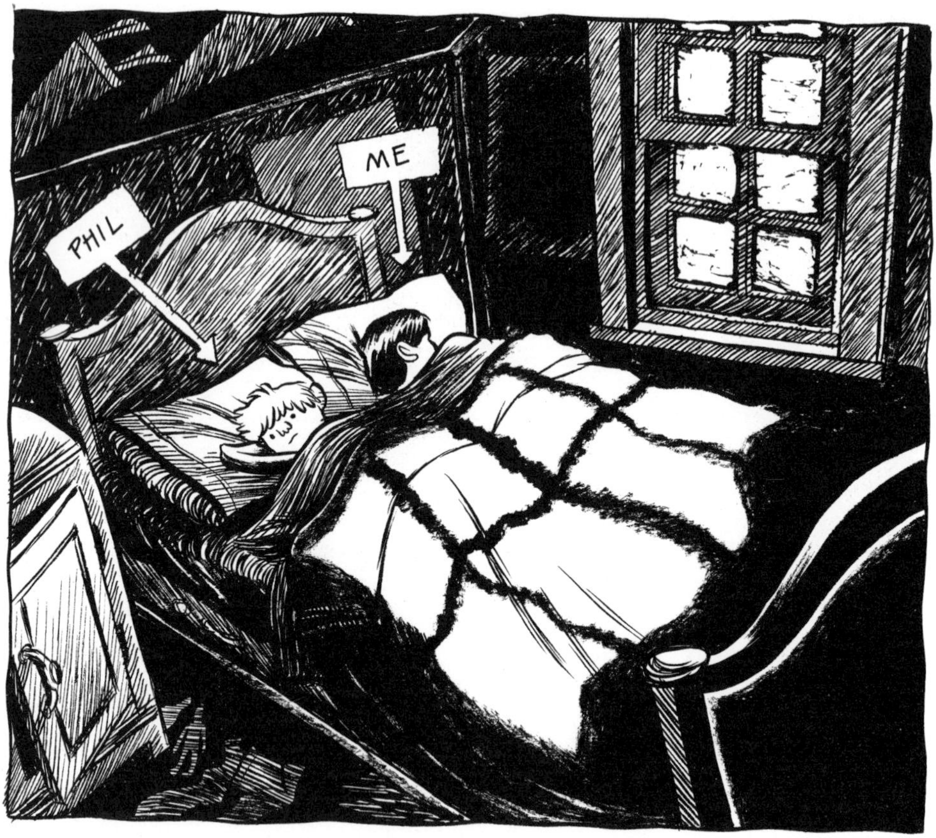
ME
PHIL

"SHARED" is the sugar-coated way of saying we were TRAPPED in the same bed, as we were children and had no say in the matter.

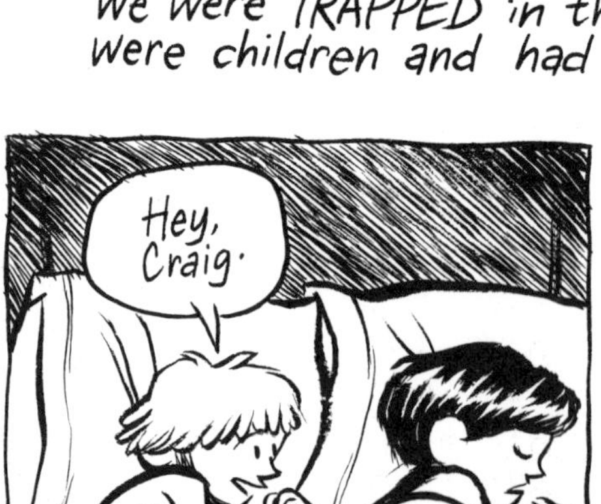
Hey, Craig.
I'm trying to sleep.

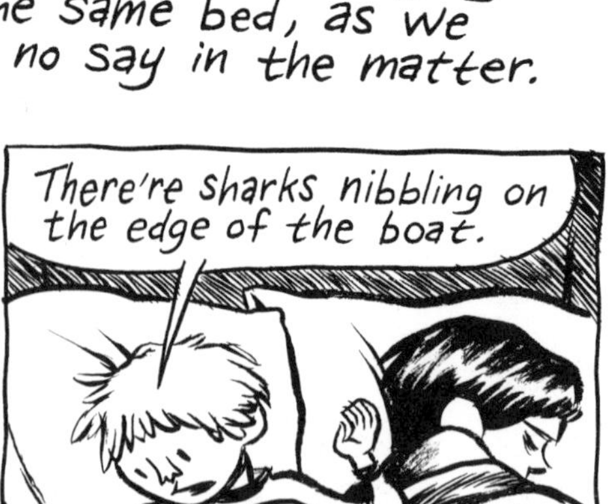
There're sharks nibbling on the edge of the boat.
It's not a boat, stupid. It's a BED. Go to sleep.

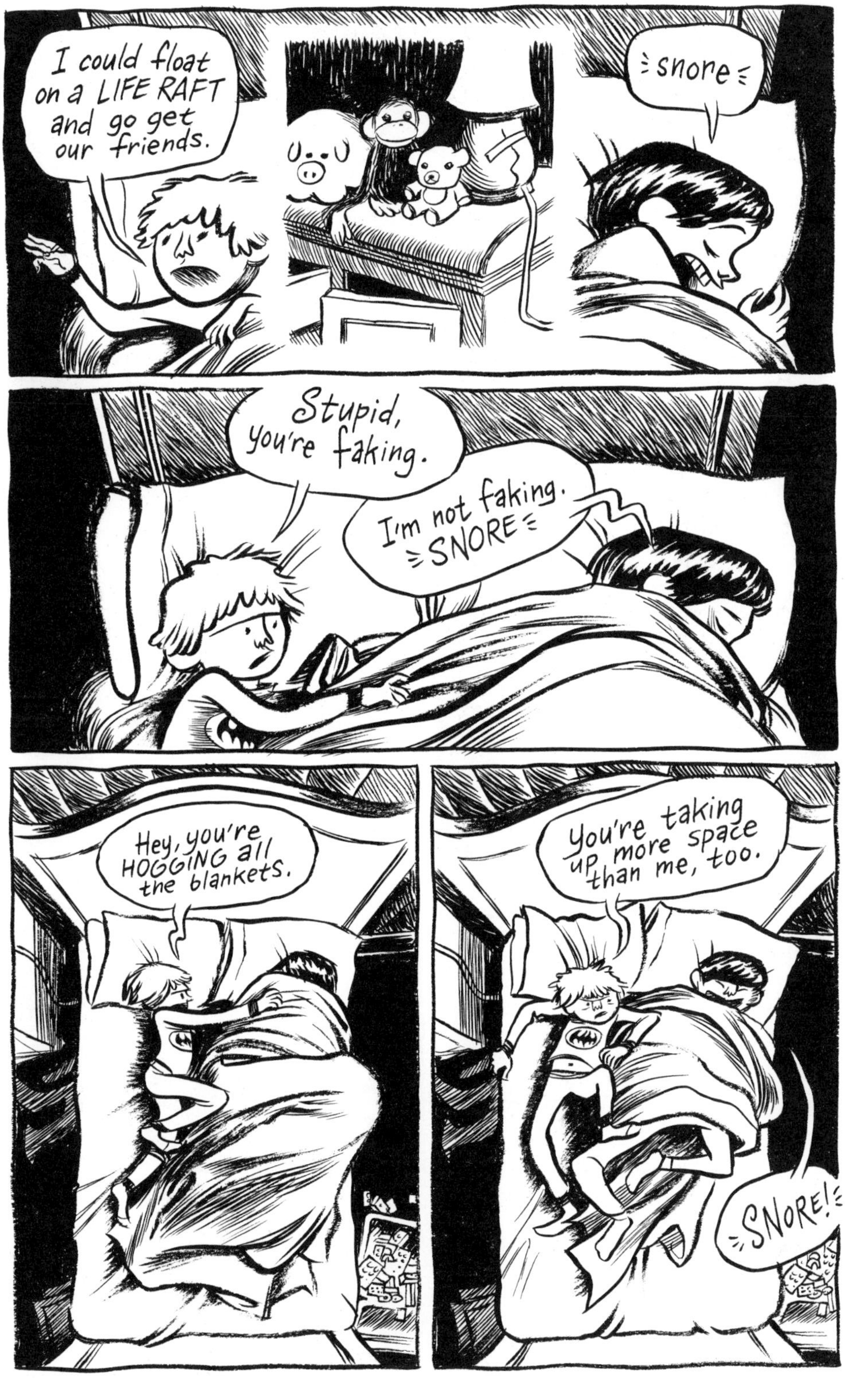
I could float on a LIFE RAFT and go get our friends.
snore
Stupid, you're faking.
I'm not faking. SNORE
Hey, you're HOGGING all the blankets.
You're taking up more space than me, too.
SNORE!

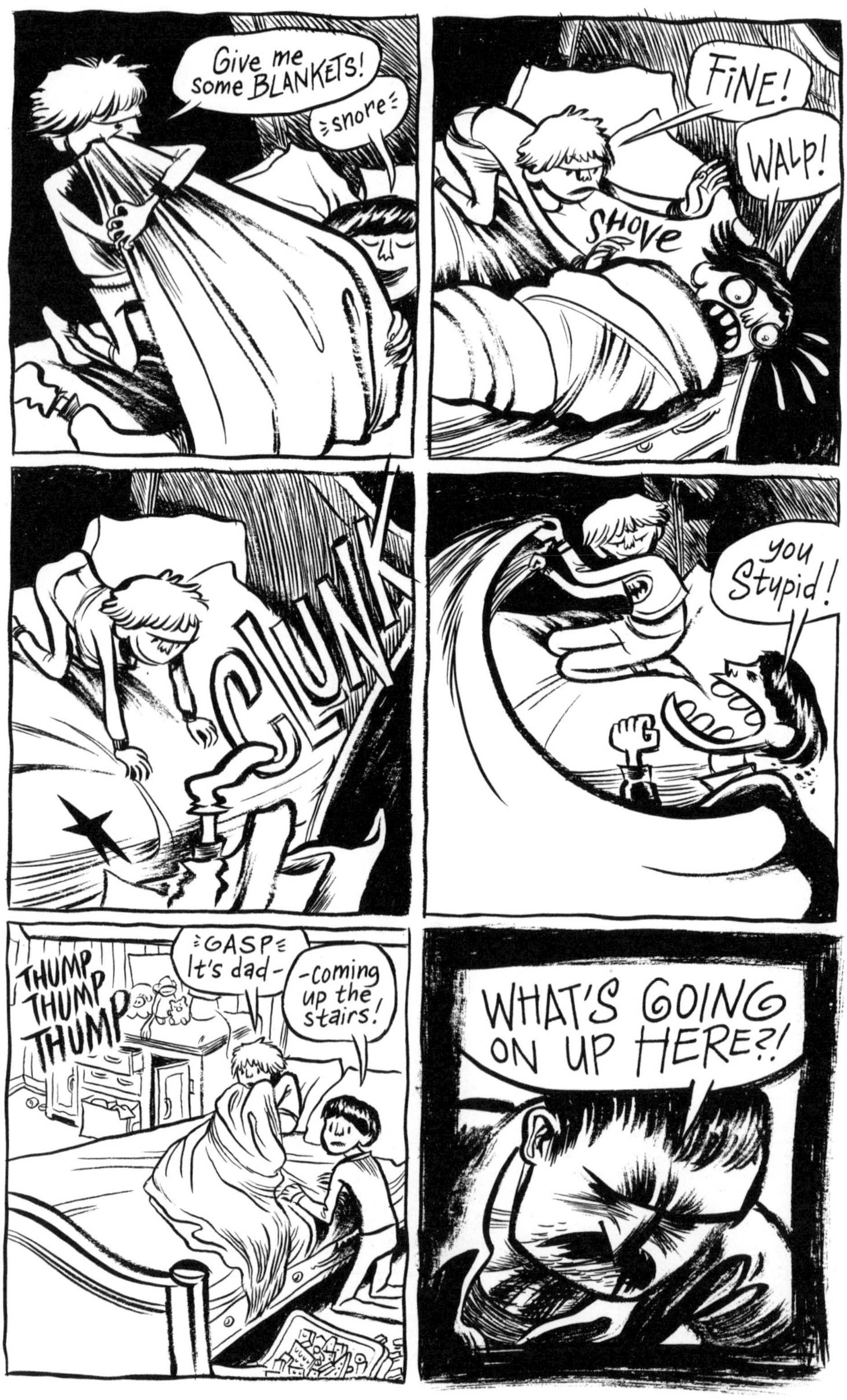
Give me some BLANKETS!
snore
FINE!
WALP!
SHOVE
CLUNK!
you Stupid!
THUMP THUMP THUMP
GASP It's dad-
-coming up the stairs!
WHAT'S GOING ON UP HERE?!

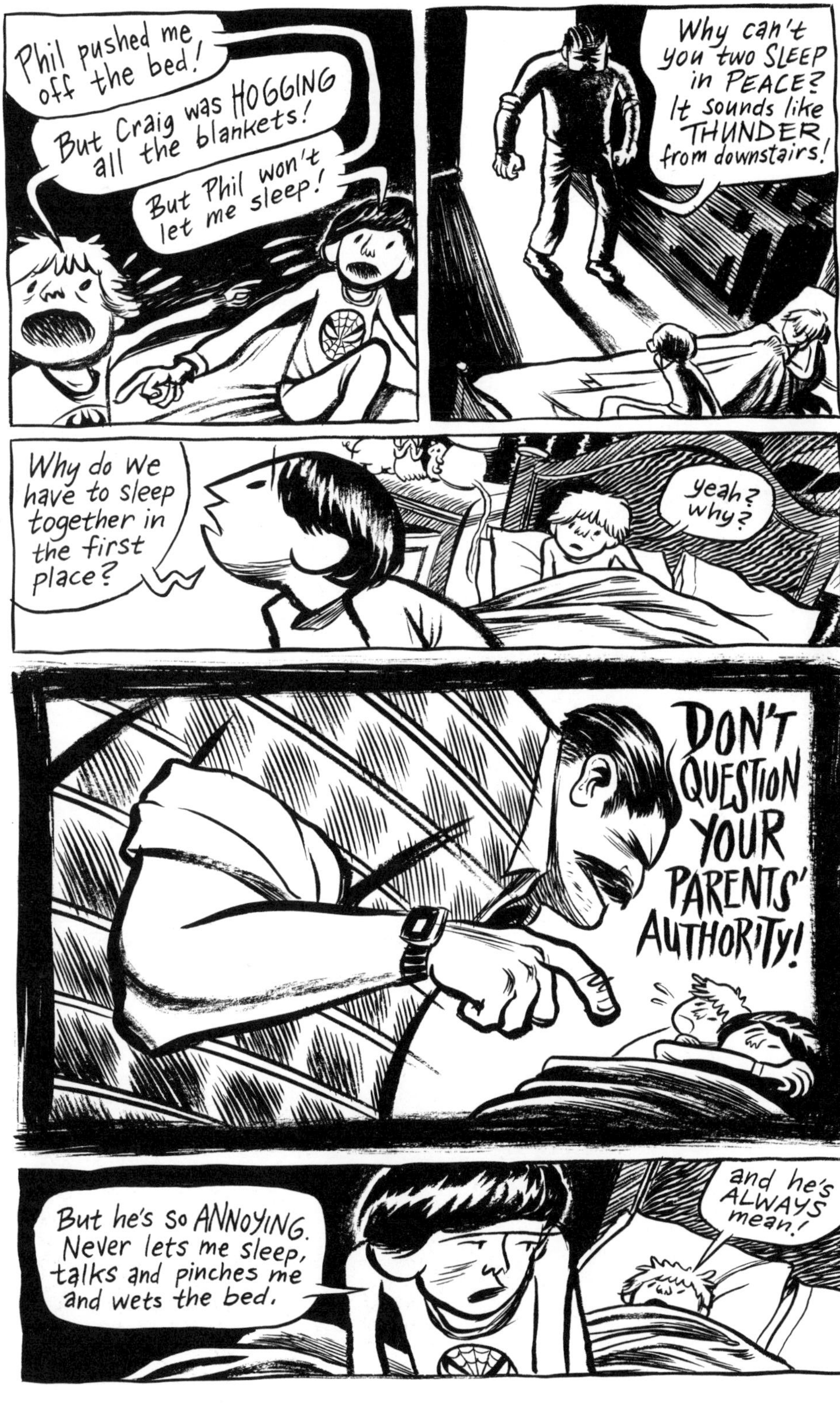
Phil pushed me off the bed!
But Craig was HOGGING all the blankets!
But Phil won't let me sleep!
Why can't you two SLEEP in PEACE? It sounds like THUNDER from downstairs!
Why do we have to sleep together in the first place?
yeah? why?
DON'T QUESTION YOUR PARENTS' AUTHORITY!
But he's so ANNOYING. Never lets me sleep, talks and pinches me and wets the bed.
and he's ALWAYS mean!

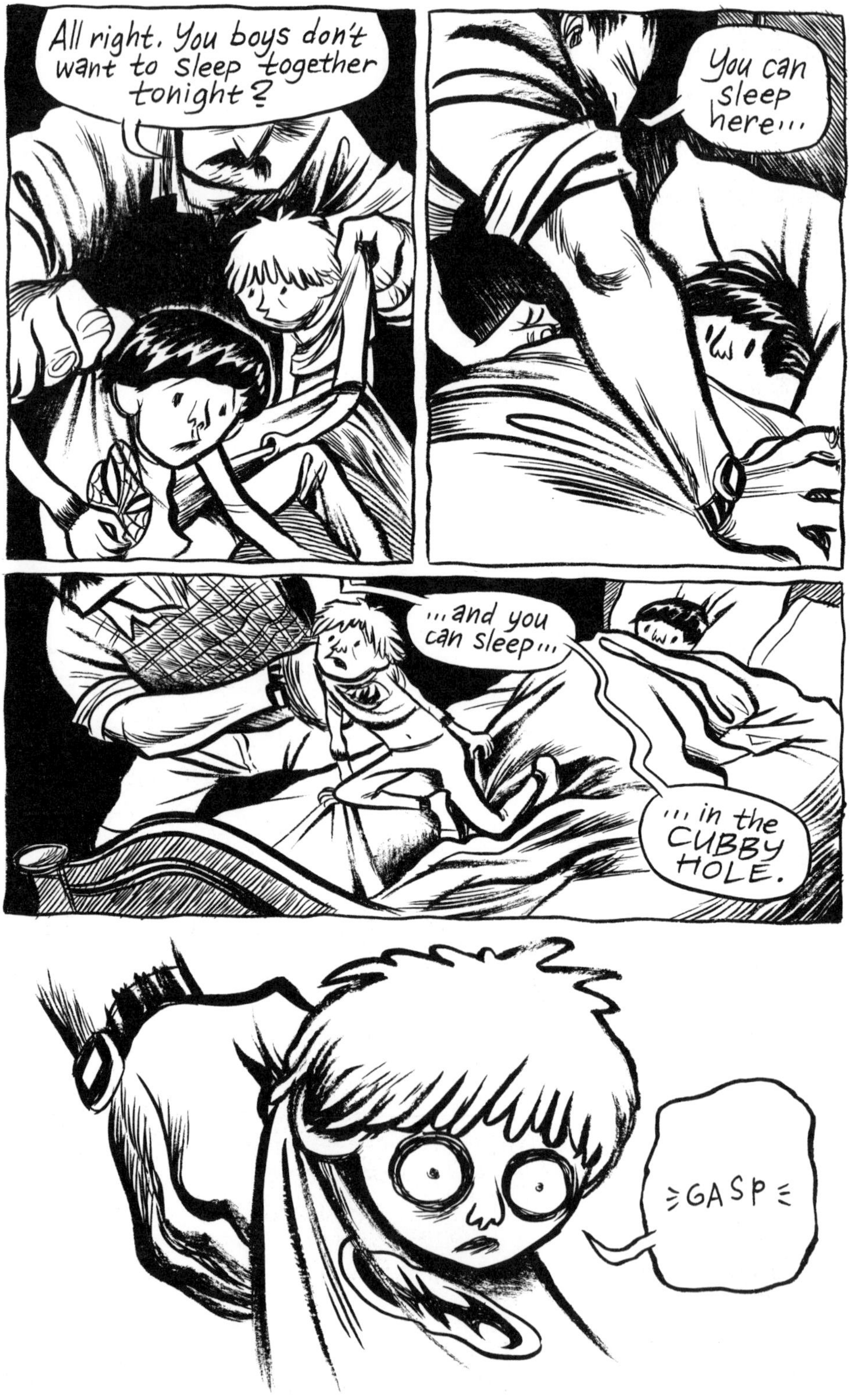
All right. You boys don't want to sleep together tonight?
You can sleep here...
...and you can sleep...
...in the CUBBY HOLE.
GASP

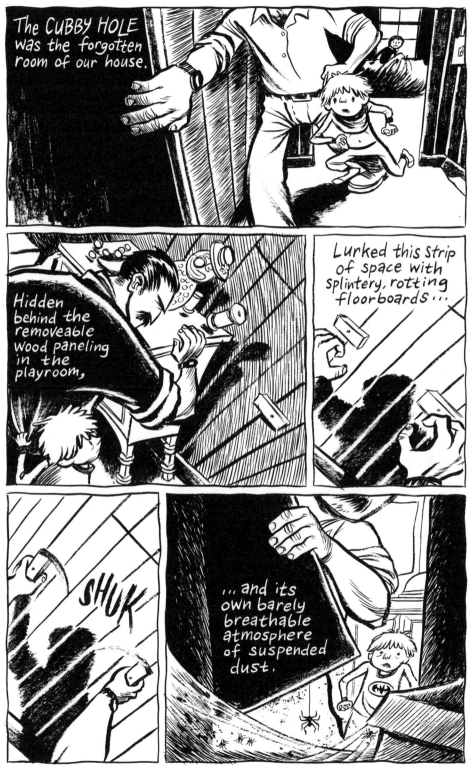

The CUBBY HOLE was the forgotten room of our house.

Hidden behind the removeable wood paneling in the playroom,

Lurked this strip of space with splintery, rotting floorboards...

SHUK

...and its own barely breathable atmosphere of suspended dust.

Uninsulated, unlit, and uninhabited – except by spiders and vermin (we heard skittering within the walls at night) and a few dust-filled cardboard boxes,

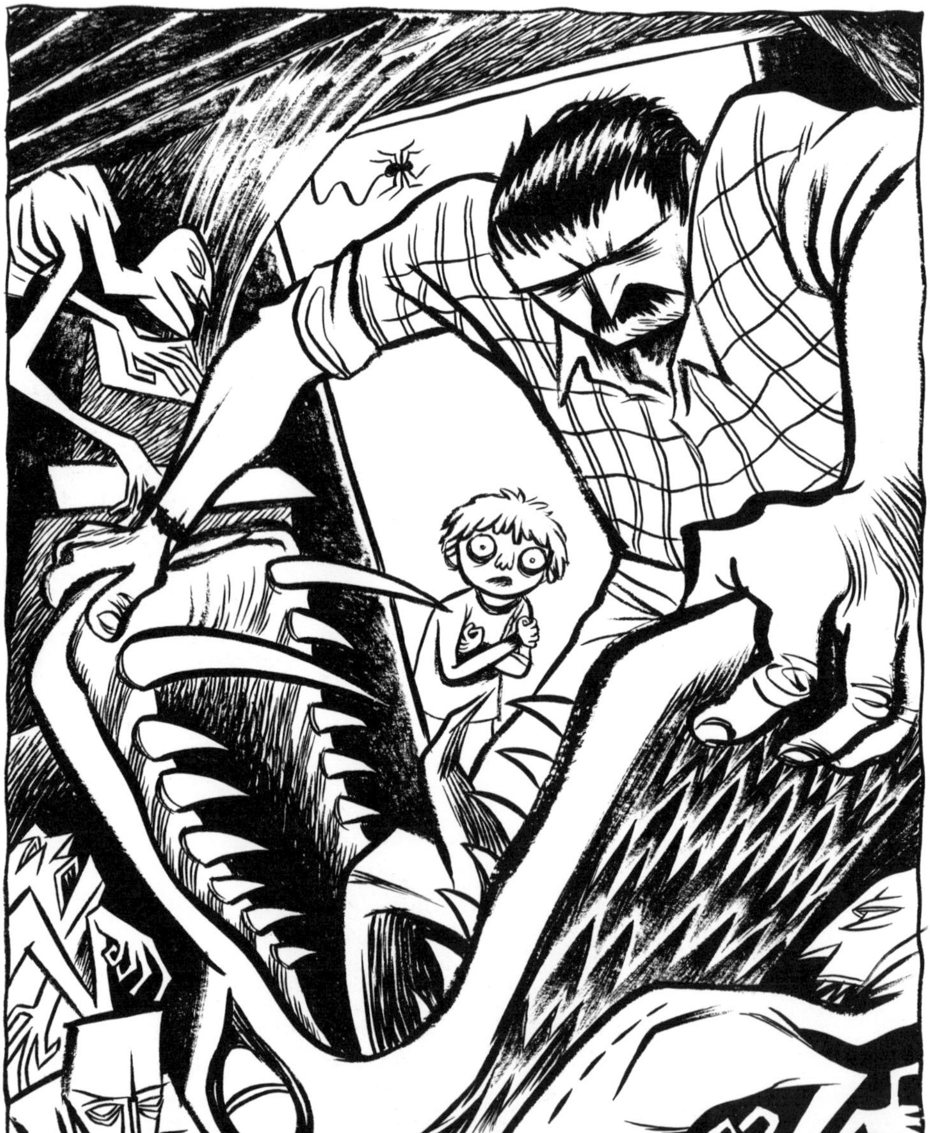

the cubby hole was best LEFT forgotten.

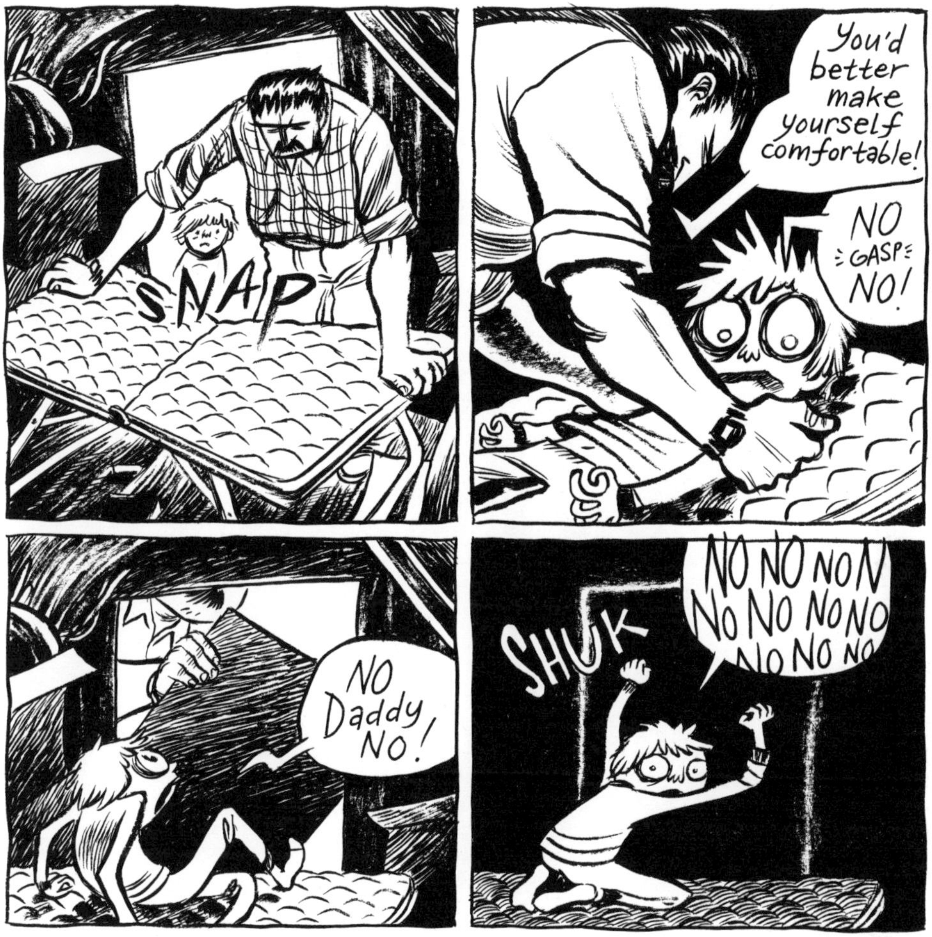
SNAP
You'd better make yourself comfortable!
NO GASP NO!
NO Daddy NO!
SHUK
NO NO NO N
No NO NO NO

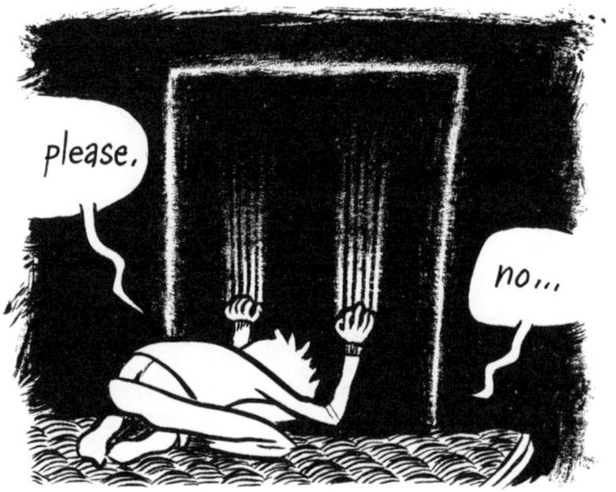
please.
no...

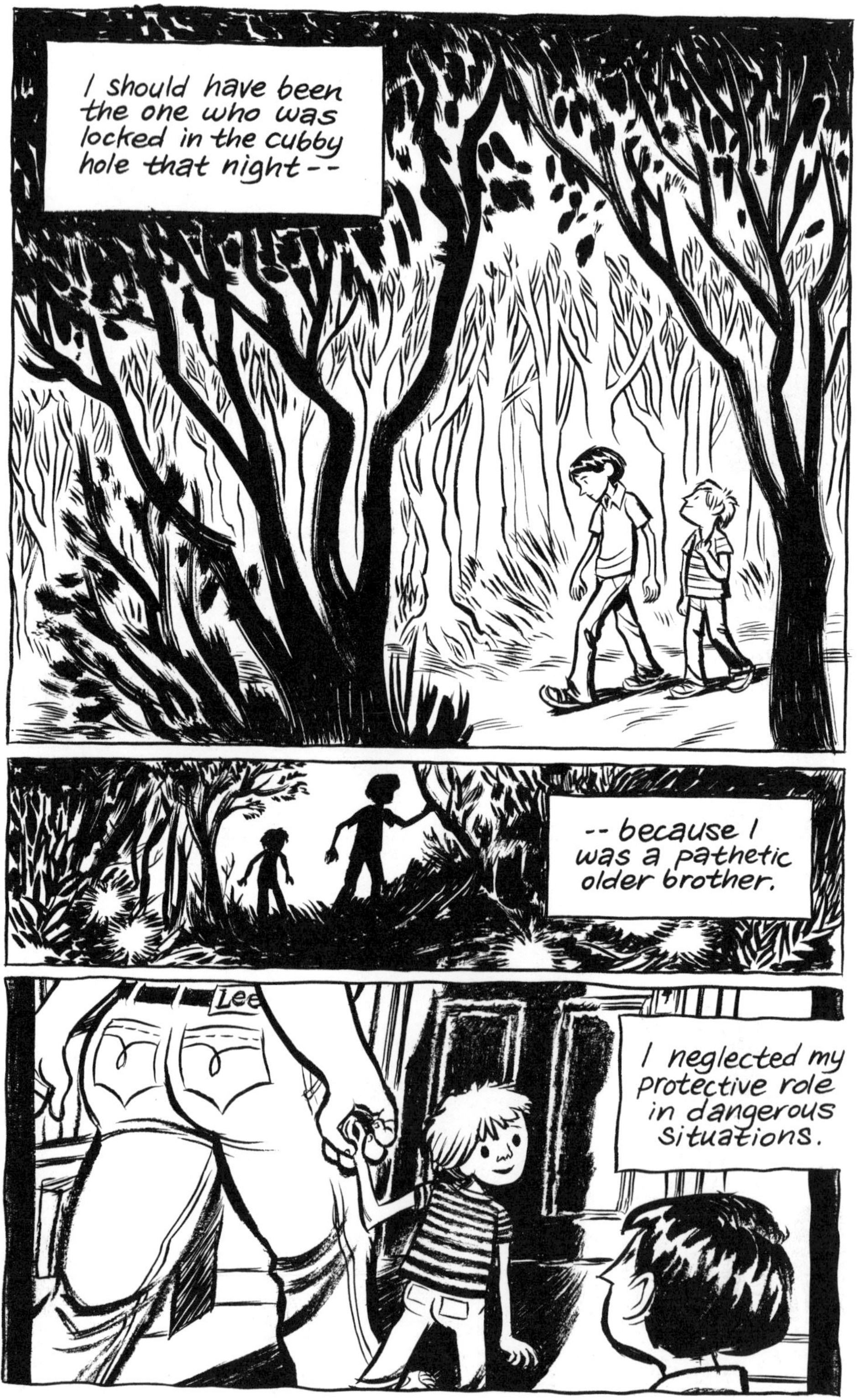
I should have been the one who was locked in the cubby hole that night --
-- because I was a pathetic older brother.
Lee
I neglected my protective role in dangerous situations.

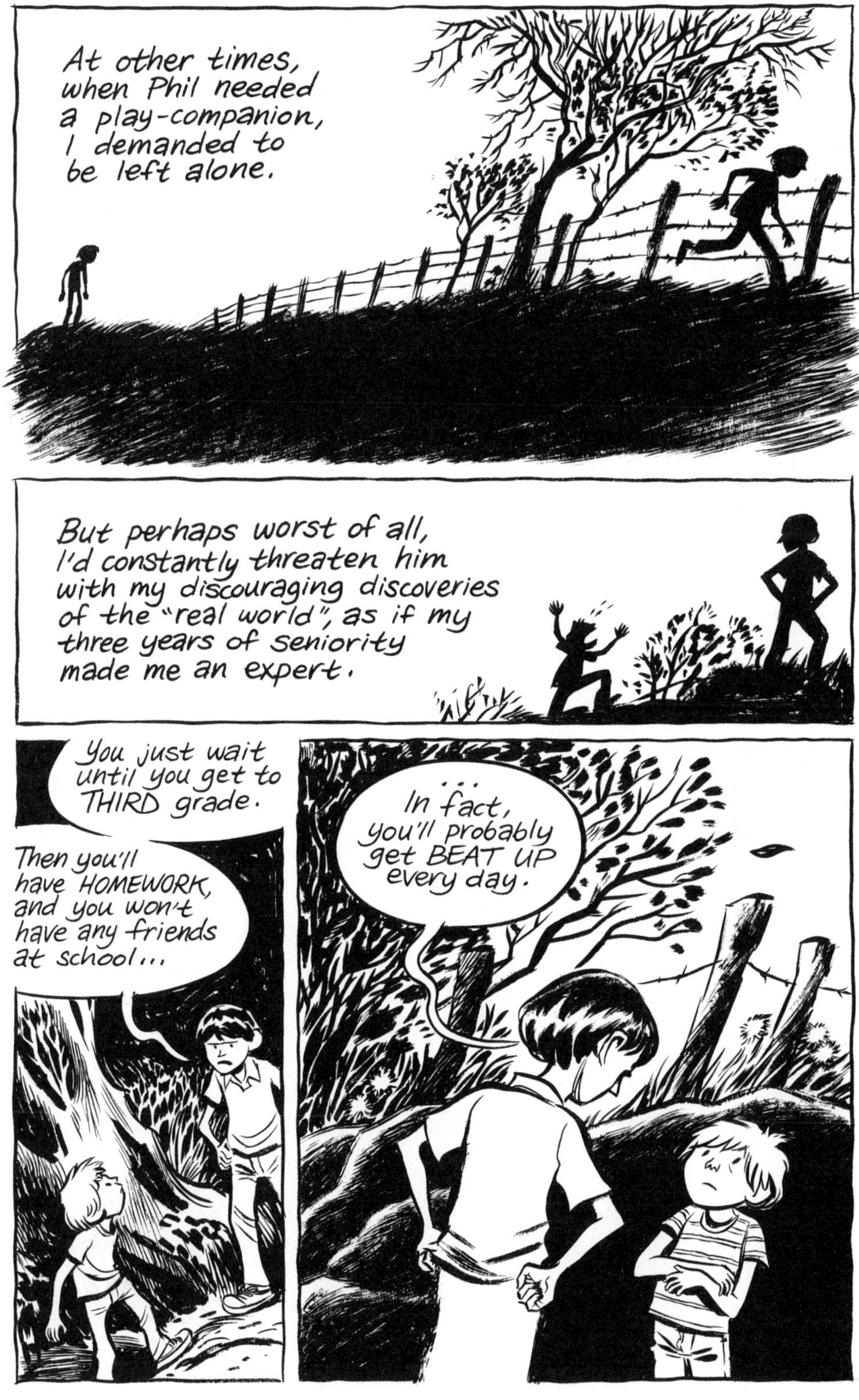

At other times, when Phil needed a play-companion, I demanded to be left alone.
But perhaps worst of all, I'd constantly threaten him with my discouraging discoveries of the "real world", as if my three years of seniority made me an expert.
You just wait until you get to THIRD grade.
Then you'll have HOMEWORK, and you won't have any friends at school...
... In fact, you'll probably get BEAT UP every day.

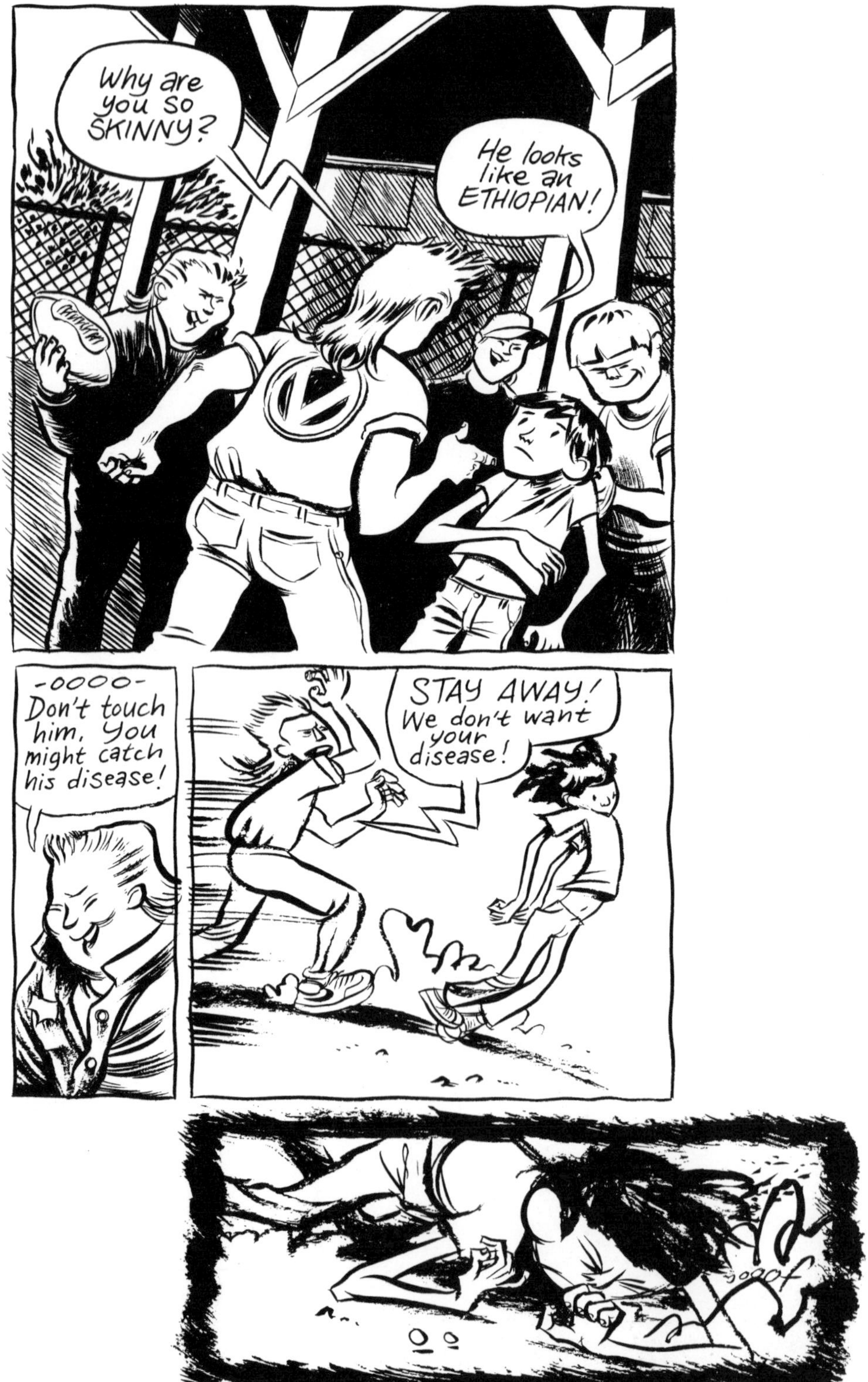
Why are you so SKINNY?
He looks like an ETHIOPIAN!
-OOOO- Don't touch him. You might catch his disease!
STAY AWAY! We don't want your disease!

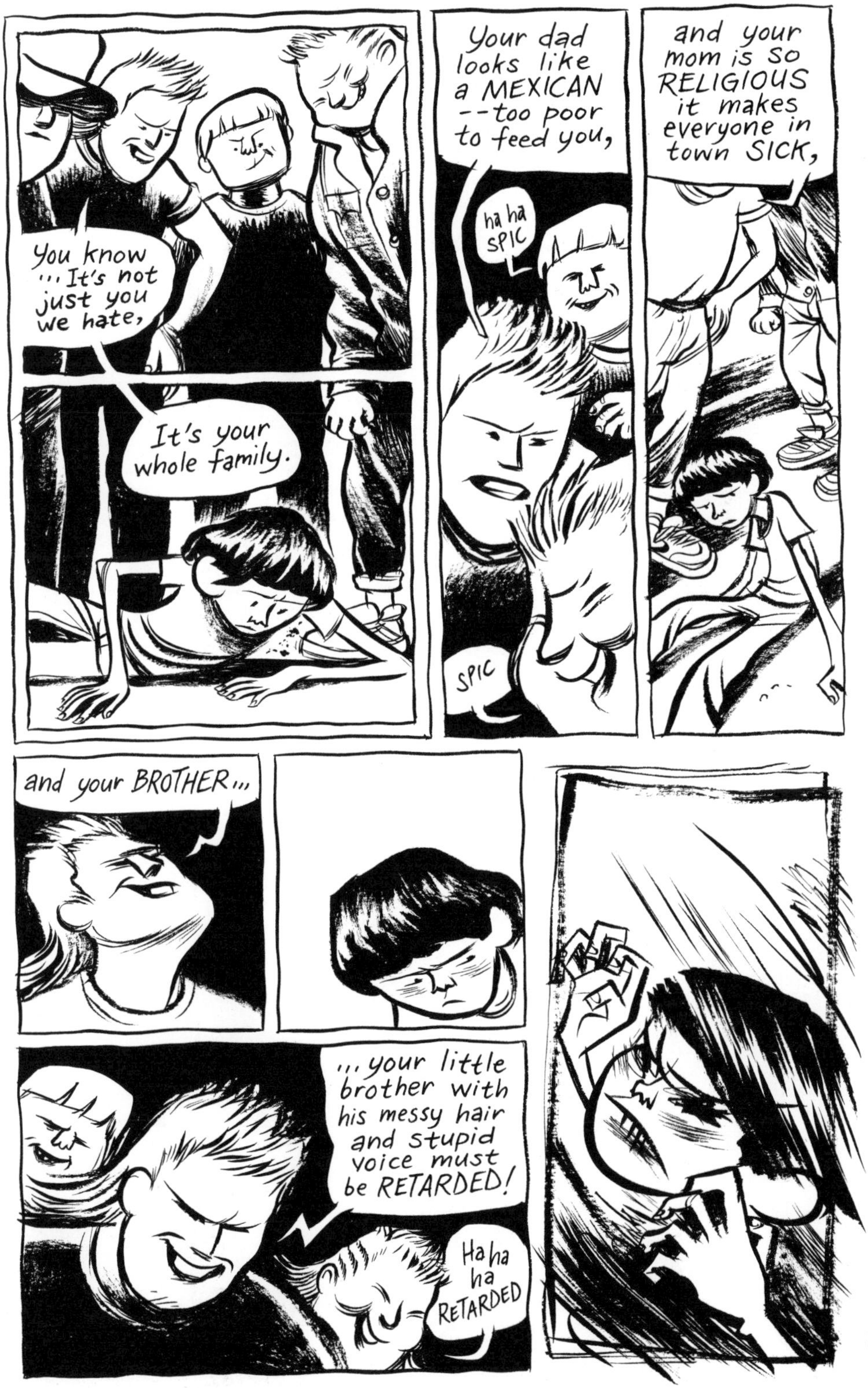
You know ... It's not just you we hate,
It's your whole family.
Your dad looks like a MEXICAN --too poor to feed you,
ha ha SPIC
SPIC
and your mom is so RELIGIOUS it makes everyone in town SICK,
and your BROTHER...
...your little brother with his messy hair and stupid voice must be RETARDED!
Ha ha ha RETARDED

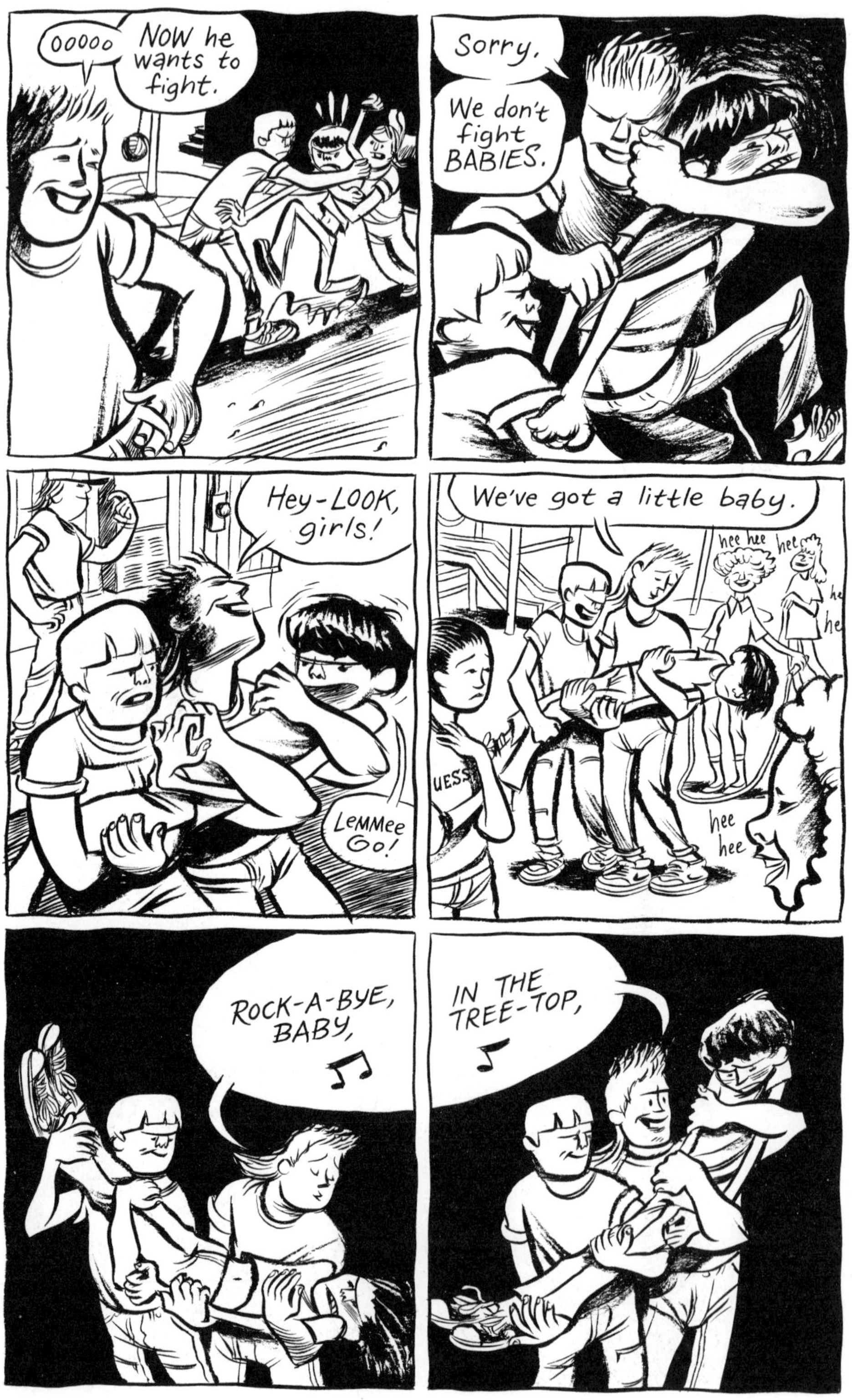
OOOOO
NOW he wants to fight.
Sorry.
We don't fight BABIES.
Hey-LOOK, girls!
LEMMEE GO!
We've got a little baby.
hee hee
hee
hee
hee
hee hee
ROCK-A-BYE, BABY,
IN THE TREE-TOP,

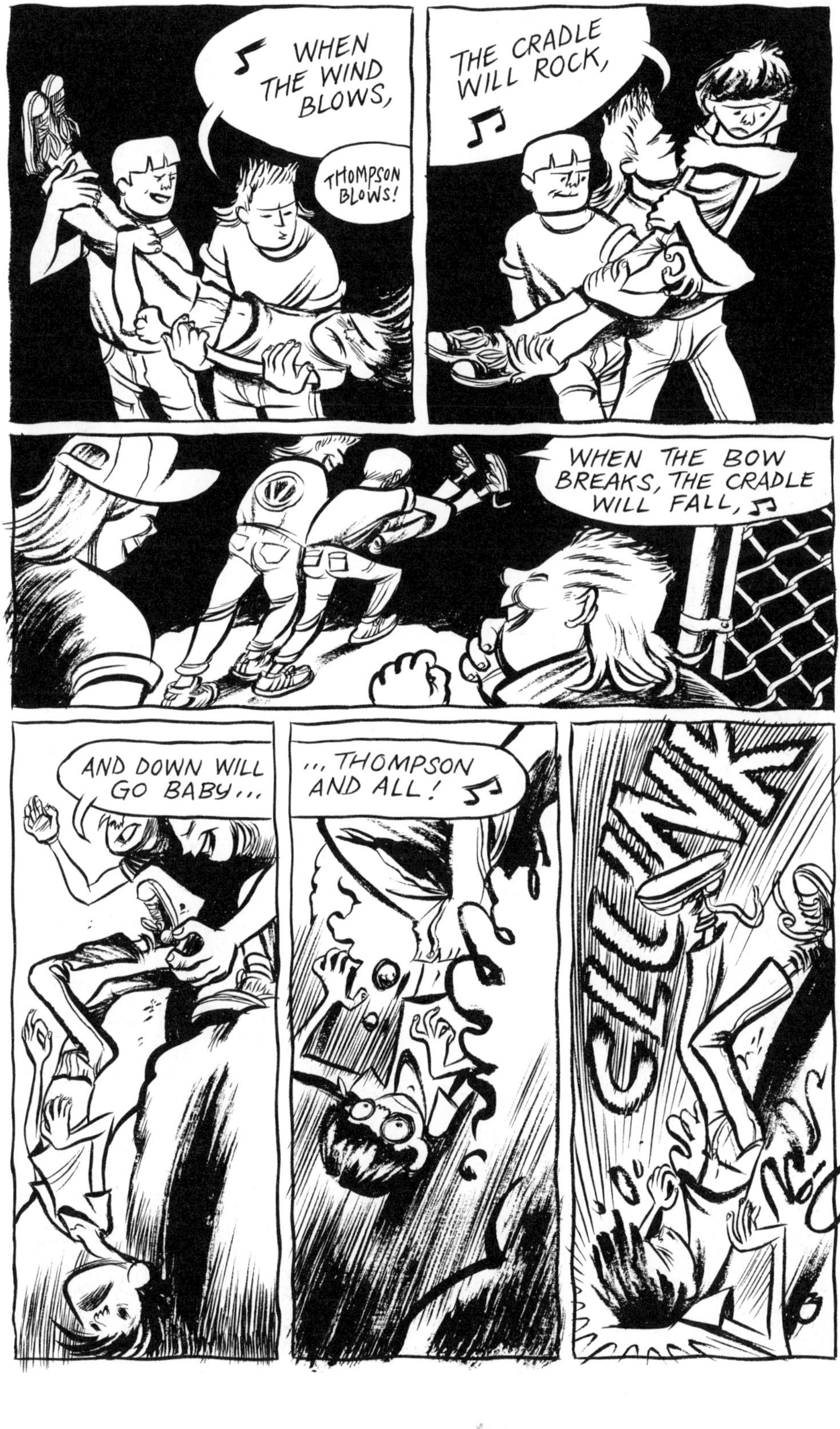
WHEN THE WIND BLOWS,
THOMPSON BLOWS!
THE CRADLE WILL ROCK,
WHEN THE BOW BREAKS, THE CRADLE WILL FALL,
AND DOWN WILL GO BABY...
...THOMPSON AND ALL!

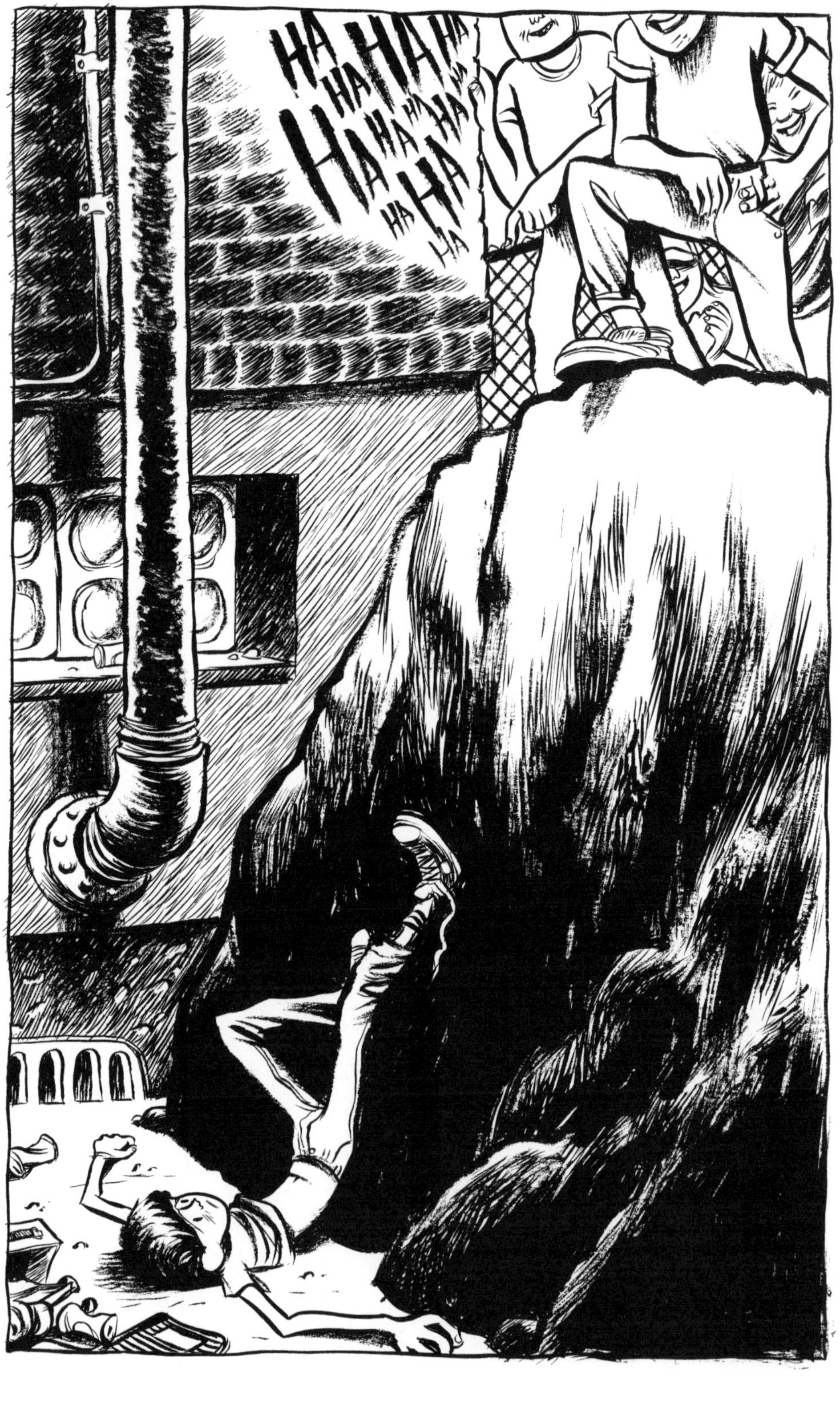
HA HA HA HA HA HA HA HA HA HA HA HA HA

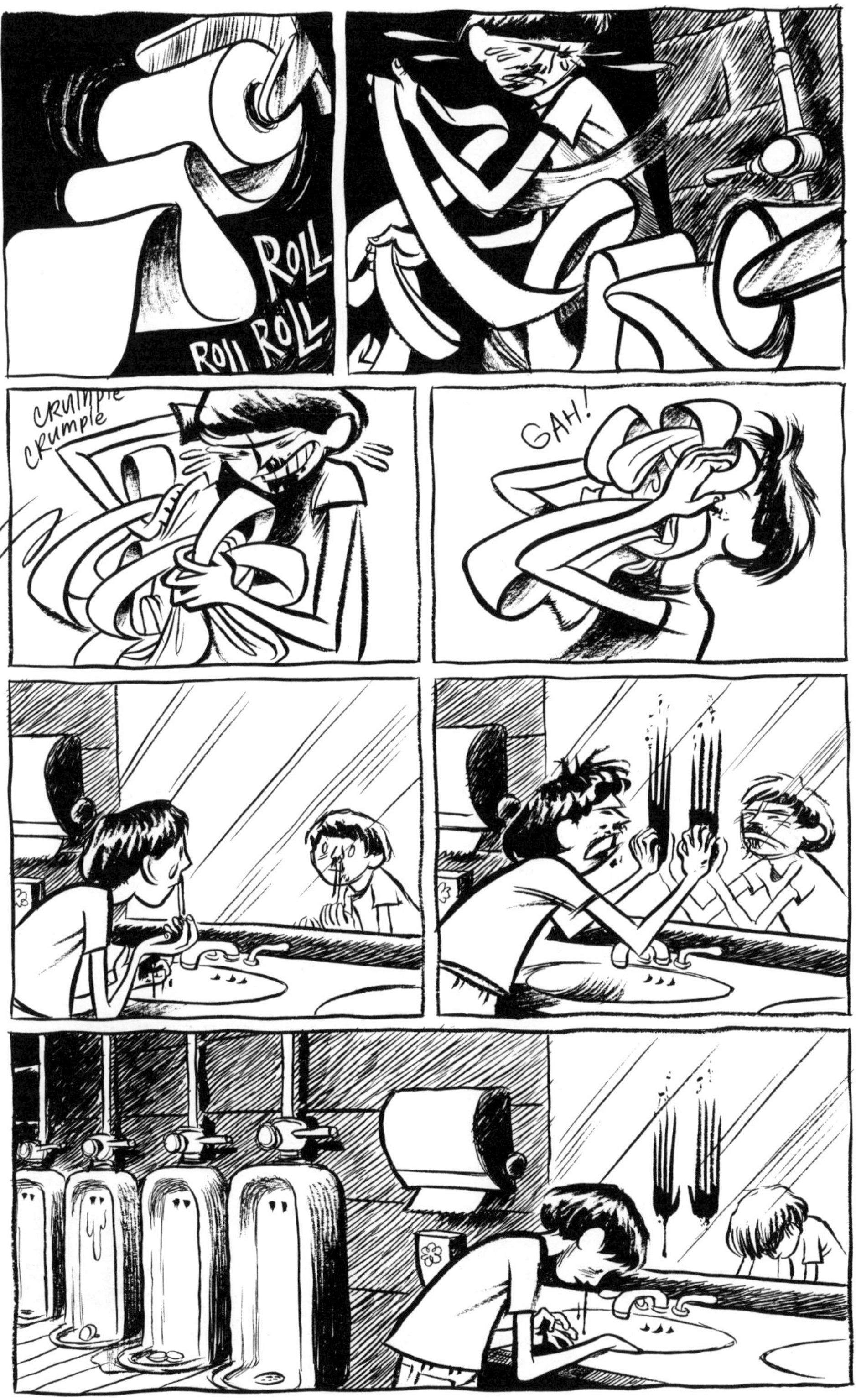
ROLL
ROLL ROLL
CRUMPLE CRUMPLE
GAH!

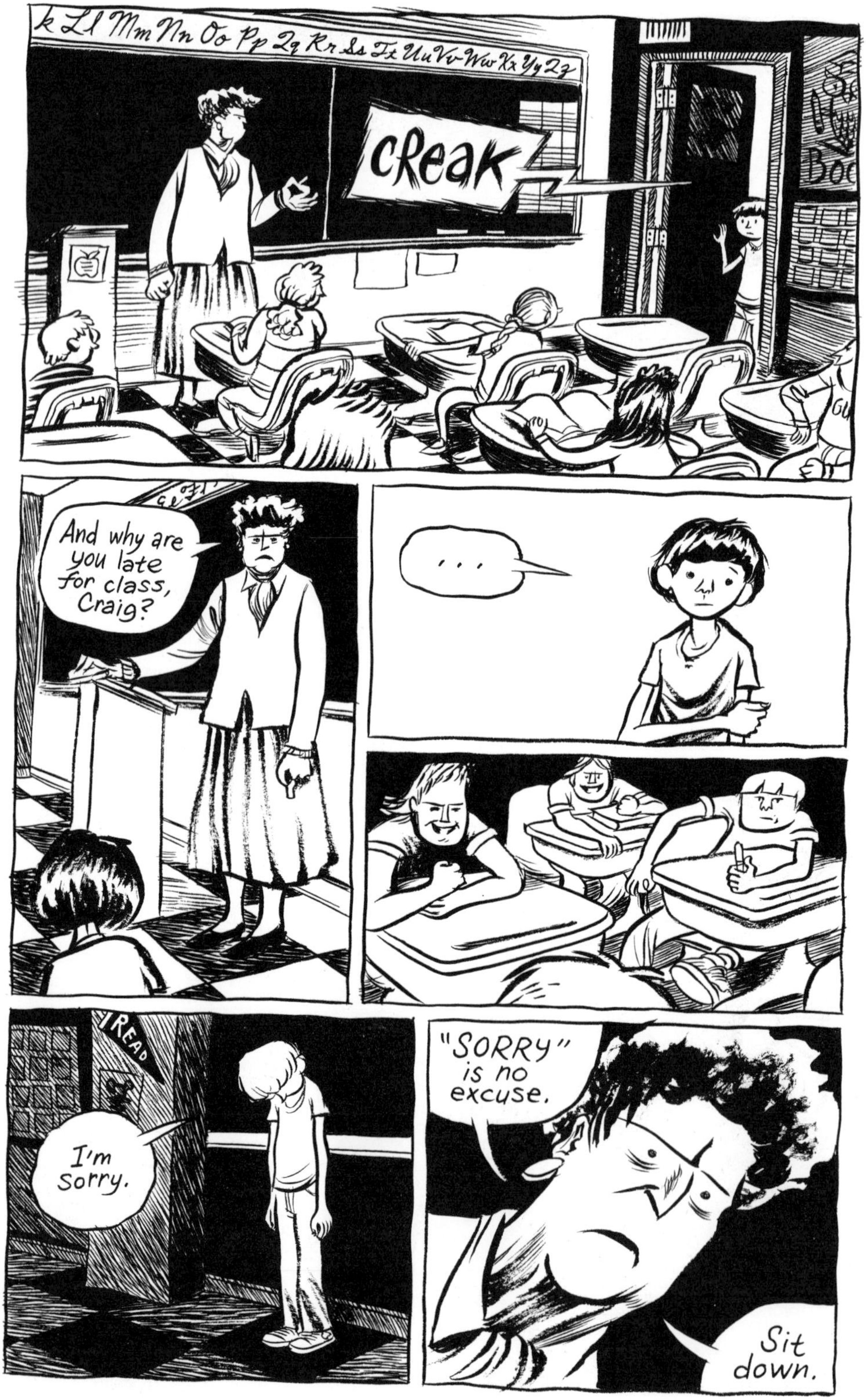
k Ll Mm Nn Oo Pp Qq Rr Ss Tt Uu Vv Ww Xx Yy Zz
CReak
And why are you late for class, Craig?
. . .
READ
I'm sorry.
"SORRY" is no excuse.
Sit down.

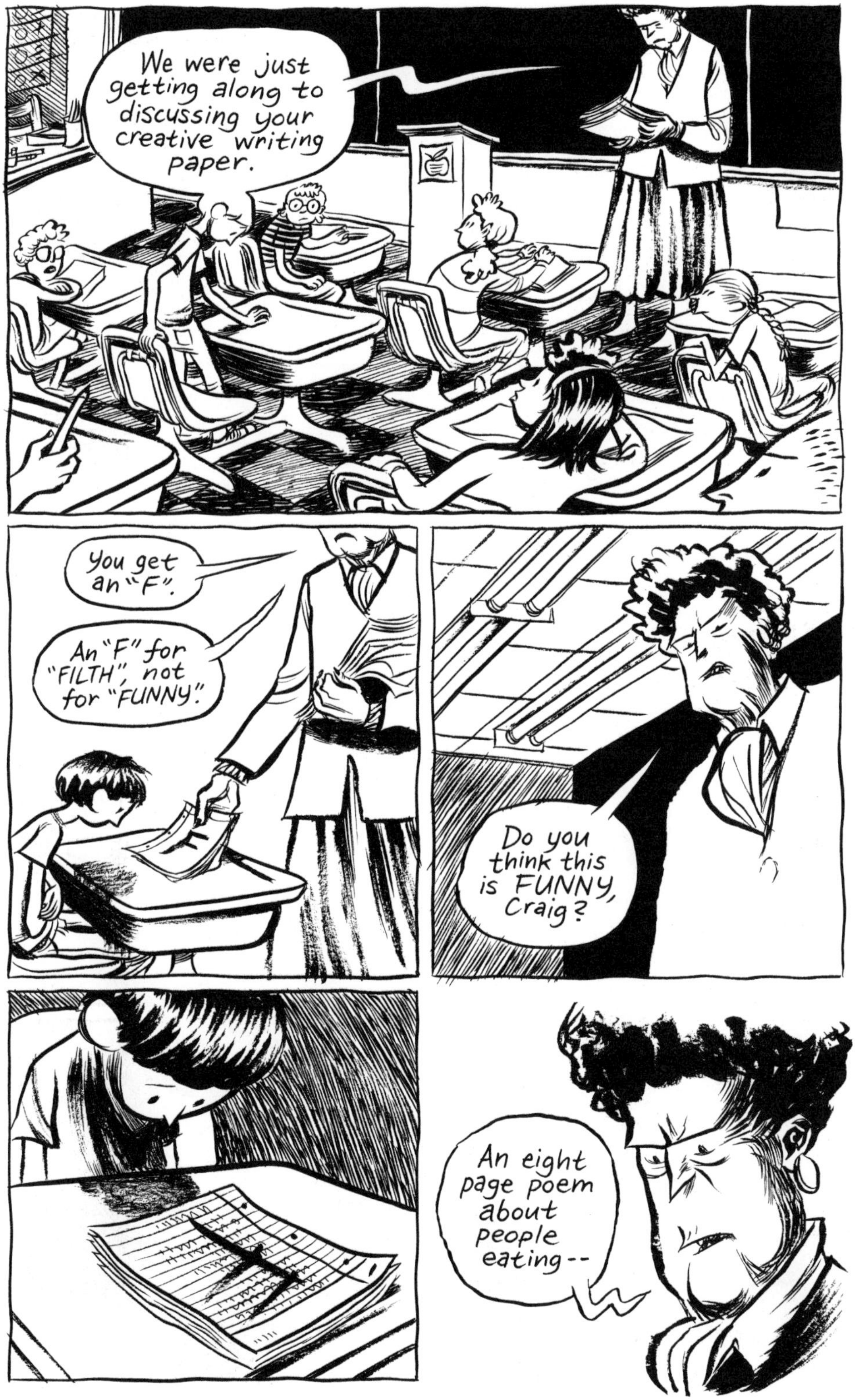
We were just getting along to discussing your creative writing paper.
You get an "F".
An "F" for "FILTH", not for "FUNNY".
Do you think this is FUNNY, Craig?
An eight page poem about people eating--

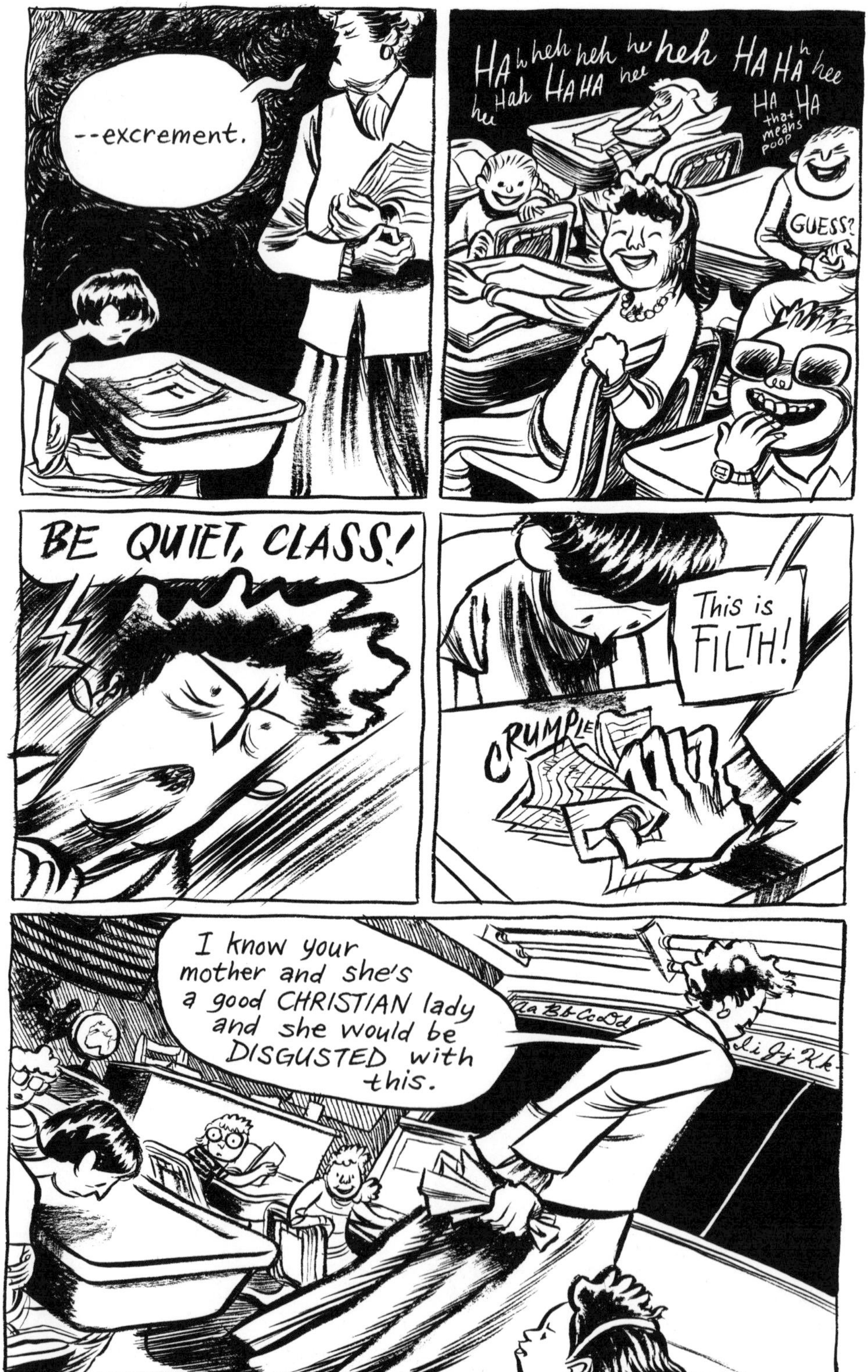
--excrement.
HA heh heh heh he heh HA HA h hee
he Hah HAHA hee
HA HA that means poop
GUESS?
BE QUIET, CLASS!
This is FILTH!
CRUMPLE
I know your mother and she's a good CHRISTIAN lady and she would be DISGUSTED with this.
Aa Bb Cc Dd
Ii Jj Kk

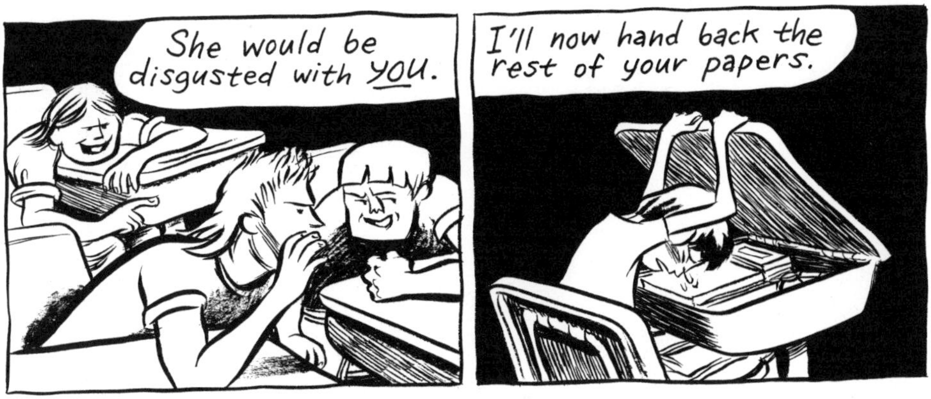
She would be disgusted with YOU.
I'll now hand back the rest of your papers.

If only God could forgive me for all the times I pictured people eating their own excrement.

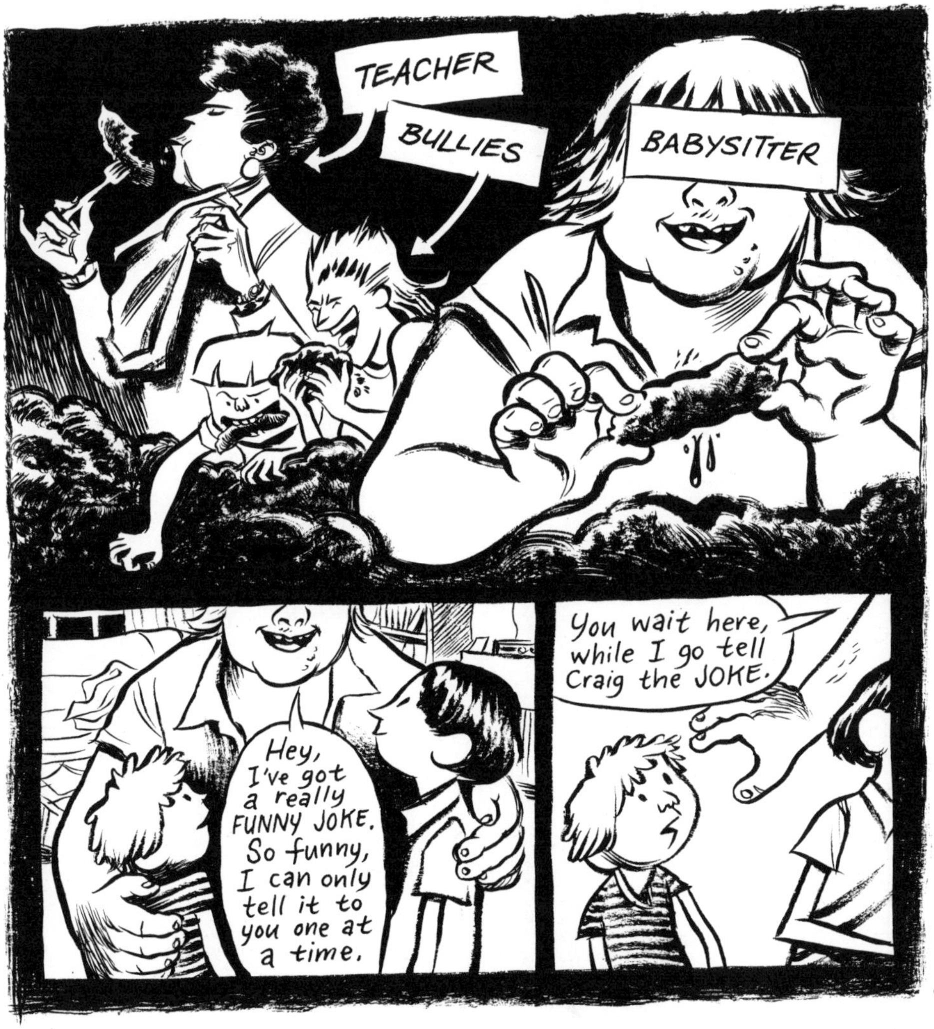
TEACHER
BULLIES
BABYSITTER
Hey, I've got a really FUNNY JOKE. So funny, I can only tell it to you one at a time.
You wait here, while I go tell Craig the JOKE.

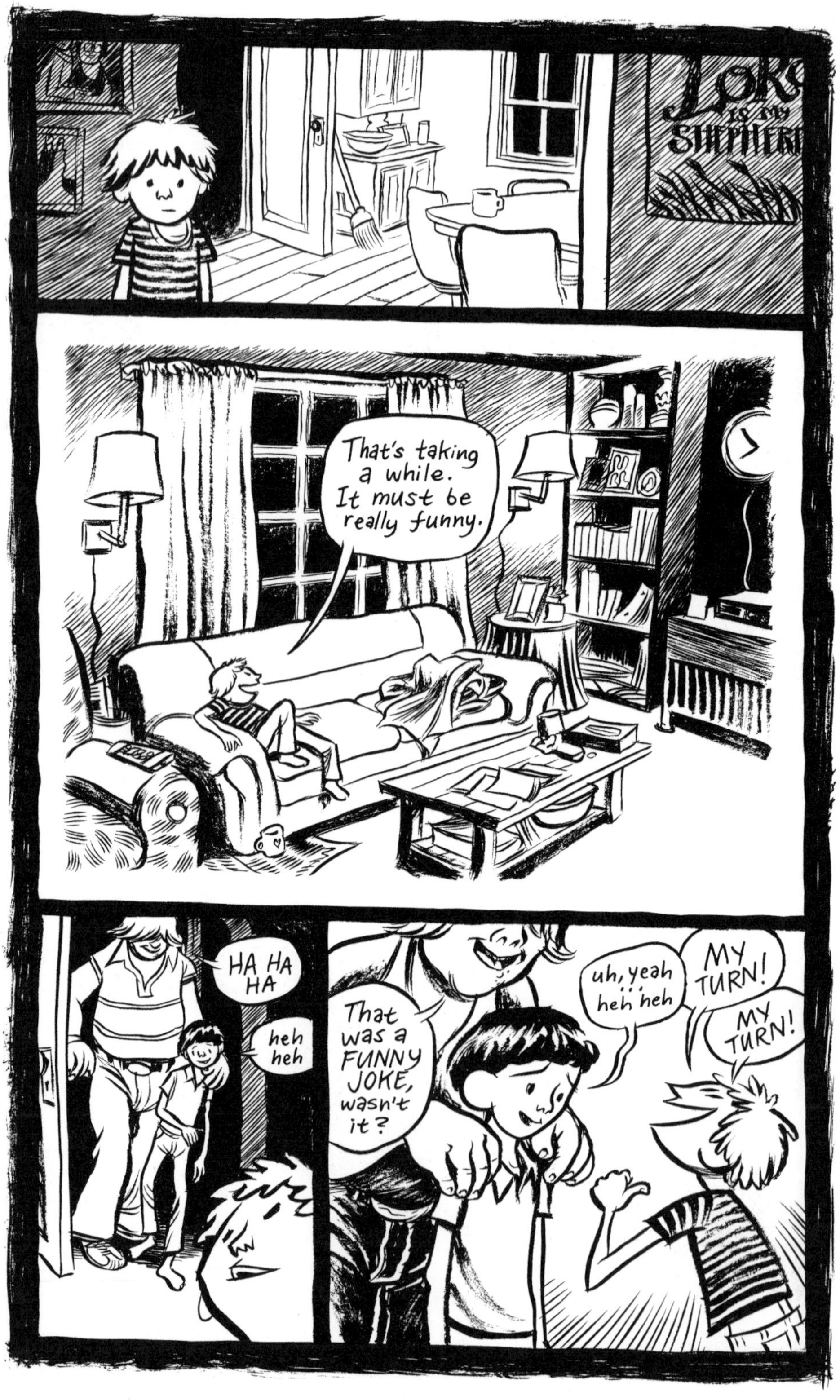

That's taking a while. It must be really funny.
HA HA HA
heh heh
That was a FUNNY JOKE, wasn't it?
uh, yeah... heh heh
MY TURN!
MY TURN!

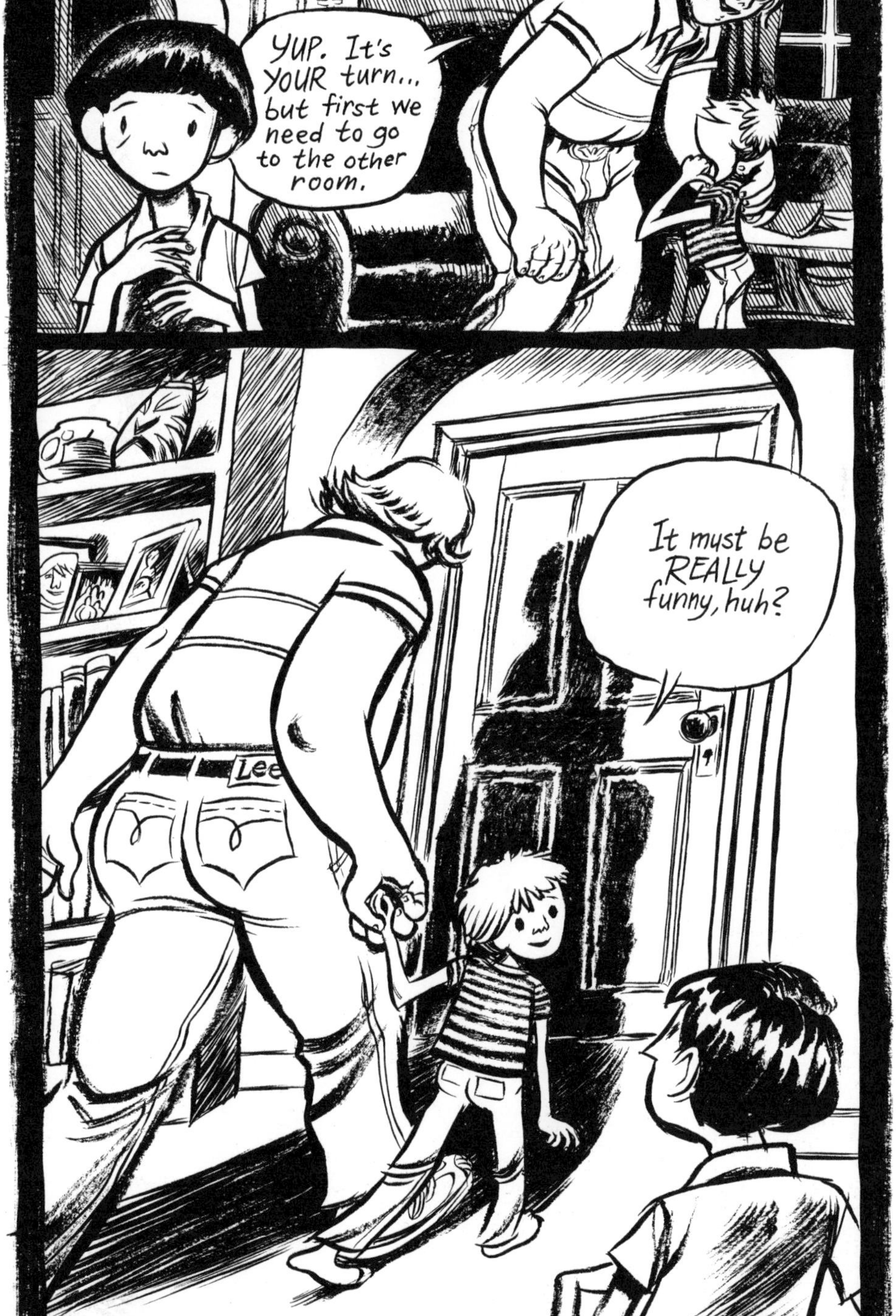
YUP. It's YOUR turn... but first we need to go to the other room.
It must be REALLY funny, huh?

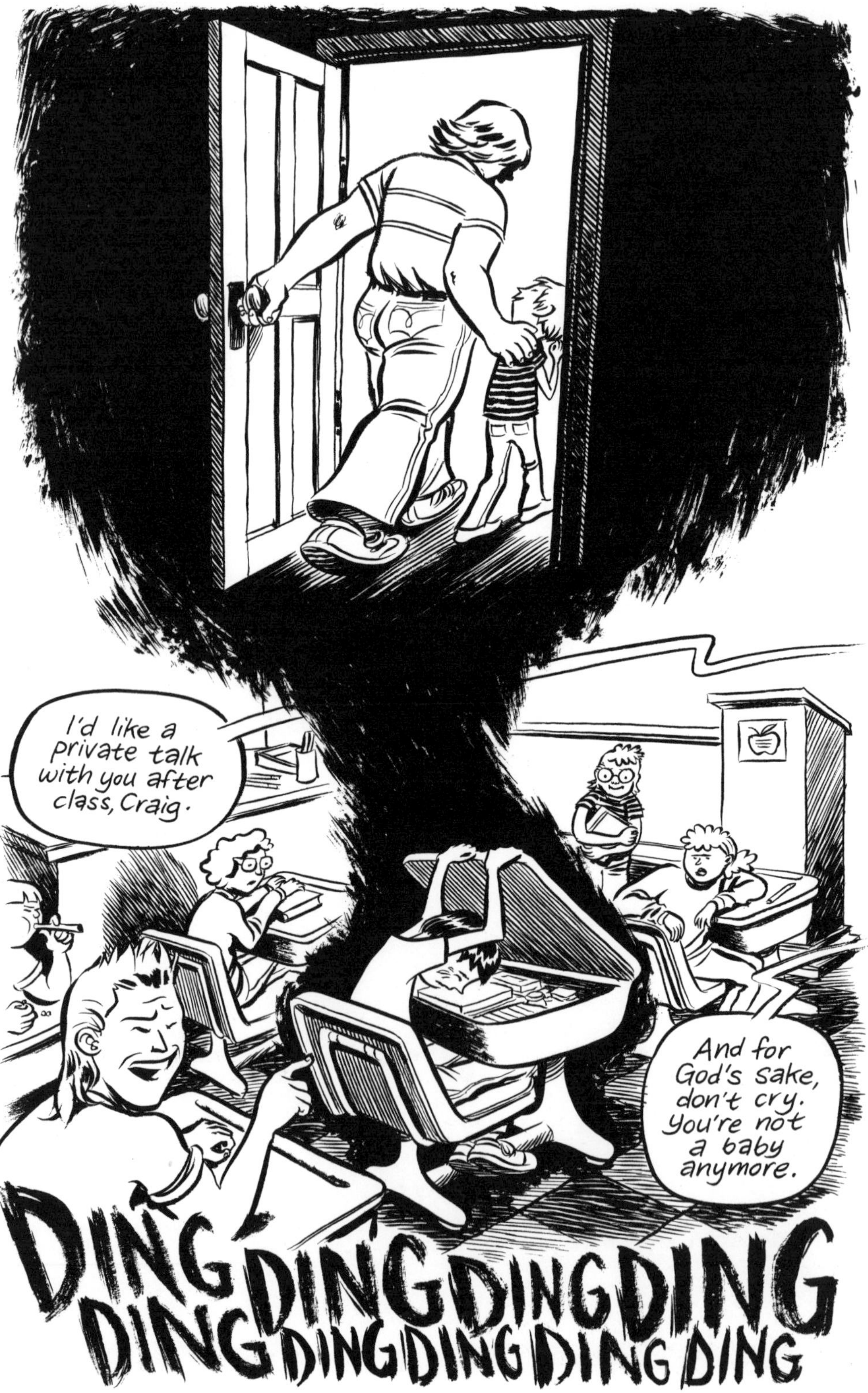

I'd like a private talk with you after class, Craig.
And for God's sake, don't cry. You're not a baby anymore.
DING DING DING DING DING DING DING DING DING DING

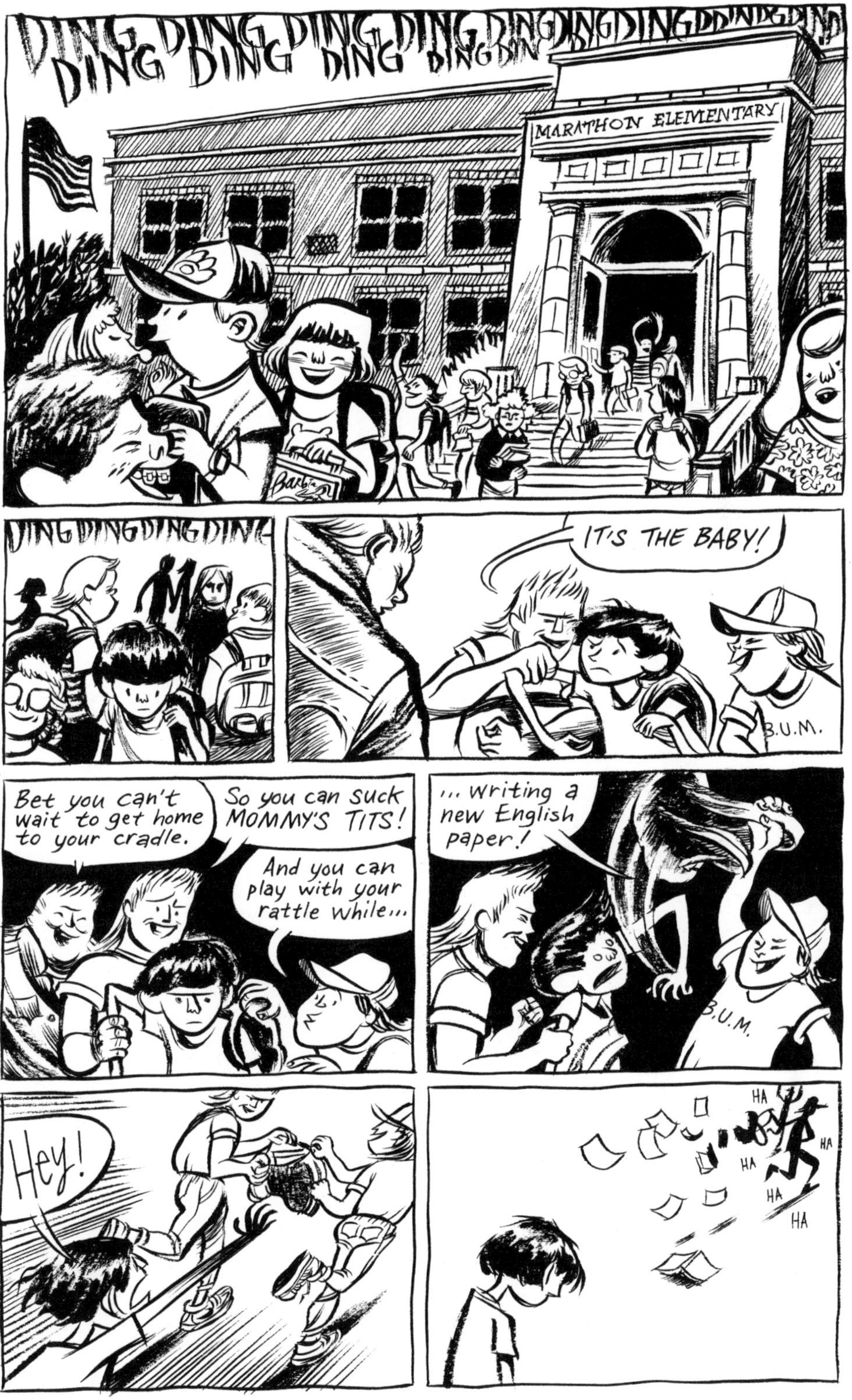
DING DING DING DING DING DING DING
DING DING DING DING DING
MARATHON ELEMENTARY
DING DING DING DING
IT'S THE BABY!
B.U.M.
Bet you can't wait to get home to your cradle.
So you can suck MOMMY'S TITS!
And you can play with your rattle while...
...writing a new English paper!
B.U.M.
Hey!
HA
HA
HA
HA
HA

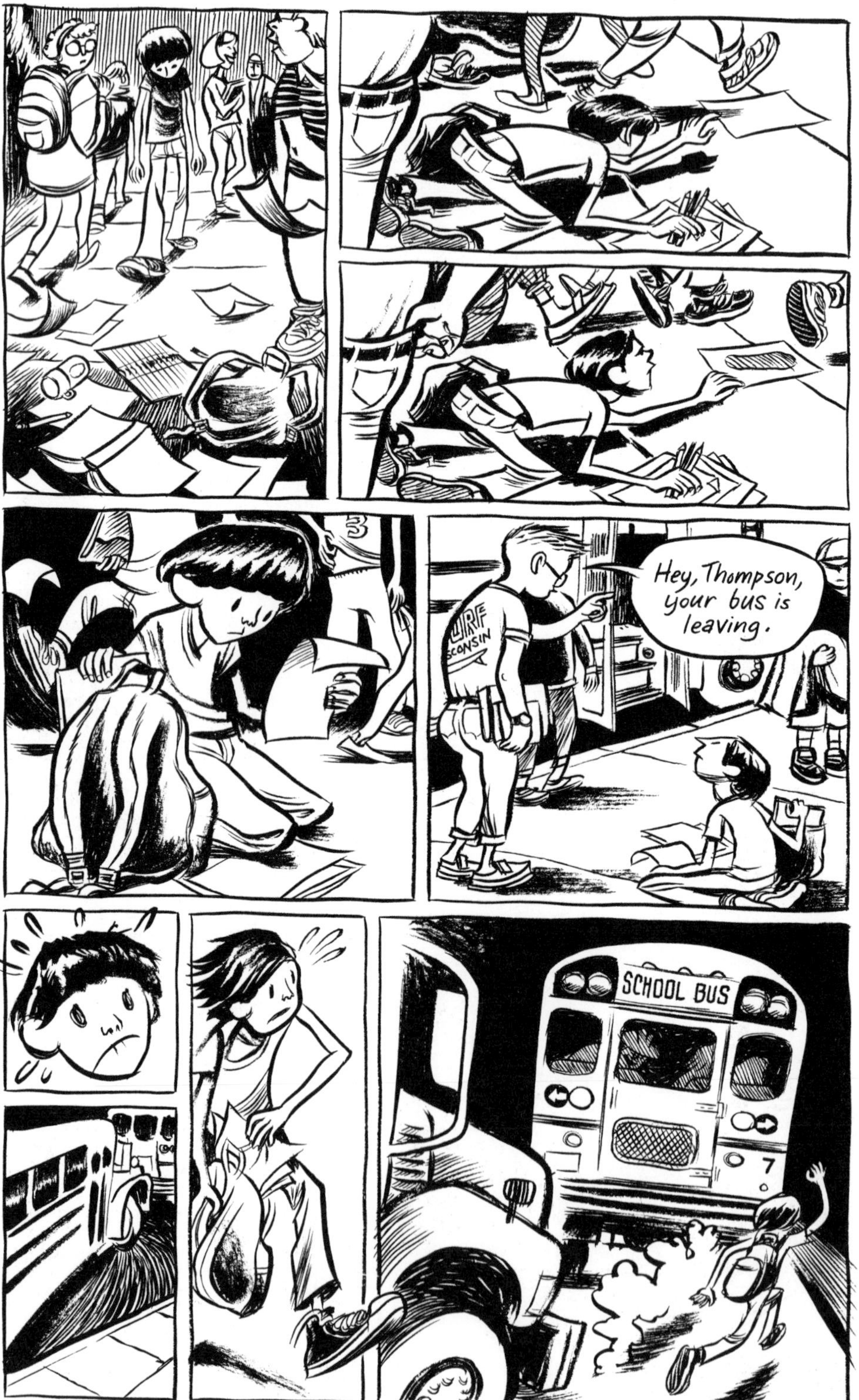
Hey, Thompson, your bus is leaving.
SURF
WISCONSIN
SCHOOL BUS
7

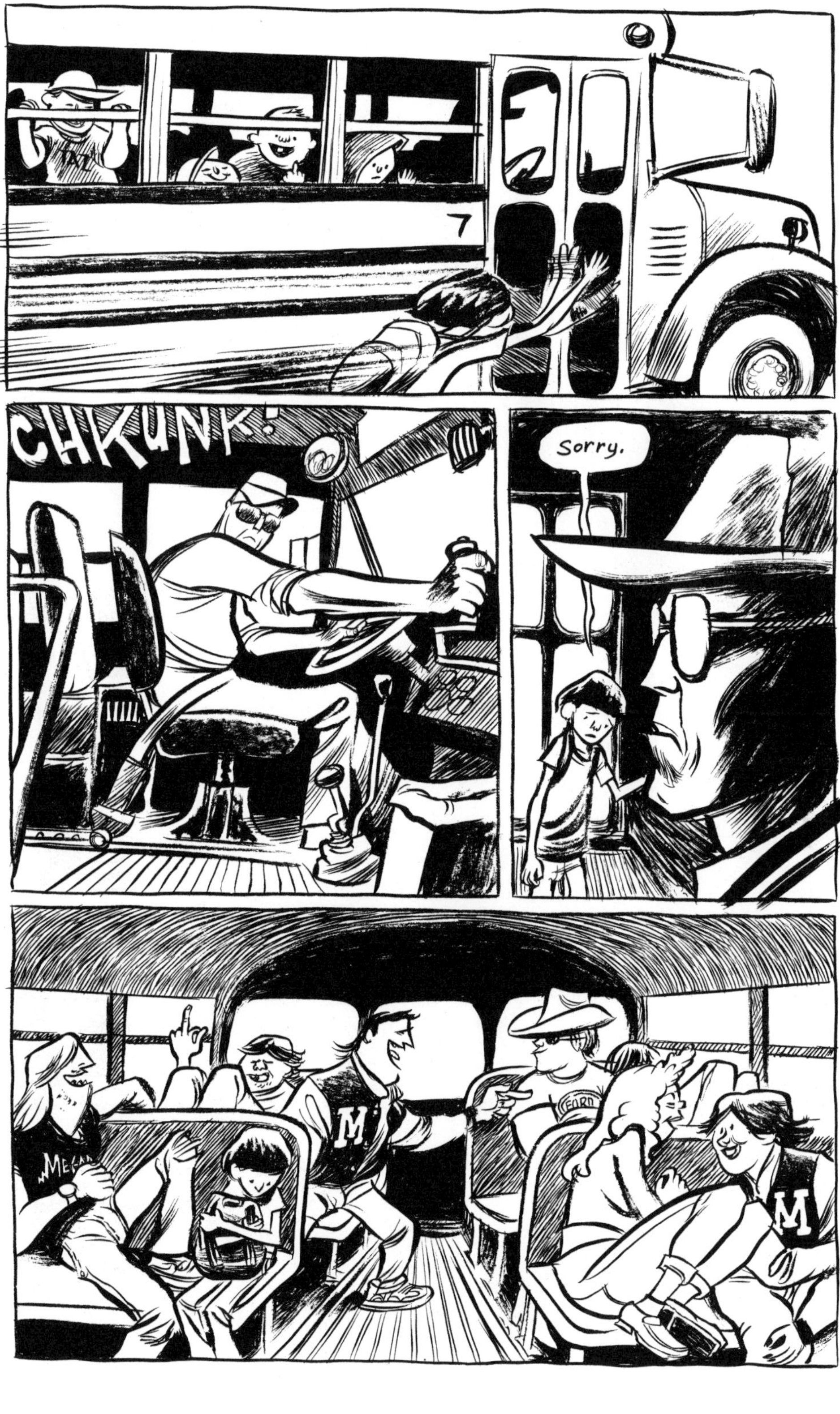
CHKUNK!
Sorry.

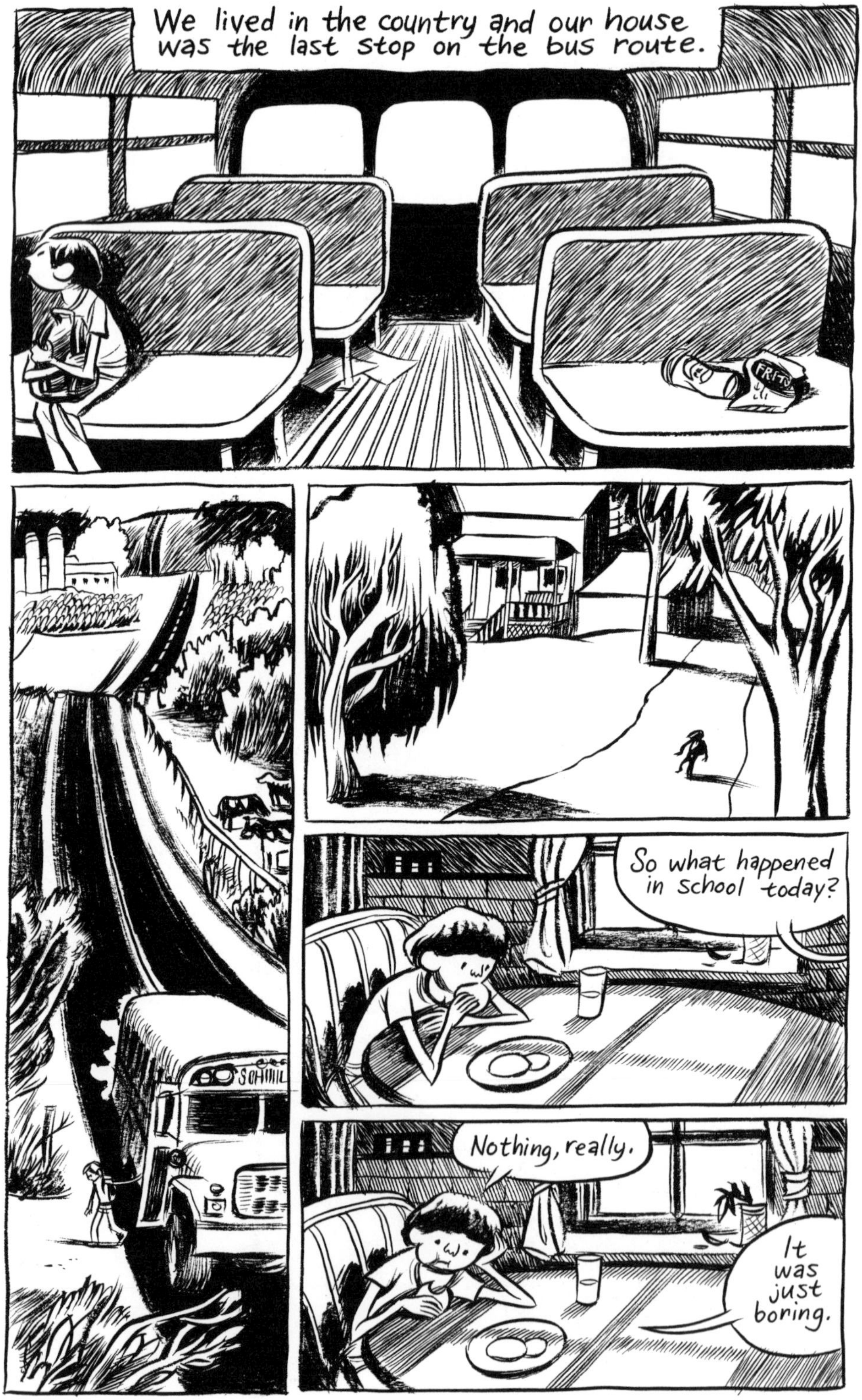
We lived in the country and our house was the last stop on the bus route.
So what happened in school today?
Nothing, really.
It was just boring.

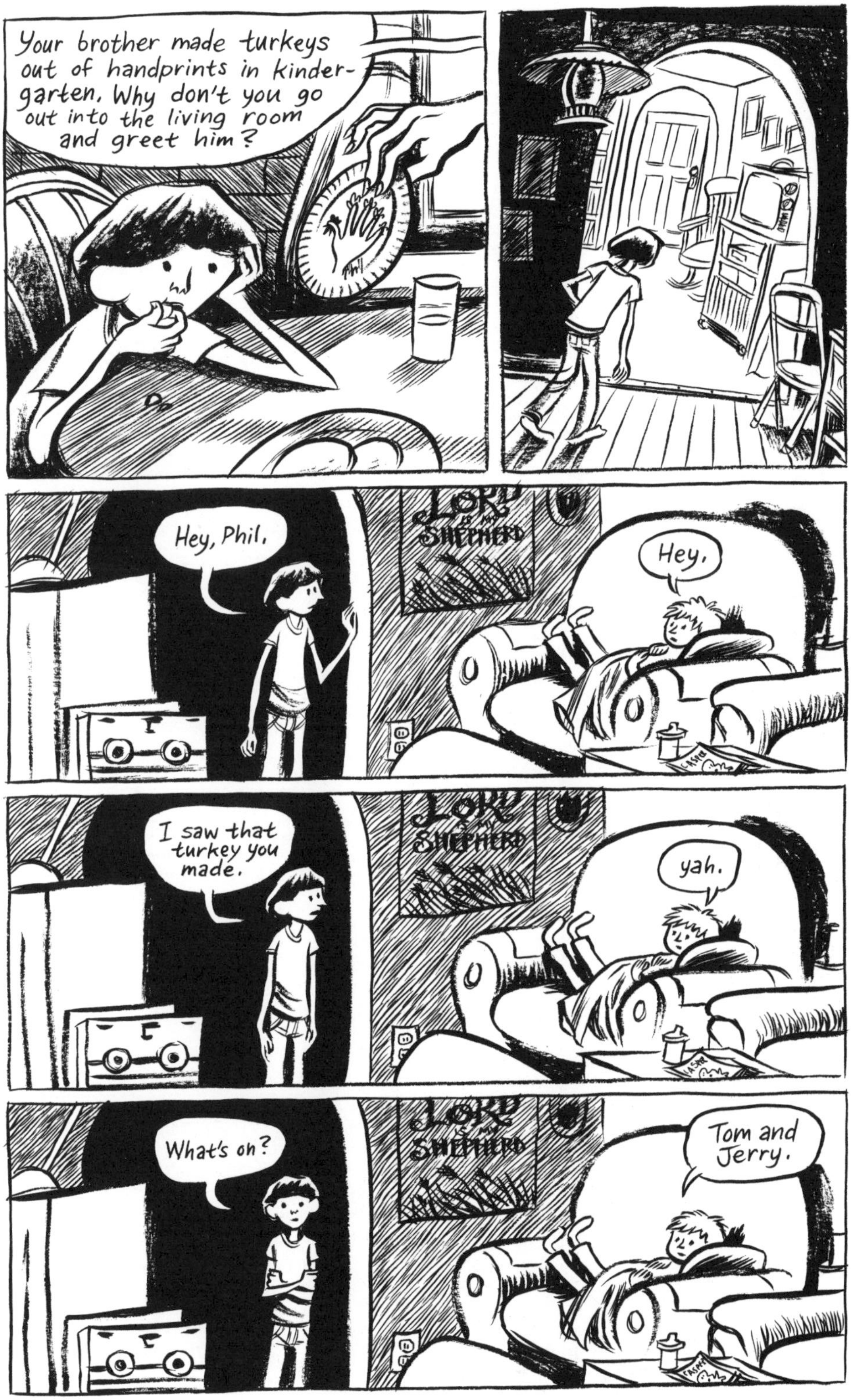
Your brother made turkeys out of handprints in kindergarten. Why don't you go out into the living room and greet him?
Hey, Phil.
Hey.
I saw that turkey you made.
yah.
What's on?
Tom and Jerry.

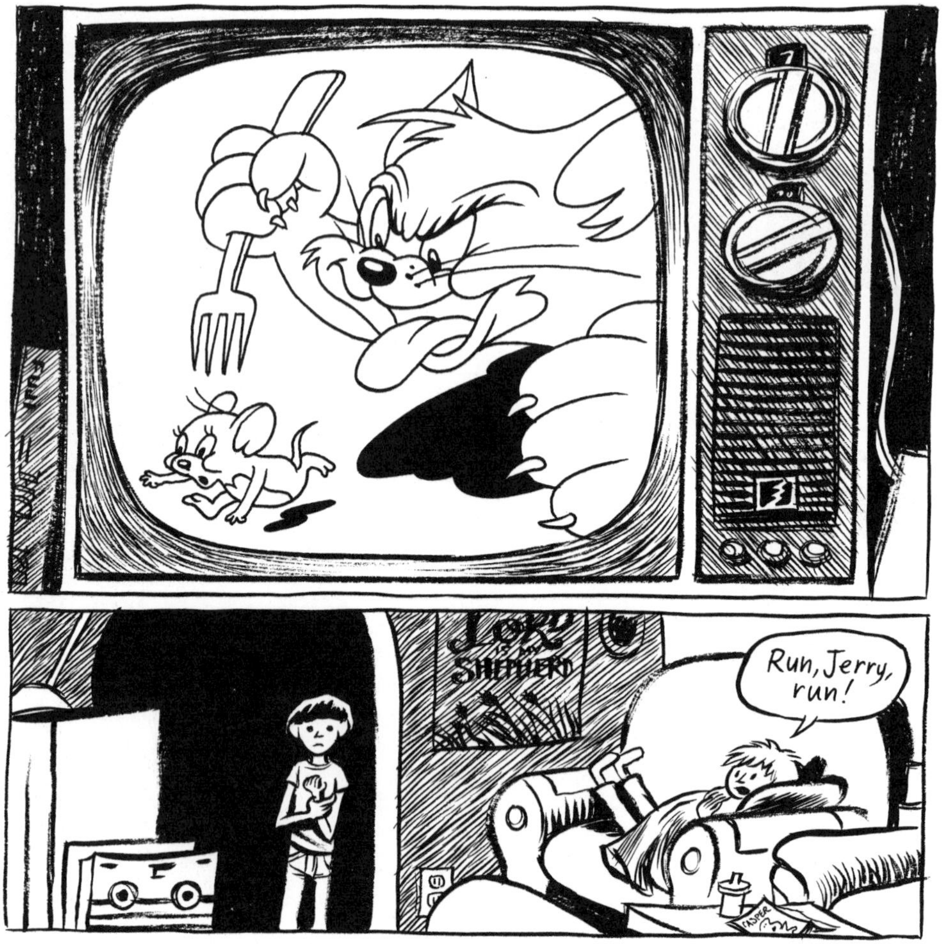
Run, Jerry, run!

As a child, I thought that life was the most horrible world anyone could ever live in, and that there HAD to be something better.

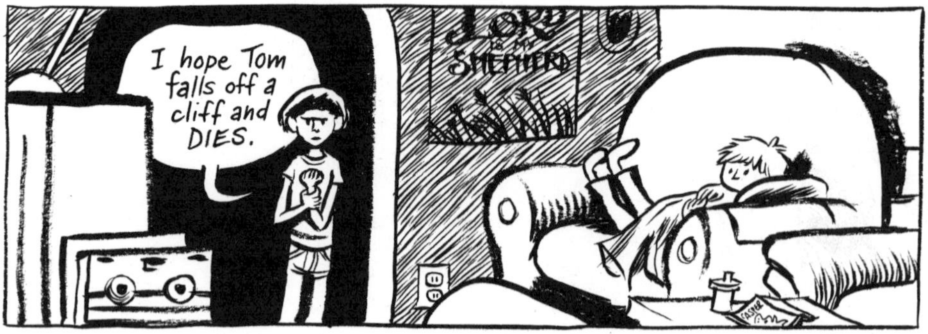
I hope Tom falls off a cliff and DIES.

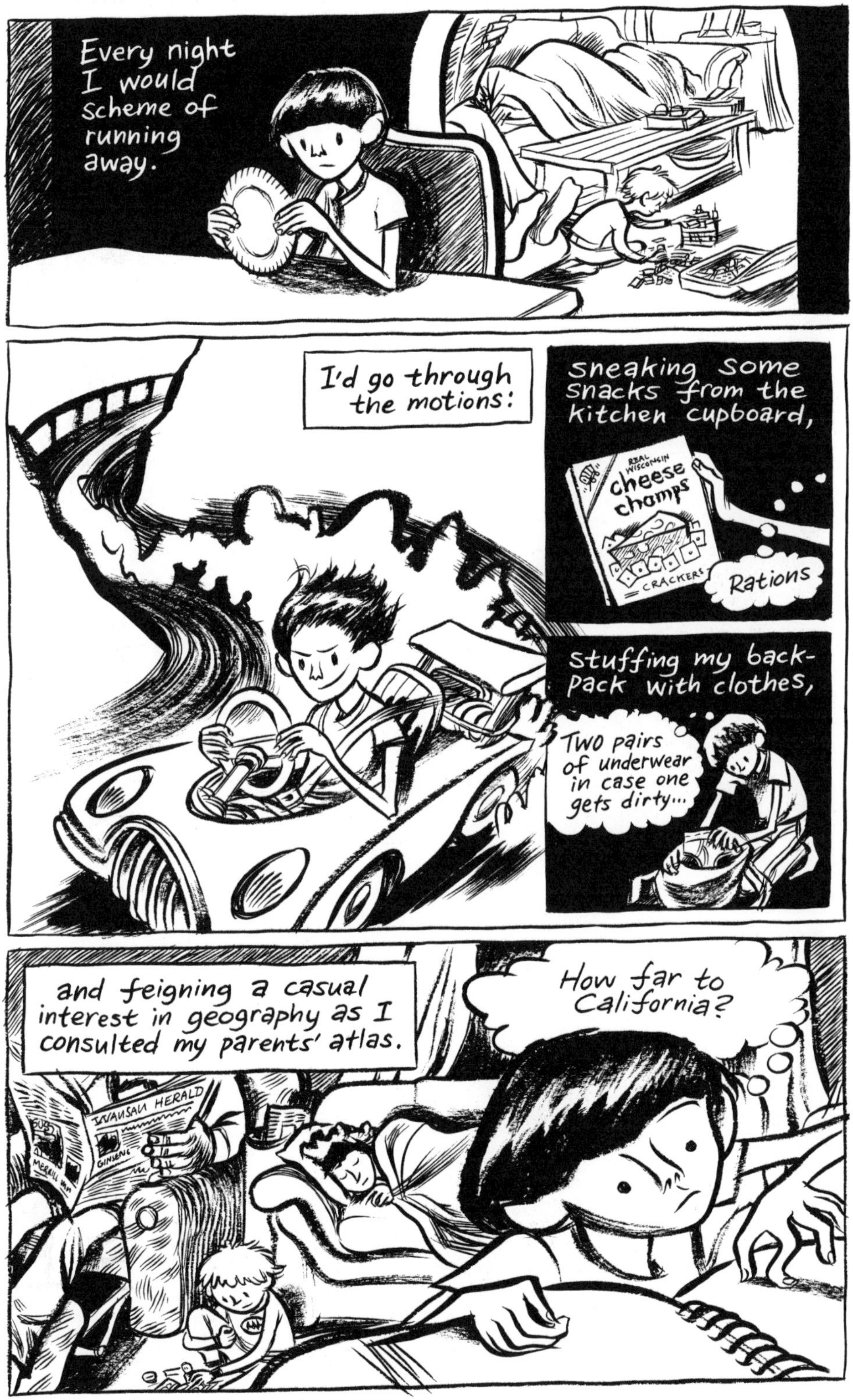
Every night I would scheme of running away.
I'd go through the motions:
sneaking some snacks from the kitchen cupboard,
REAL WISCONSIN
cheese champs
CRACKERS
Rations
stuffing my back-pack with clothes,
Two pairs of underwear in case one gets dirty...
and feigning a casual interest in geography as I consulted my parents' atlas.
How far to California?
WAUSAU HERALD

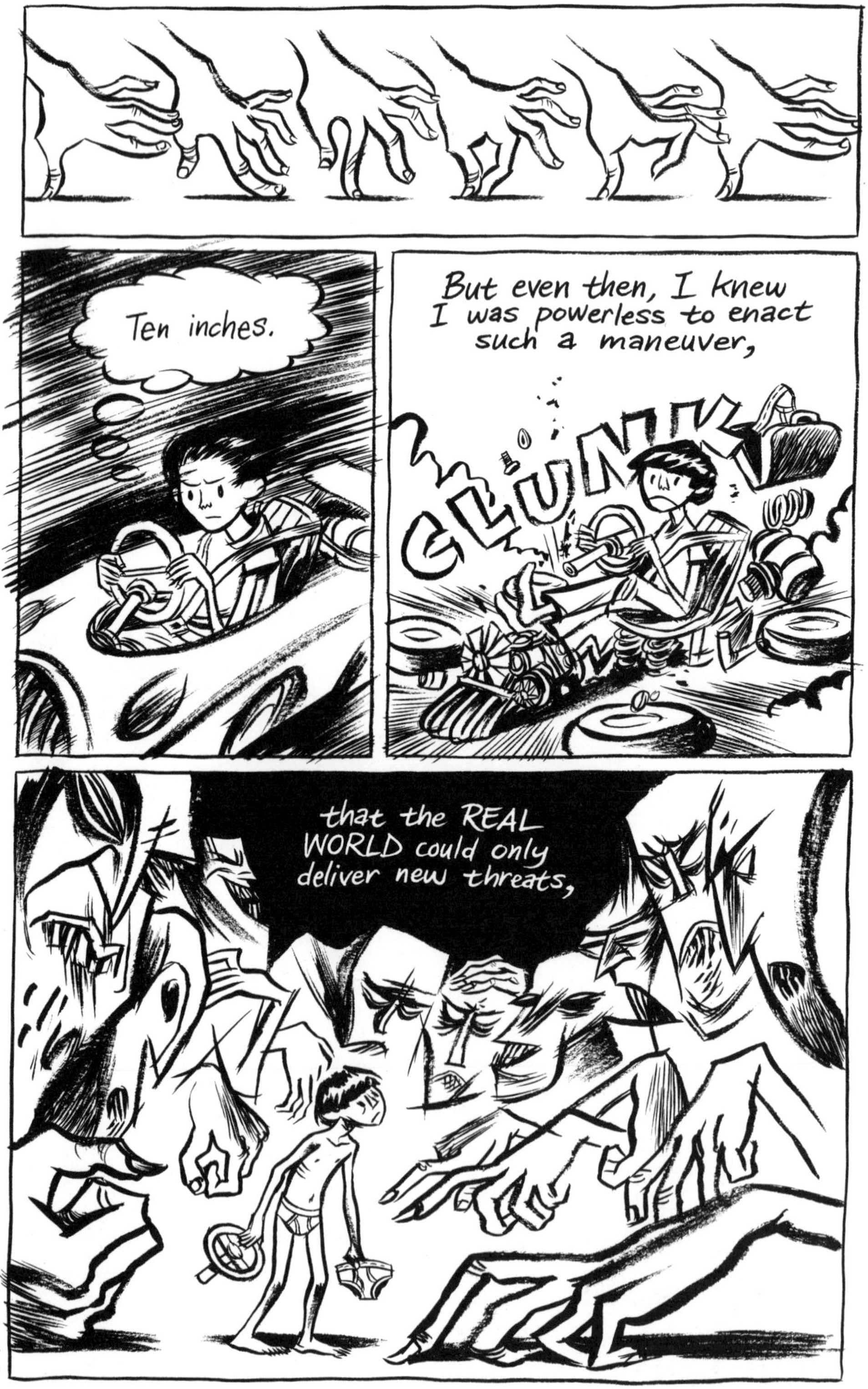
Ten inches.
But even then, I knew I was powerless to enact such a maneuver,
CLUNK
that the REAL WORLD could only deliver new threats,

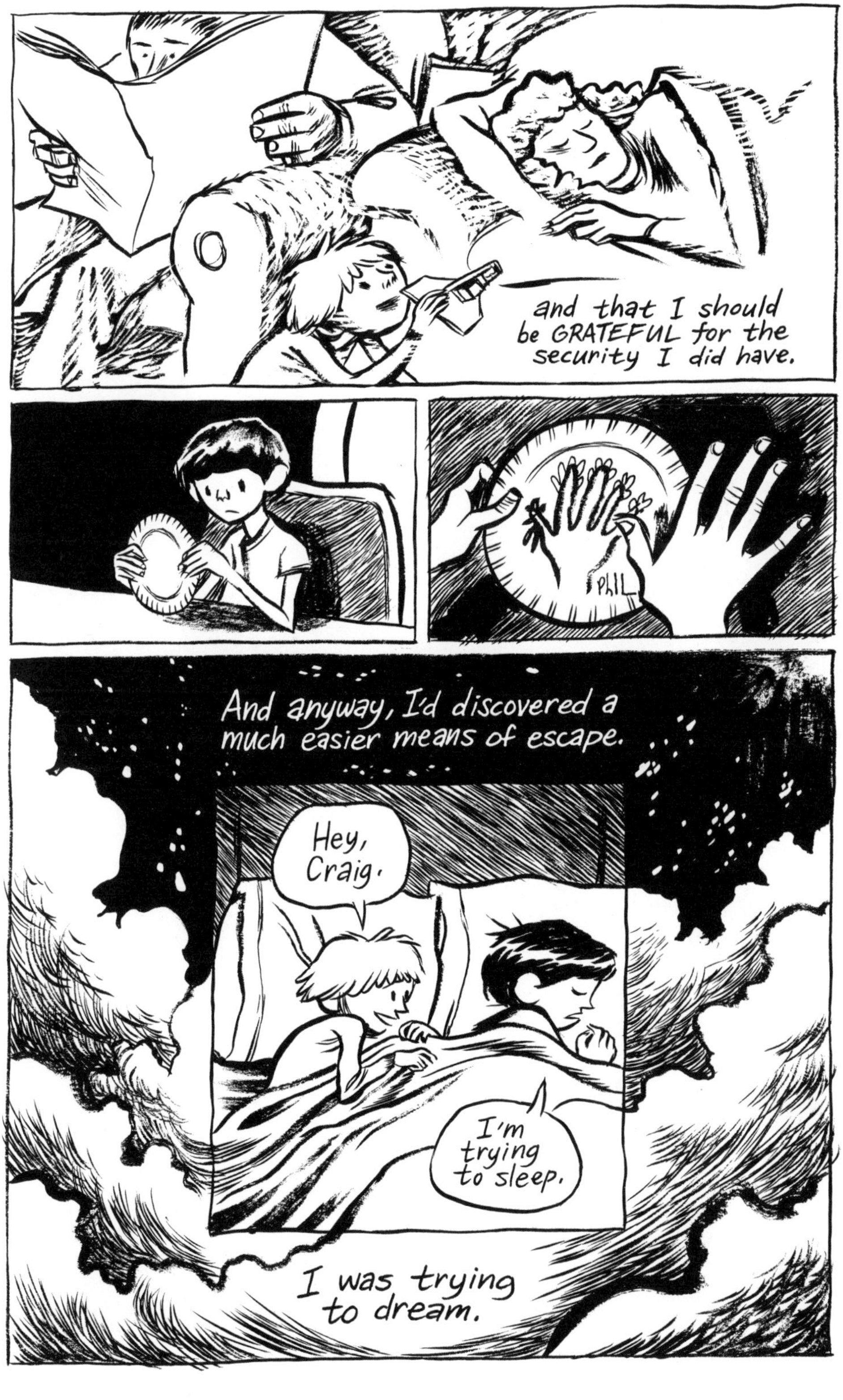
and that I should be GRATEFUL for the security I did have.
PHIL
And anyway, I'd discovered a much easier means of escape.
Hey, Craig.
I'm trying to sleep.
I was trying to dream.

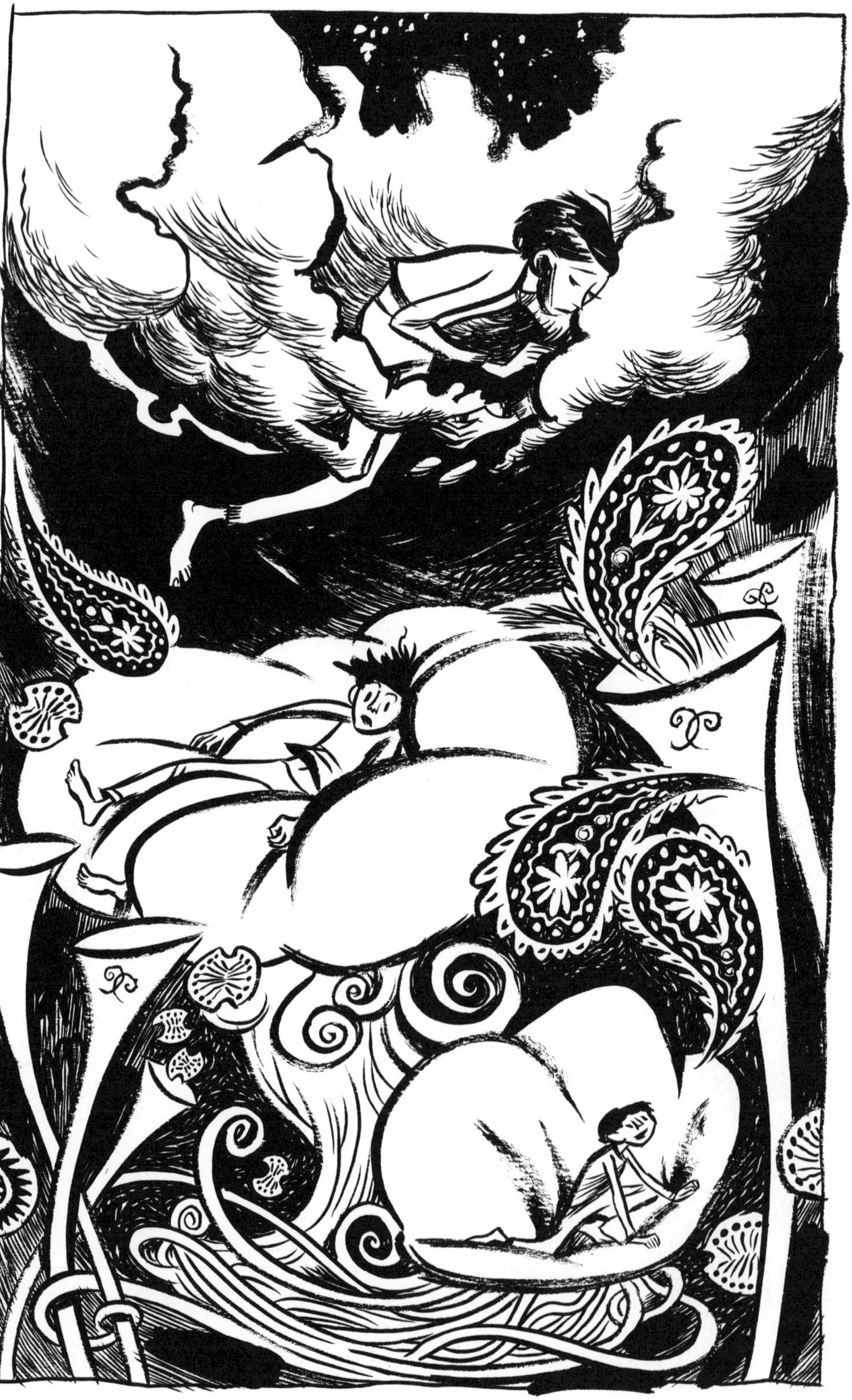

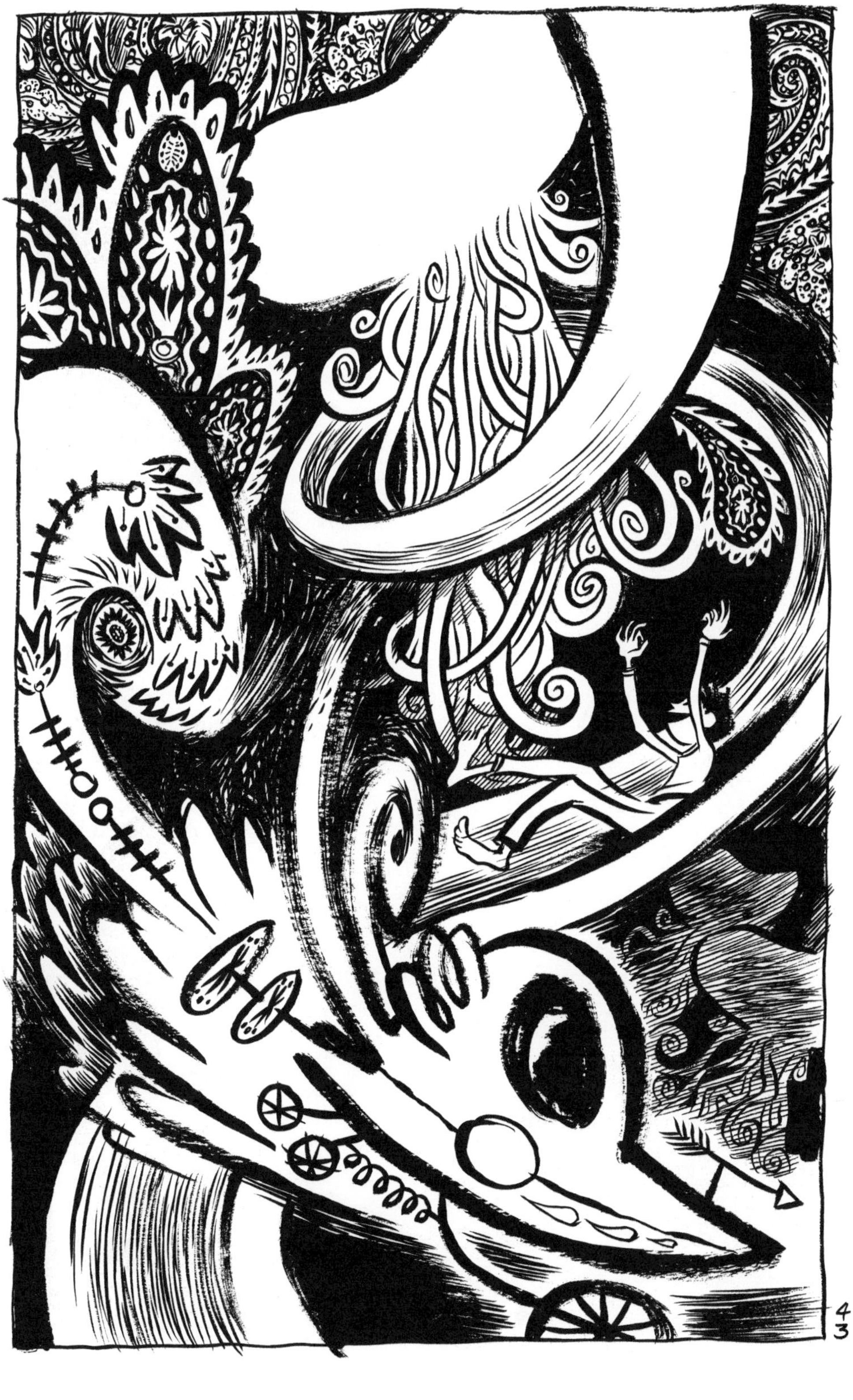

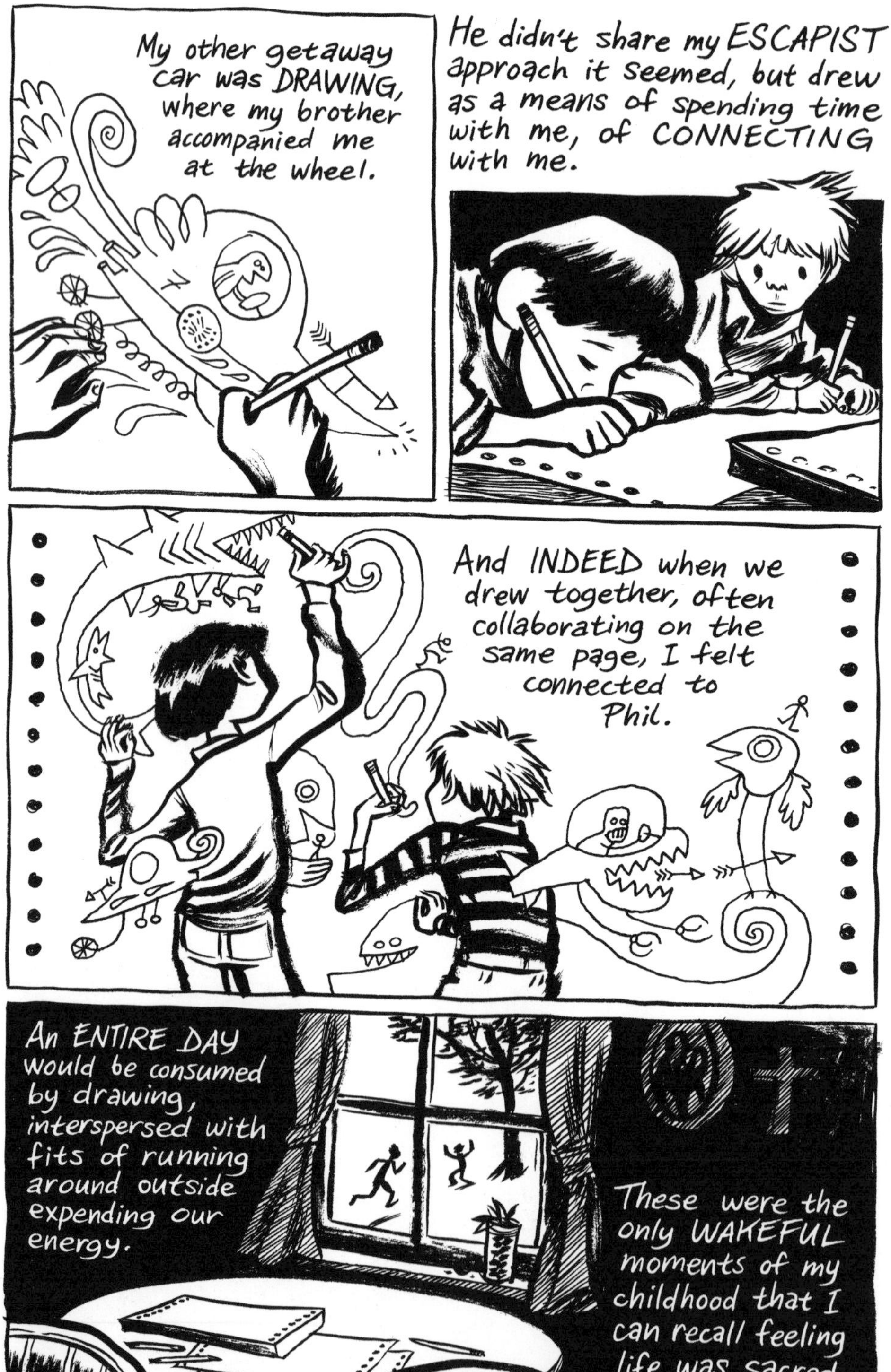
My other getaway car was DRAWING, where my brother accompanied me at the wheel.
He didn't share my ESCAPIST approach it seemed, but drew as a means of spending time with me, of CONNECTING with me.
And INDEED when we drew together, often collaborating on the same page, I felt connected to Phil.
An ENTIRE DAY would be consumed by drawing, interspersed with fits of running around outside expending our energy.
These were the only WAKEFUL moments of my childhood that I can recall feeling life was sacred or worthwhile.

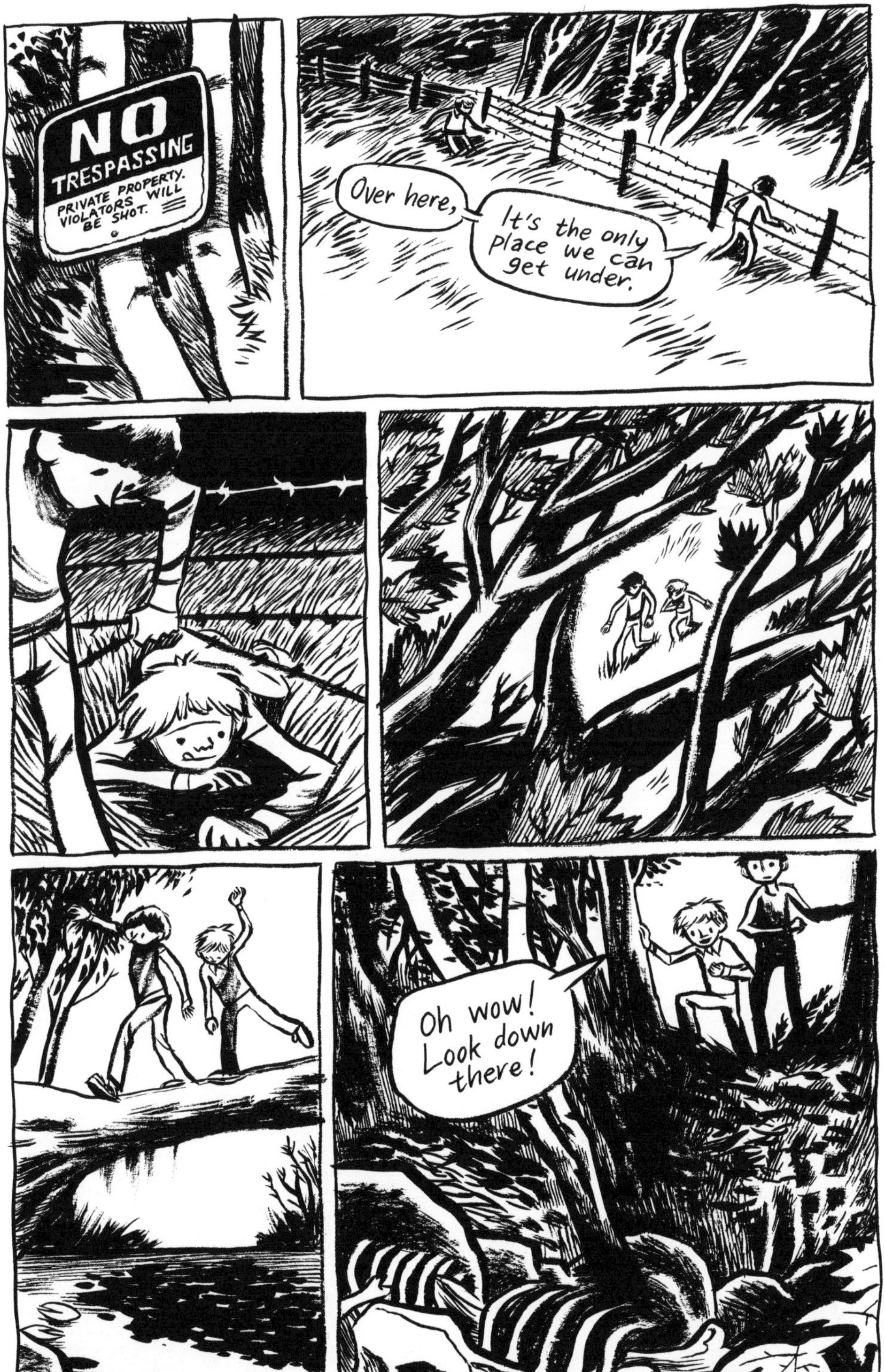
NO TRESPASSING
PRIVATE PROPERTY. VIOLATORS WILL BE SHOT.
Over here,
It's the only place we can get under.
Oh wow! Look down there!

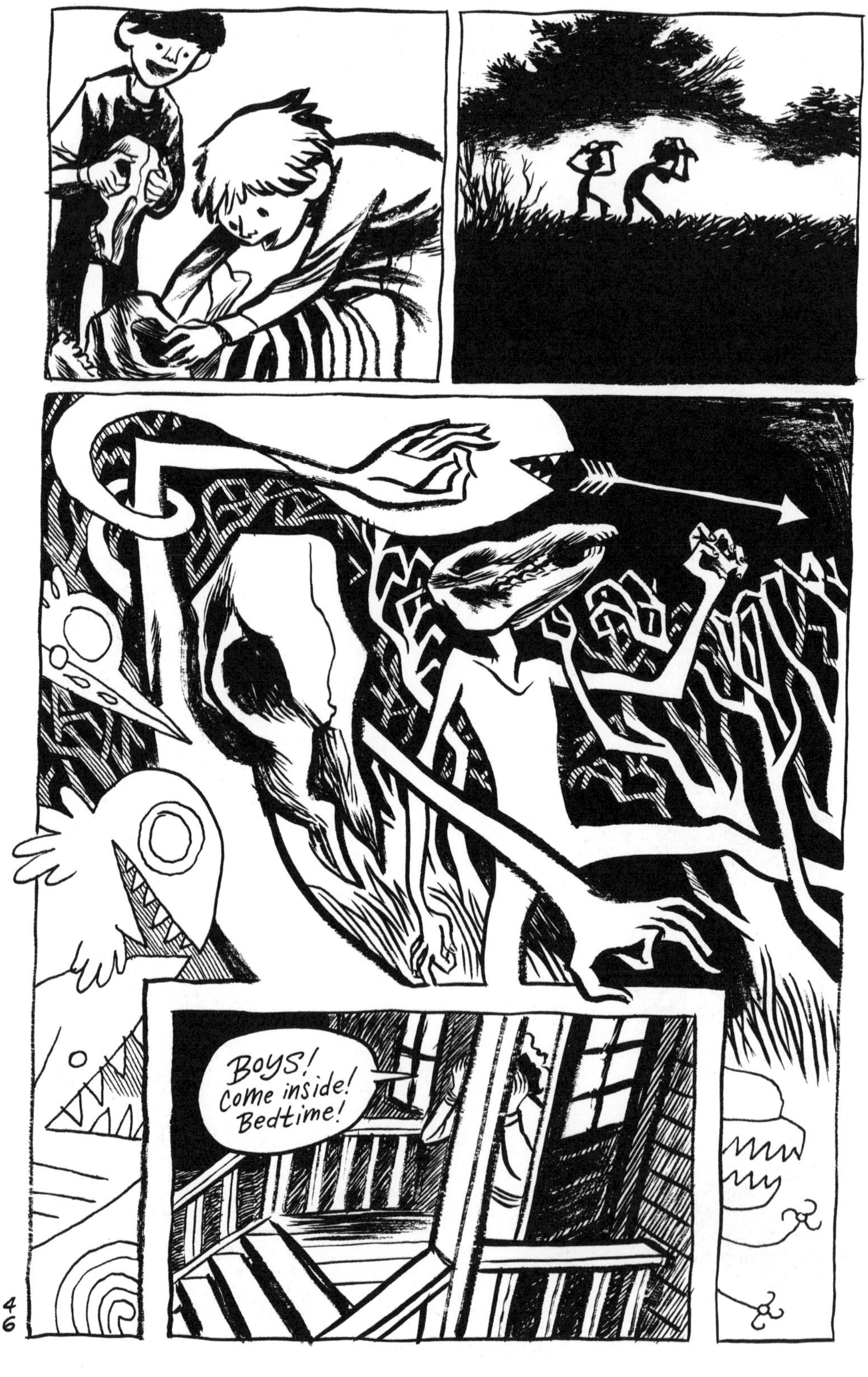
Boys! Come inside! Bedtime!

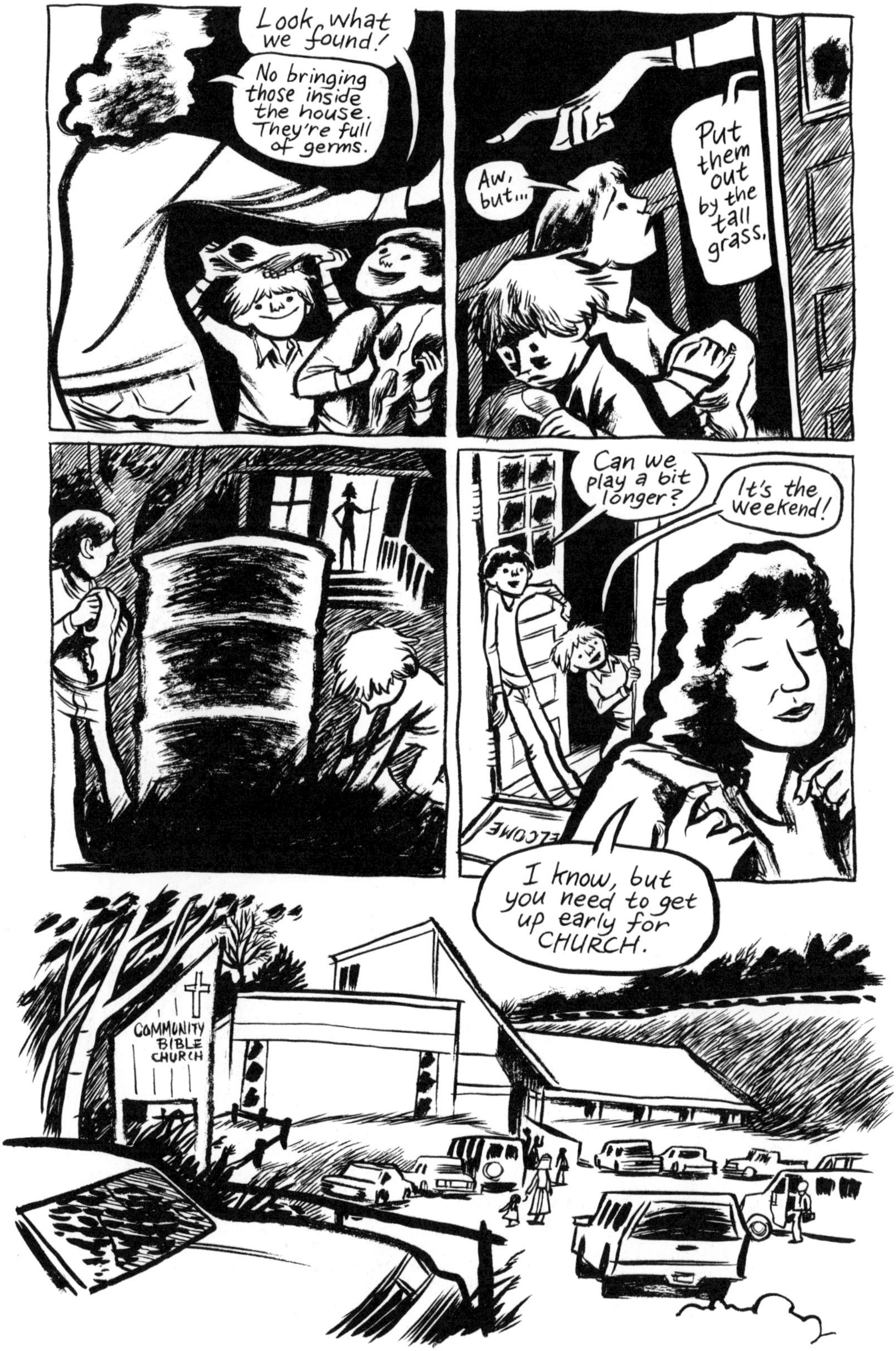
Look what we found!
No bringing those inside the house. They're full of germs.
Aw, but...
Put them out by the tall grass.
Can we play a bit longer?
It's the weekend!
I know, but you need to get up early for CHURCH.
WELCOME
COMMUNITY BIBLE CHURCH

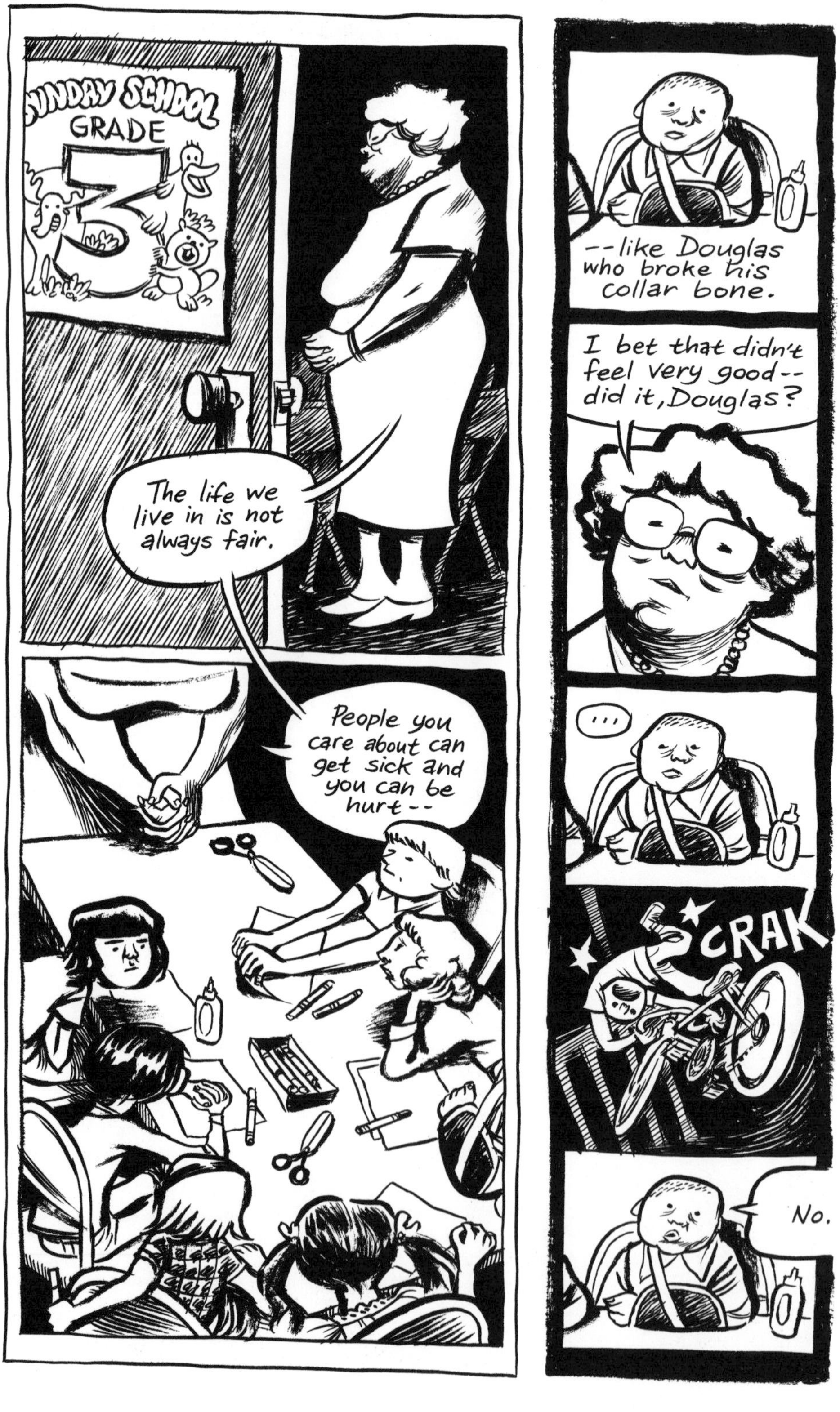

SUNDAY SCHOOL GRADE 3
The life we live in is not always fair.
People you care about can get sick and you can be hurt --
-- like Douglas who broke his collar bone.
I bet that didn't feel very good -- did it, Douglas?
...
CRAK
No.

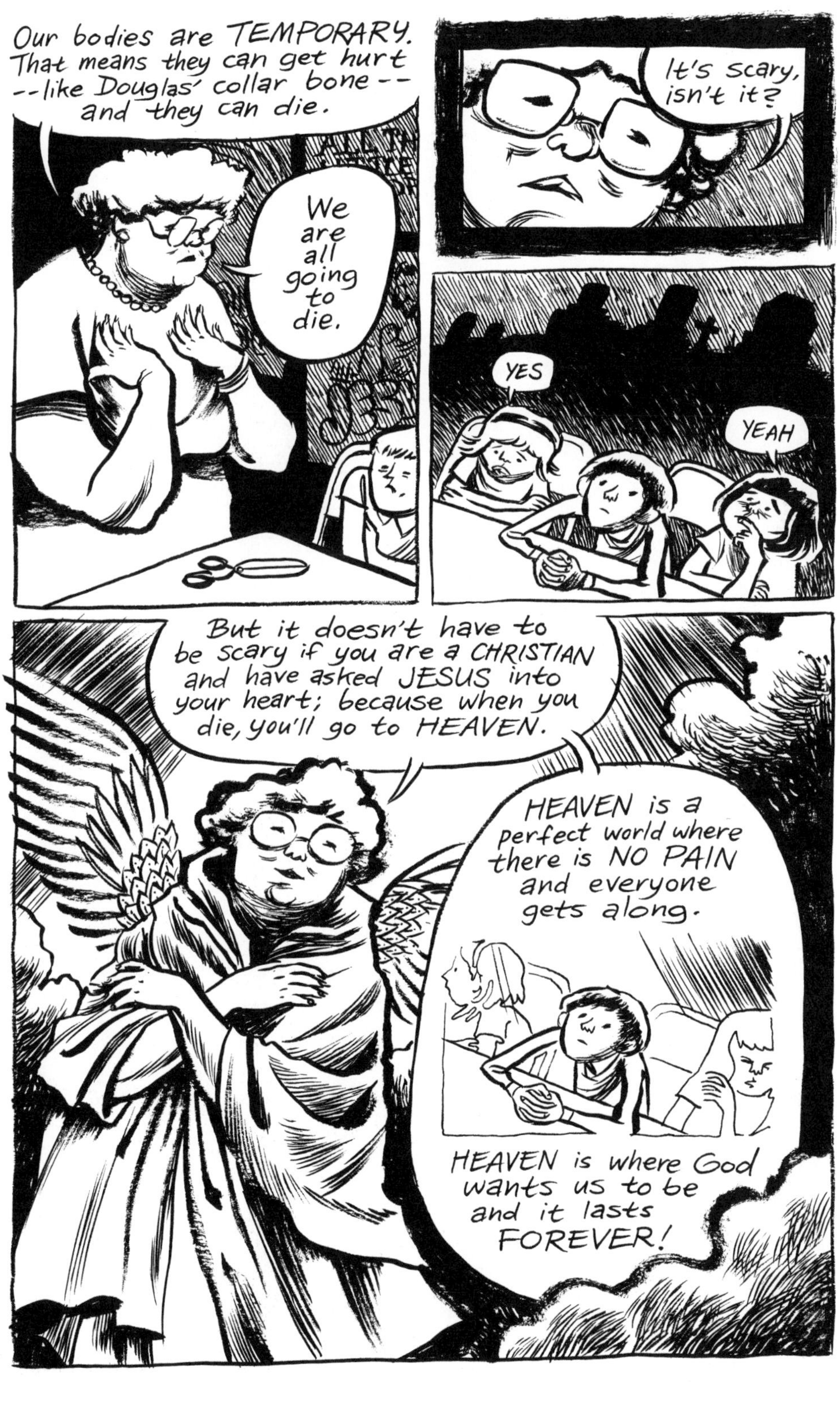

Our bodies are TEMPORARY. That means they can get hurt --like Douglas' collar bone-- and they can die.
We are all going to die.
It's scary, isn't it?
YES
YEAH
But it doesn't have to be scary if you are a CHRISTIAN and have asked JESUS into your heart; because when you die, you'll go to HEAVEN.
HEAVEN is a perfect world where there is NO PAIN and everyone gets along.
HEAVEN is where God wants us to be and it lasts FOREVER!

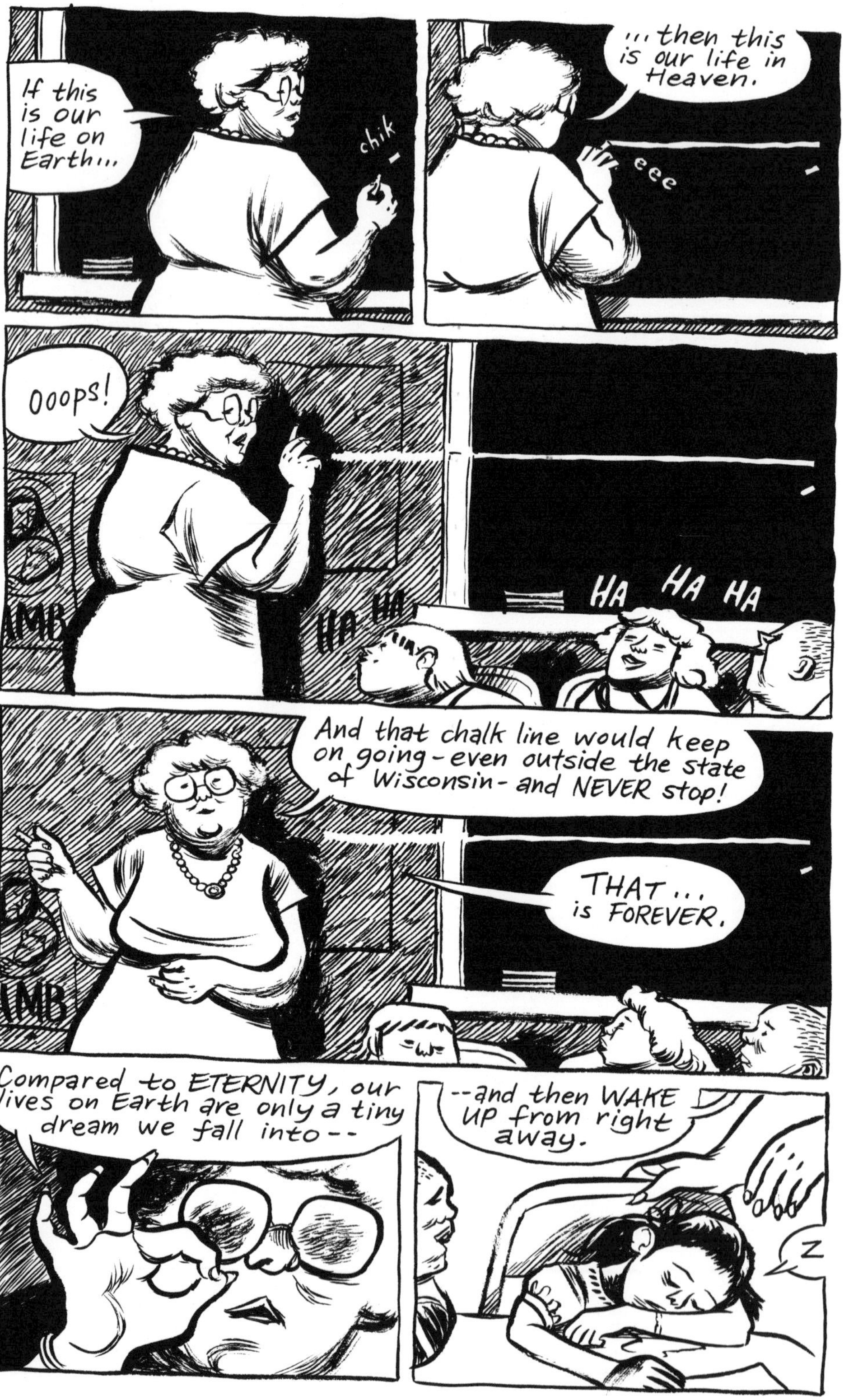
If this is our life on Earth...
chik
...then this is our life in Heaven.
eee
Ooops!
HA HA
HA HA HA
And that chalk line would keep on going - even outside the state of Wisconsin - and NEVER stop!
THAT... is FOREVER.
Compared to ETERNITY, our lives on Earth are only a tiny dream we fall into--
--and then WAKE UP from right away.
Z

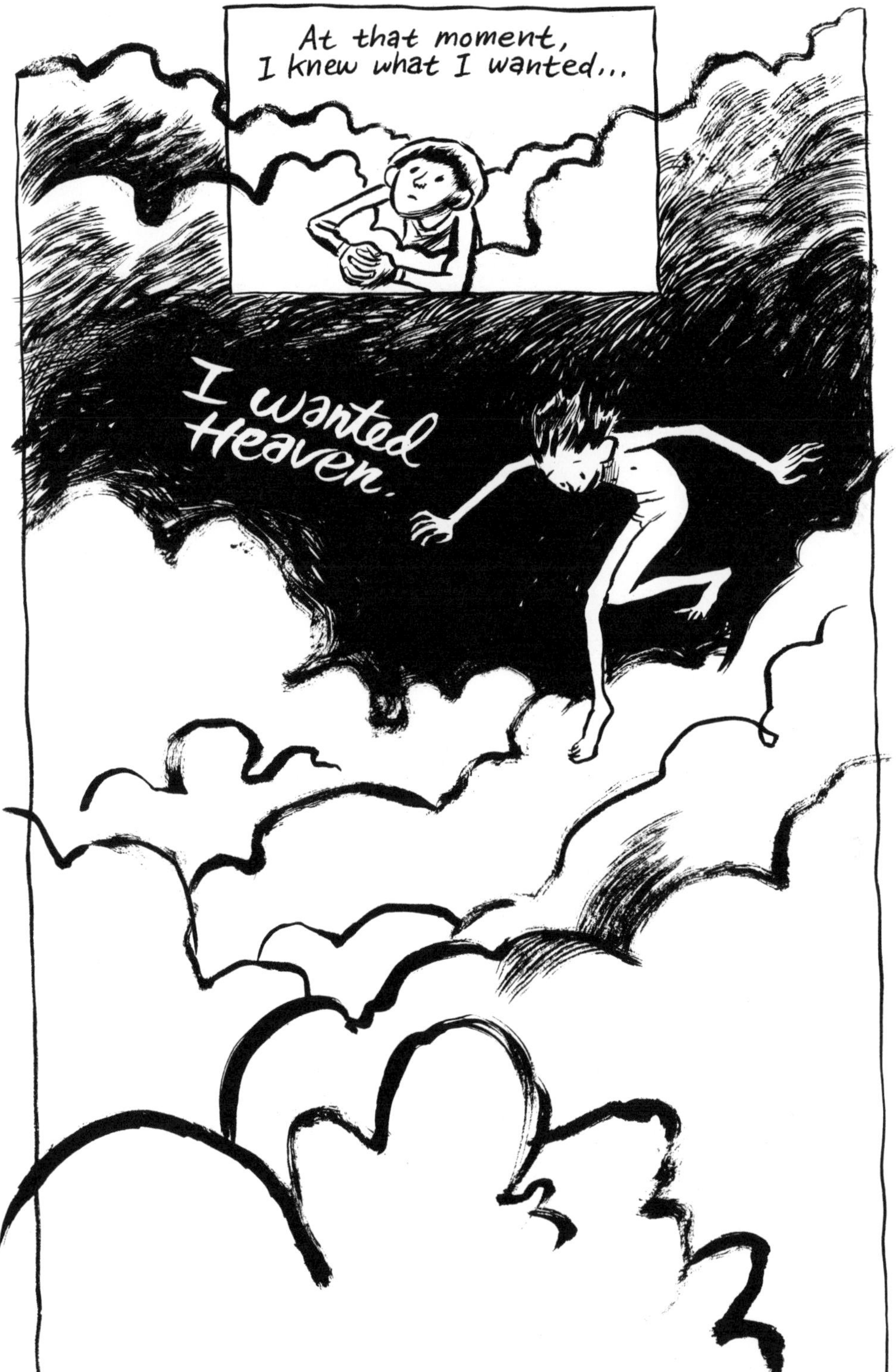
At that moment, I knew what I wanted...
I wanted Heaven.

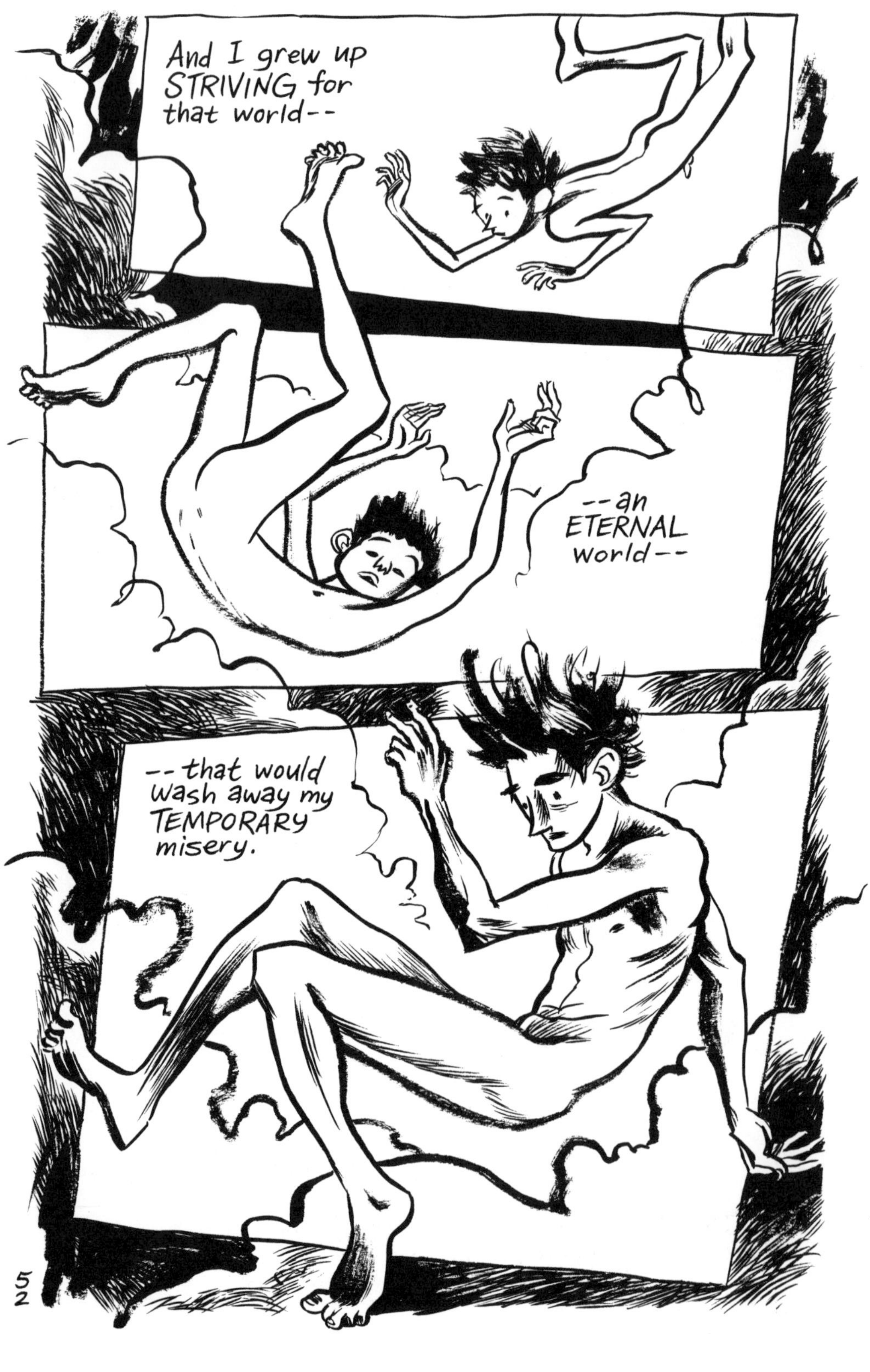
And I grew up STRIVING for that world--
--an ETERNAL world--
--that would wash away my TEMPORARY misery.

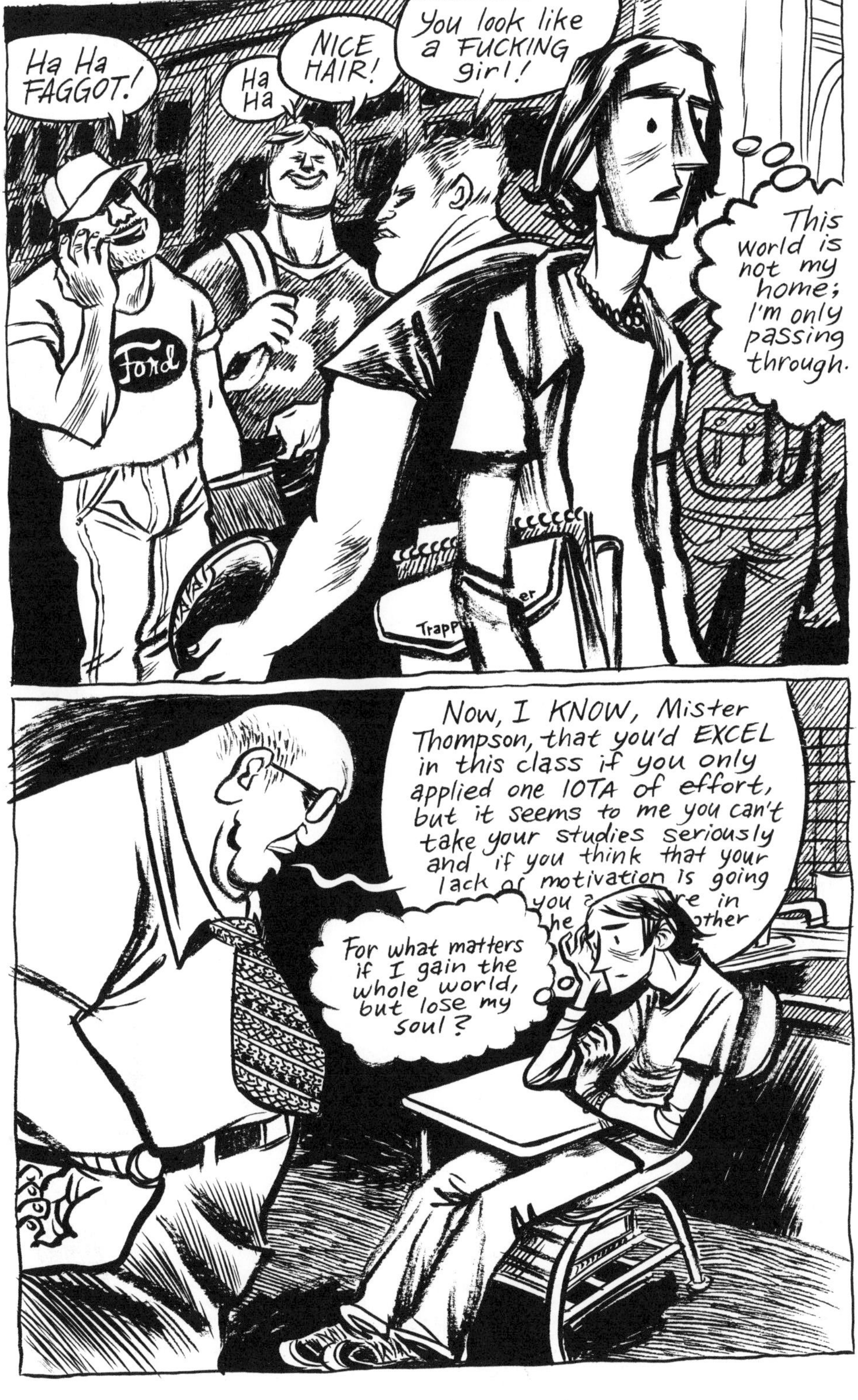
Ha Ha FAGGOT!
Ha Ha
NICE HAIR!
You look like a FUCKING girl!
This world is not my home; I'm only passing through.
Ford
Trapp
Now, I KNOW, Mister Thompson, that you'd EXCEL in this class if you only applied one IOTA of effort, but it seems to me you can't take your studies seriously and if you think that your lack of motivation is going
For what matters if I gain the whole world, but lose my soul?

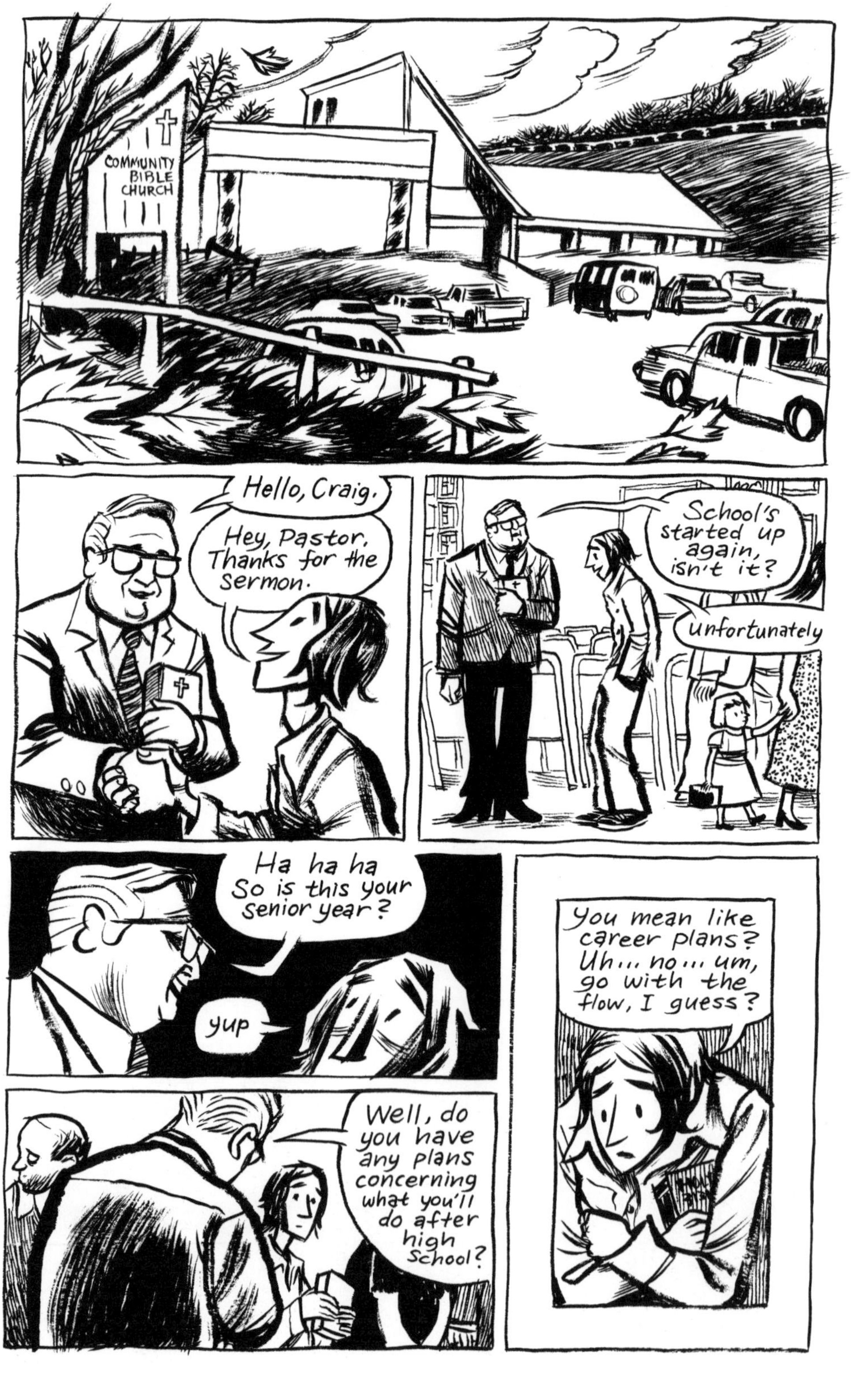
COMMUNITY BIBLE CHURCH
Hello, Craig.
Hey, Pastor. Thanks for the sermon.
School's started up again, isn't it?
unfortunately
Ha ha ha So is this your senior year?
yup
Well, do you have any plans concerning what you'll do after high school?
You mean like career plans? Uh... no... um, go with the flow, I guess?

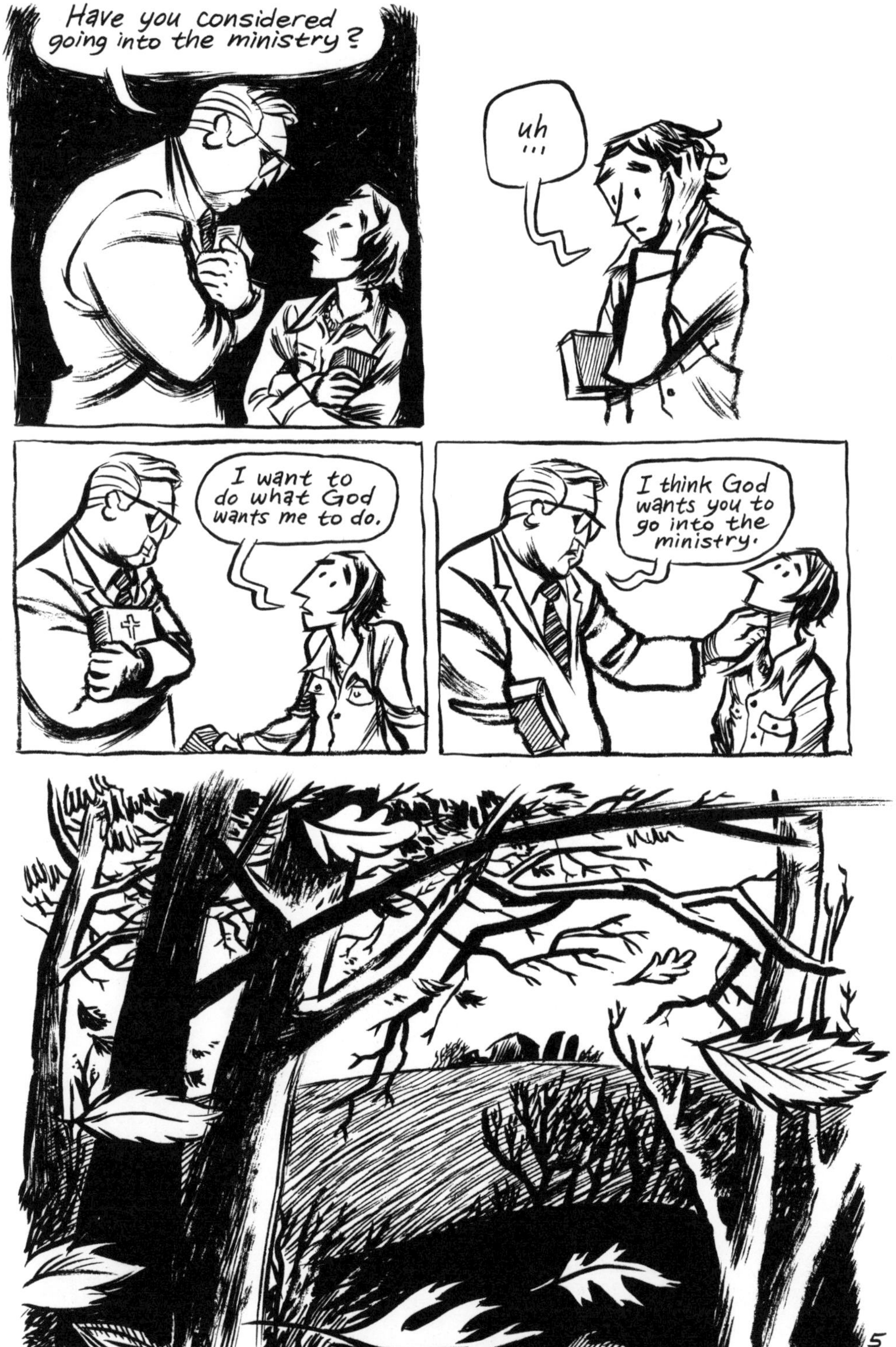
Have you considered going into the ministry?
uh ...
I want to do what God wants me to do.
I think God wants you to go into the ministry.

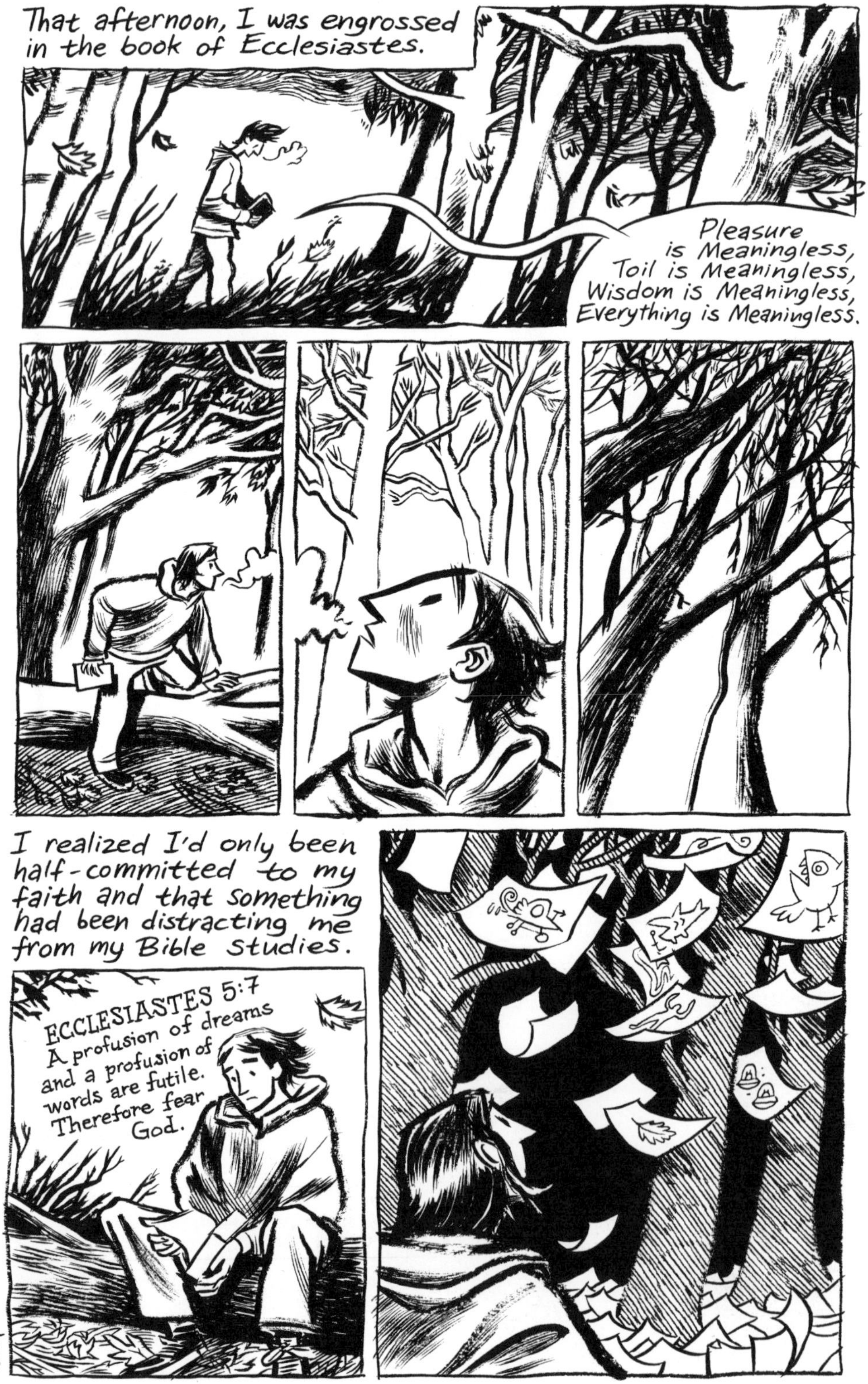
That afternoon, I was engrossed in the book of Ecclesiastes.
Pleasure is Meaningless, Toil is Meaningless, Wisdom is Meaningless, Everything is Meaningless.
I realized I'd only been half-committed to my faith and that something had been distracting me from my Bible studies.
ECCLESIASTES 5:7
A profusion of dreams and a profusion of words are futile. Therefore fear God.

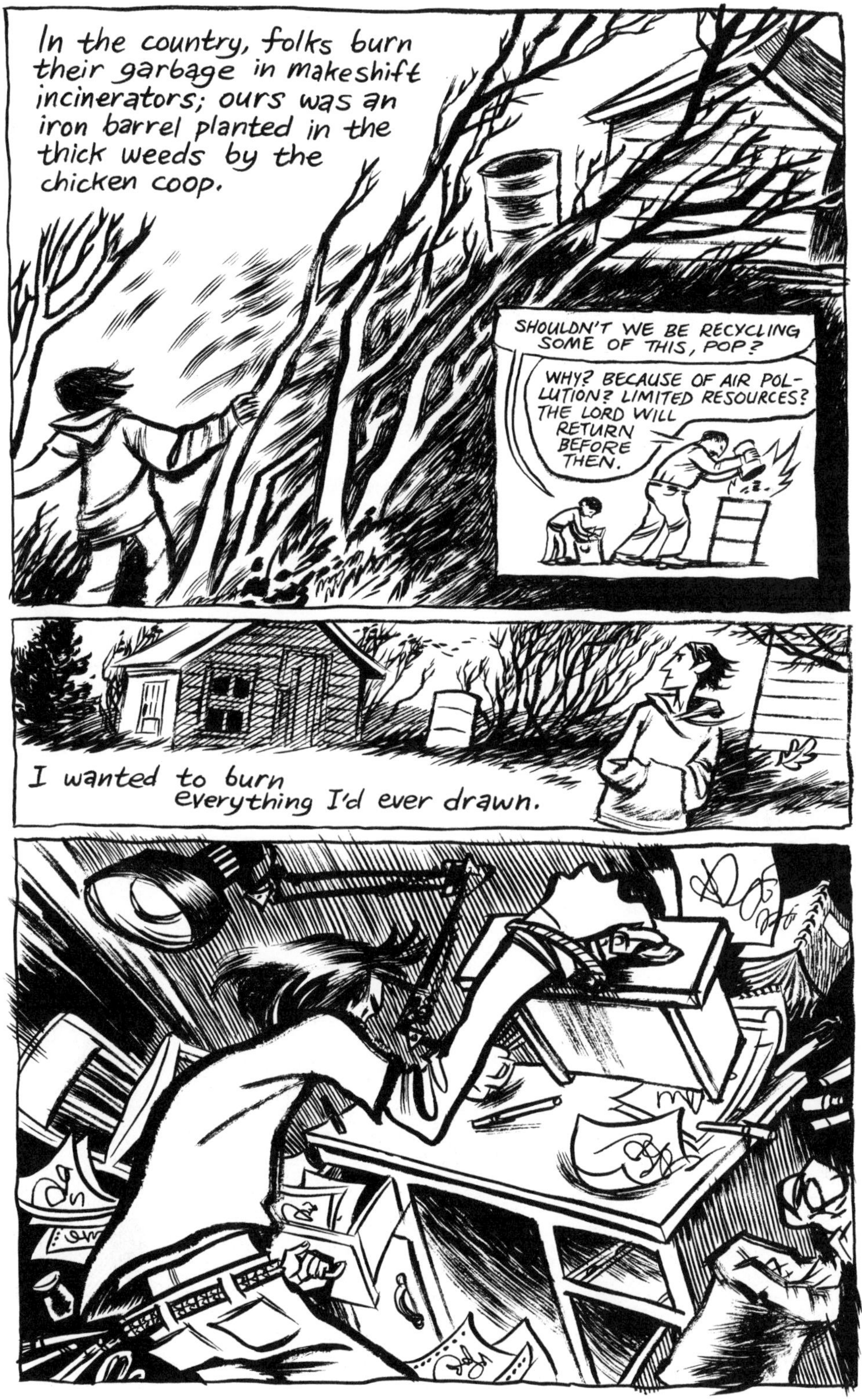
In the country, folks burn their garbage in makeshift incinerators; ours was an iron barrel planted in the thick weeds by the chicken coop.
SHOULDN'T WE BE RECYCLING SOME OF THIS, POP?
WHY? BECAUSE OF AIR POLLUTION? LIMITED RESOURCES? THE LORD WILL RETURN BEFORE THEN.
I wanted to burn everything I'd ever drawn.

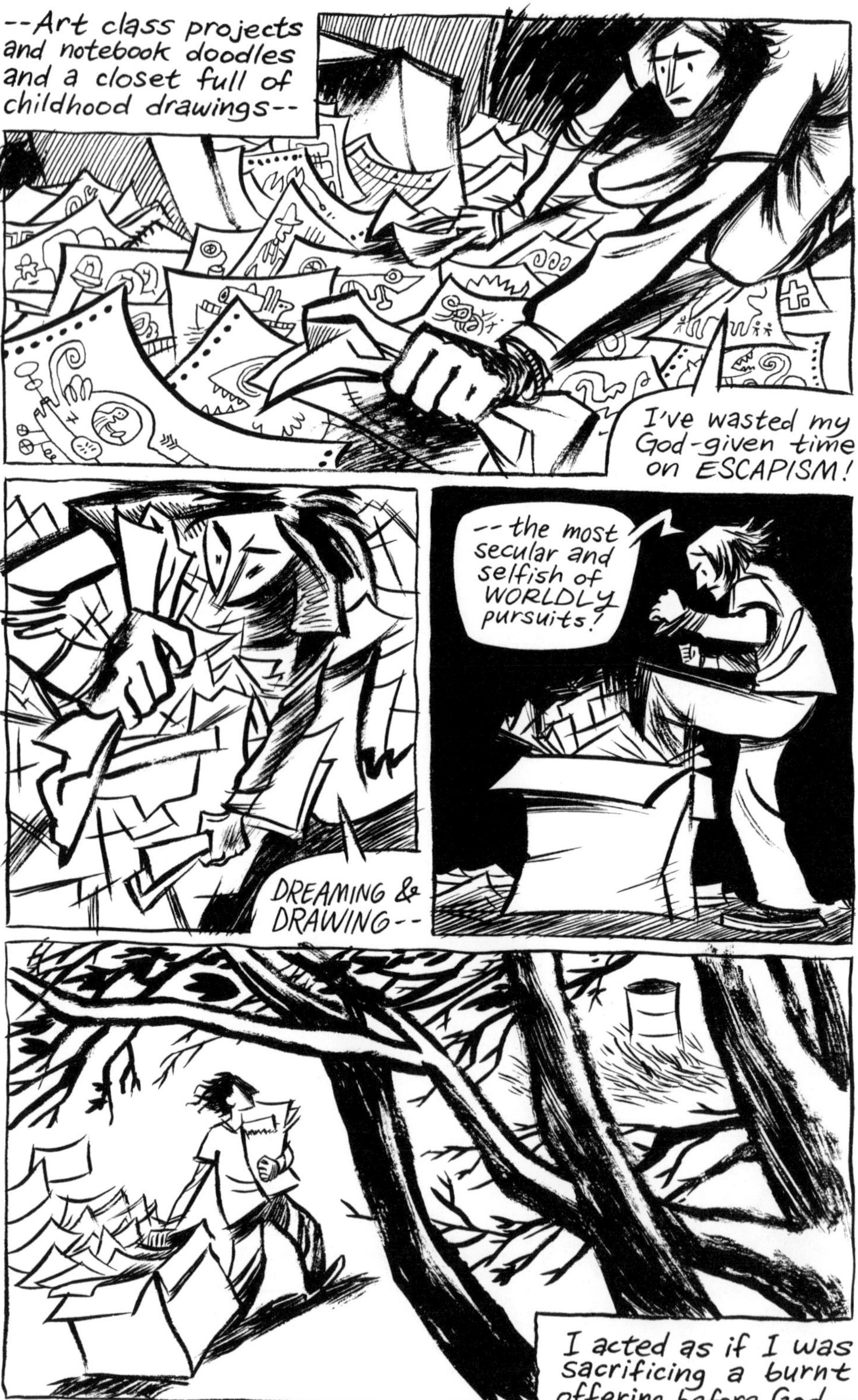
--Art class projects and notebook doodles and a closet full of childhood drawings--
I've wasted my God-given time on ESCAPISM!
DREAMING & DRAWING--
--the most secular and selfish of WORLDLY pursuits!
I acted as if I was sacrificing a burnt offering before God--

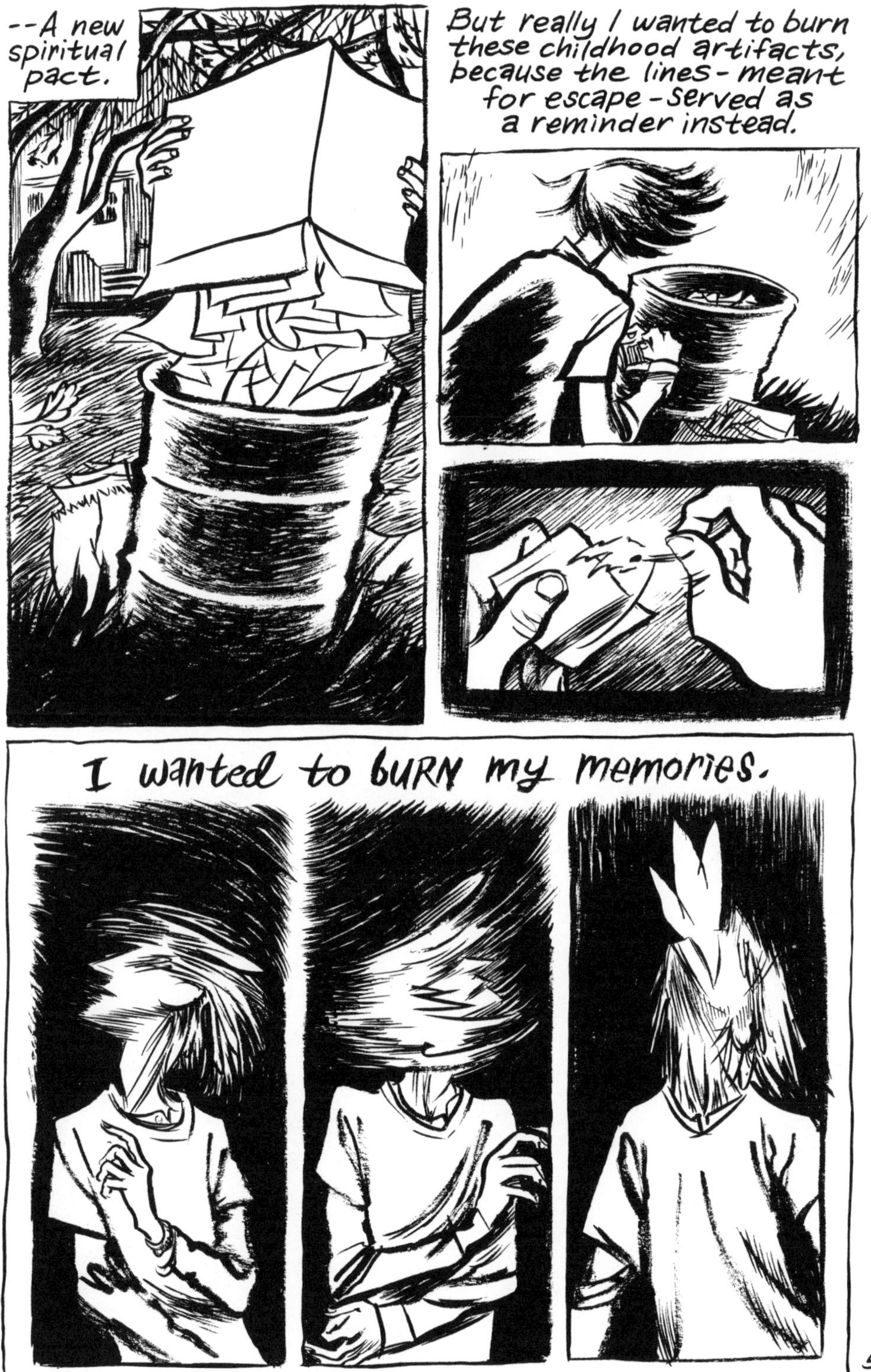
--A new spiritual pact.
But really I wanted to burn these childhood artifacts, because the lines- meant for escape - served as a reminder instead.
I wanted to burn my memories.

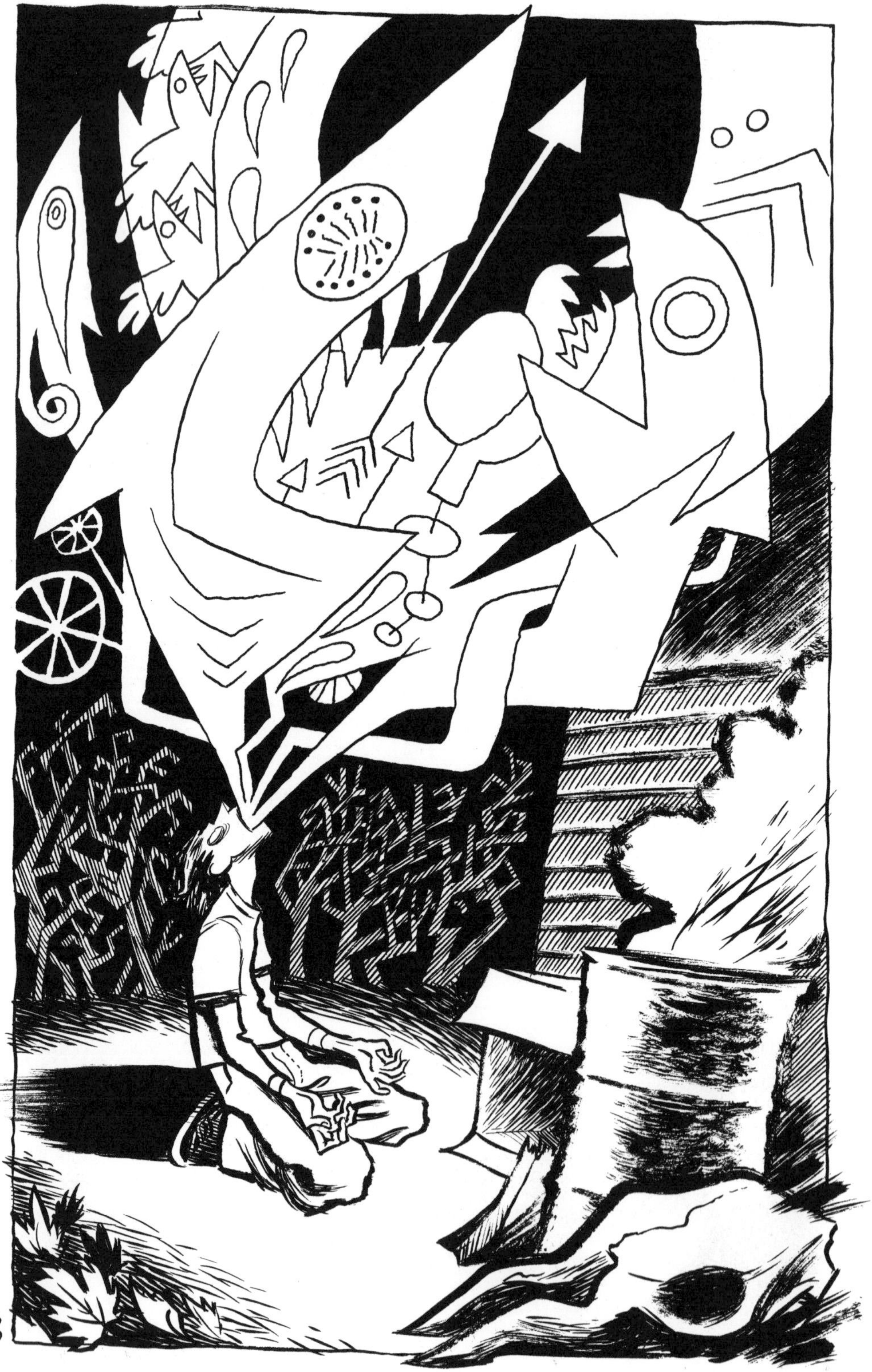

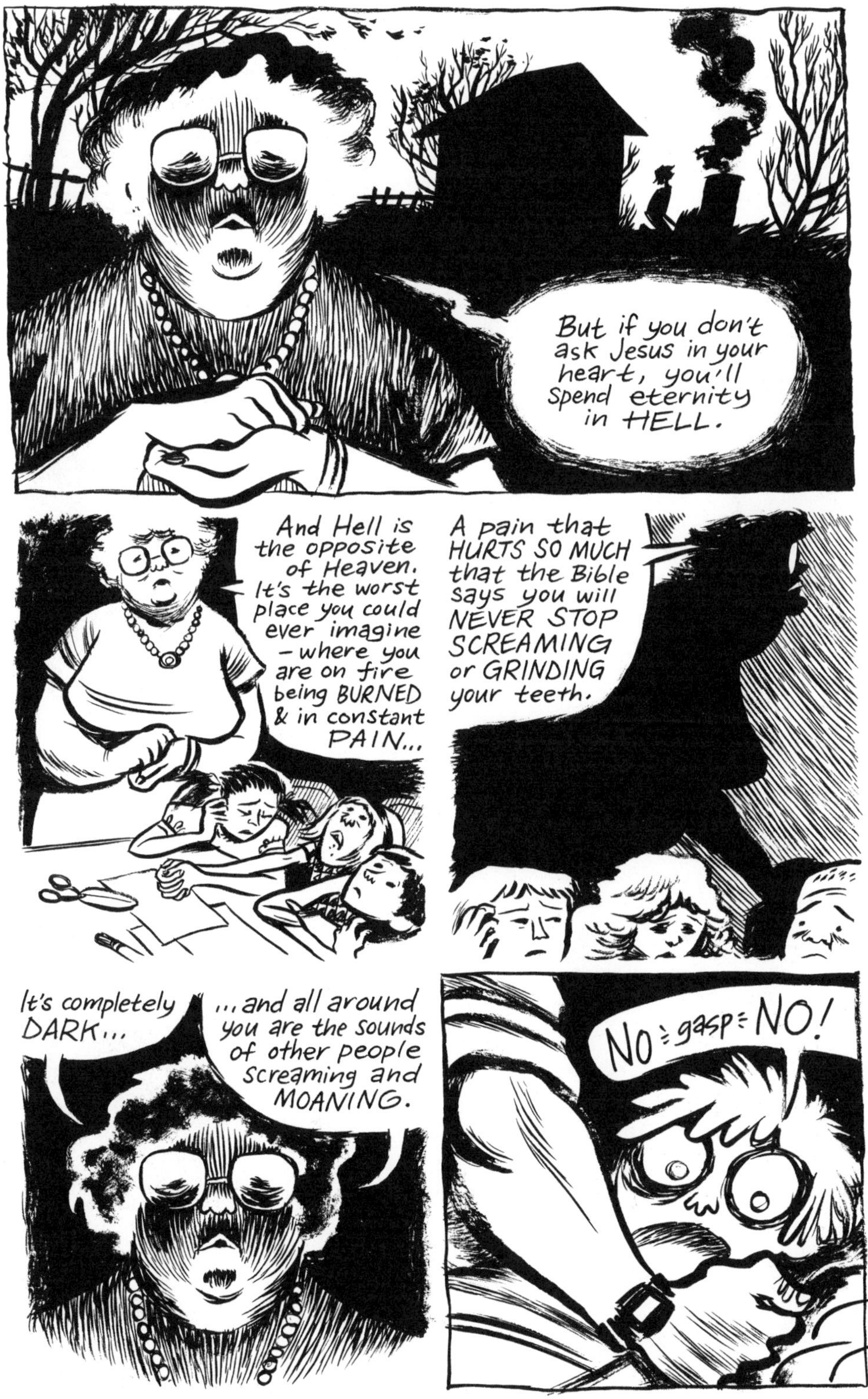
But if you don't ask Jesus in your heart, you'll spend eternity in HELL.
And Hell is the opposite of Heaven. It's the worst place you could ever imagine —where you are on fire being BURNED & in constant PAIN...
A pain that HURTS SO MUCH that the Bible says you will NEVER STOP SCREAMING or GRINDING your teeth.
It's completely DARK...
...and all around you are the sounds of other people screaming and MOANING.
No gasp NO!

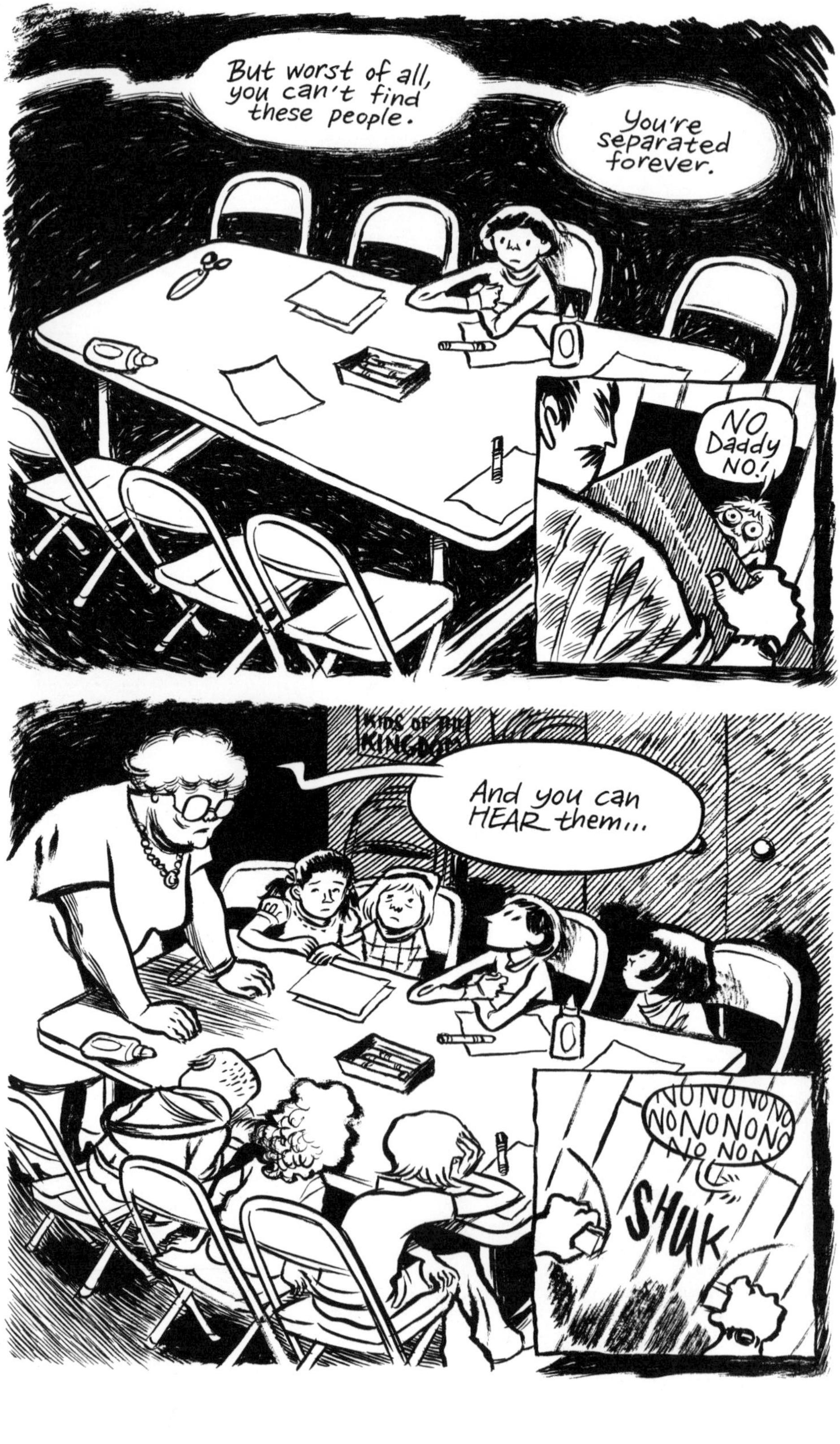
But worst of all, you can't find these people.
You're separated forever.
NO Daddy NO!
KIDS OF THE KINGDOM
And you can HEAR them...
NONONONO NONONONO NO NON
SHUK

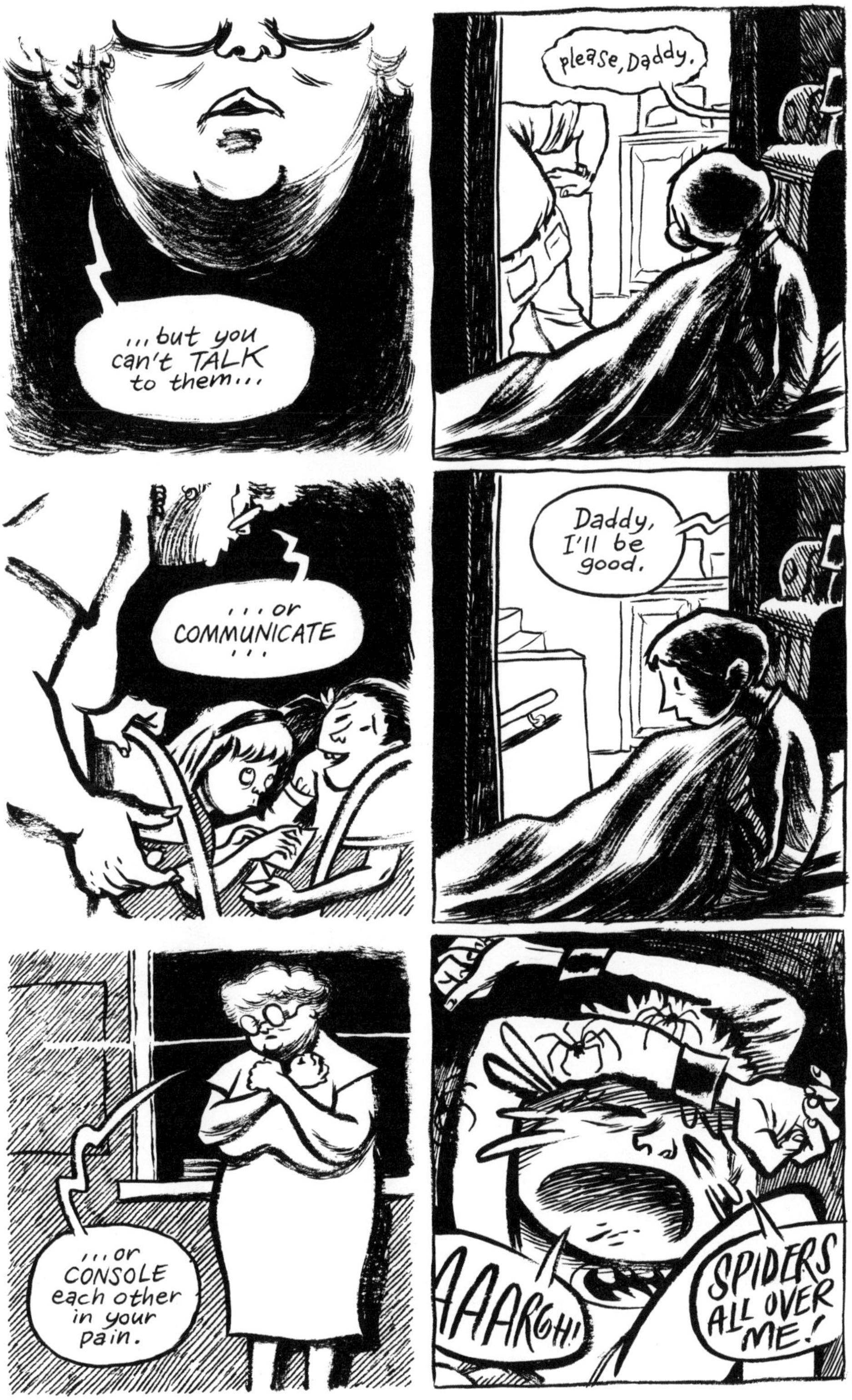
...but you can't TALK to them...
please, Daddy.
...or COMMUNICATE...
Daddy, I'll be good.
...or CONSOLE each other in your pain.
AAARGH!
SPIDERS ALL OVER ME!

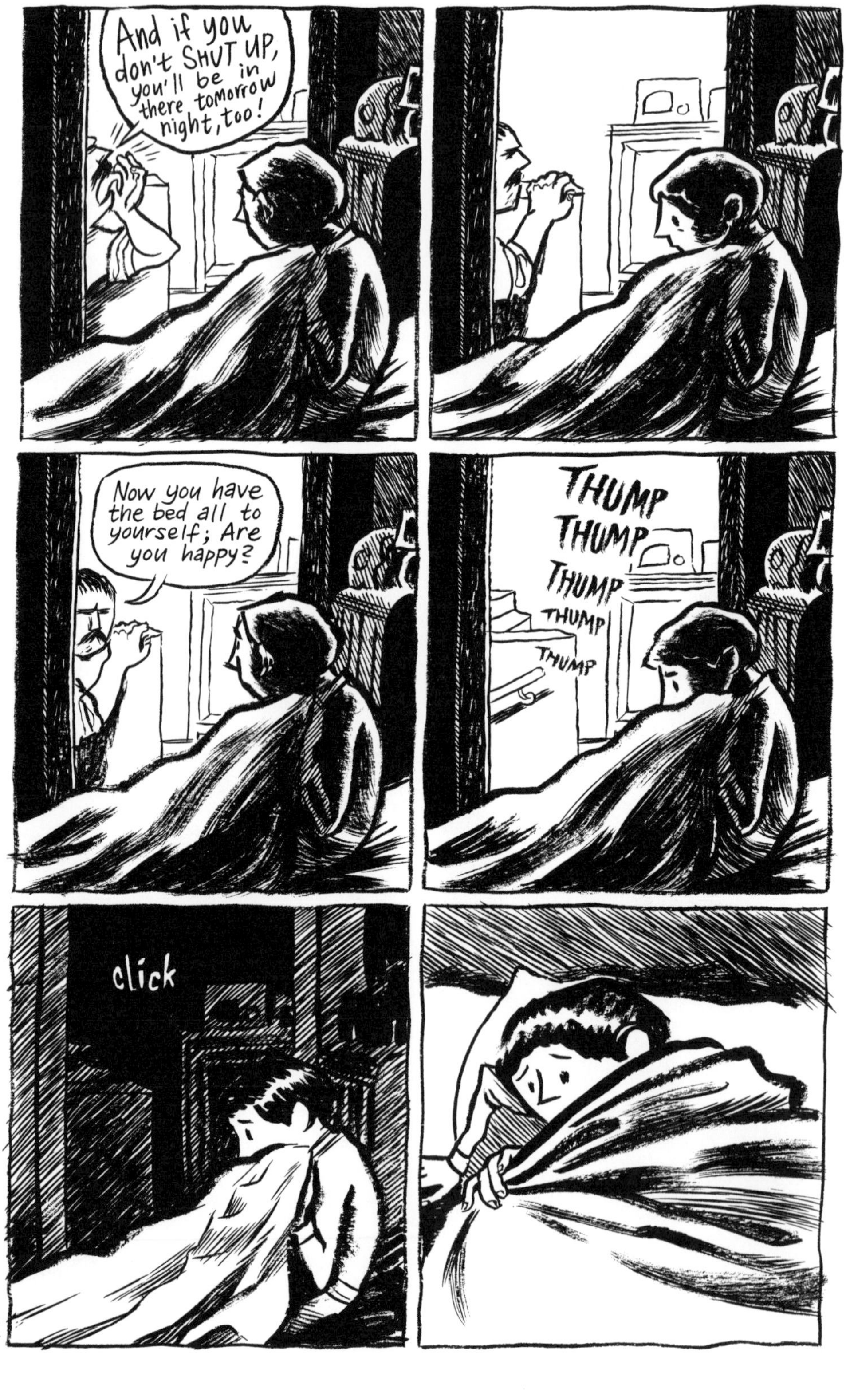
And if you don't SHUT UP, you'll be in there tomorrow night, too!
Now you have the bed all to yourself; Are you happy?
THUMP
THUMP
THUMP
THUMP
THUMP
click

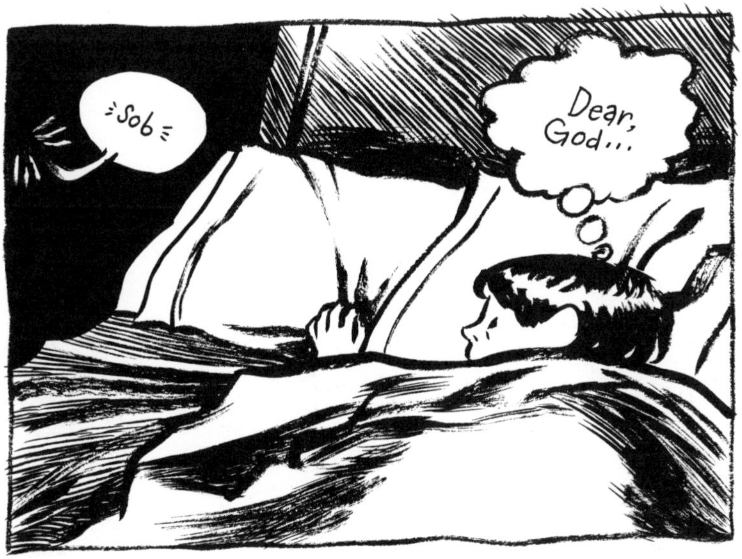
sob
Dear, God...

II

Stirring Furnace

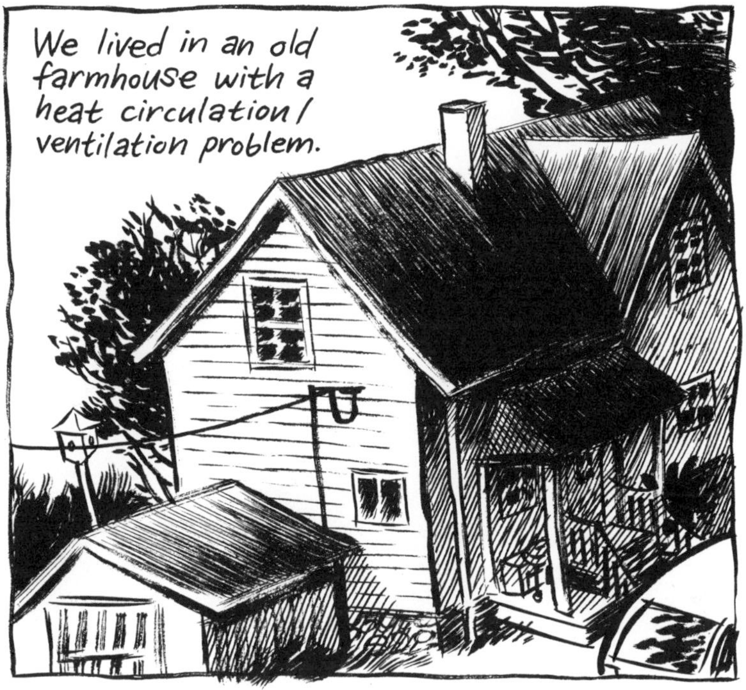
We lived in an old farmhouse with a heat circulation/ ventilation problem.

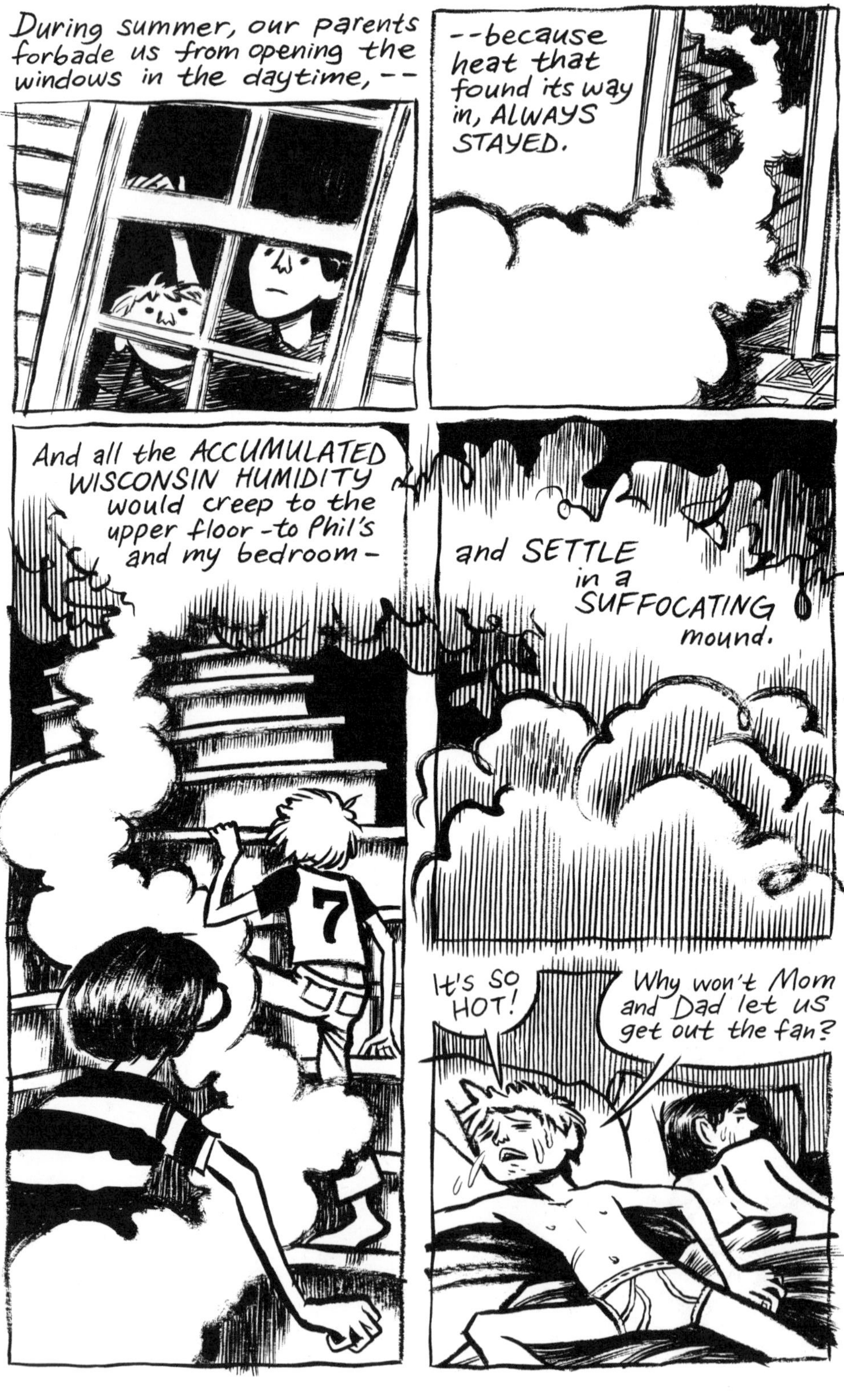

During summer, our parents forbade us from opening the windows in the daytime, --
--because heat that found its way in, ALWAYS STAYED.
And all the ACCUMULATED WISCONSIN HUMIDITY would creep to the upper floor - to Phil's and my bedroom -
and SETTLE in a SUFFOCATING mound.
It's SO HOT!
Why won't Mom and Dad let us get out the fan?
7

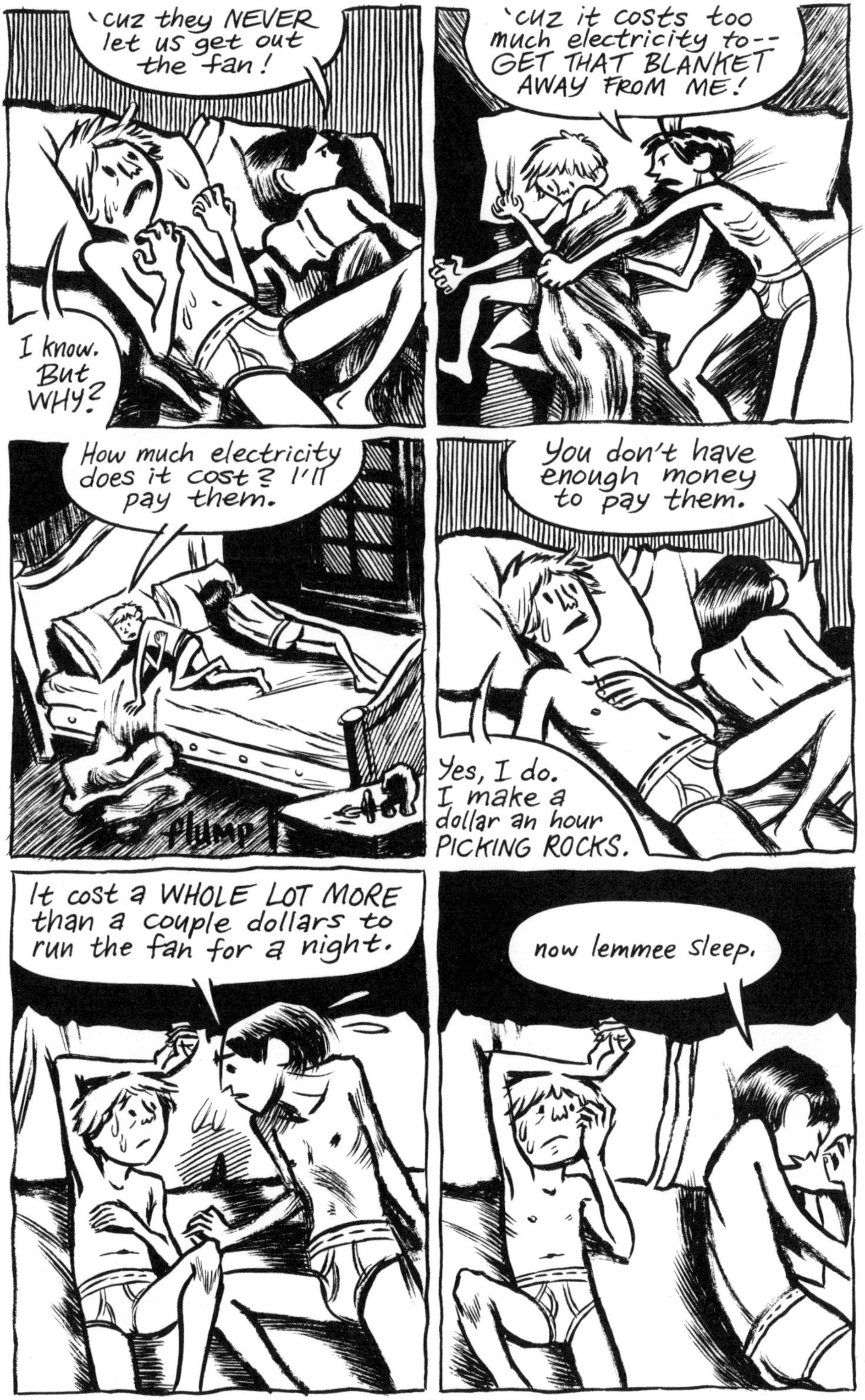
`cuz they NEVER let us get out the fan!
I know. But WHY?
`cuz it costs too much electricity to-- GET THAT BLANKET AWAY FROM ME!
How much electricity does it cost? I'll pay them.
flump!
You don't have enough money to pay them.
Yes, I do. I make a dollar an hour PICKING ROCKS.
It cost a WHOLE LOT MORE than a couple dollars to run the fan for a night.
now lemmee sleep.

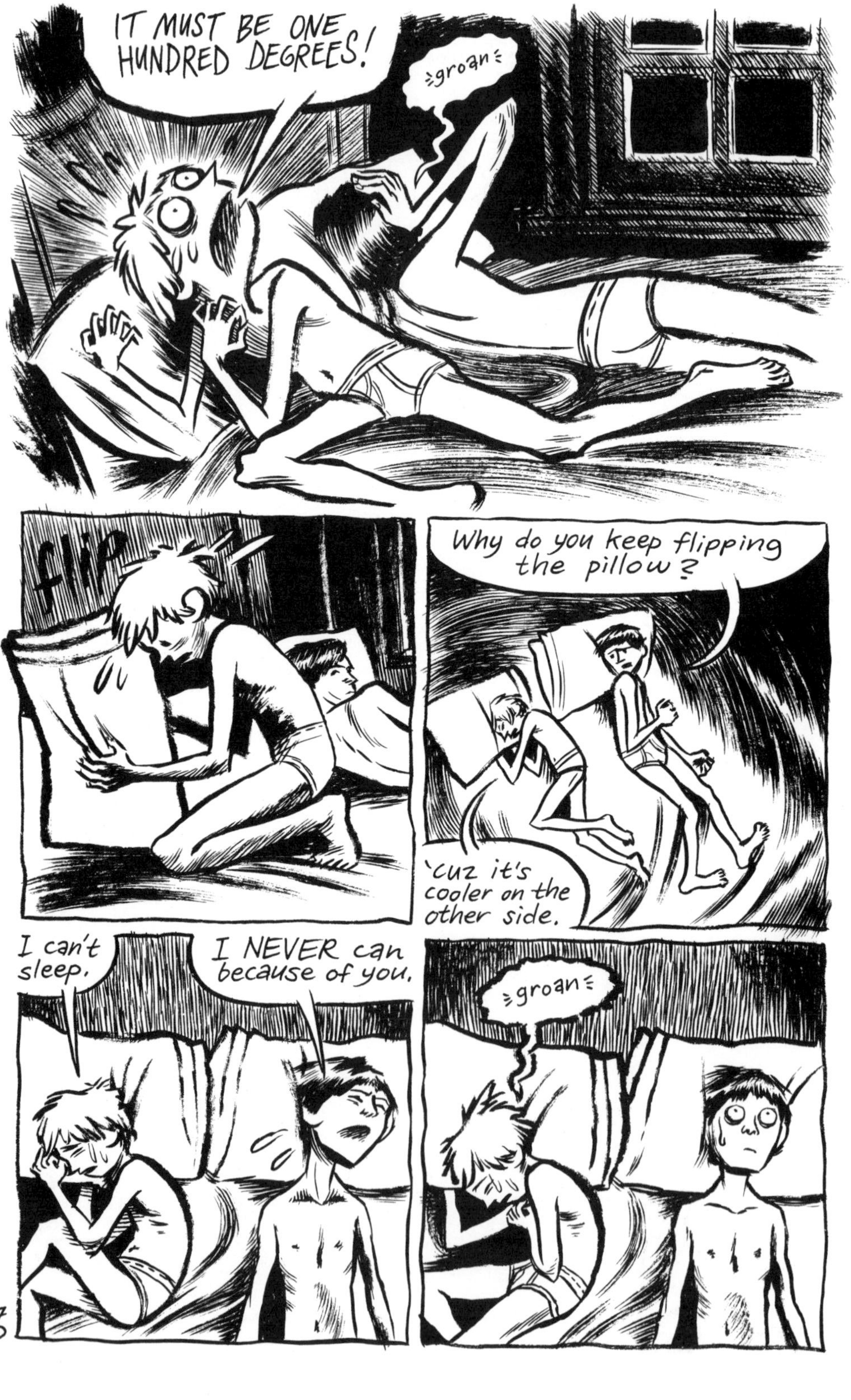
IT MUST BE ONE HUNDRED DEGREES!
groan
flip
Why do you keep flipping the pillow?
'cuz it's cooler on the other side.
I can't sleep.
I NEVER can because of you.
groan

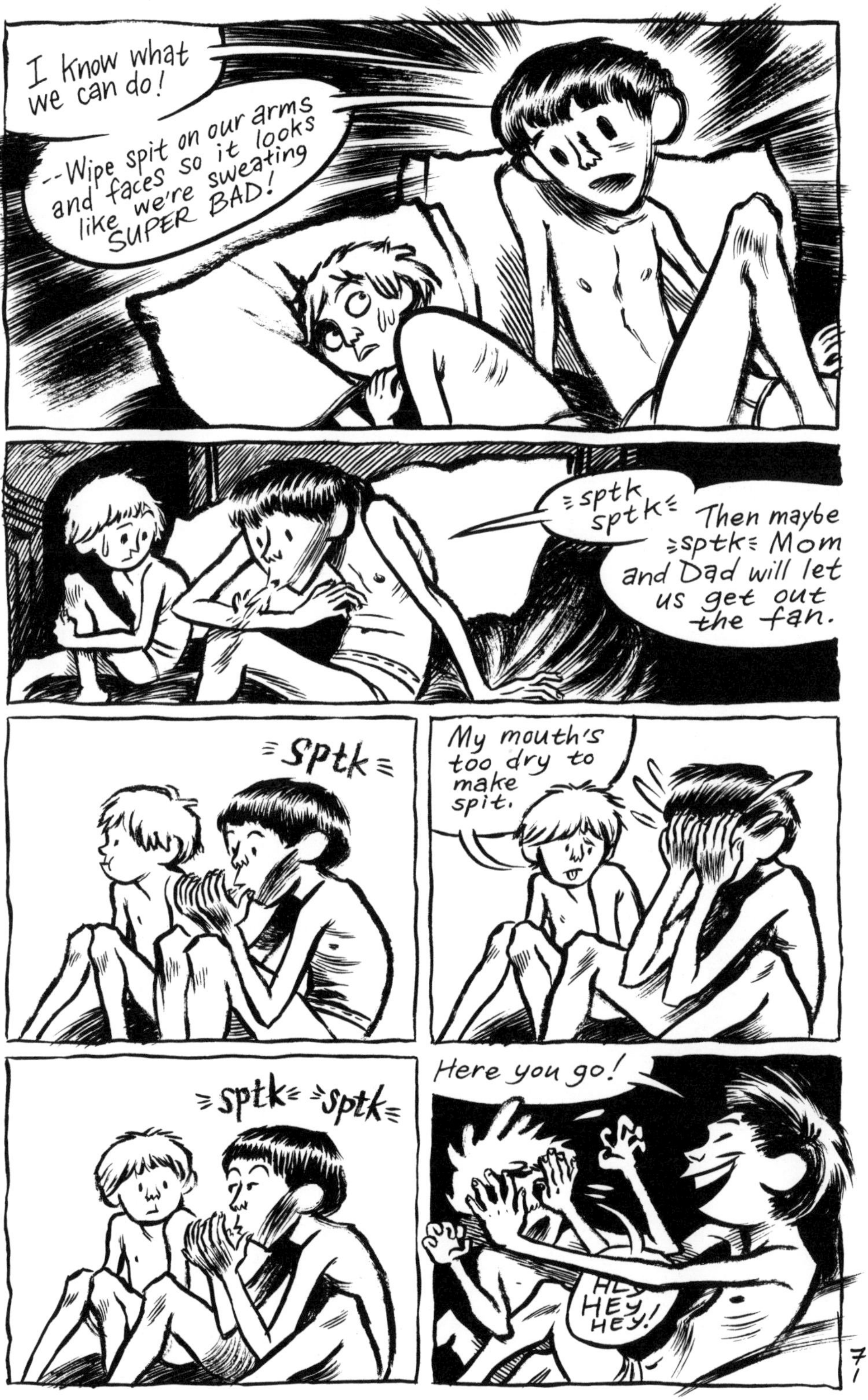
I know what we can do!
--Wipe spit on our arms and faces so it looks like we're sweating like we're SUPER BAD!
sptk sptk
Then maybe sptk Mom and Dad will let us get out the fan.
Sptk
My mouth's too dry to make spit.
sptk sptk
Here you go!
HEY HEY HEY!

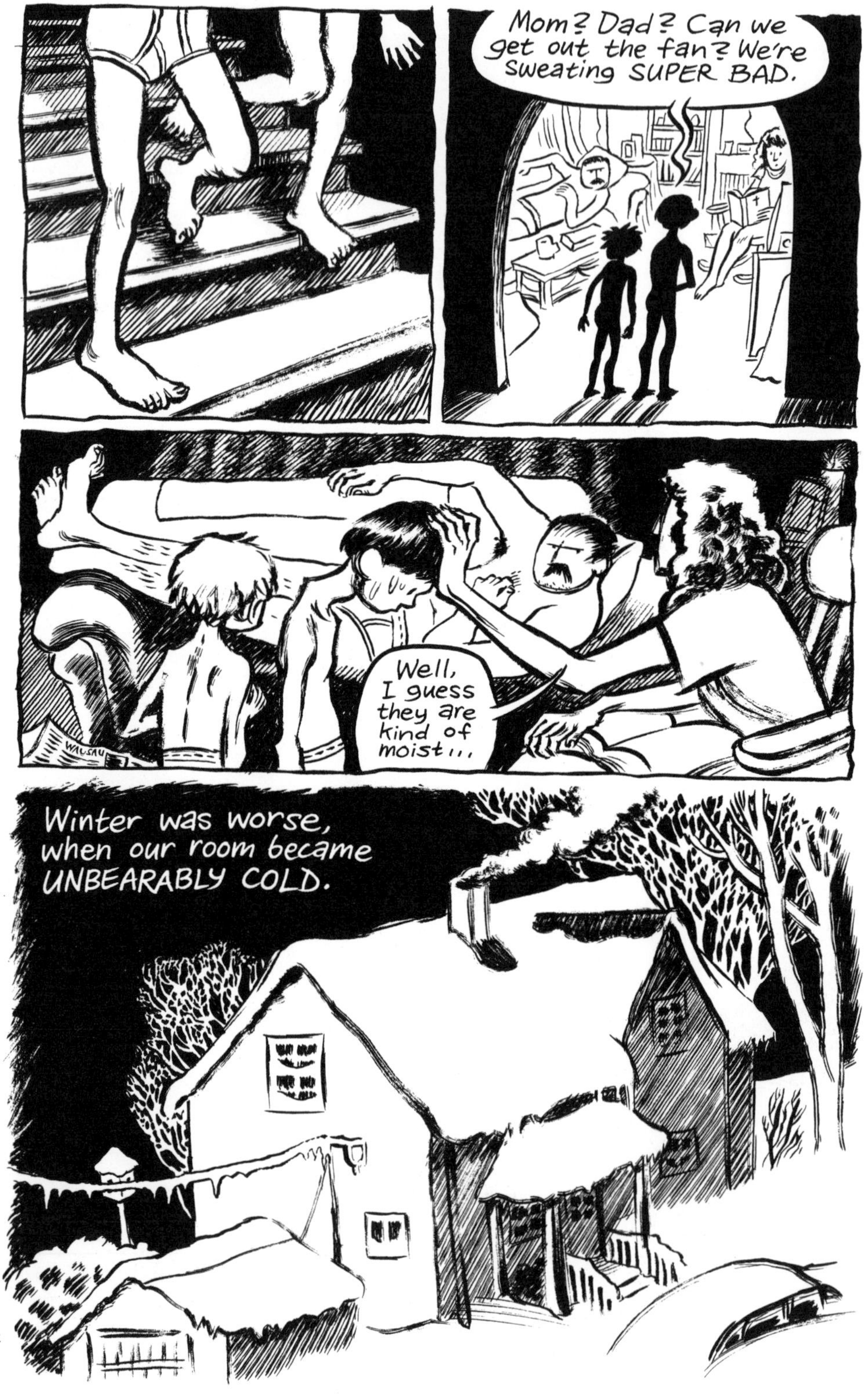
Mom? Dad? Can we get out the fan? We're Sweating SUPER BAD.
WAUSAU
Well, I guess they are kind of moist...
Winter was worse, when our room became UNBEARABLY COLD.

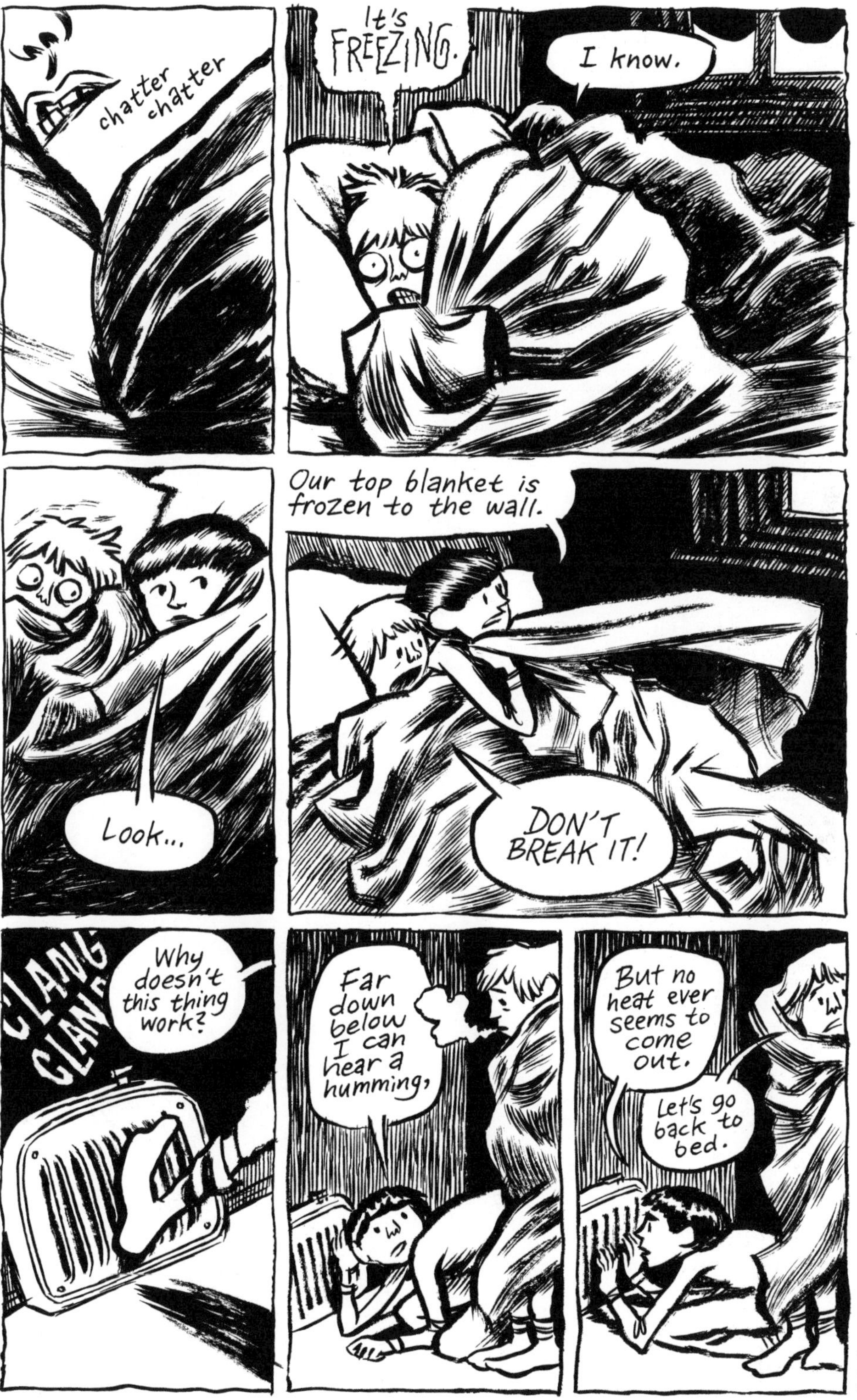
chatter chatter
It's FREEZING.
I know.
Look...
Our top blanket is frozen to the wall.
DON'T BREAK IT!
CLANG CLANG
Why doesn't this thing work?
Far down below I can hear a humming,
But no heat ever seems to come out.
Let's go back to bed.

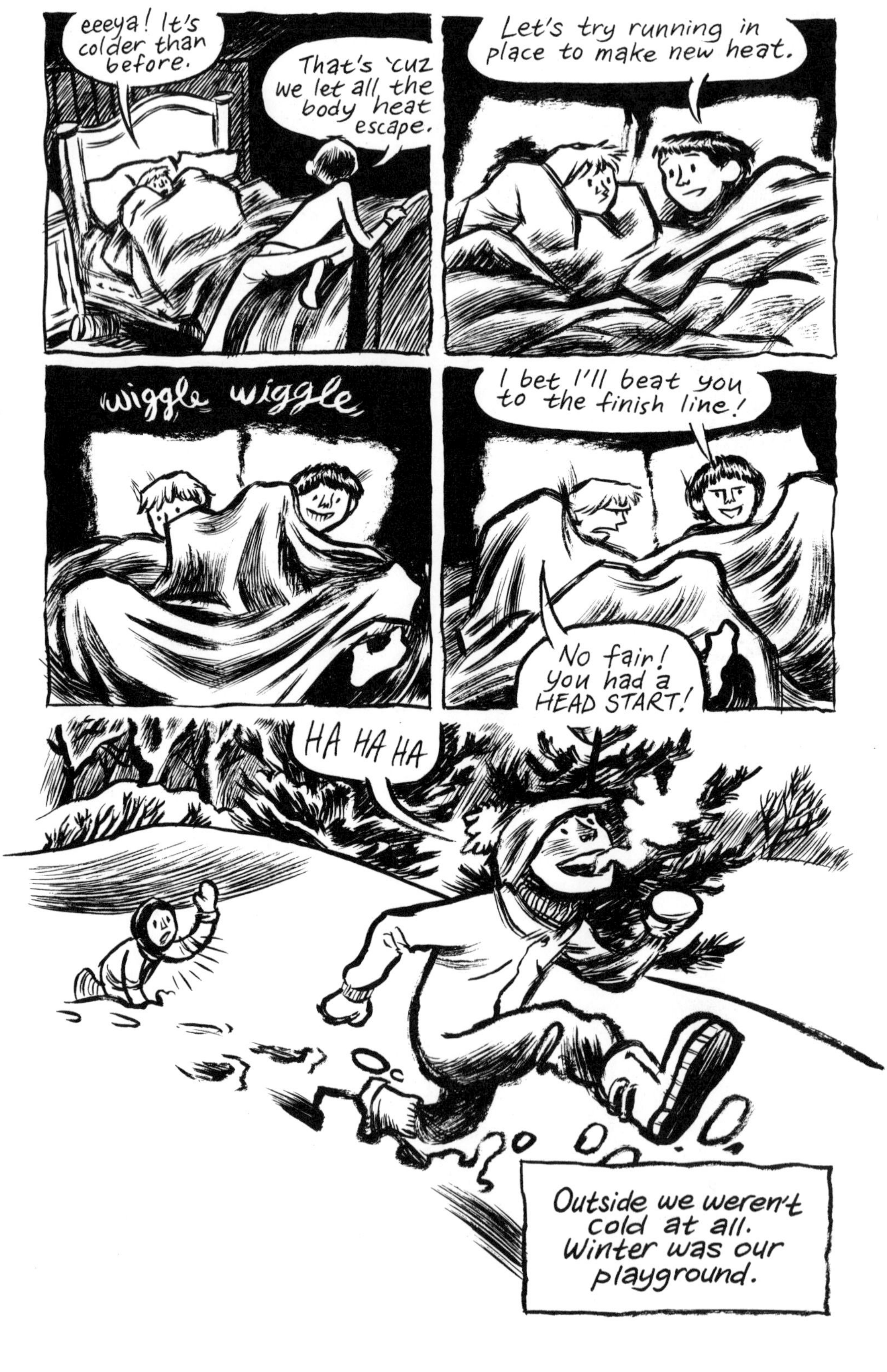
eeeya! It's colder than before.
That's 'cuz we let all the body heat escape.
Let's try running in place to make new heat.
wiggle wiggle
I bet I'll beat you to the finish line!
No fair! You had a HEAD START!
HA HA HA
Outside we weren't cold at all. Winter was our playground.

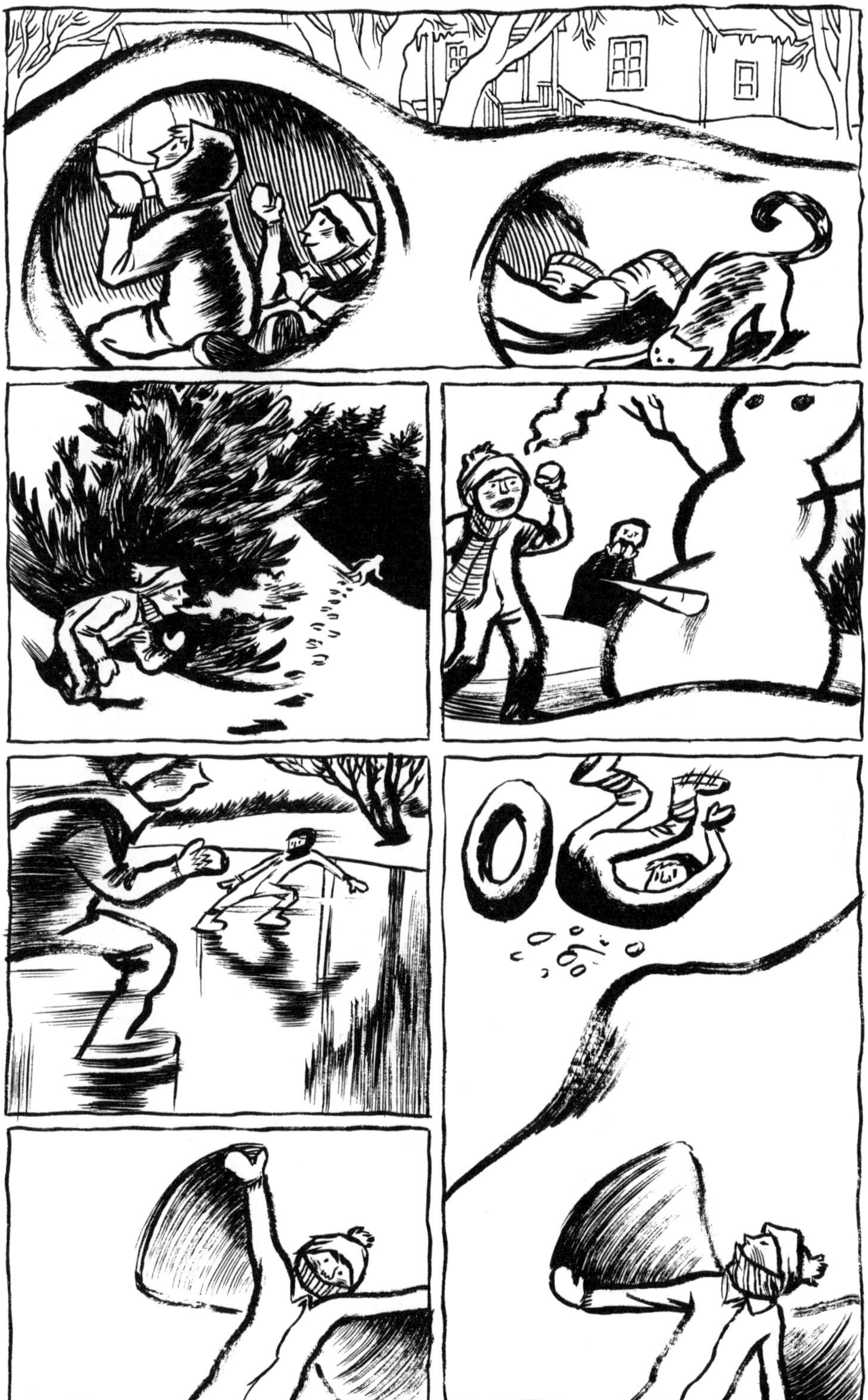

And winter's greatest treasure--
(other than the fact that snow cushioned one's fall)
HA HA HA
--was Christmas break.

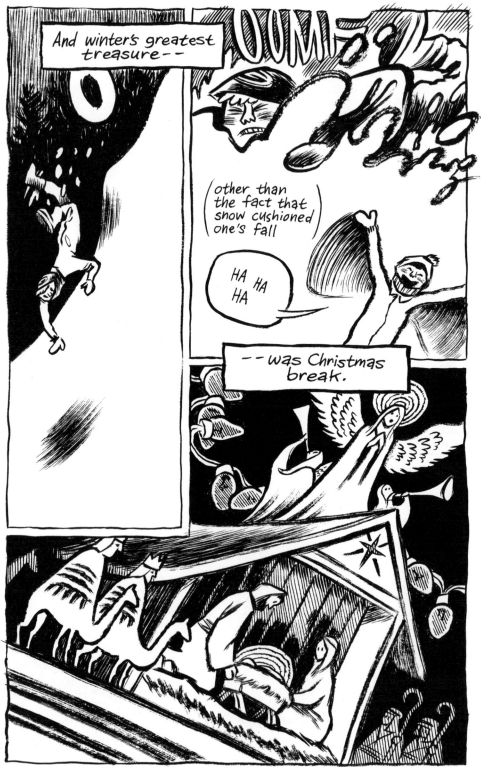

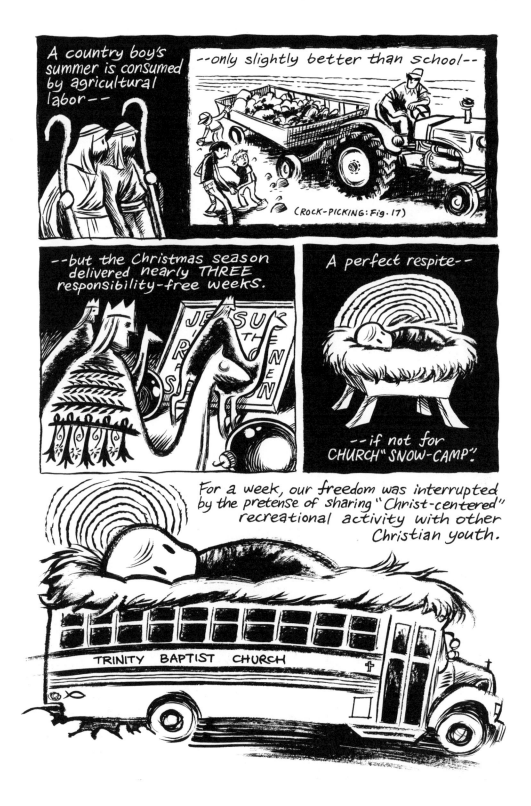

A country boy's summer is consumed by agricultural labor--

--only slightly better than school--

(ROCK-PICKING: Fig. 17)

--but the Christmas season delivered nearly THREE responsibility-free weeks.

A perfect respite--

--if not for CHURCH "SNOW-CAMP".

For a week, our freedom was interrupted by the pretense of sharing "Christ-centered" recreational activity with other Christian youth.

TRINITY BAPTIST CHURCH

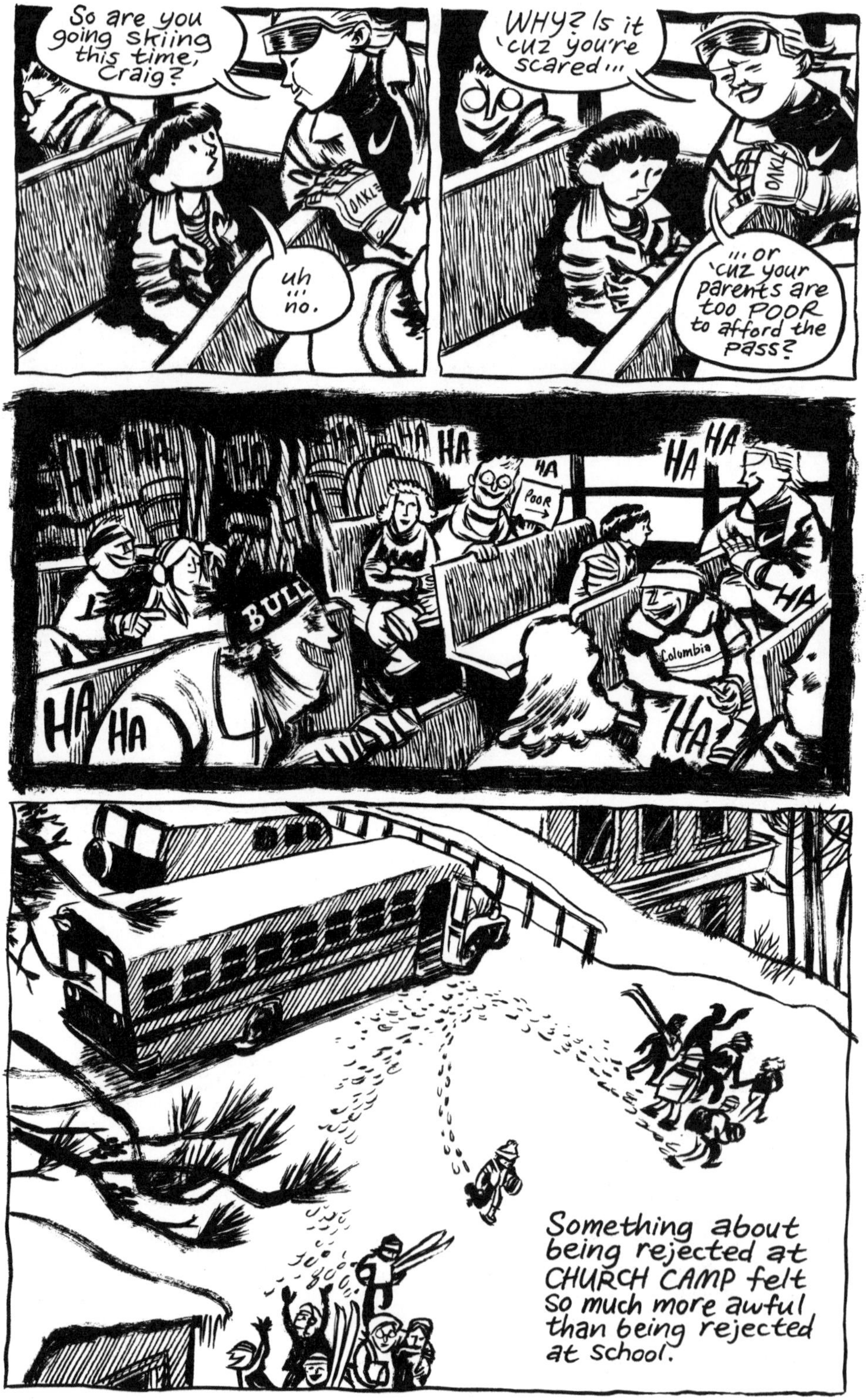
So are you going skiing this time, Craig?
uh ... no.
WHY? Is it 'cuz you're scared...
...or 'cuz your parents are too POOR to afford the pass?
HA HA HA HA HA HA HA HA HA HA HA HA HA HA
POOR
BULL
Columbia
Something about being rejected at CHURCH CAMP felt so much more awful than being rejected at school.

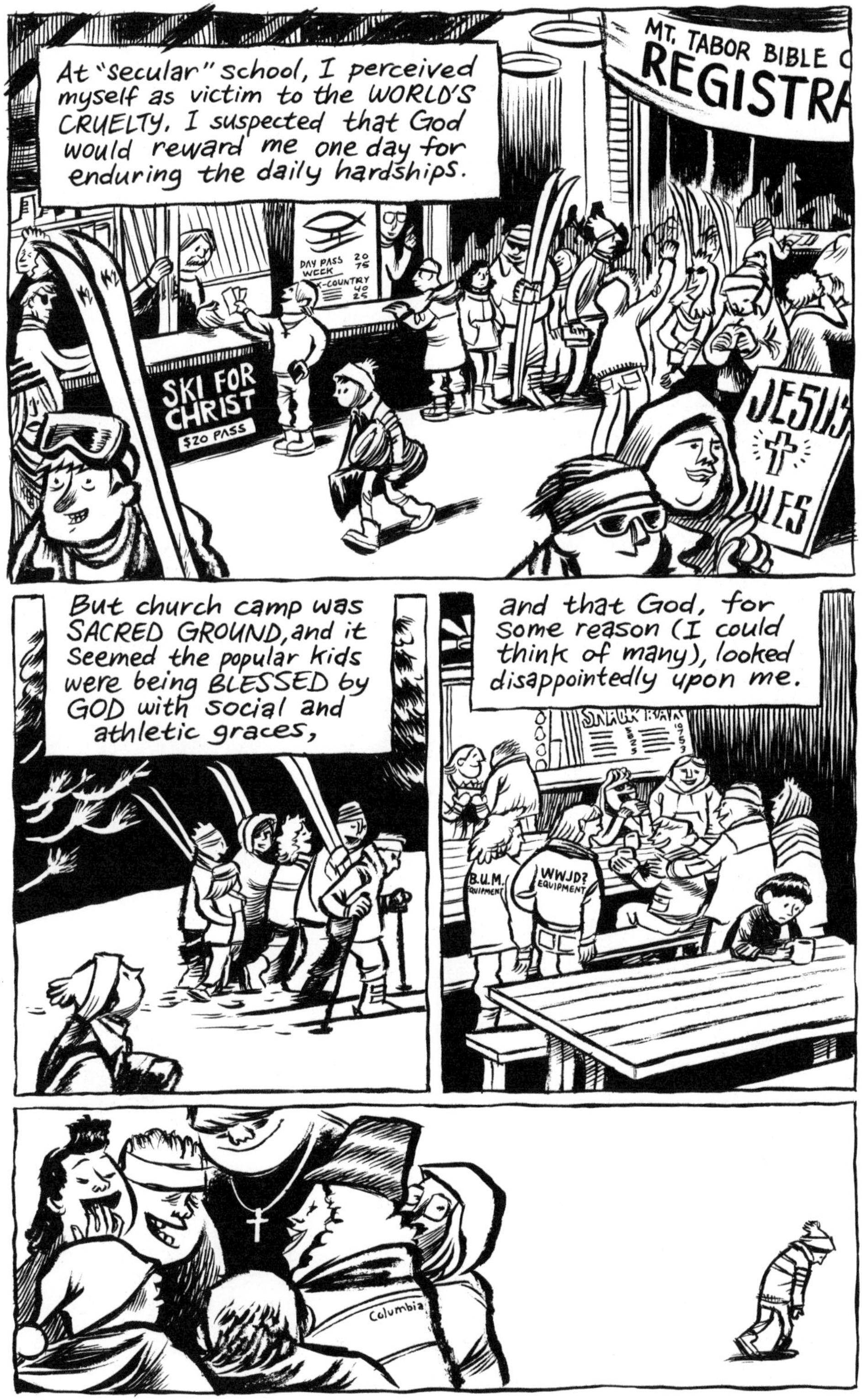
At "secular" school, I perceived myself as victim to the WORLD'S CRUELTY. I suspected that God would reward me one day for enduring the daily hardships.
MT. TABOR BIBLE C
REGISTRA
DAY PASS 20
WEEK 75
SKI FOR CHRIST
$20 PASS
JESUS
But church camp was SACRED GROUND, and it seemed the popular kids were being BLESSED by GOD with social and athletic graces,
and that God, for some reason (I could think of many), looked disappointedly upon me.
B.U.M. EQUIPMENT
WWJD? EQUIPMENT
Columbia

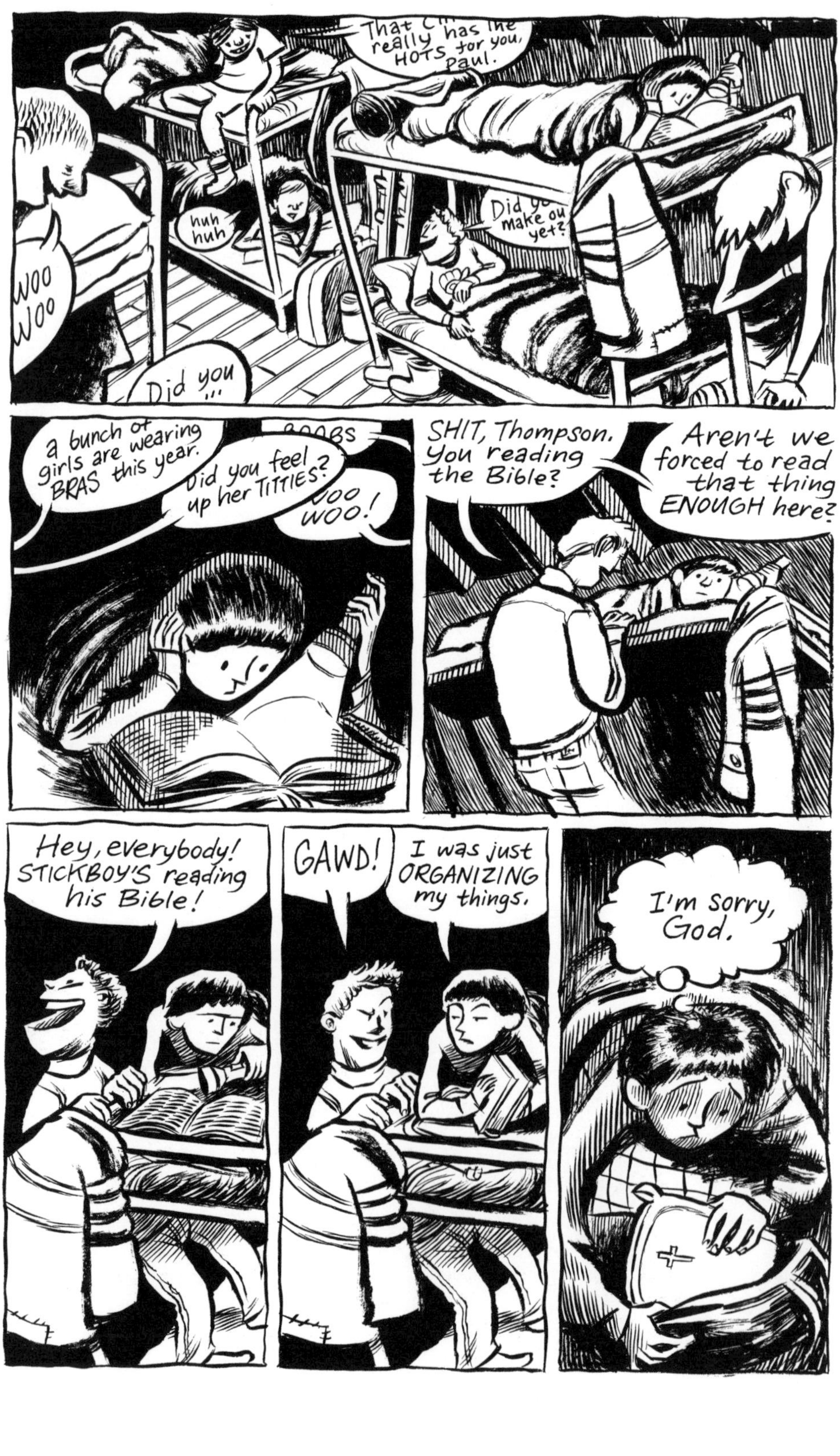
That Ch... really has the HOTS for you, Paul.
huh huh
Did yo... make ou... yet?
WOO WOO
Did you ...
a bunch of girls are wearing BRAS this year.
BOOBS
Did you feel up her TITTIES?
WOO WOO!
SHIT, Thompson. You reading the Bible?
Aren't we forced to read that thing ENOUGH here?
Hey, everybody! STICKBOY'S reading his Bible!
GAWD!
I was just ORGANIZING my things.
I'm sorry, God.

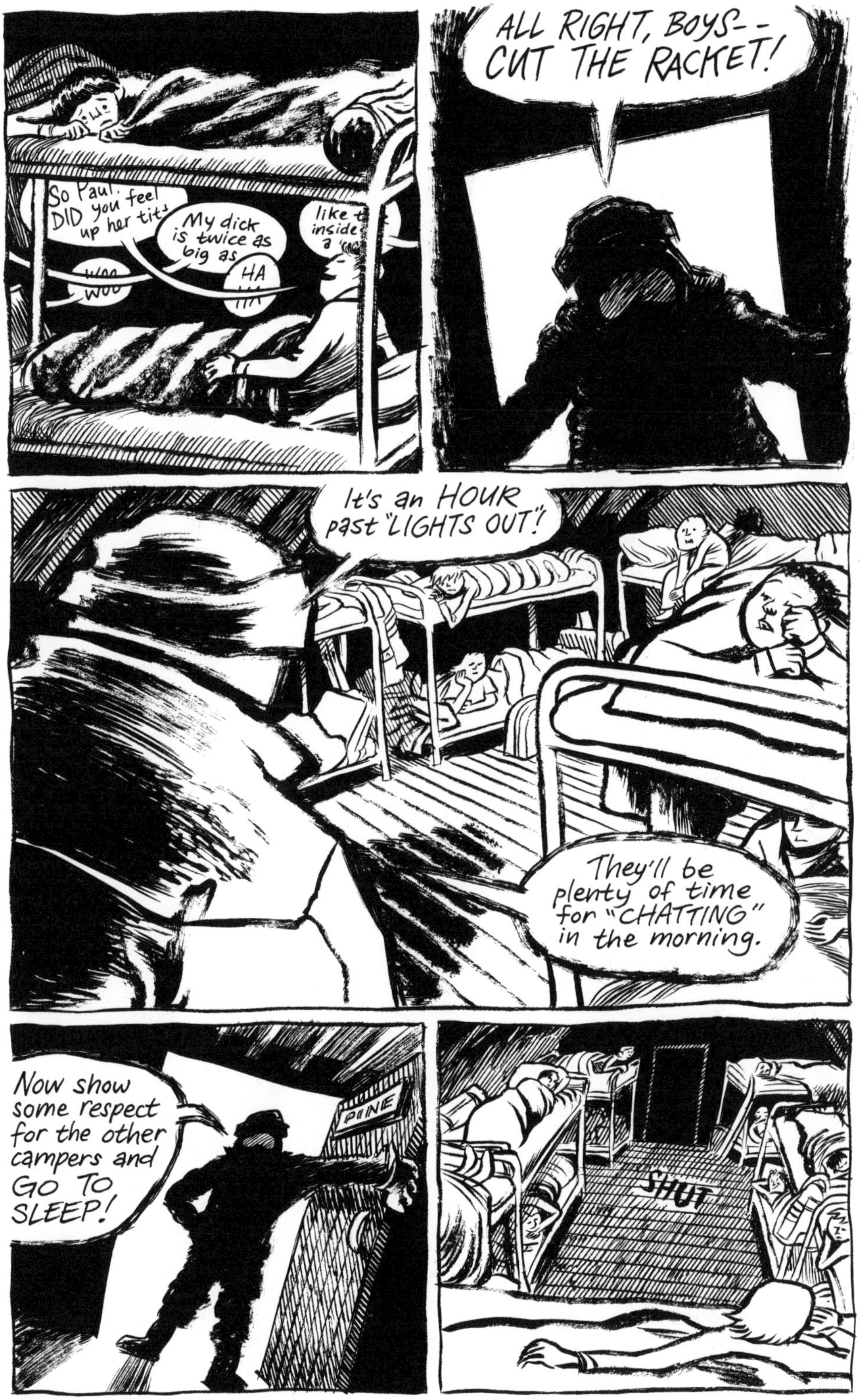
So Paul! DID you feel up her tits
My dick is twice as big as
like
inside
HA
ALL RIGHT, BOYS--
CUT THE RACKET!
It's an HOUR past "LIGHTS OUT"!
They'll be plenty of time for "CHATTING" in the morning.
Now show some respect for the other campers and GO TO SLEEP!
PINE
SHUT

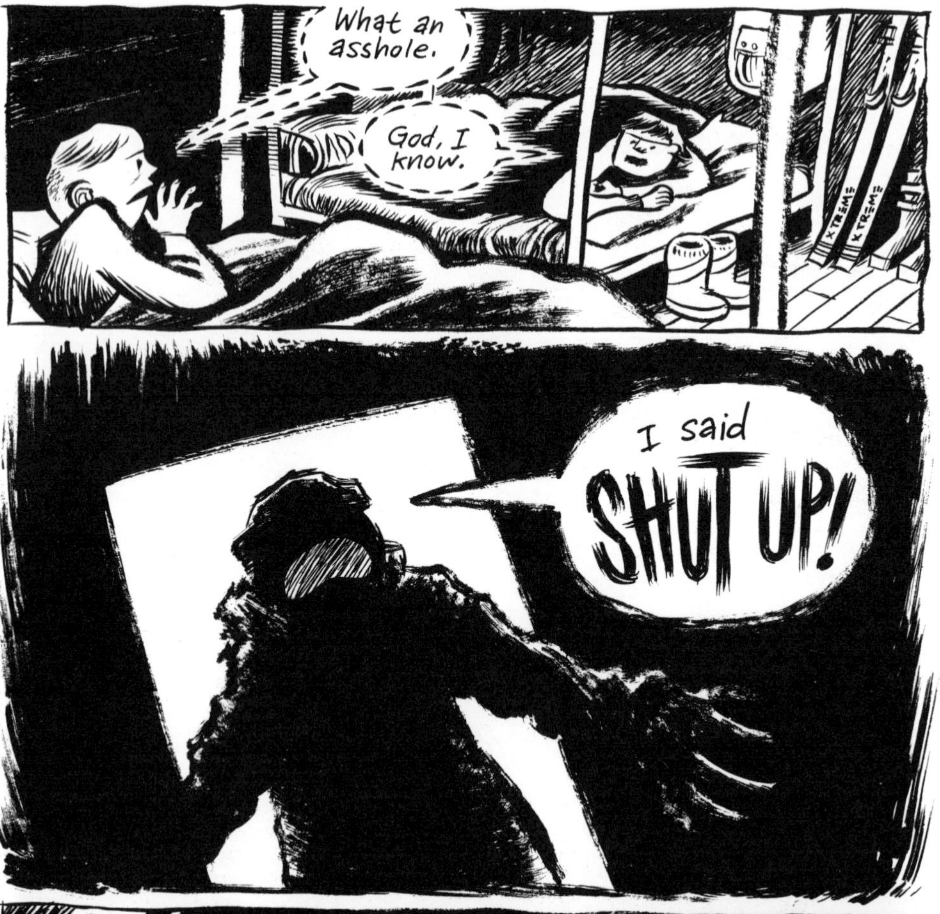
What an asshole.
God, I know.
I said SHUT UP!

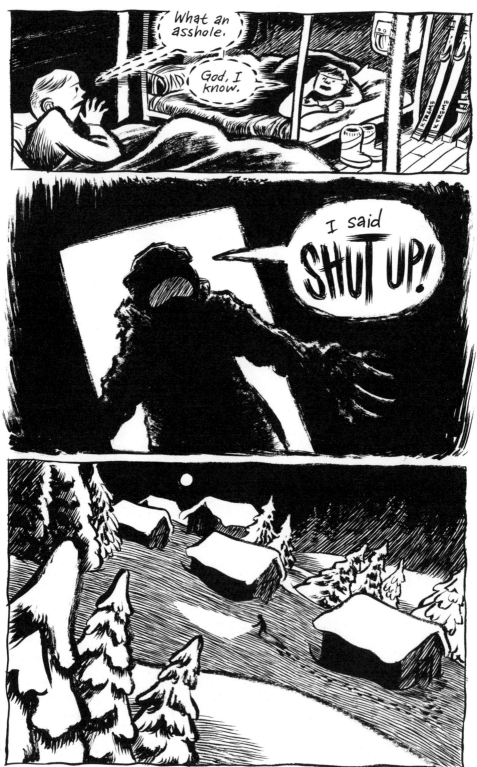

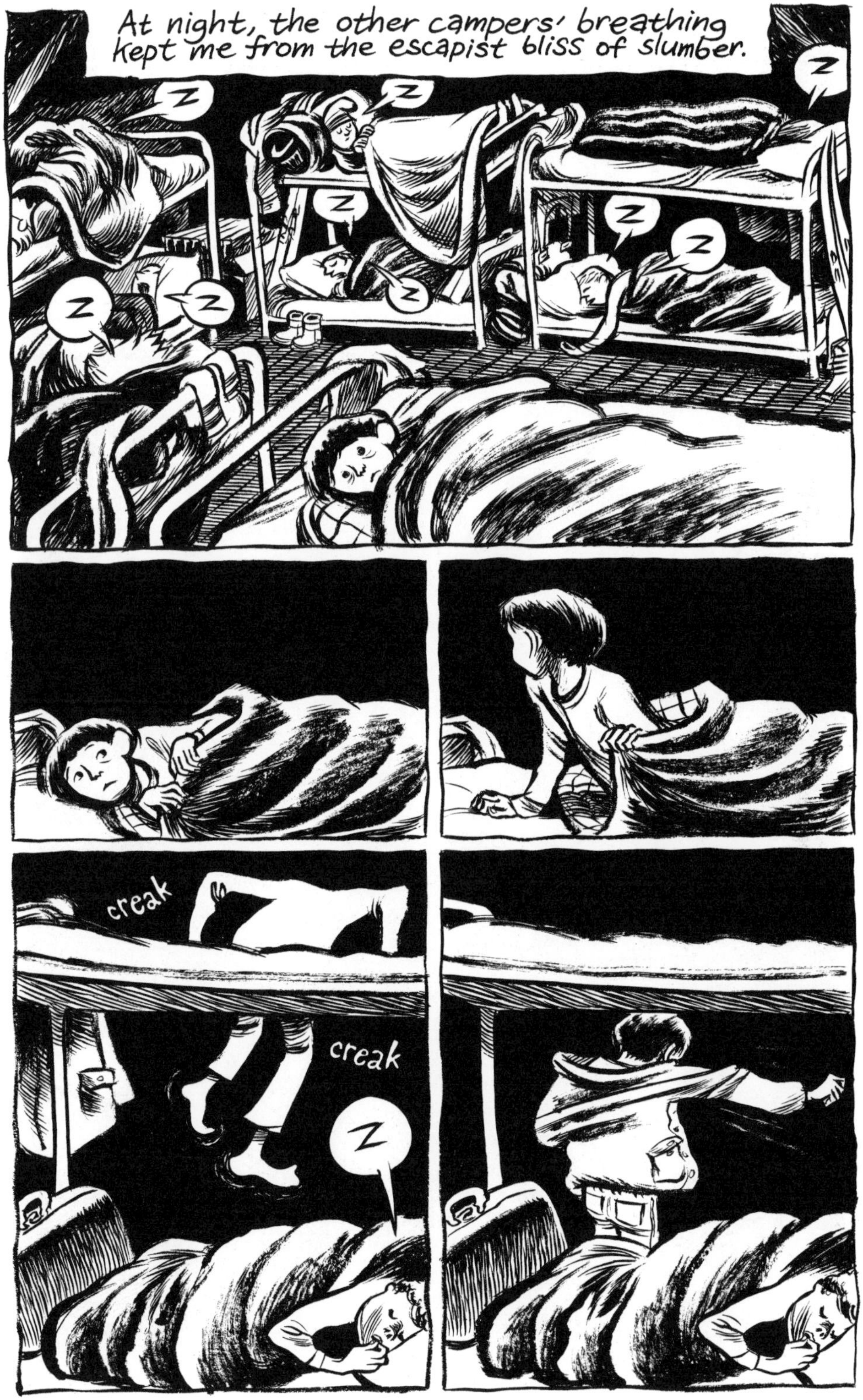
At night, the other campers' breathing kept me from the escapist bliss of slumber.
Z
Z
Z
Z
Z
Z
Z
Z
Z
creak
creak
Z

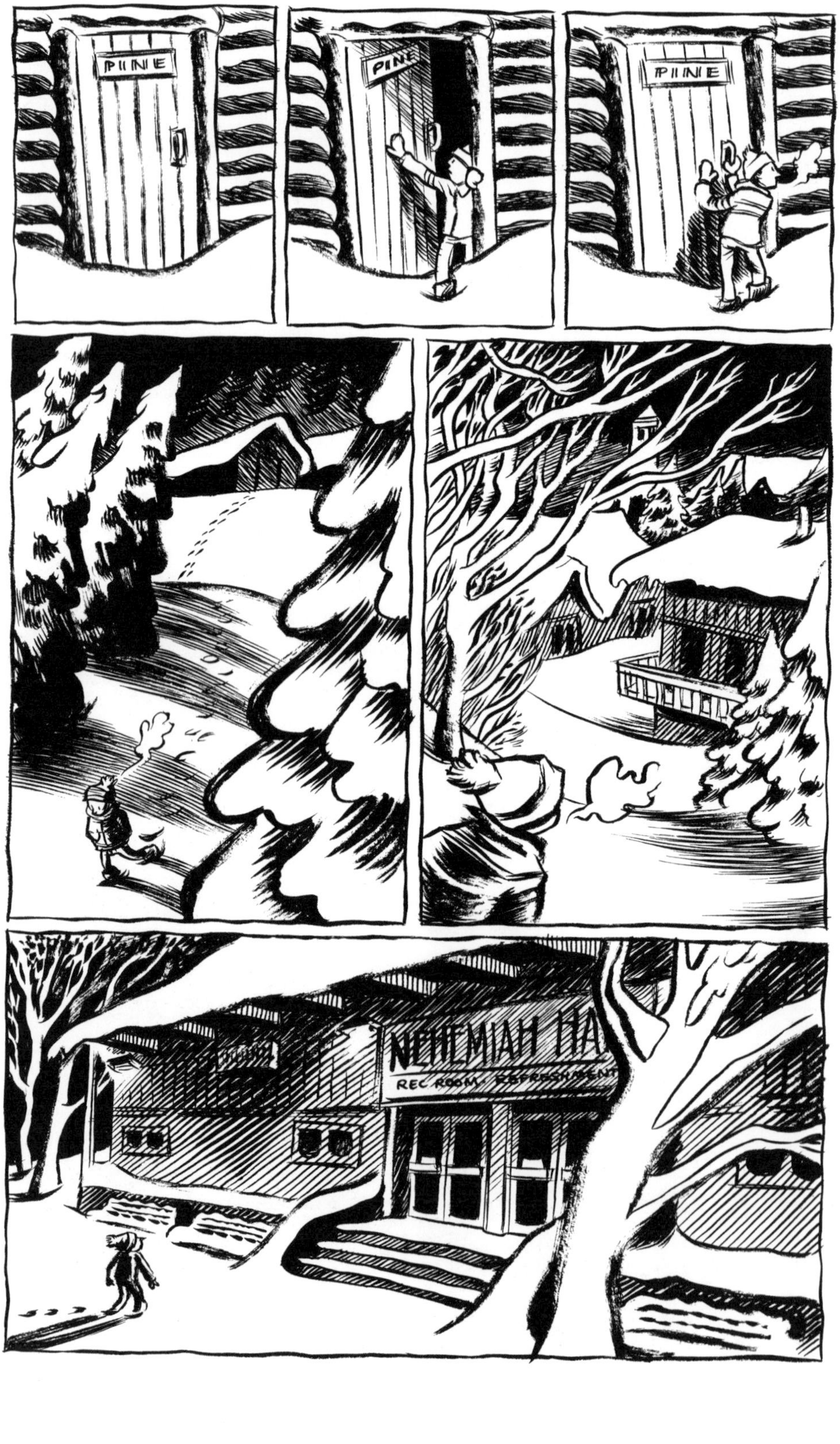
PINE
PINE
PINE
NEHEMIAH HA
REC ROOM · REFRESHMENT

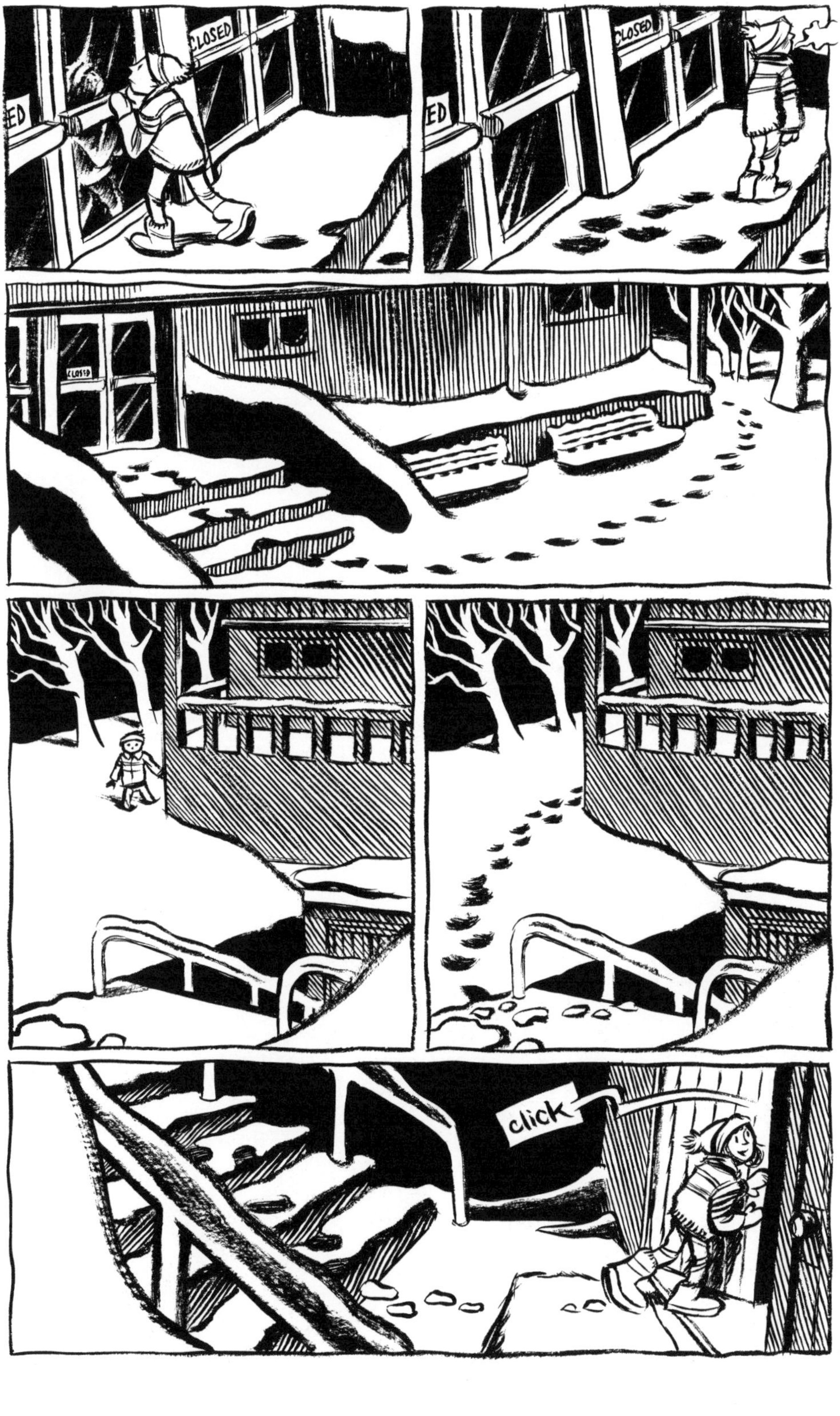
CLOSED
ED
CLOSED
ED
CLOSED
click

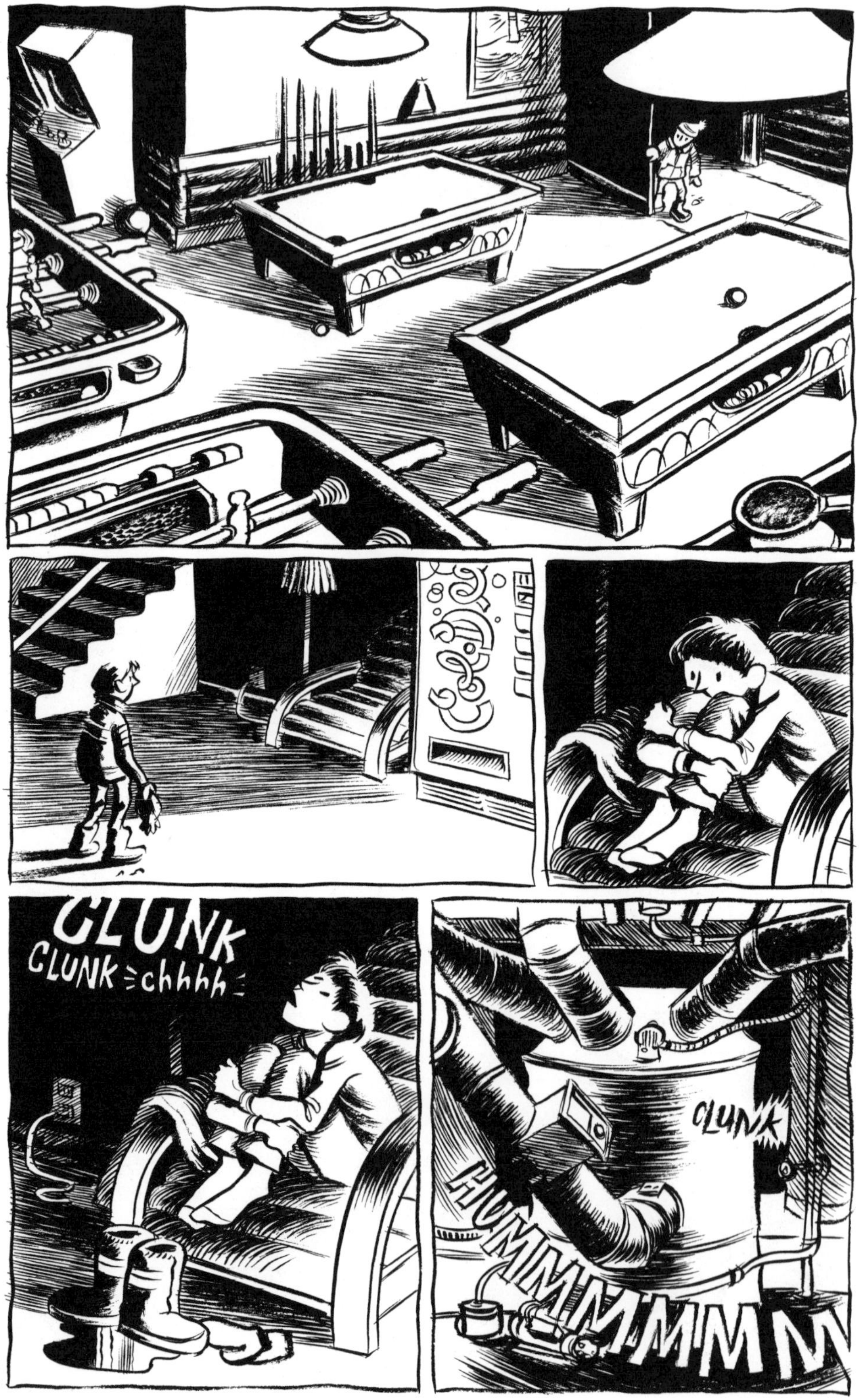
CLUNK
CLUNK =chhhh=
CLUNK
HUMMMMMMMM

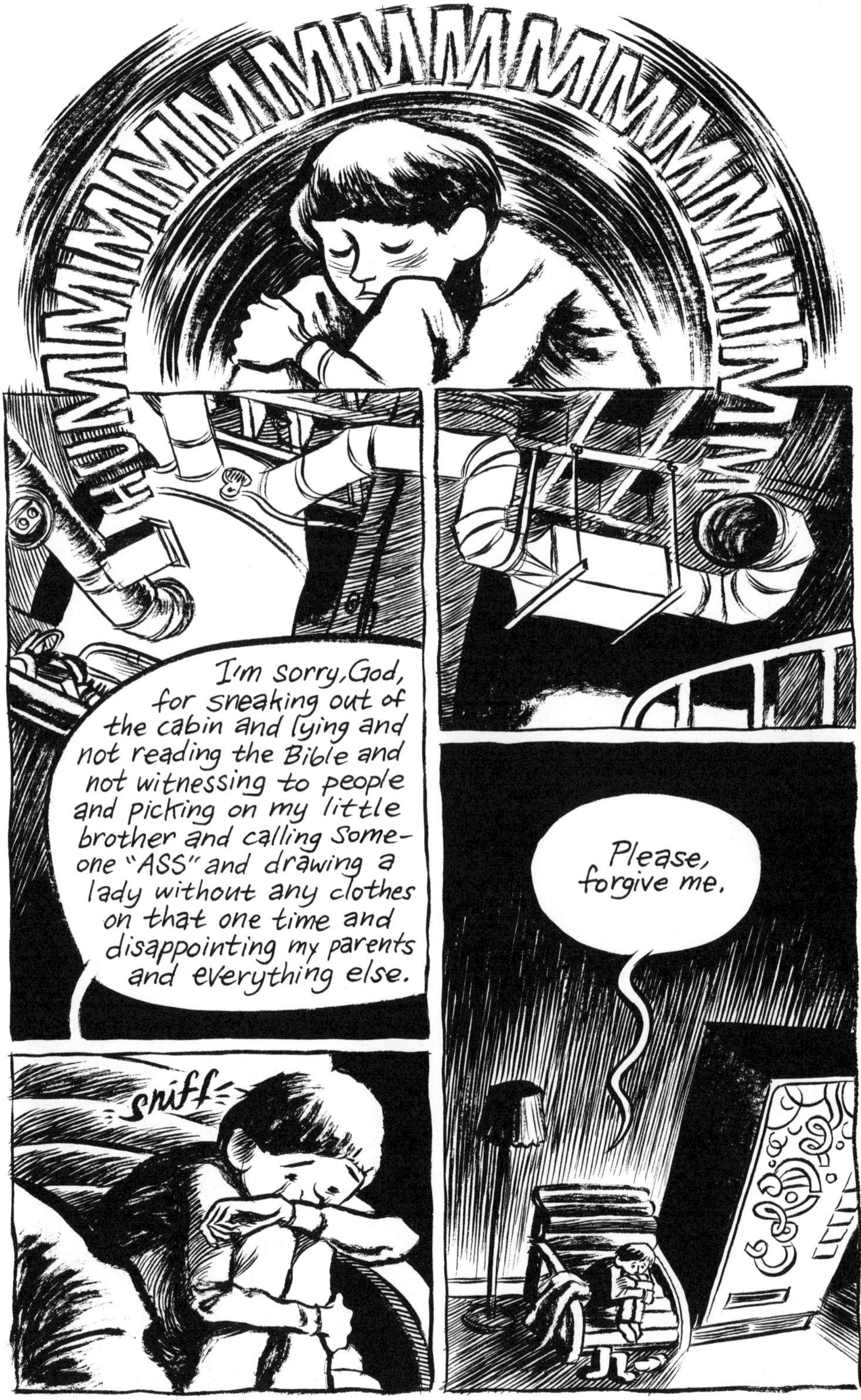
HUMMMMMMMMMMMMMMMMM
I'm sorry, God, for sneaking out of the cabin and lying and not reading the Bible and not witnessing to people and picking on my little brother and calling Someone "ASS" and drawing a lady without any clothes on that one time and disappointing my parents and everything else.
Please, forgive me.
sniff

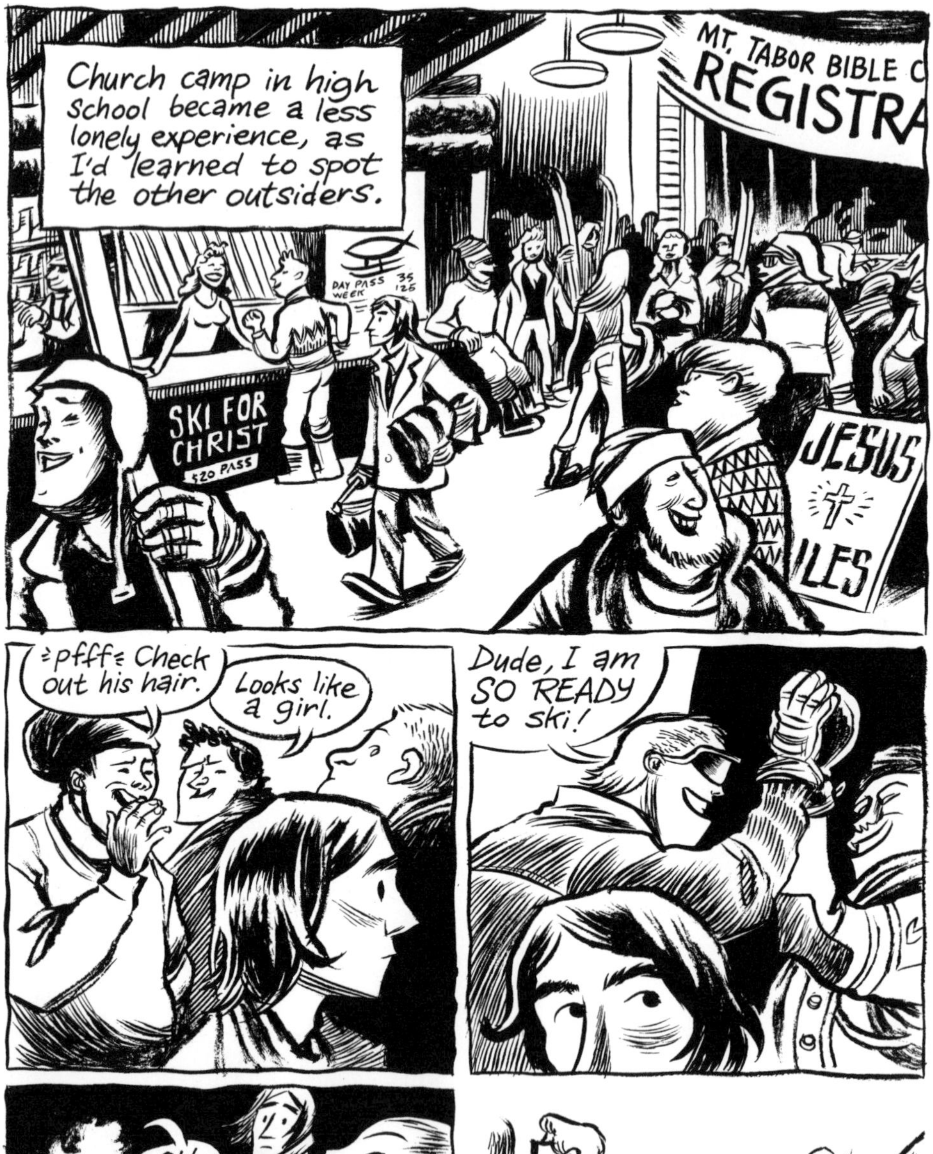

Church camp in high school became a less lonely experience, as I'd learned to spot the other outsiders.
MT. TABOR BIBLE C
REGISTRA
DAY PASS 35
WEEK 125
SKI FOR CHRIST
$20 PASS
JESUS
ILES
≥pfff≤ Check out his hair.
Looks like a girl.
Dude, I am SO READY to ski!
OH-MY-GAWD!
I LOVE your sweater!

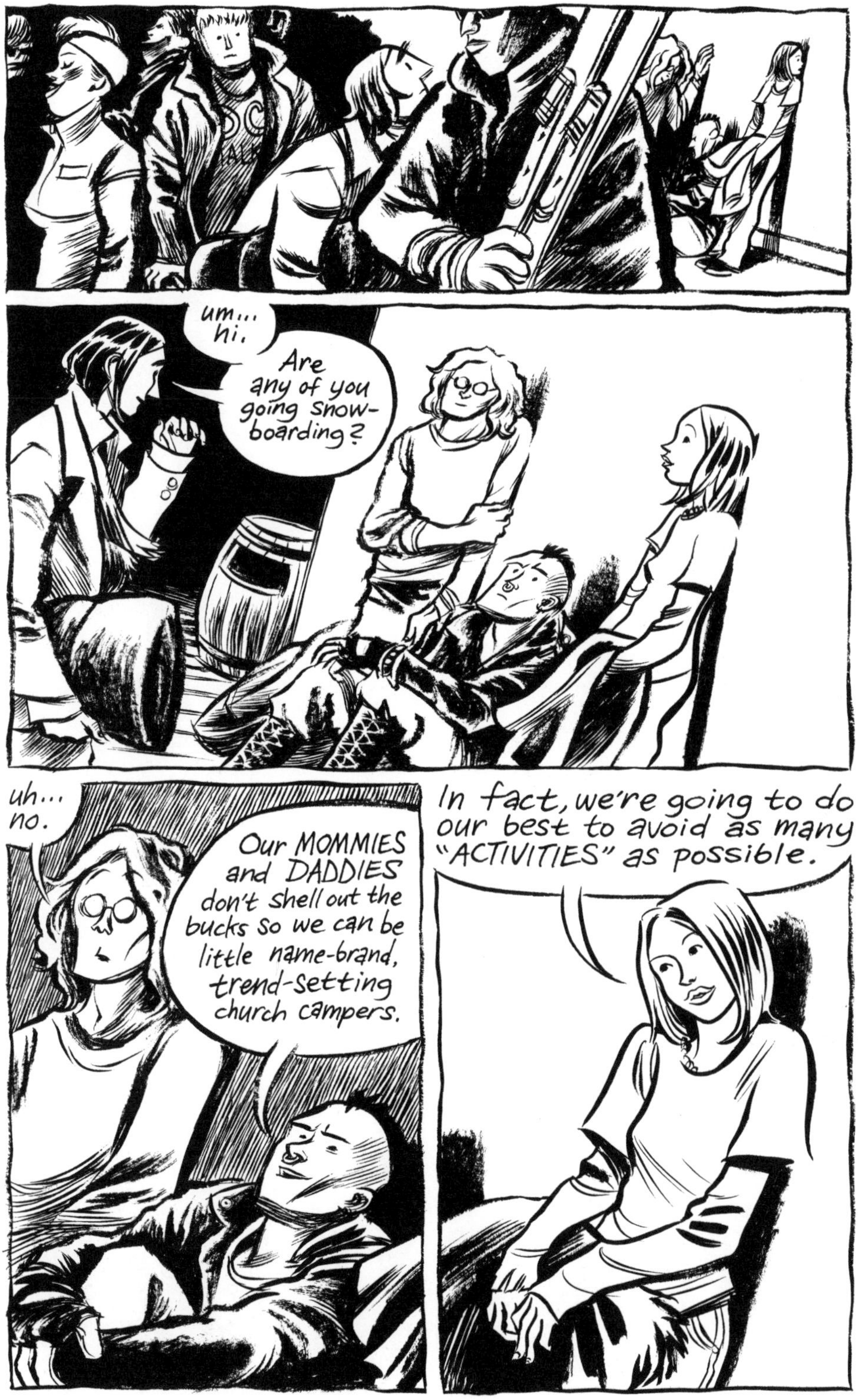
um... hi.
Are any of you going snow-boarding?
uh... no.
Our MOMMIES and DADDIES don't shell out the bucks so we can be little name-brand, trend-setting church campers.
In fact, we're going to do our best to avoid as many "ACTIVITIES" as possible.

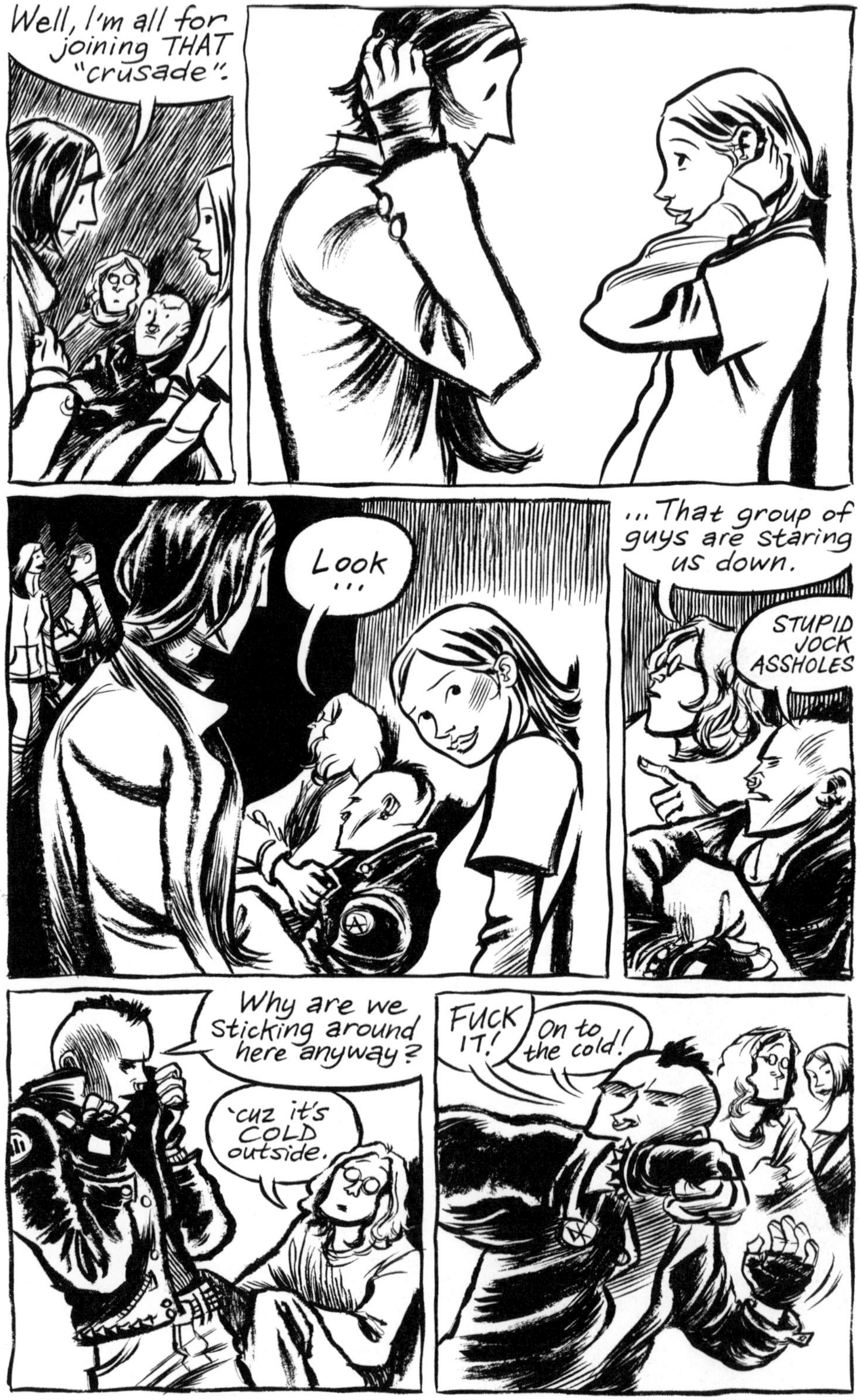
Well, I'm all for joining THAT "crusade".
Look ...
... That group of guys are staring us down.
STUPID JOCK ASSHOLES
Why are we sticking around here anyway?
`cuz it's COLD outside.
FUCK IT!
On to the cold!

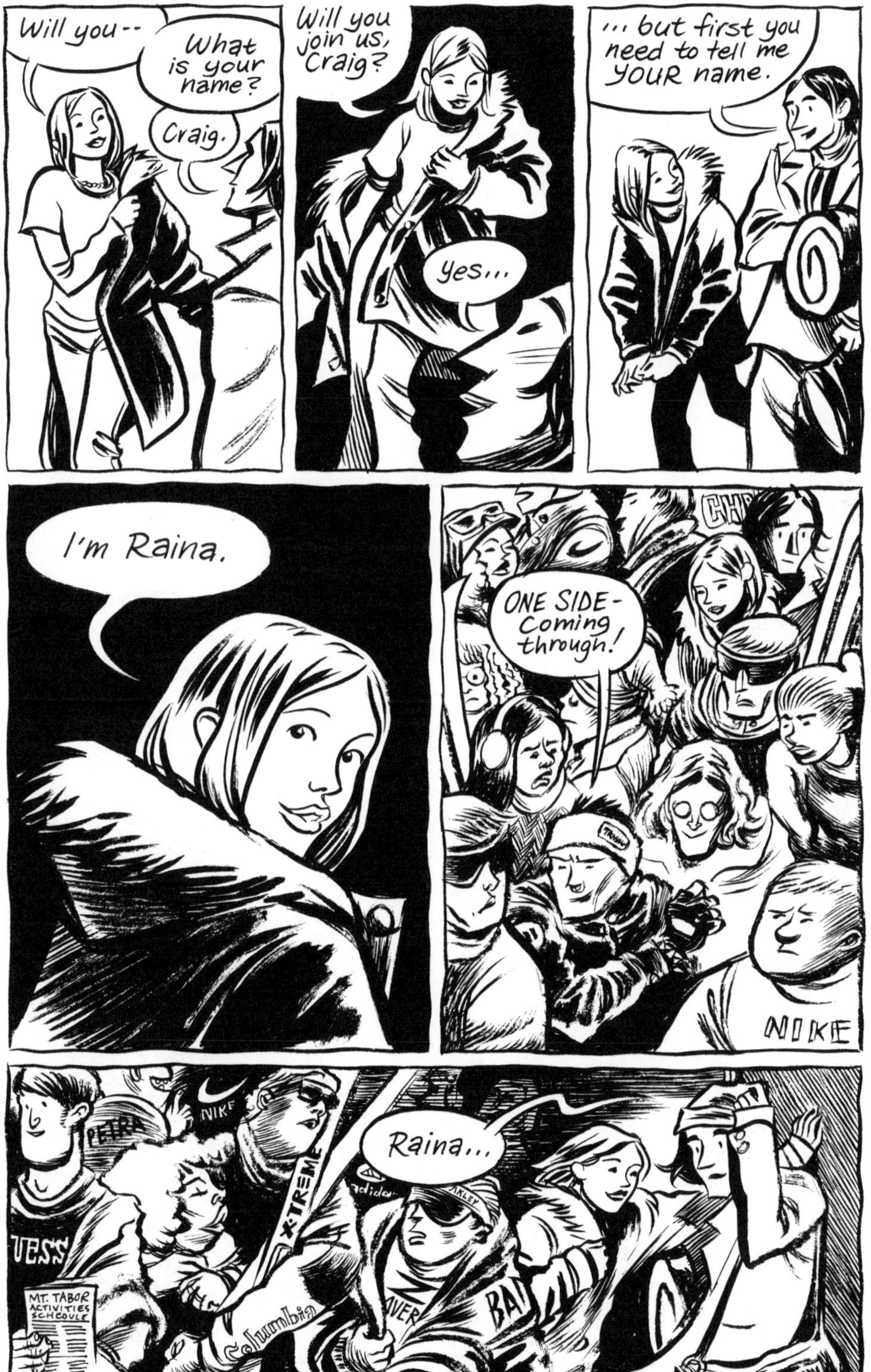
Will you--
What is your name?
Craig.
Will you join us, Craig?
Yes...
... but first you need to tell me YOUR name.
I'm Raina.
ONE SIDE- Coming through!
NIKE
Raina...
PETRA
NIKE
X-TREME
adidas
OAKLEY
UESS
MT. TABOR ACTIVITIES SCHEDULE
Columbia

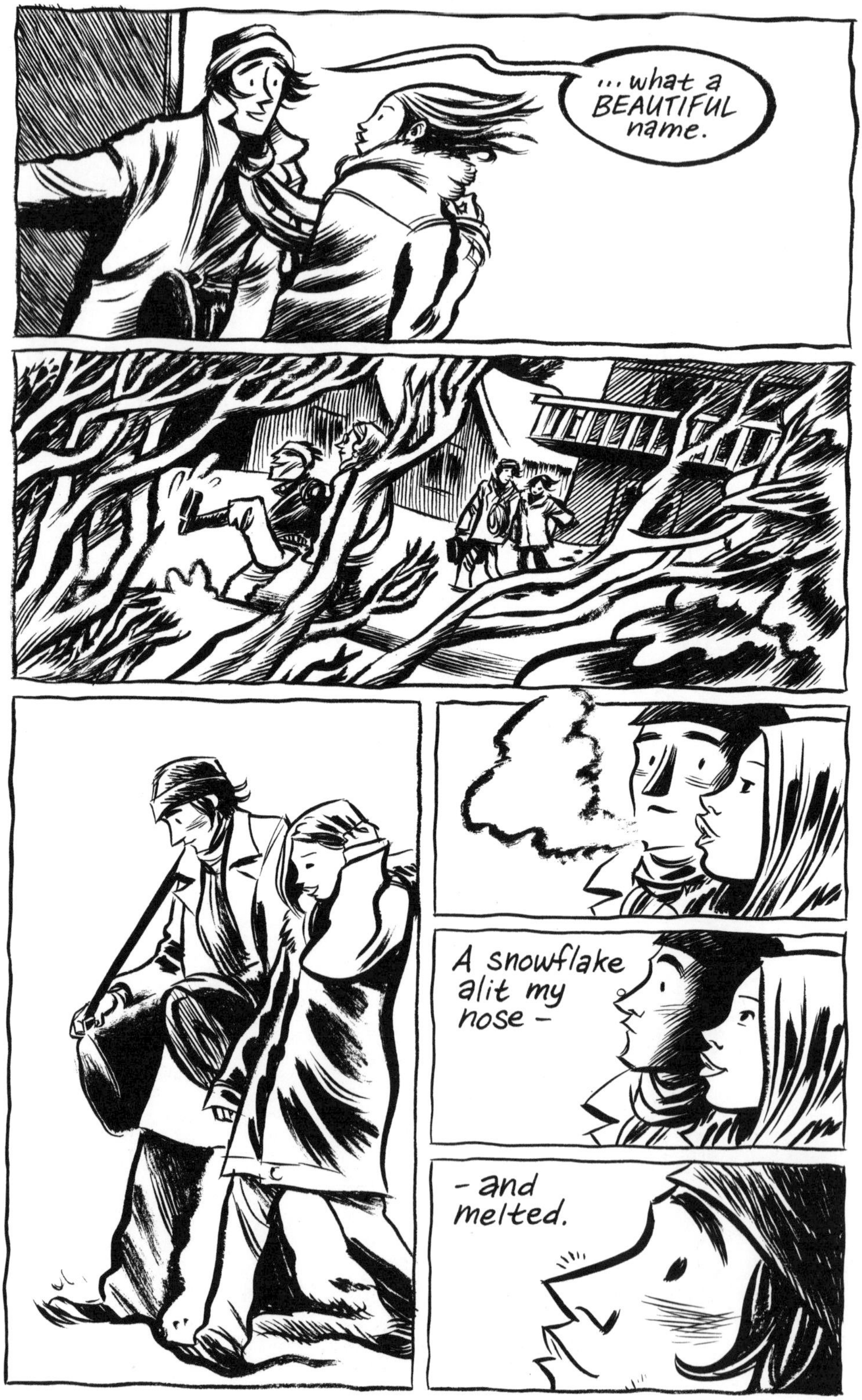
...what a BEAUTIFUL name.
A snowflake alit my nose -
- and melted.

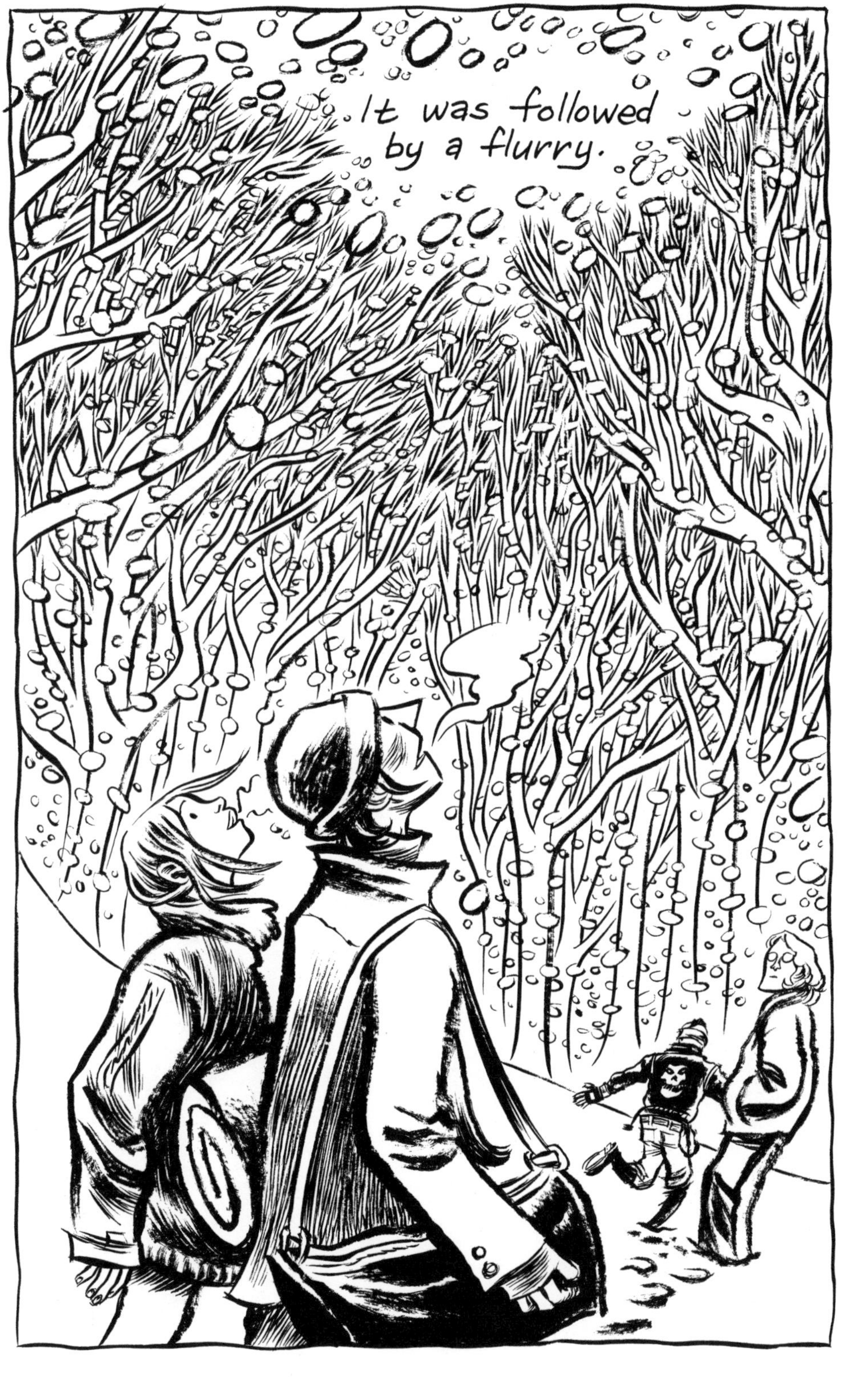
It was followed by a flurry.

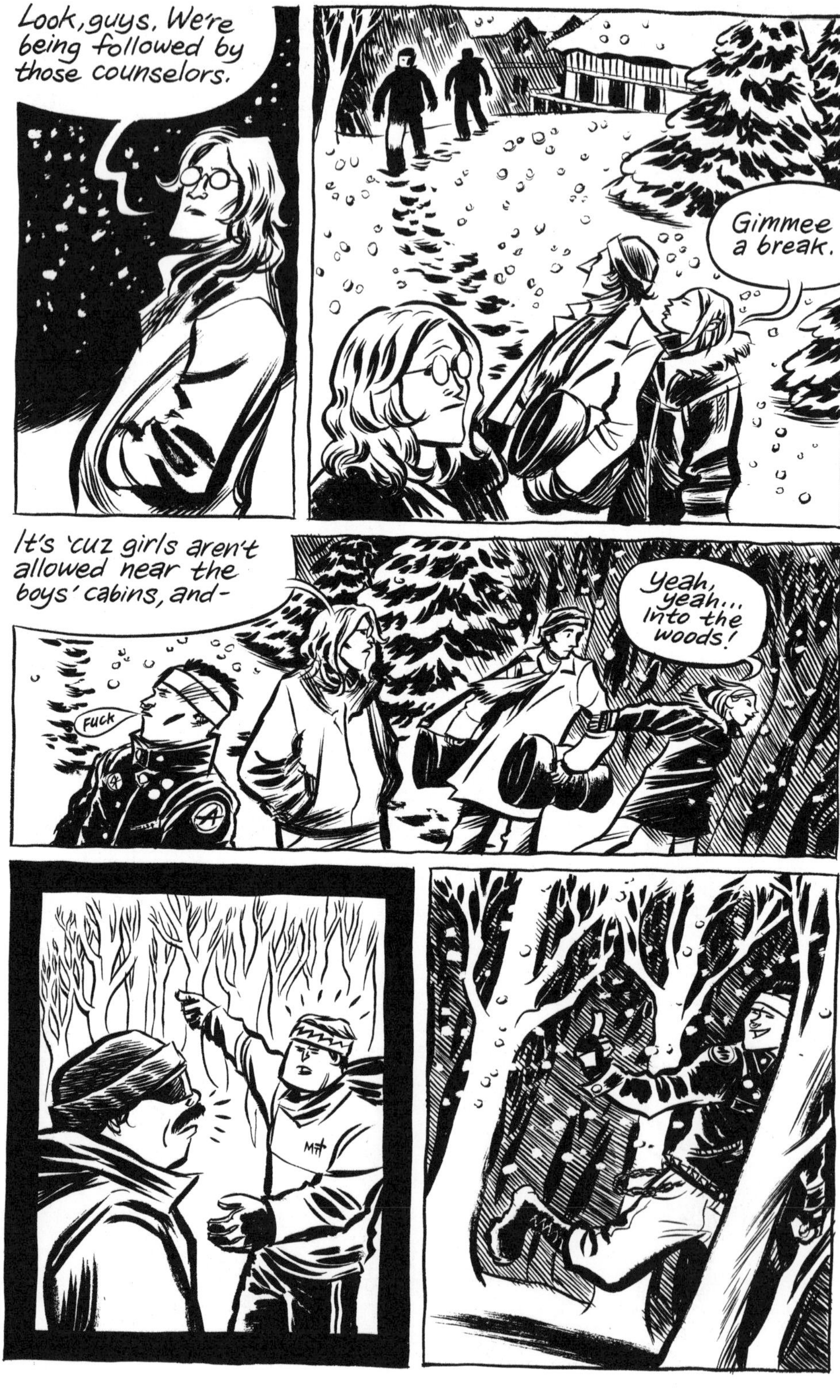
Look, guys. We're being followed by those counselors.
Gimmee a break.
It's 'cuz girls aren't allowed near the boys' cabins, and-
FUCK
Yeah, yeah... Into the woods!

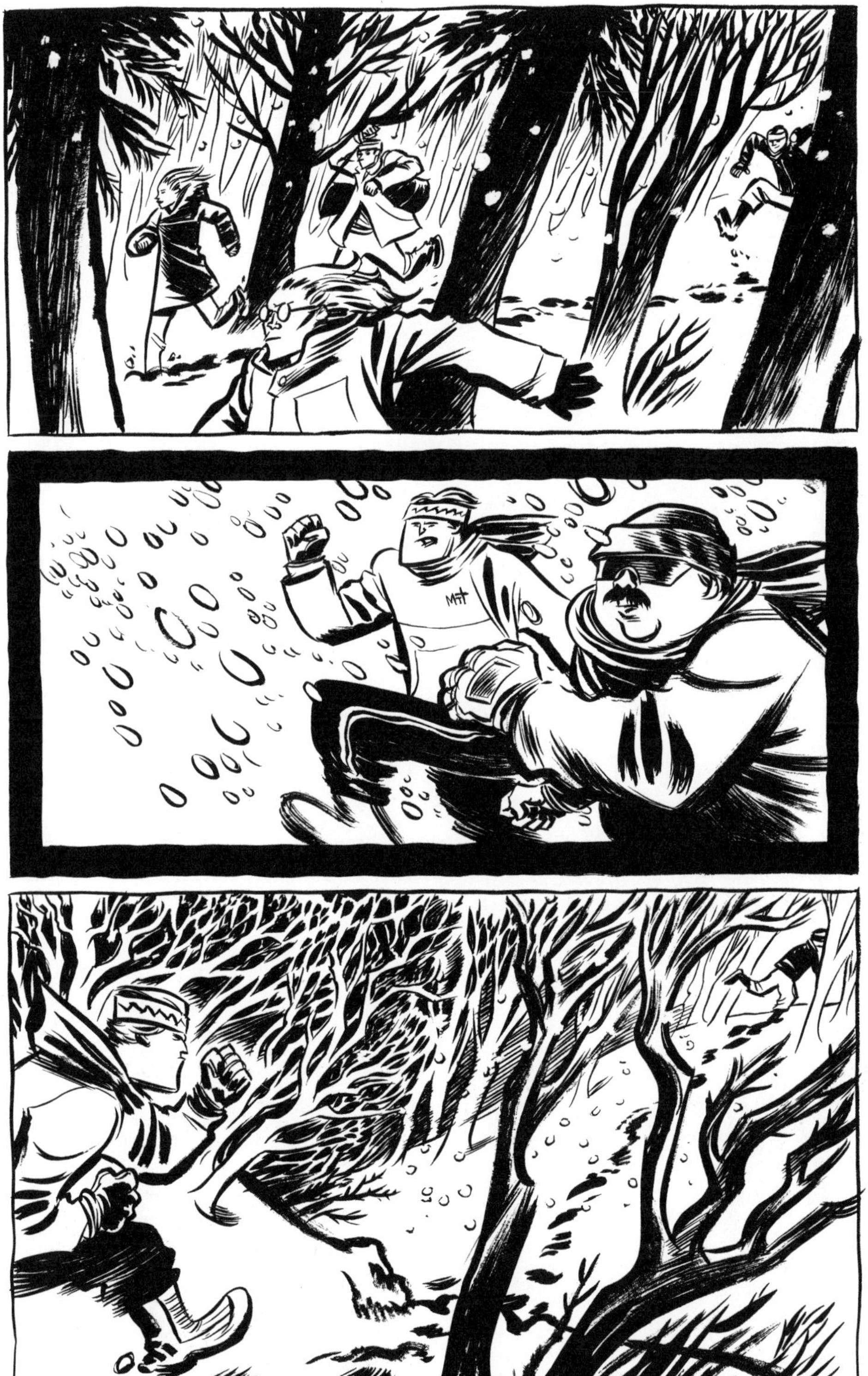

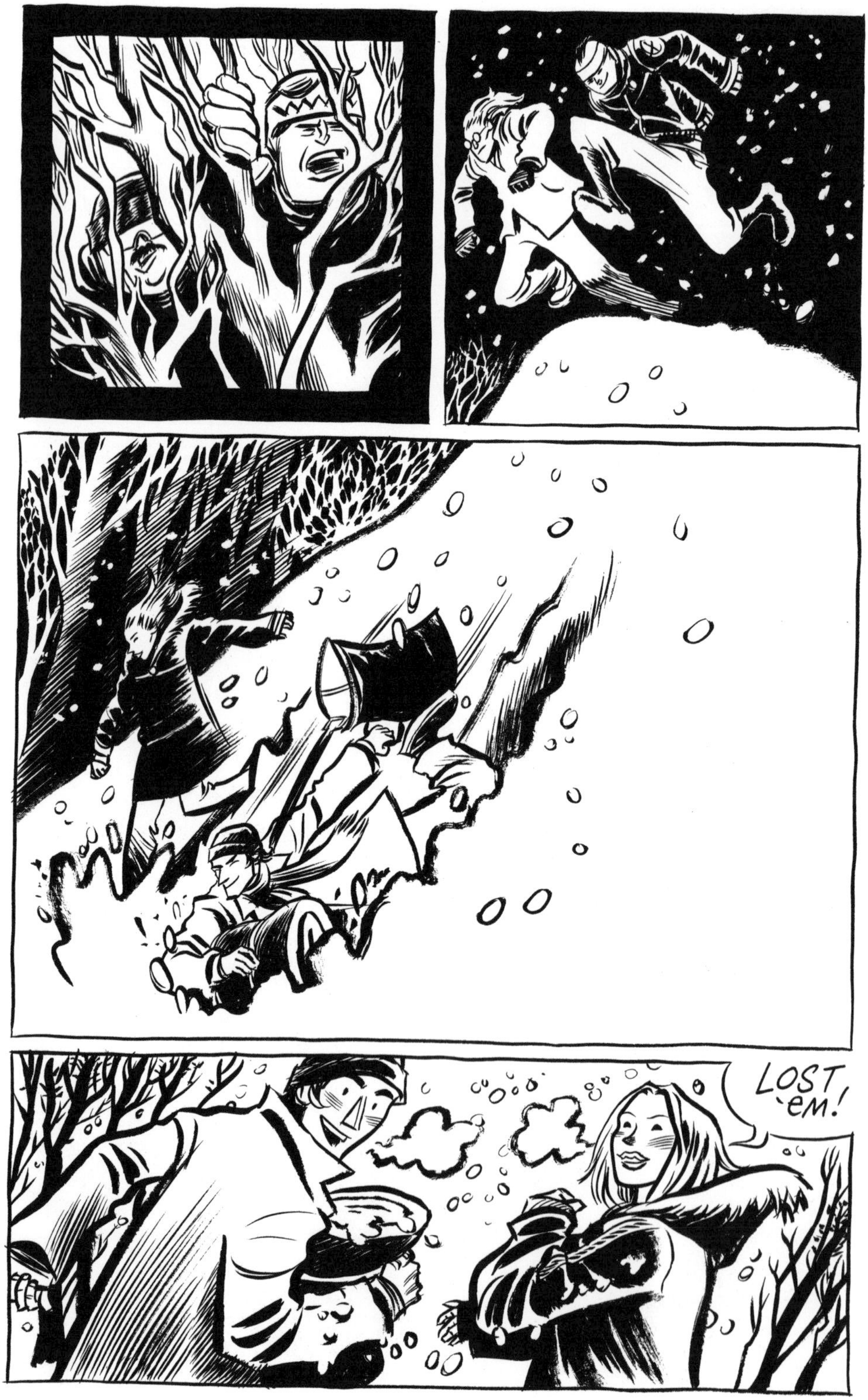
LOST 'EM!

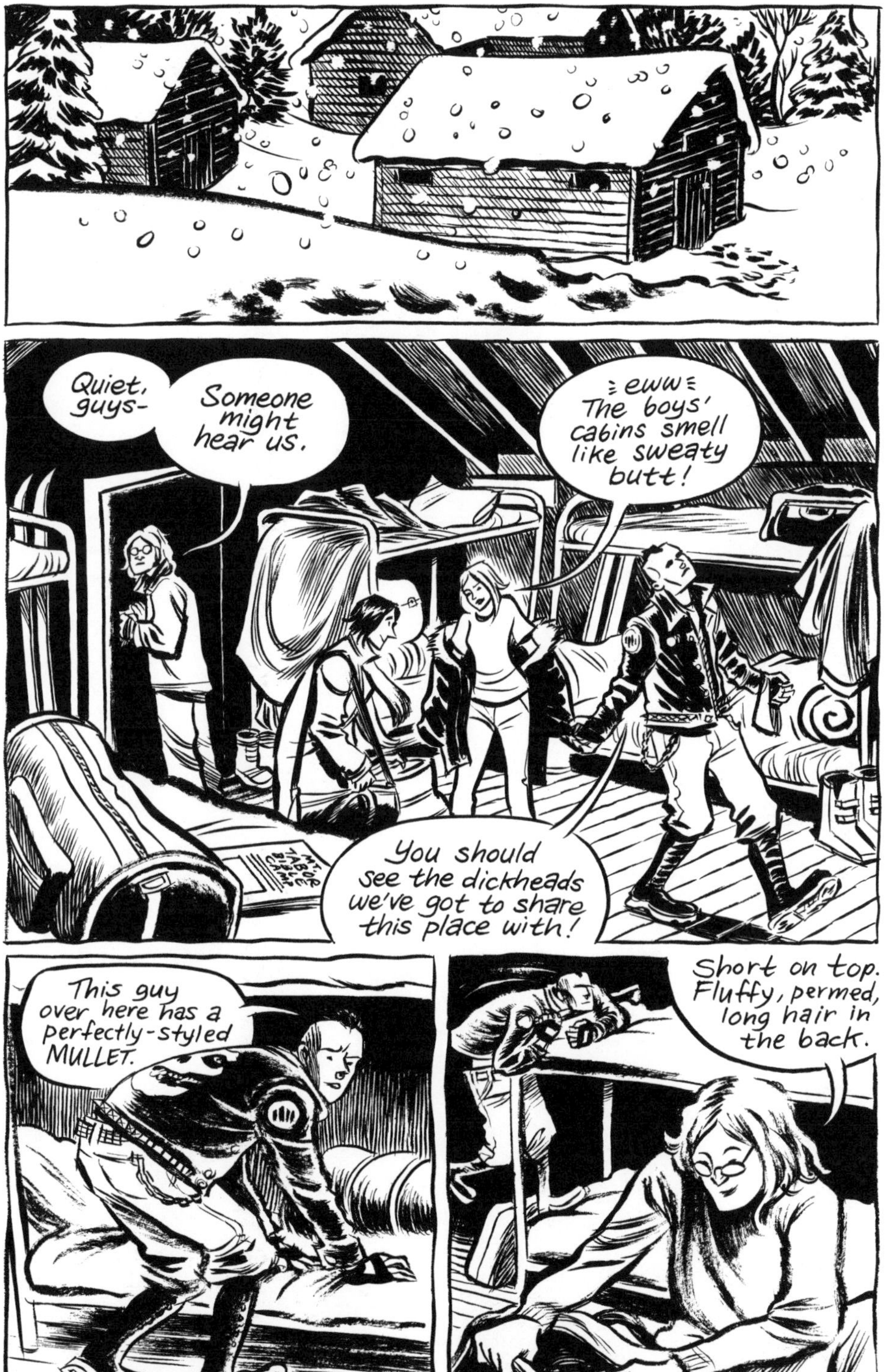
Quiet, guys-
Someone might hear us.
≡eww≡ The boys' cabins smell like sweaty butt!
MT. TABOR BIBLE CAMP
You should see the dickheads we've got to share this place with!
This guy over here has a perfectly-styled MULLET.
Short on top. Fluffy, permed, long hair in the back.

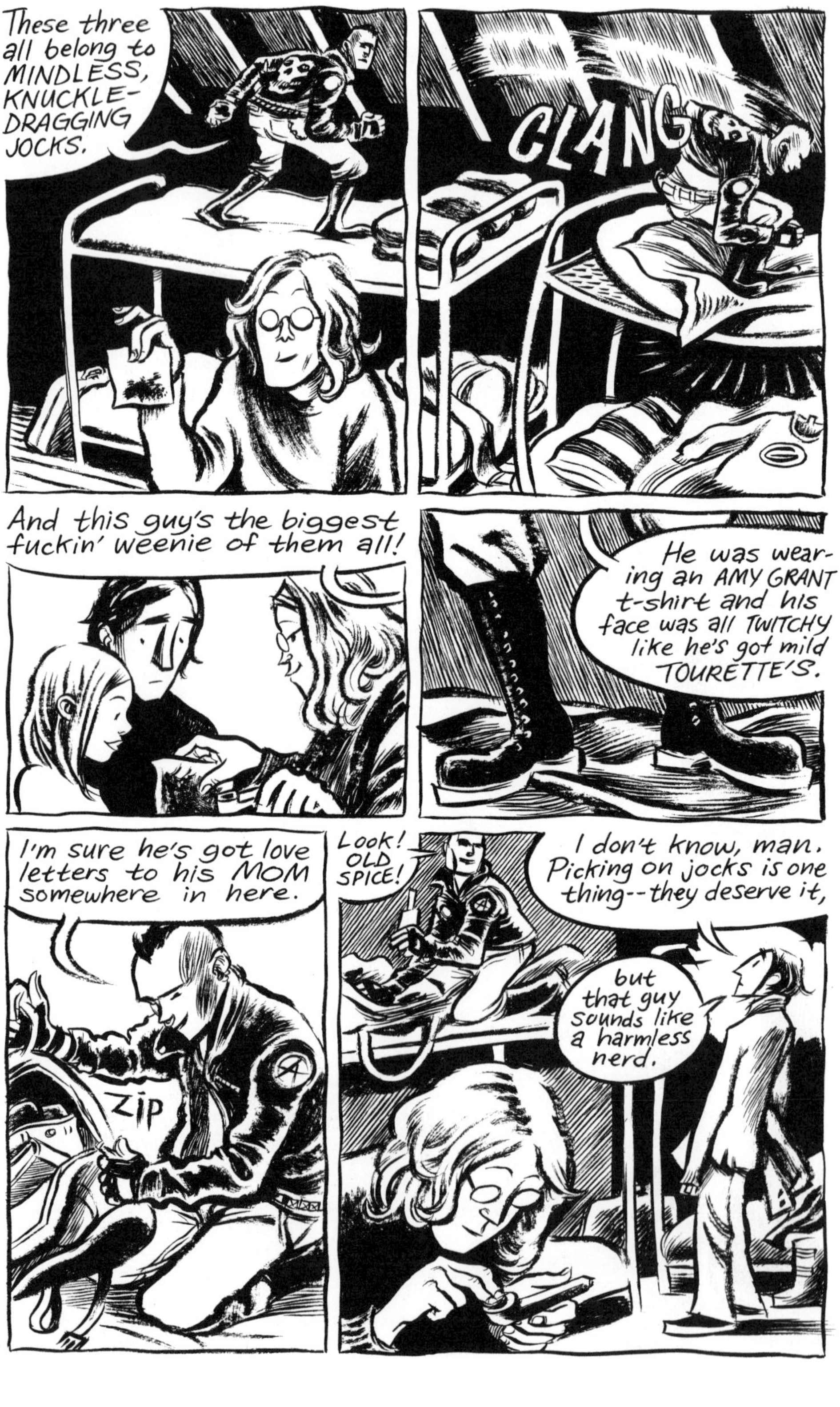
These three all belong to MINDLESS, KNUCKLE-DRAGGING JOCKS.
CLANG
And this guy's the biggest fuckin' weenie of them all!
He was wearing an AMY GRANT t-shirt and his face was all TWITCHY like he's got mild TOURETTE'S.
I'm sure he's got love letters to his MOM somewhere in here.
ZIP
Look! OLD SPICE!
I don't know, man. Picking on jocks is one thing--they deserve it,
but that guy sounds like a harmless nerd.

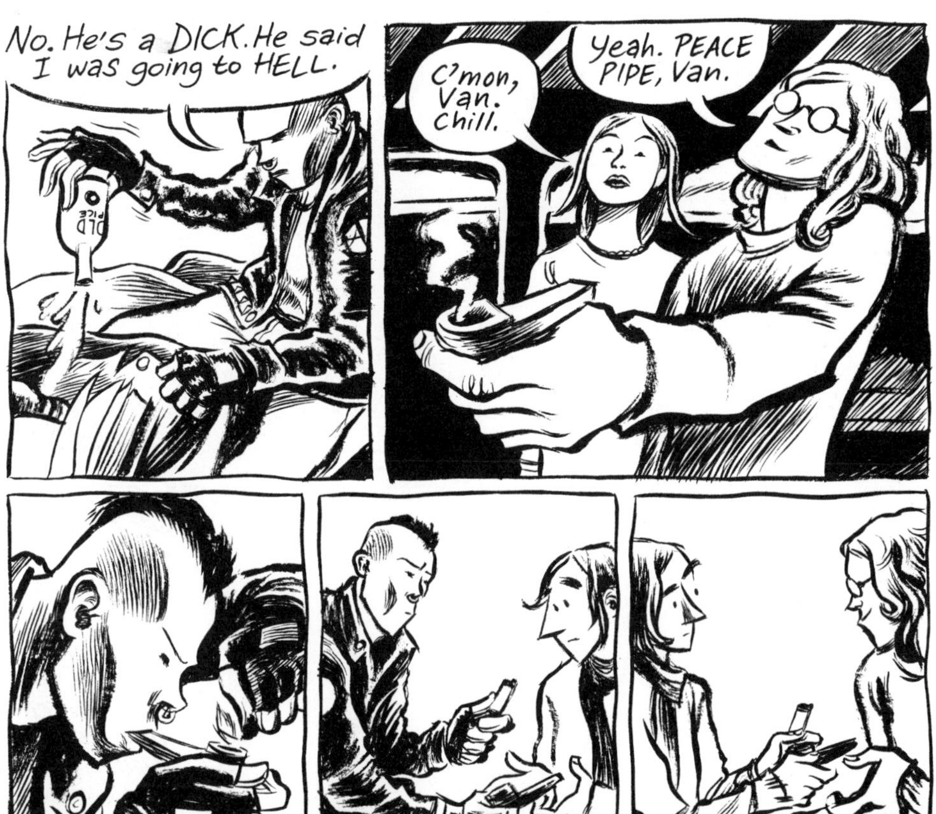
No. He's a DICK. He said I was going to HELL.
C'mon, Van. Chill.
Yeah. PEACE PIPE, Van.
SSSYOK
Don't you smoke?
uh... no.
Why? You think it's WRONG? You know, like BIBLICALLY wrong?
Not at all,
It's just not for me.

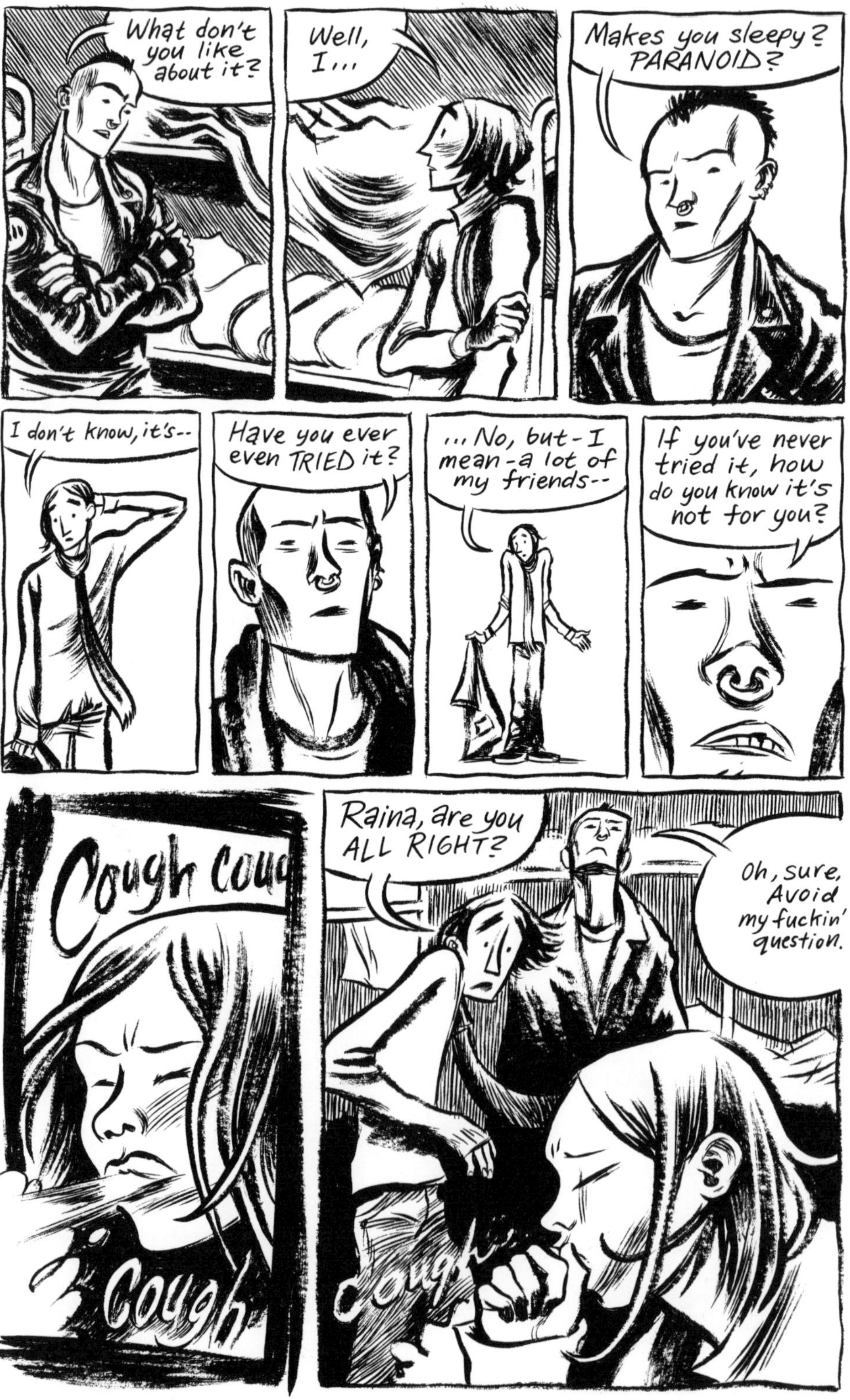
What don't you like about it?
Well, I...
Makes you sleepy? PARANOID?
I don't know, it's--
Have you ever even TRIED it?
...No, but-I mean-a lot of my friends--
If you've never tried it, how do you know it's not for you?
Cough couc
Cough
Raina, are you ALL RIGHT?
Oh, sure, Avoid my fuckin' question.
Cough

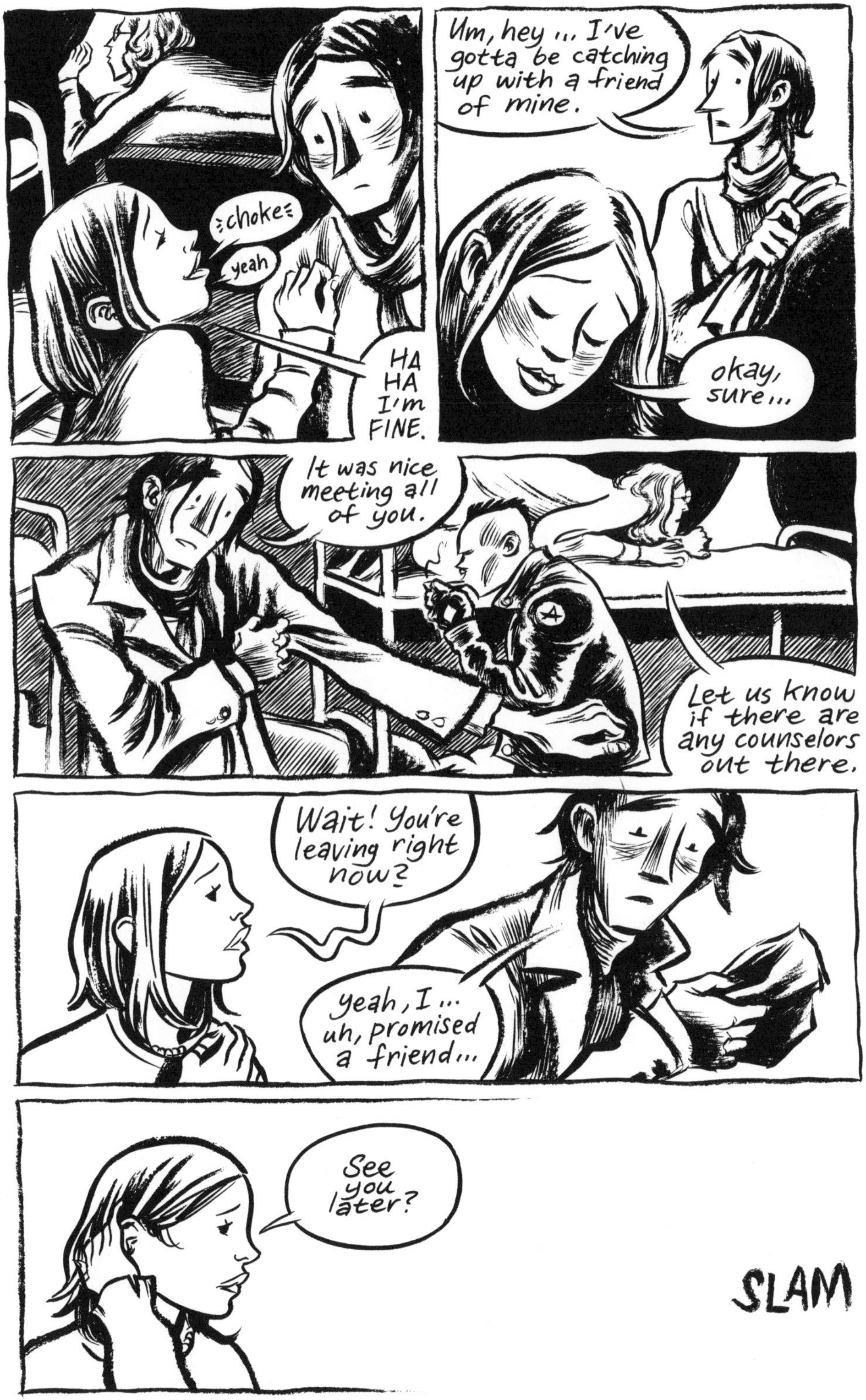

choke
yeah
HA HA I'm FINE.
Um, hey ... I've gotta be catching up with a friend of mine.
okay, sure...
It was nice meeting all of you.
Let us know if there are any counselors out there.
Wait! You're leaving right now?
Yeah, I... uh, promised a friend...
See you later?
SLAM

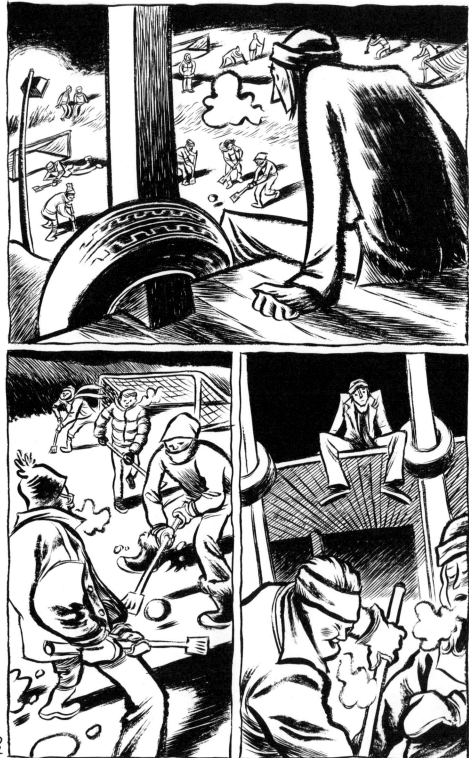

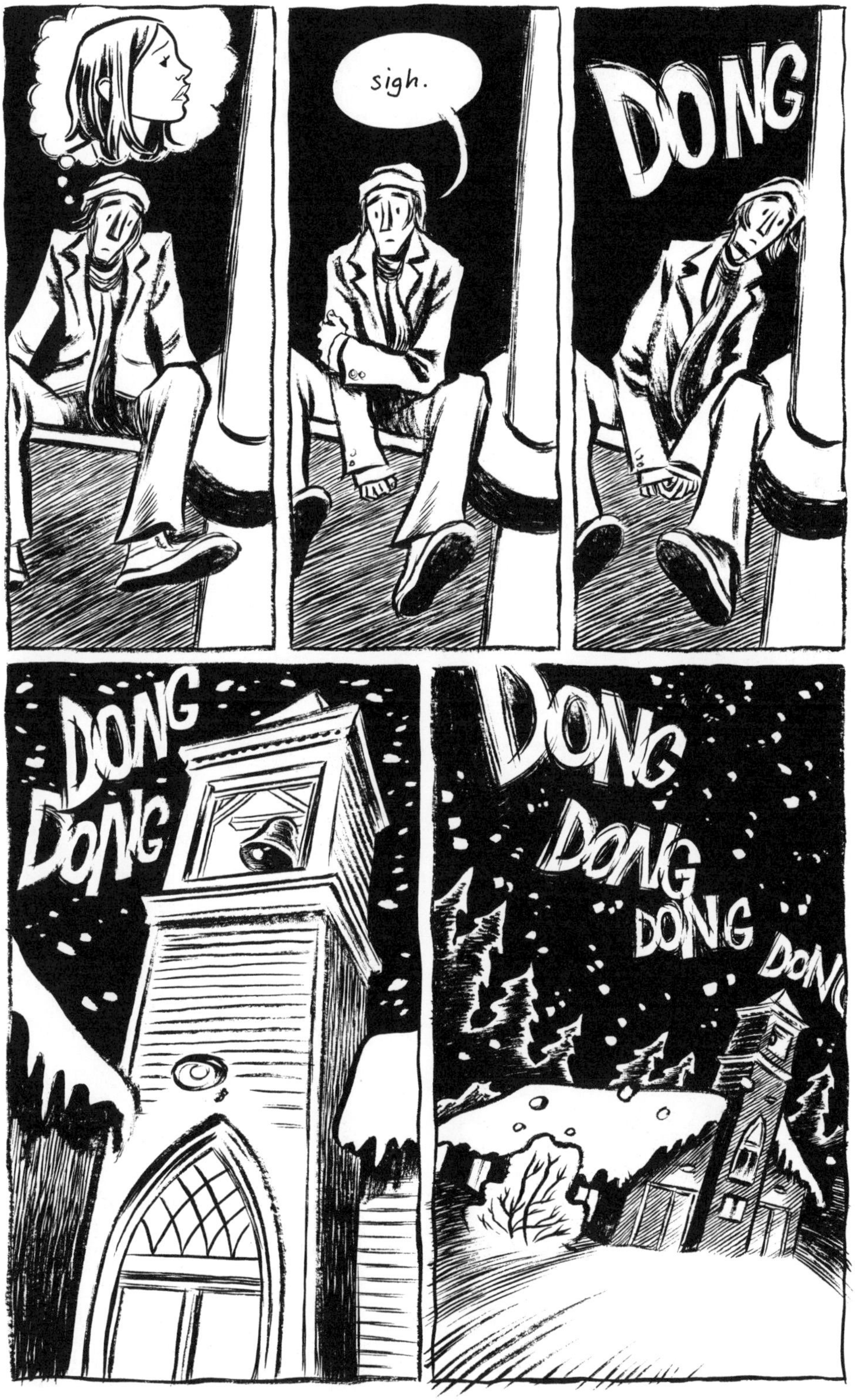
sigh.
DONG
DONG
DONG
DONG
DONG
DONG
DONG

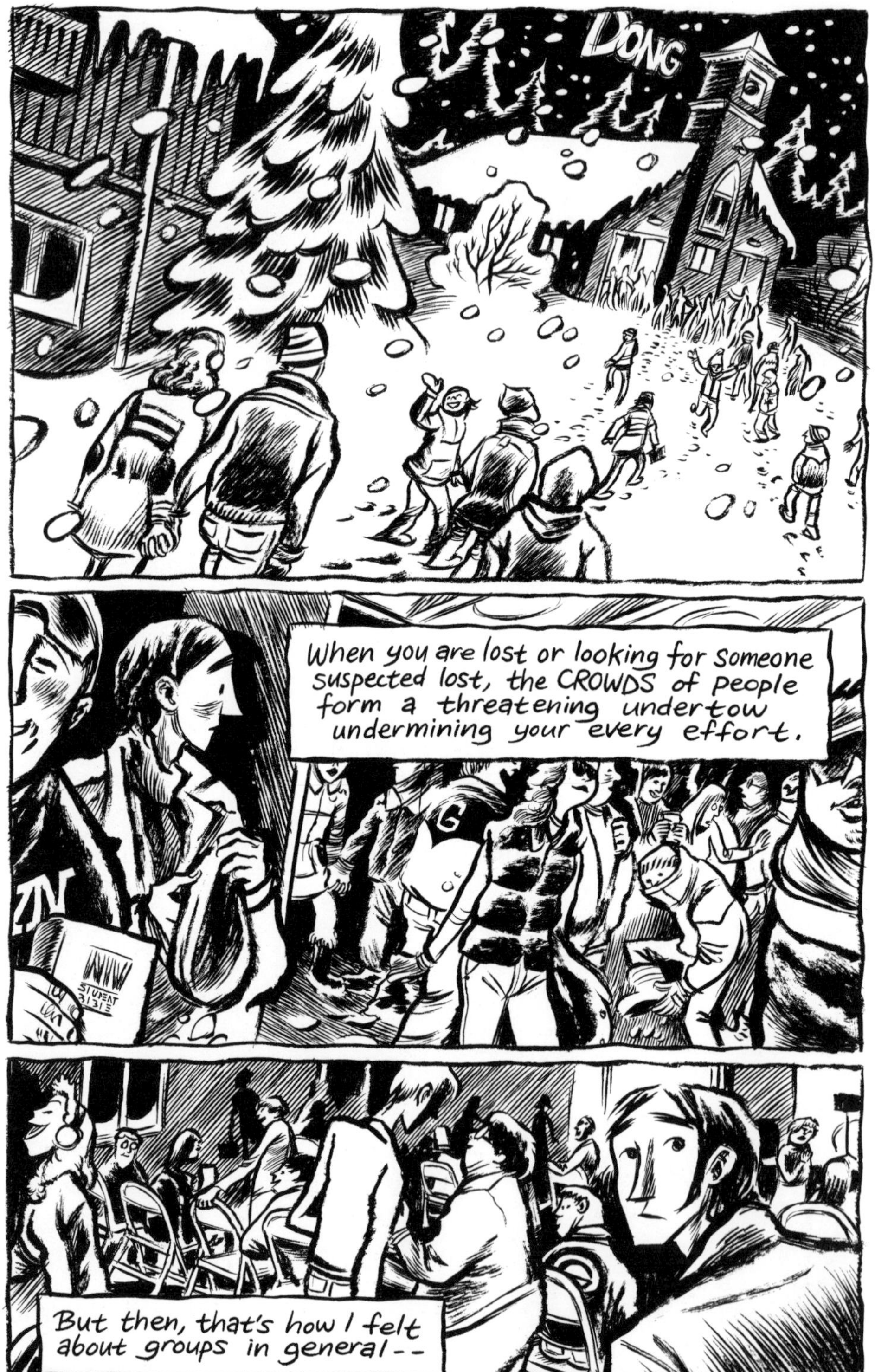
DONG
When you are lost or looking for someone suspected lost, the CROWDS of people form a threatening undertow undermining your every effort.
But then, that's how I felt about groups in general--

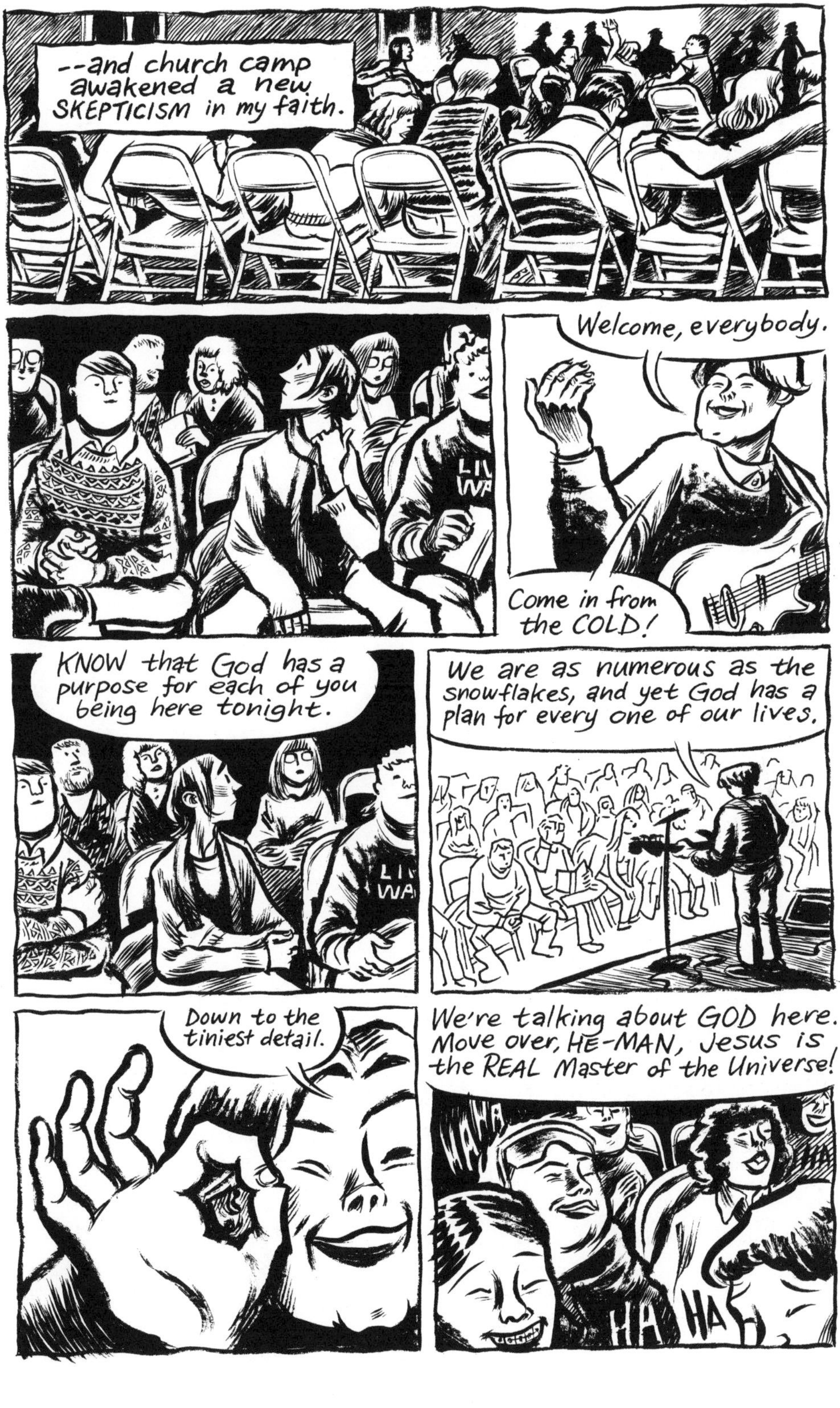
--and church camp awakened a new SKEPTICISM in my faith.
Welcome, everybody.
Come in from the COLD!
KNOW that God has a purpose for each of you being here tonight.
We are as numerous as the snowflakes, and yet God has a plan for every one of our lives.
Down to the tiniest detail.
We're talking about GOD here. Move over, HE-MAN, Jesus is the REAL Master of the Universe!
HA HA
HA HA
HA HA

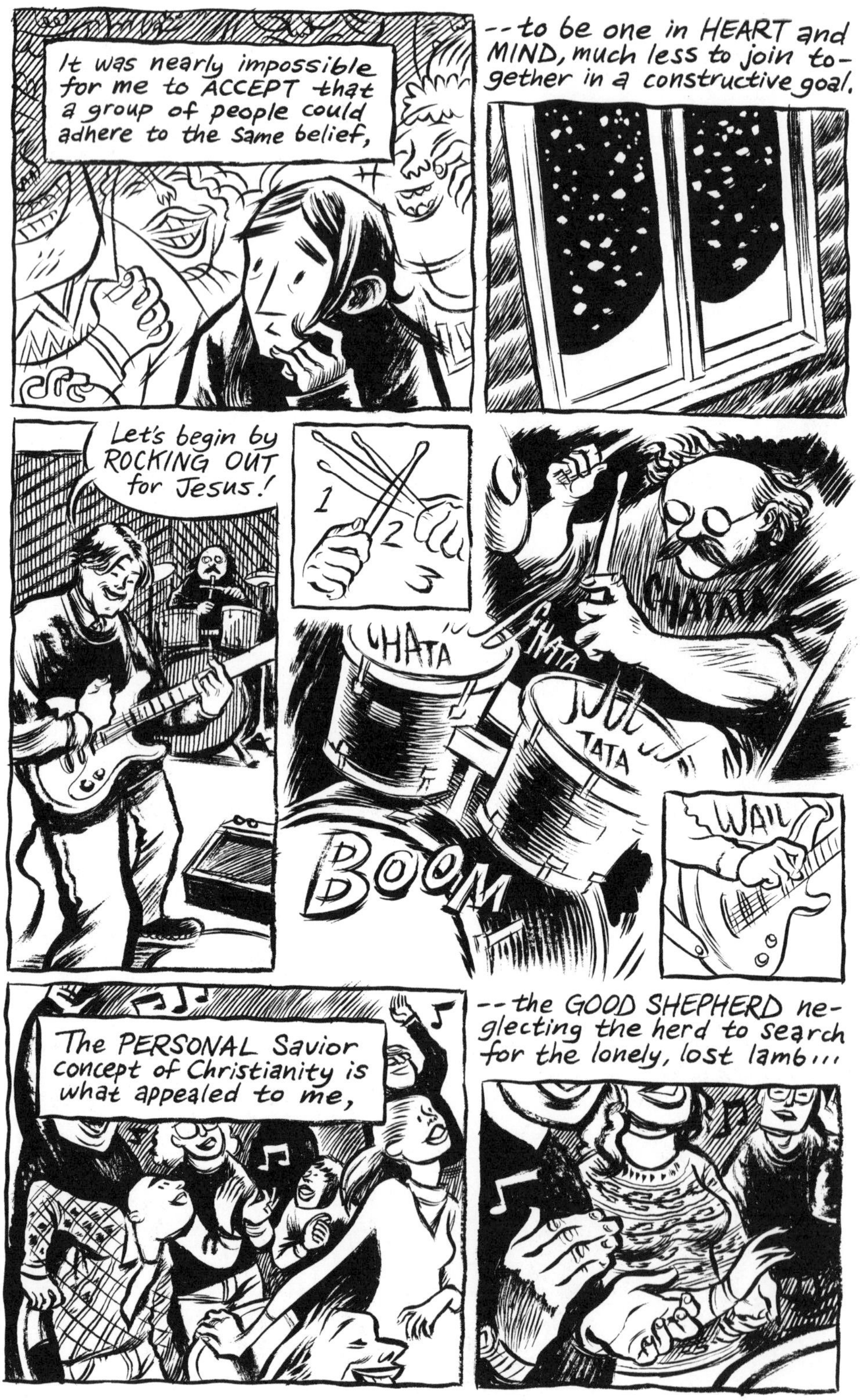
It was nearly impossible for me to ACCEPT that a group of people could adhere to the same belief,
-- to be one in HEART and MIND, much less to join together in a constructive goal.
Let's begin by ROCKING OUT for Jesus!
1
2
CHATA
CHATA
CHATA
TATA
BOOM
WAIL
The PERSONAL Savior concept of Christianity is what appealed to me,
-- the GOOD SHEPHERD neglecting the herd to search for the lonely, lost lamb...

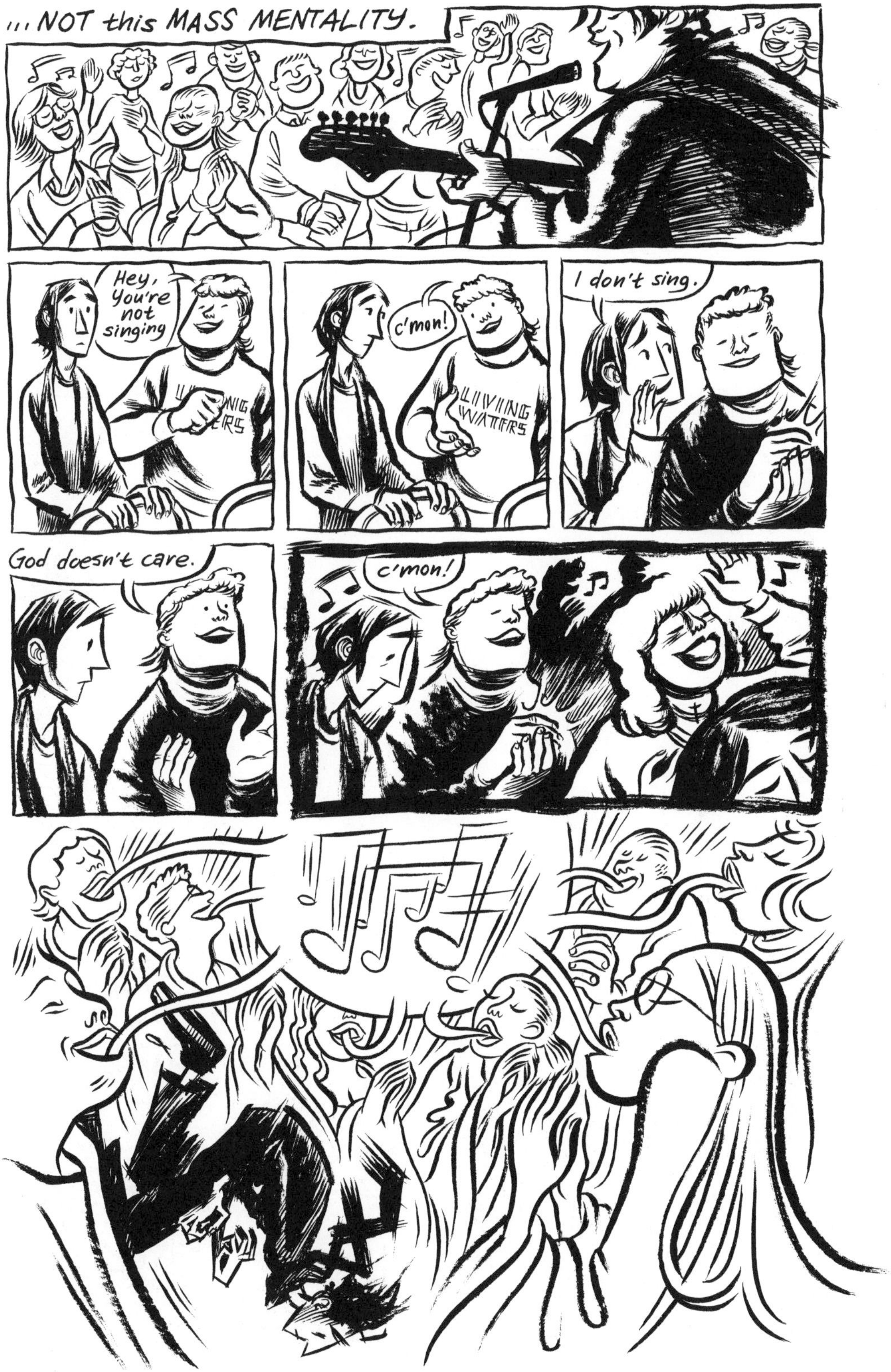

... NOT this MASS MENTALITY.
Hey, you're not singing
LIVING WATERS
c'mon!
LIVING WATERS
I don't sing.
God doesn't care.
c'mon!

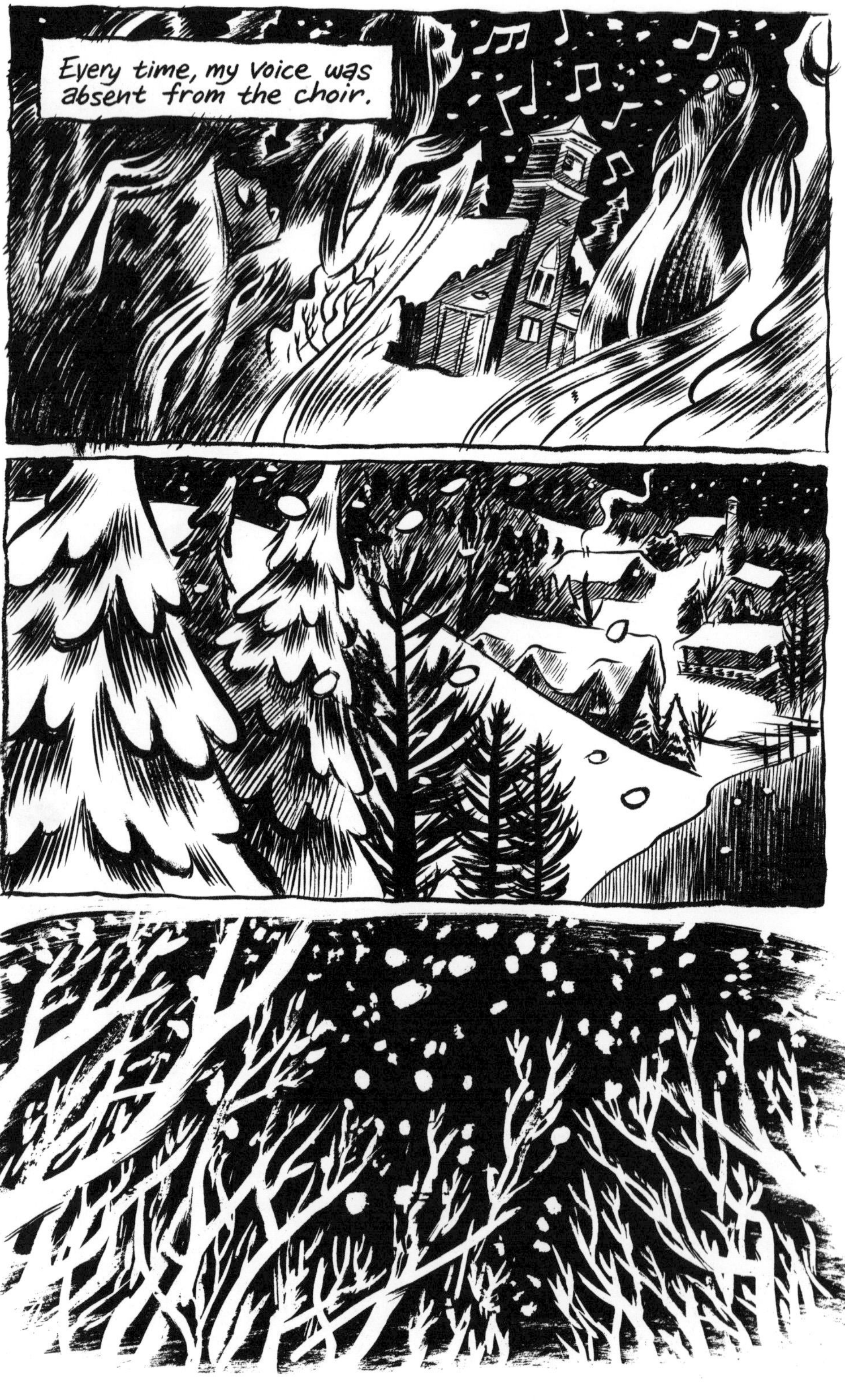
Every time, my voice was absent from the choir.

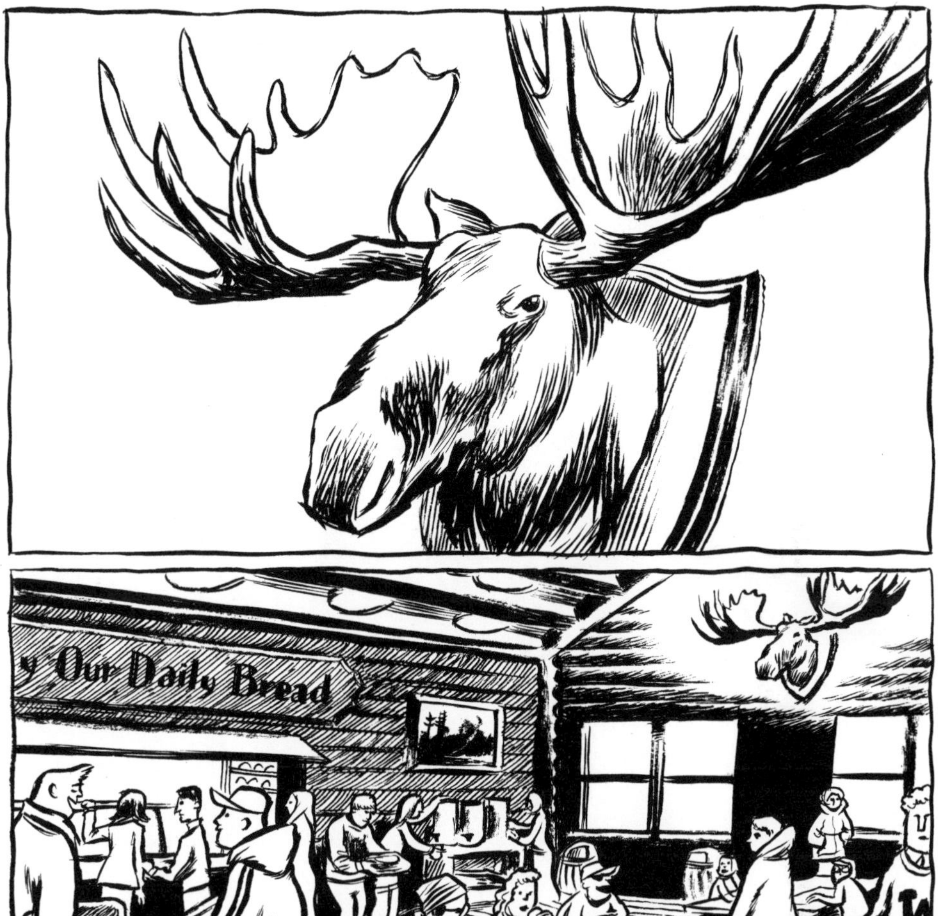
y Our Daily Bread

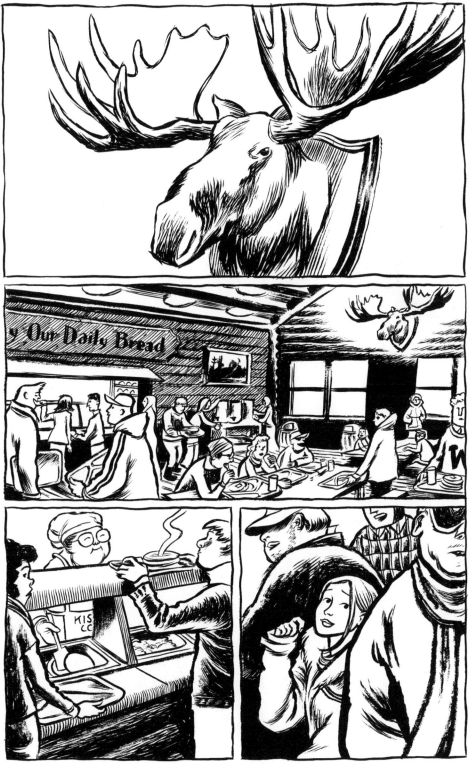

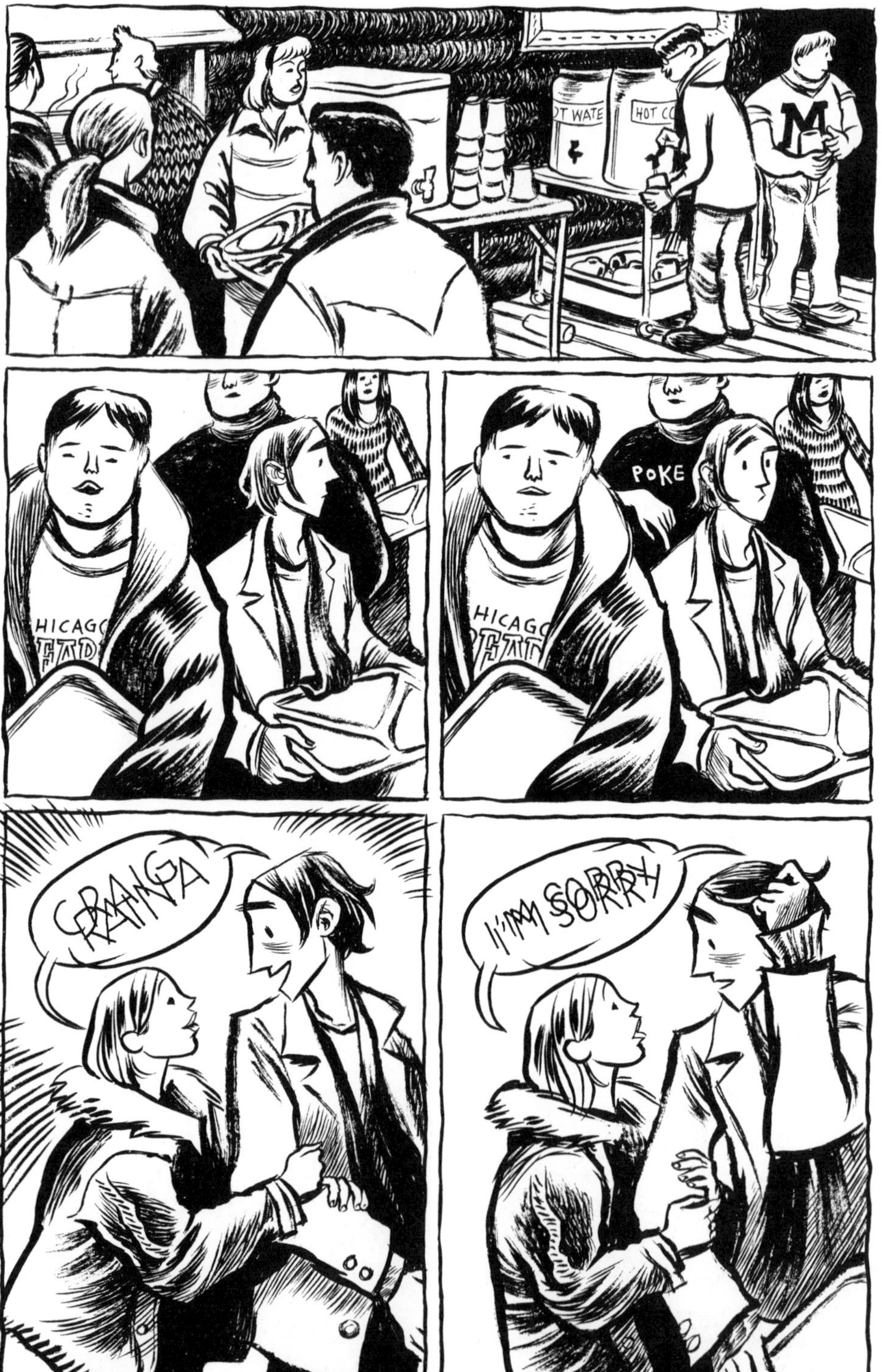
HOT WATE
HOT CO
M
HICAGO
POKE
HICAGO
CRAIG / RAINA
I'M SORRY

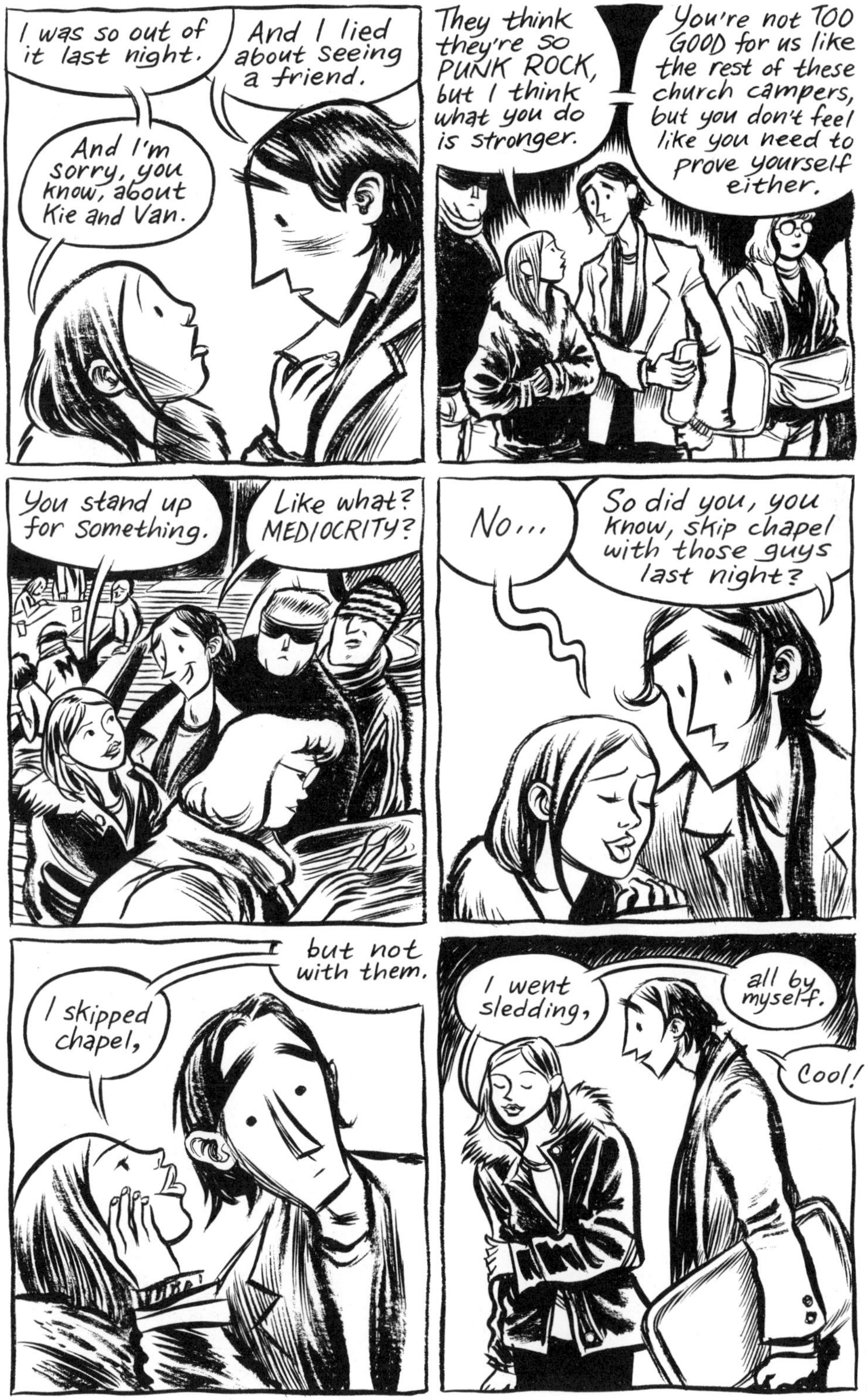
I was so out of it last night.
And I'm sorry, you know, about Kie and Van.
And I lied about seeing a friend.
They think they're so PUNK ROCK, but I think what you do is stronger.
You're not TOO GOOD for us like the rest of these church campers, but you don't feel like you need to prove yourself either.
You stand up for something.
Like what? MEDIOCRITY?
No...
So did you, you know, skip chapel with those guys last night?
I skipped chapel,
but not with them.
I went sledding,
all by myself.
Cool!

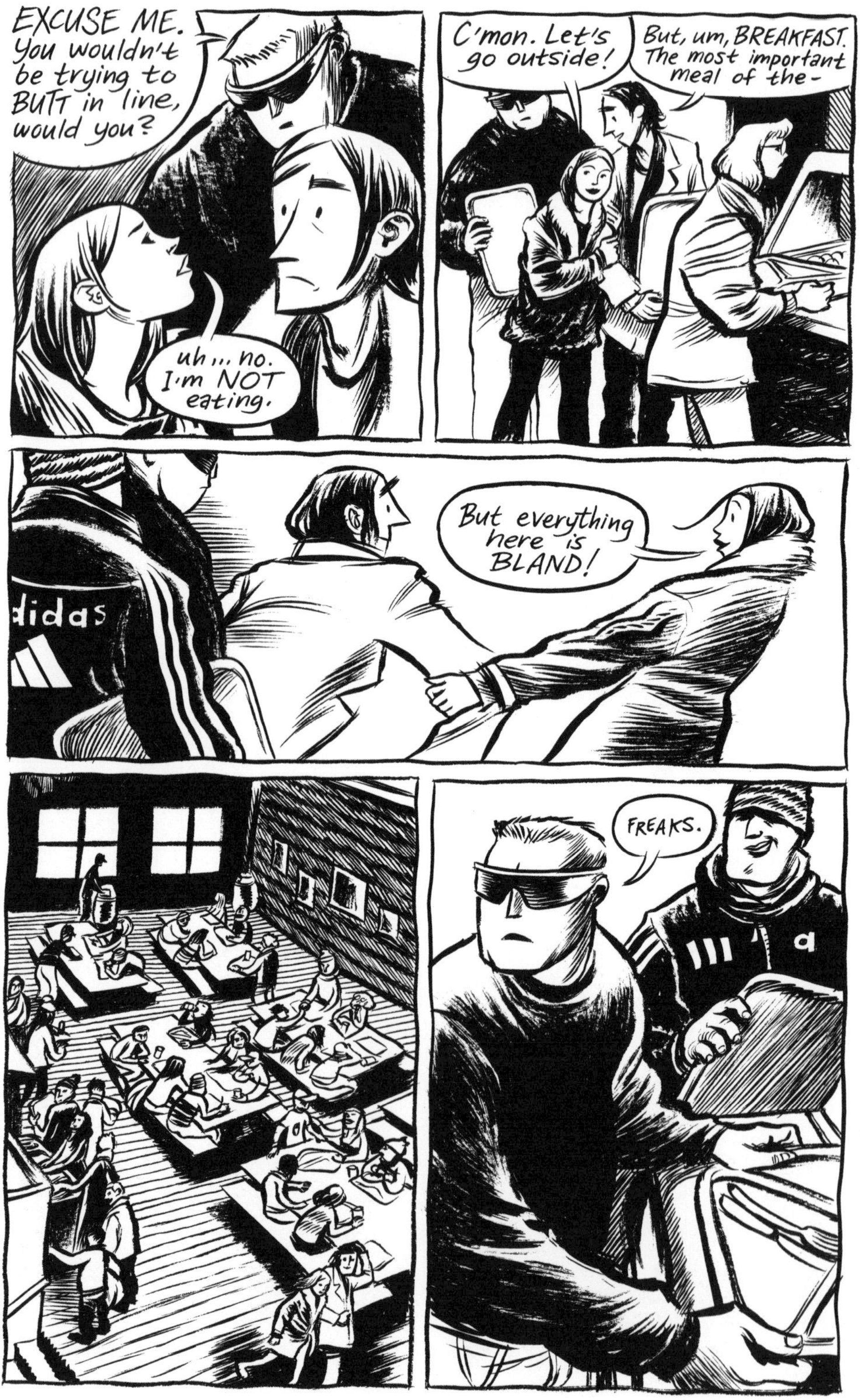
EXCUSE ME. You wouldn't be trying to BUTT in line, would you?
uh... no. I'm NOT eating.
C'mon. Let's go outside!
But, um, BREAKFAST. The most important meal of the-
didas
But everything here is BLAND!
FREAKS.

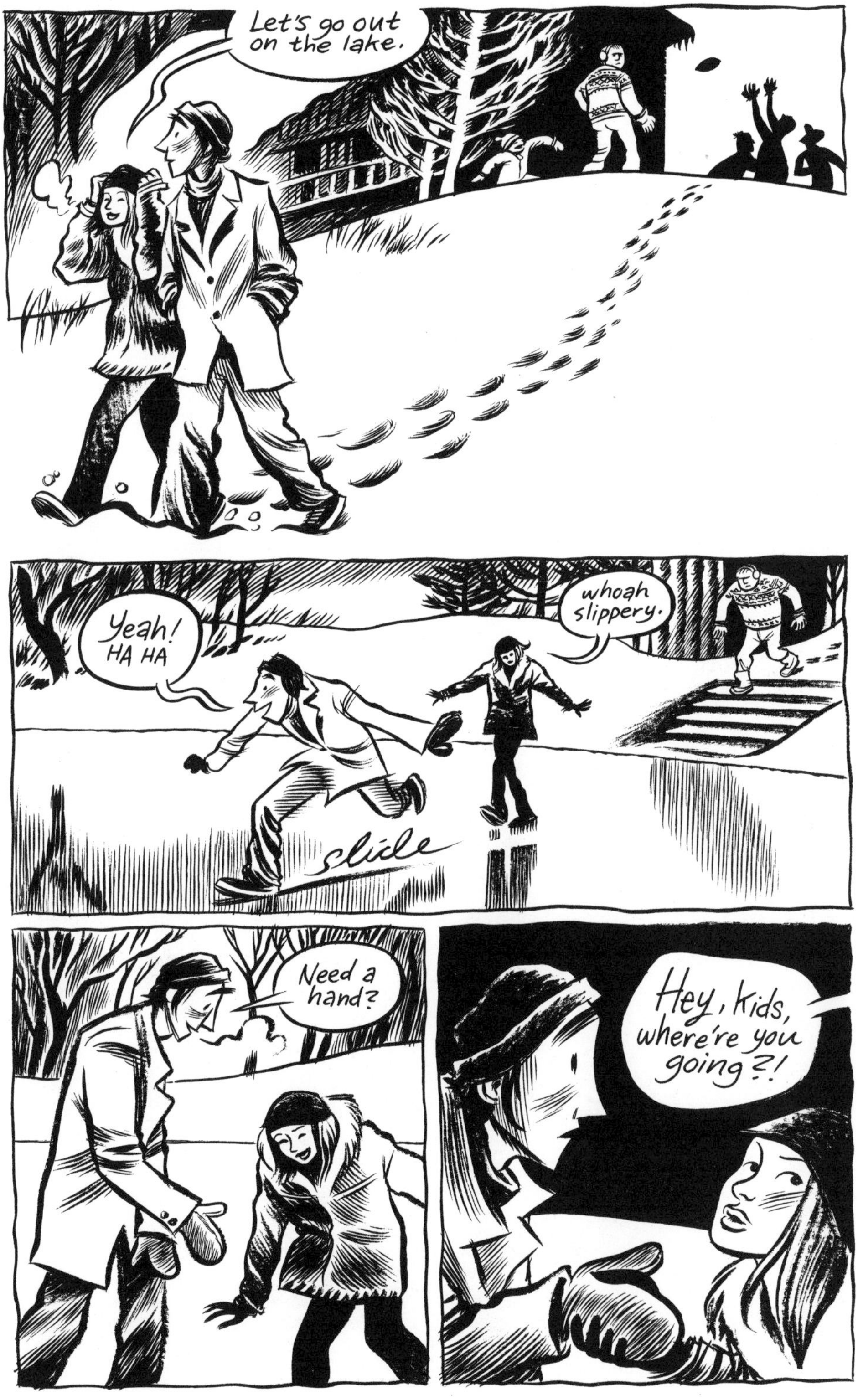
Let's go out on the lake.
Yeah! HA HA
whoah slippery.
slide
Need a hand?
Hey, kids, where're you going?!

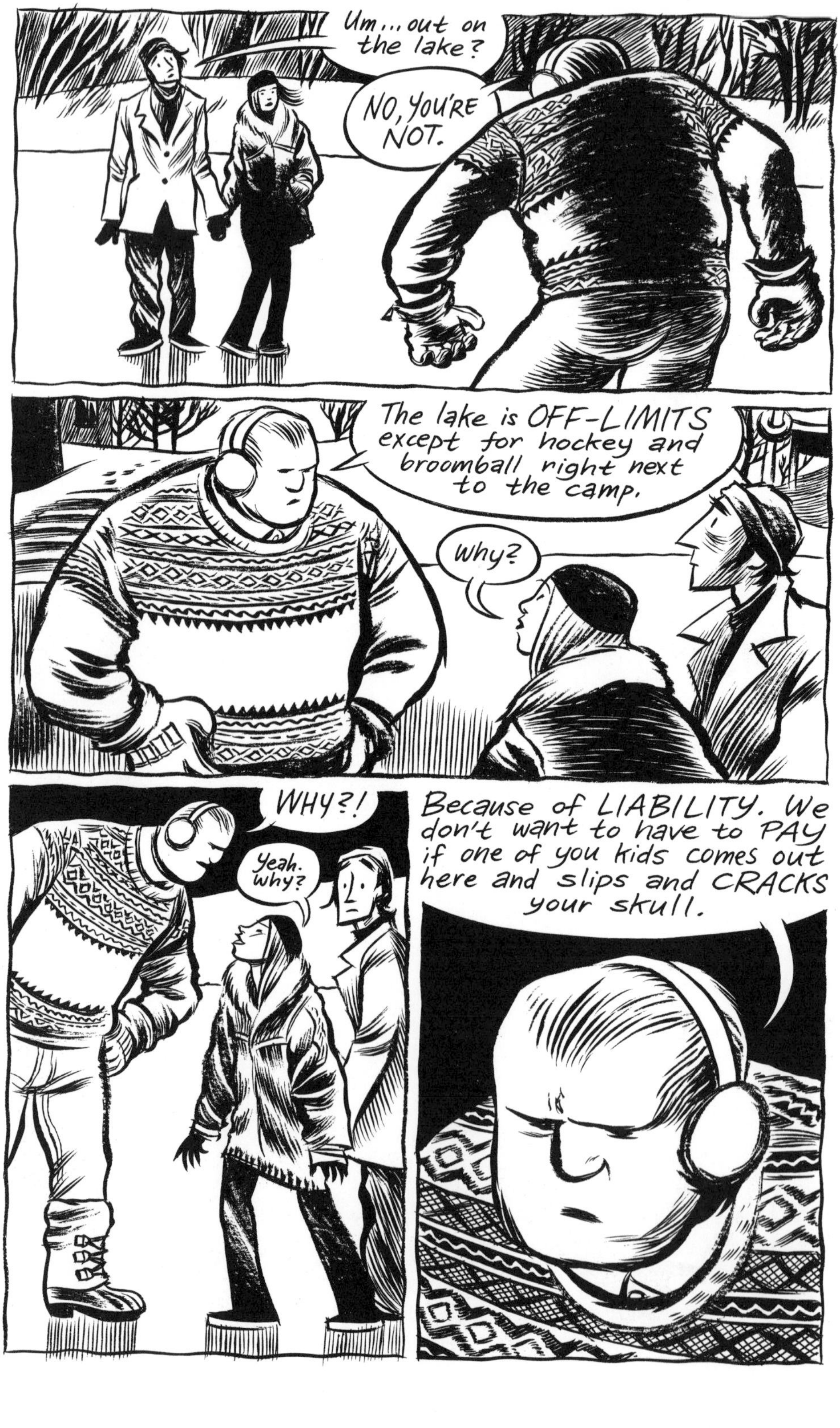
Um... out on the lake?
NO, YOU'RE NOT.
The lake is OFF-LIMITS except for hockey and broomball right next to the camp.
Why?
WHY?!
Yeah. Why?
Because of LIABILITY. We don't want to have to PAY if one of you kids comes out here and slips and CRACKS your skull.

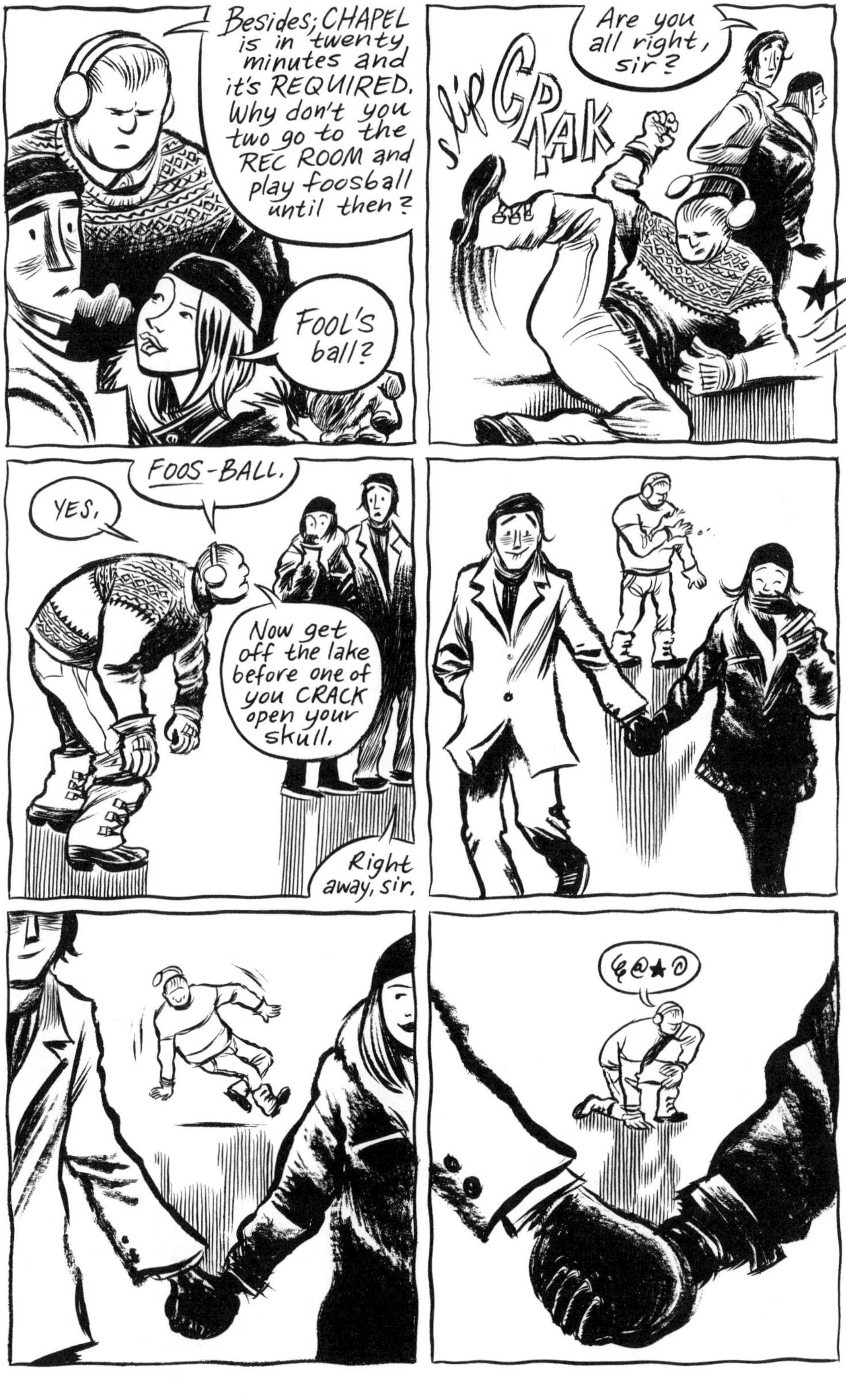
Besides; CHAPEL is in twenty minutes and it's REQUIRED. Why don't you two go to the REC ROOM and play foosball until then?
FOOL'S ball?
Are you all right, sir?
slip
CRAK
YES.
FOOS-BALL.
Now get off the lake before one of you CRACK open your skull.
Right away, sir.

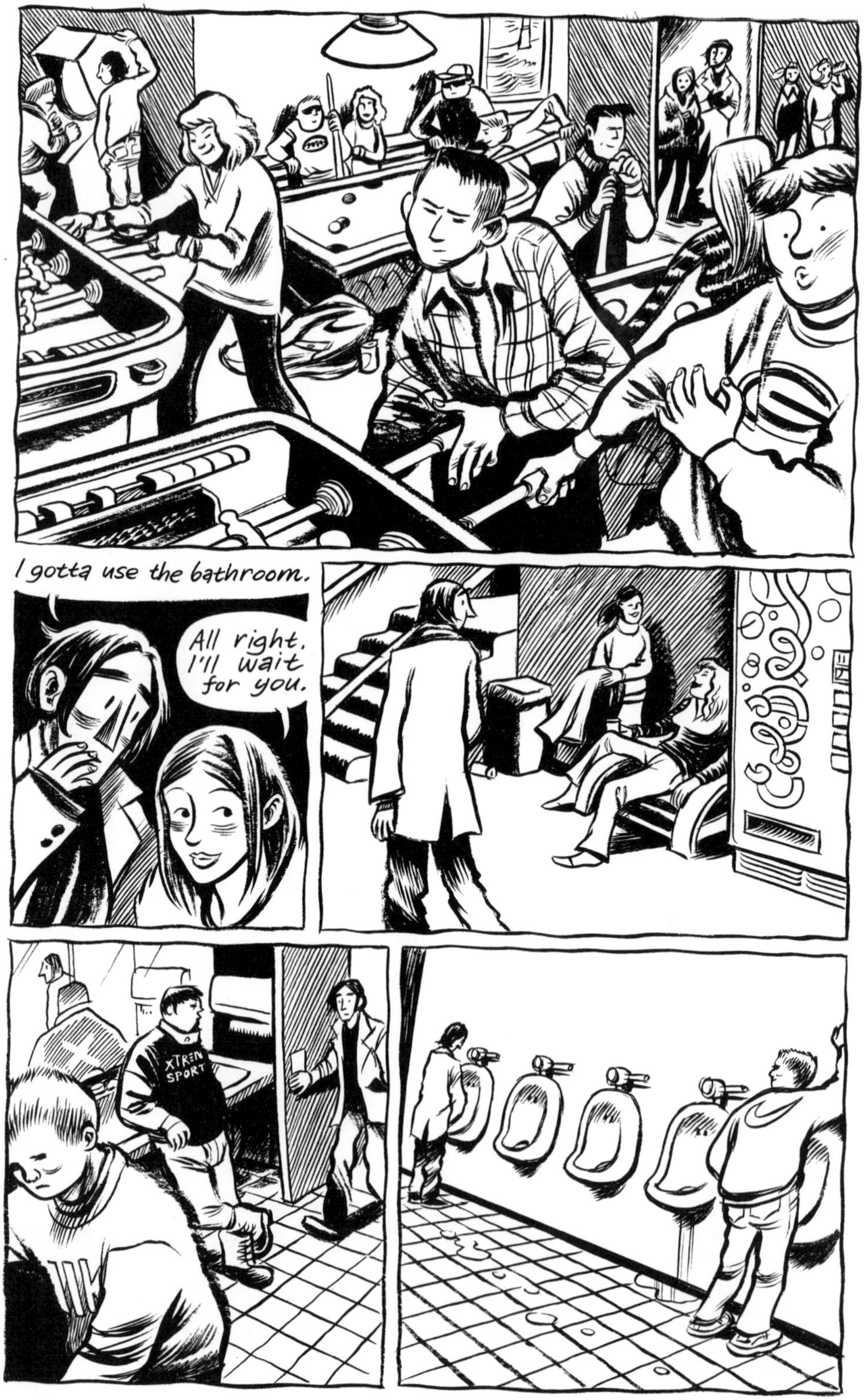
I gotta use the bathroom.
All right, I'll wait for you.
XTREM SPORT

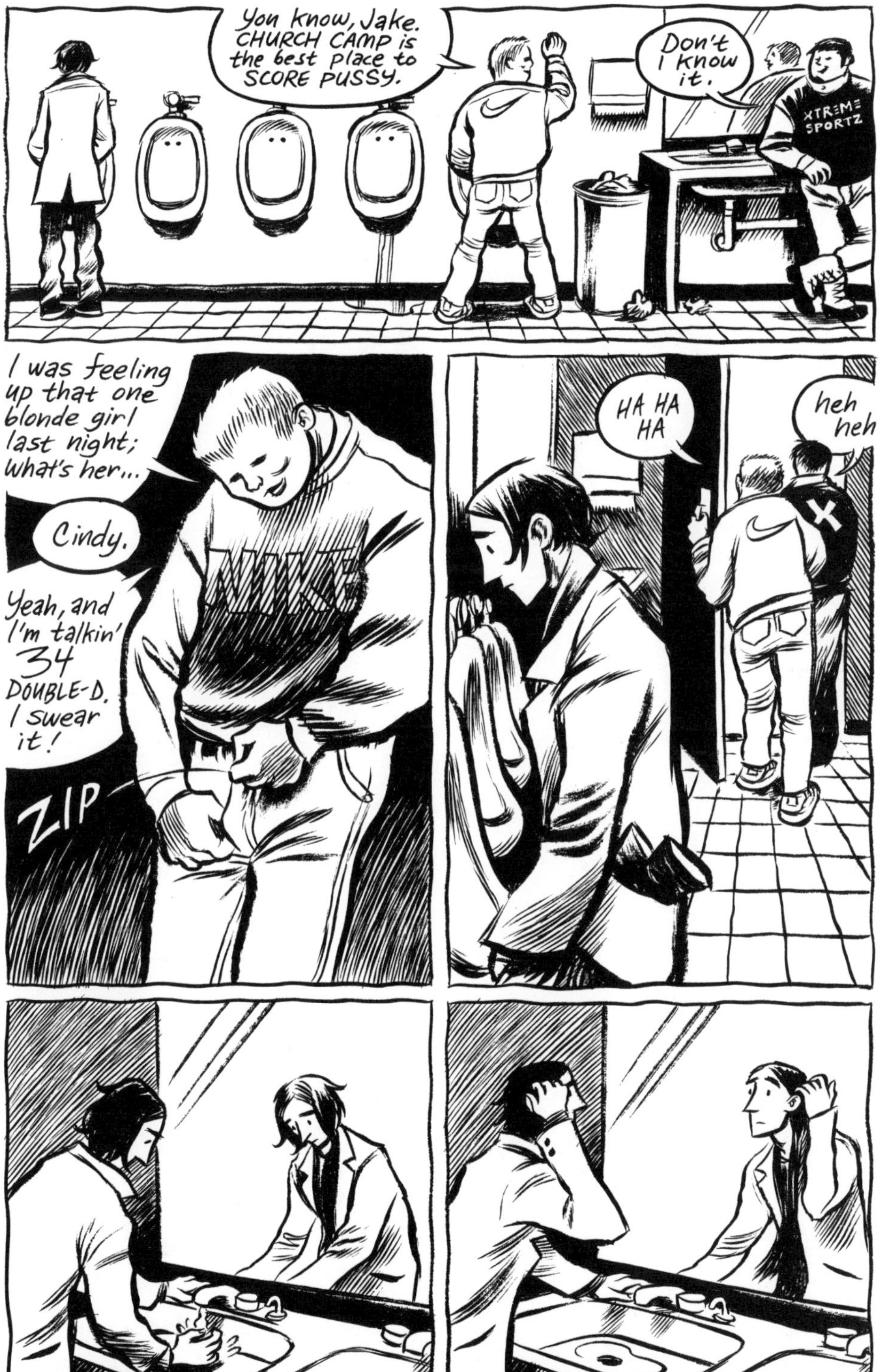

You know, Jake. CHURCH CAMP is the best place to SCORE PUSSY.
Don't I know it.
XTREME SPORTZ
I was feeling up that one blonde girl last night; what's her...
Cindy.
Yeah, and I'm talkin' 34 DOUBLE-D. I swear it!
ZIP
NIKE
HA HA HA
heh heh

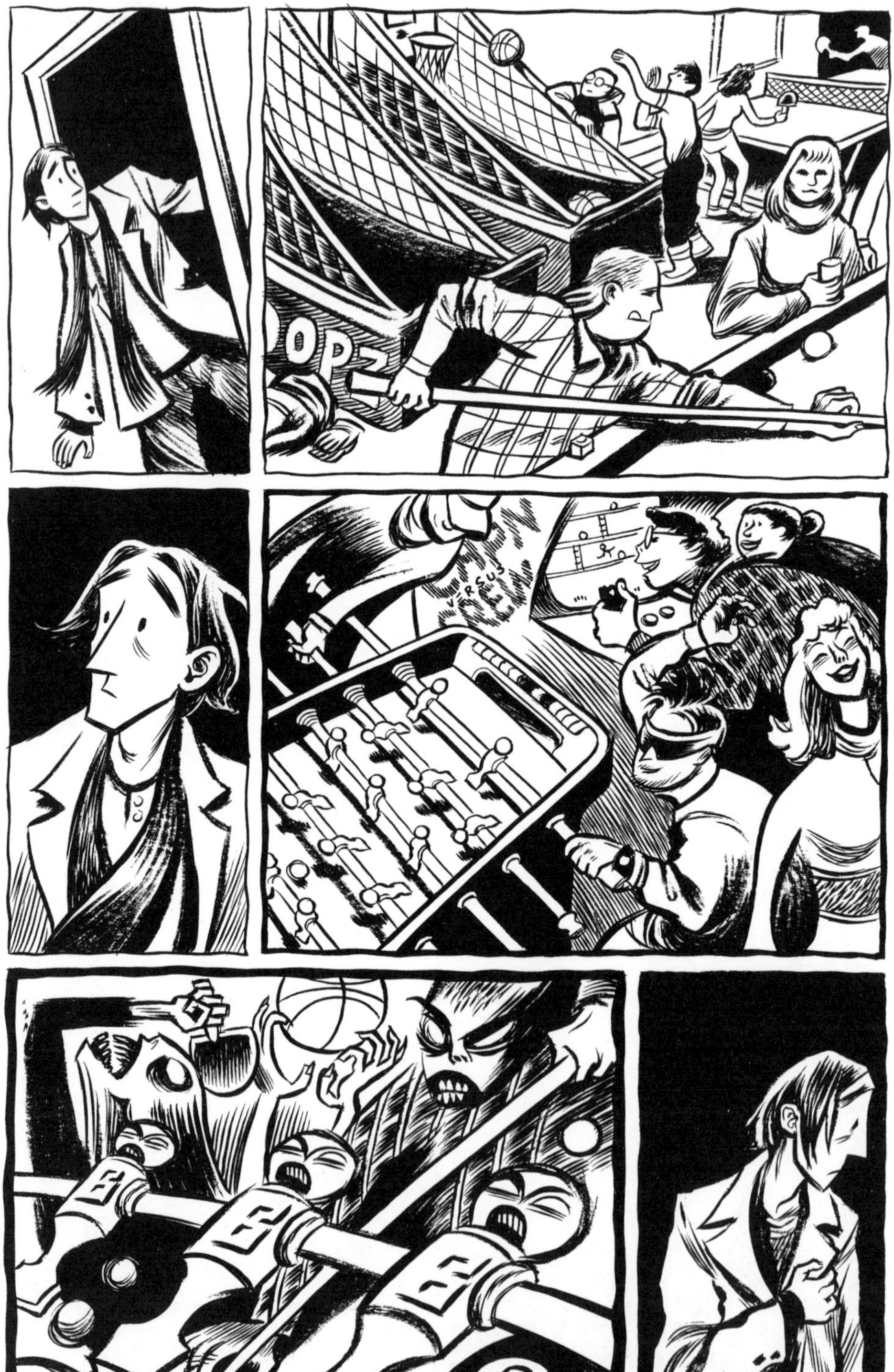
VERSUS

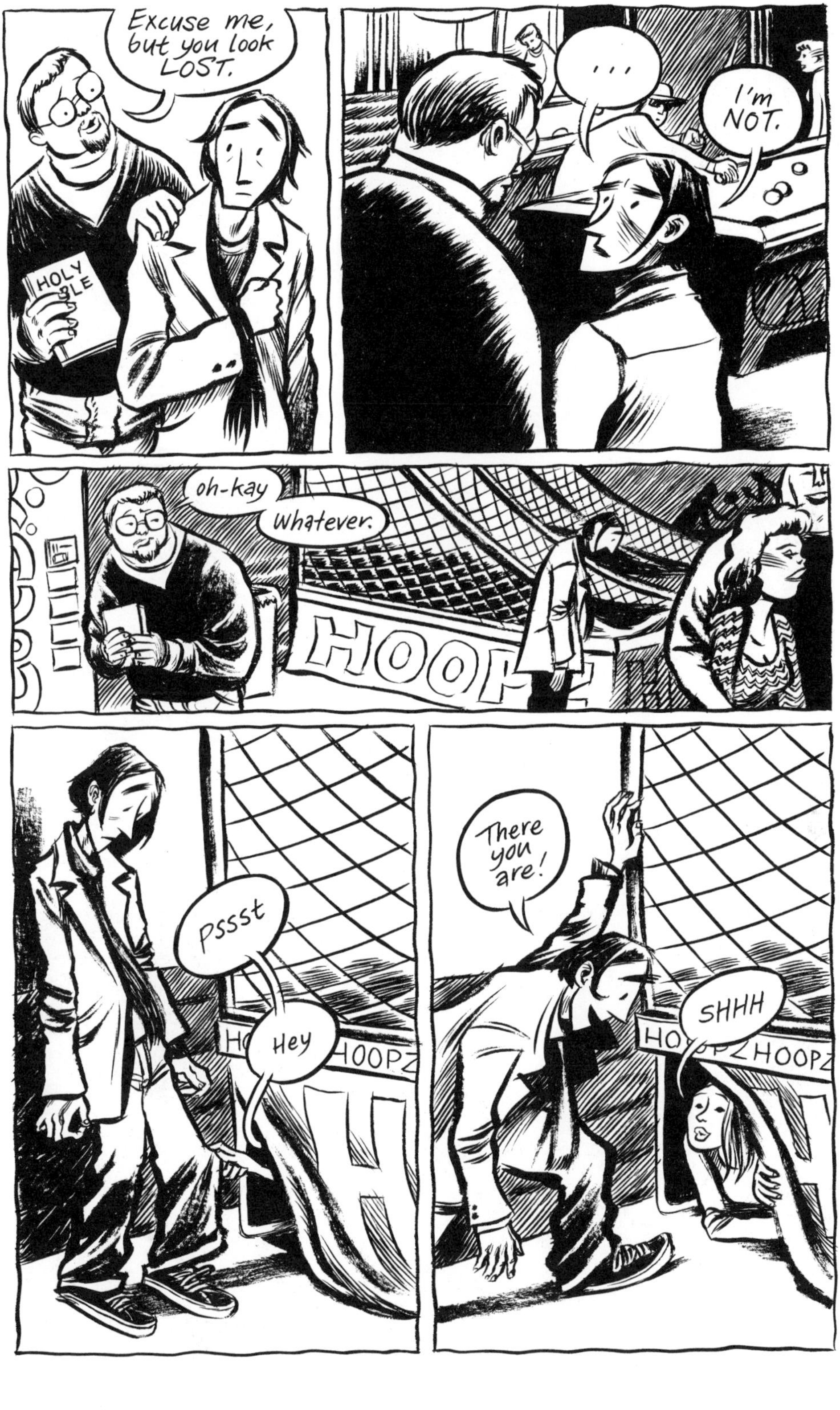
Excuse me, but you look LOST.
HOLY BLE
. . .
I'm NOT.
oh-kay
whatever.
HOOP
Pssst
Hey
HOOPZ
There you are!
SHHH
HOOPZ HOOPZ

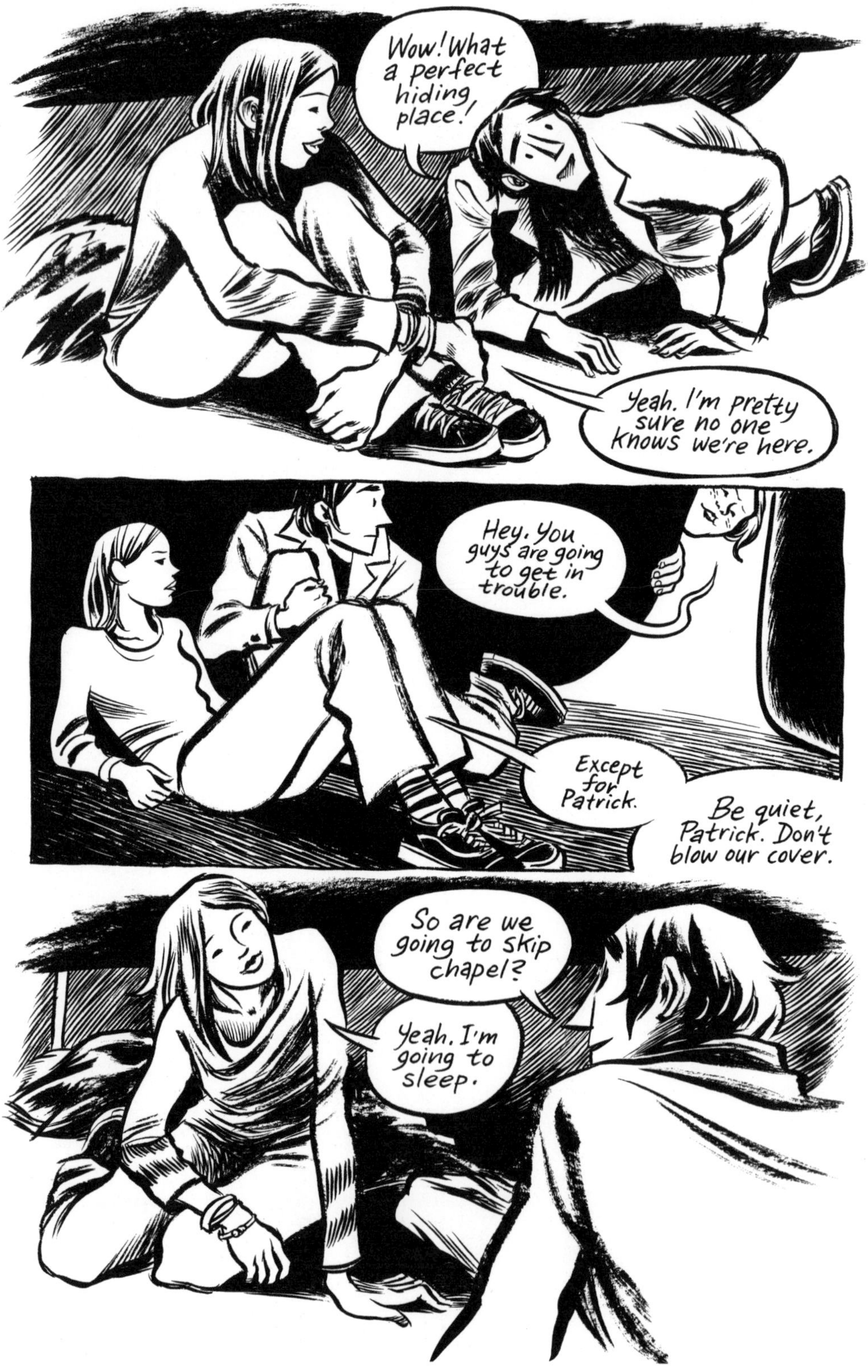

Wow! What a perfect hiding place!
Yeah. I'm pretty sure no one knows we're here.
Hey. You guys are going to get in trouble.
Except for Patrick.
Be quiet, Patrick. Don't blow our cover.
So are we going to skip chapel?
Yeah. I'm going to sleep.

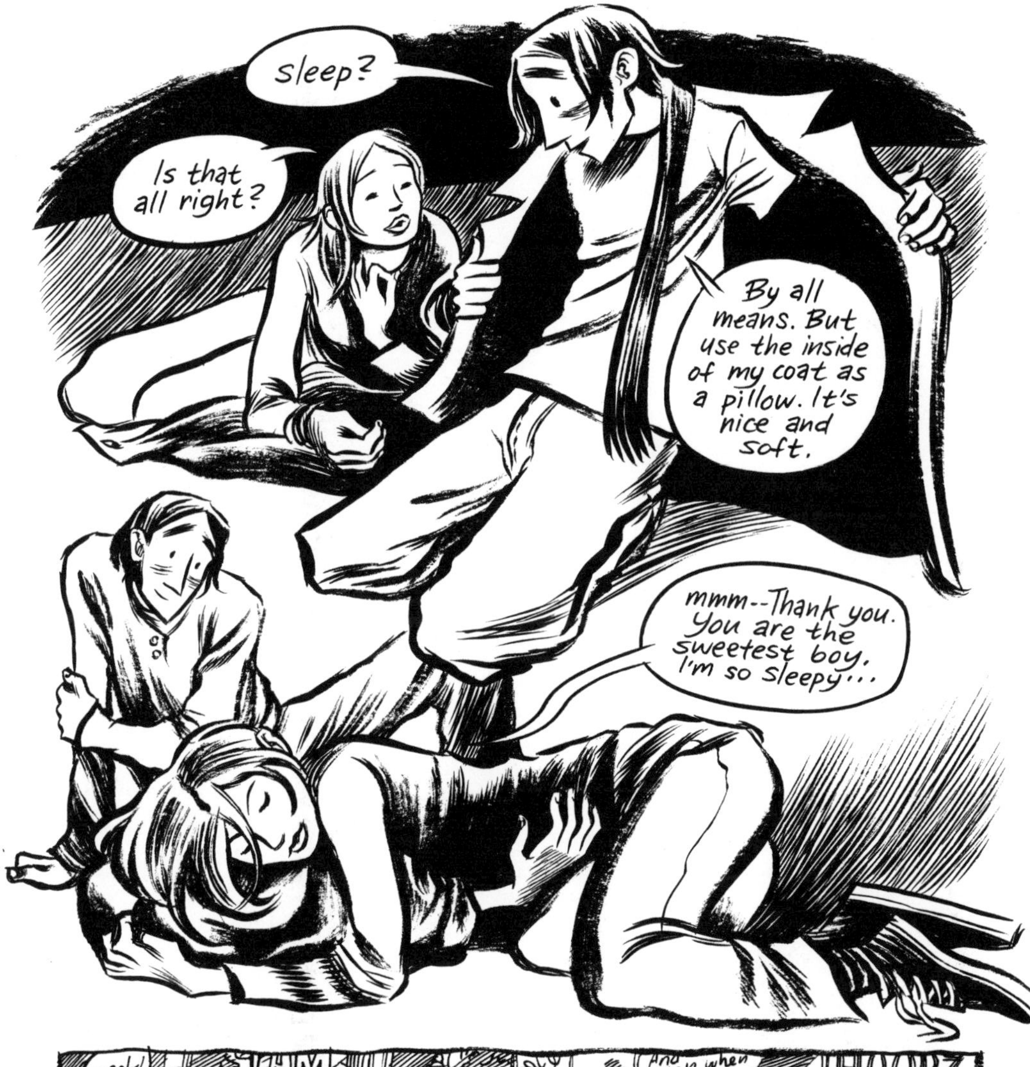
sleep?
Is that all right?
By all means. But use the inside of my coat as a pillow. It's nice and soft.
mmm--Thank you. You are the sweetest boy. I'm so sleepy...

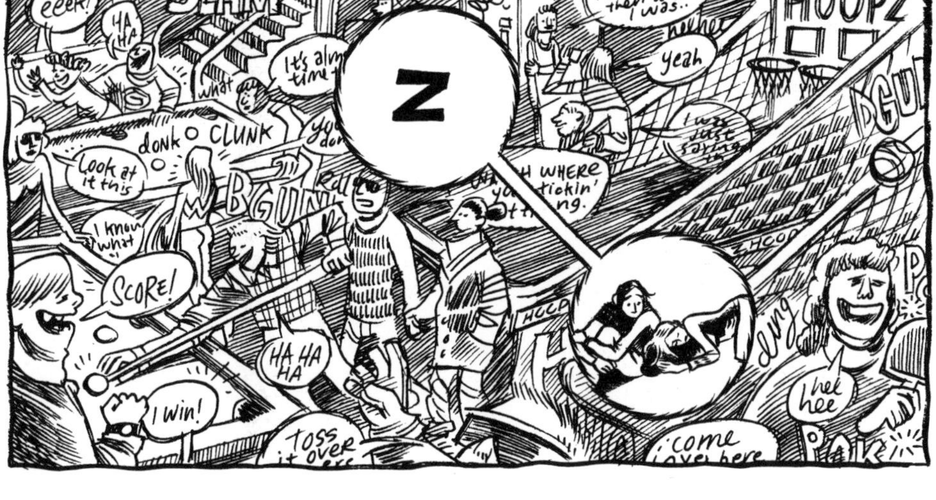
eeek!
HA HA
SLAM
Z
And then when I was..
HOOPZ
yeah
donk
CLUNK
Look at it this
I know what
SCORE!
HA HA HA
I win!
hee hee
come over here

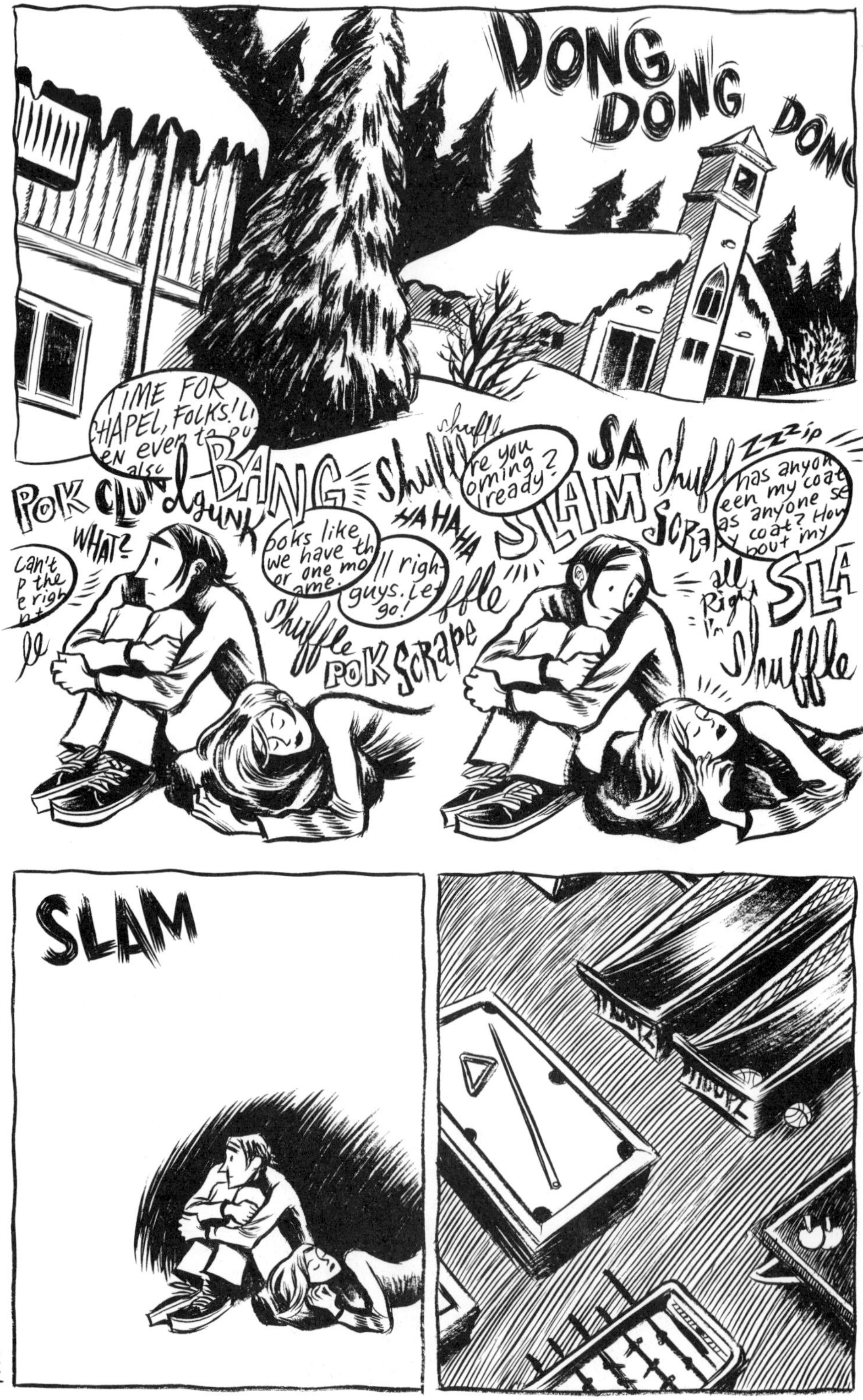
DONG DONG DONG
TIME FOR CHAPEL, FOLKS!
POK CLUNG BANG GUNK
WHAT?
Shuffle
re you oming? ready?
SA SLAM
Shuff
SCRAP
ZZZip
has anyon een my coat as anyone se coat? How bout my
Looks like we have th one mo ame.
HAHAHA
ll righ guys. Let go!
Shuffle
POK SCRAPE
all Right I'm
SLA
Shuffle
SLAM

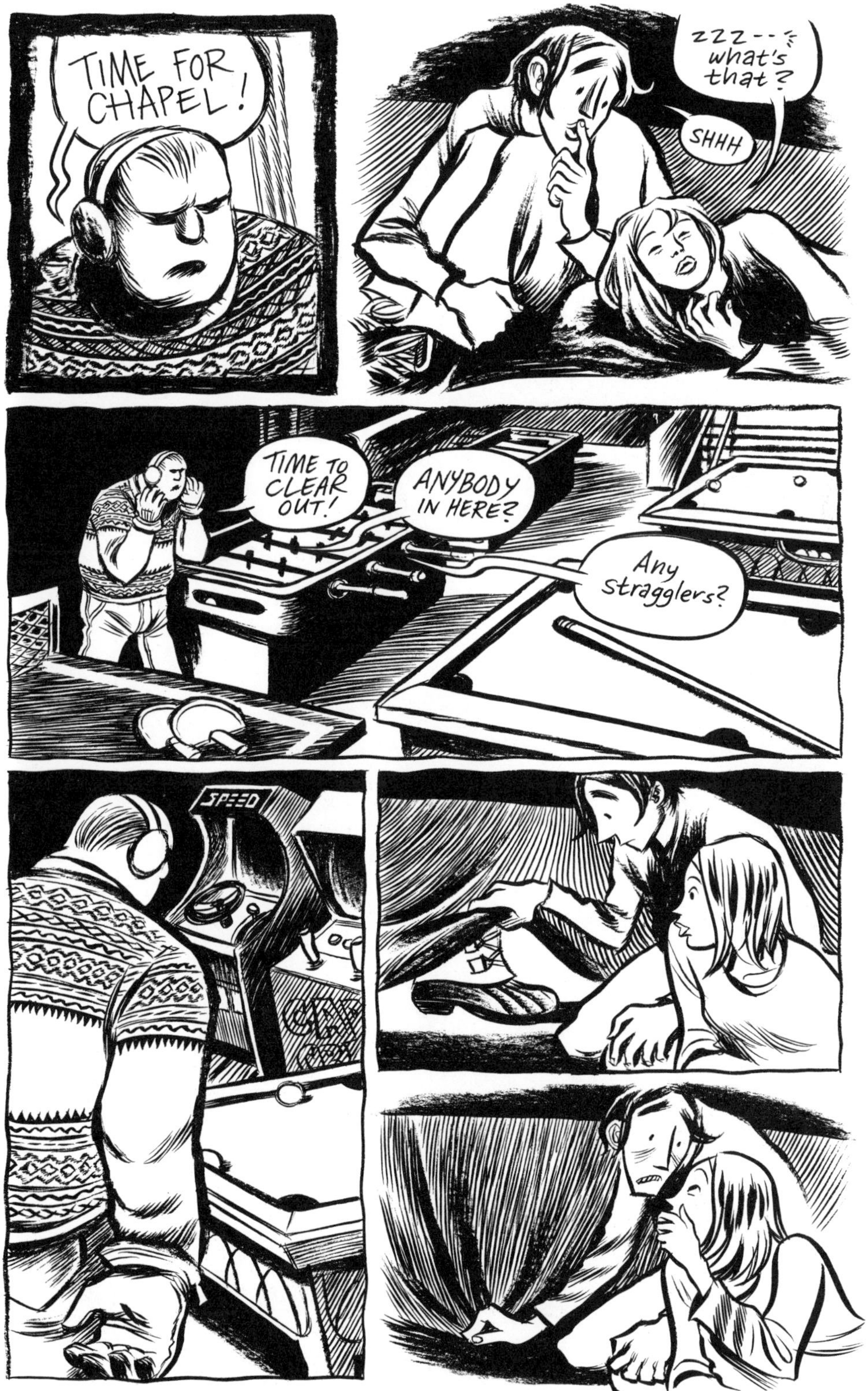
TIME FOR CHAPEL!
ZZZ-- what's that?
SHHH
TIME TO CLEAR OUT!
ANYBODY IN HERE?
Any stragglers?
SPEED

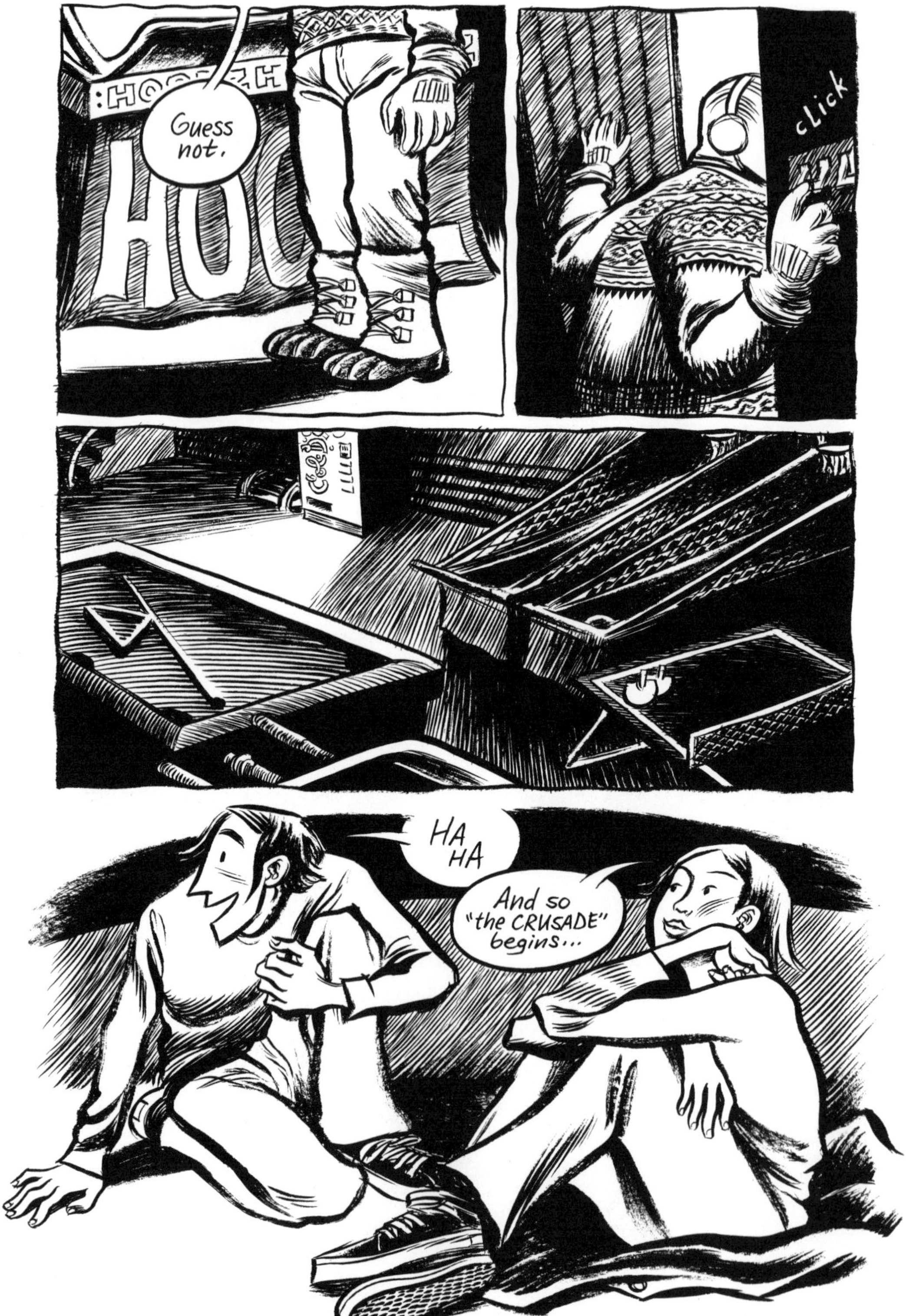
Guess not.
click
HA HA
And so "the CRUSADE" begins...

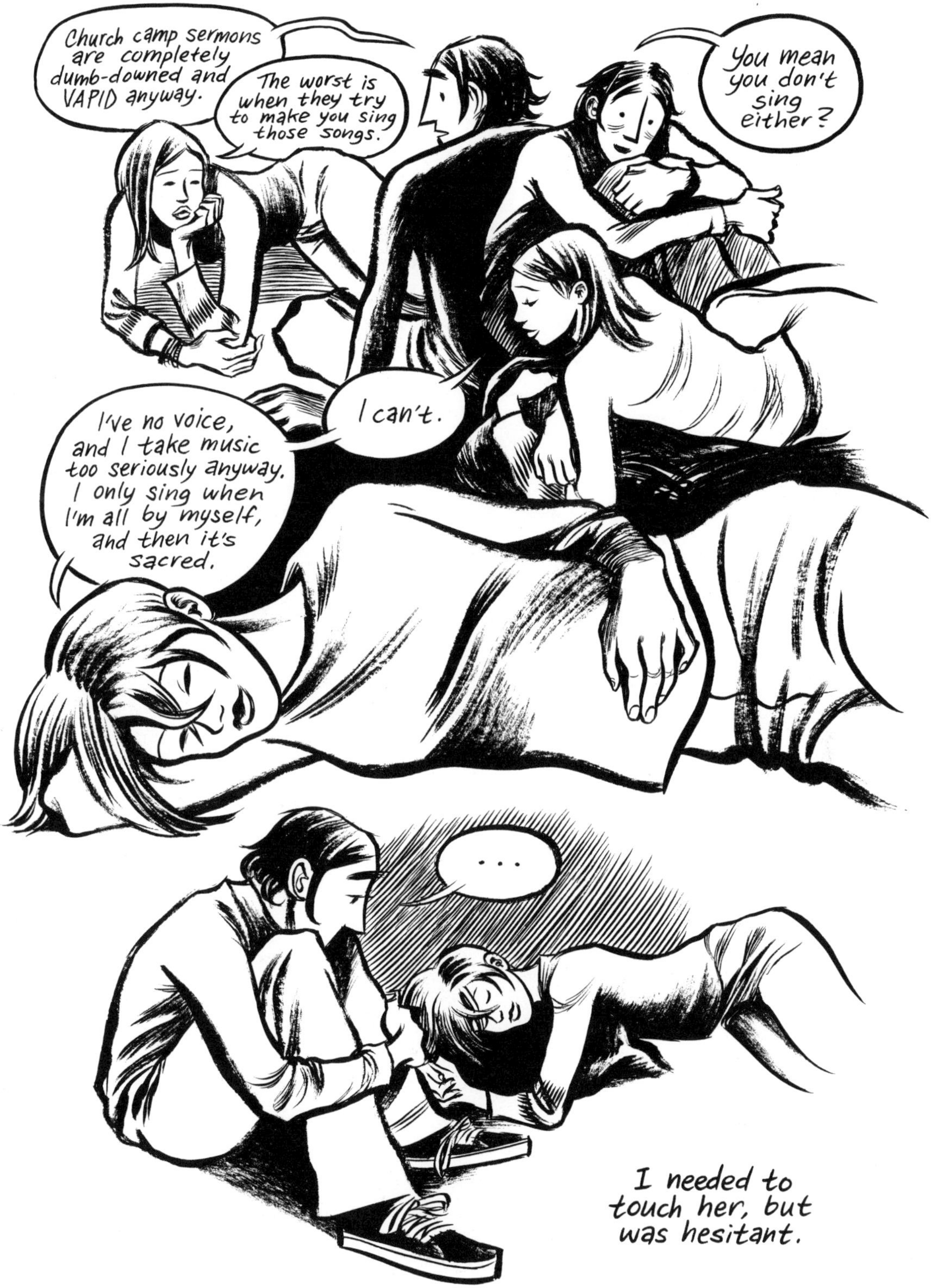

Church camp sermons are completely dumb-downed and VAPID anyway.
The worst is when they try to make you sing those songs.
You mean you don't sing either?
I can't.
I've no voice, and I take music too seriously anyway. I only sing when I'm all by myself, and then it's sacred.
...
I needed to touch her, but was hesitant.

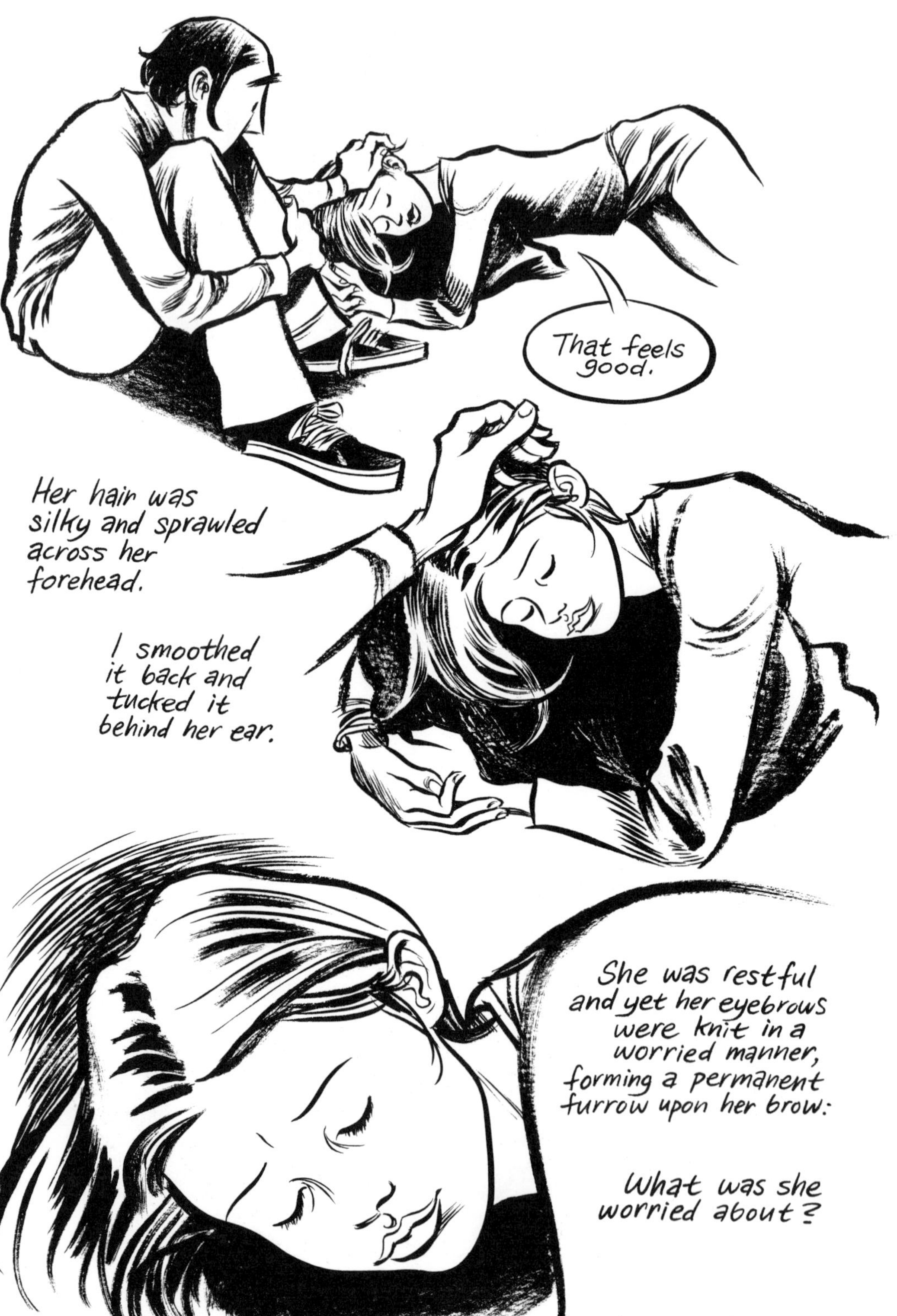
That feels good.
Her hair was silky and sprawled across her forehead.
I smoothed it back and tucked it behind her ear.
She was restful and yet her eyebrows were knit in a worried manner, forming a permanent furrow upon her brow:
What was she worried about?

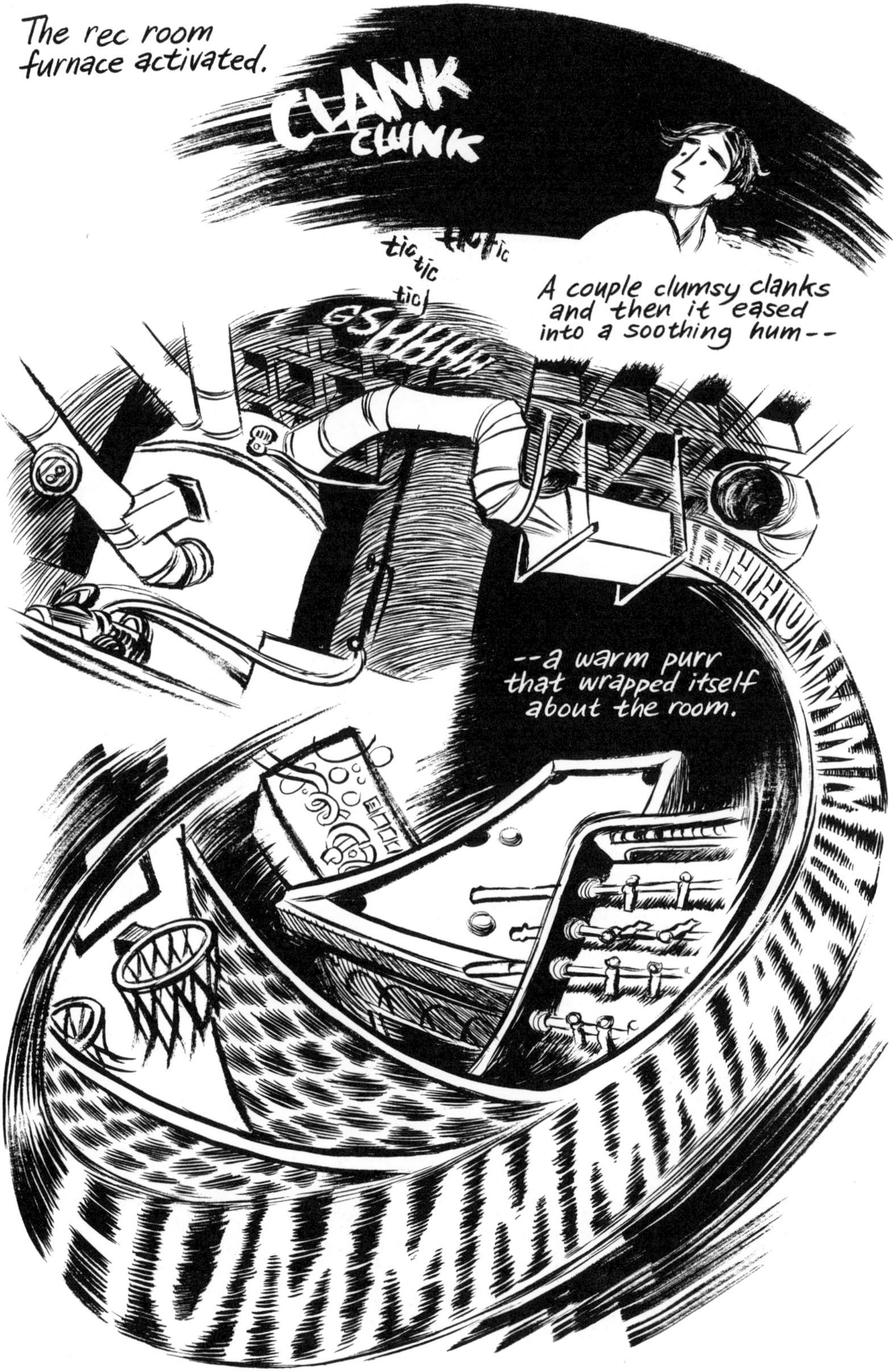
The rec room furnace activated.
CLANK
CLUNK
A couple clumsy clanks and then it eased into a soothing hum--
--a warm purr that wrapped itself about the room.

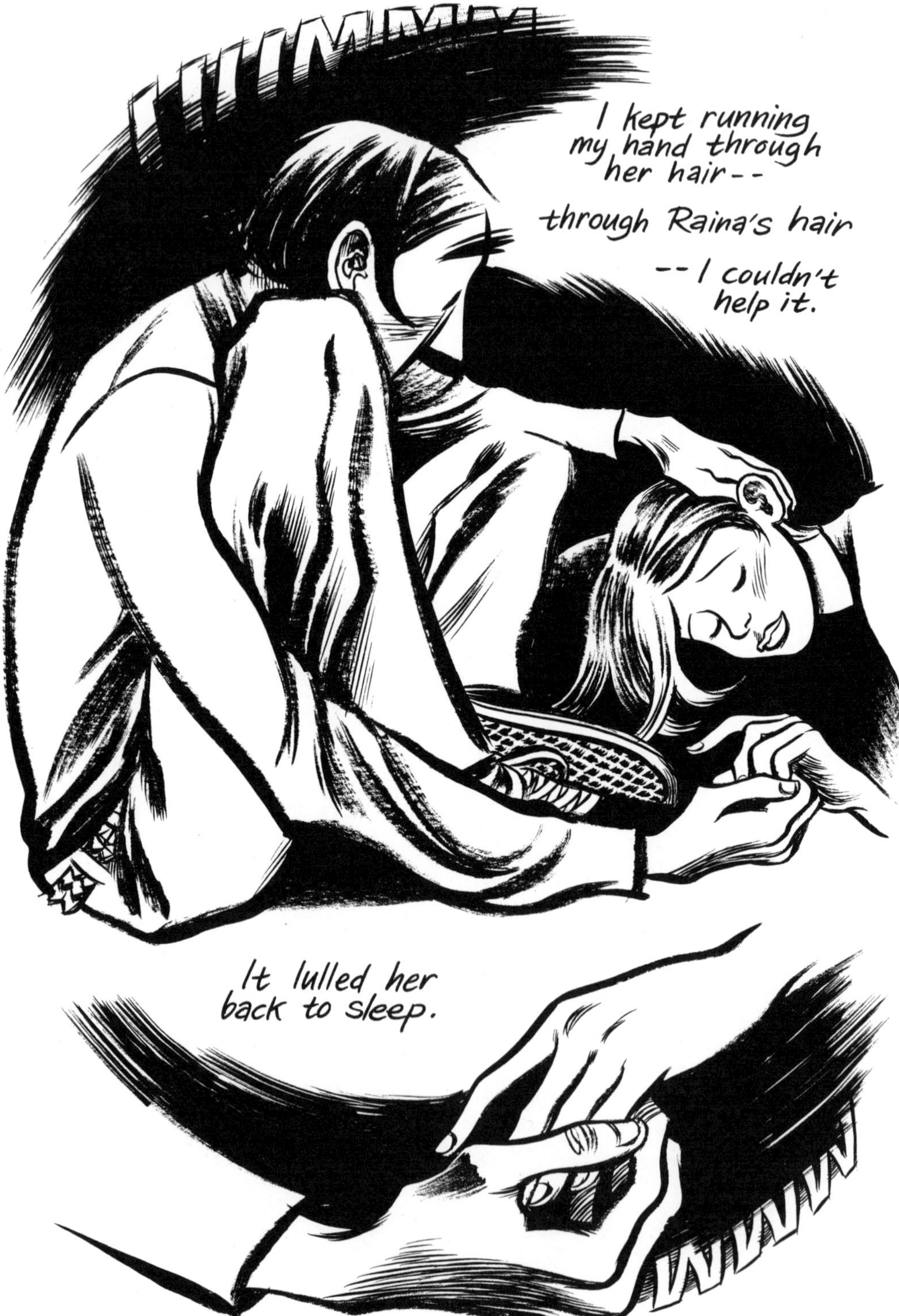
I kept running my hand through her hair--
through Raina's hair
--I couldn't help it.
It lulled her back to sleep.

III

Blank
Sheet

There was a certain
challenge Phil and I
would undertake
each winter.

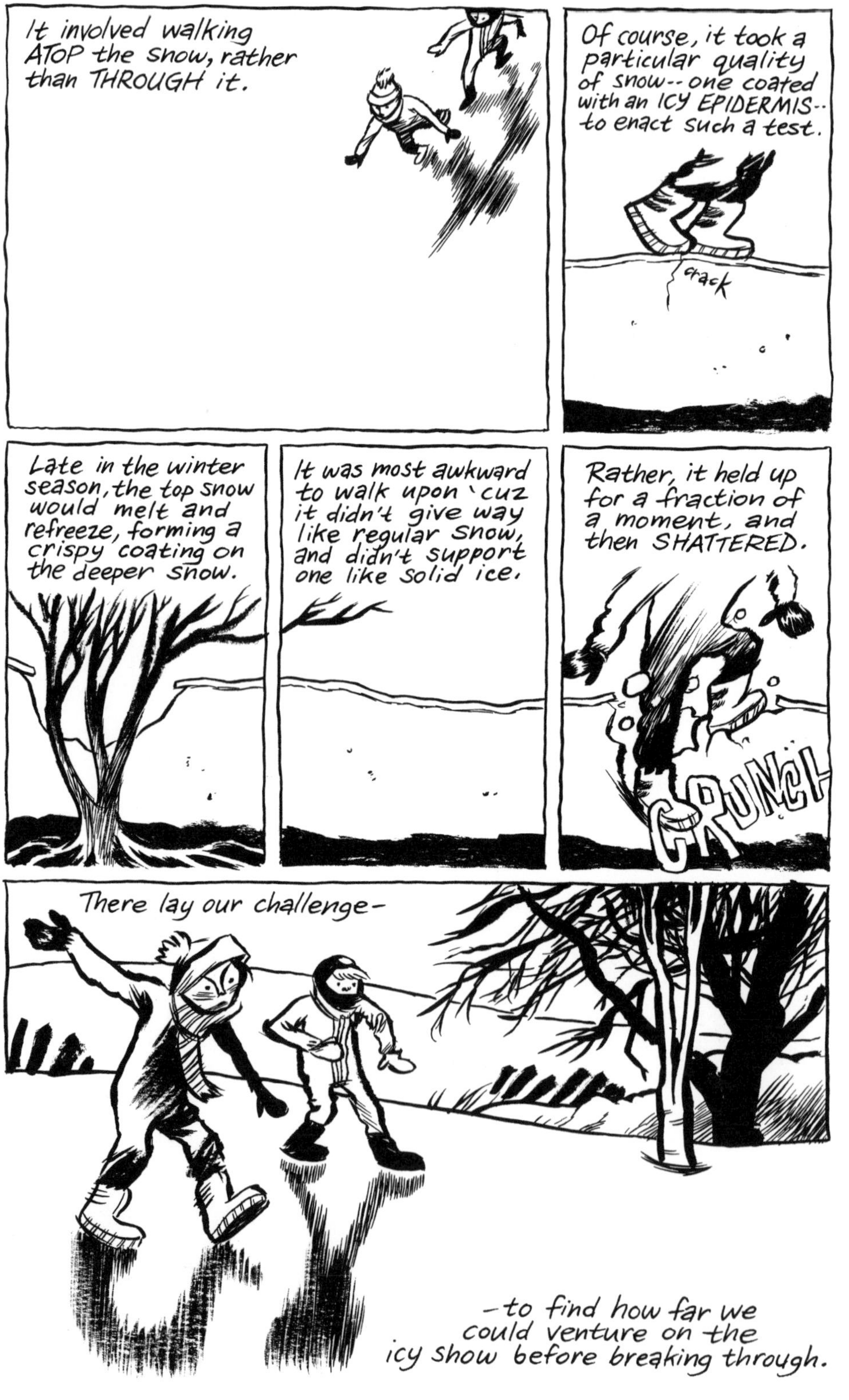
It involved walking ATOP the snow, rather than THROUGH it.
Of course, it took a particular quality of snow-- one coated with an ICY EPIDERMIS-- to enact such a test.
crack
Late in the winter season, the top snow would melt and refreeze, forming a crispy coating on the deeper snow.
It was most awkward to walk upon 'cuz it didn't give way like regular snow, and didn't support one like solid ice.
Rather, it held up for a fraction of a moment, and then SHATTERED.
CRUNCH
There lay our challenge-
-to find how far we could venture on the icy snow before breaking through.

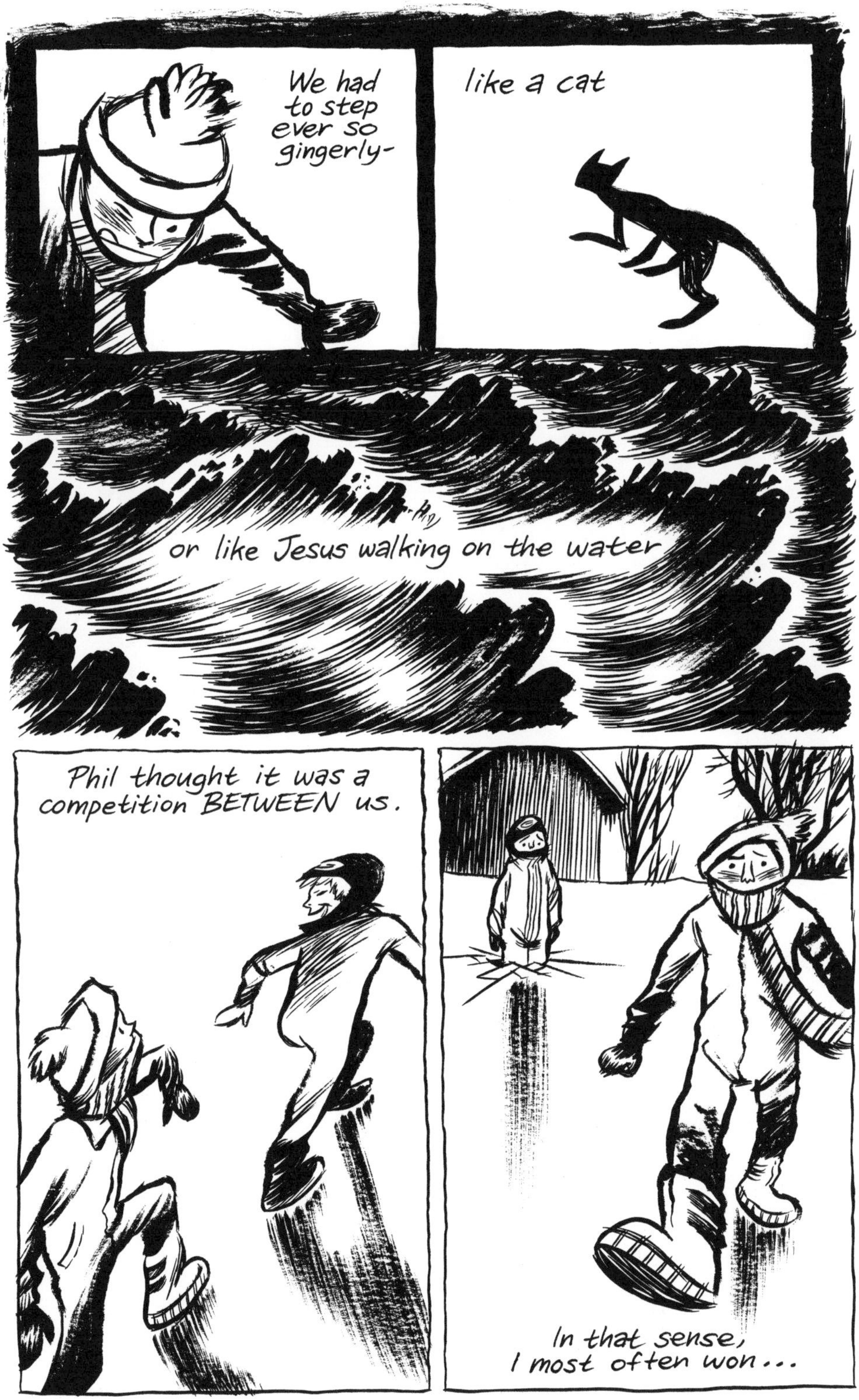
We had to step ever so gingerly-
like a cat
or like Jesus walking on the water
Phil thought it was a competition BETWEEN us.
In that sense, I most often won...

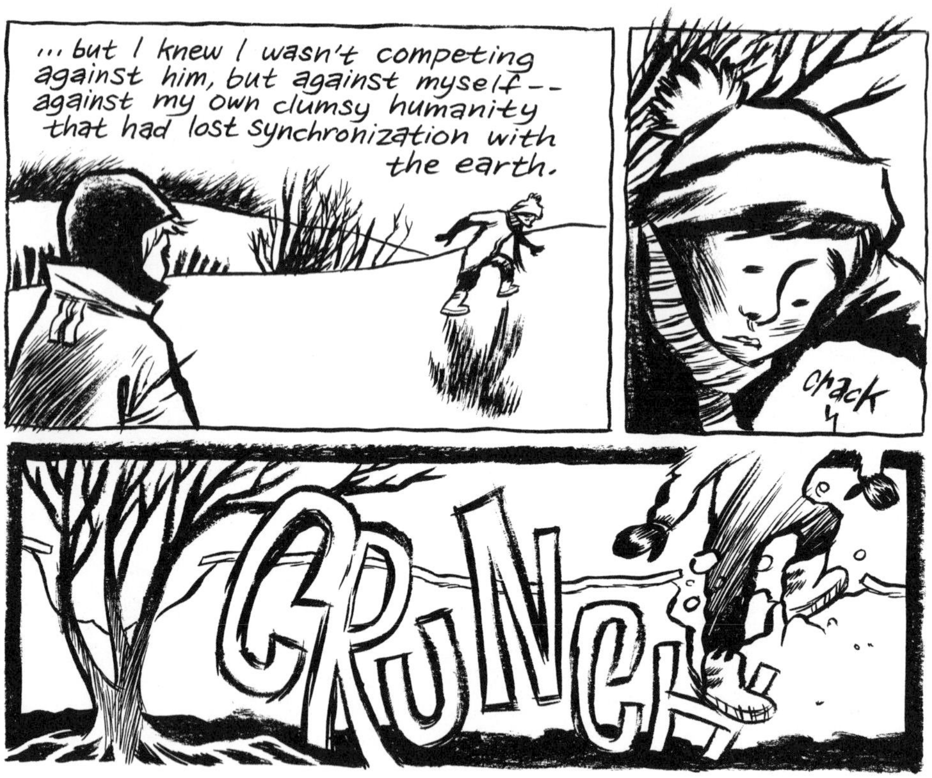
...but I knew I wasn't competing against him, but against myself-- against my own clumsy humanity that had lost synchronization with the earth.
crack
CRUNCH

In that sense,
I always lost.

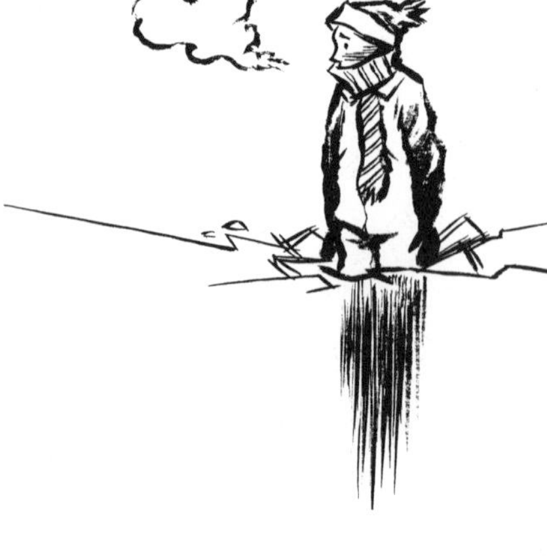

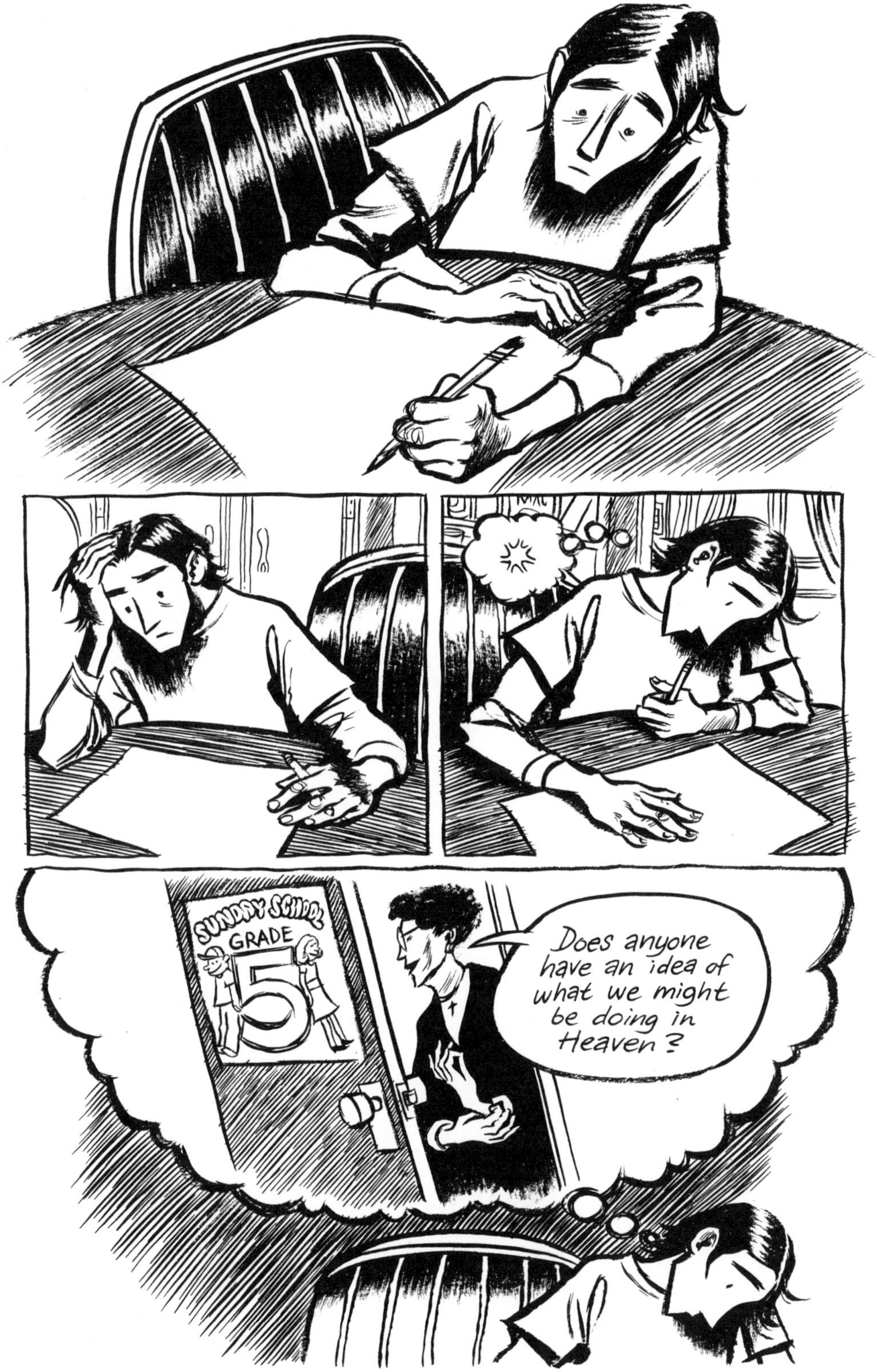
SUNDAY SCHOOL
GRADE
5
Does anyone have an idea of what we might be doing in Heaven?

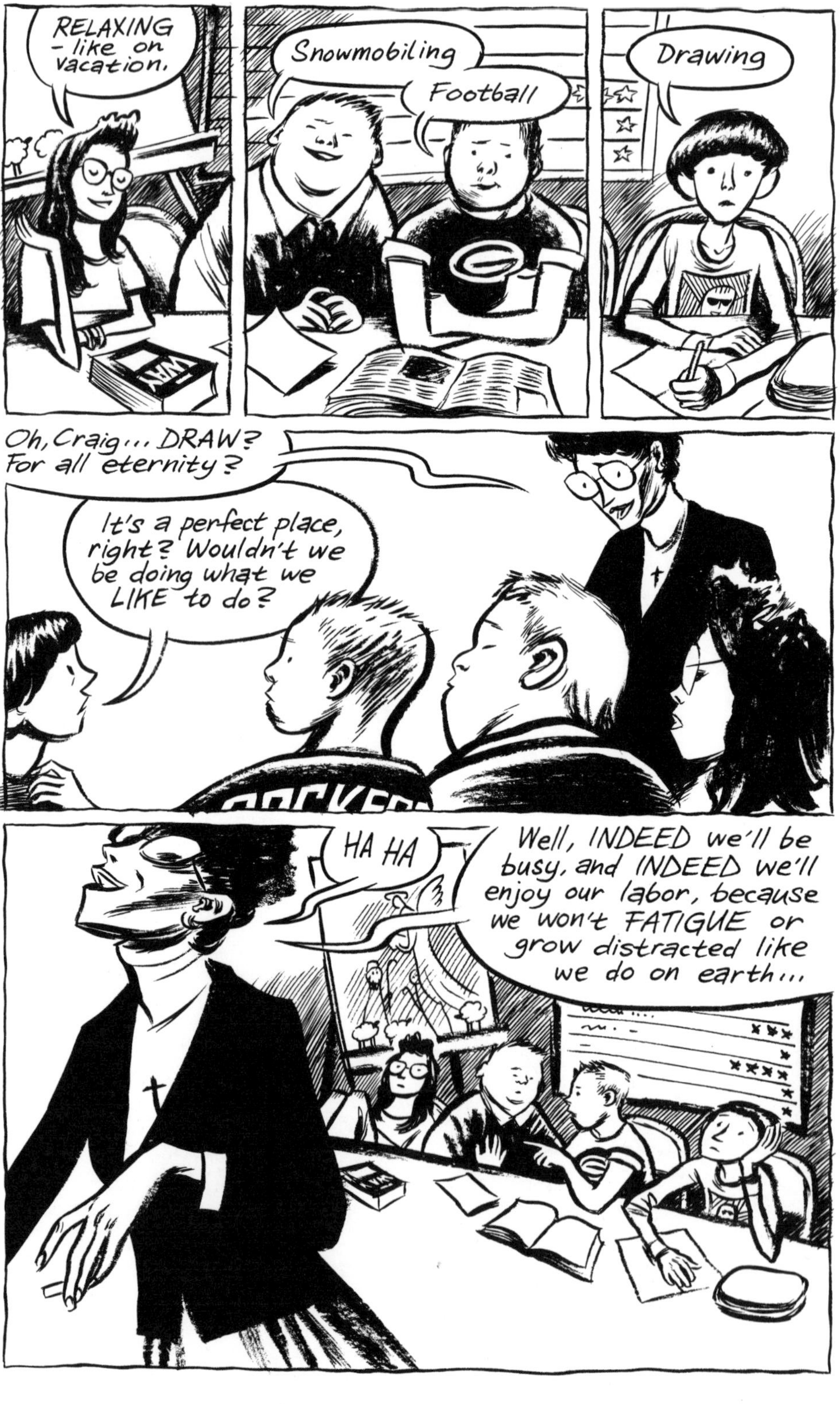
RELAXING - like on vacation.
Snowmobiling
Football
Drawing
Oh, Craig... DRAW? For all eternity?
It's a perfect place, right? Wouldn't we be doing what we LIKE to do?
HA HA
Well, INDEED we'll be busy, and INDEED we'll enjoy our labor, because we won't FATIGUE or grow distracted like we do on earth...

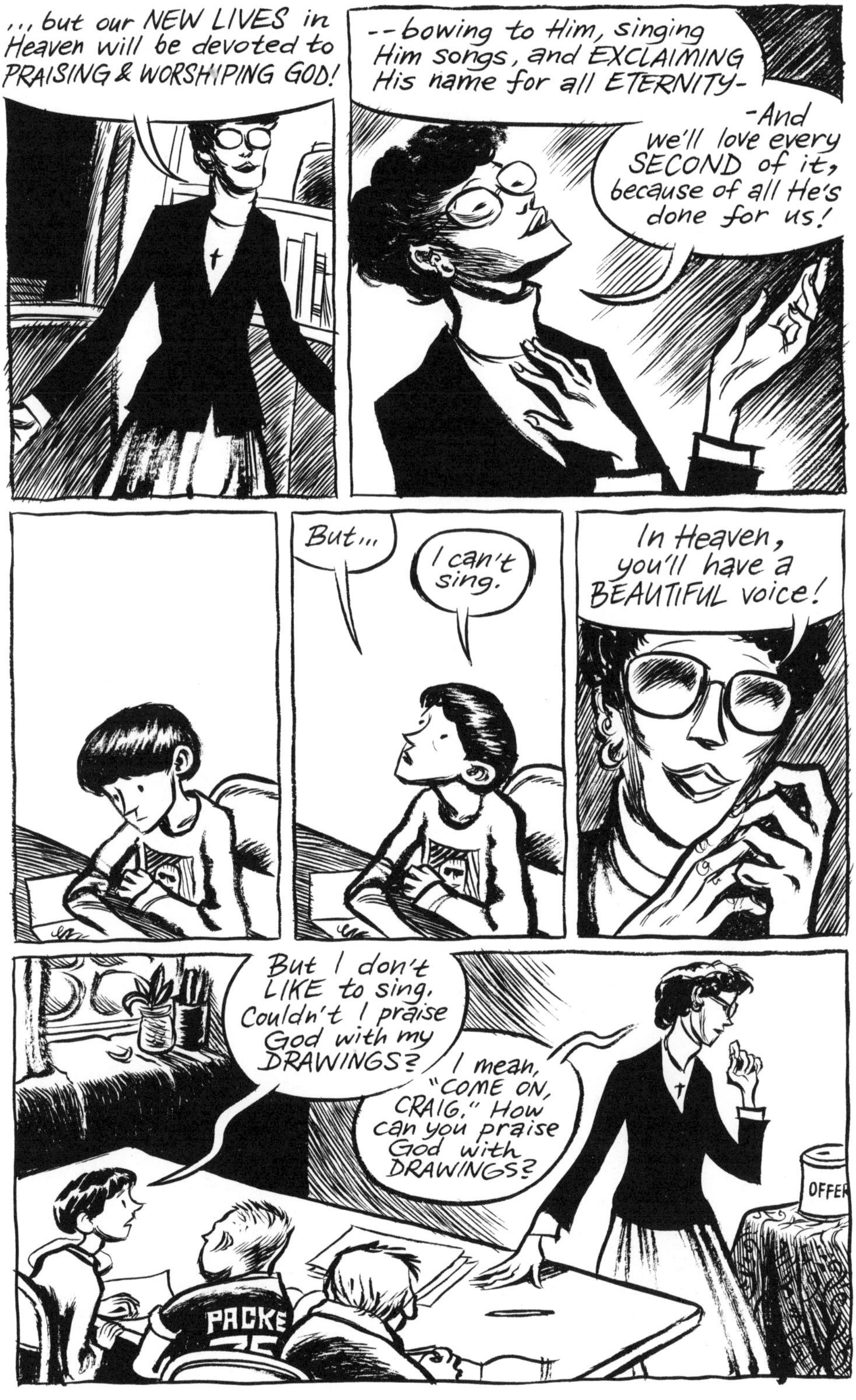

..., but our NEW LIVES in Heaven will be devoted to PRAISING & WORSHIPING GOD!
--bowing to Him, singing Him songs, and EXCLAIMING His name for all ETERNITY-
-And we'll love every SECOND of it, because of all He's done for us!
But...
I can't sing.
In Heaven, you'll have a BEAUTIFUL voice!
But I don't LIKE to sing. Couldn't I praise God with my DRAWINGS?
I mean, "COME ON, CRAIG." How can you praise God with DRAWINGS?
OFFER
PACKE

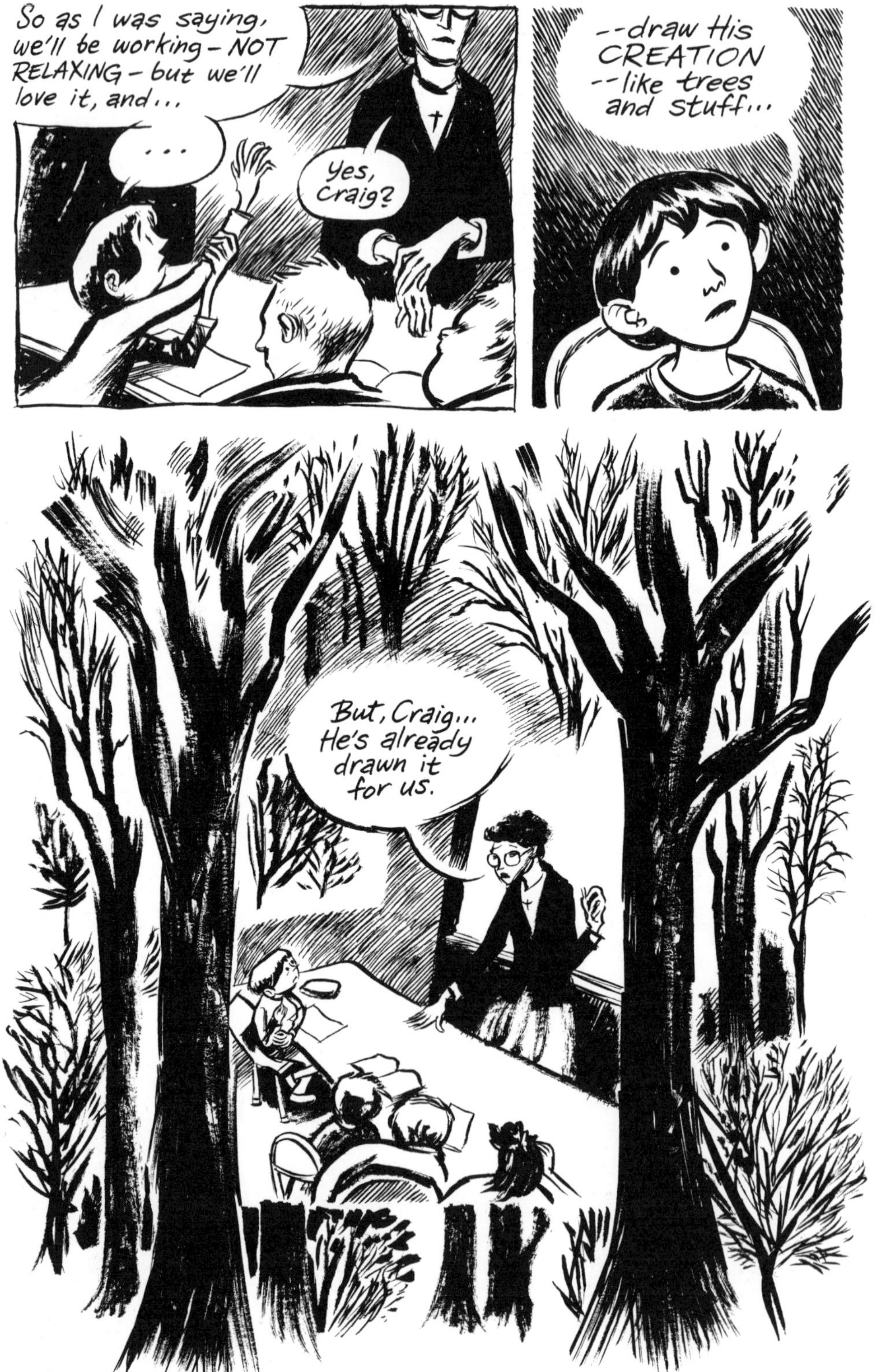
So as I was saying, we'll be working – NOT RELAXING – but we'll love it, and...
...
Yes, Craig?
--draw His CREATION --like trees and stuff...
But, Craig... He's already drawn it for us.

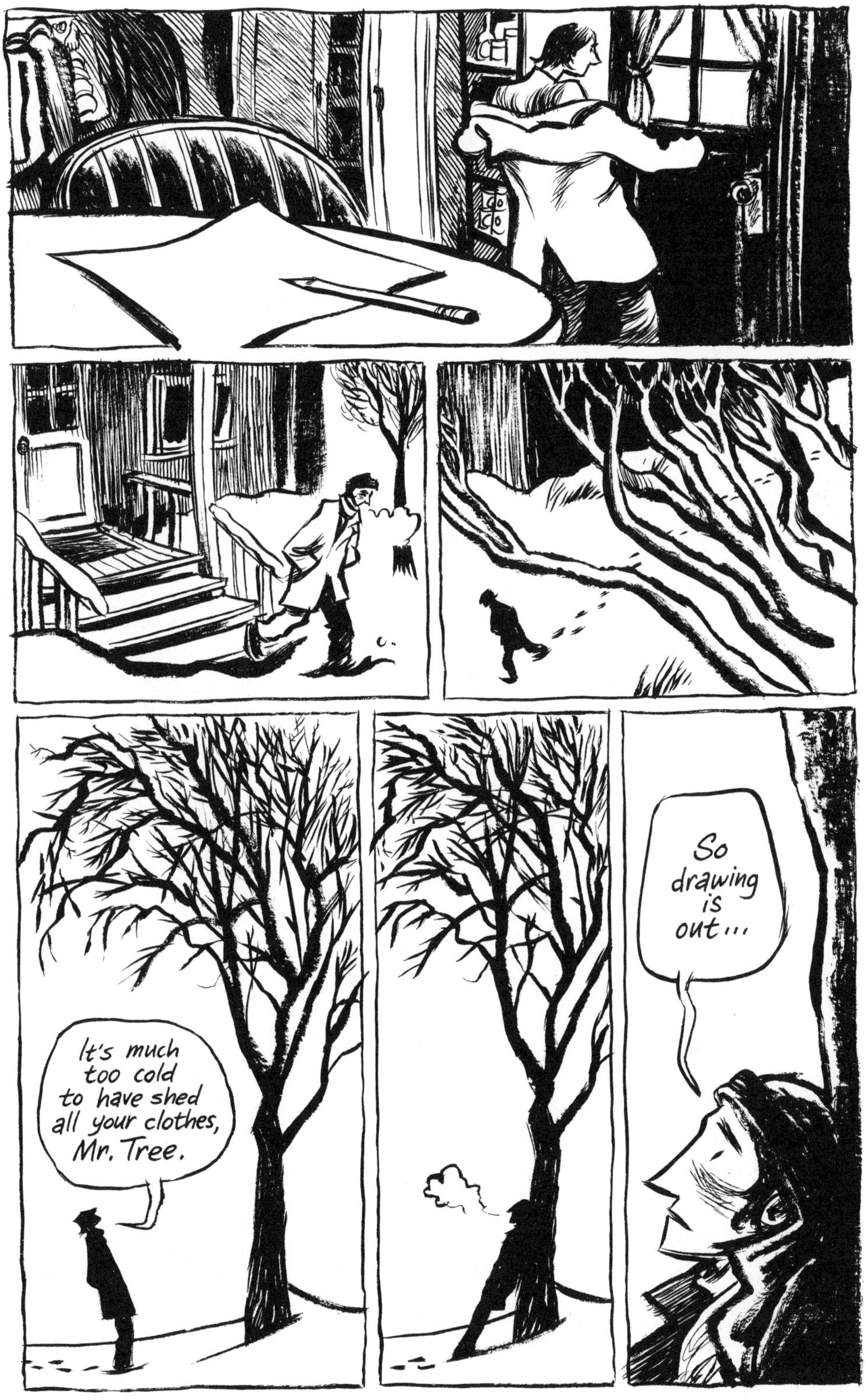
It's much too cold to have shed all your clothes, Mr. Tree.
So drawing is out...

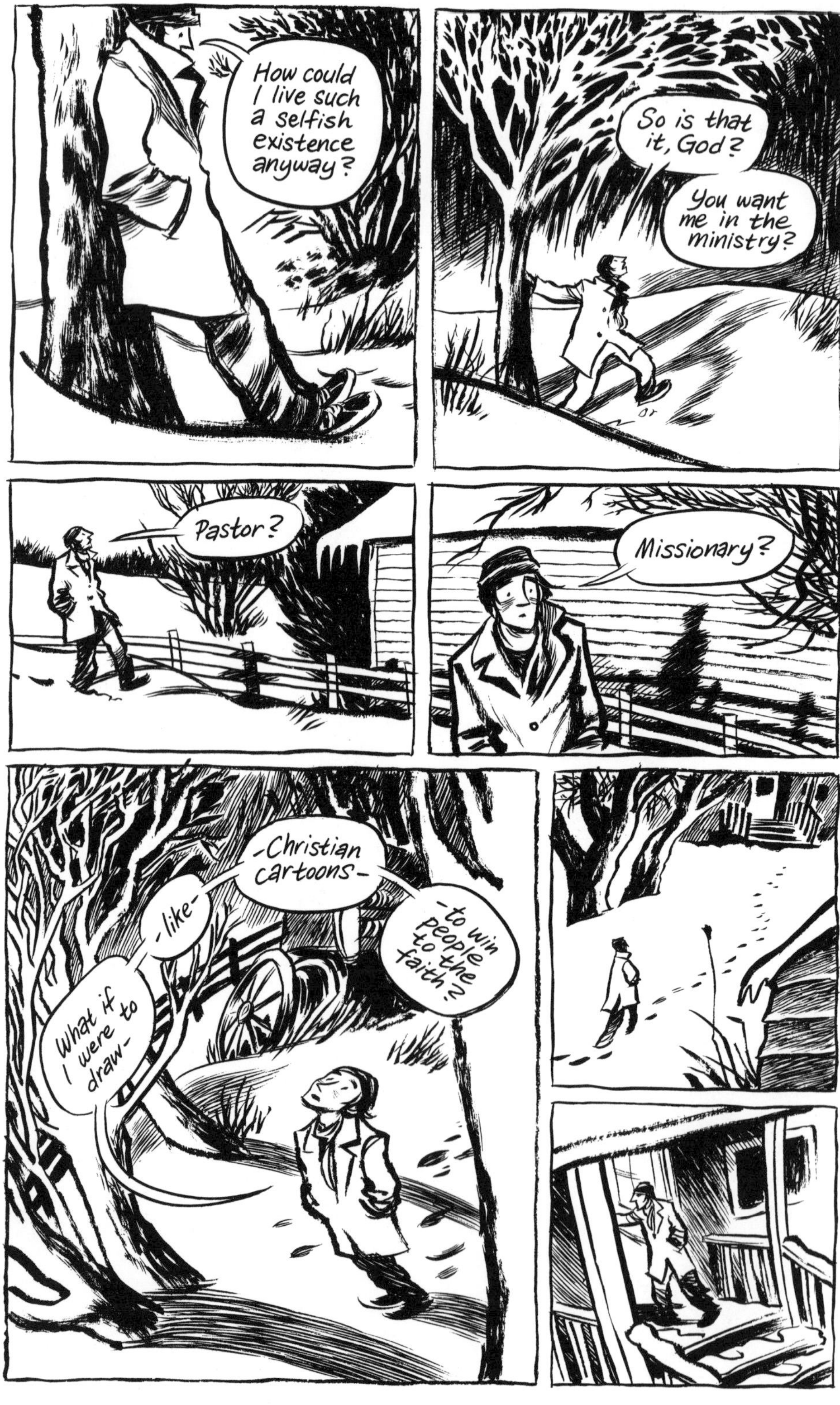
How could I live such a selfish existence anyway?
So is that it, God?
You want me in the ministry?
Pastor?
Missionary?
What if I were to draw-
-like-
-Christian cartoons-
-to win people to the faith?

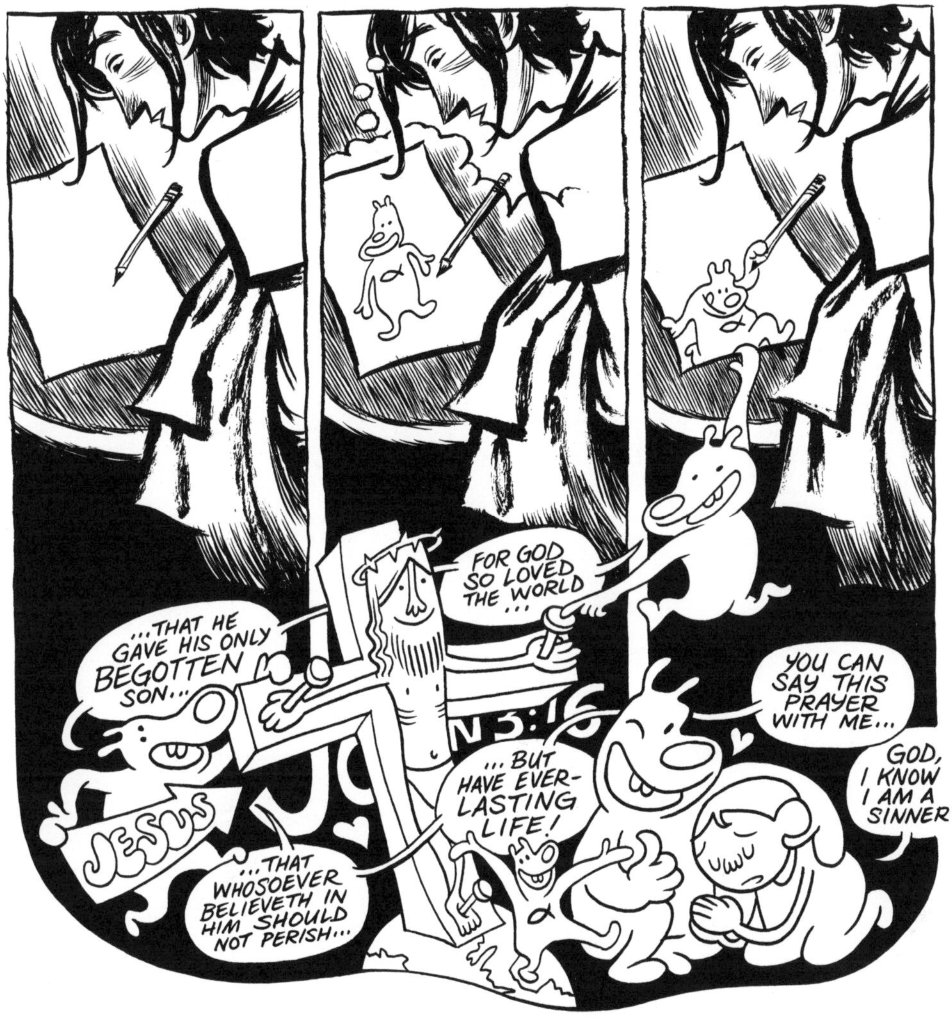
FOR GOD SO LOVED THE WORLD...
...THAT HE GAVE HIS ONLY BEGOTTEN SON...
...THAT WHOSOEVER BELIEVETH IN HIM SHOULD NOT PERISH...
...BUT HAVE EVER-LASTING LIFE!
JESUS
YOU CAN SAY THIS PRAYER WITH ME...
GOD, I KNOW I AM A SINNER...

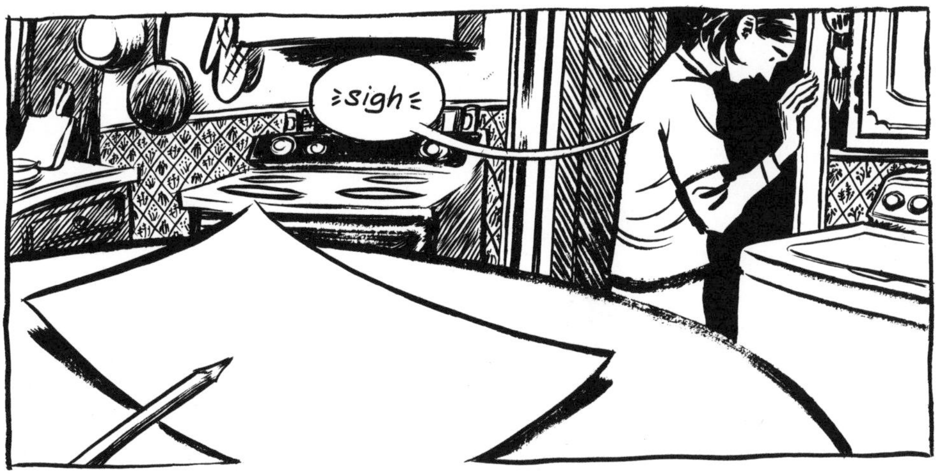
sigh

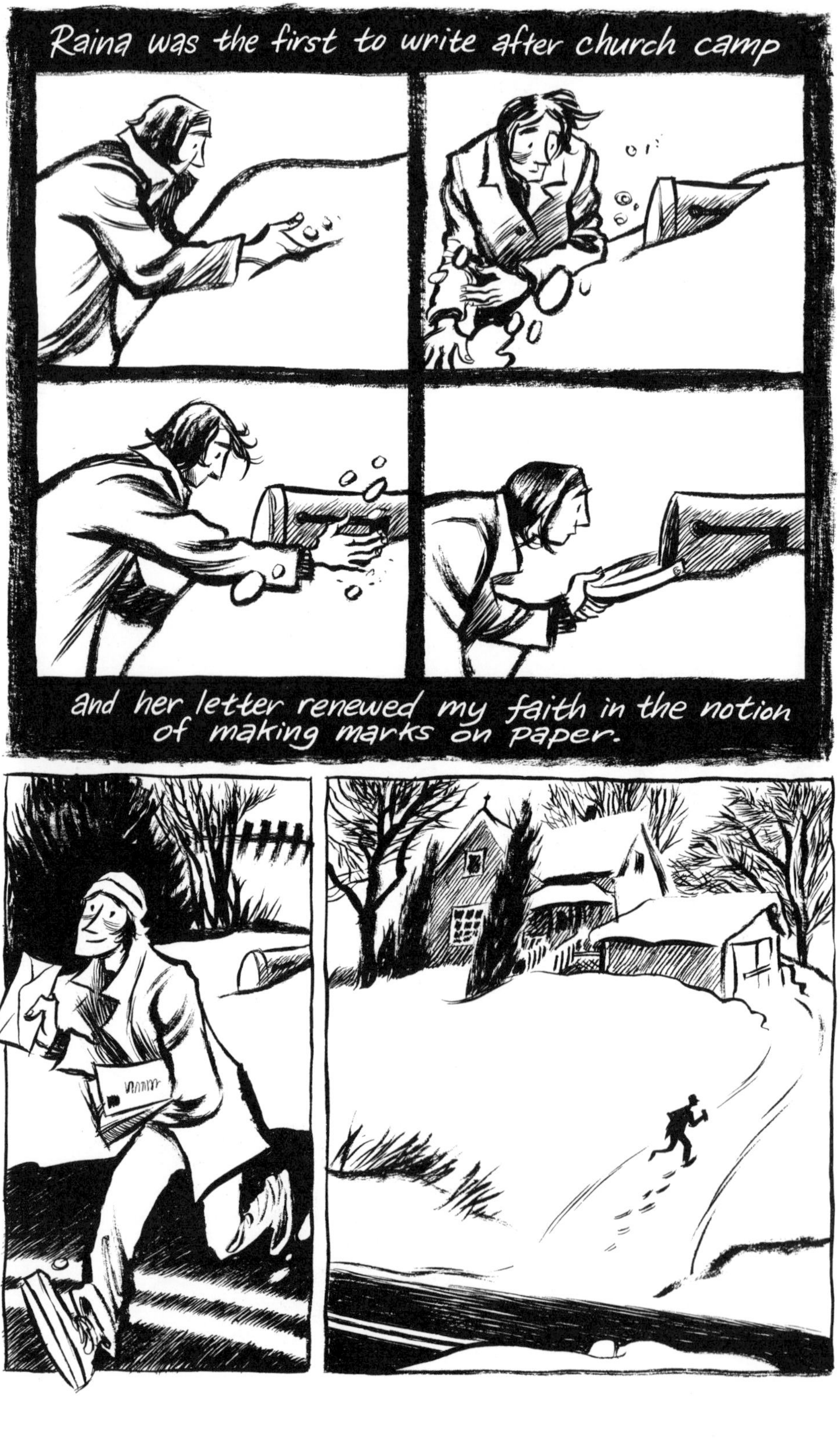
Raina was the first to write after church camp
and her letter renewed my faith in the notion of making marks on paper.

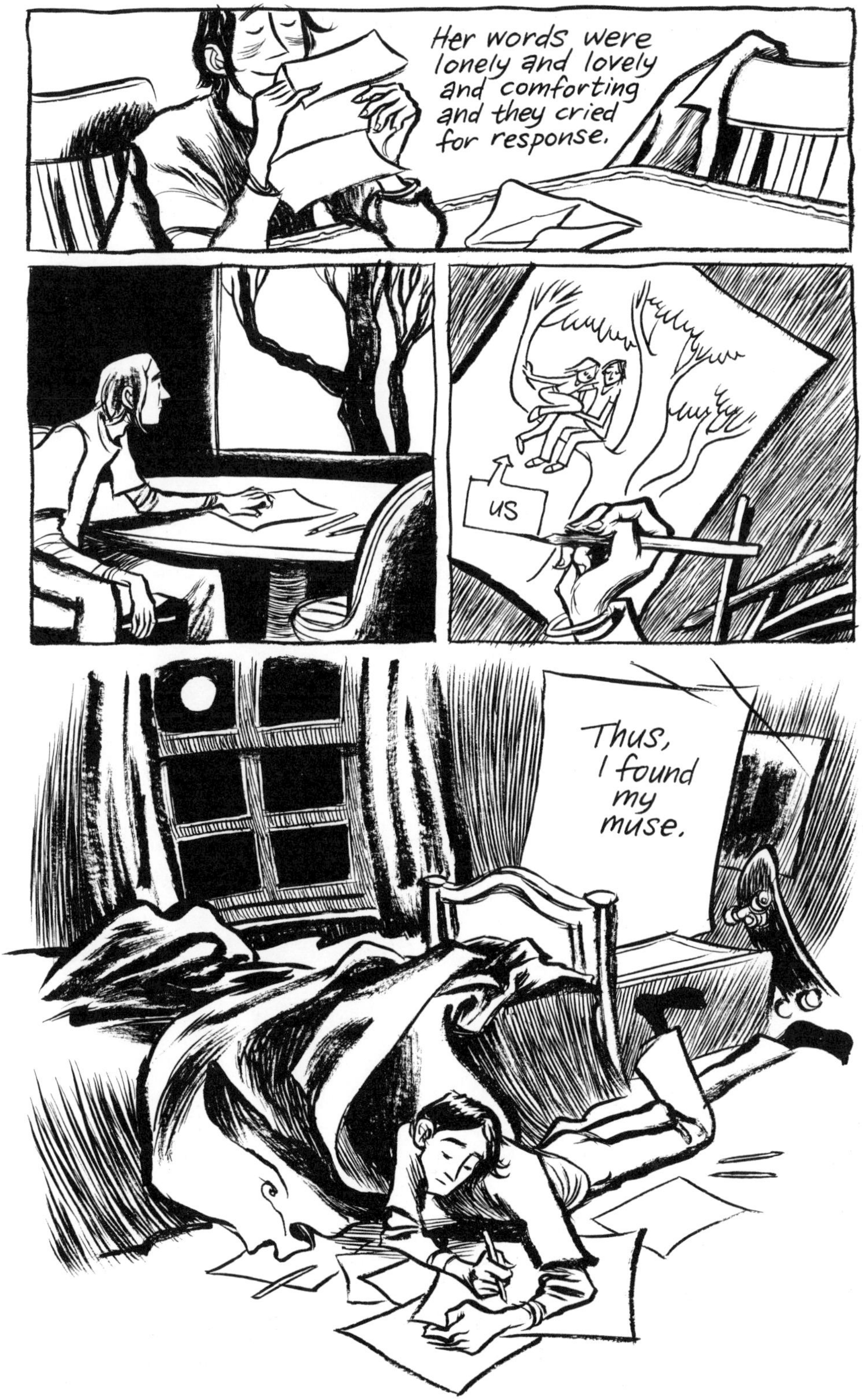
Her words were lonely and lovely and comforting and they cried for response.
US
Thus, I found my muse.

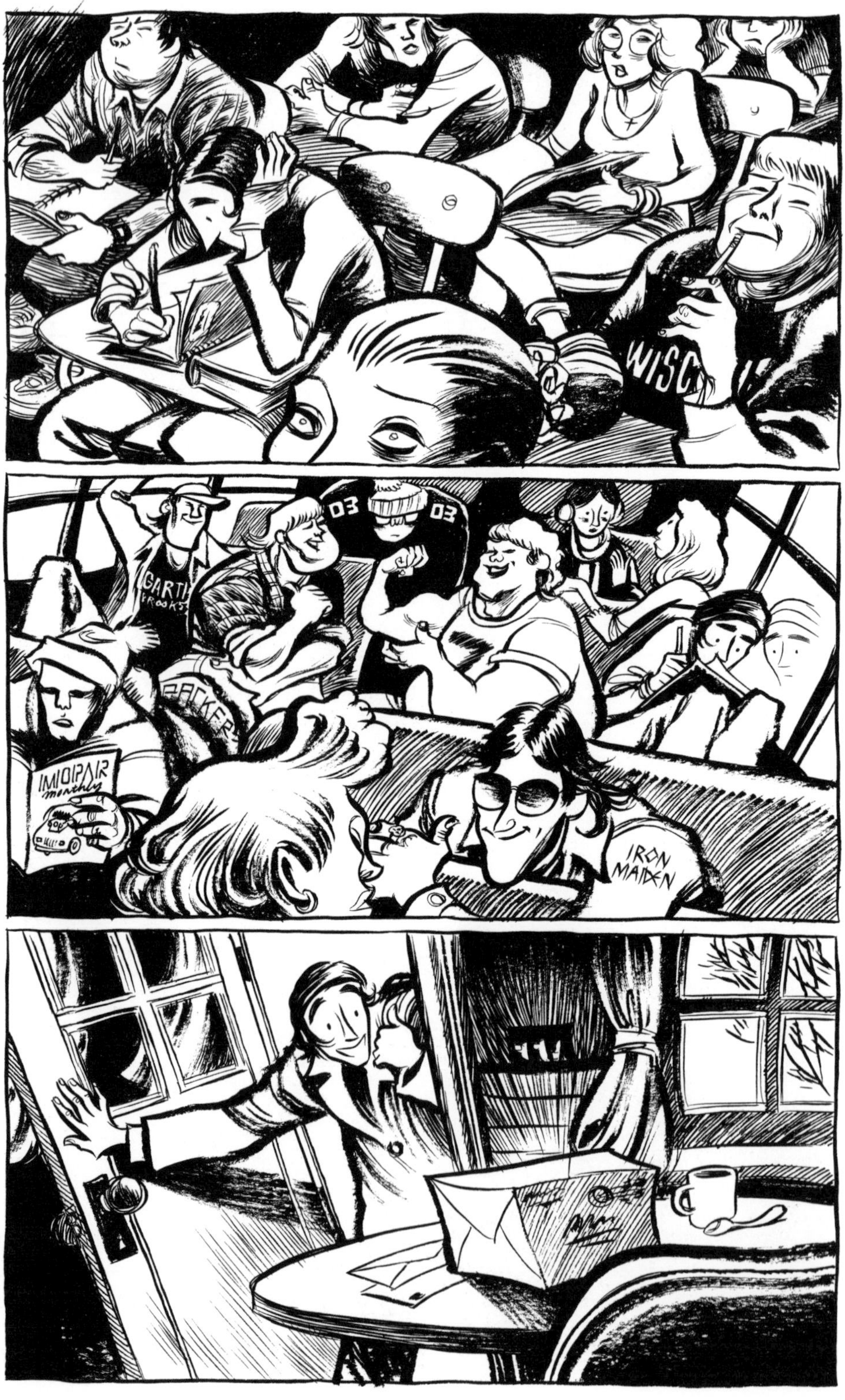
WISC
03
03
GARTH
BROOKS
MOPAR
monthly
IRON MAIDEN

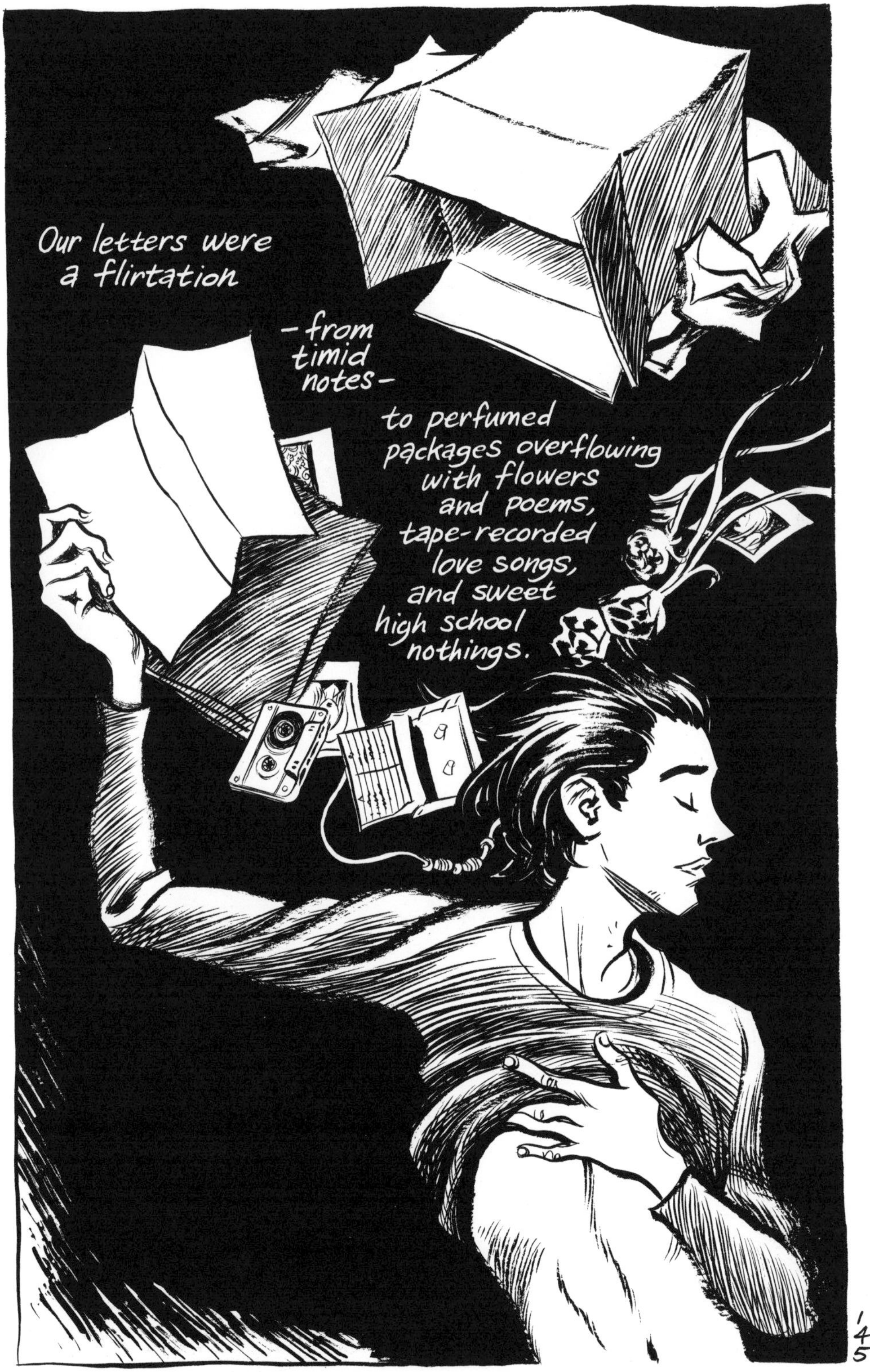
Our letters were a flirtation
-from timid notes-
to perfumed packages overflowing with flowers and poems, tape-recorded love songs, and sweet high school nothings.

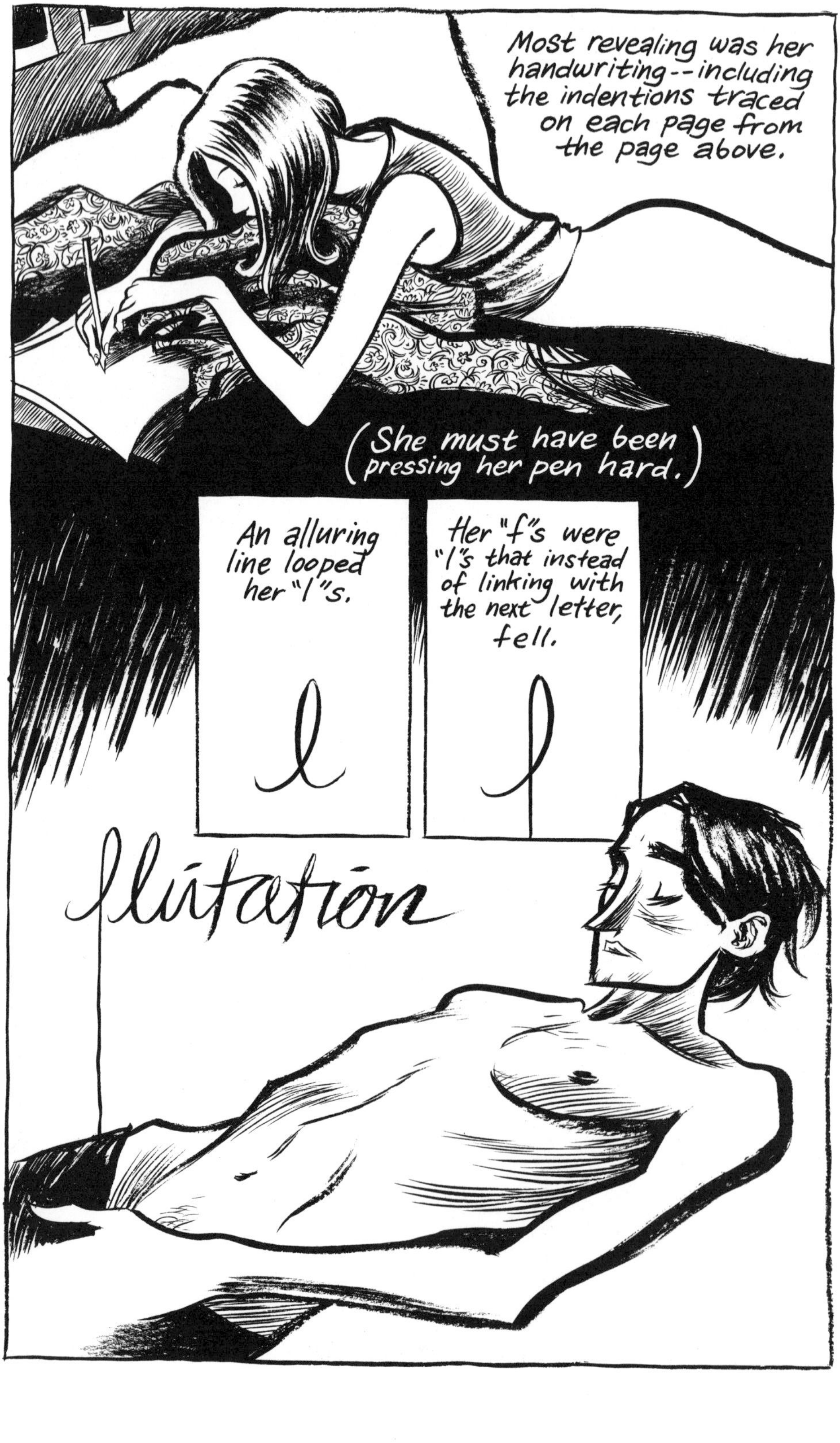
Most revealing was her handwriting--including the indentions traced on each page from the page above.
(She must have been pressing her pen hard.)
An alluring line looped her "l"s.
Her "f"s were "l"s that instead of linking with the next letter, fell.
llutation

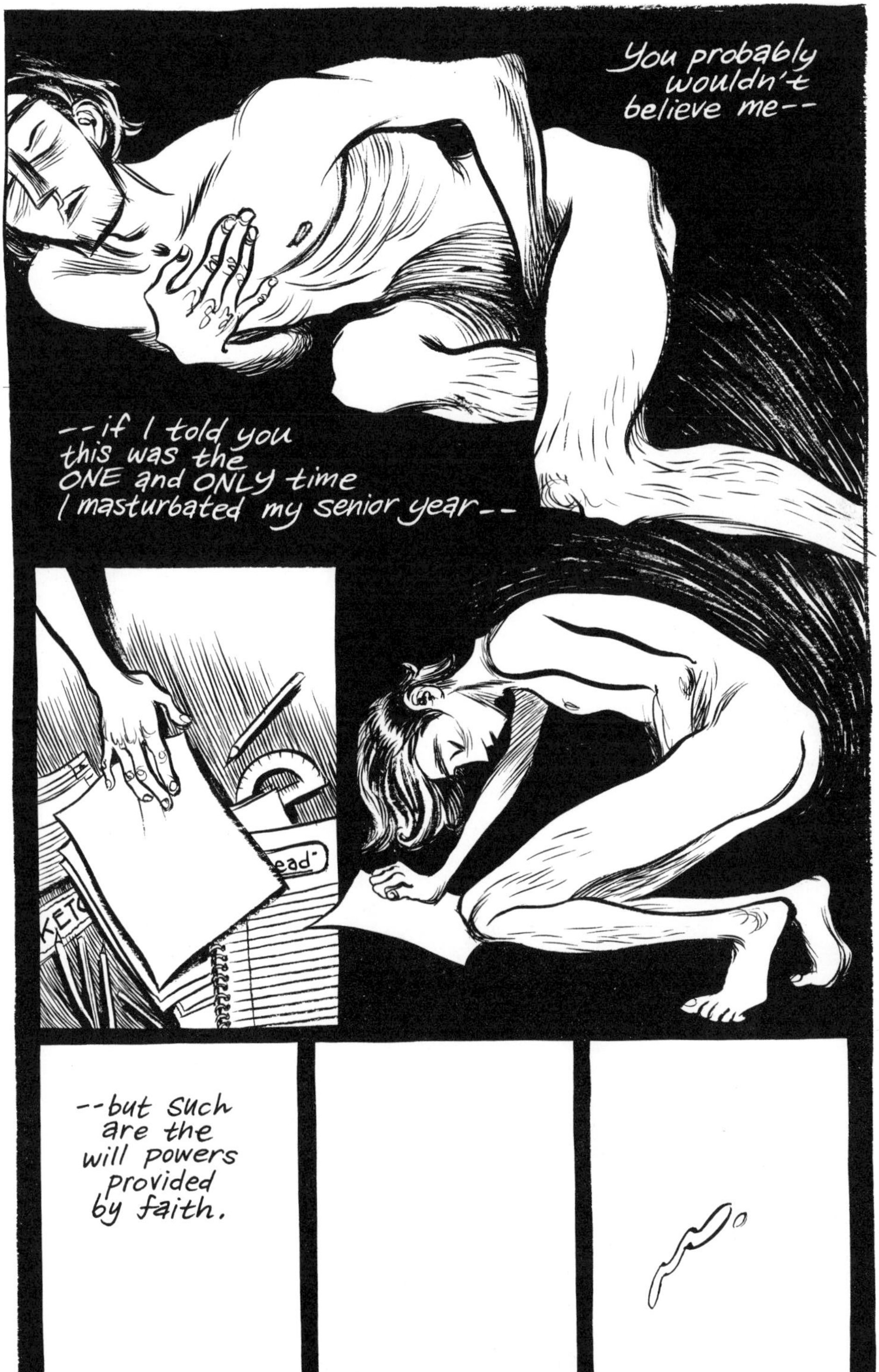
You probably wouldn't believe me--
--if I told you this was the ONE and ONLY time I masturbated my senior year--
ead
KETC
--but such are the will powers provided by faith.

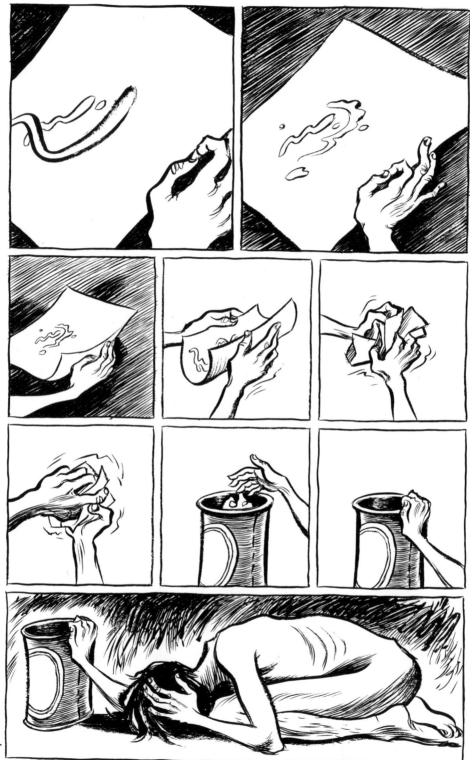

148

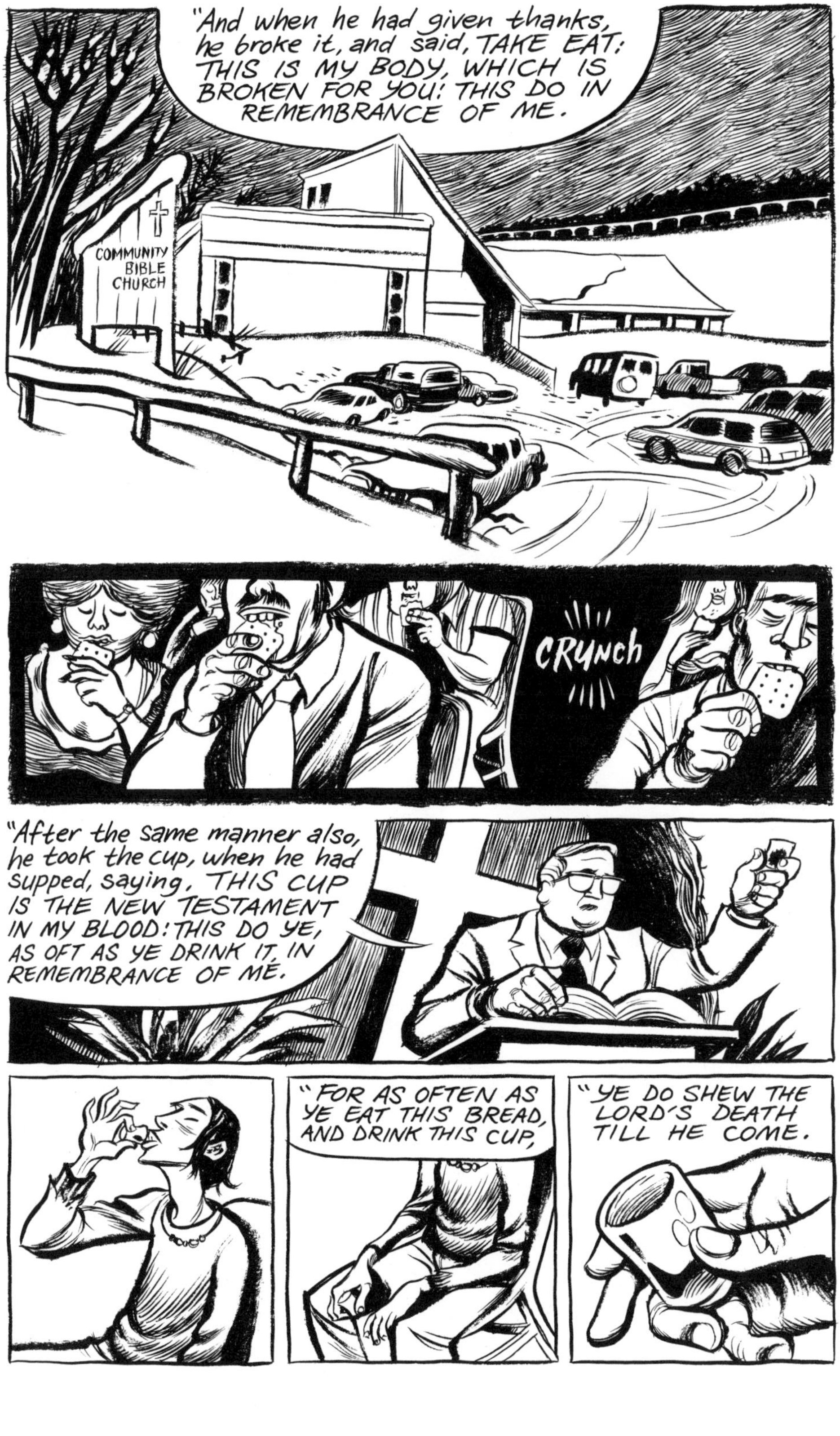
"And when he had given thanks, he broke it, and said, TAKE EAT: THIS IS MY BODY, WHICH IS BROKEN FOR YOU: THIS DO IN REMEMBRANCE OF ME.
COMMUNITY BIBLE CHURCH
CRUNCH
"After the same manner also, he took the cup, when he had supped, saying, THIS CUP IS THE NEW TESTAMENT IN MY BLOOD: THIS DO YE, AS OFT AS YE DRINK IT, IN REMEMBRANCE OF ME.
"FOR AS OFTEN AS YE EAT THIS BREAD, AND DRINK THIS CUP,
"YE DO SHEW THE LORD'S DEATH TILL HE COME.

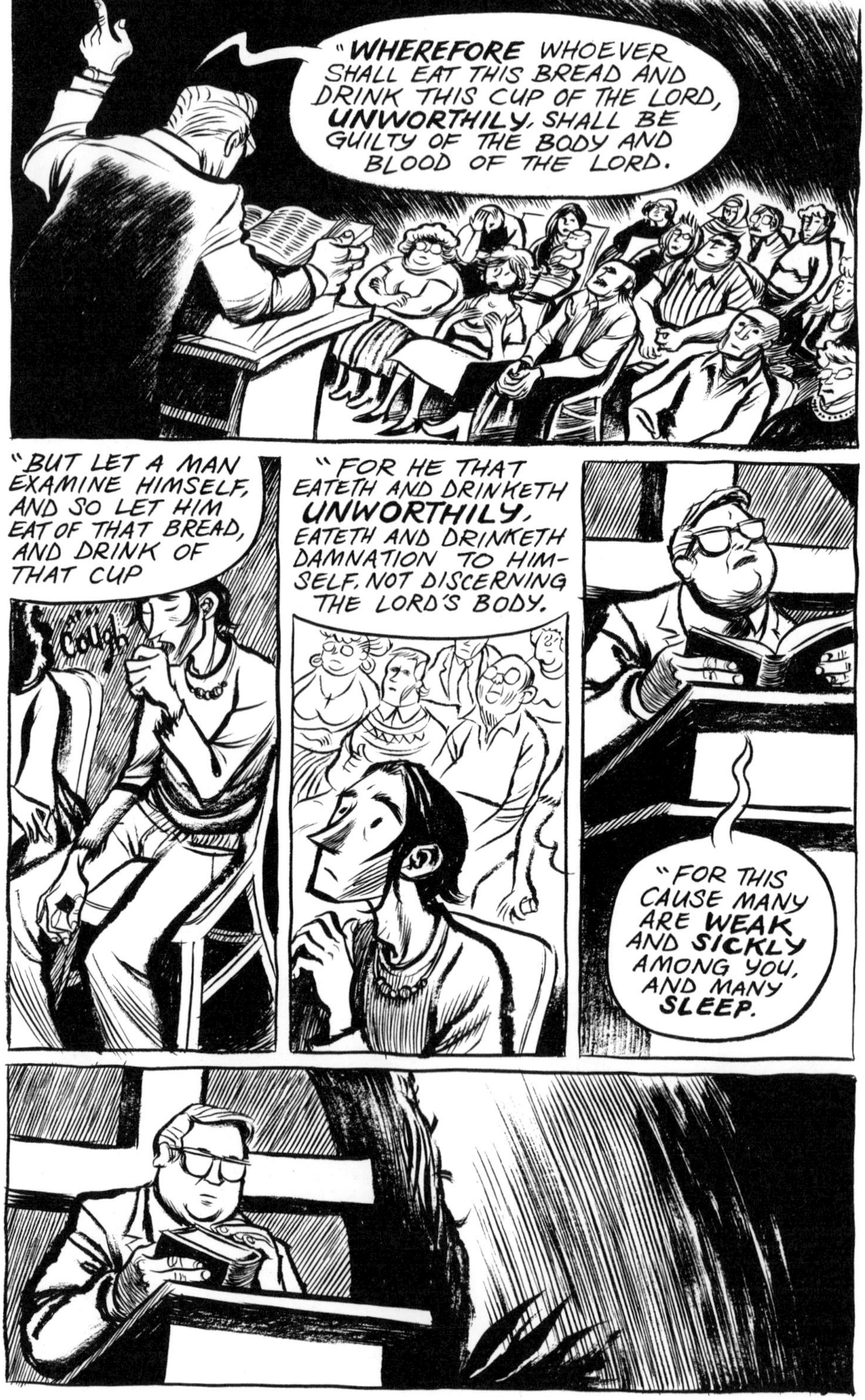

"WHEREFORE WHOEVER SHALL EAT THIS BREAD AND DRINK THIS CUP OF THE LORD, UNWORTHILY, SHALL BE GUILTY OF THE BODY AND BLOOD OF THE LORD.
"BUT LET A MAN EXAMINE HIMSELF, AND SO LET HIM EAT OF THAT BREAD, AND DRINK OF THAT CUP
...Cough
"FOR HE THAT EATETH AND DRINKETH UNWORTHILY, EATETH AND DRINKETH DAMNATION TO HIMSELF, NOT DISCERNING THE LORD'S BODY.
"FOR THIS CAUSE MANY ARE WEAK AND SICKLY AMONG YOU, AND MANY SLEEP.

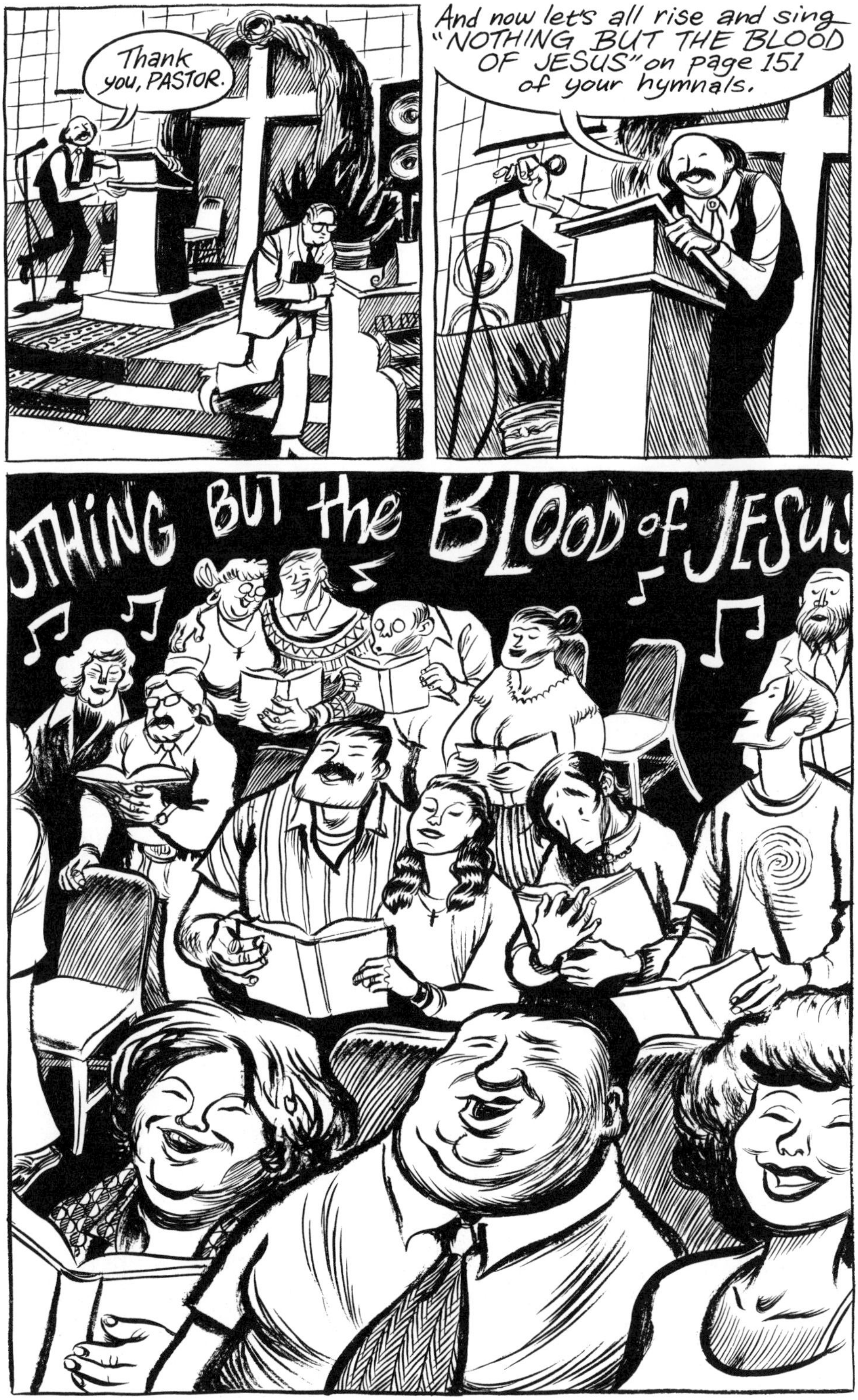
Thank you, PASTOR.
And now let's all rise and sing "NOTHING BUT THE BLOOD OF JESUS" on page 151 of your hymnals.
OTHING BUT the BLOOD of JESUS

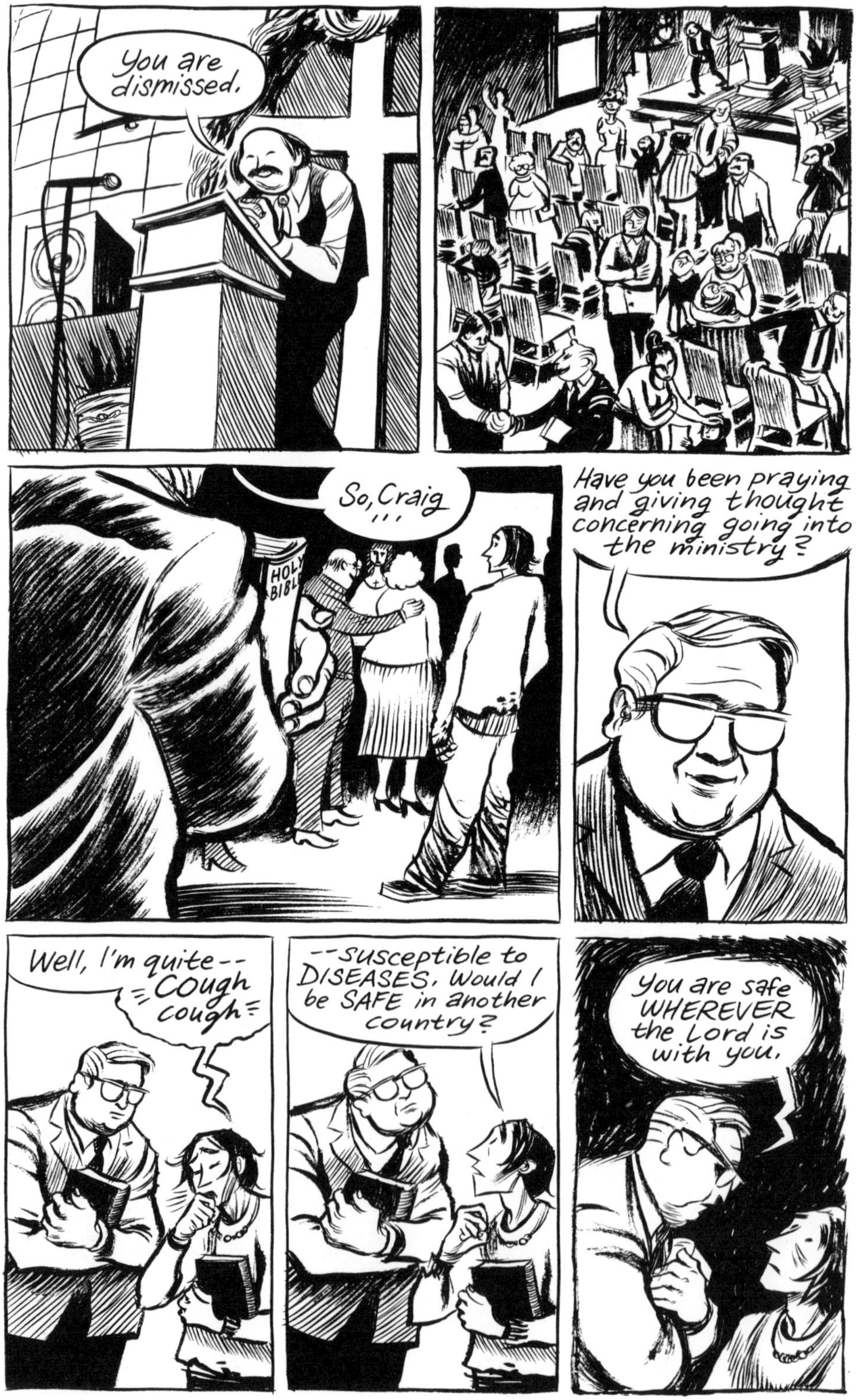
You are dismissed.
So, Craig ...
Have you been praying and giving thought concerning going into the ministry?
HOLY BIBLE
Well, I'm quite--
COUGH cough
--susceptible to DISEASES. Would I be SAFE in another country?
You are safe WHEREVER the Lord is with you.

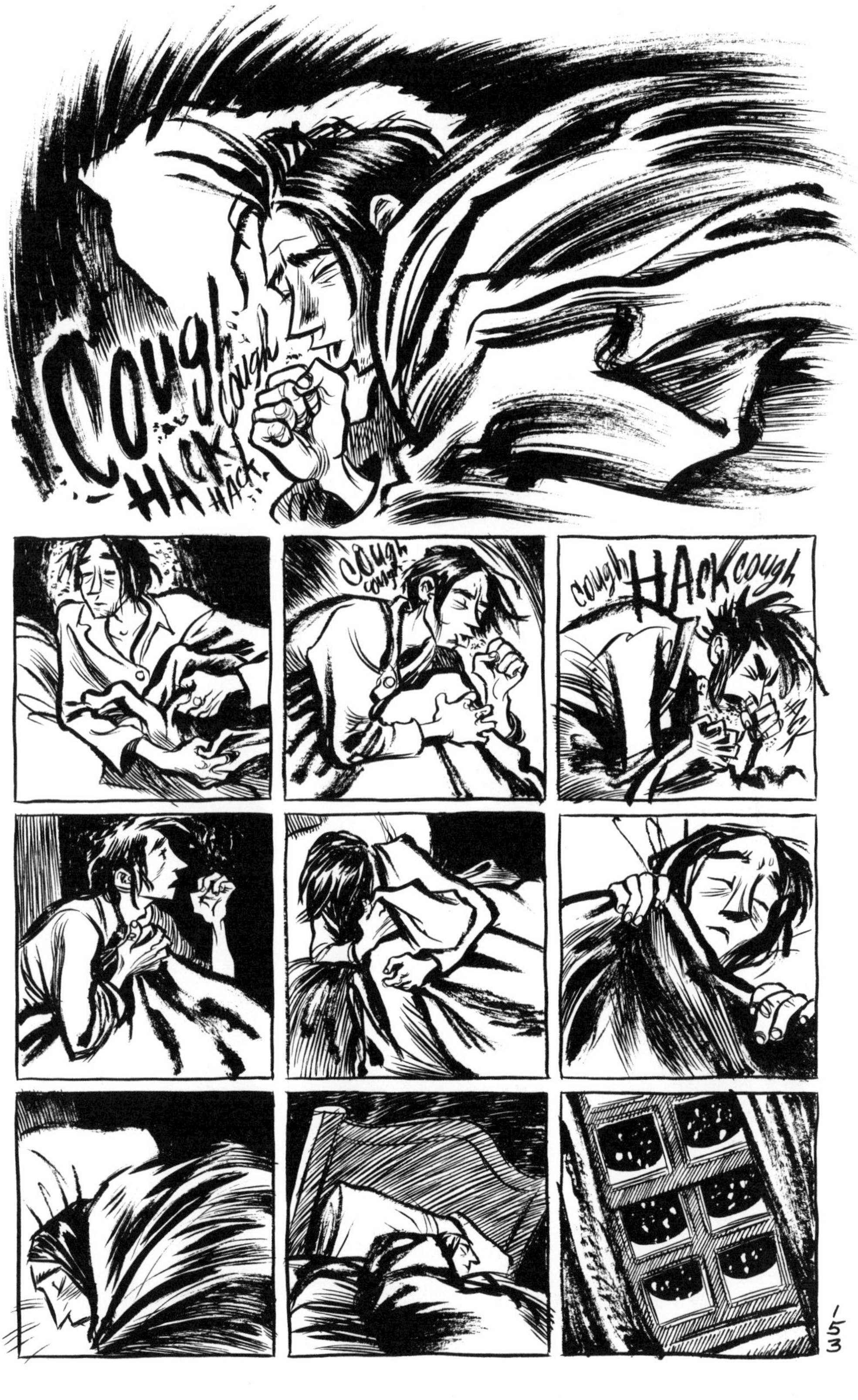

Cough
cough
HACK
HACK
cough
cough
cough HACK cough

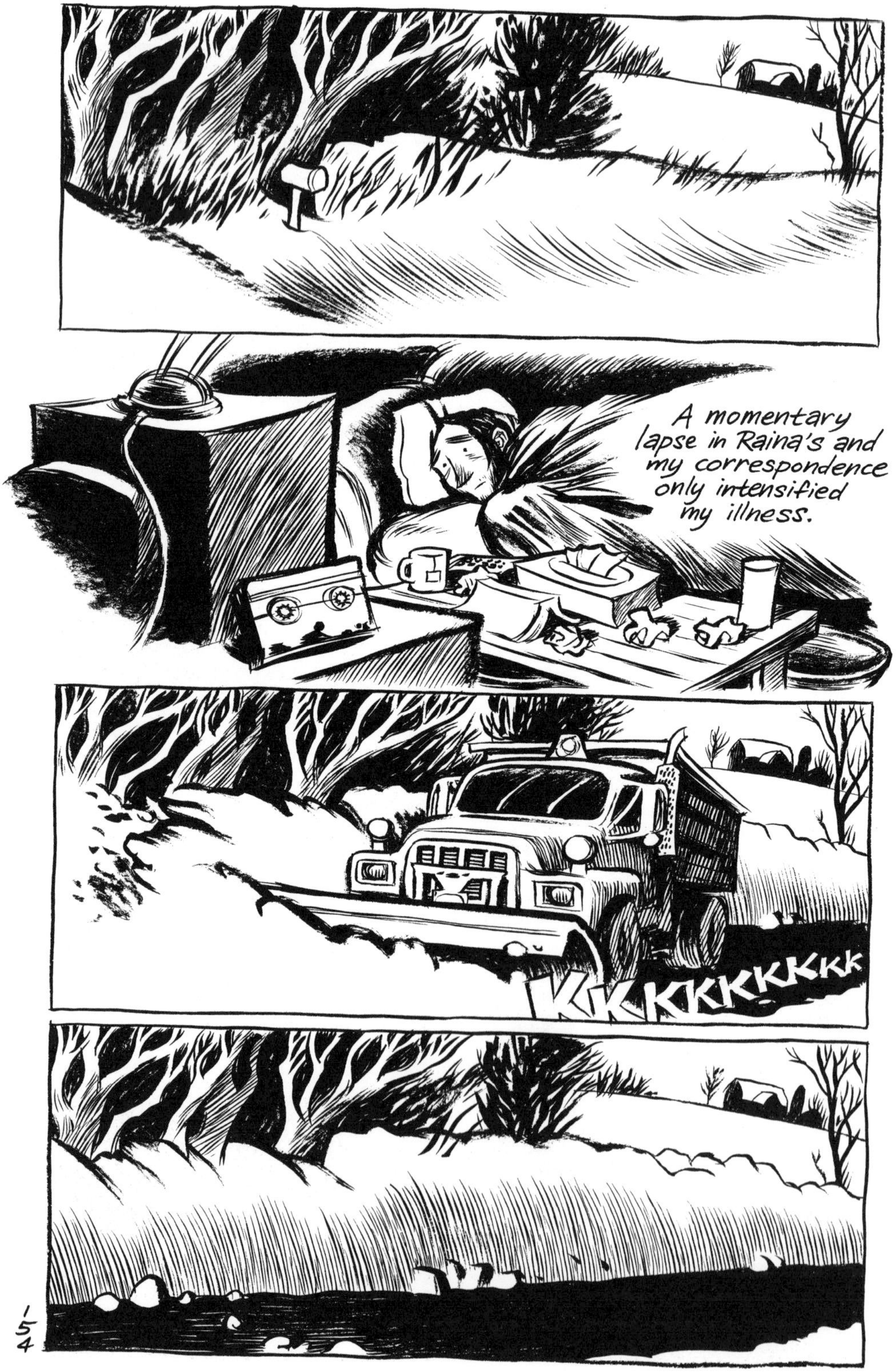
A momentary lapse in Raina's and my correspondence only intensified my illness.
KKKKKKKKK

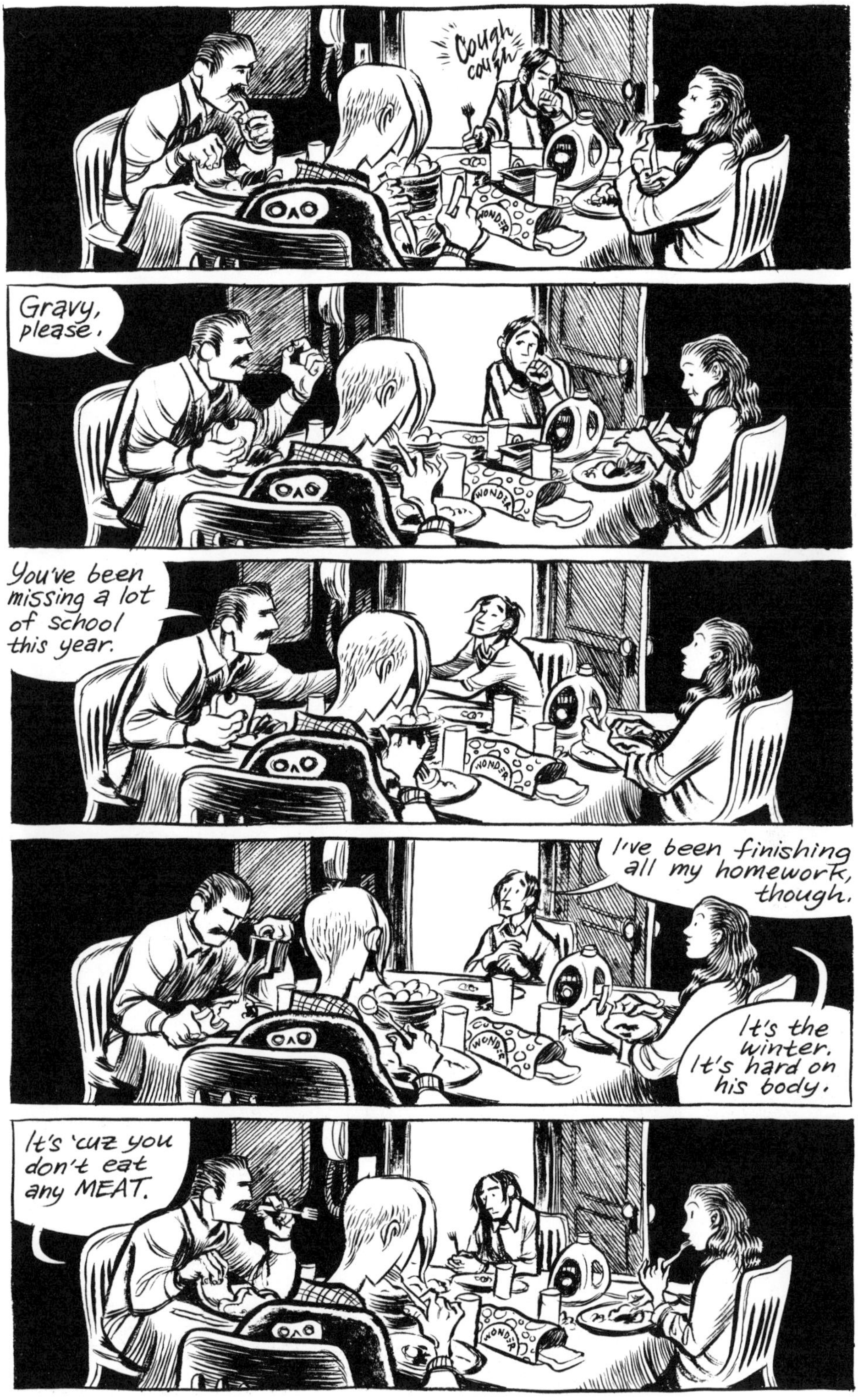

Cough cough
WONDER
Gravy, please.
You've been missing a lot of school this year.
I've been finishing all my homework, though.
It's the winter. It's hard on his body.
It's 'cuz you don't eat any MEAT.

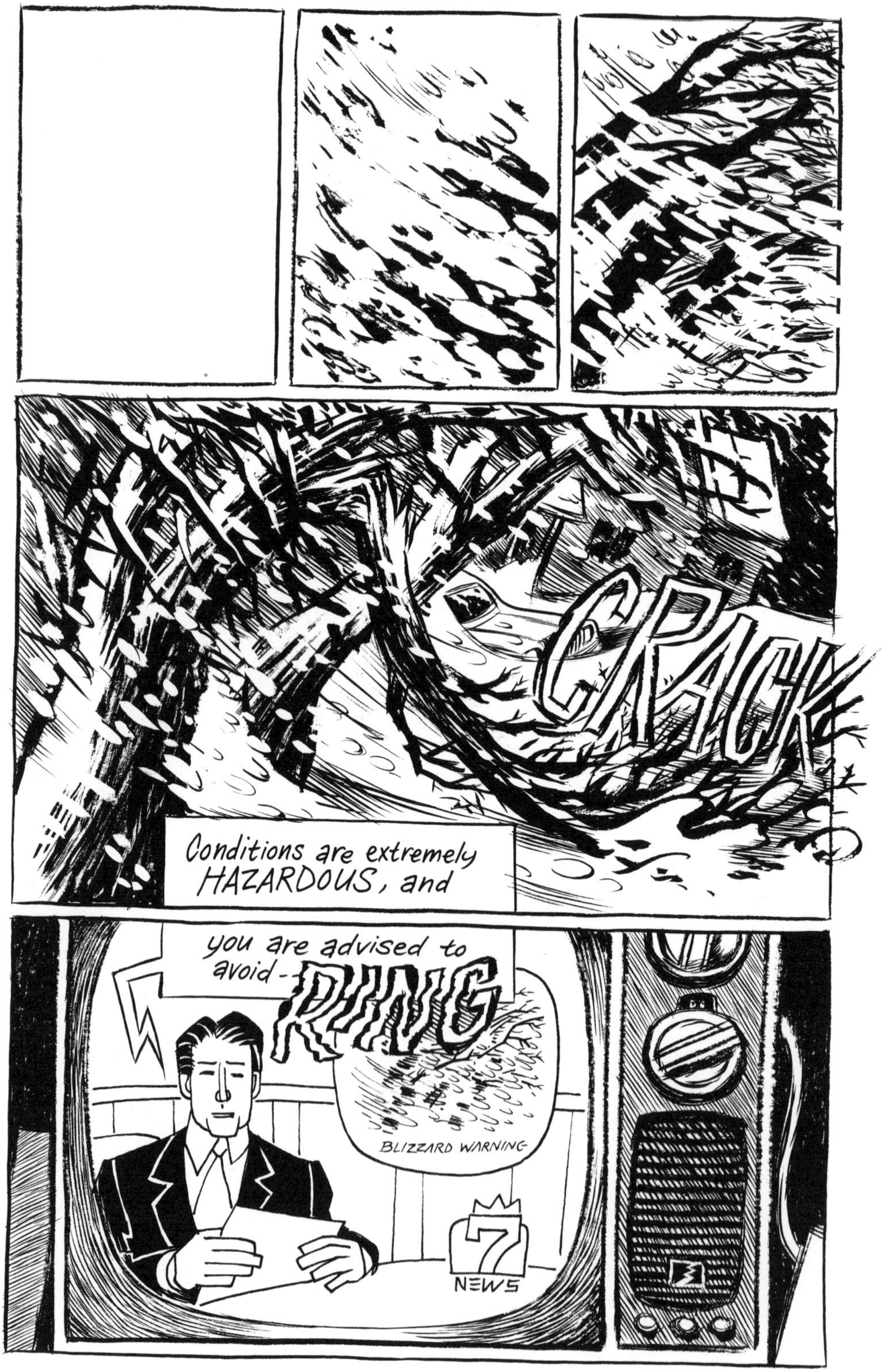
CRACK
Conditions are extremely HAZARDOUS, and
you are advised to avoid--
RING
BLIZZARD WARNING
7
NEWS

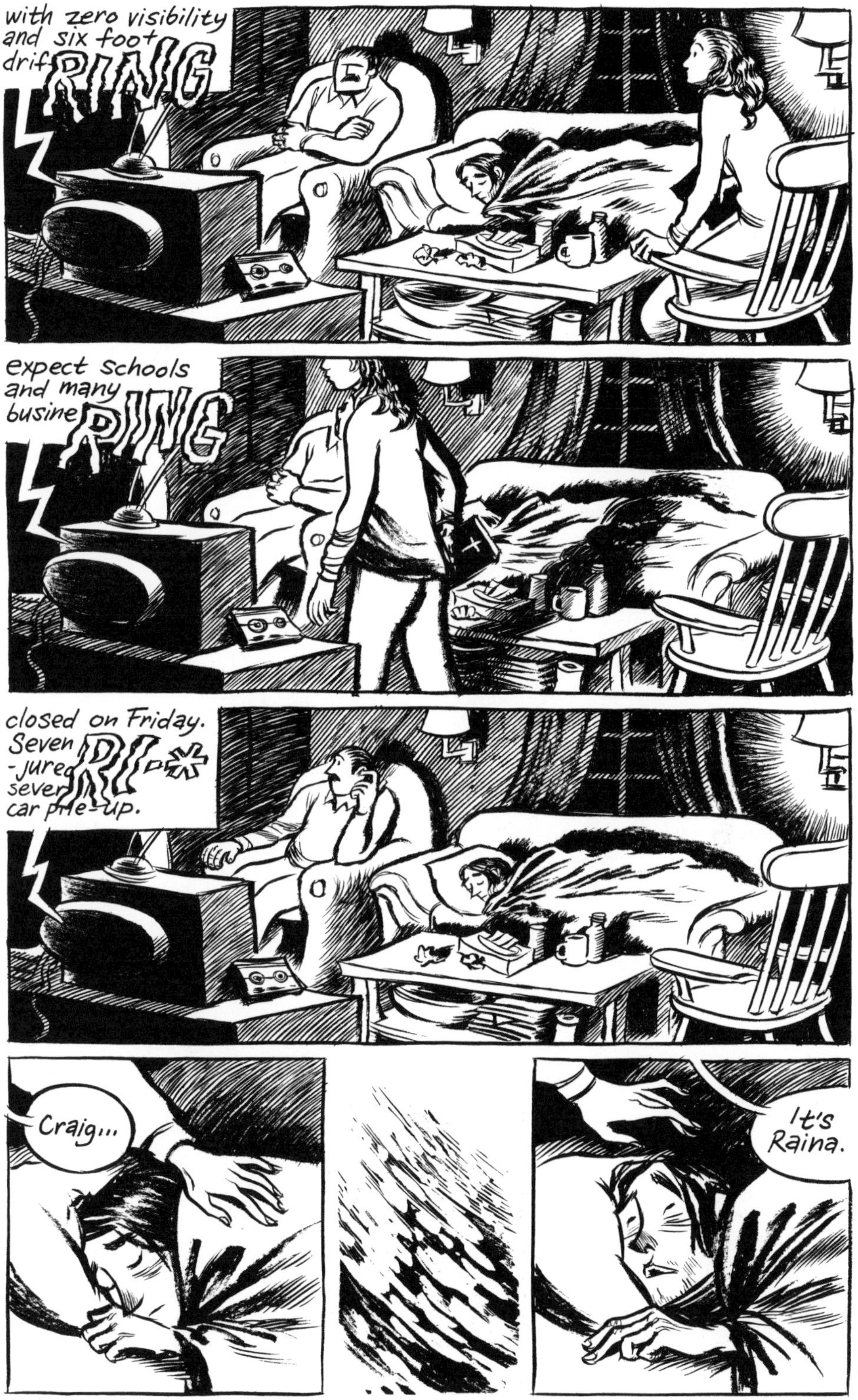
with zero visibility
and six foot
drif
RING
expect schools
and many
busine
RING
closed on Friday.
Seven
-jured
sever
car pile-up.
RI
Craig...
It's
Raina.

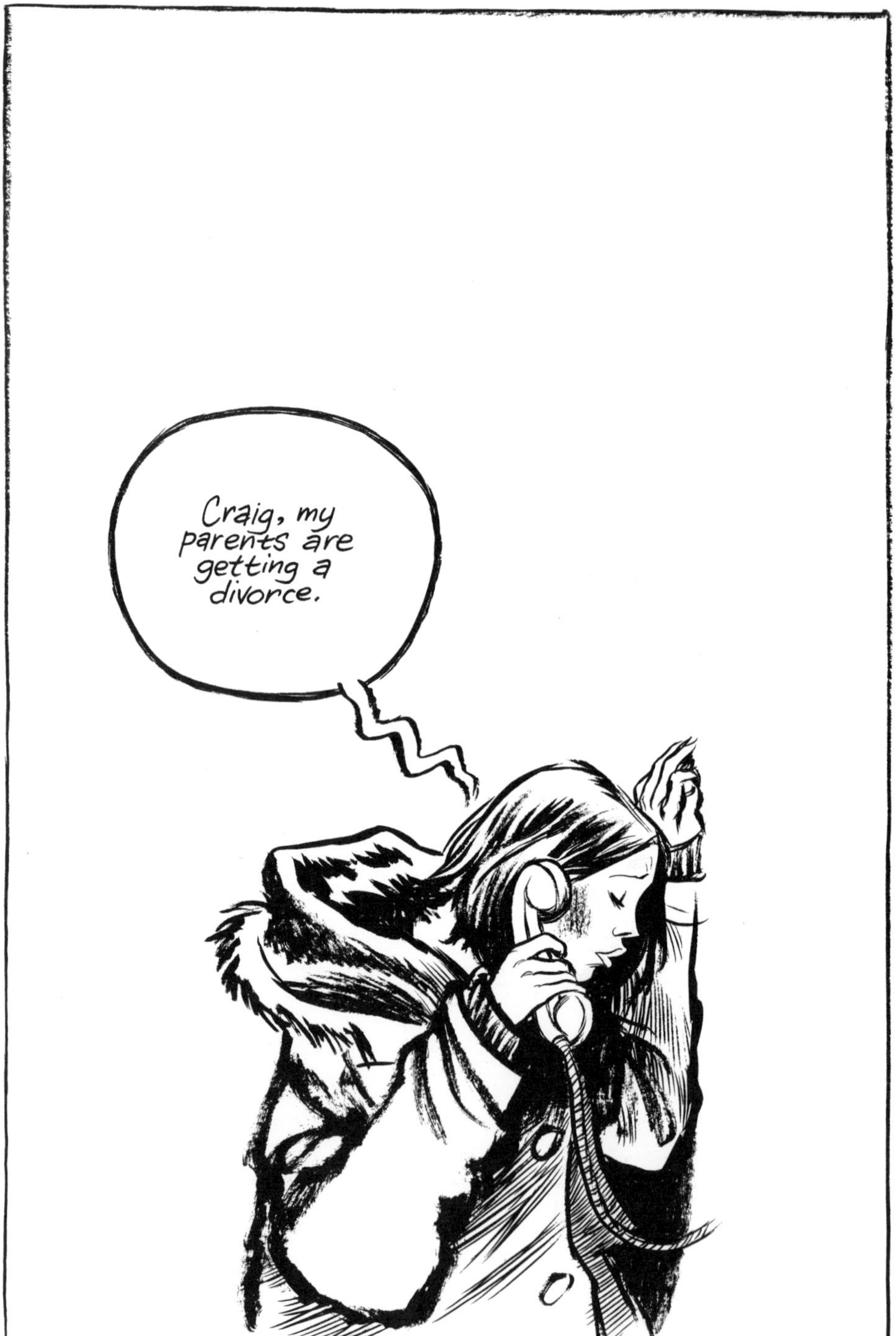
Craig, my parents are getting a divorce.

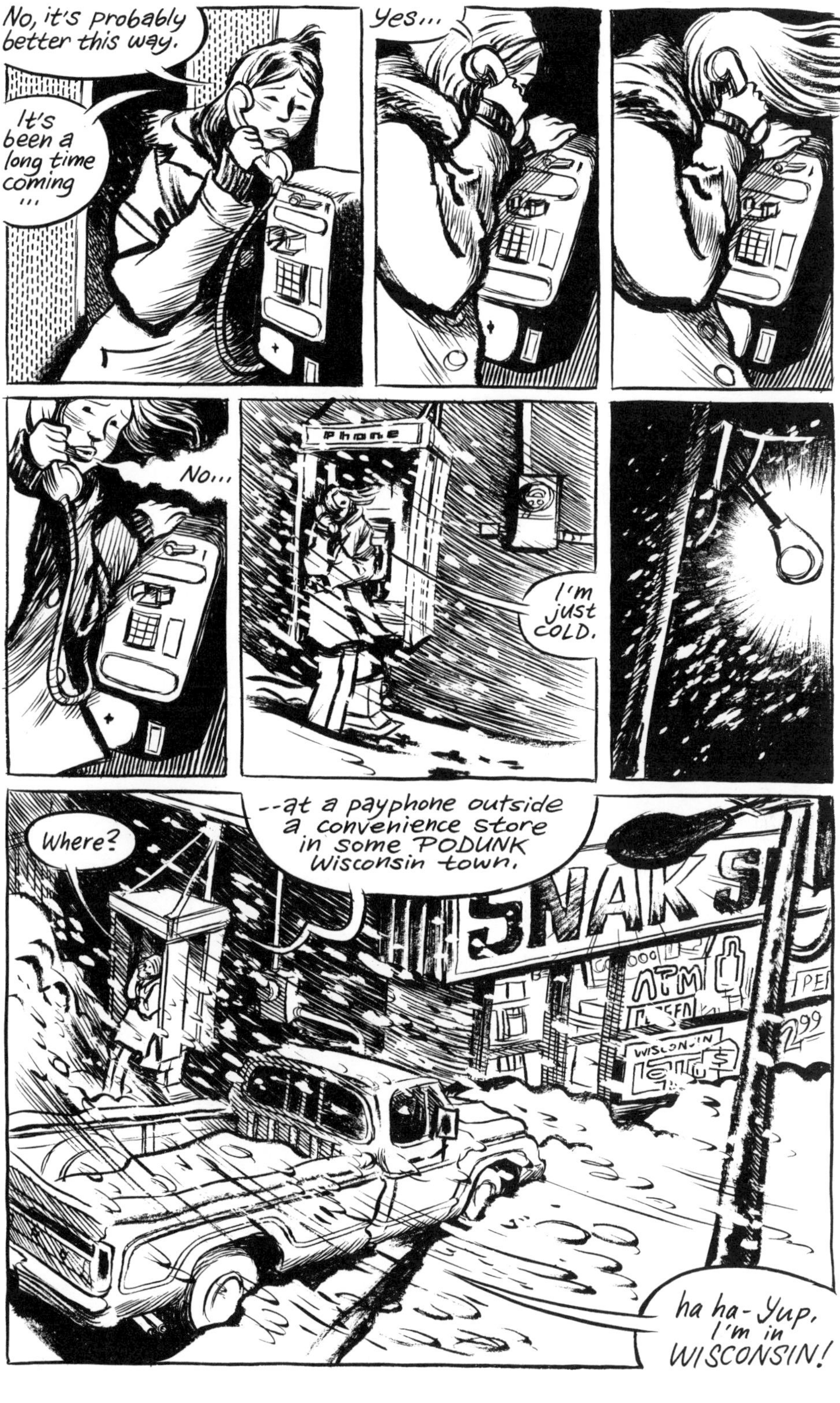
No, it's probably better this way.
It's been a long time coming ...
Yes...
No...
Phone
I'm just COLD.
Where?
--at a payphone outside a convenience store in some PODUNK Wisconsin town.
SNAKS
ATM
ha ha- Yup, I'm in WISCONSIN!

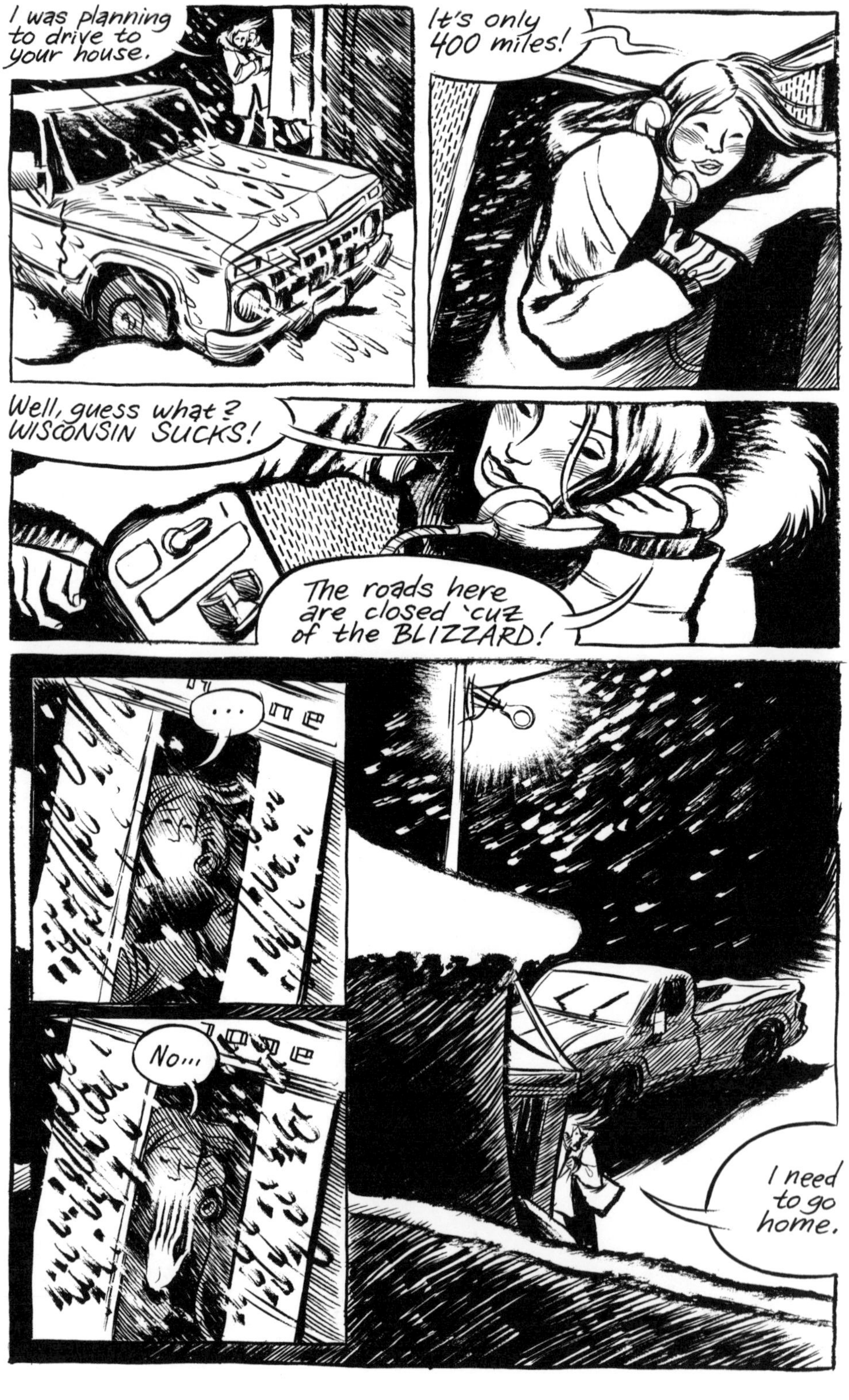
I was planning to drive to your house.
It's only 400 miles!
Well, guess what? WISCONSIN SUCKS!
The roads here are closed 'cuz of the BLIZZARD!
...
No...
I need to go home.

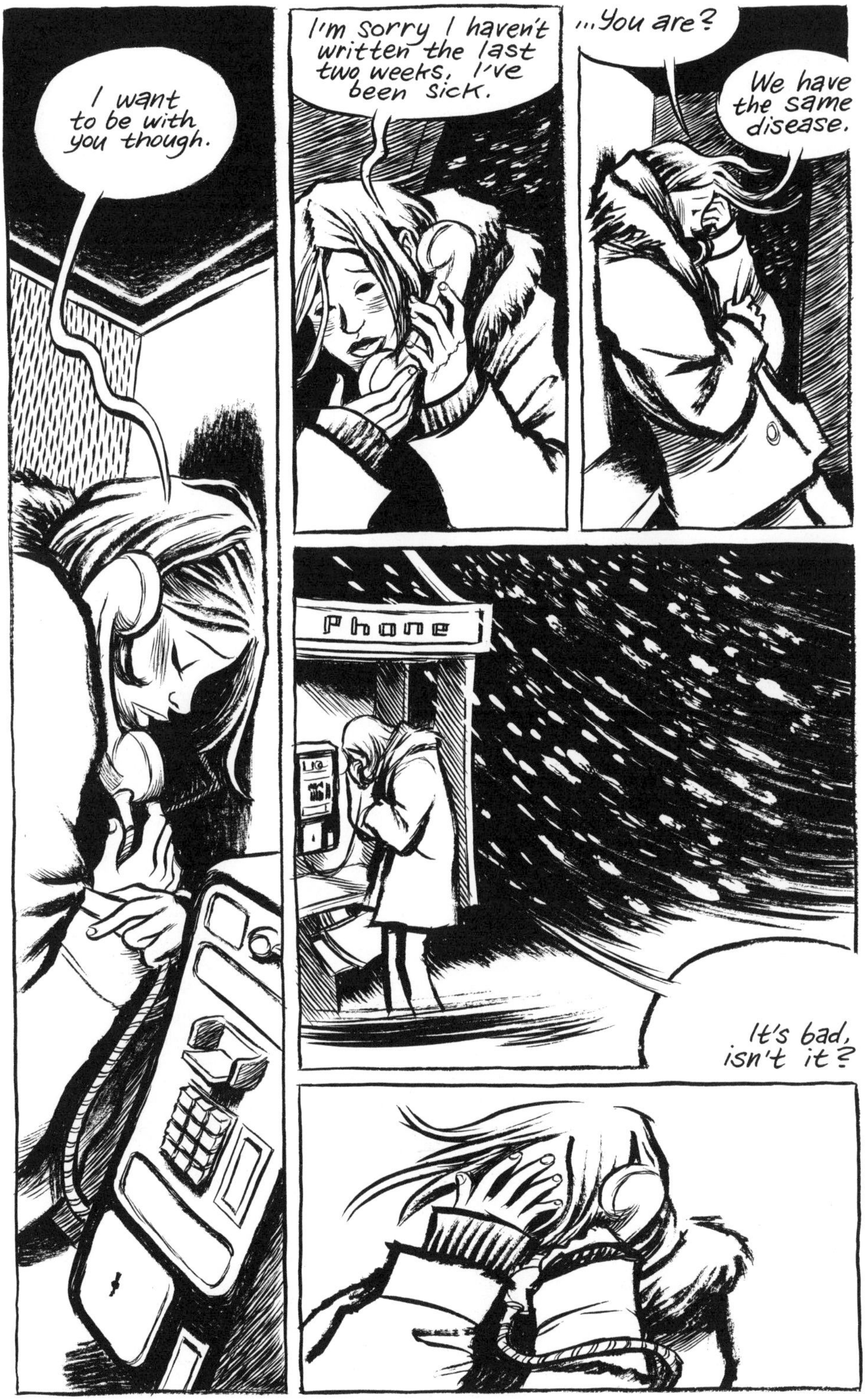
I want to be with you though.
I'm sorry I haven't written the last two weeks, I've been sick.
...You are?
We have the same disease.
Phone
It's bad, isn't it?

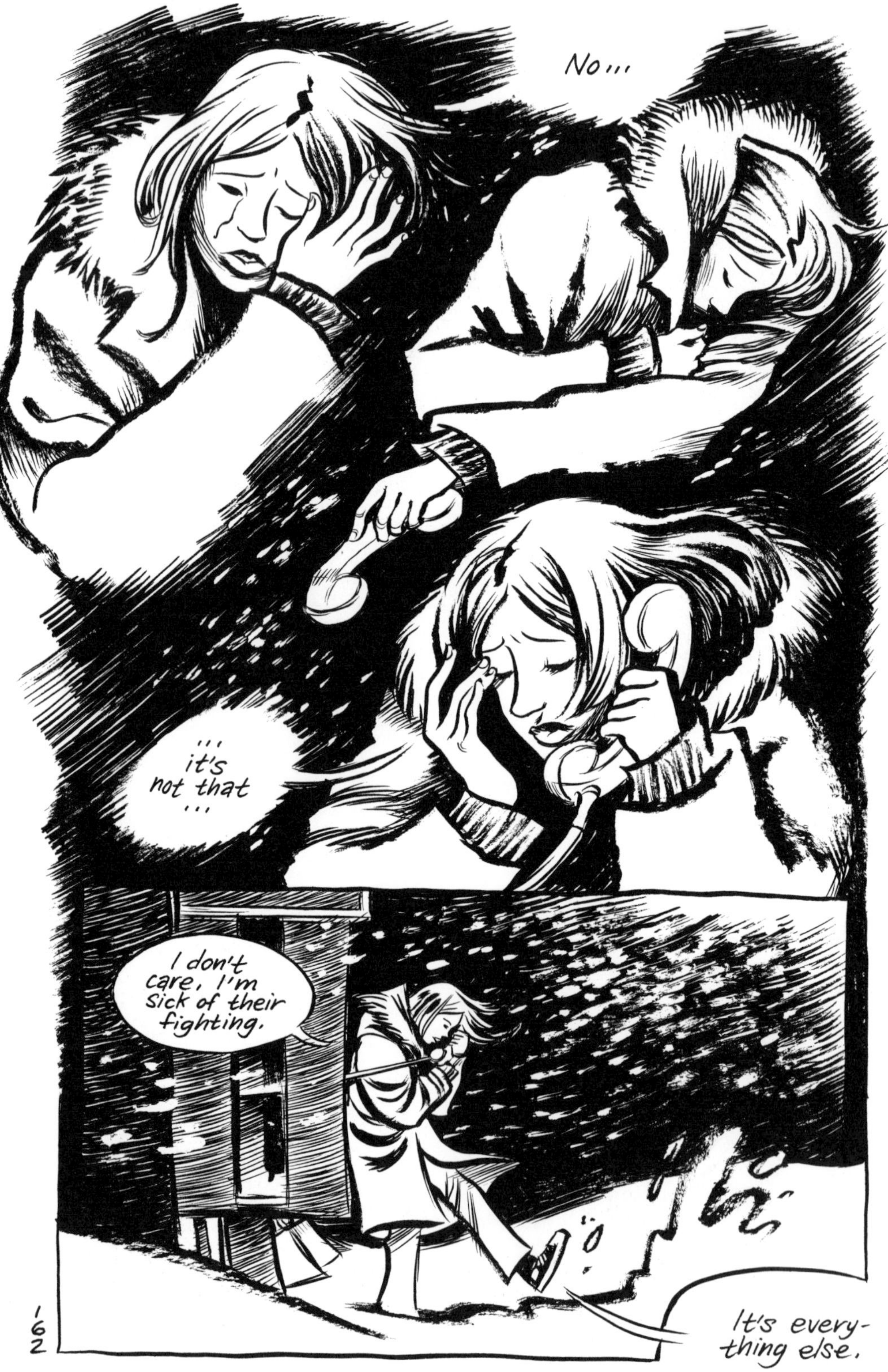
No...
... it's not that ...
I don't care, I'm sick of their fighting.
It's every-thing else.

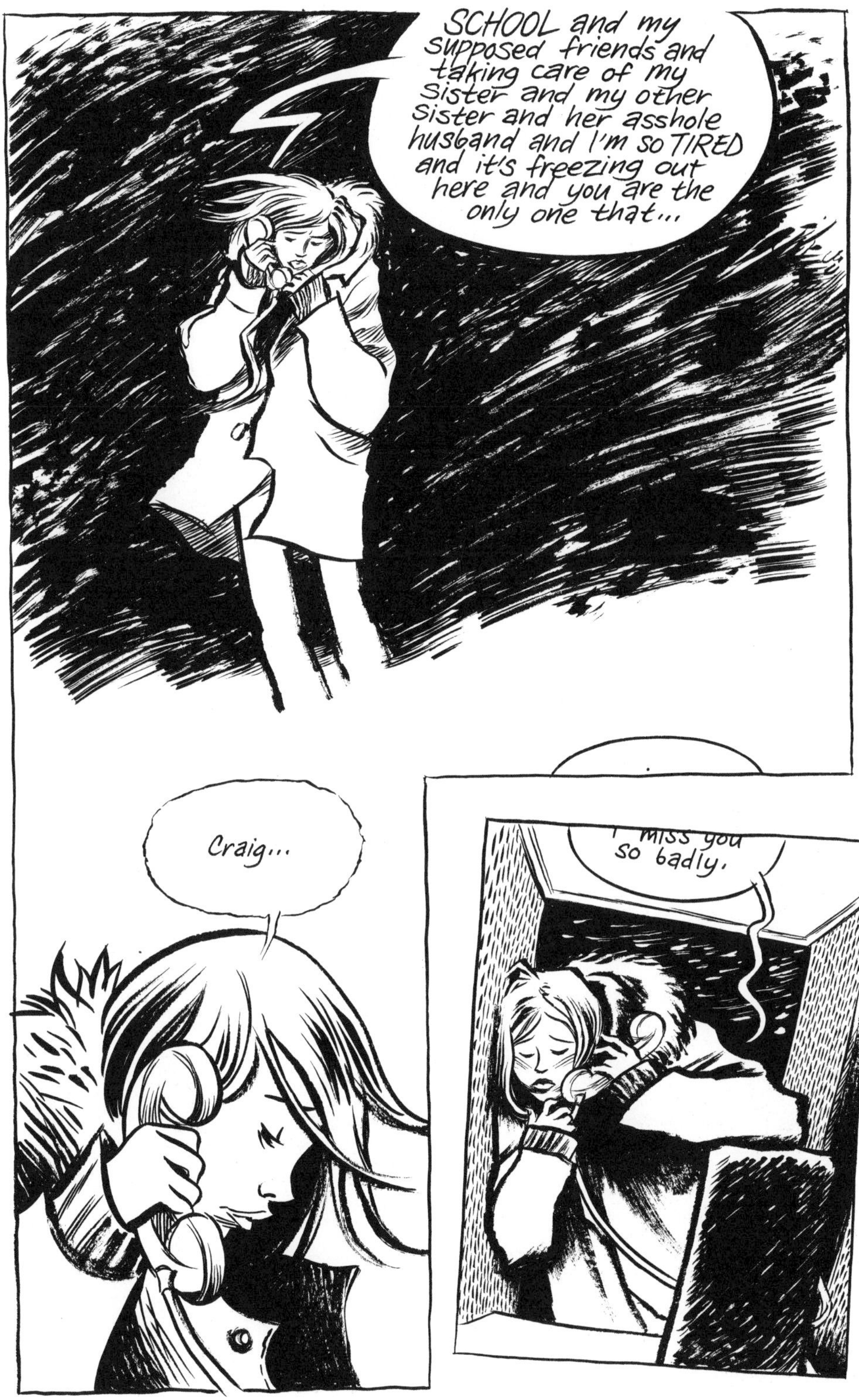
SCHOOL and my supposed friends and taking care of my sister and my other sister and her asshole husband and I'm SO TIRED and it's freezing out here and you are the only one that...
Craig...
I miss you so badly.

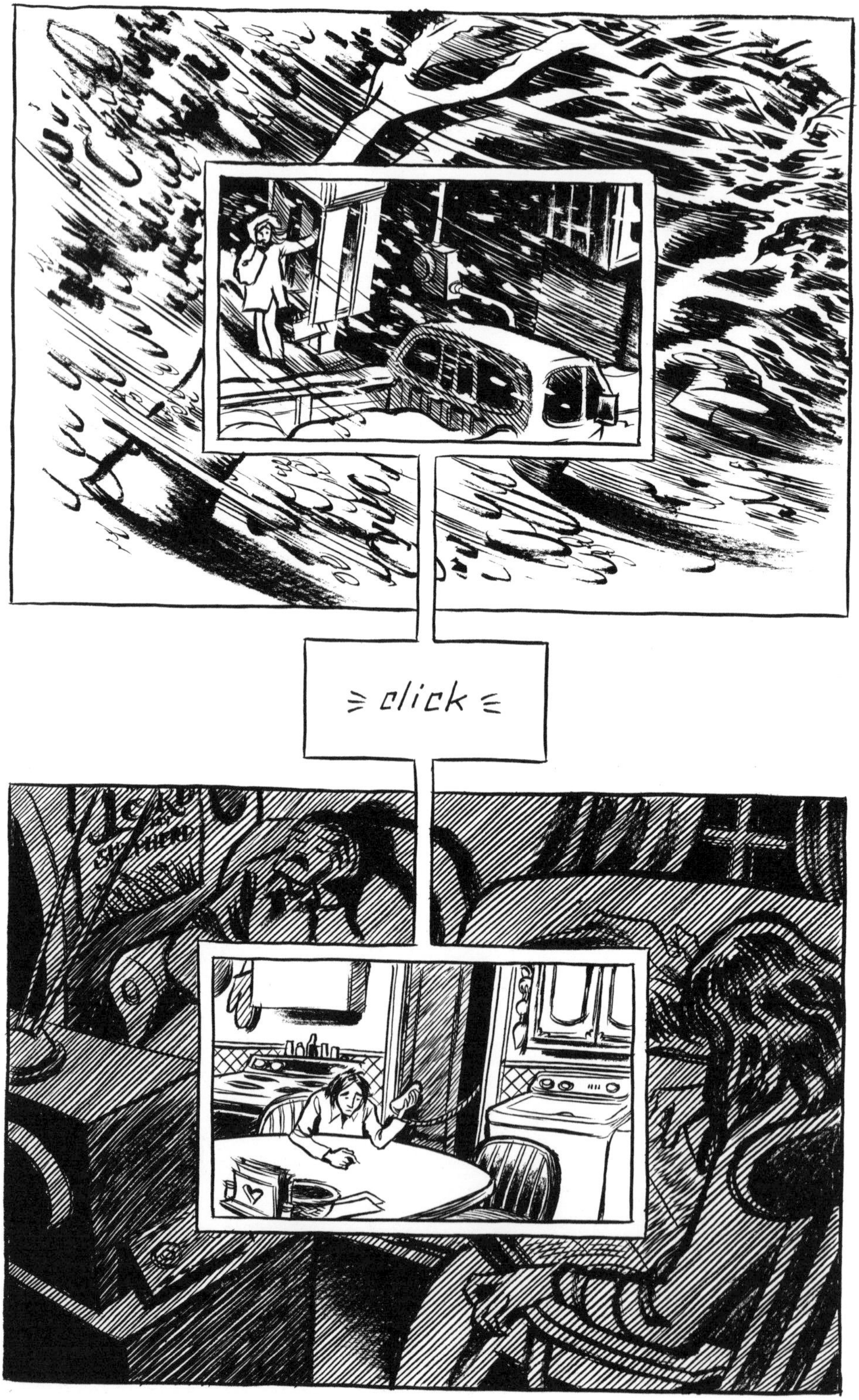
click

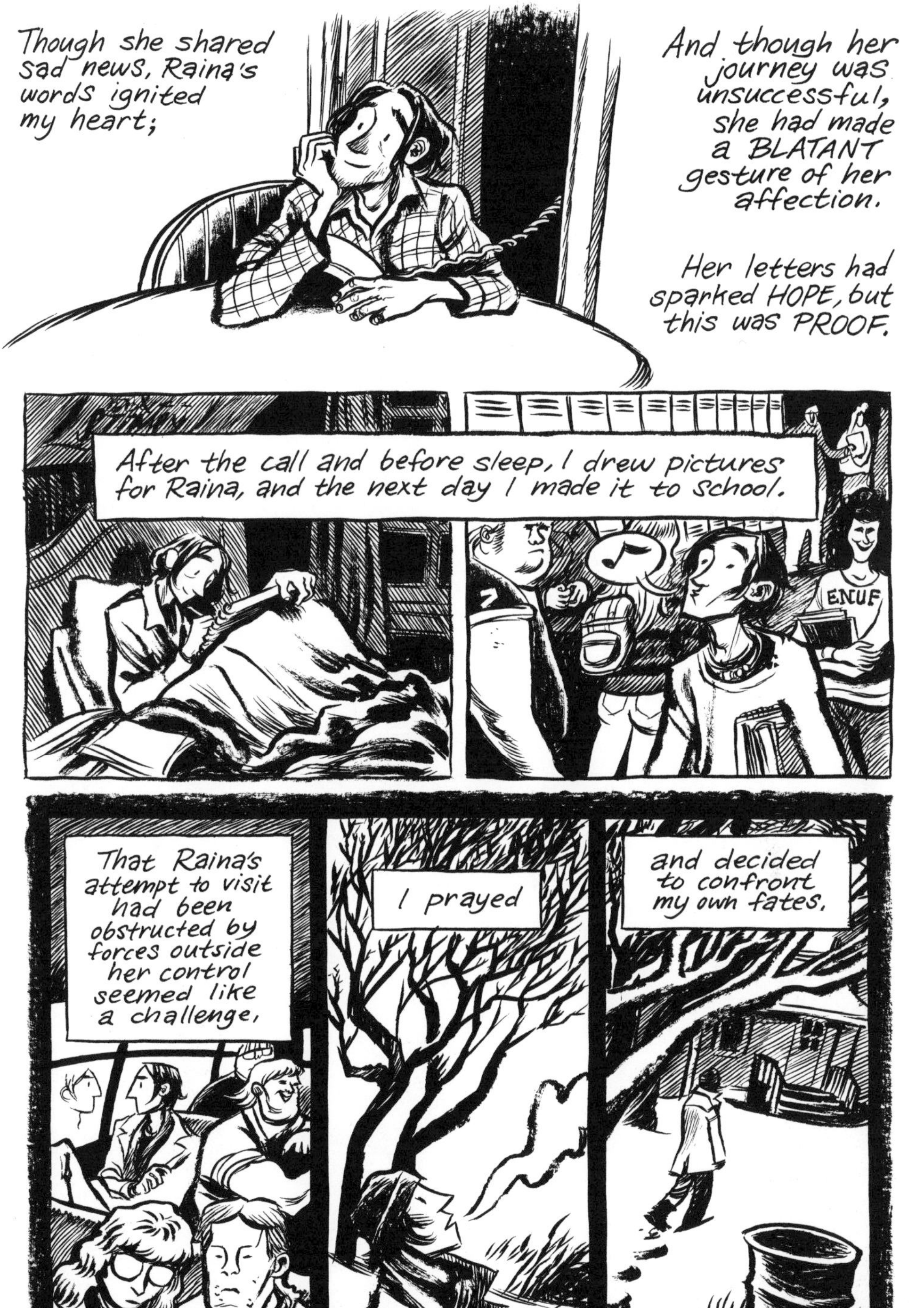
Though she shared sad news, Raina's words ignited my heart;
And though her journey was unsuccessful, she had made a BLATANT gesture of her affection.
Her letters had sparked HOPE, but this was PROOF.
After the call and before sleep, I drew pictures for Raina, and the next day I made it to school.
ENUF
That Raina's attempt to visit had been obstructed by forces outside her control seemed like a challenge,
MOERAE
MOIRAI
I prayed
and decided to confront my own fates.

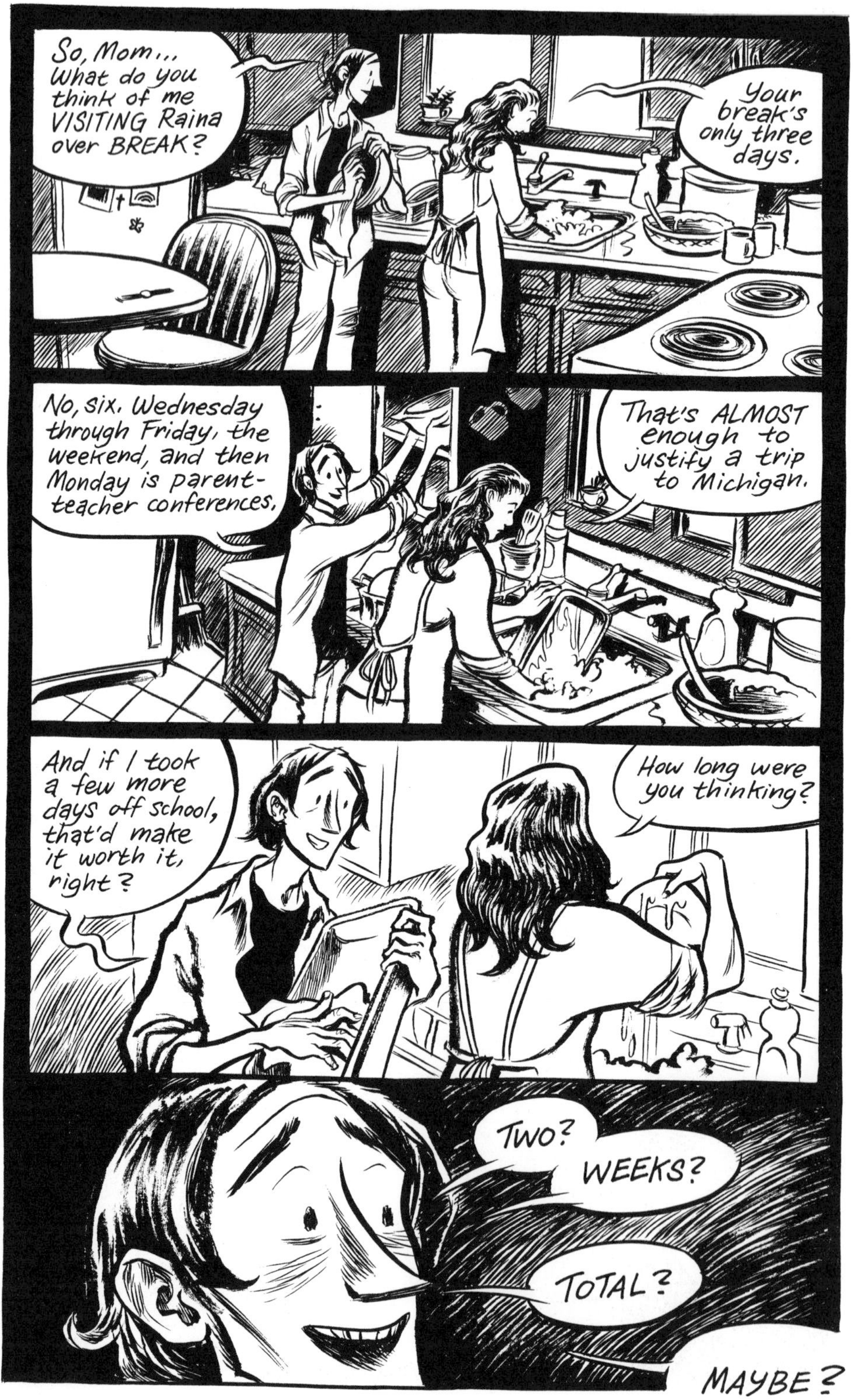
So, Mom... What do you think of me VISITING Raina over BREAK?
Your break's only three days.
No, six. Wednesday through Friday, the weekend, and then Monday is parent-teacher conferences.
That's ALMOST enough to justify a trip to Michigan.
And if I took a few more days off school, that'd make it worth it, right?
How long were you thinking?
TWO?
WEEKS?
TOTAL?
MAYBE?

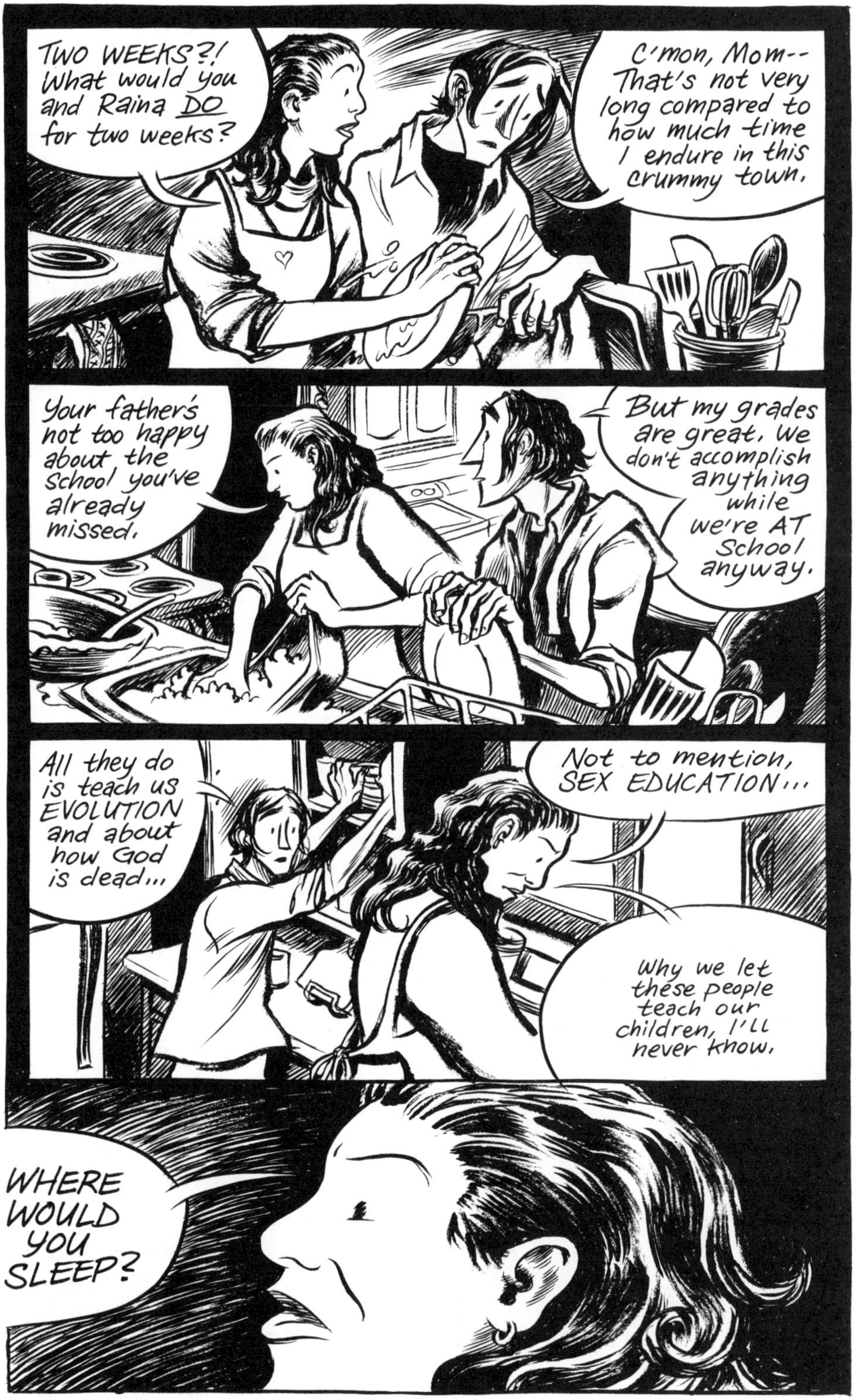
TWO WEEKS?! What would you and Raina DO for two weeks?
C'mon, Mom-- That's not very long compared to how much time I endure in this crummy town.
Your father's not too happy about the school you've already missed.
But my grades are great. We don't accomplish anything while we're AT school anyway.
All they do is teach us EVOLUTION and about how God is dead...
Not to mention, SEX EDUCATION...
Why we let these people teach our children, I'll never know.
WHERE WOULD YOU SLEEP?

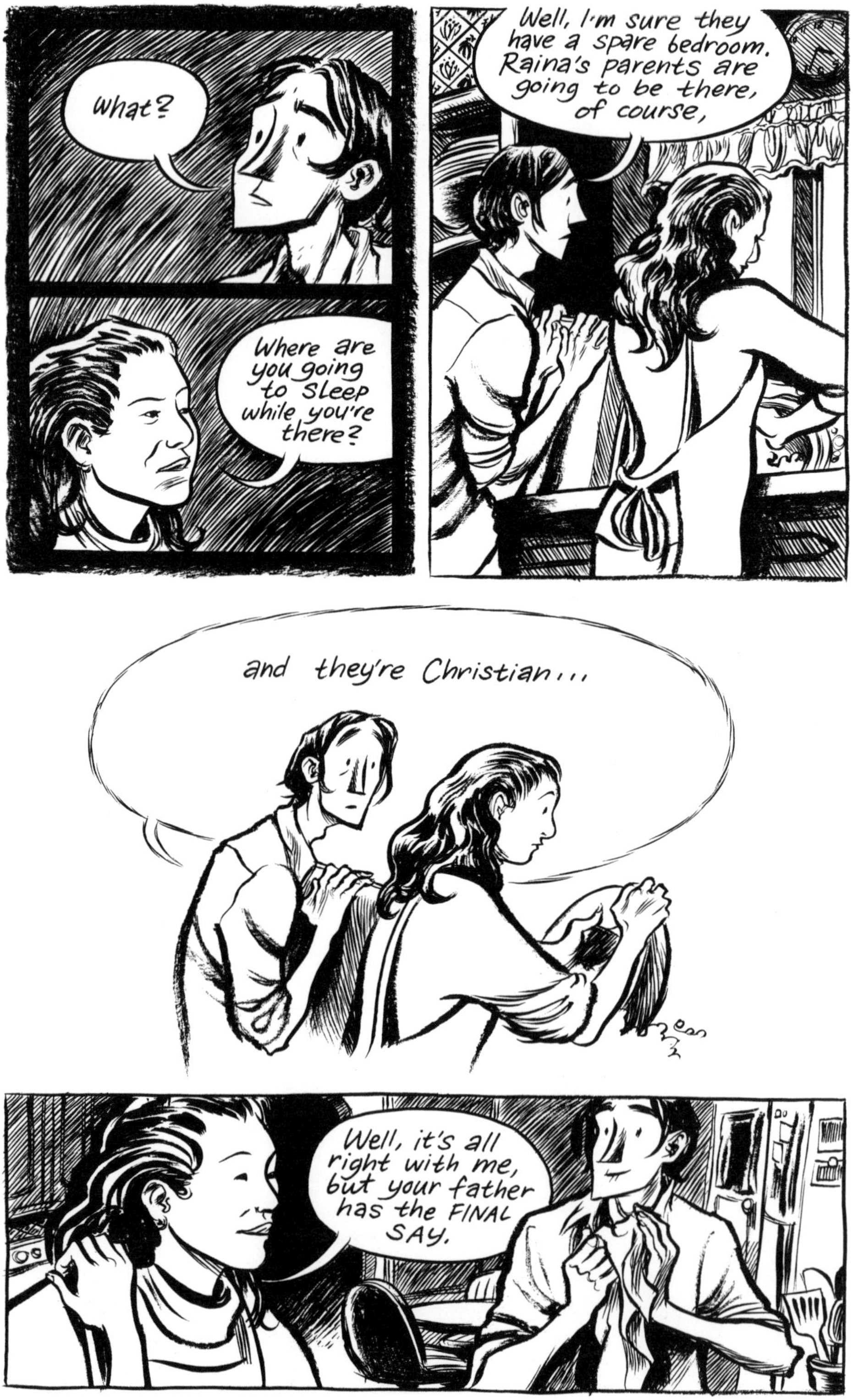
What?
Well, I'm sure they have a spare bedroom. Raina's parents are going to be there, of course,
Where are you going to sleep while you're there?
and they're Christian...
Well, it's all right with me, but your father has the FINAL SAY.

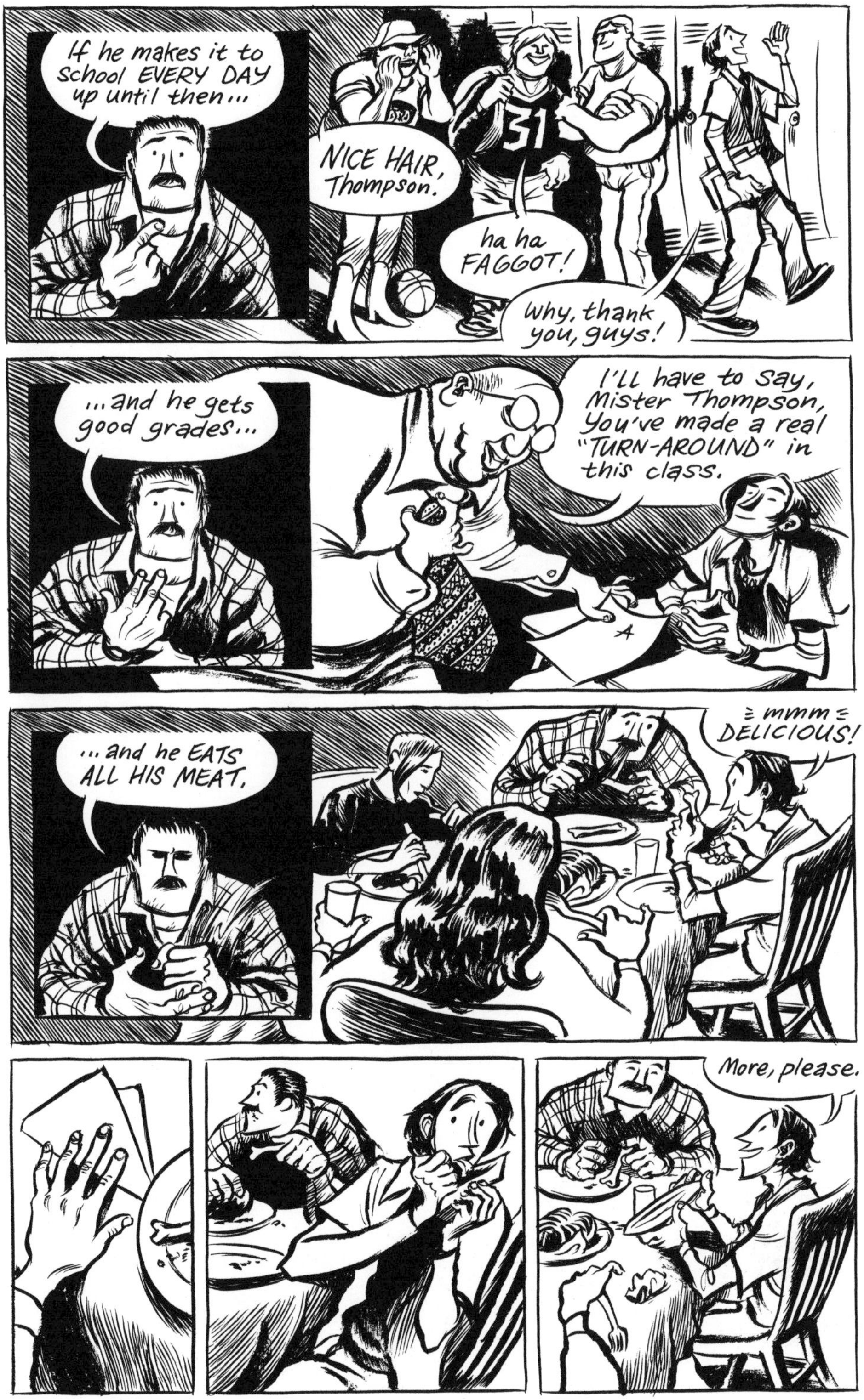
If he makes it to school EVERY DAY up until then...
NICE HAIR, Thompson.
ha ha FAGGOT!
Why, thank you, guys!
...and he gets good grades...
I'll have to say, Mister Thompson, You've made a real "TURN-AROUND" in this class.
...and he EATS ALL HIS MEAT.
mmm DELICIOUS!
More, please.

My mother drove me; her father drove her; and we planned to meet HALFWAY, at the border of Wisconsin and Michigan.

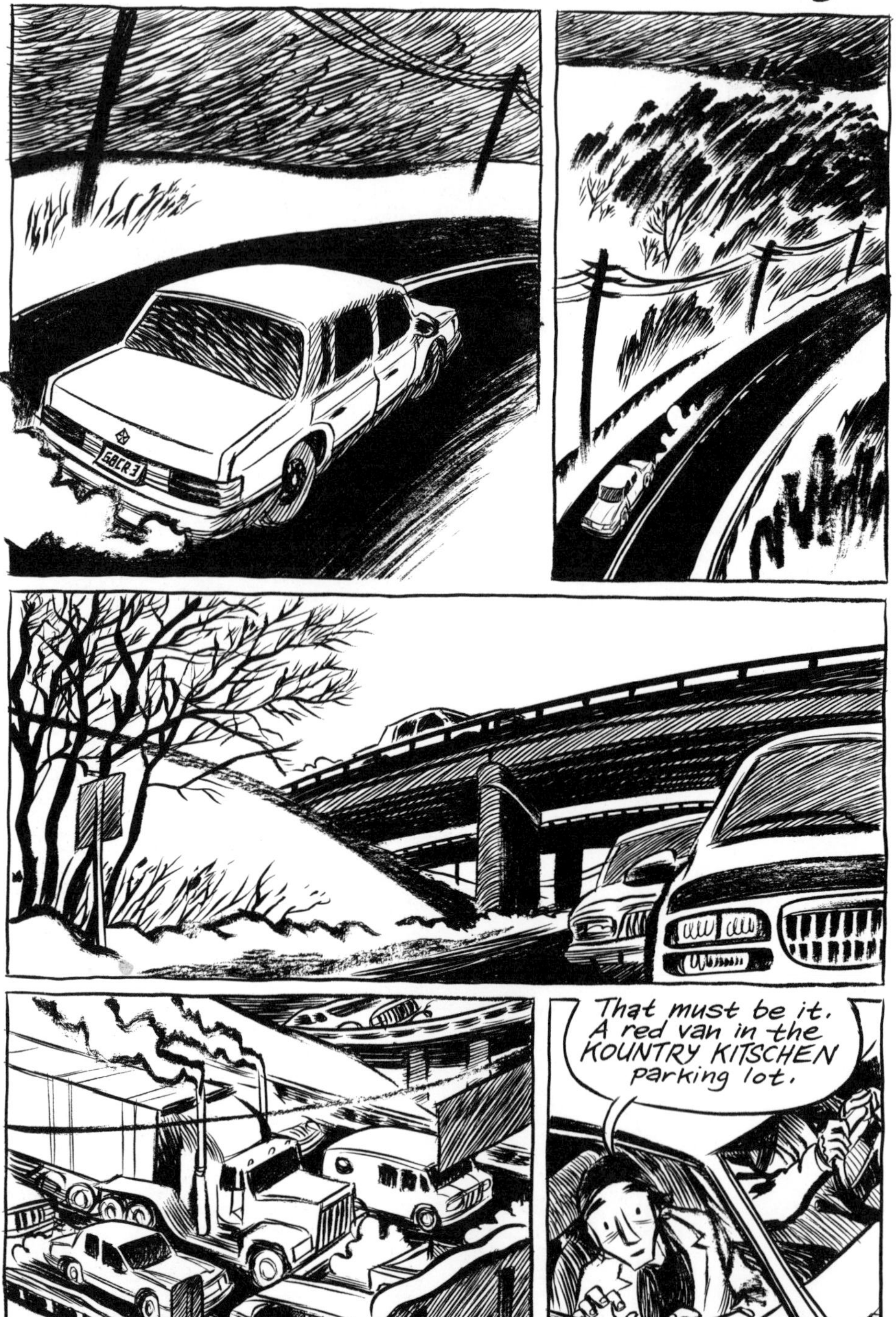
That must be it. A red van in the KOUNTRY KITSCHEN parking lot.

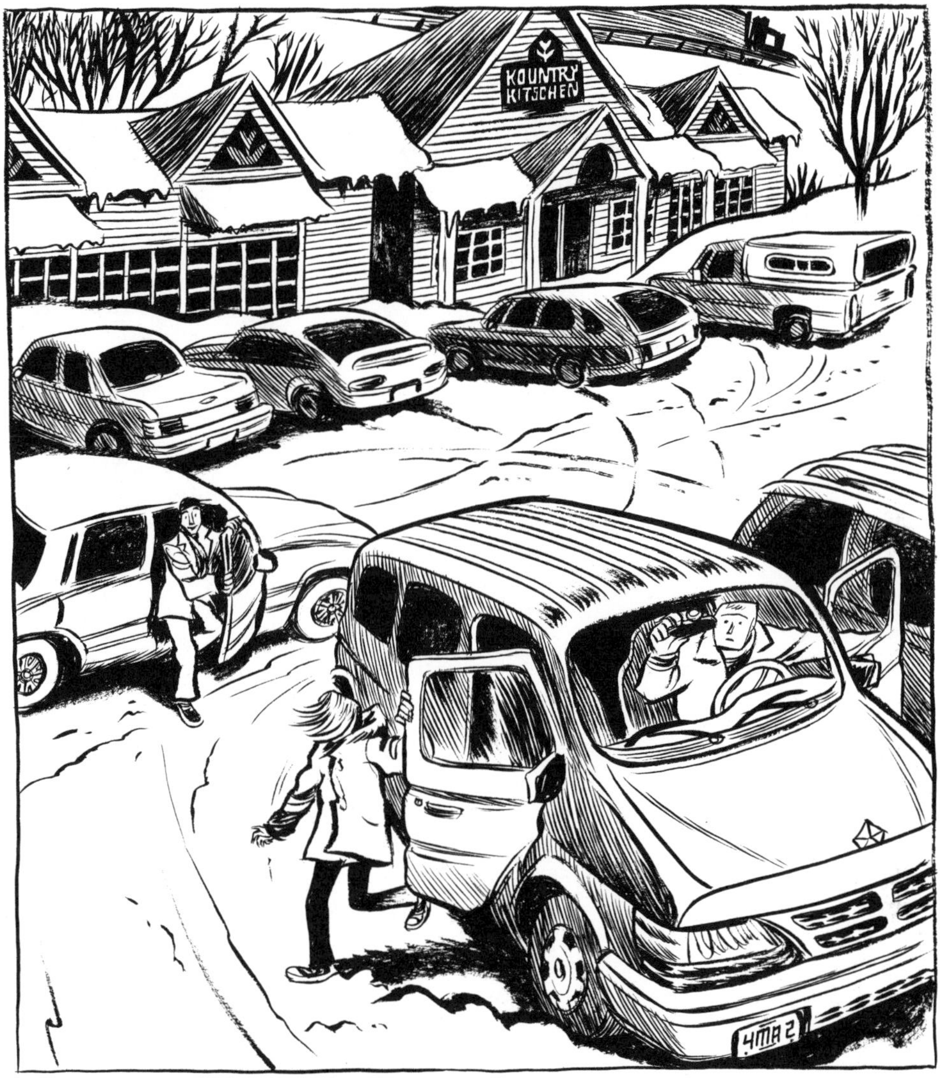
KOUNTRY
KITSCHEN

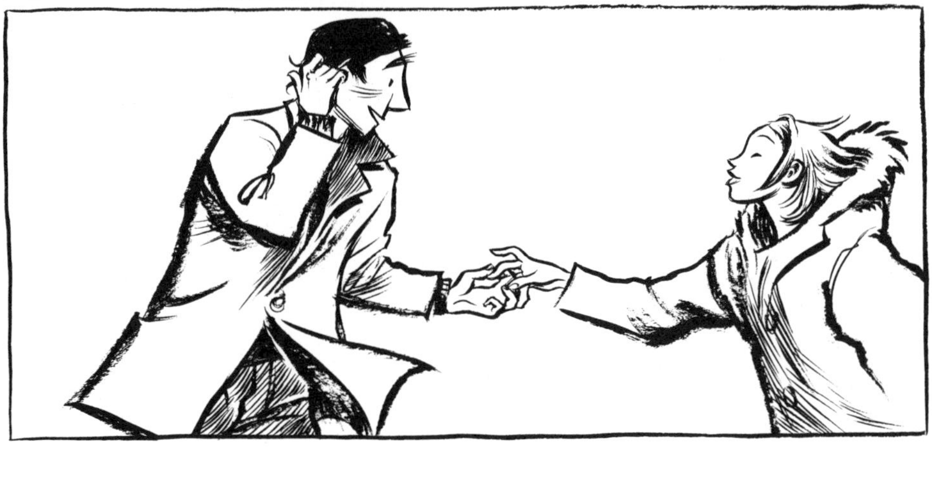

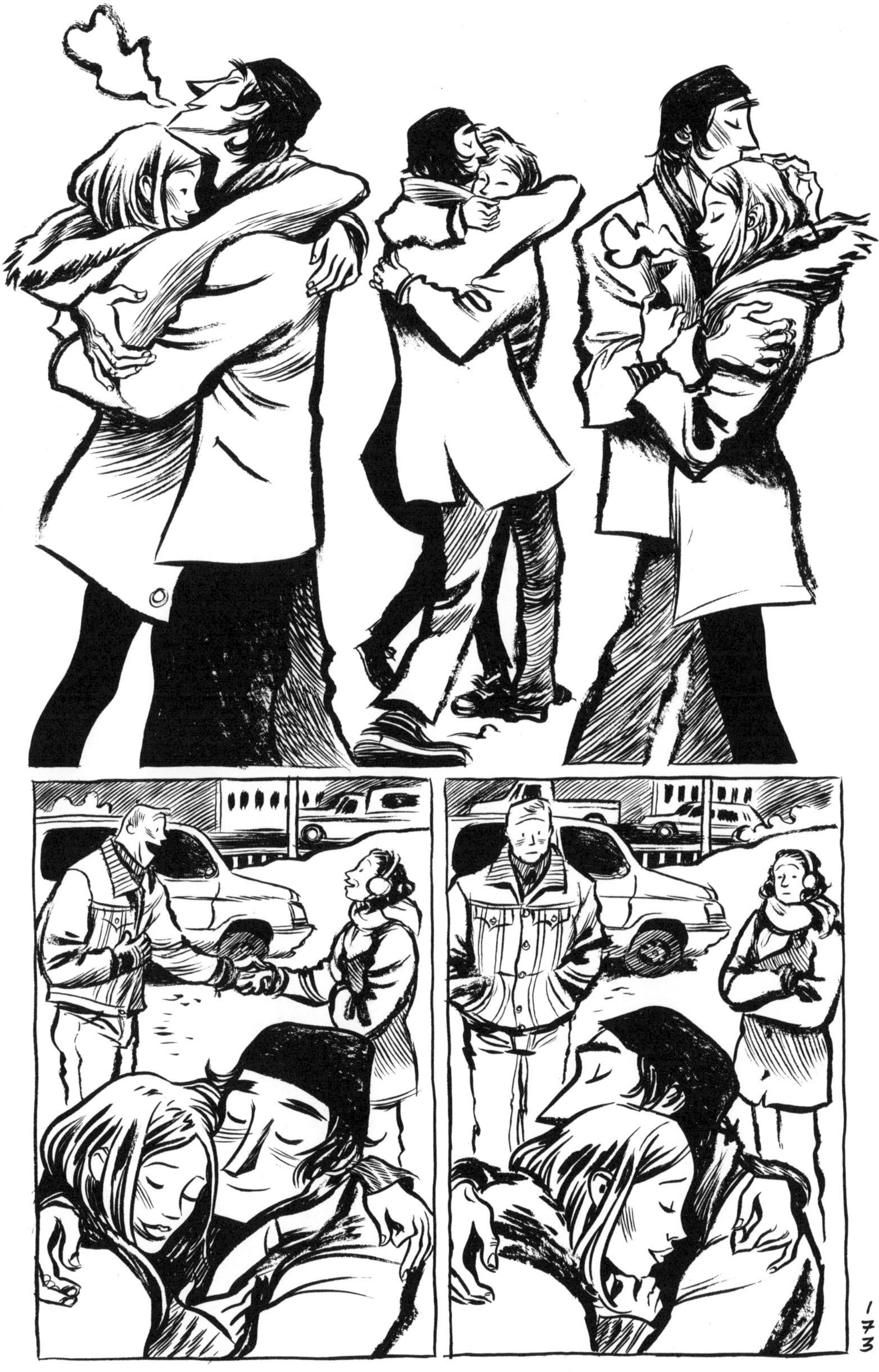

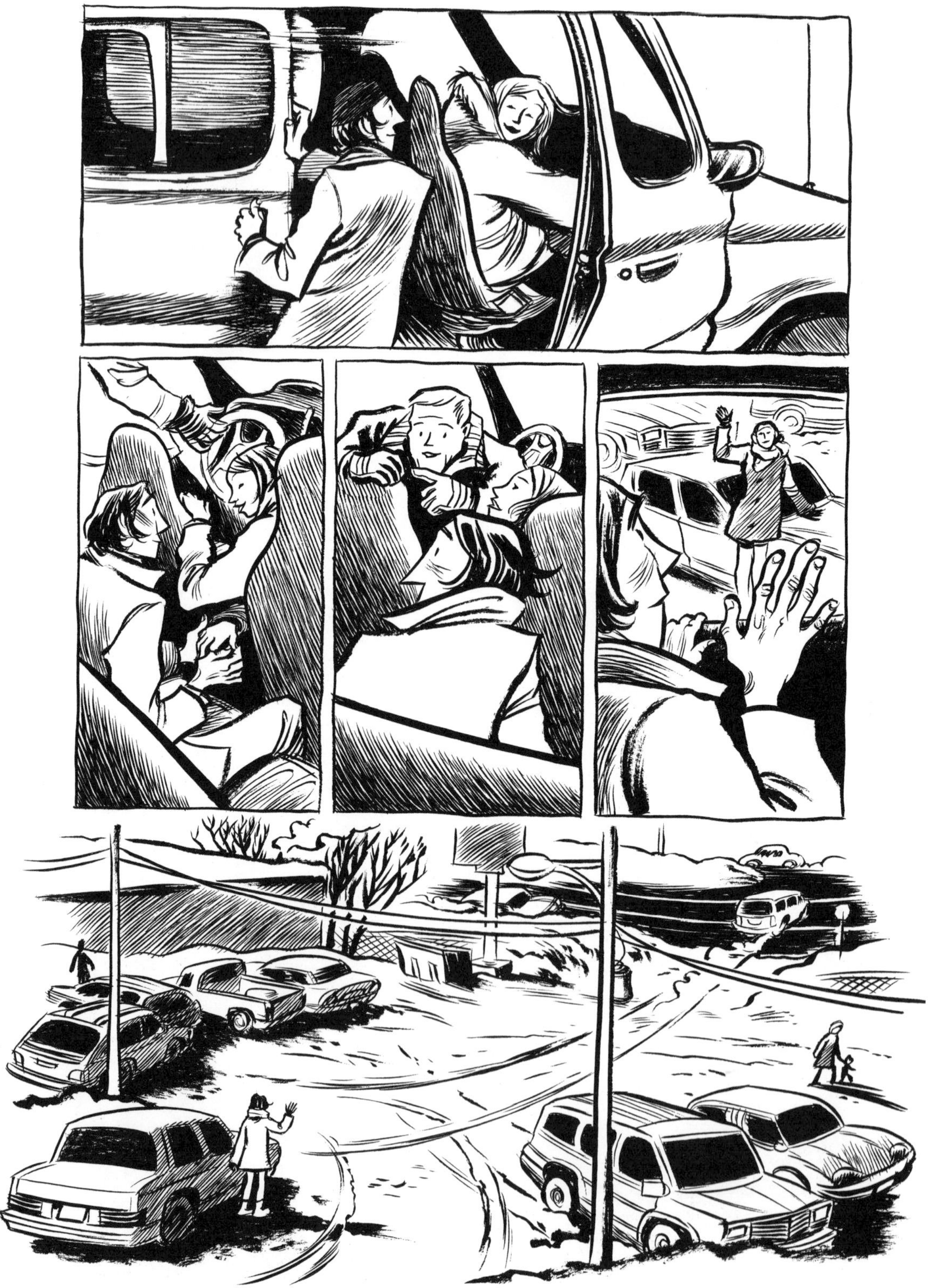

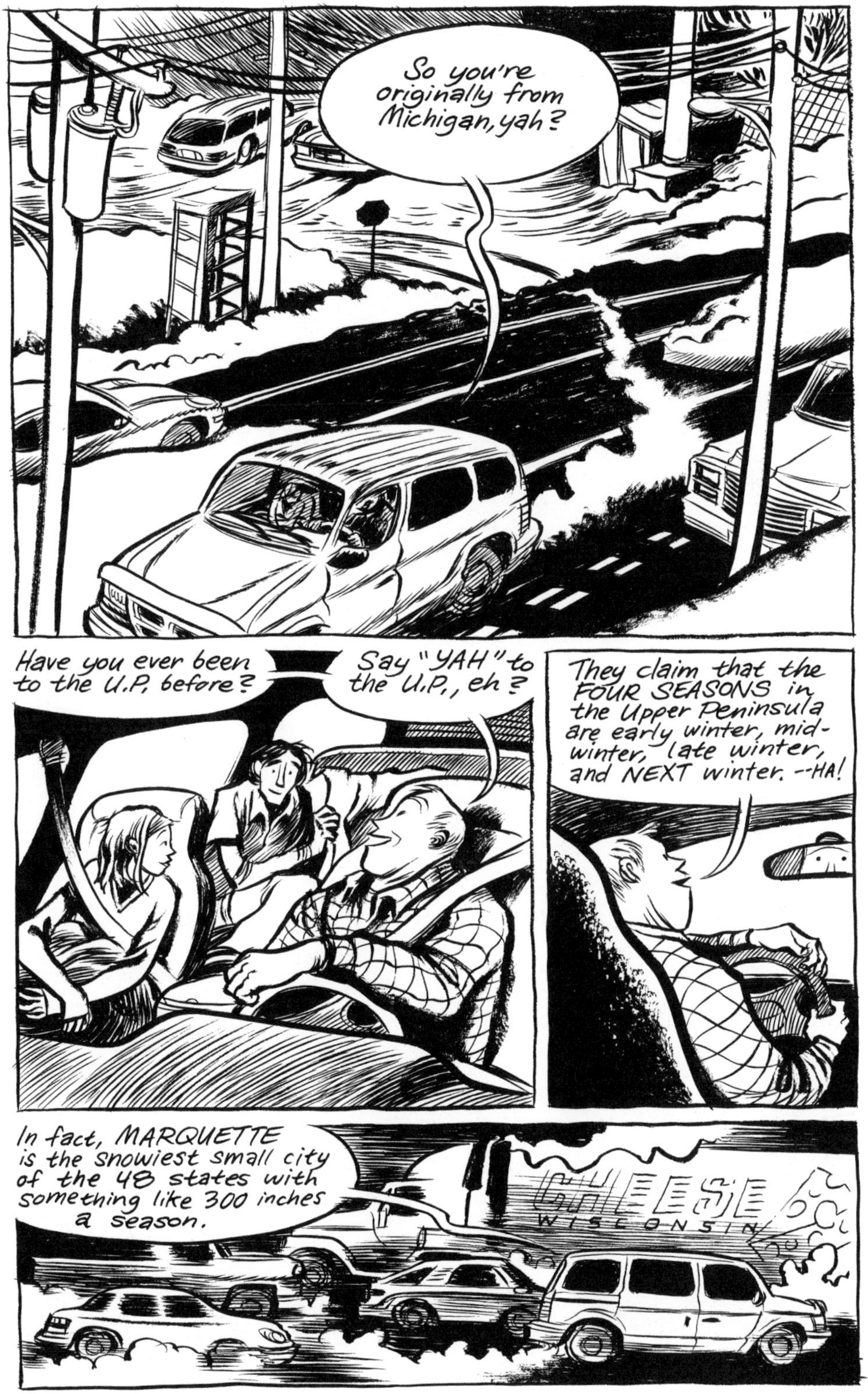
So you're originally from Michigan, yah?
Have you ever been to the U.P. before?
Say "YAH" to the U.P., eh?
They claim that the FOUR SEASONS in the Upper Peninsula are early winter, mid-winter, late winter, and NEXT winter. --HA!
In fact, MARQUETTE is the snowiest small city of the 48 states with something like 300 inches a season.
CHEESE
WISCONSIN

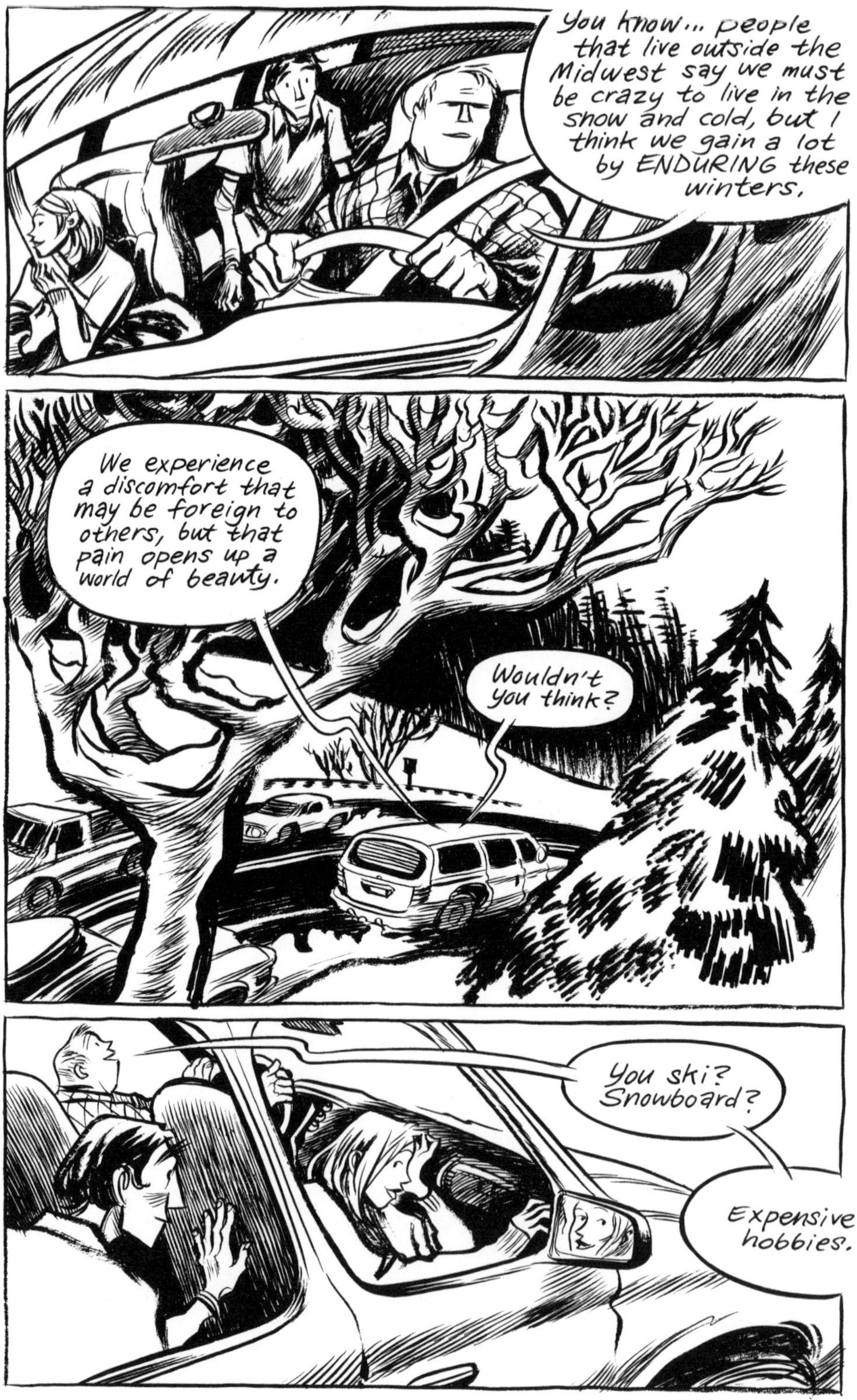
You know... people that live outside the Midwest say we must be crazy to live in the snow and cold, but I think we gain a lot by ENDURING these winters.
We experience a discomfort that may be foreign to others, but that pain opens up a world of beauty.
Wouldn't you think?
You ski? Snowboard?
Expensive hobbies.

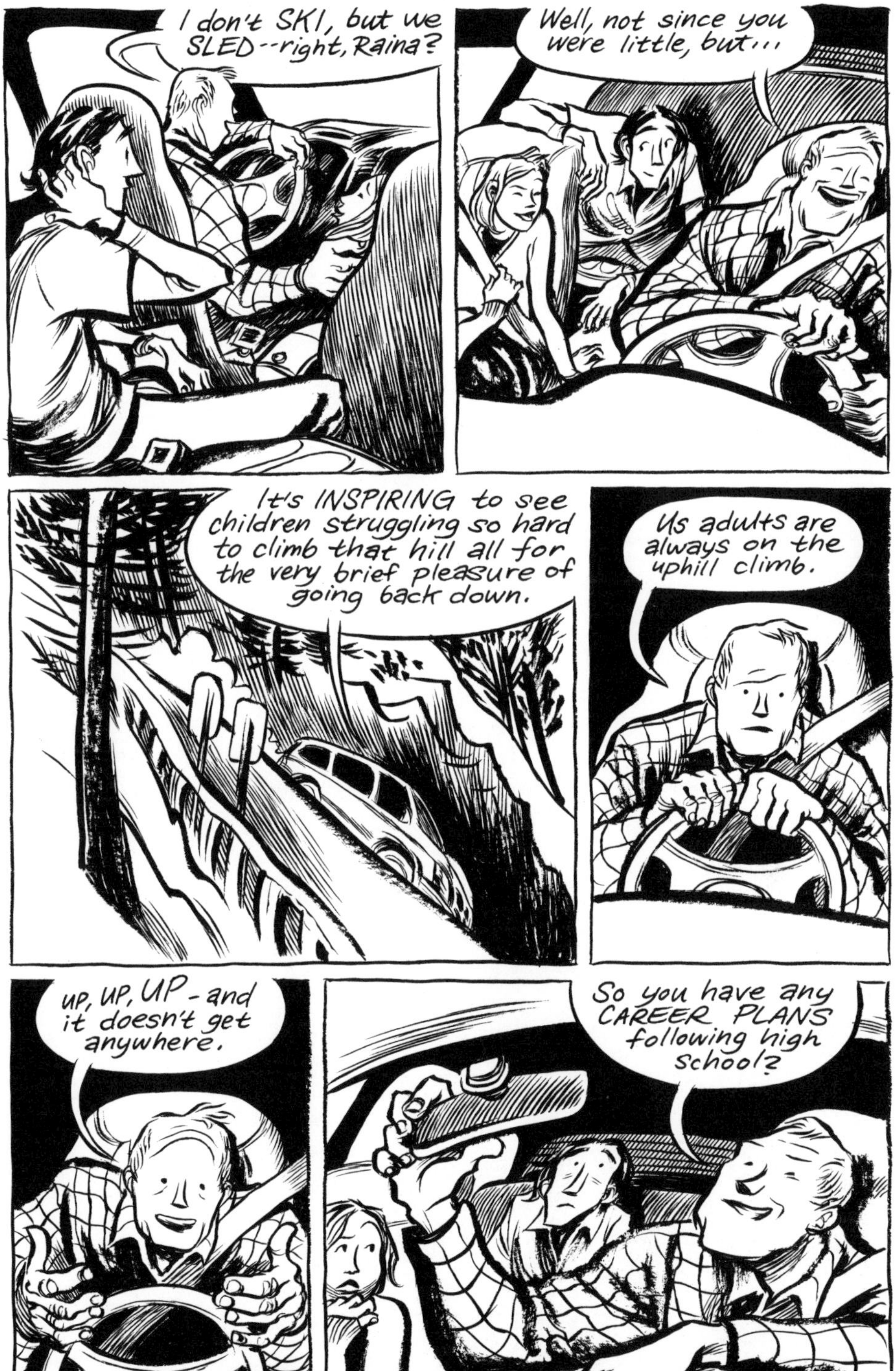
I don't SKI, but we SLED--right, Raina?
Well, not since you were little, but...
It's INSPIRING to see children struggling so hard to climb that hill all for the very brief pleasure of going back down.
Us adults are always on the uphill climb.
up, up, UP - and it doesn't get anywhere.
So you have any CAREER PLANS following high school?

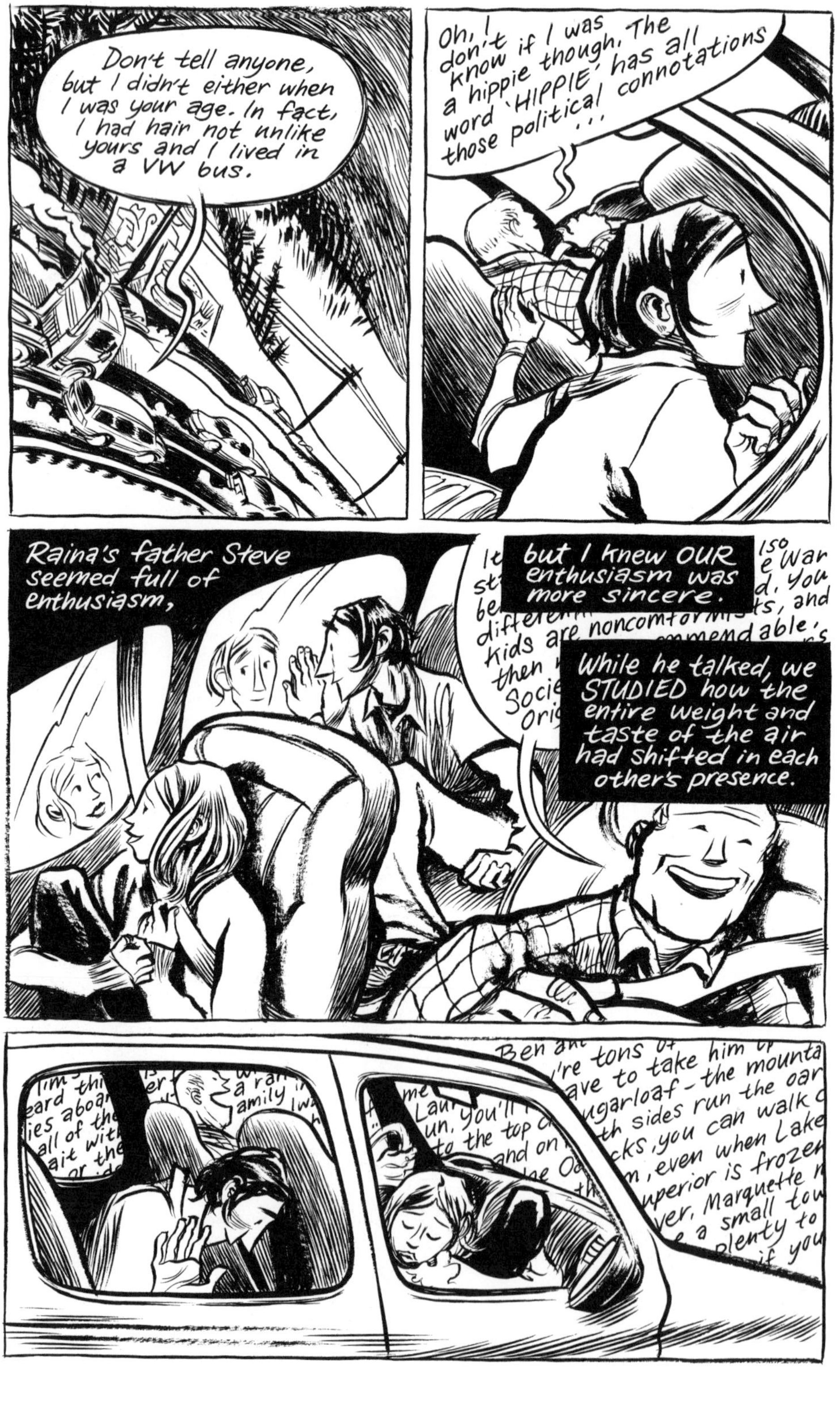
Don't tell anyone, but I didn't either when I was your age. In fact, I had hair not unlike yours and I lived in a VW bus.
Oh, I don't know if I was a hippie though. The word 'HIPPIE' has all those political connotations ...
Raina's father Steve seemed full of enthusiasm,
but I knew OUR enthusiasm was more sincere.
While he talked, we STUDIED how the entire weight and taste of the air had shifted in each other's presence.

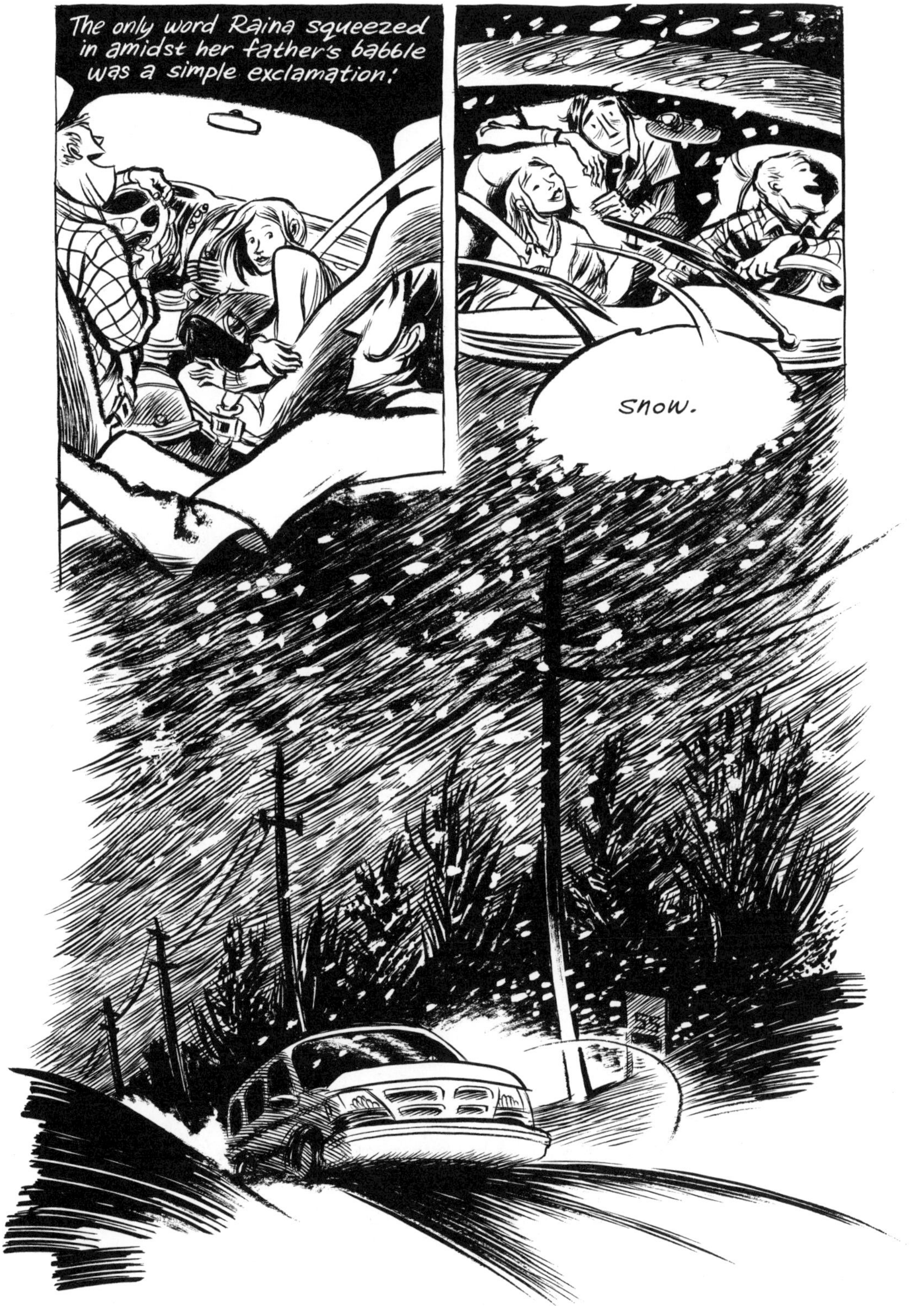
The only word Raina squeezed in amidst her father's babble was a simple exclamation:
Snow.

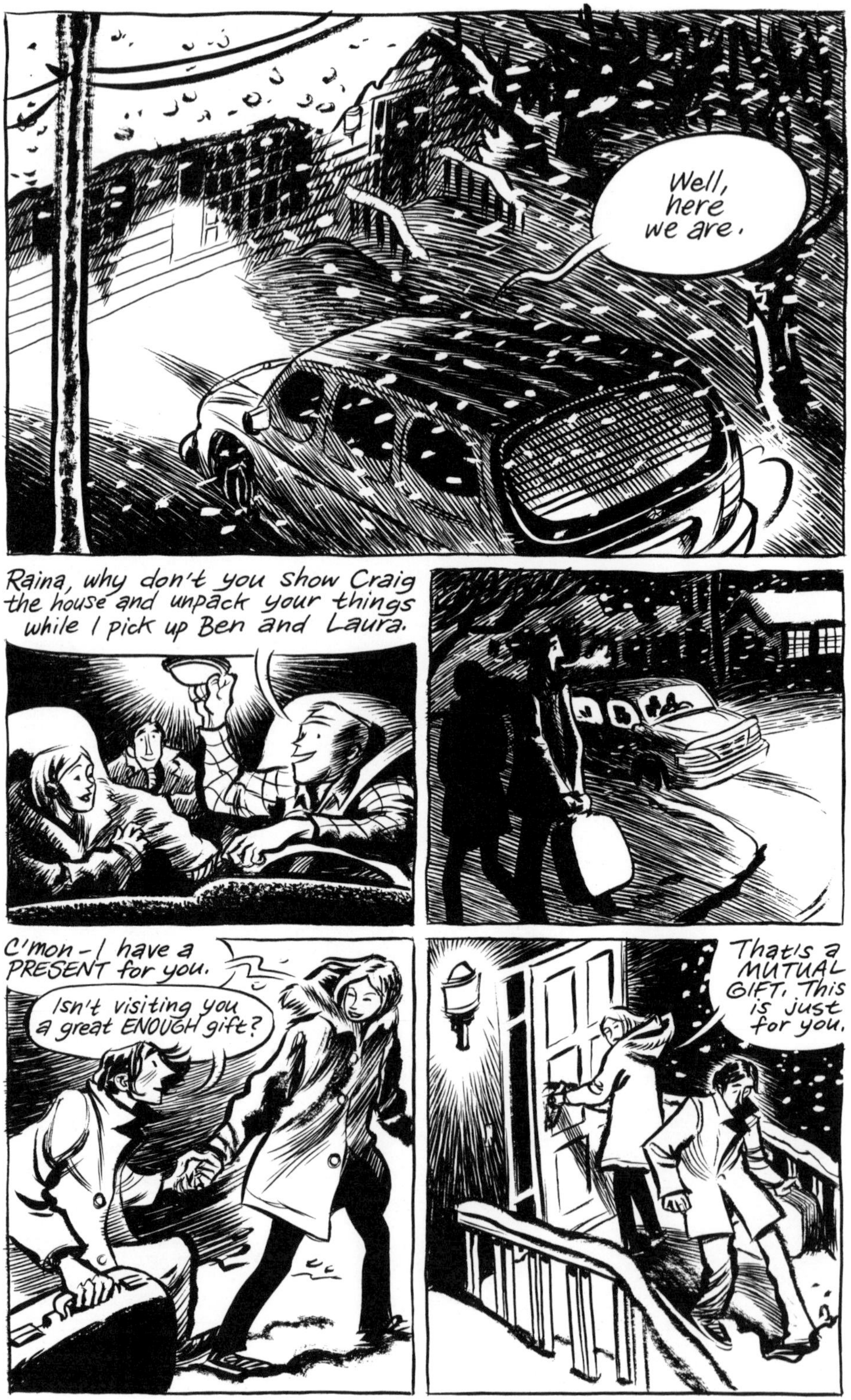
Well, here we are.
Raina, why don't you show Craig the house and unpack your things while I pick up Ben and Laura.
C'mon - I have a PRESENT for you.
Isn't visiting you a great ENOUGH gift?
That's a MUTUAL GIFT. This is just for you.

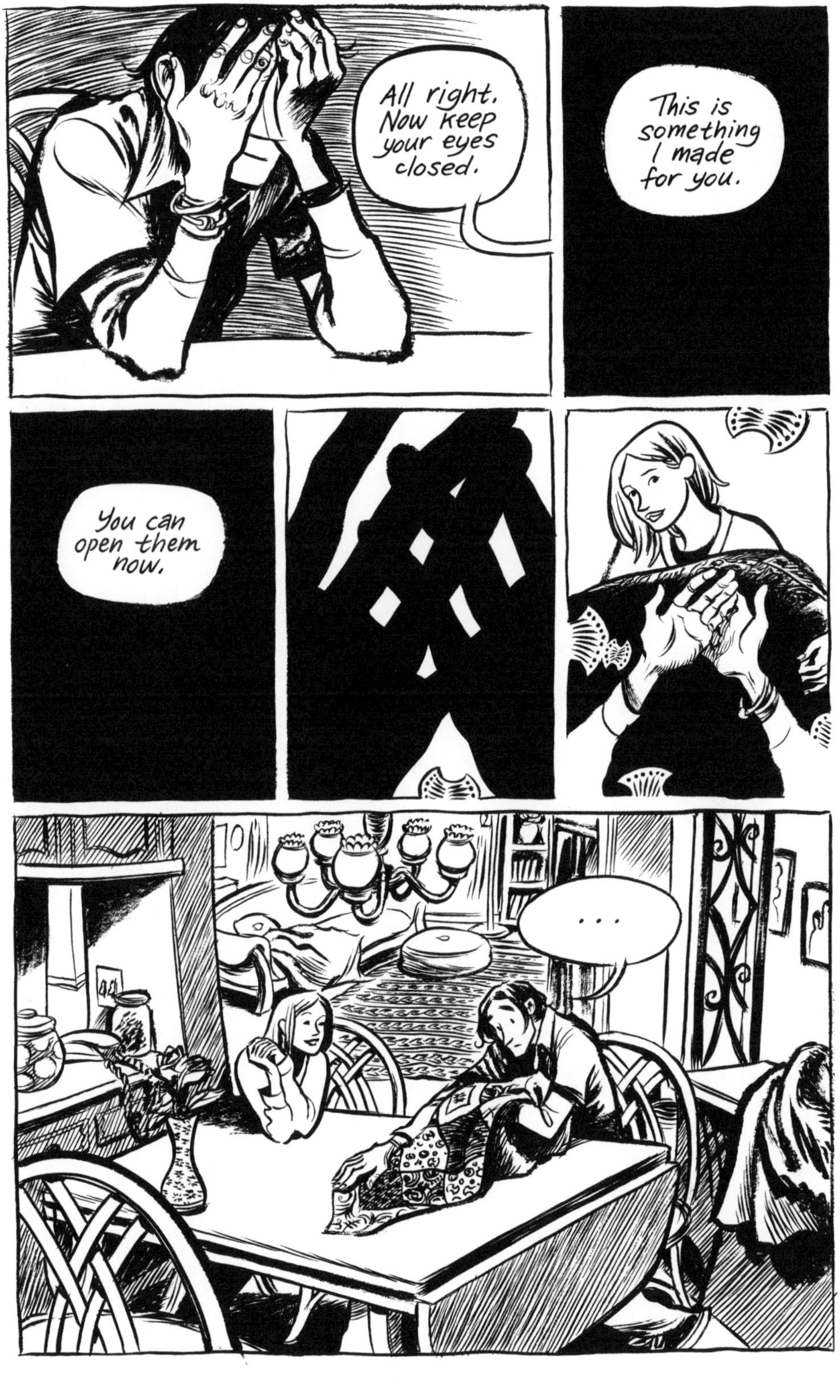
All right. Now keep your eyes closed.
This is something I made for you.
You can open them now.
. . .

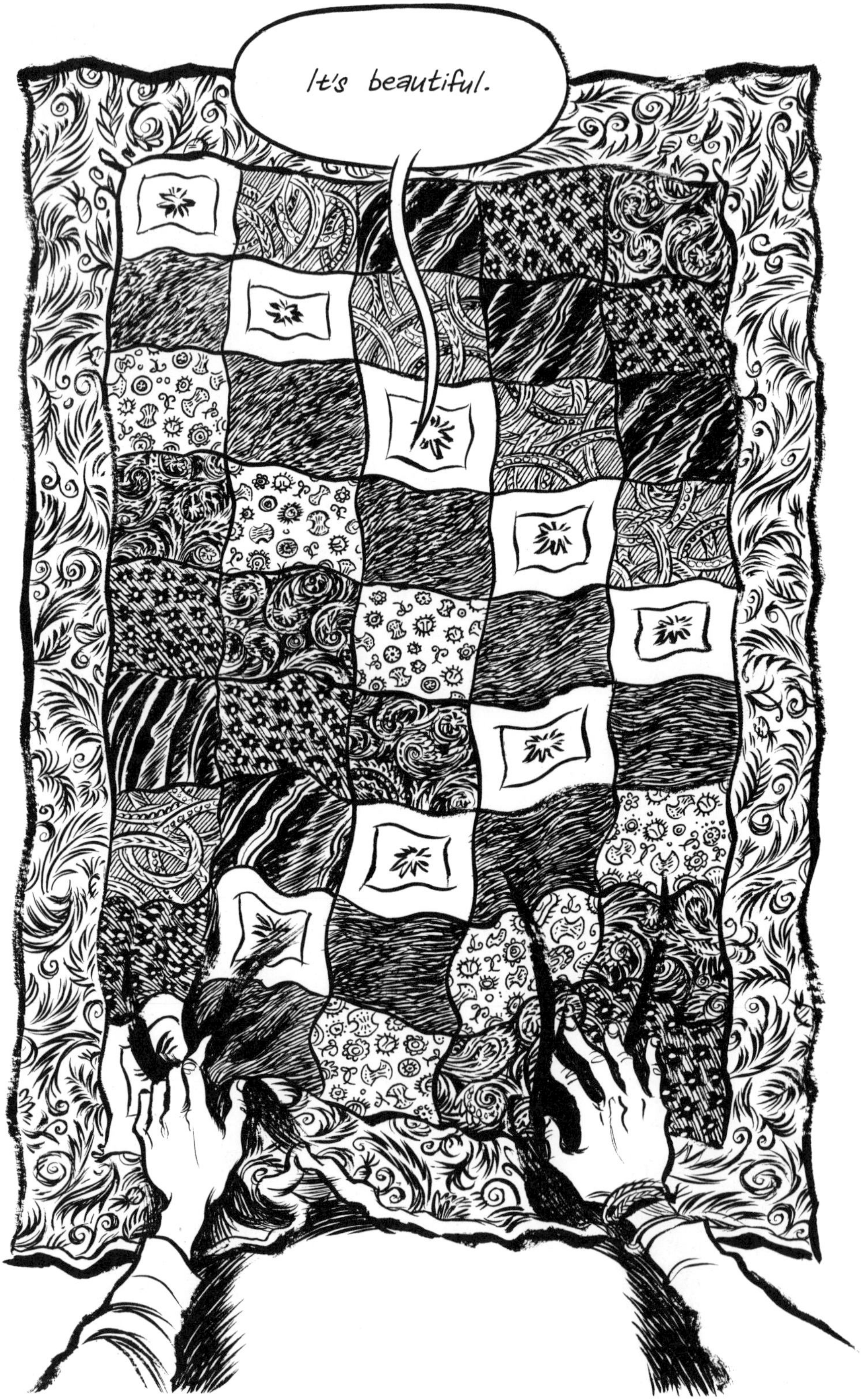
It's beautiful.

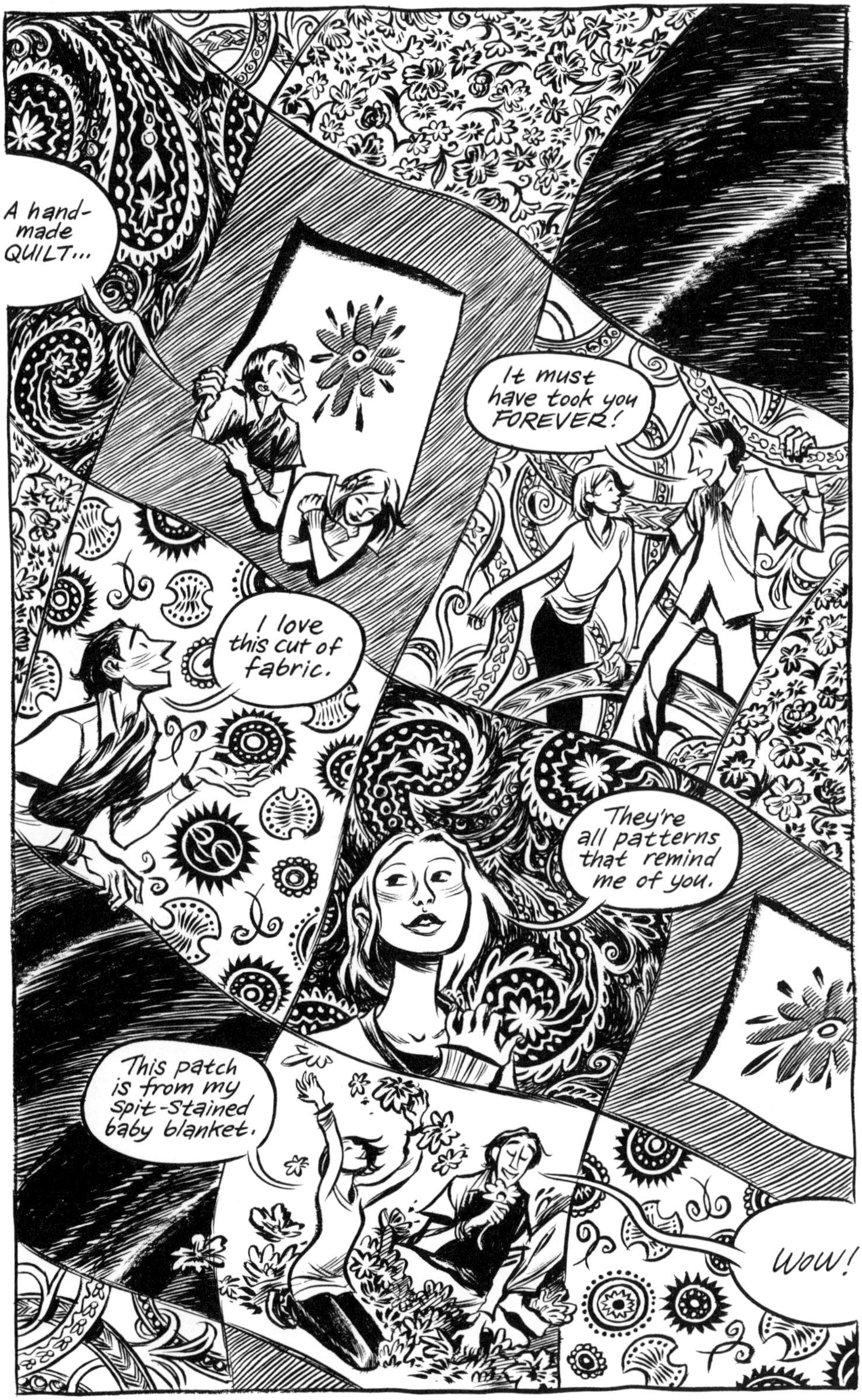
A hand-made QUILT...
It must have took you FOREVER!
I love this cut of fabric.
They're all patterns that remind me of you.
This patch is from my spit-Stained baby blanket.
WOW!

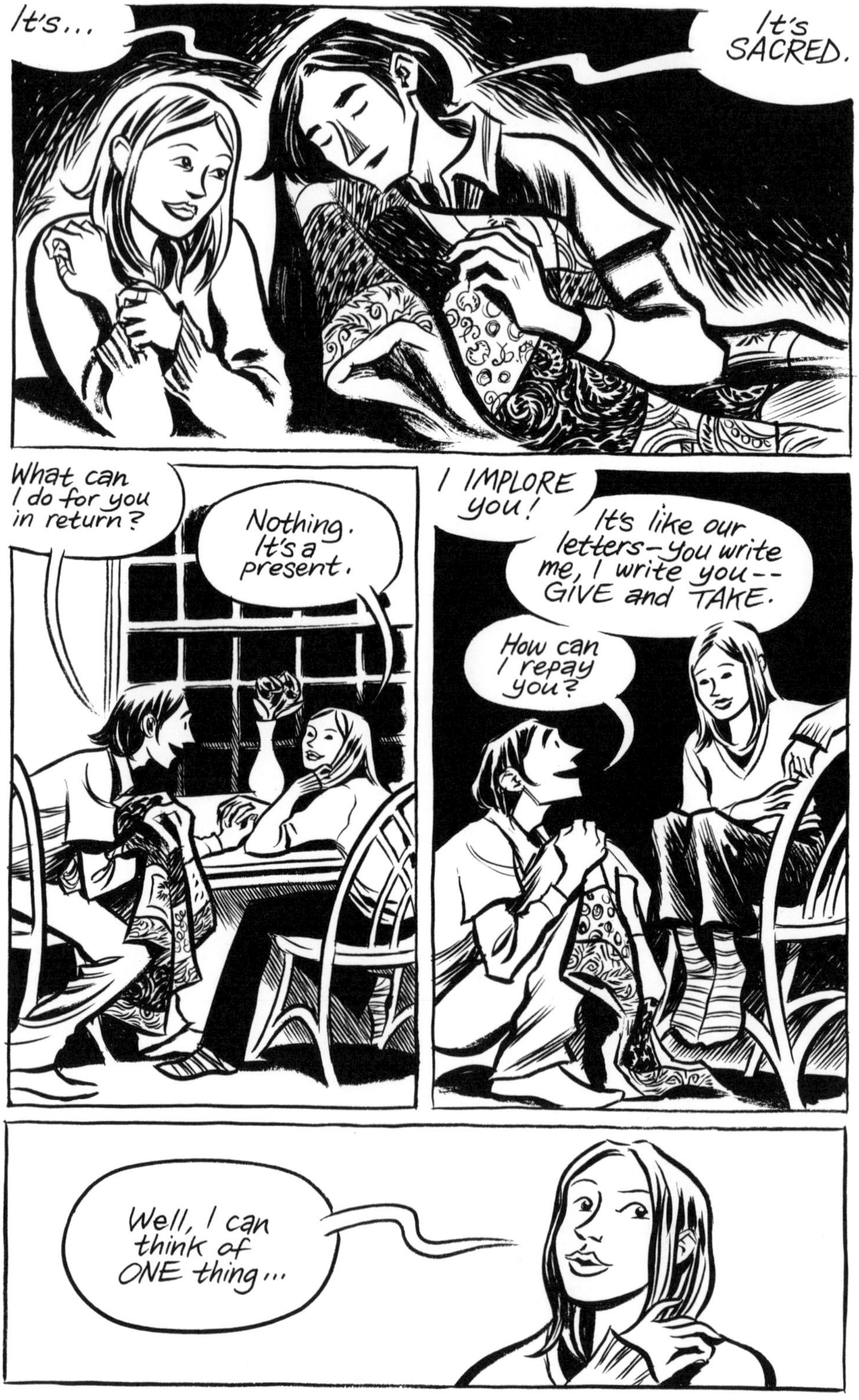
It's...
It's SACRED.
What can I do for you in return?
Nothing. It's a present.
I IMPLORE you!
It's like our letters-- You write me, I write you-- GIVE and TAKE.
How can I repay you?
Well, I can think of ONE thing...

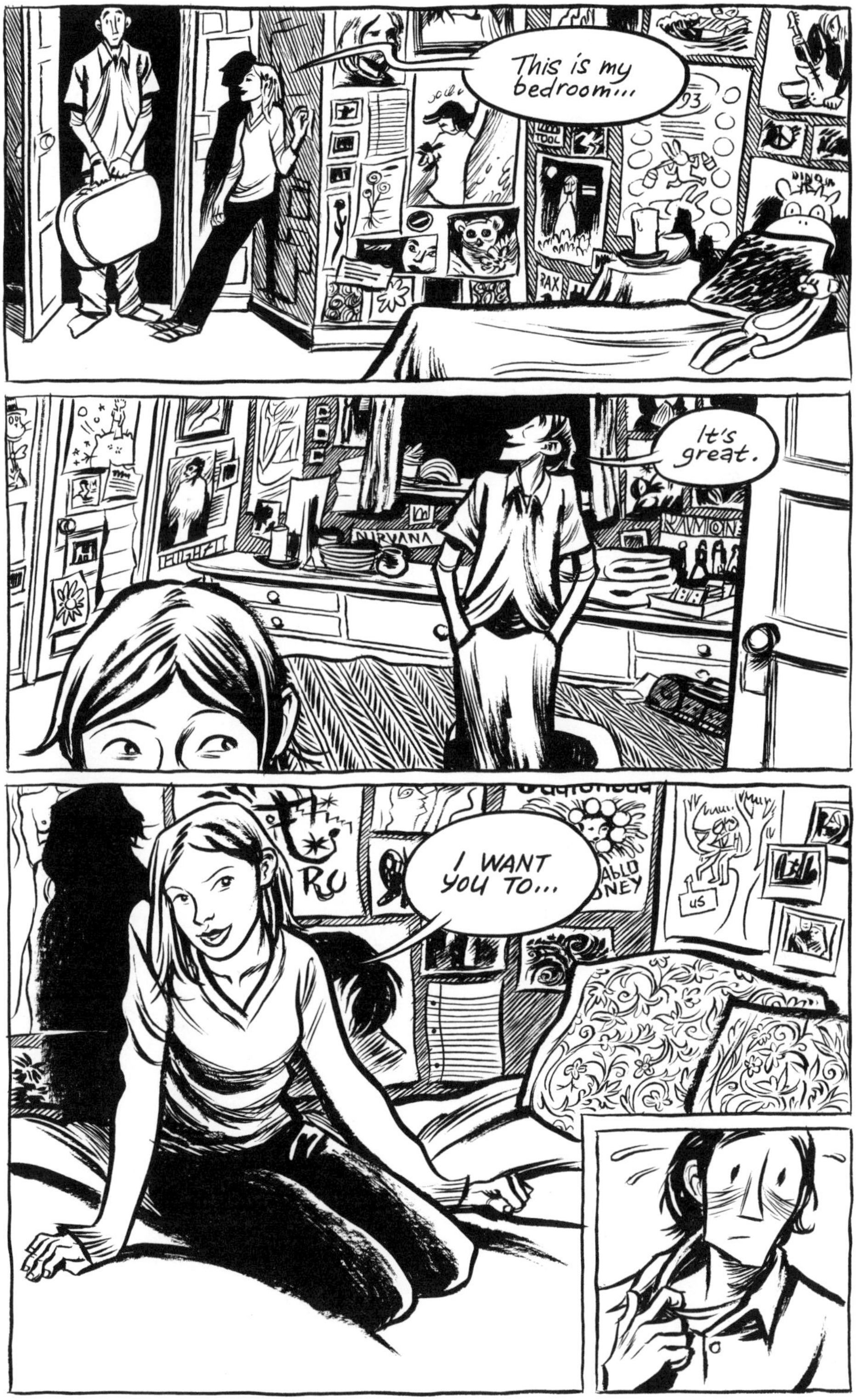
This is my bedroom...
It's great.
I WANT YOU TO...

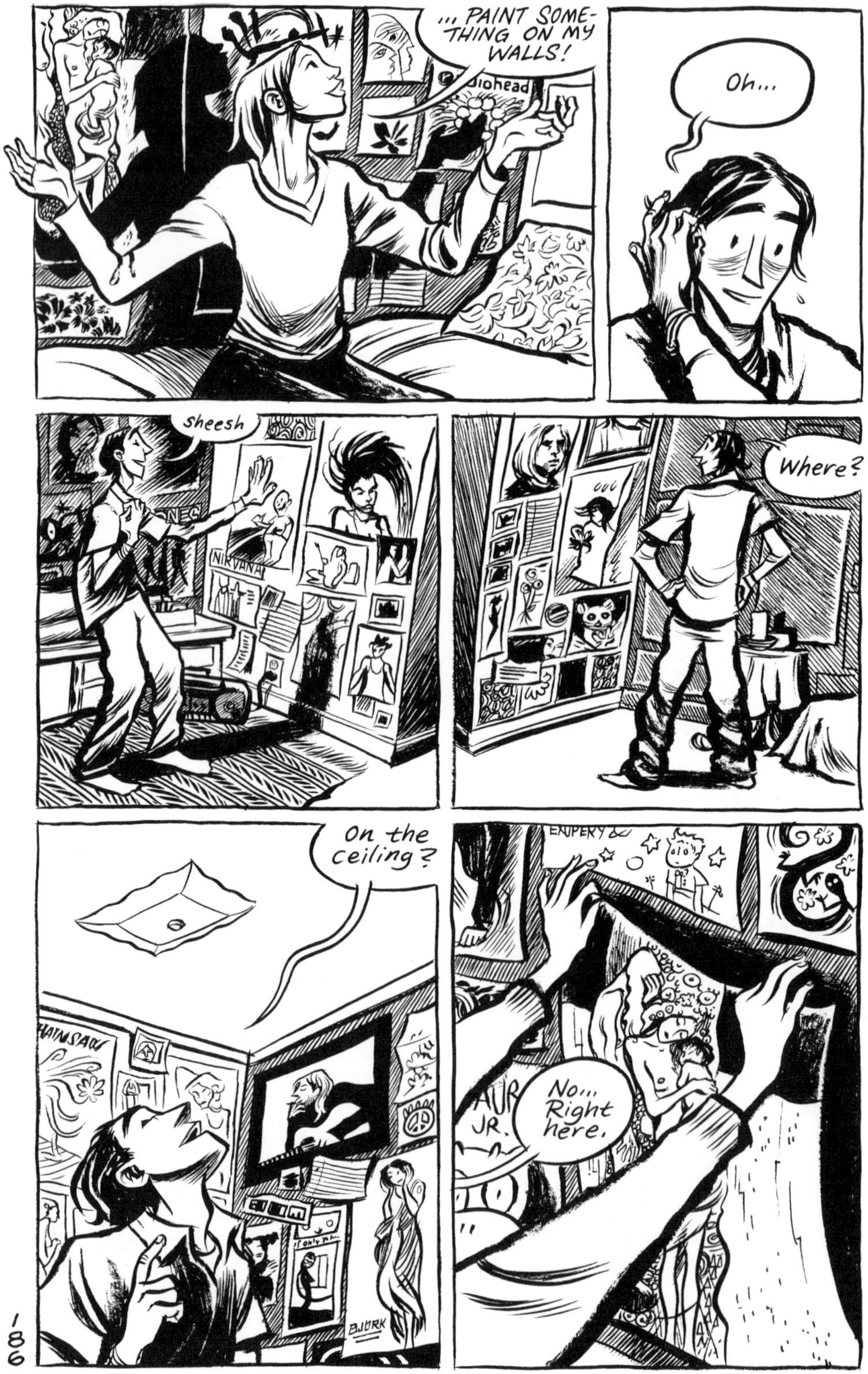
... PAINT SOME-THING ON MY WALLS!
Oh...
sheesh
Where?
On the ceiling?
No... Right here.

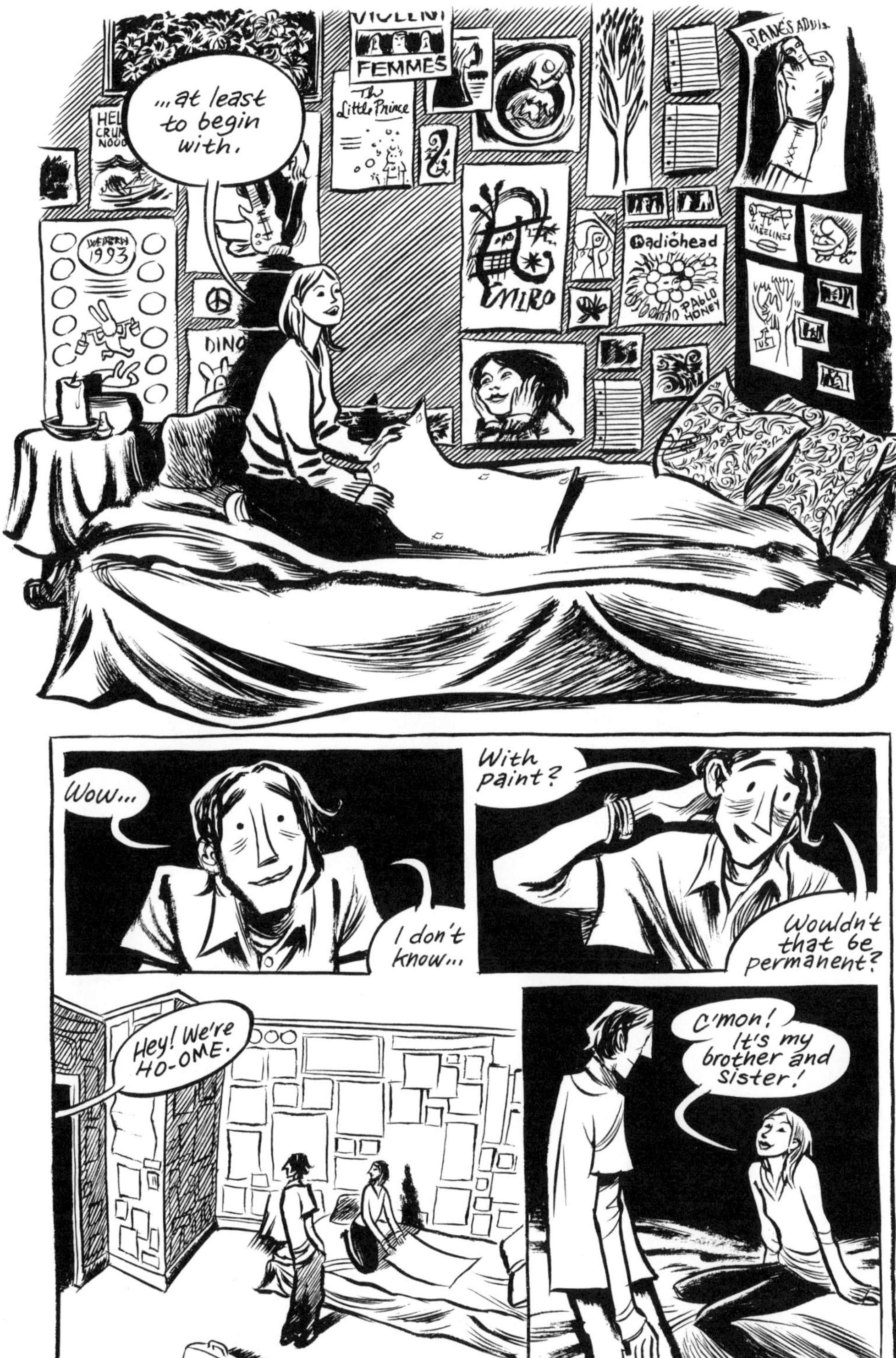

...at least to begin with.
FEMMES
The Little Prince
MIRO
Radiohead
PABLO HONEY
Wow...
I don't know...
With paint?
Wouldn't that be permanent?
Hey! We're HO-OME.
C'mon! It's my brother and sister!

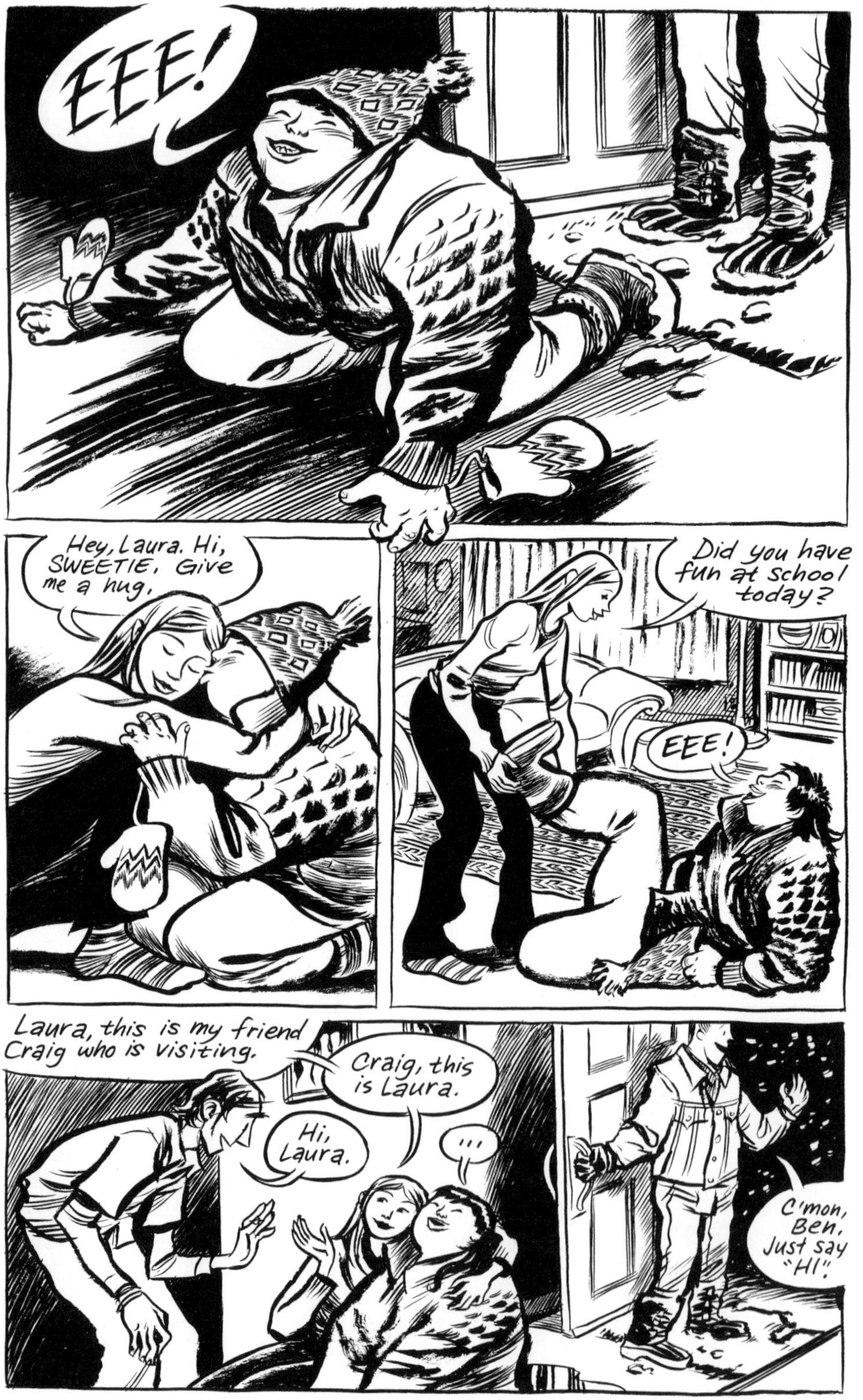
EEE!
Hey, Laura. Hi, SWEETIE. Give me a hug.
Did you have fun at school today?
EEE!
Laura, this is my friend Craig who is visiting.
Craig, this is Laura.
Hi, Laura.
...
C'mon, Ben. Just say "HI."

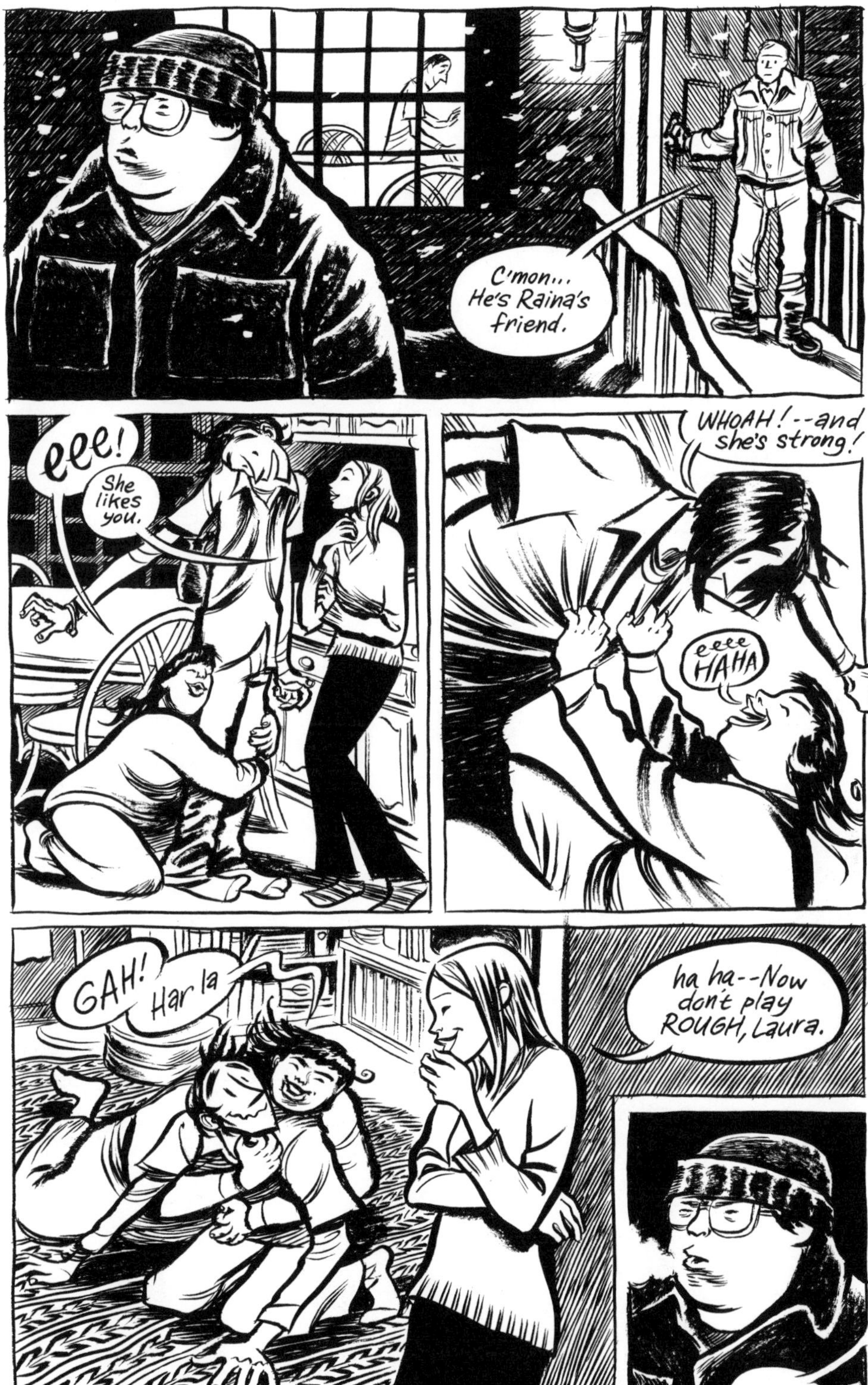
C'mon... He's Raina's friend.
eee!
She likes you.
WHOAH! --and she's strong!
eeee HAHA
GAH!
Har la
ha ha--Now don't play ROUGH, Laura.
Ben...

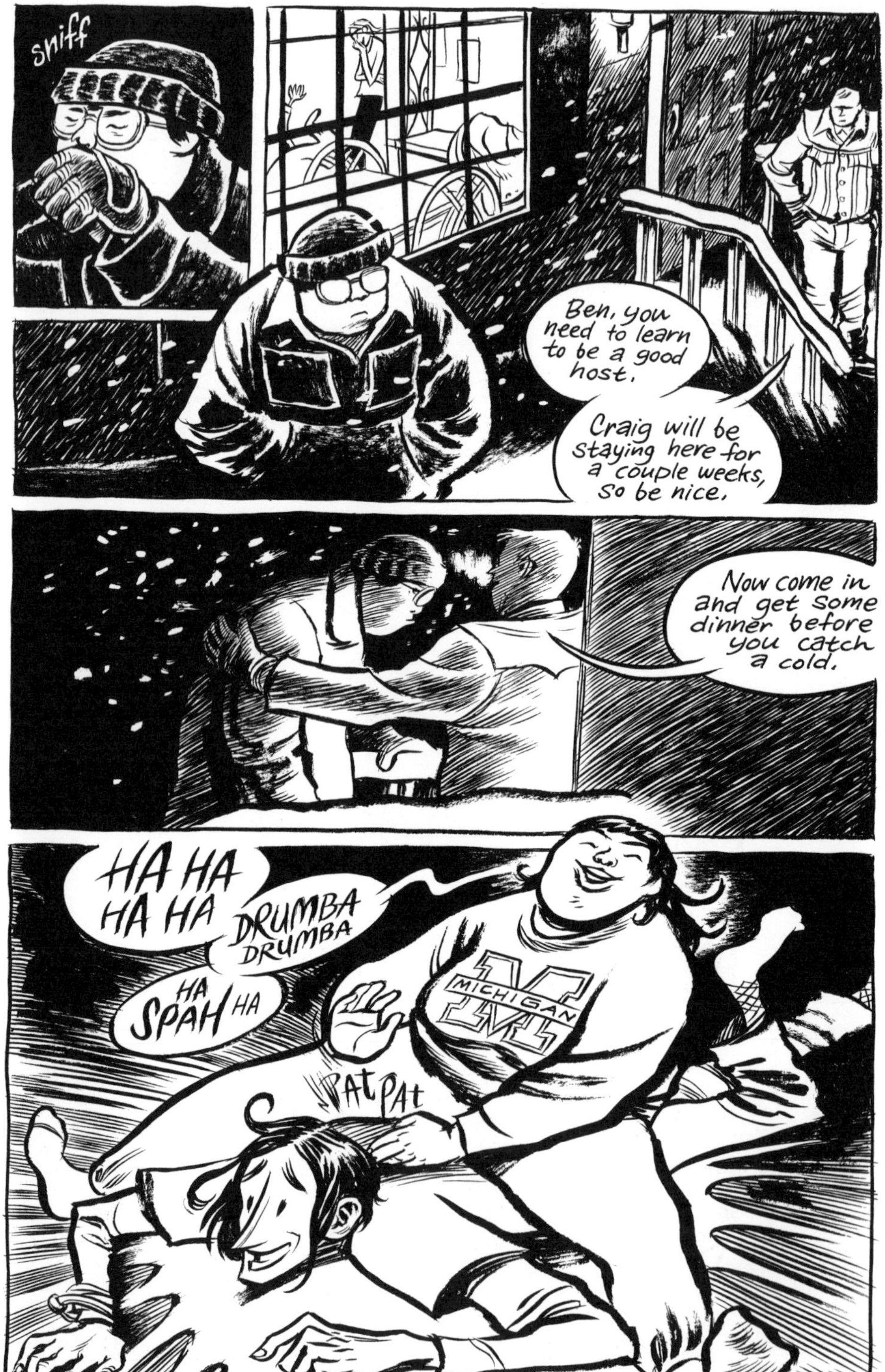
sniff
Ben, you need to learn to be a good host.
Craig will be staying here for a couple weeks, so be nice.
Now come in and get some dinner before you catch a cold.
HA HA HA HA
DRUMBA DRUMBA
HA SPAH HA
MICHIGAN
PAT PAT

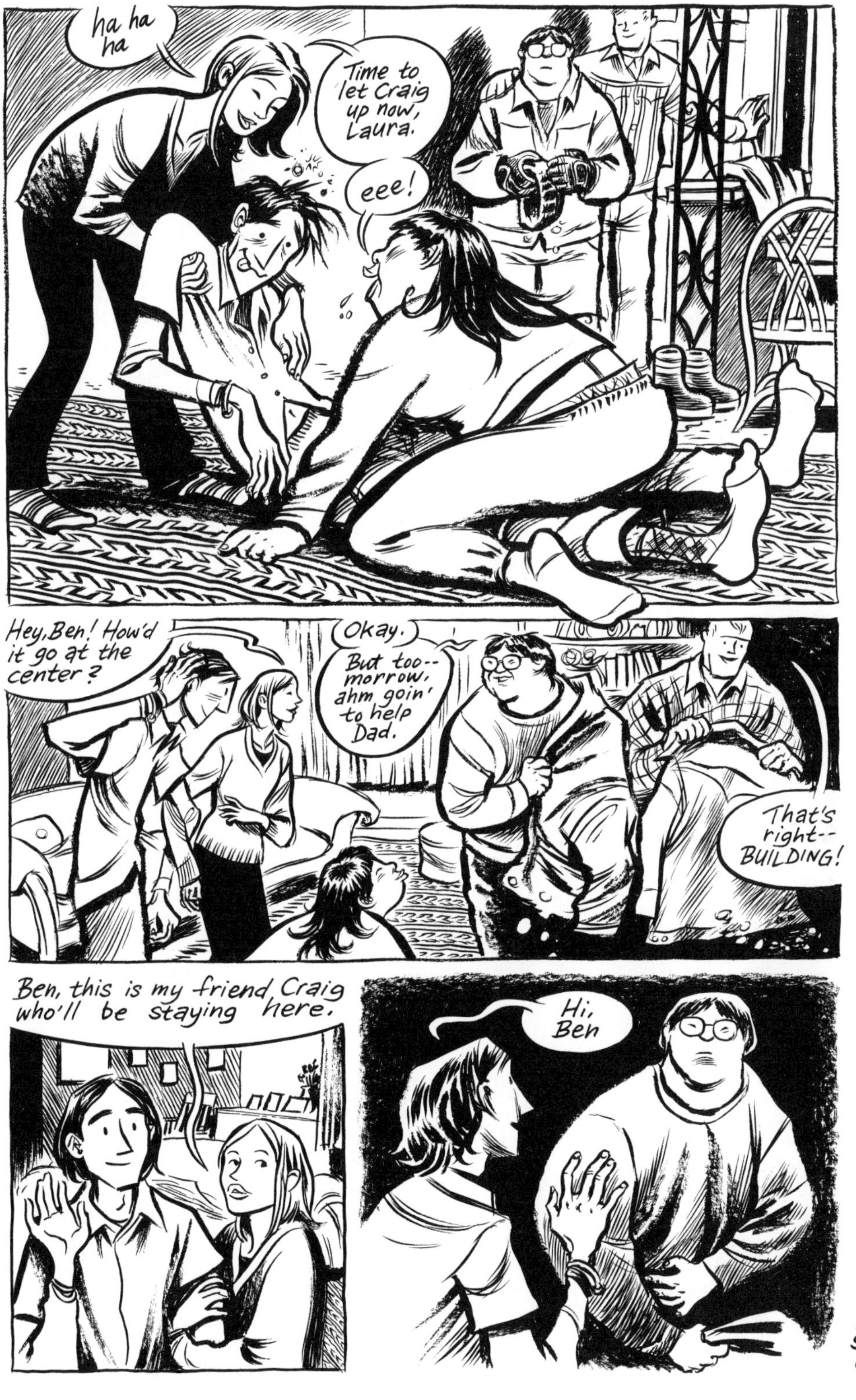
ha ha ha
Time to let Craig up now, Laura.
eee!
Hey, Ben! How'd it go at the center?
Okay.
But too-- morrow, ahm goin' to help Dad.
That's right-- BUILDING!
Ben, this is my friend Craig who'll be staying here.
Hi, Ben

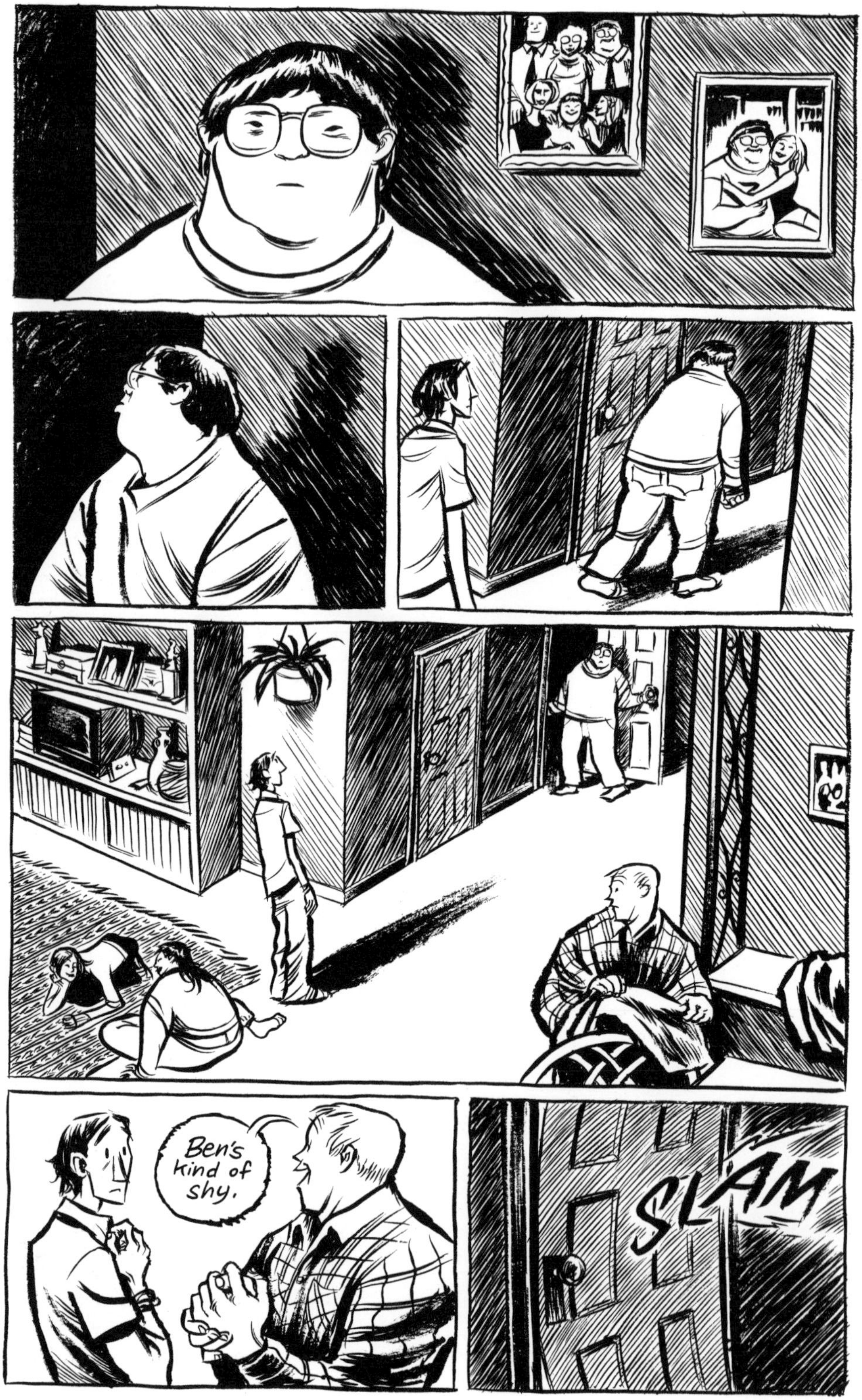
Ben's kind of shy.
SLAM

193

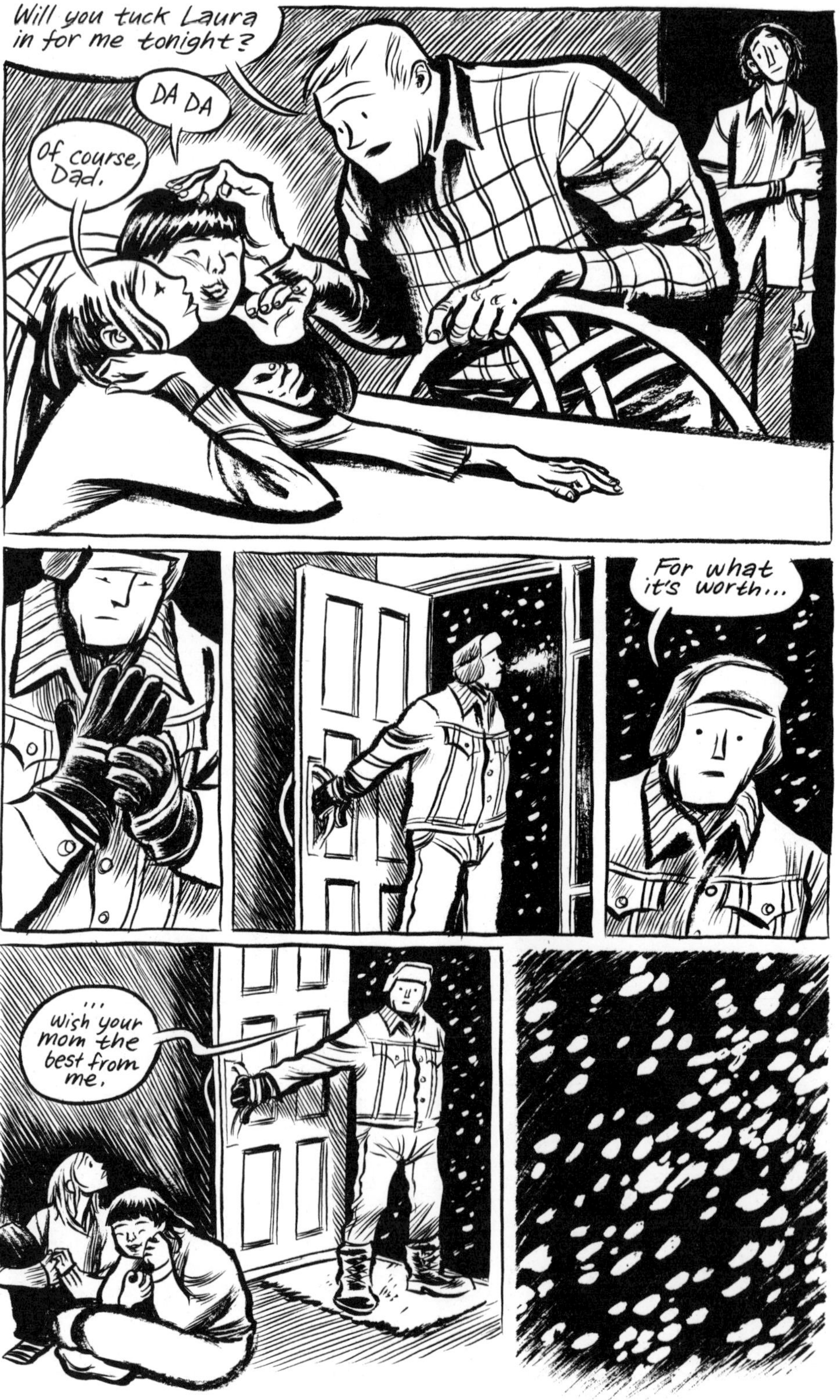
Will you tuck Laura in for me tonight?
DA DA
Of course, Dad.
For what it's worth...
... wish your mom the best from me.

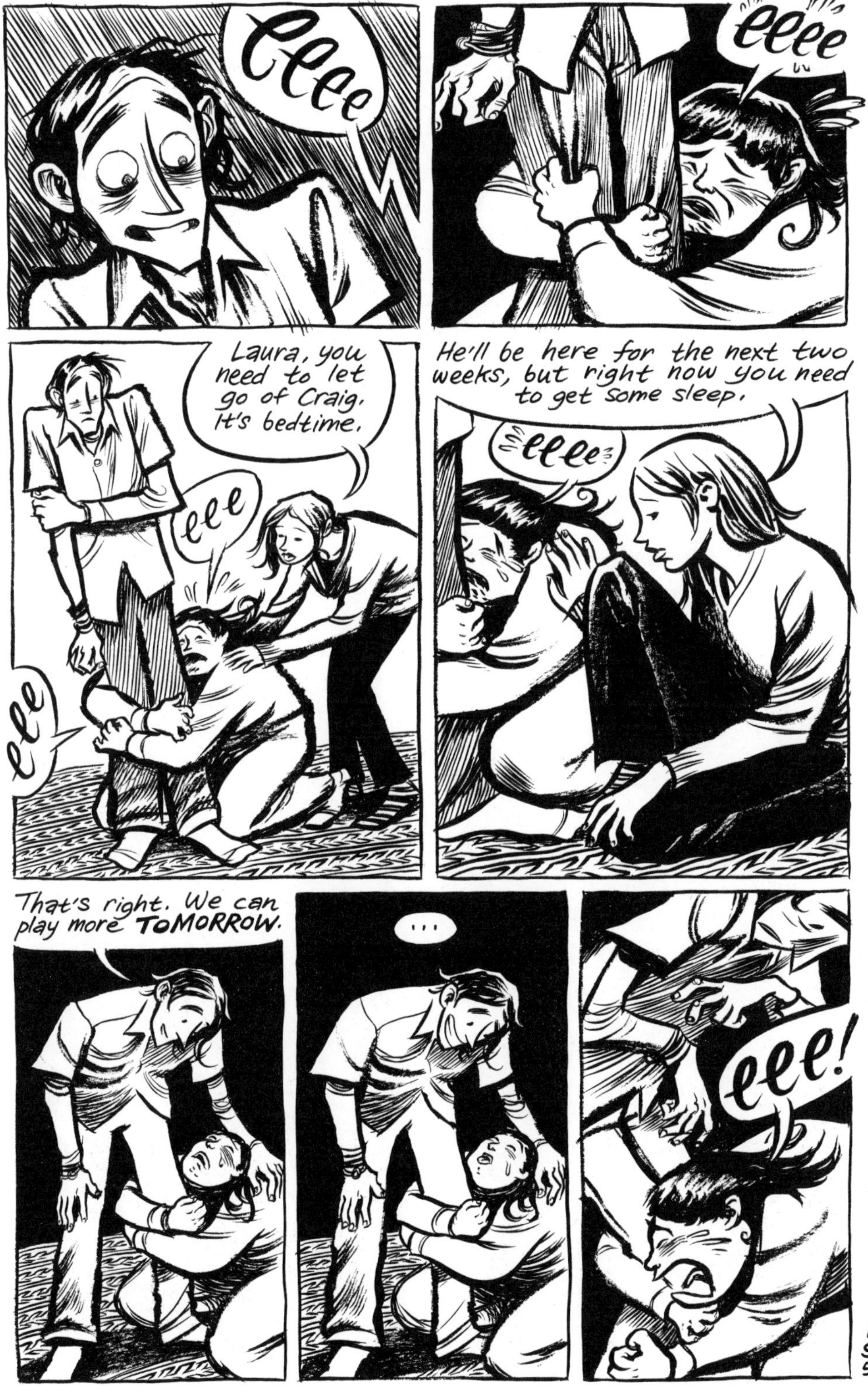
eeee
eeee
Laura, you need to let go of Craig. It's bedtime.
eee
eee
He'll be here for the next two weeks, but right now you need to get some sleep.
eeee
That's right. We can play more TOMORROW.
...
eee!

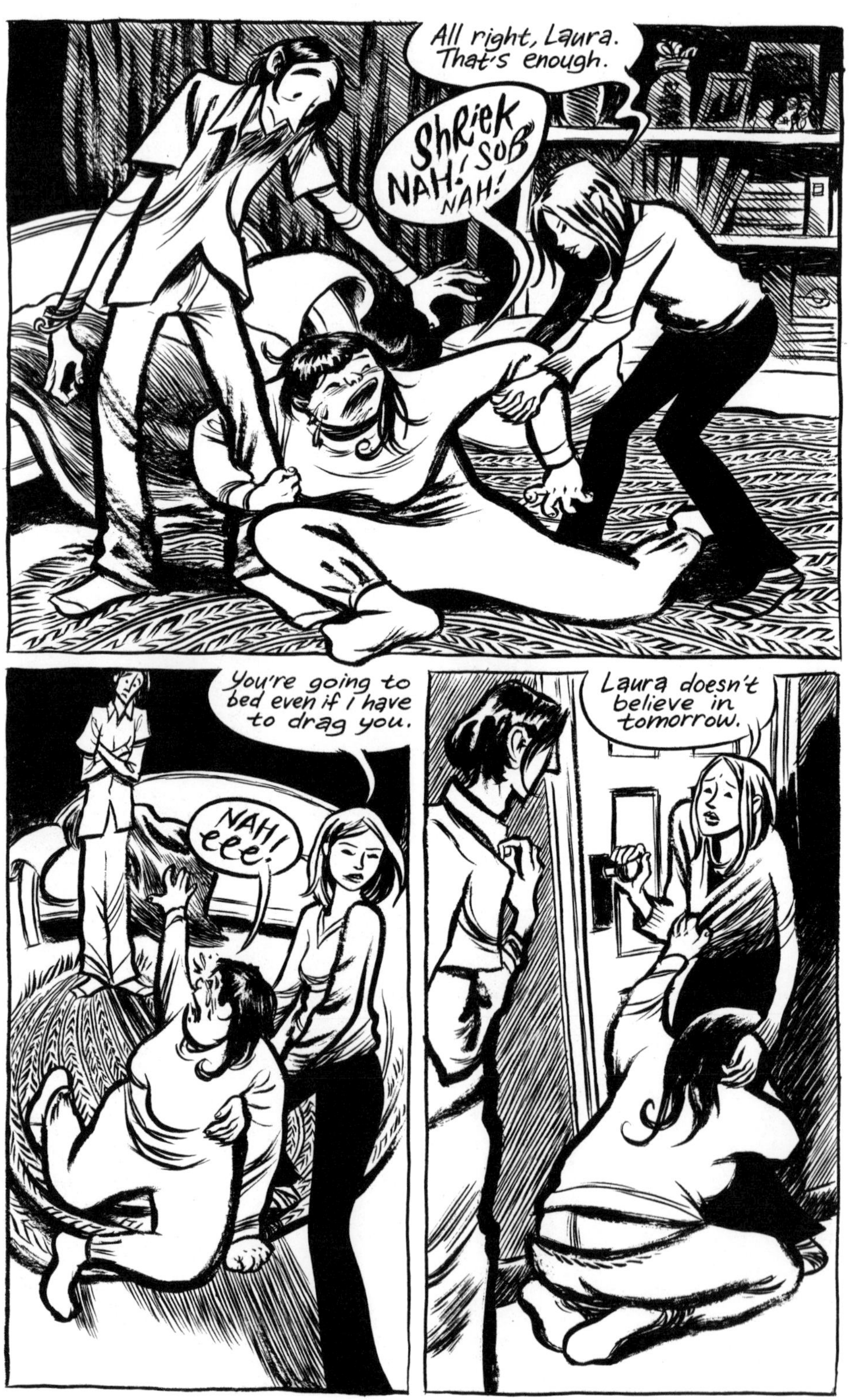
All right, Laura. That's enough.
Shriek! Sob NAH! NAH!
You're going to bed even if I have to drag you.
NAH! eee!
Laura doesn't believe in tomorrow.

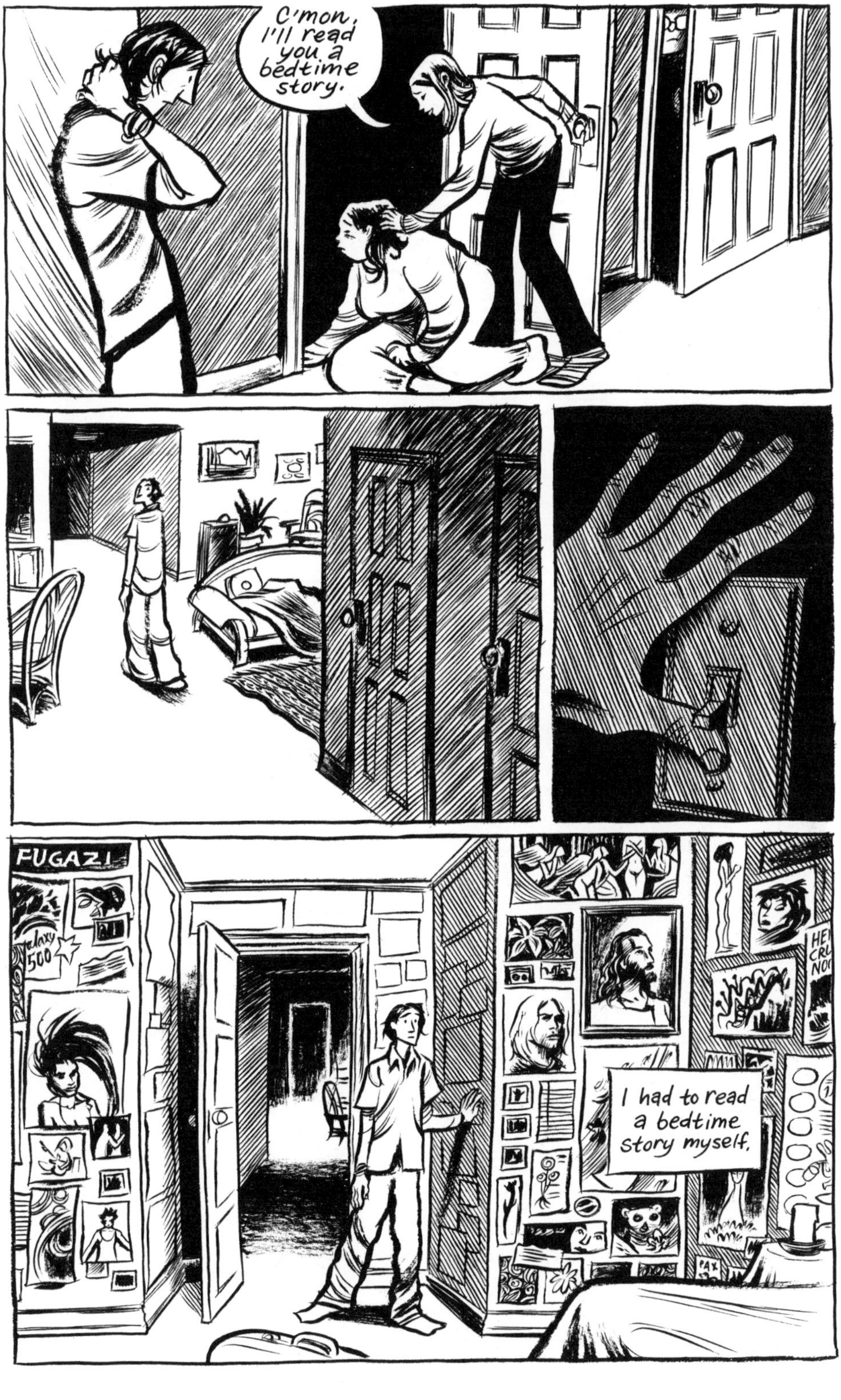
C'mon, I'll read you a bedtime story.
FUGAZI
galaxy 500
I had to read a bedtime story myself.

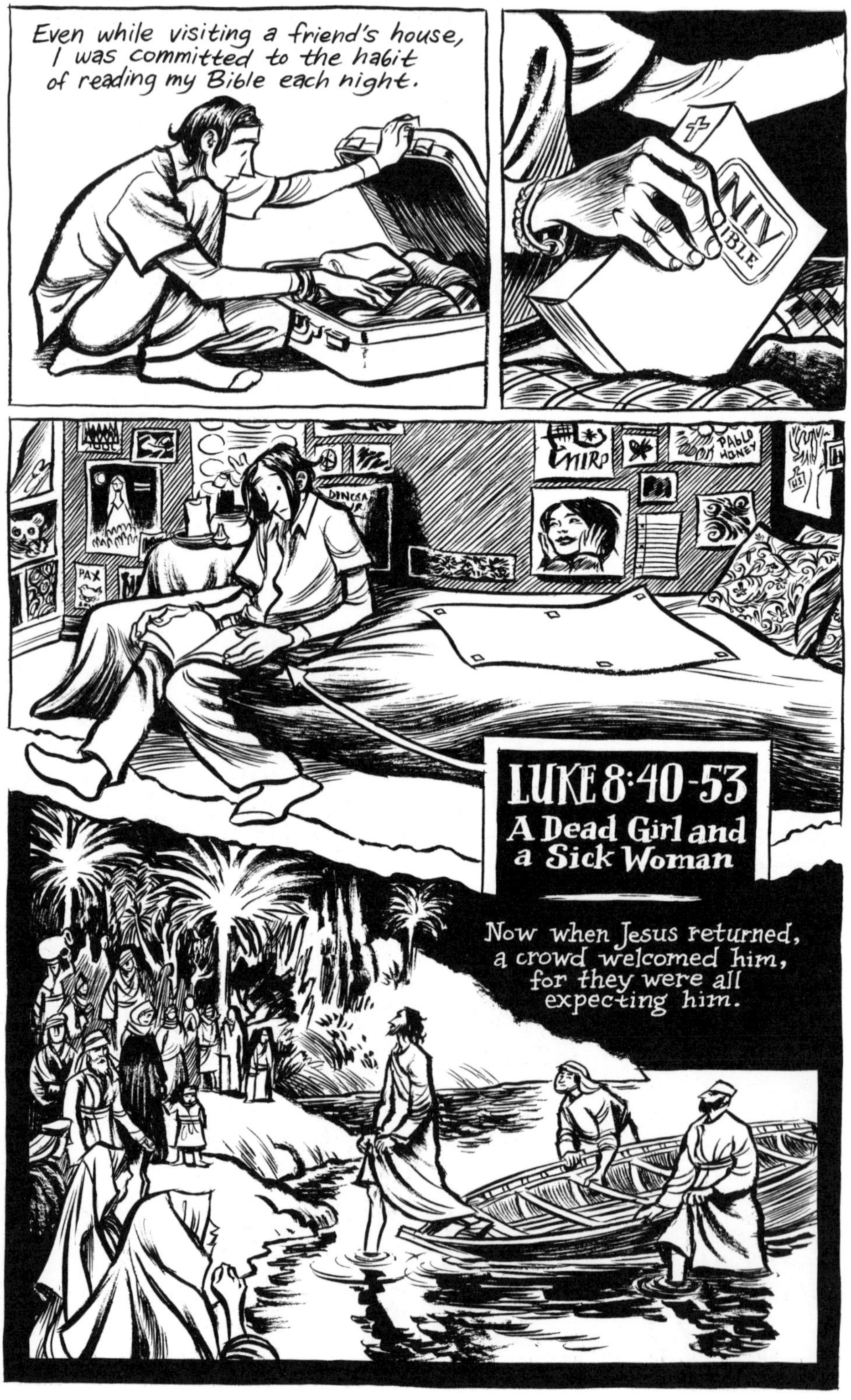
Even while visiting a friend's house, I was committed to the habit of reading my Bible each night.
NIV
PABLO HONEY
PAX
LUKE 8:40-53
A Dead Girl and a Sick Woman
Now when Jesus returned, a crowd welcomed him, for they were all expecting him.

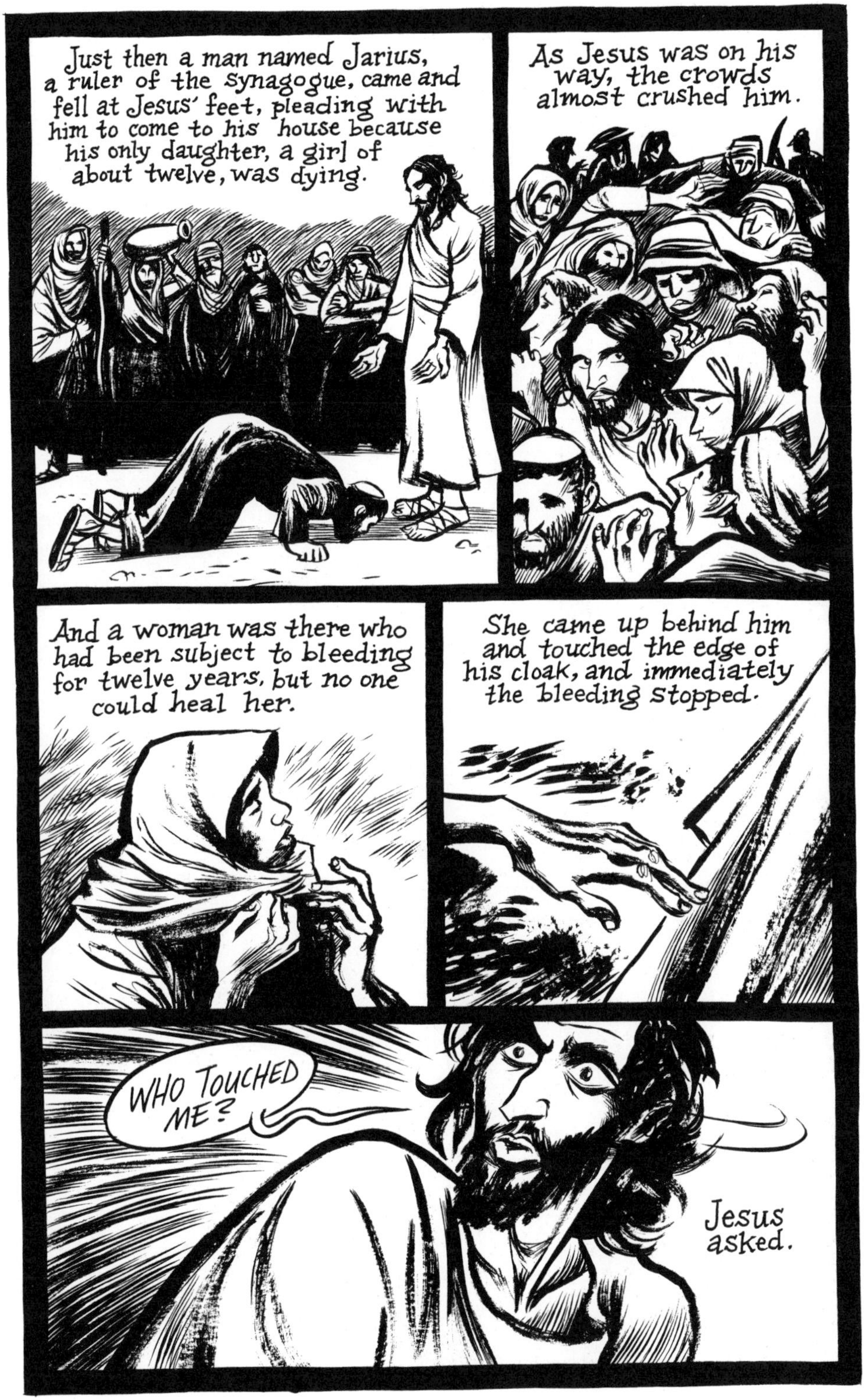
Just then a man named Jarius, a ruler of the synagogue, came and fell at Jesus' feet, pleading with him to come to his house because his only daughter, a girl of about twelve, was dying.
As Jesus was on his way, the crowds almost crushed him.
And a woman was there who had been subject to bleeding for twelve years, but no one could heal her.
She came up behind him and touched the edge of his cloak, and immediately the bleeding stopped.
WHO TOUCHED ME?
Jesus asked.

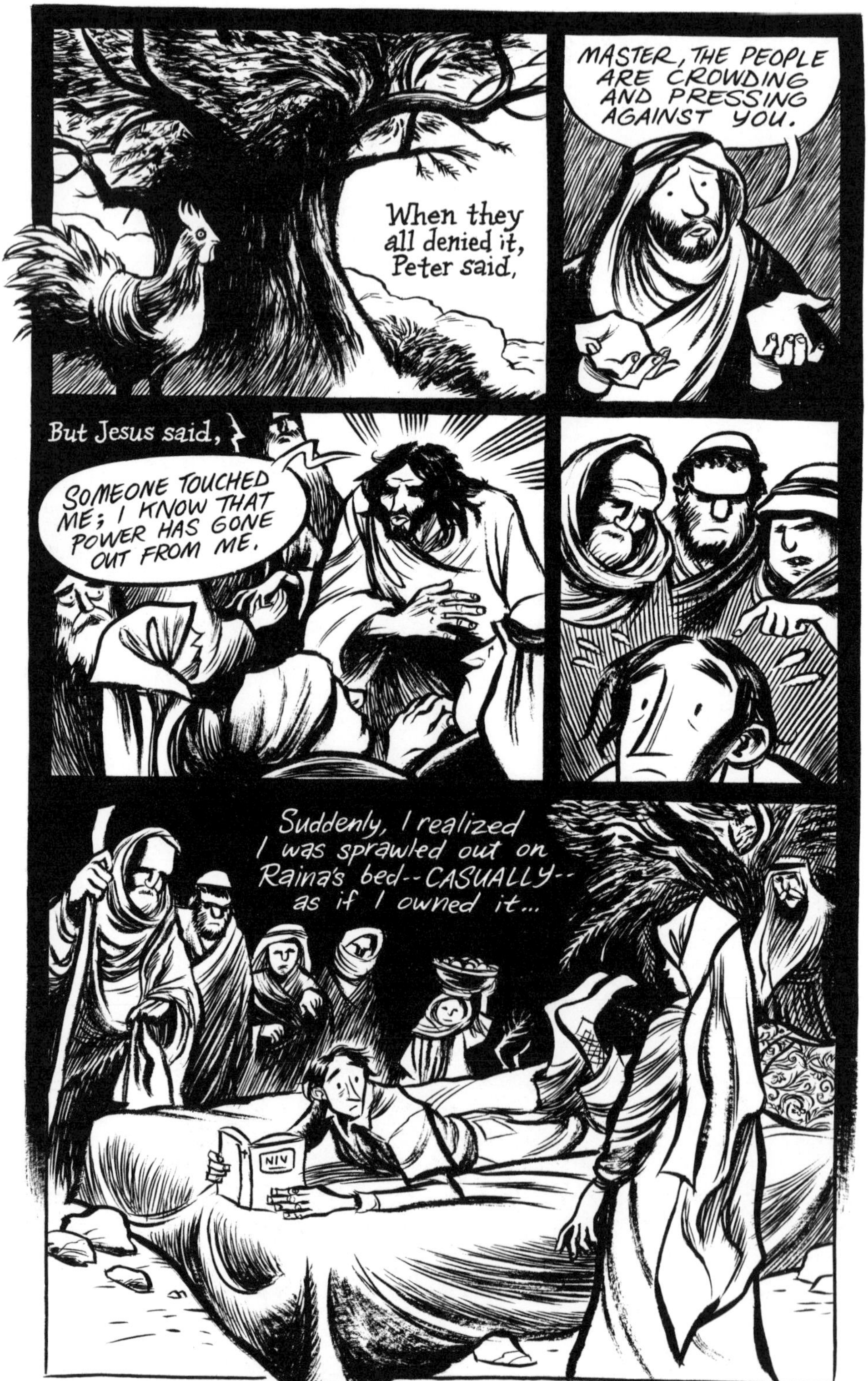
When they all denied it, Peter said,
MASTER, THE PEOPLE ARE CROWDING AND PRESSING AGAINST YOU.
But Jesus said,
SOMEONE TOUCHED ME; I KNOW THAT POWER HAS GONE OUT FROM ME.
Suddenly, I realized I was sprawled out on Raina's bed--CASUALLY--as if I owned it...
NIV

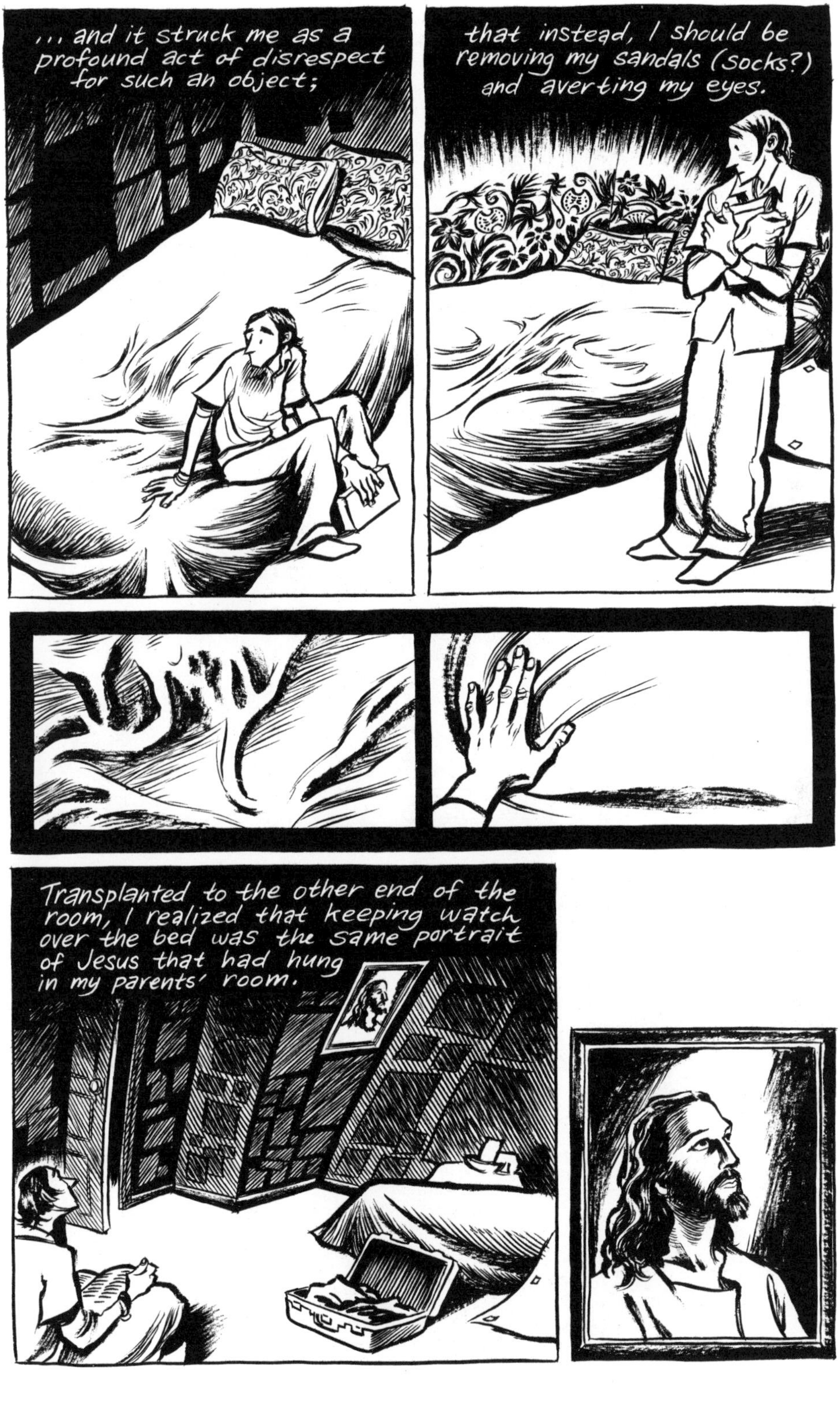

... and it struck me as a profound act of disrespect for such an object;
that instead, I should be removing my sandals (socks?) and averting my eyes.
Transplanted to the other end of the room, I realized that keeping watch over the bed was the same portrait of Jesus that had hung in my parents' room.

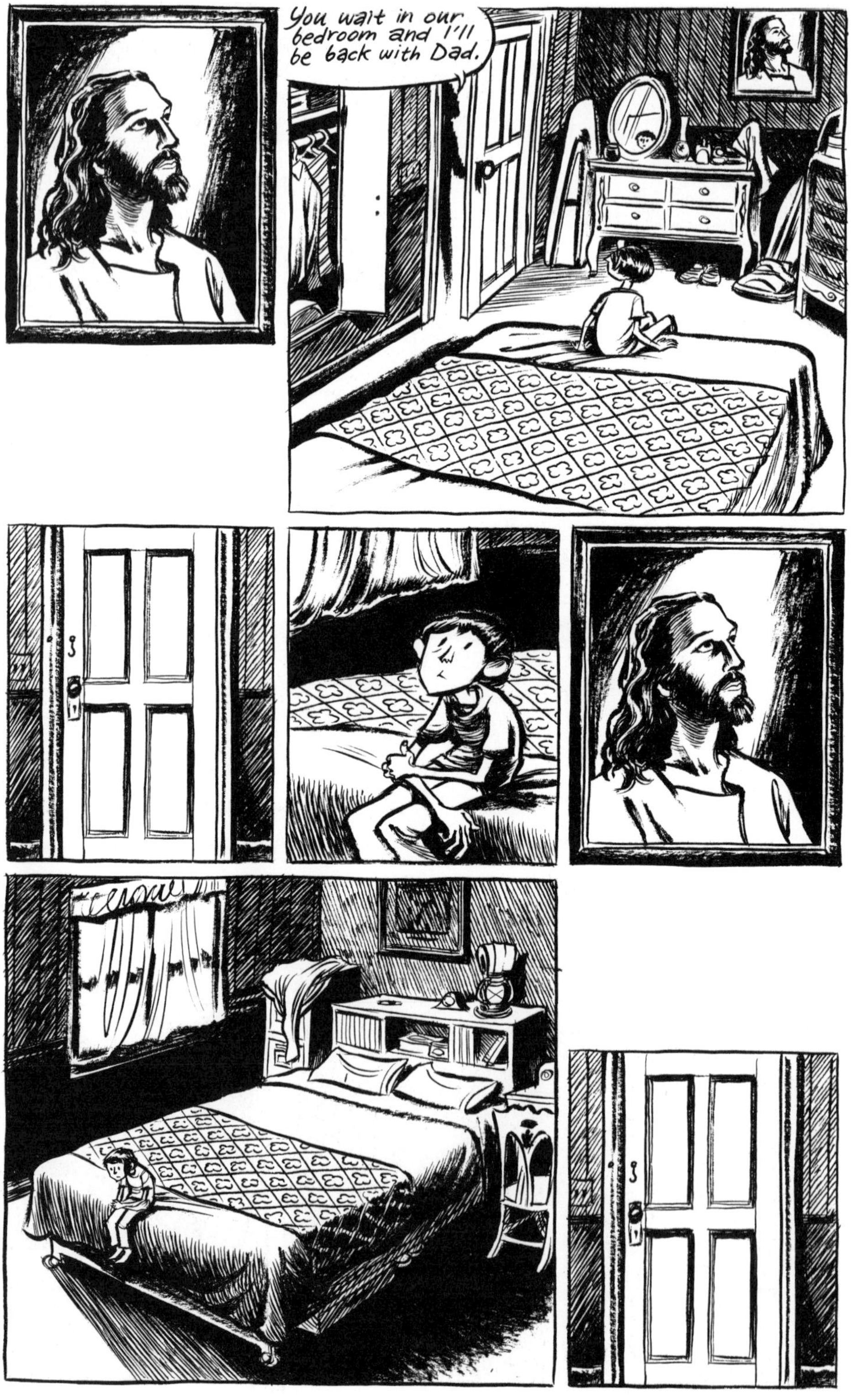
You wait in our bedroom and I'll be back with Dad.

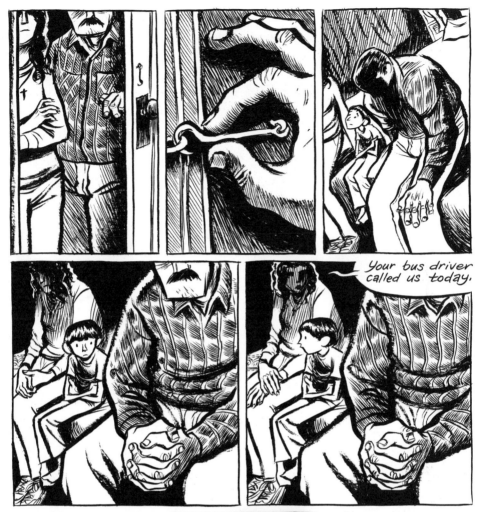

Your bus driver called us today.

She said you were drawing on the bus and you threw something in the waste basket.

Do you remember what it was?

203

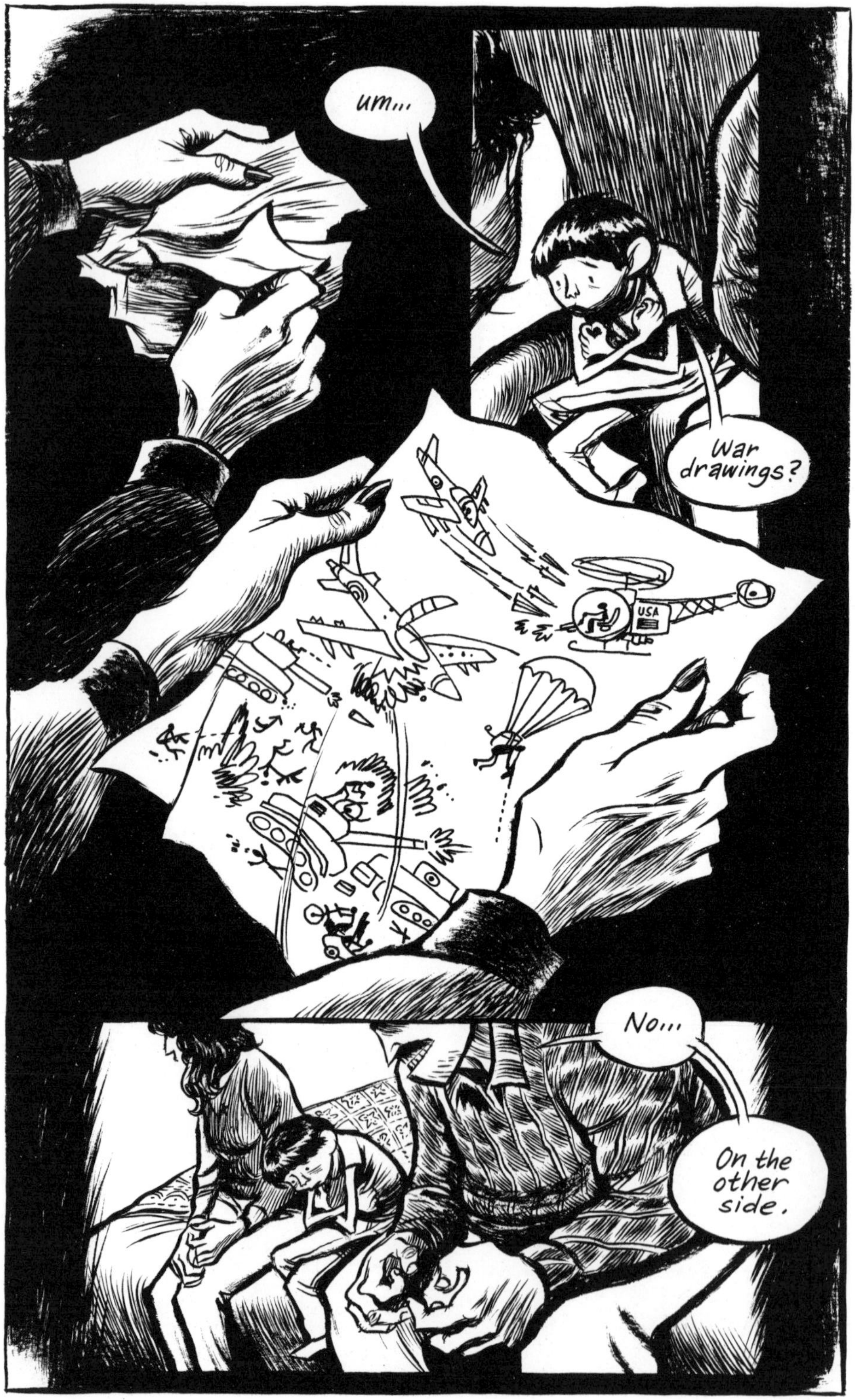
um...
War drawings?
USA
No...
On the other side.

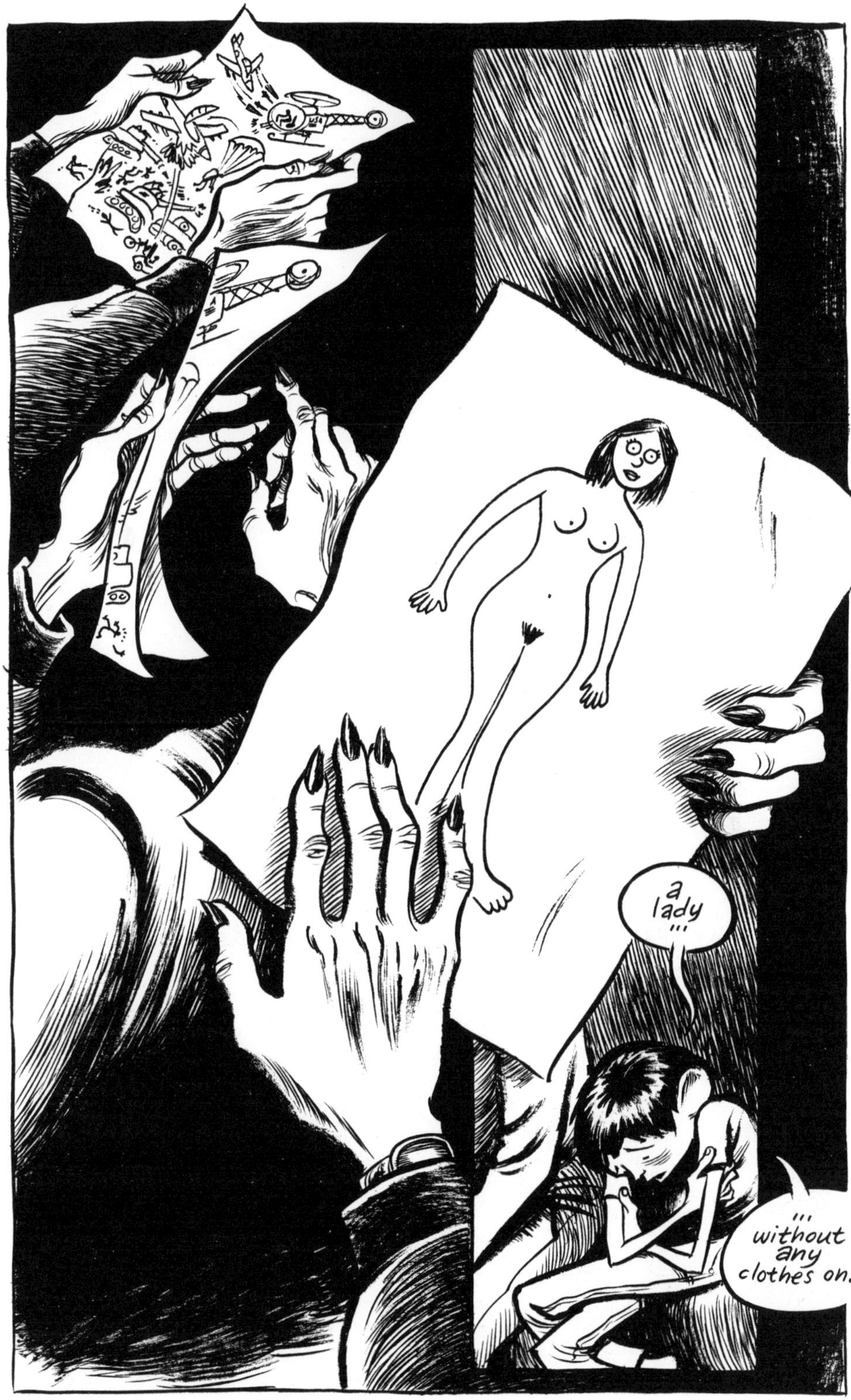
a lady ...
... without any clothes on.

206

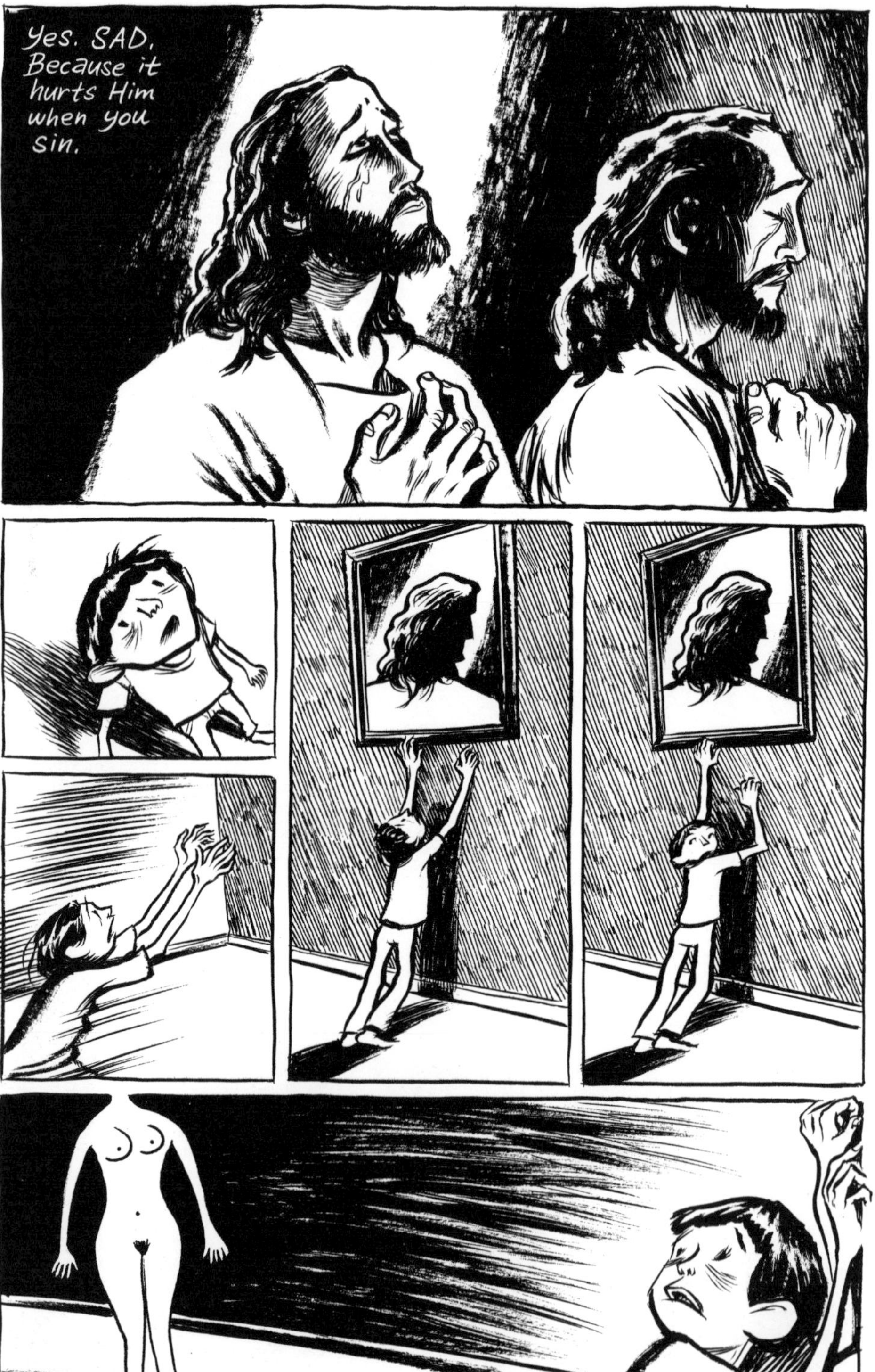
Yes. SAD. Because it hurts Him when you sin.

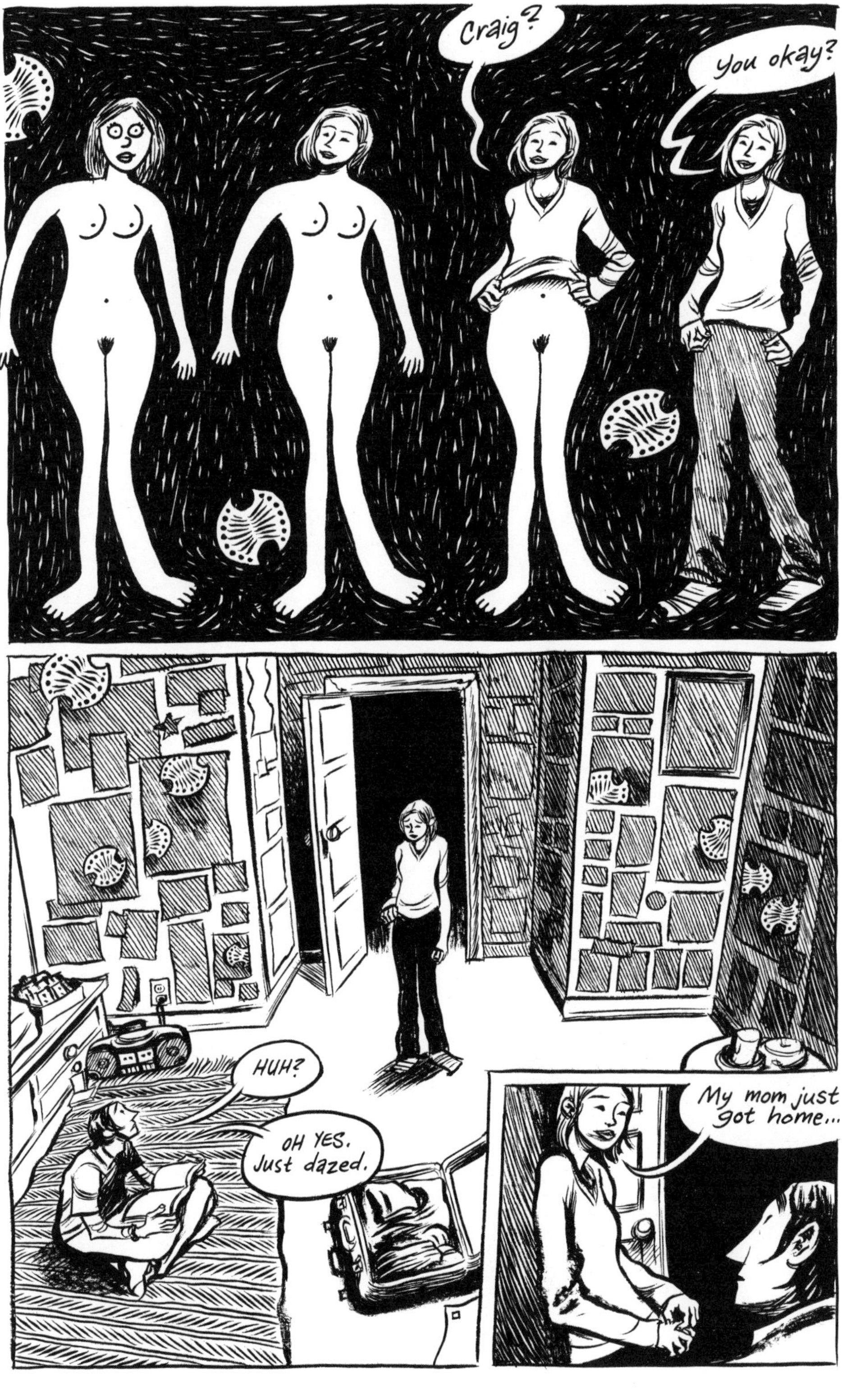
Craig?
You okay?
HUH?
OH YES. Just dazed.
My mom just got home...

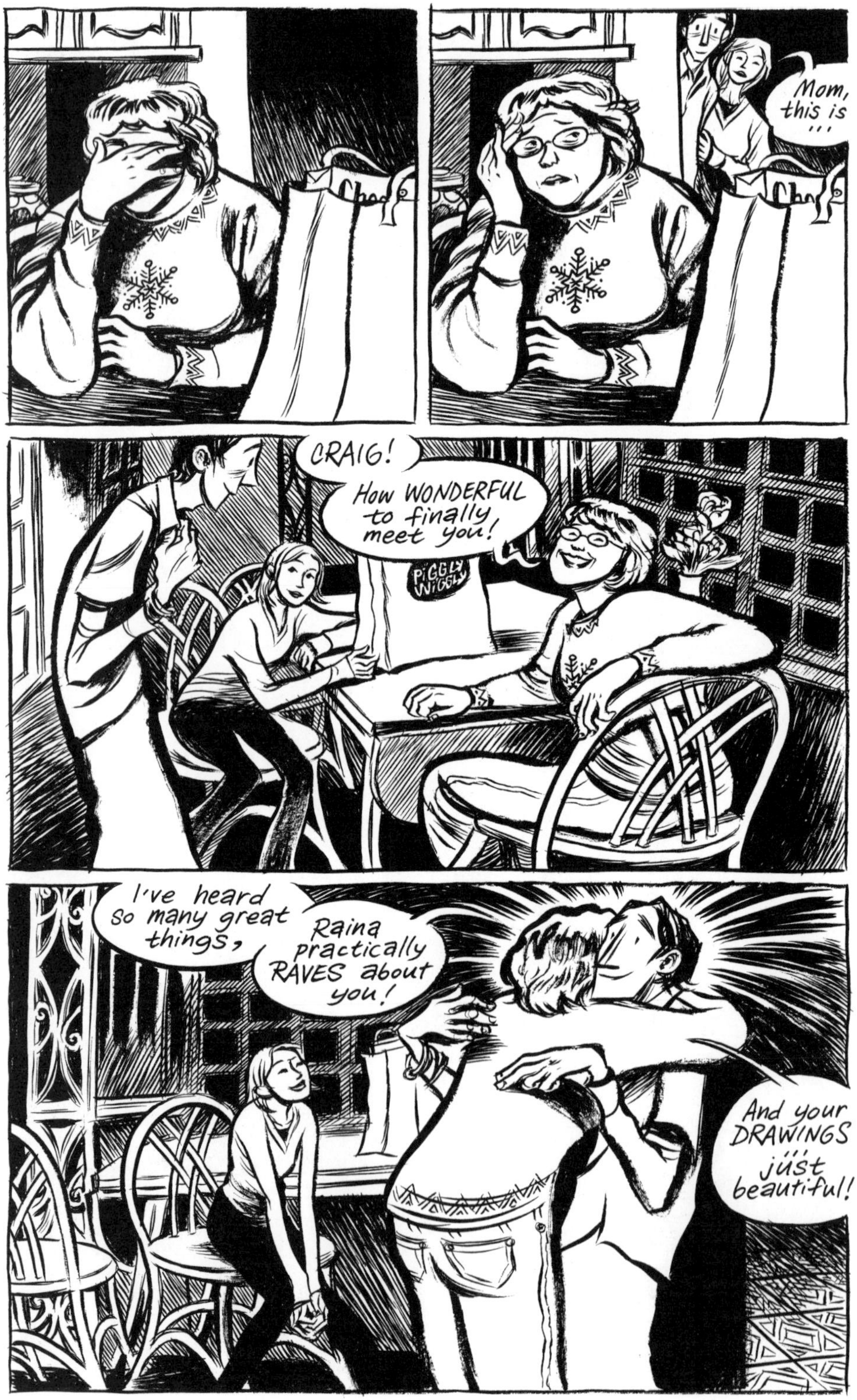
Mom, this is ...
CRAIG!
How WONDERFUL to finally meet you!
PIGGLY WIGGLY
I've heard so many great things,
Raina practically RAVES about you!
And your DRAWINGS ... just beautiful!

2
1
3

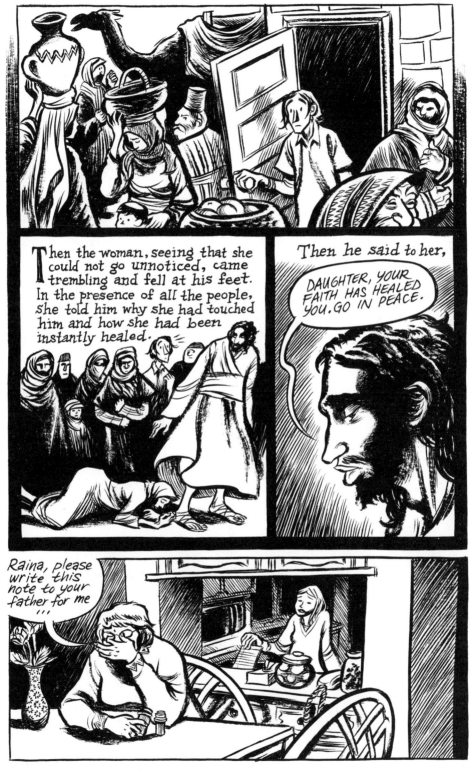

Then the woman, seeing that she could not go unnoticed, came trembling and fell at his feet. In the presence of all the people, she told him why she had touched him and how she had been instantly healed.

Then he said to her,

DAUGHTER, YOUR FAITH HAS HEALED YOU. GO IN PEACE.

Raina, please write this note to your father for me ...

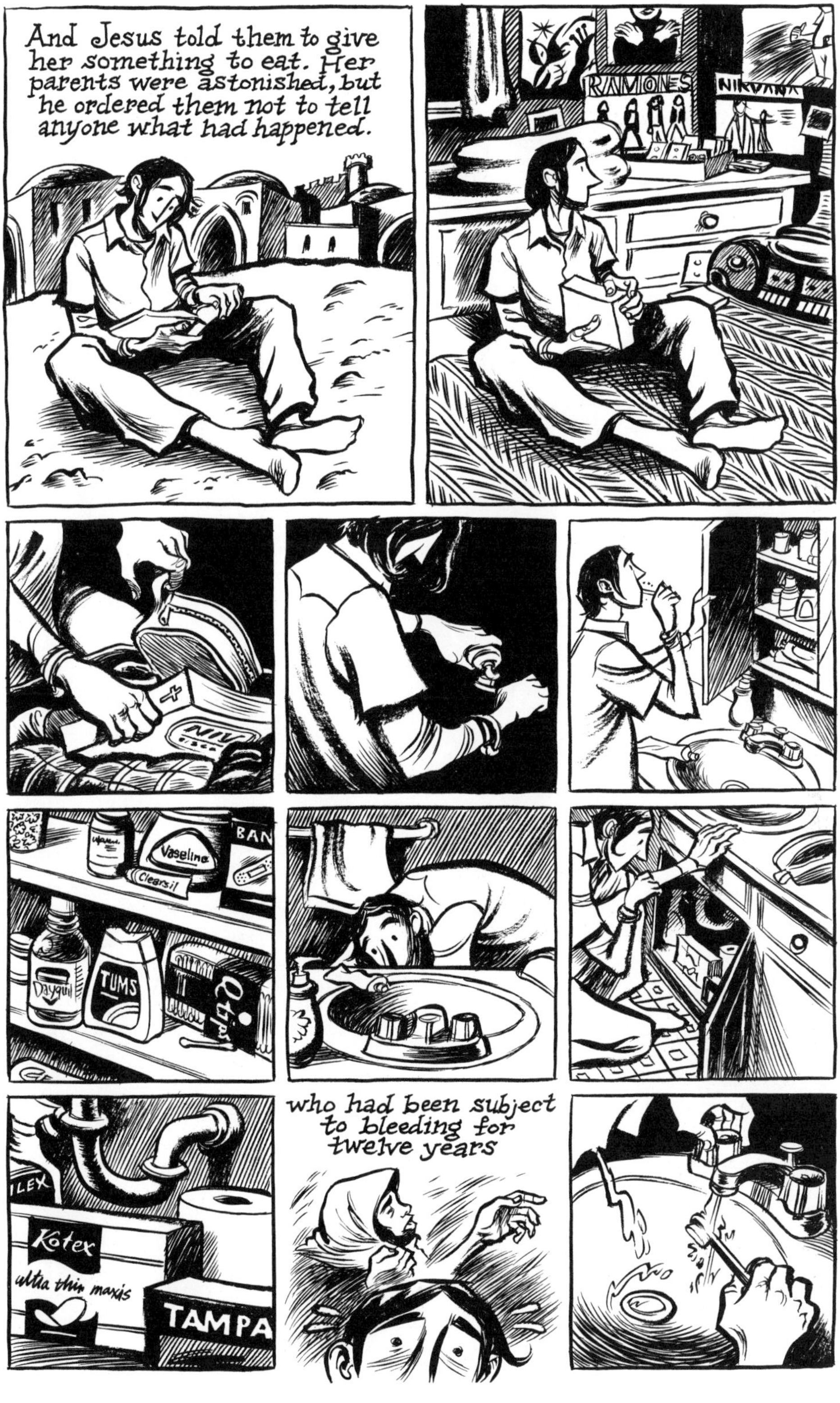
And Jesus told them to give her something to eat. Her parents were astonished, but he ordered them not to tell anyone what had happened.
RAMONES
NIRVANA
Vaseline
Clearsil
BAN
Dayquil
TUMS
Q-tips
ILEX
Kotex
ultra thin maxis
TAMPA
who had been subject to bleeding for twelve years

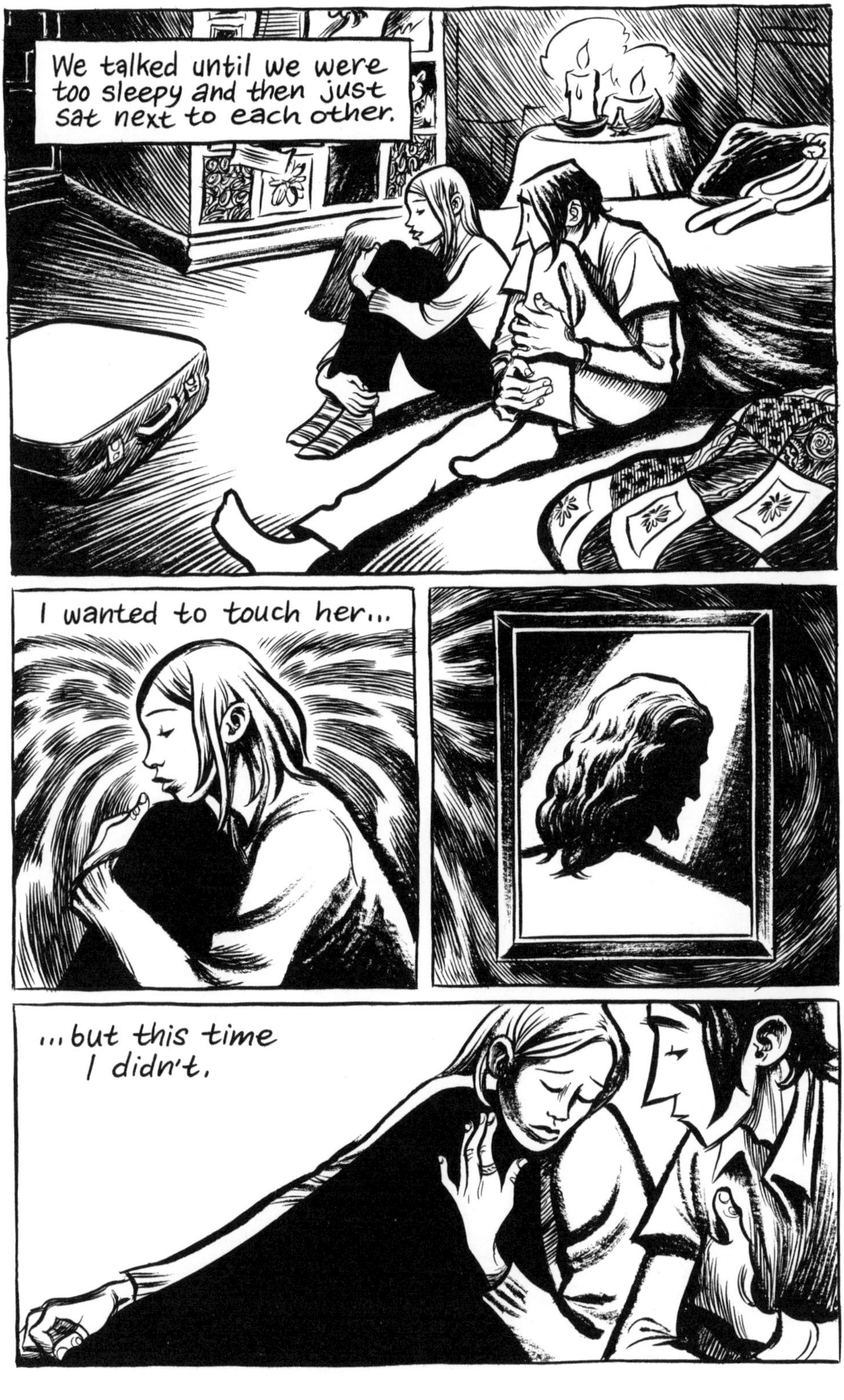
We talked until we were too sleepy and then just sat next to each other.
I wanted to touch her...
...but this time I didn't.

223

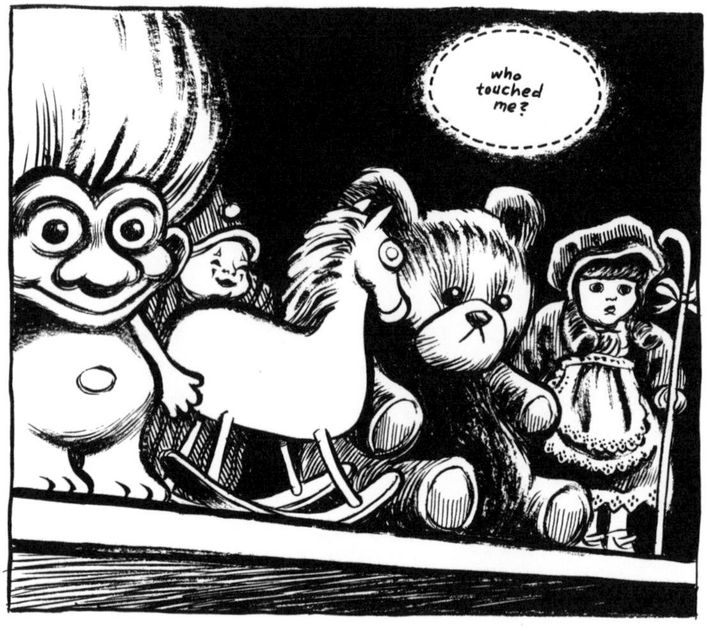
who touched me?

IV

Static

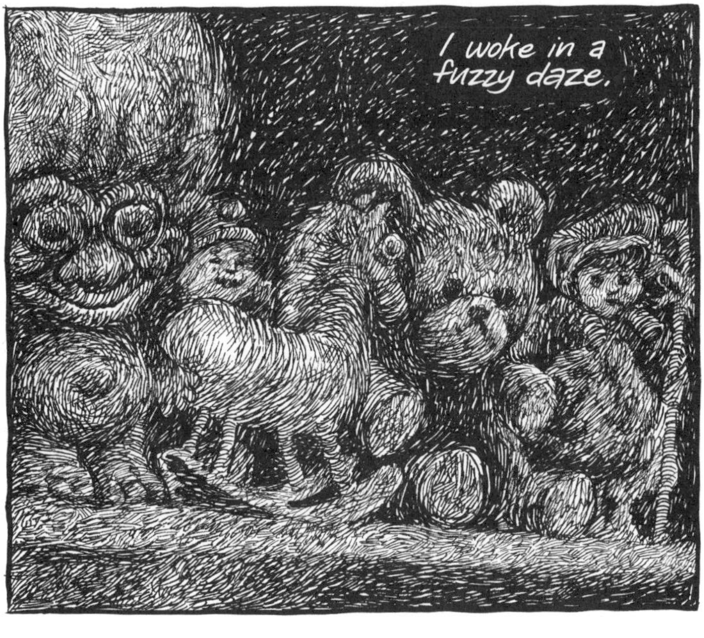
I woke in a fuzzy daze.

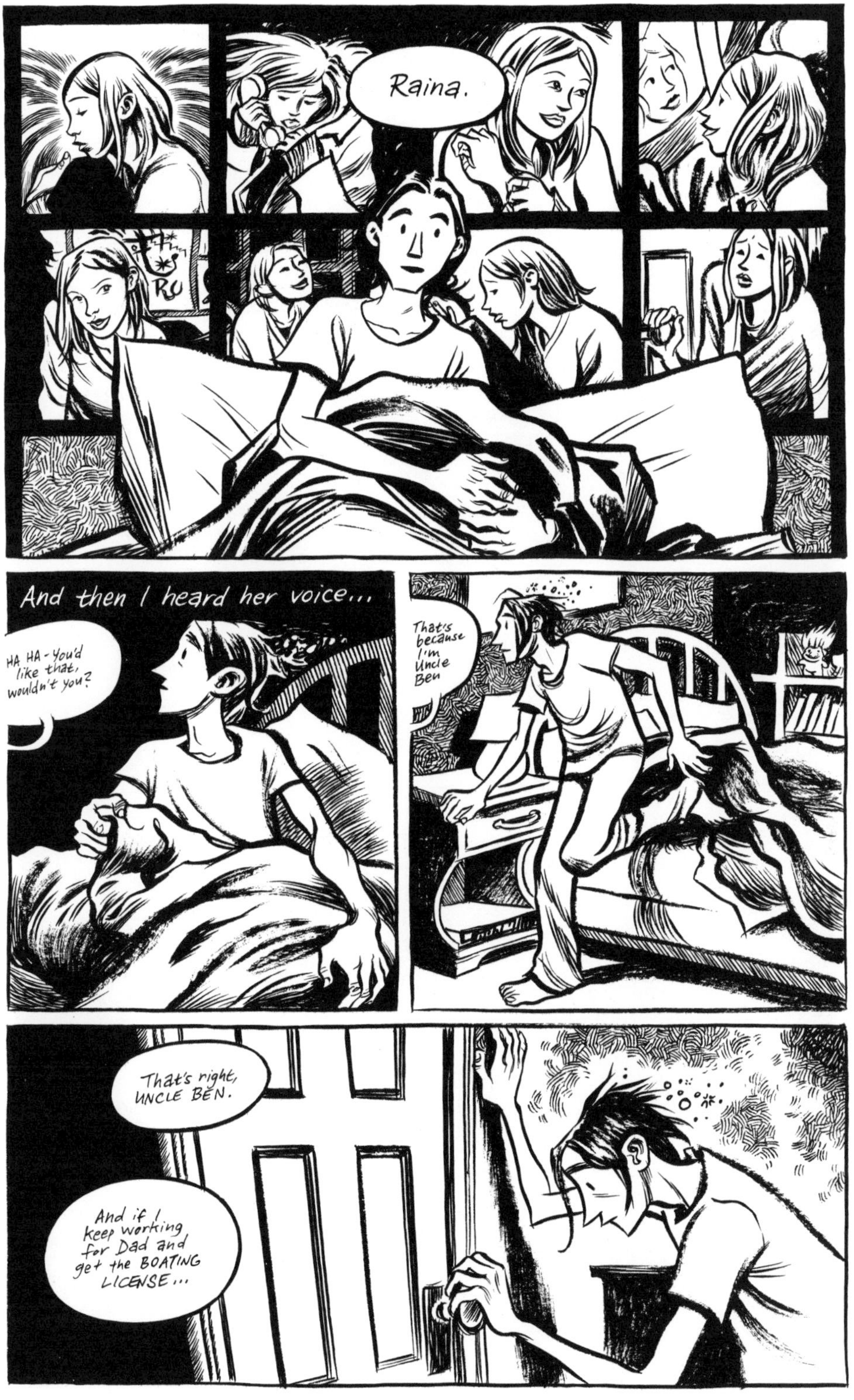
Raina.
And then I heard her voice...
HA HA - You'd like that, wouldn't you?
That's because I'm Uncle Ben
That's right, UNCLE BEN.
And if I keep working for Dad and get the BOATING LICENSE...

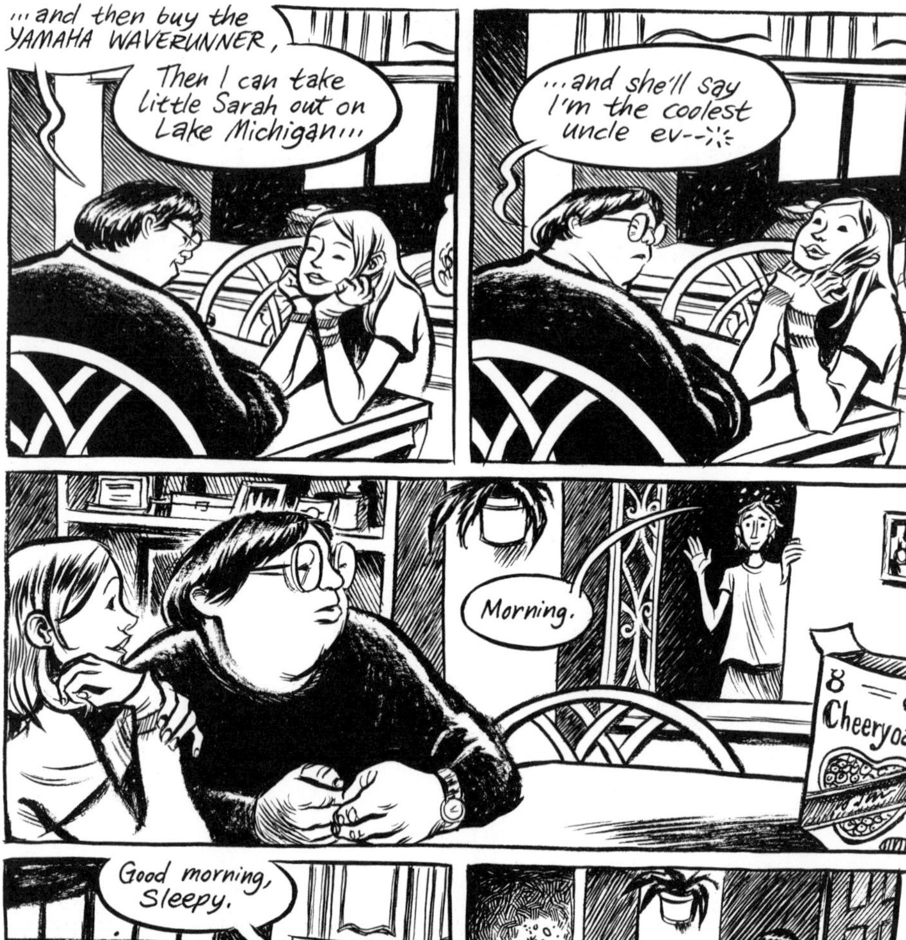
...and then buy the YAMAHA WAVERUNNER,
Then I can take little Sarah out on Lake Michigan...
...and she'll say I'm the coolest uncle ev--
Morning.
Cheeryoat
Good morning, Sleepy.
Ben...

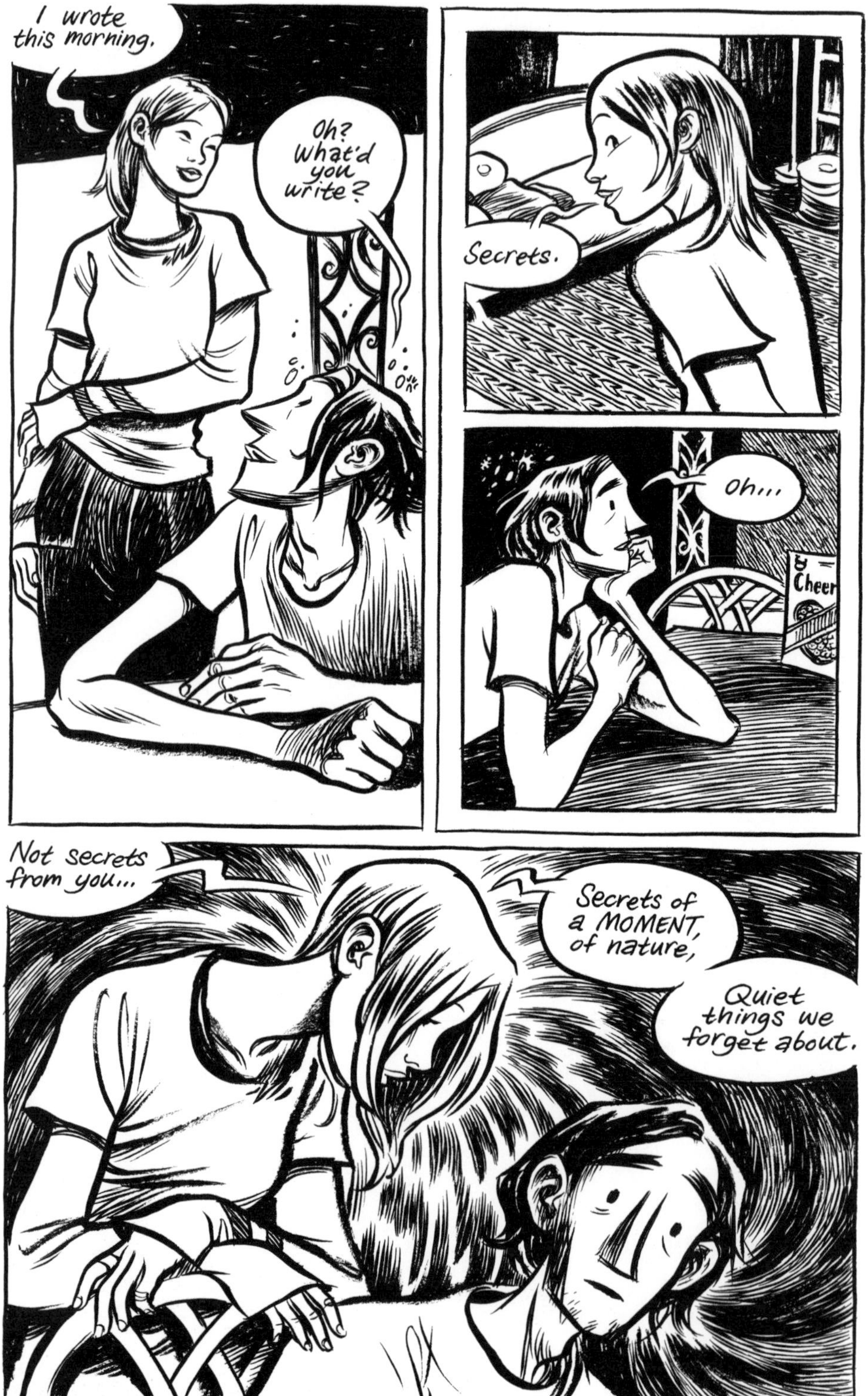
I wrote this morning.
Oh? What'd you write?
Secrets.
Oh...
Cheer
Not secrets from you...
Secrets of a MOMENT, of nature,
Quiet things we forget about.

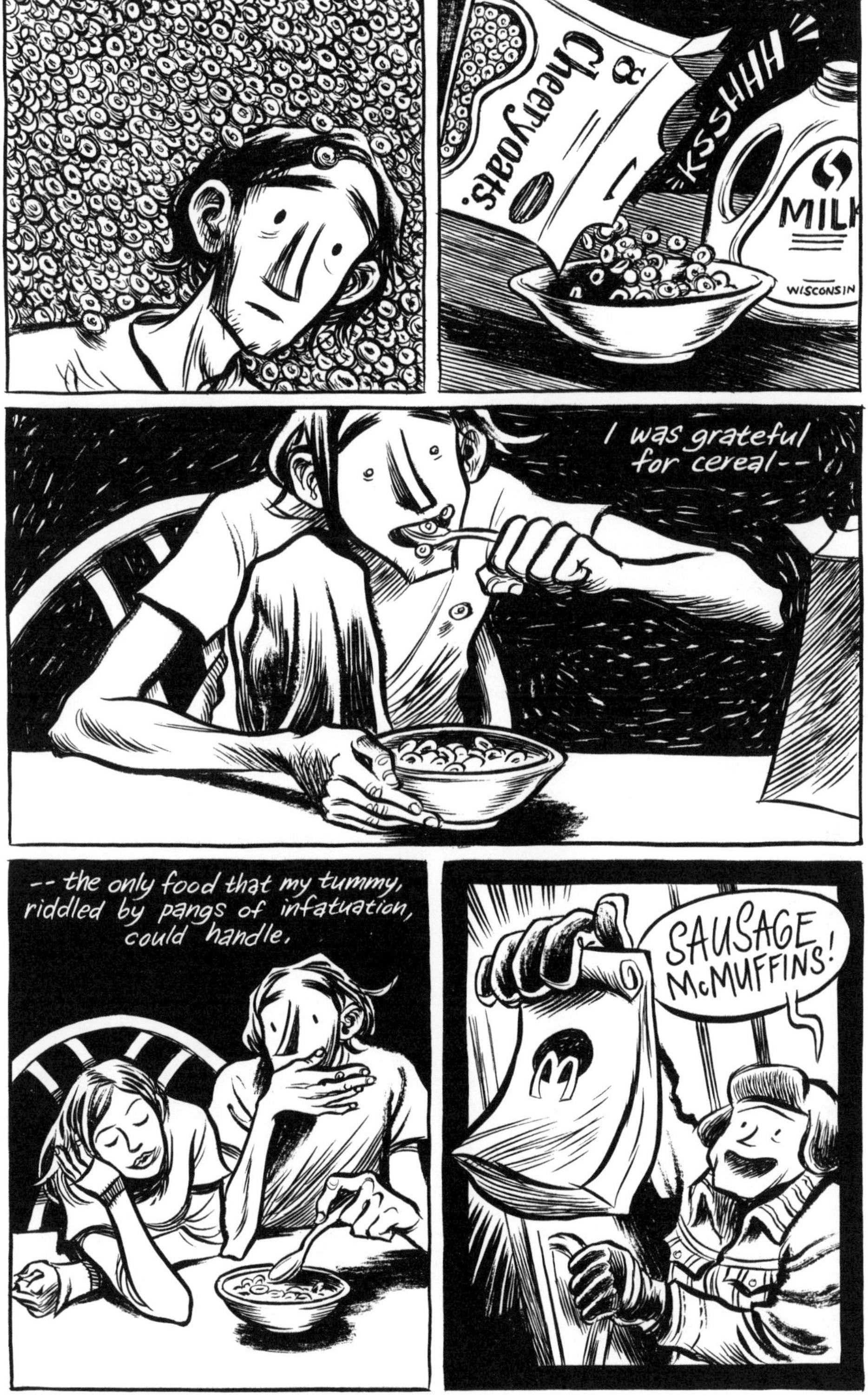
Cheeryoats.
KSSHHH
MILK
WISCONSIN
I was grateful for cereal--
-- the only food that my tummy, riddled by pangs of infatuation, could handle.
SAUSAGE McMUFFINS!

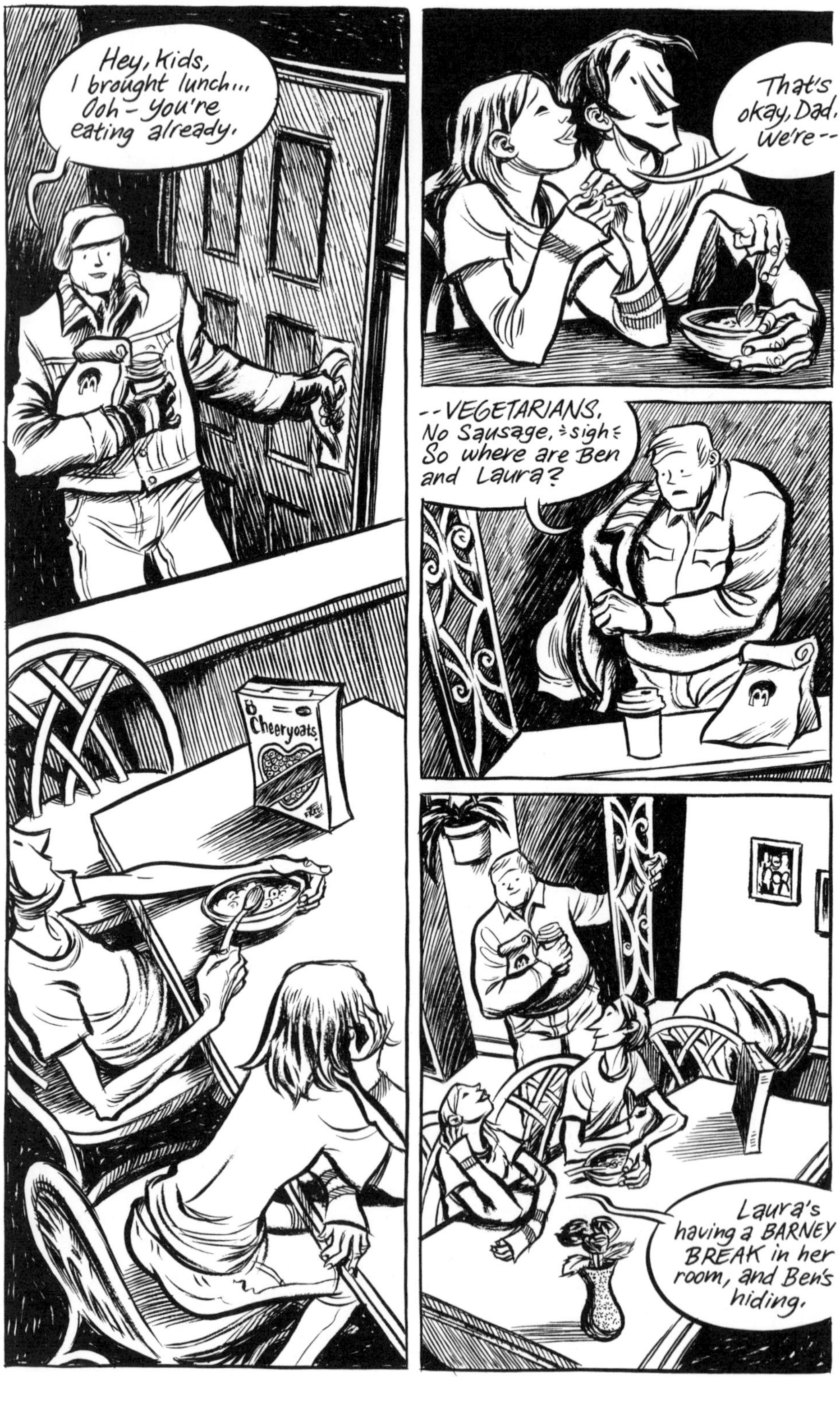
Hey, kids, I brought lunch... Ooh – You're eating already.
That's okay, Dad, We're --
--VEGETARIANS. No Sausage. ⸗sigh⸗ So where are Ben and Laura?
Cheeryoats
Laura's having a BARNEY BREAK in her room, and Ben's hiding.

235

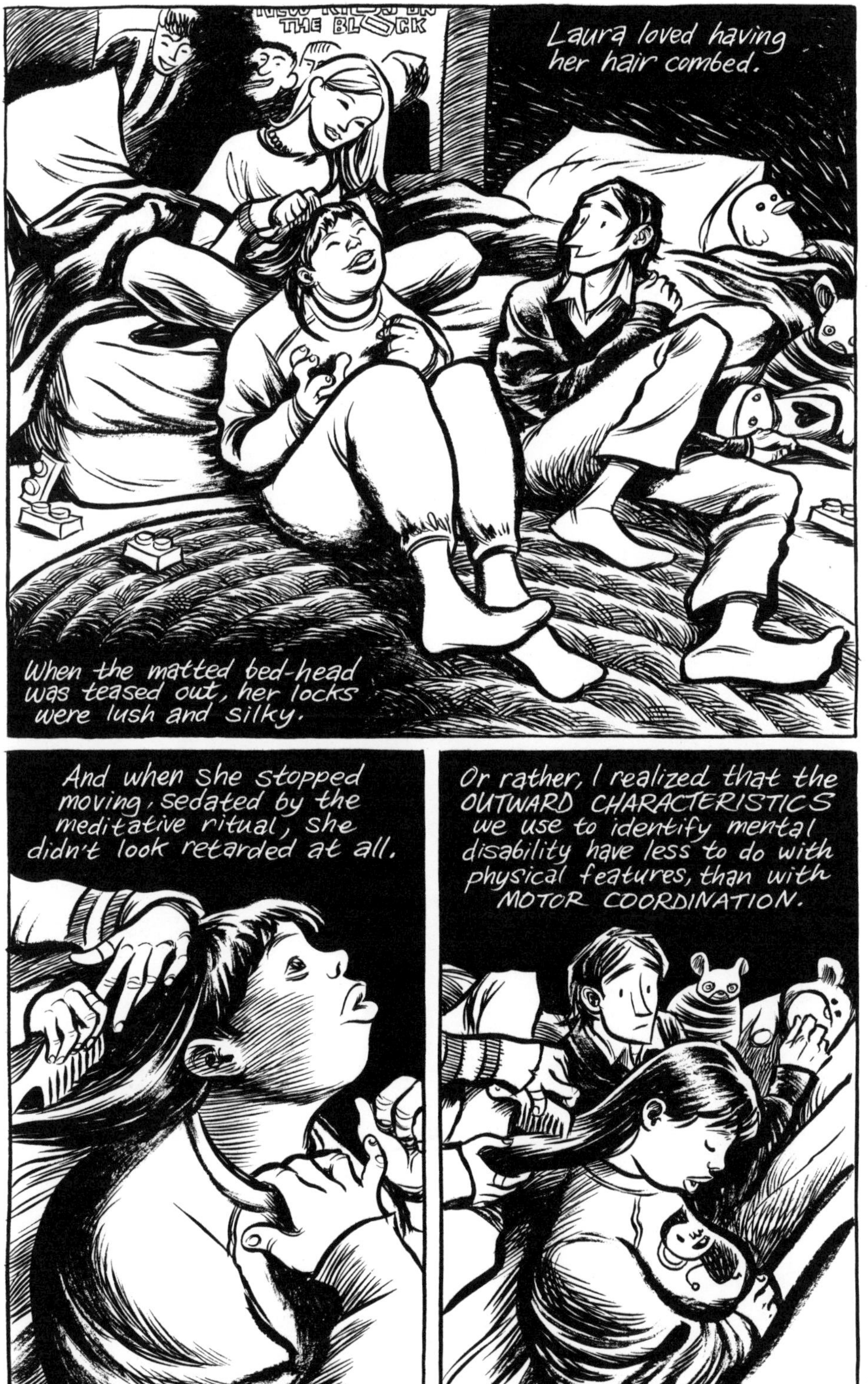
Laura loved having her hair combed.
When the matted bed-head was teased out, her locks were lush and silky.
And when she stopped moving, sedated by the meditative ritual, she didn't look retarded at all.
Or rather, I realized that the OUTWARD CHARACTERISTICS we use to identify mental disability have less to do with physical features, than with MOTOR COORDINATION.

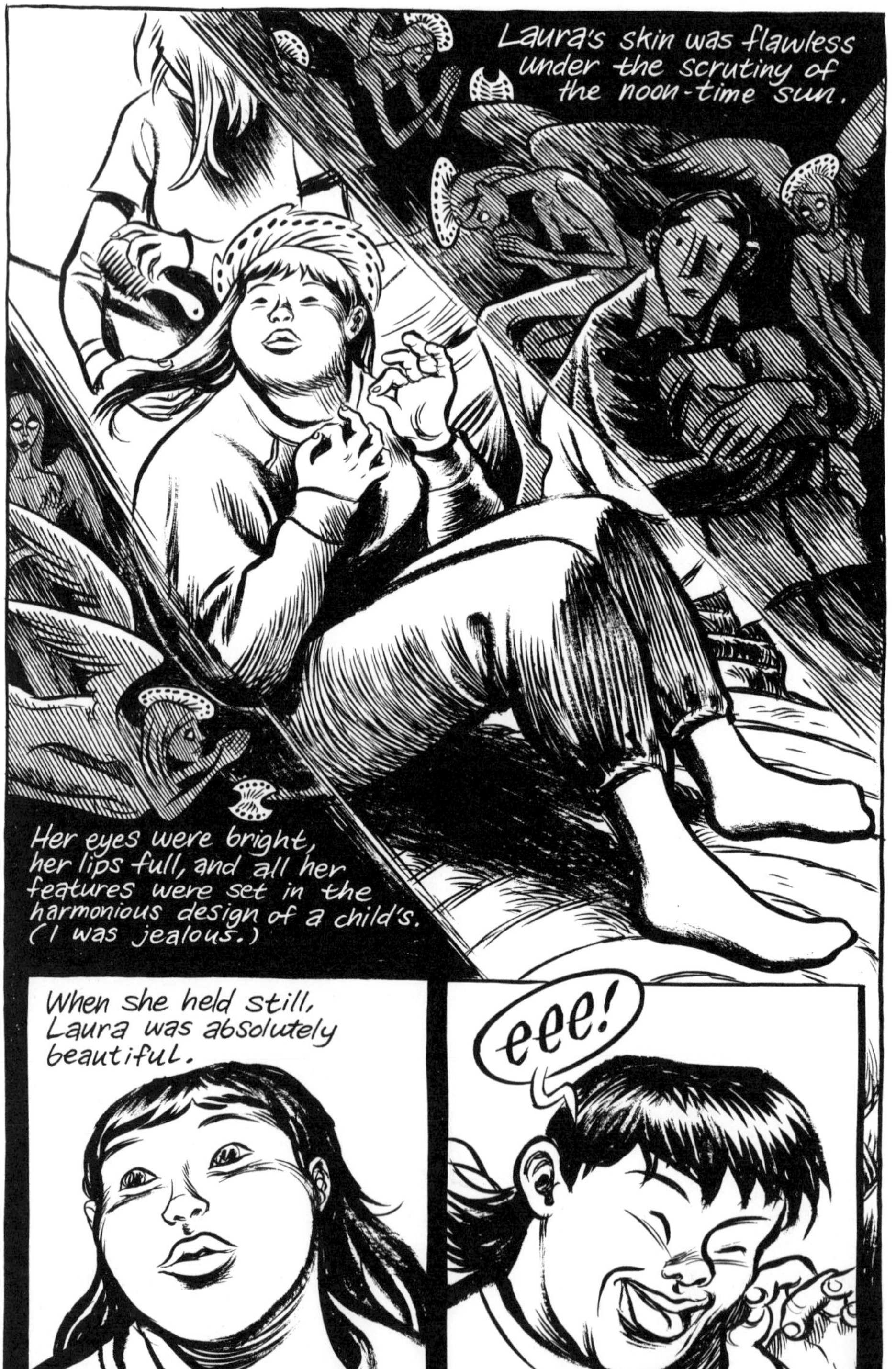
Laura's skin was flawless under the scrutiny of the noon-time sun.
Her eyes were bright, her lips full, and all her features were set in the harmonious design of a child's. (I was jealous.)
When she held still, Laura was absolutely beautiful.
eee!

239

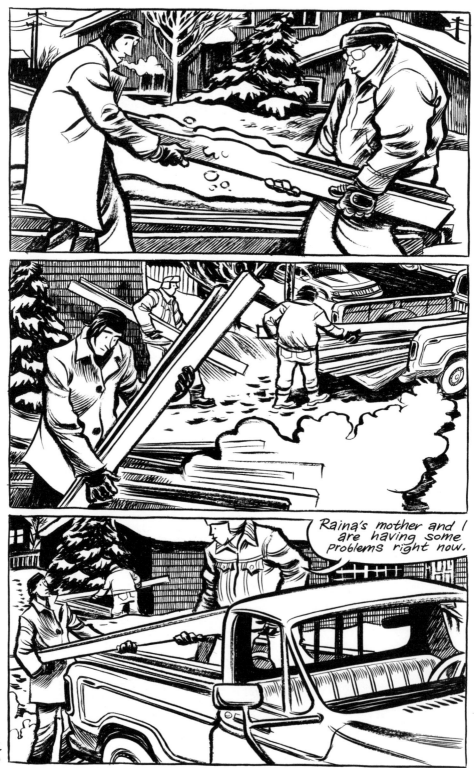

Raina's mother and I are having some problems right now.

240

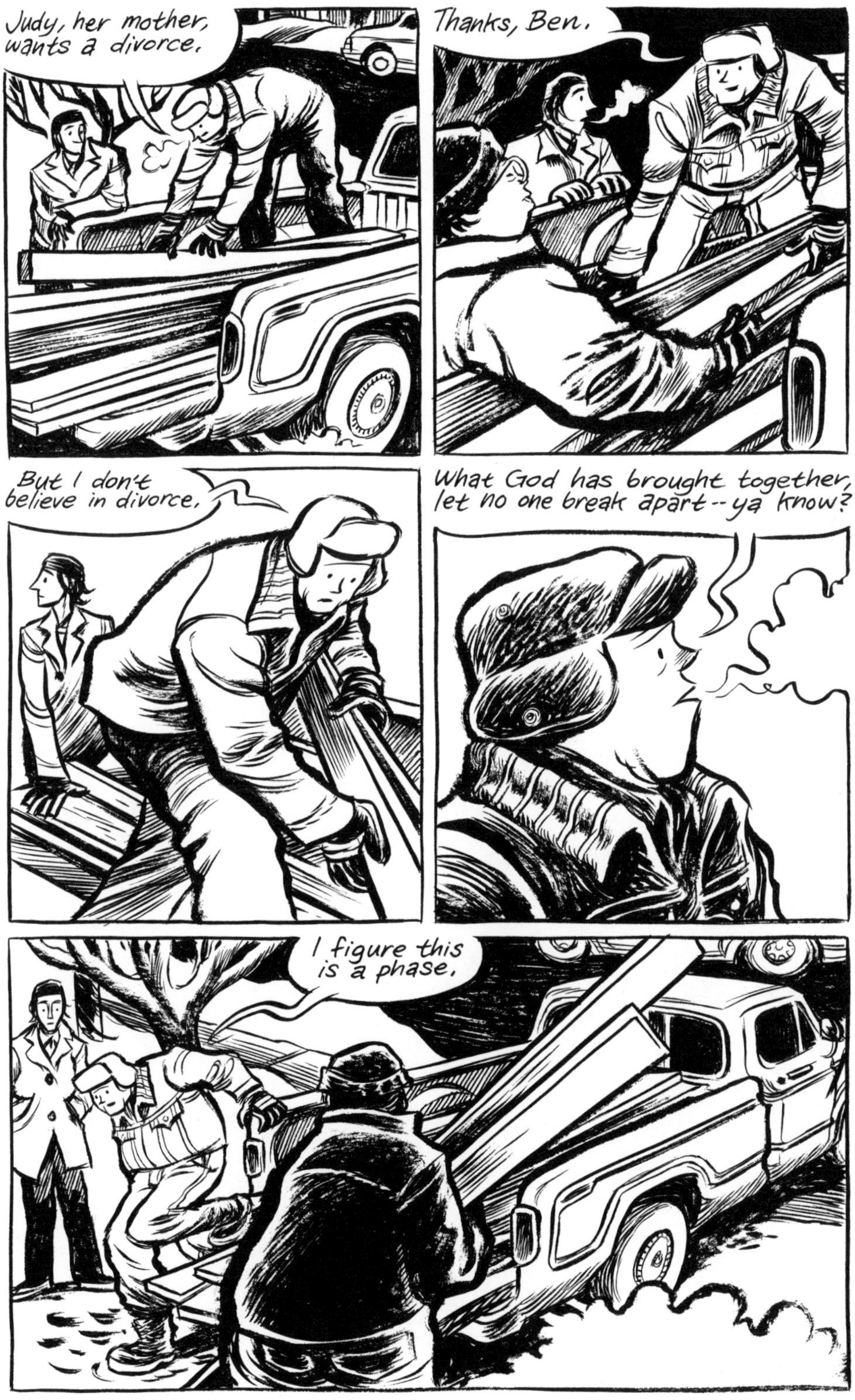
Judy, her mother, wants a divorce.
Thanks, Ben.
But I don't believe in divorce.
What God has brought together, let no one break apart--ya know?
I figure this is a phase.

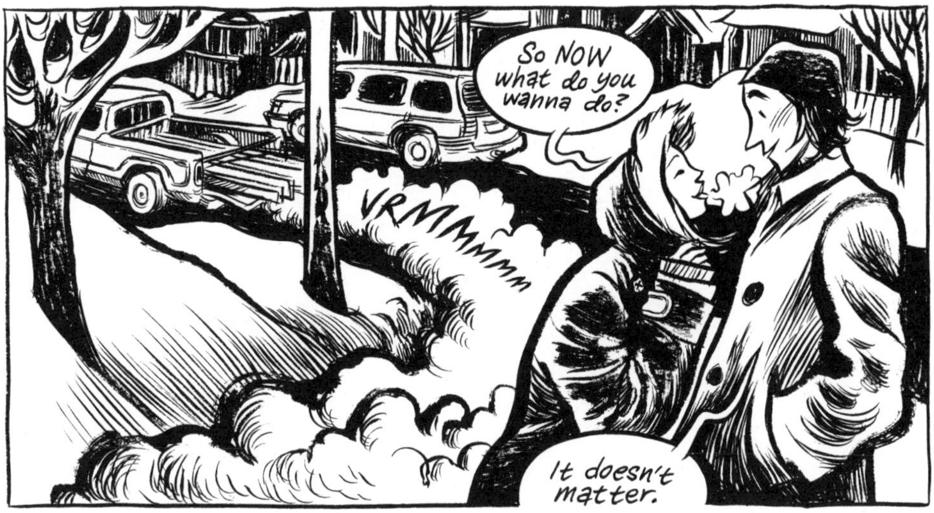
So NOW what do you wanna do?
VRMMMMMMM
It doesn't matter.

And so we drove about town.

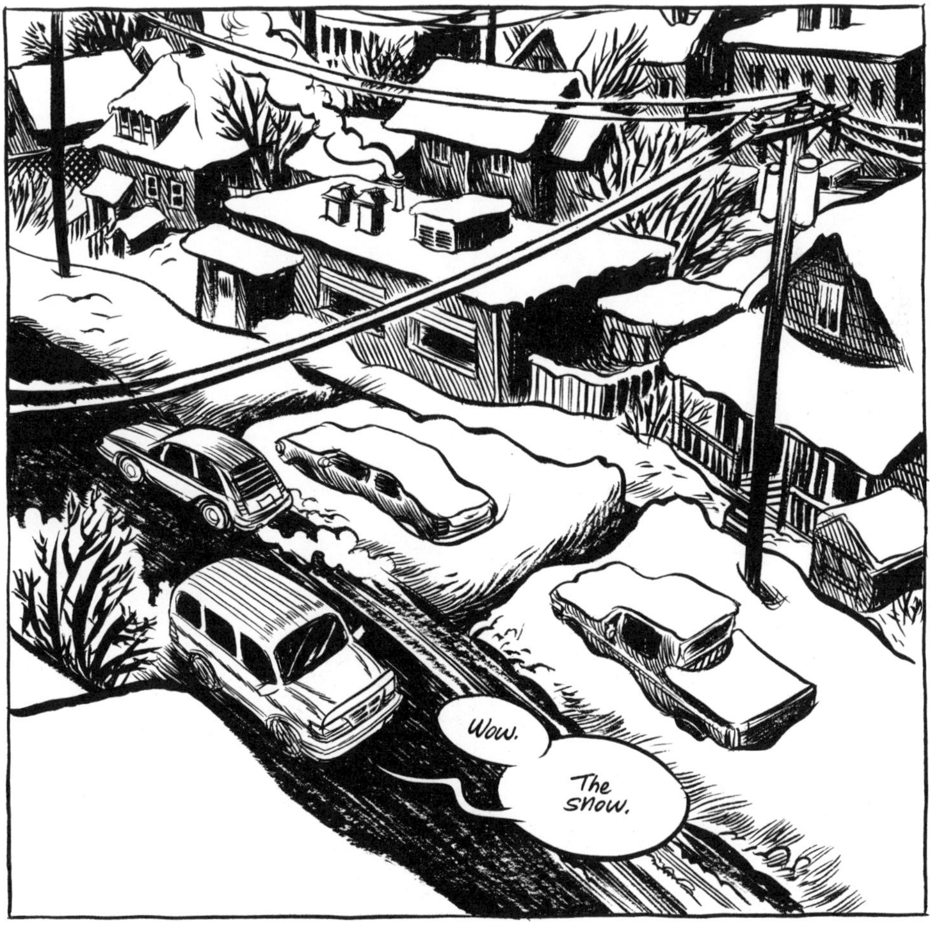
Wow.
The snow.

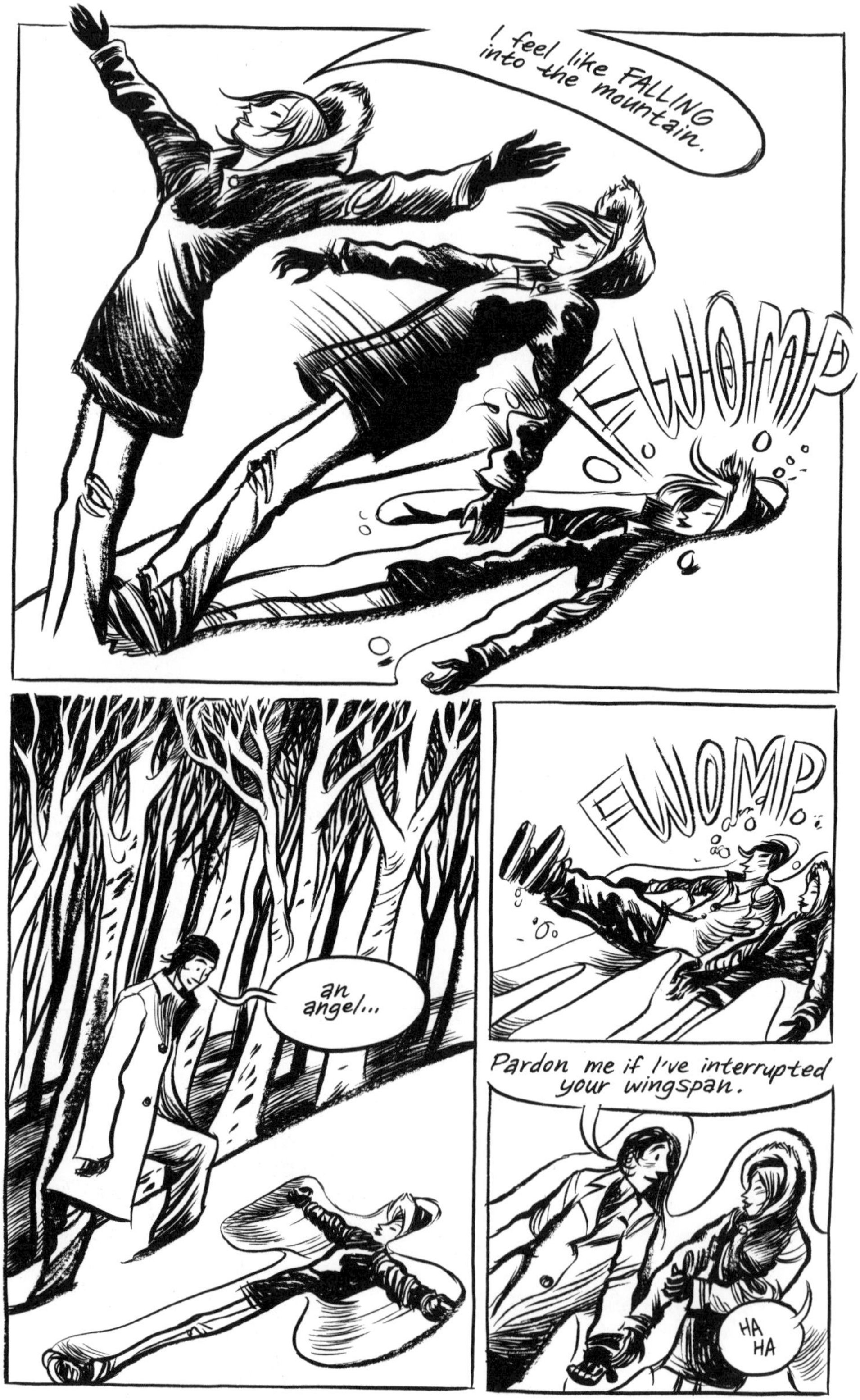
I feel like FALLING into the mountain.
FWOMP
an angel...
FWOMP
Pardon me if I've interrupted your wingspan.
HA HA

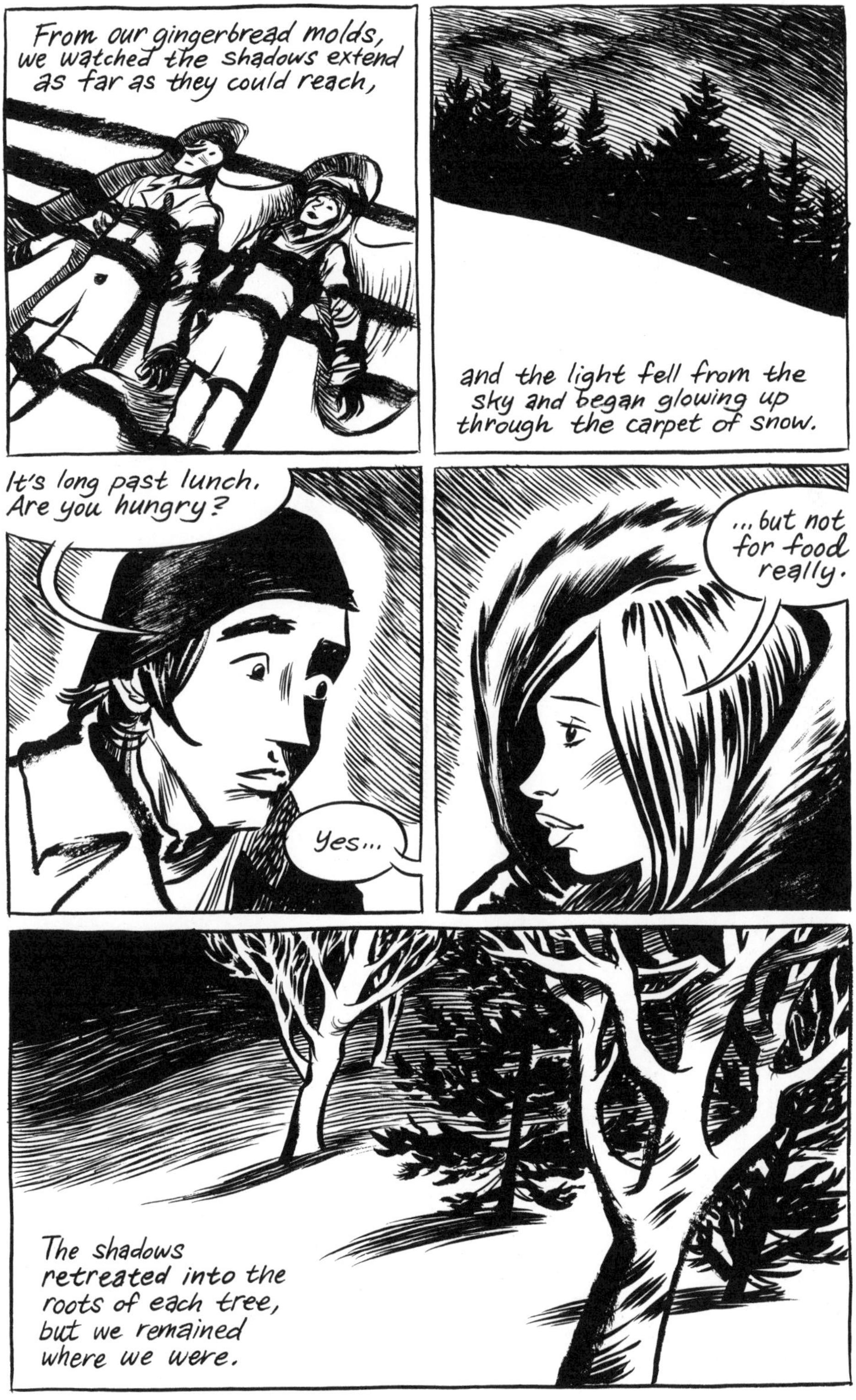

From our gingerbread molds, we watched the shadows extend as far as they could reach,
and the light fell from the sky and began glowing up through the carpet of snow.
It's long past lunch. Are you hungry?
Yes...
...but not for food really.
The shadows retreated into the roots of each tree, but we remained where we were.

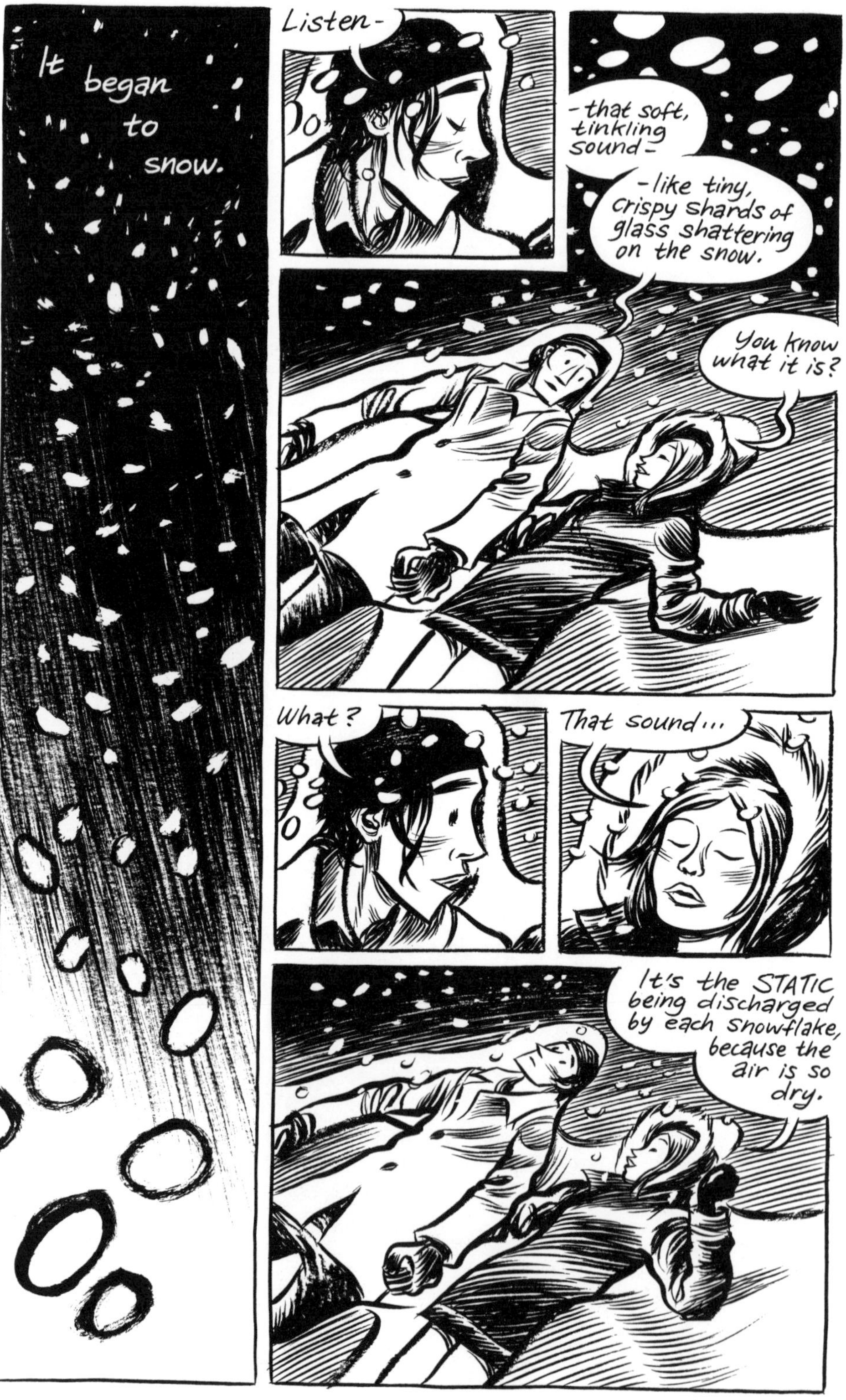
It began to snow.
Listen-
-that soft, tinkling sound-
-like tiny, crispy shards of glass shattering on the snow.
You know what it is?
What?
That sound...
It's the STATIC being discharged by each snowflake, because the air is so dry.

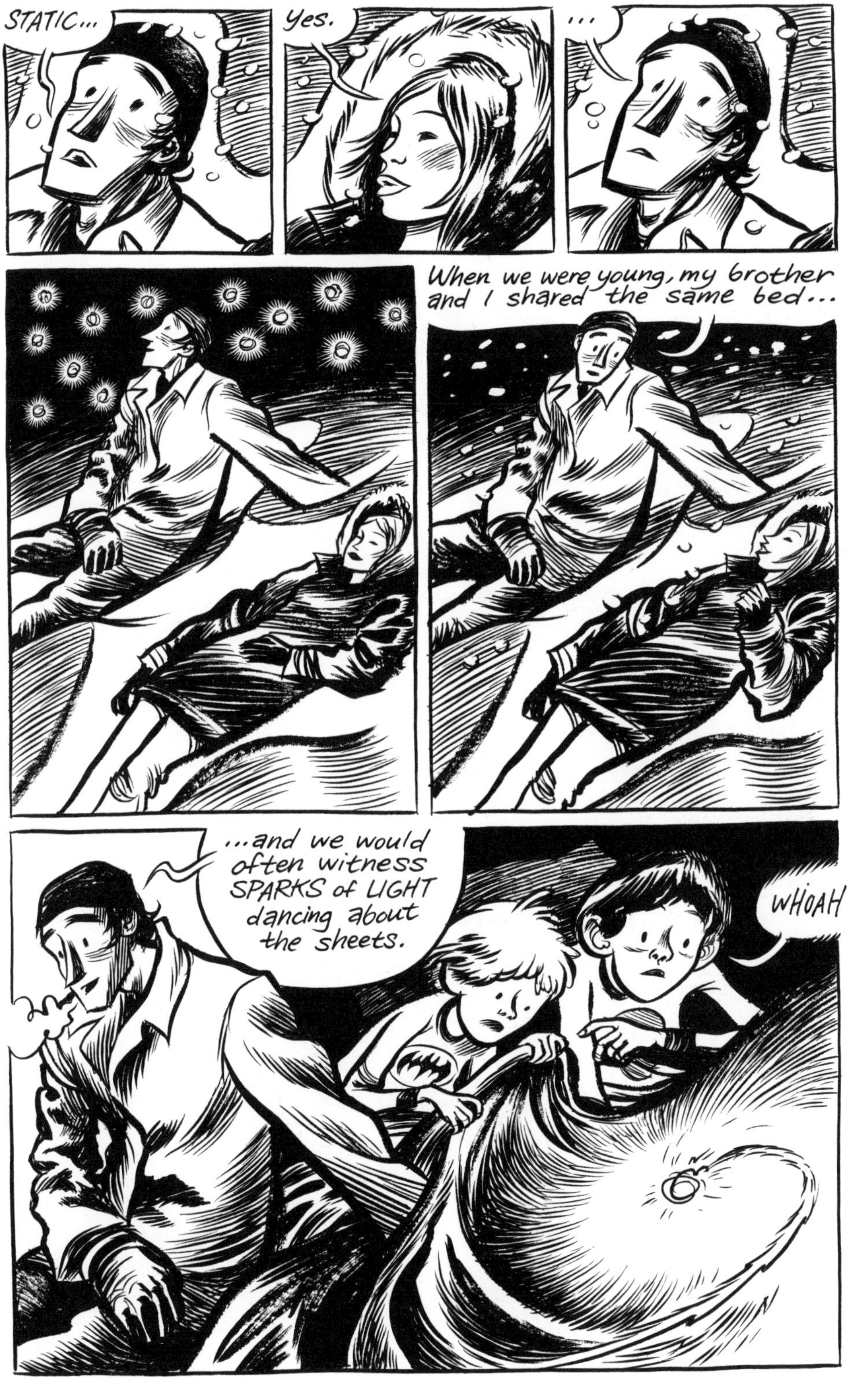
STATIC...
Yes.
...
When we were young, my brother and I shared the same bed...
...and we would often witness SPARKS of LIGHT dancing about the sheets.
WHOAH

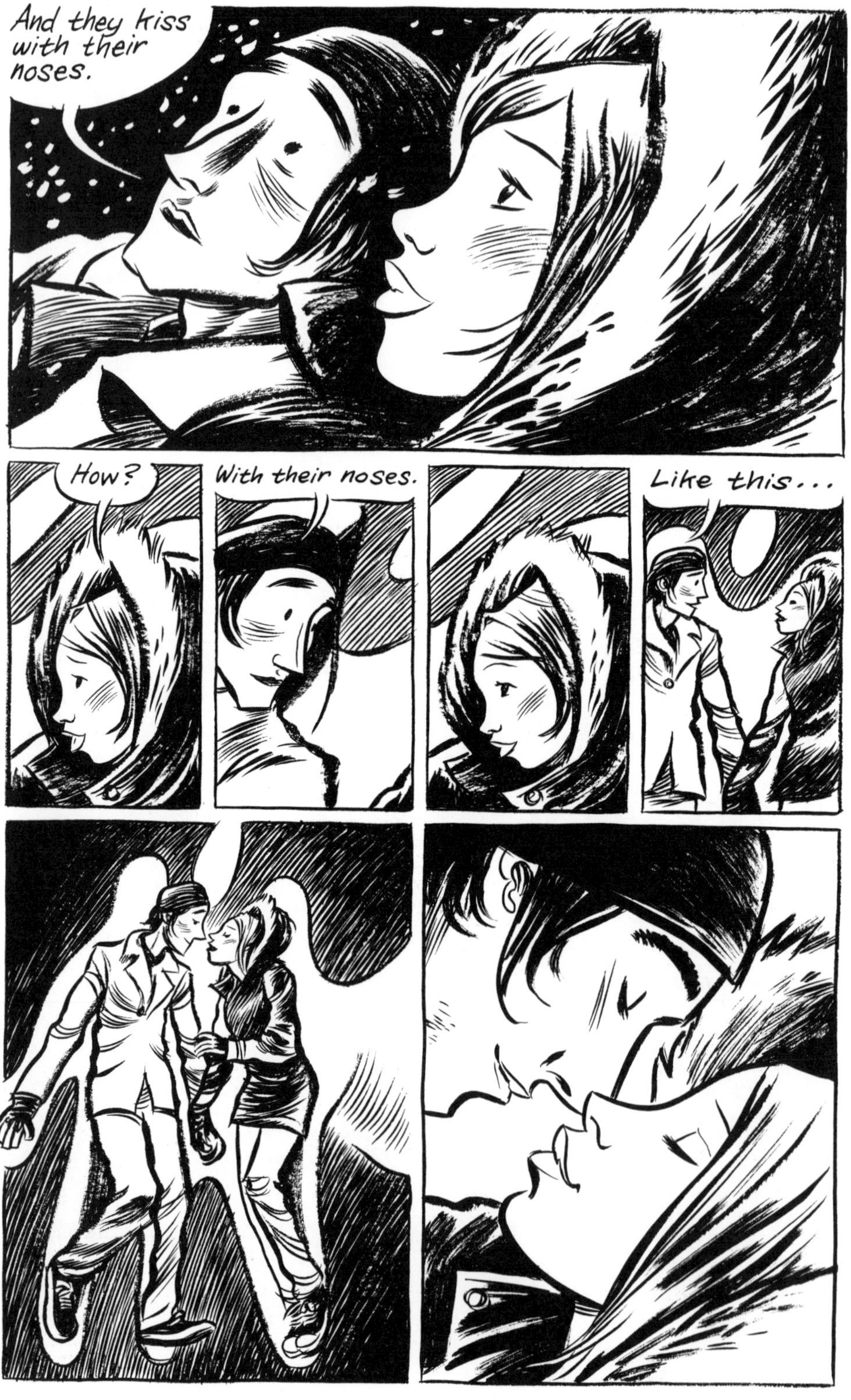
And they kiss with their noses.
How?
With their noses.
Like this...

255

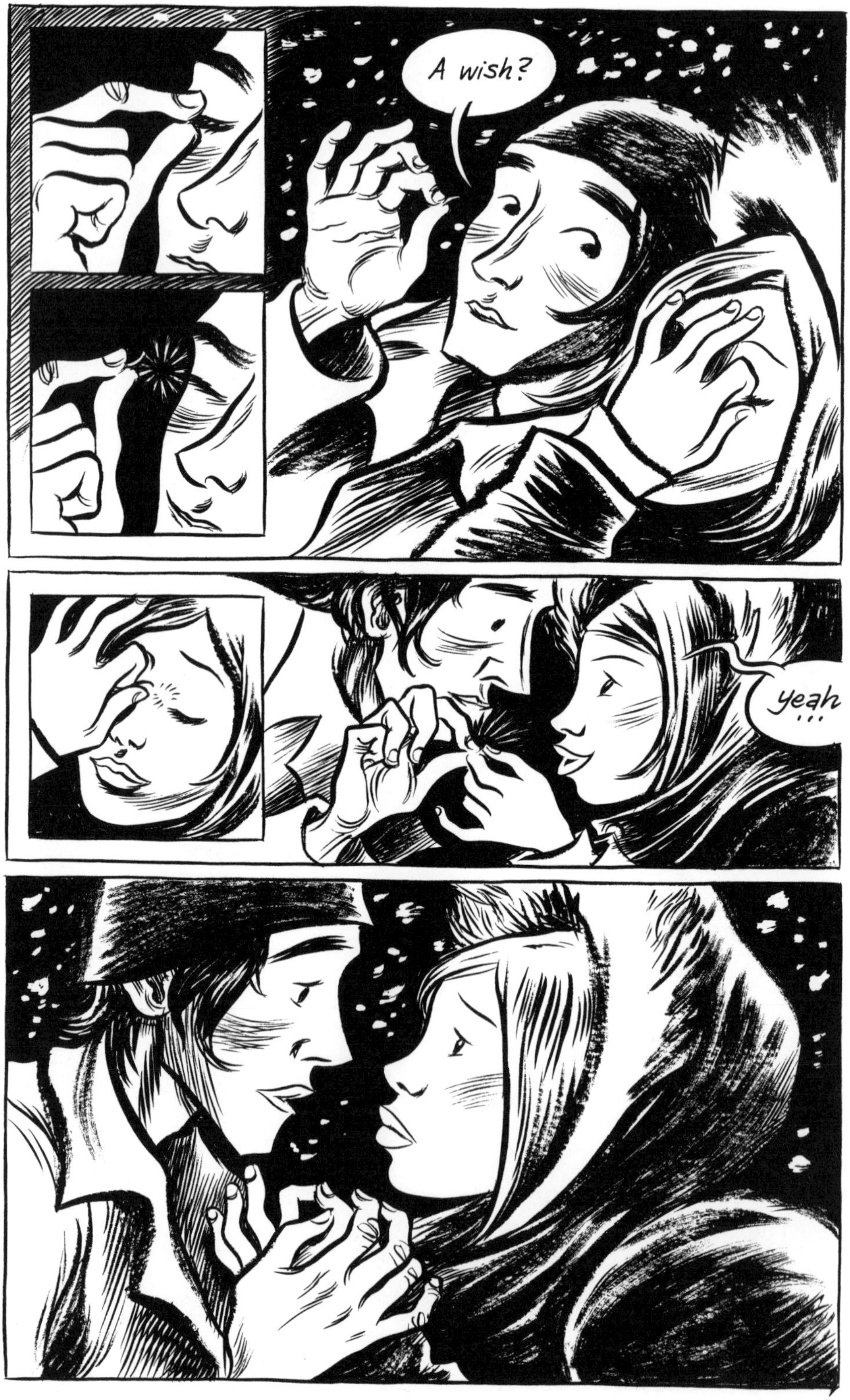
A wish?
yeah
...

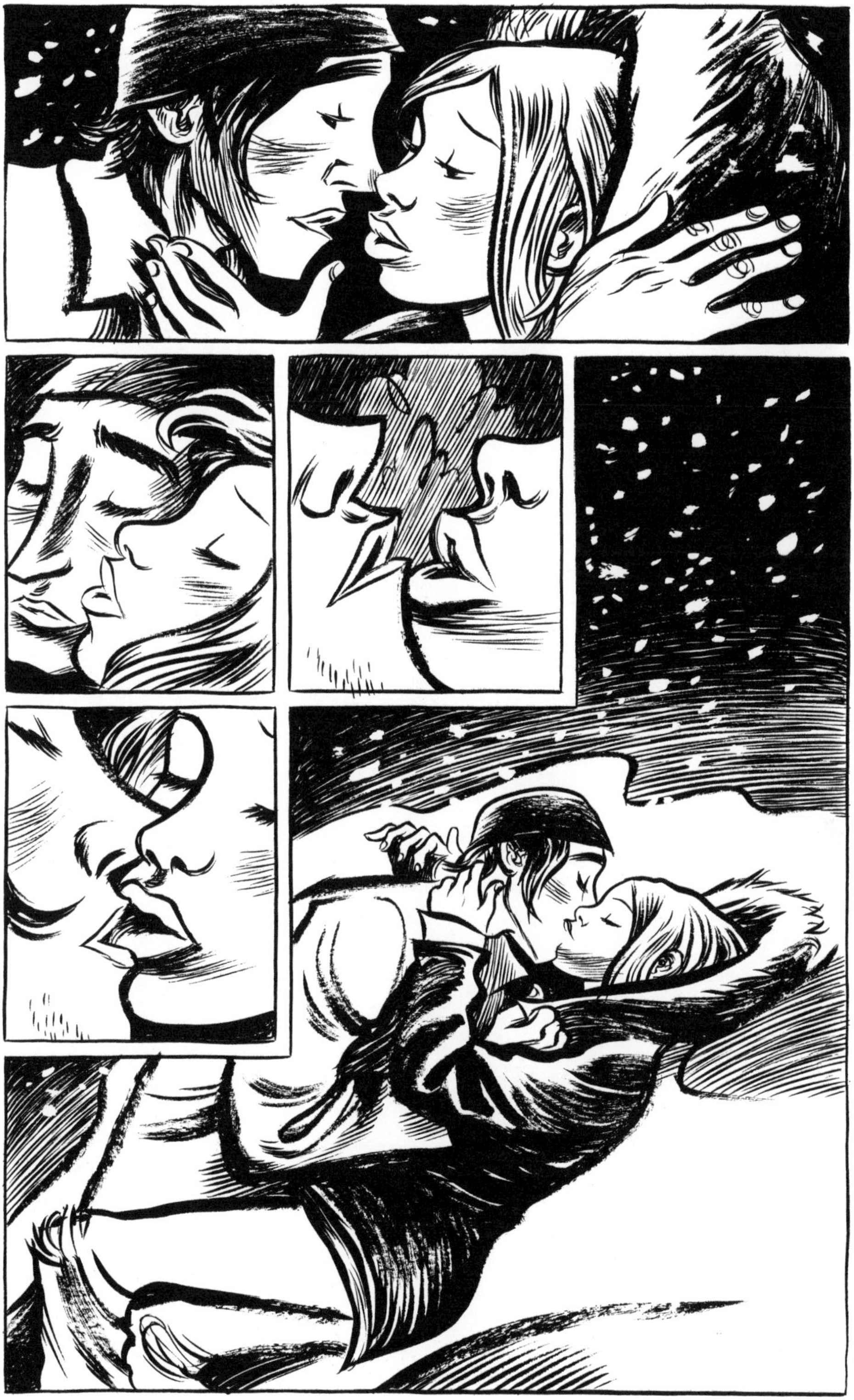

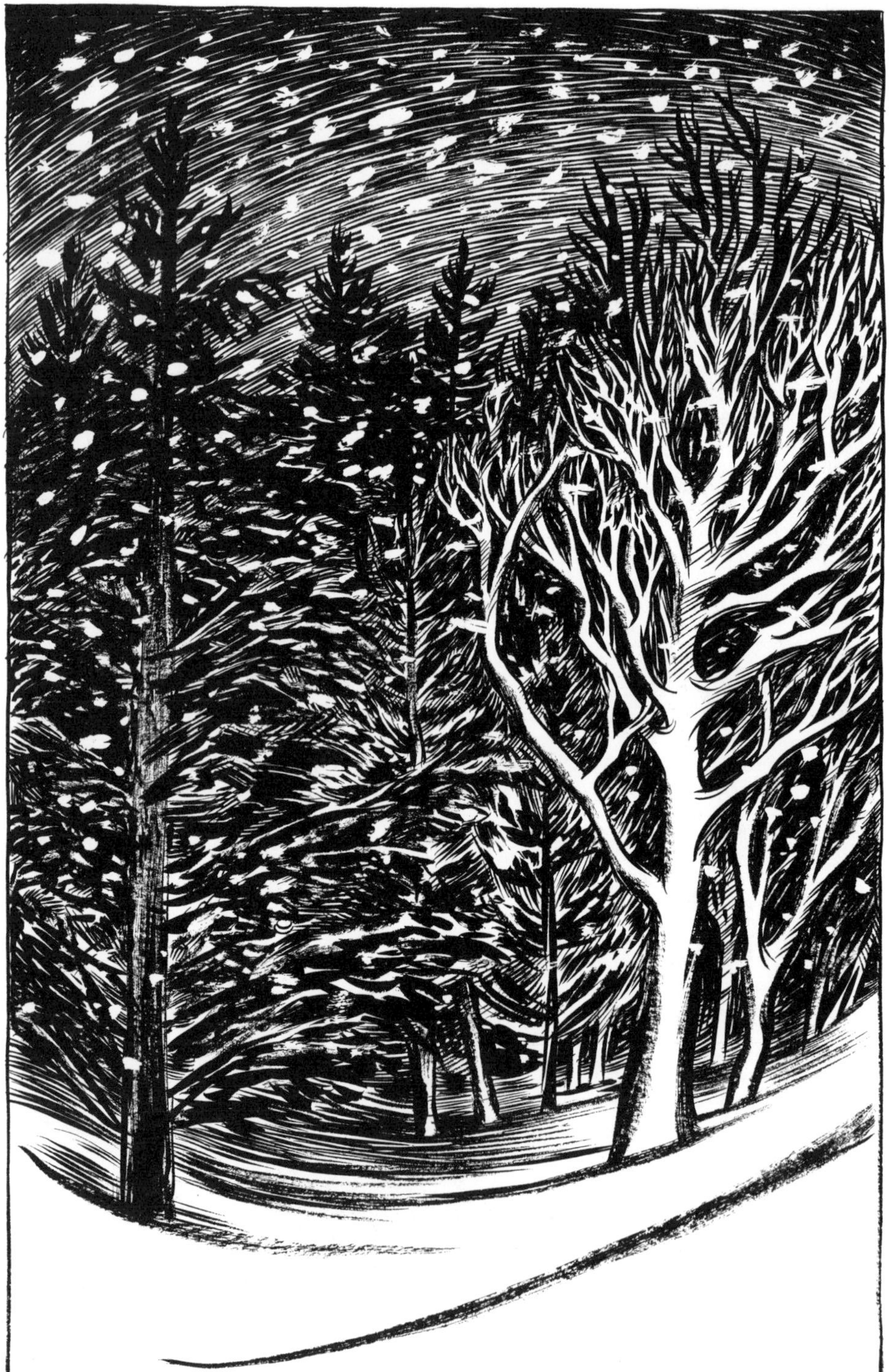

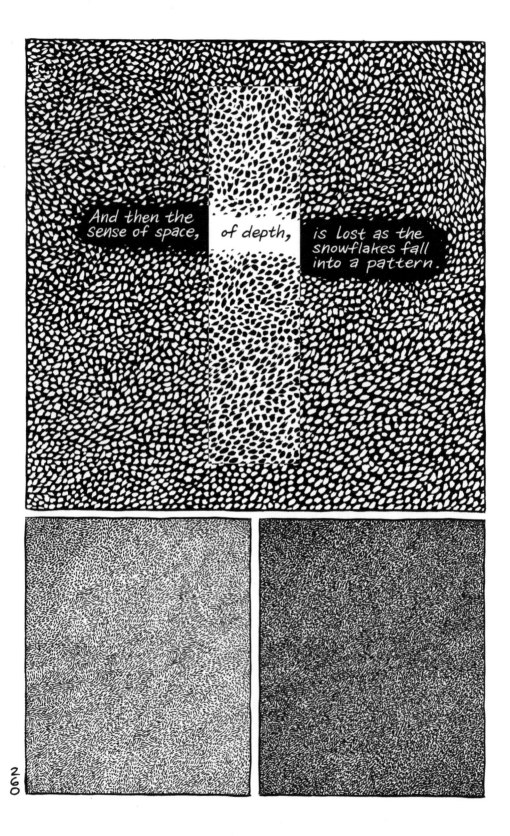

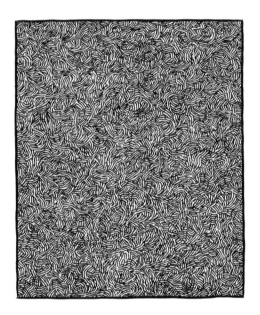

V

*I Don't
Wanna
Grow
Up*

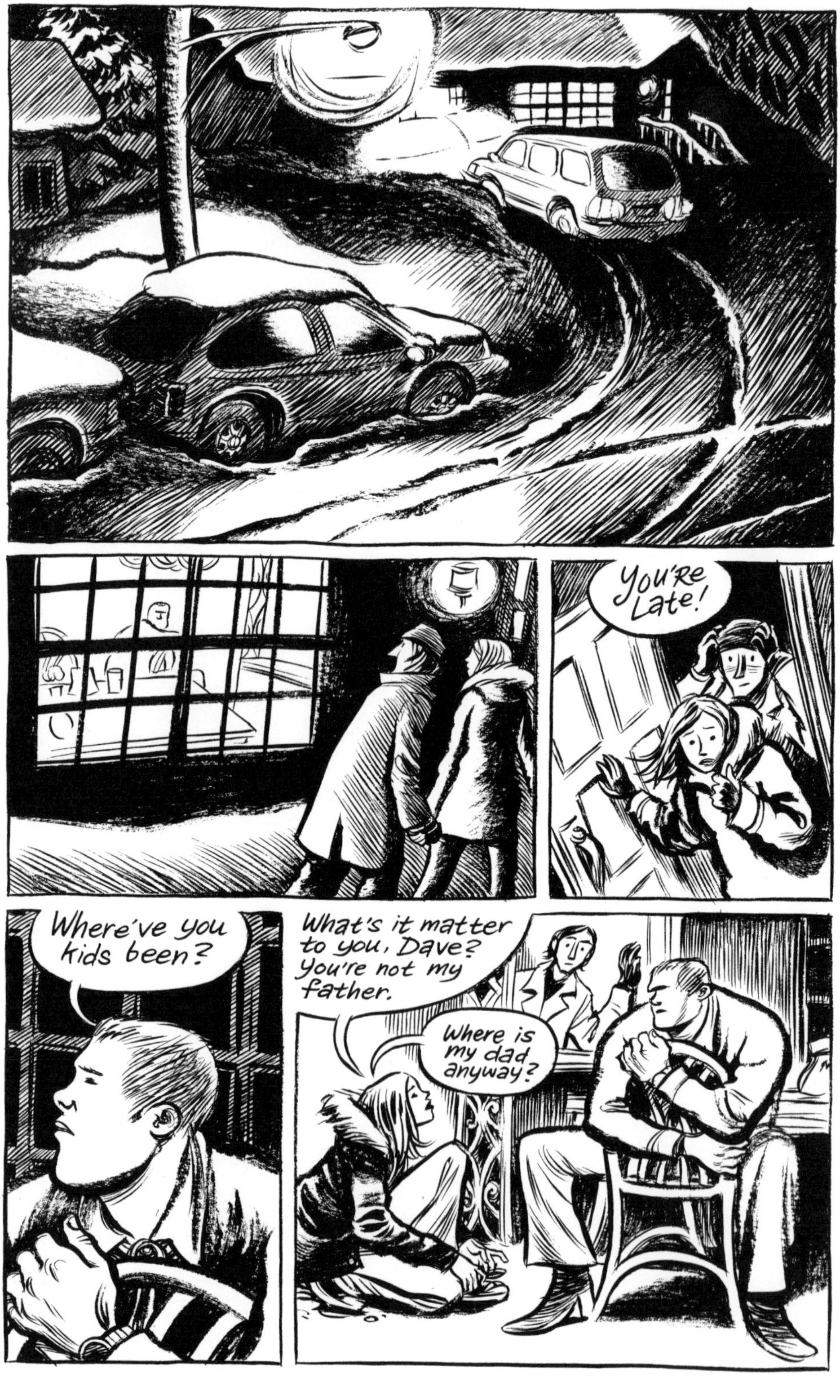
You're Late!
Where've you kids been?
What's it matter to you, Dave? You're not my father.
Where is my dad anyway?

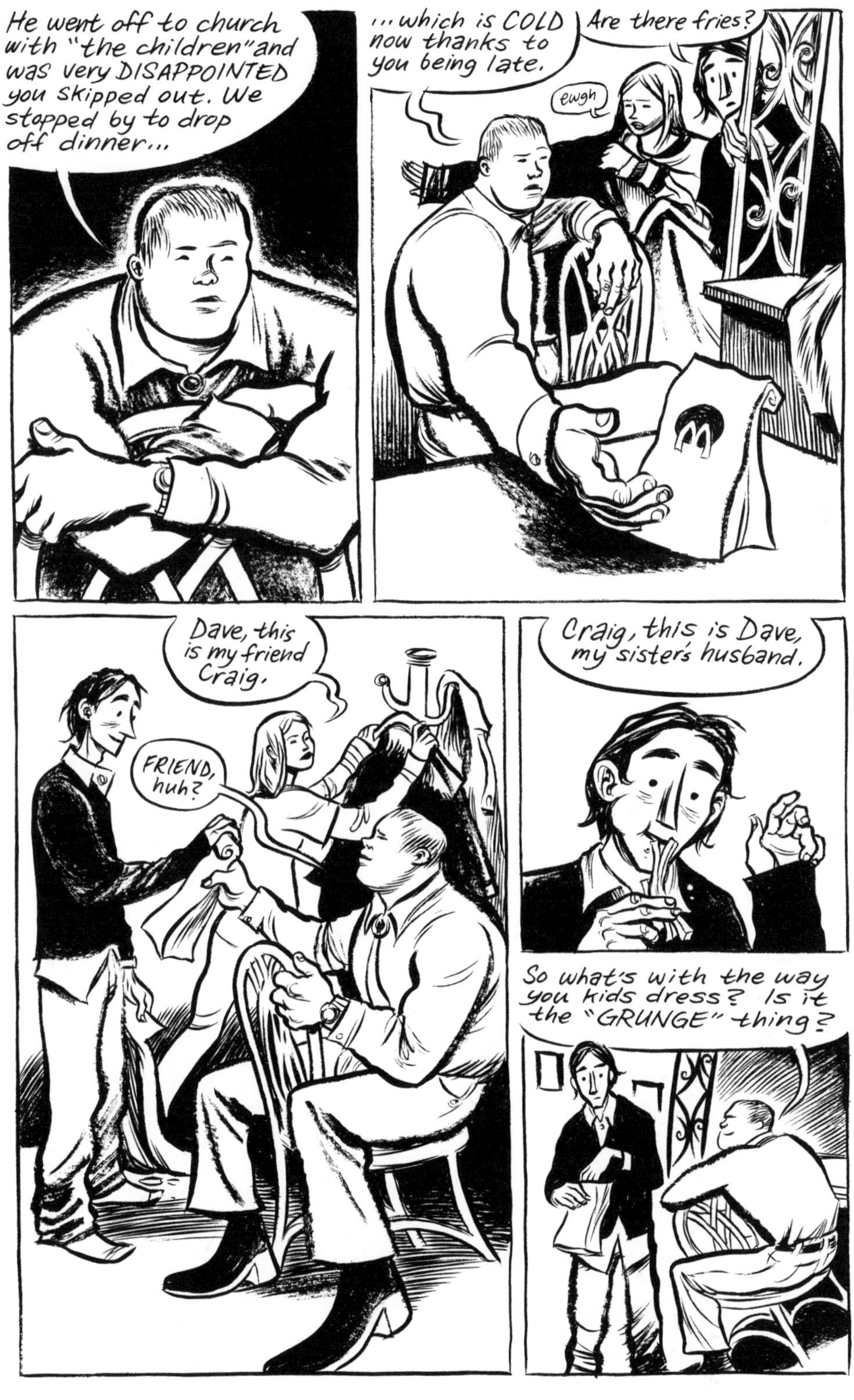

He went off to church with "the children" and was very DISAPPOINTED you skipped out. We stopped by to drop off dinner...
...which is COLD now thanks to you being late.
Are there fries?
ewgh
Dave, this is my friend Craig.
FRIEND, huh?
Craig, this is Dave, my sister's husband.
So what's with the way you kids dress? Is it the "GRUNGE" thing?

267

269

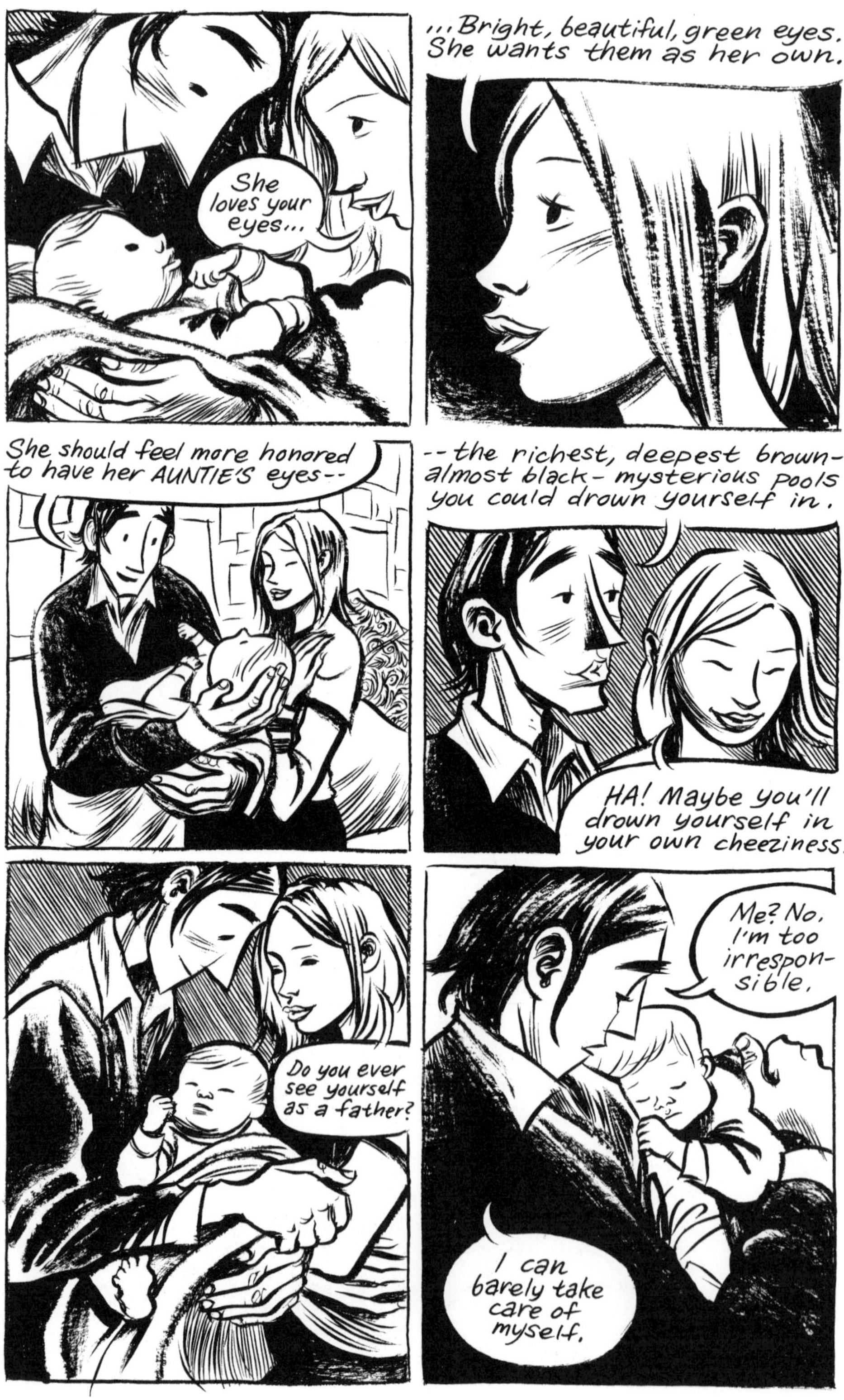
She loves your eyes...
...Bright, beautiful, green eyes. She wants them as her own.
She should feel more honored to have her AUNTIE'S eyes--
--the richest, deepest brown-almost black-mysterious pools you could drown yourself in.
HA! Maybe you'll drown yourself in your own cheeziness!
Do you ever see yourself as a father?
Me? No. I'm too irrespon-sible.
I can barely take care of myself.

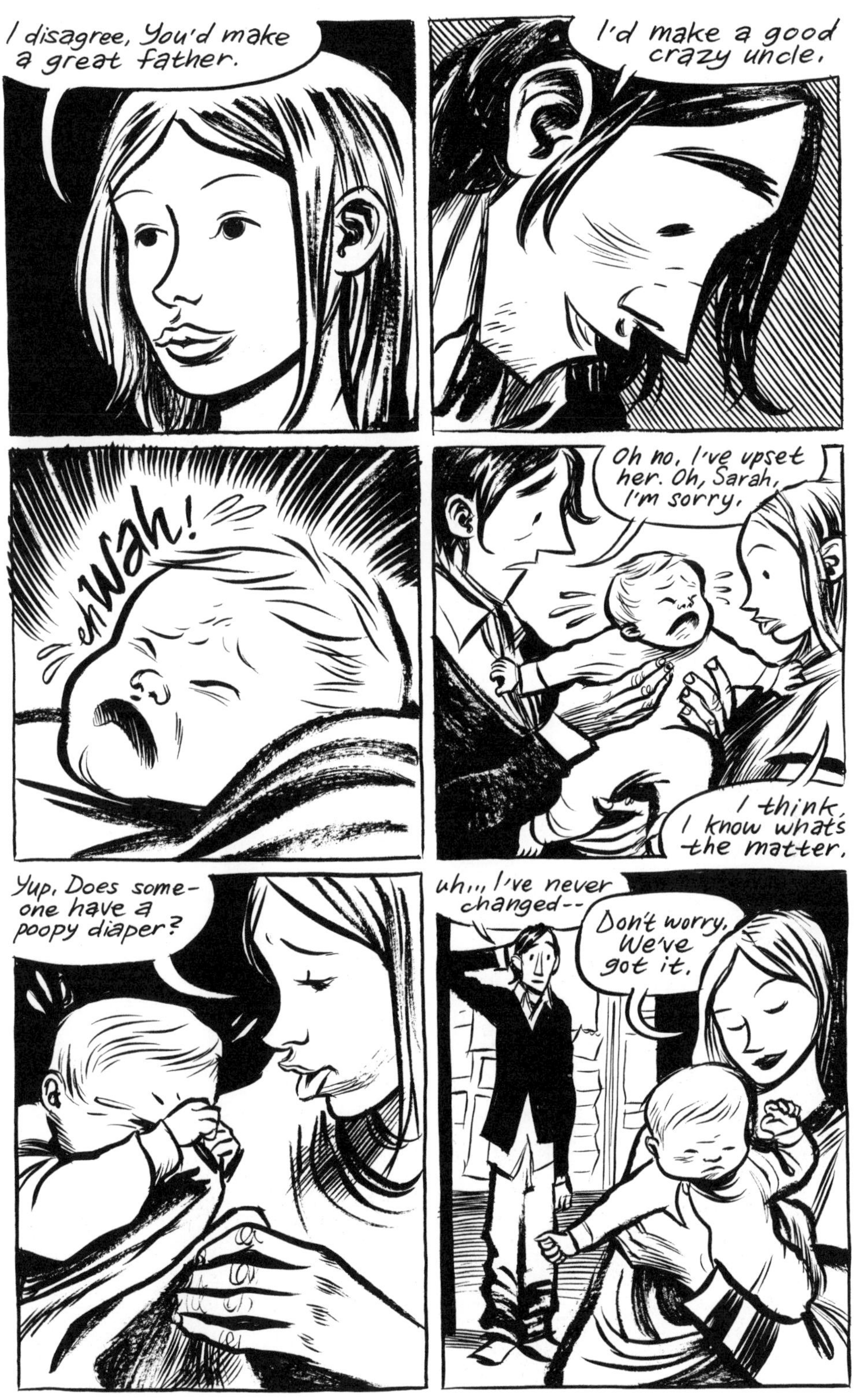
I disagree. You'd make a great father.
I'd make a good crazy uncle.
ehWah!
Oh no, I've upset her. Oh, Sarah, I'm sorry.
I think I know what's the matter.
Yup. Does some-one have a poopy diaper?
uh... I've never changed--
Don't worry. We've got it.

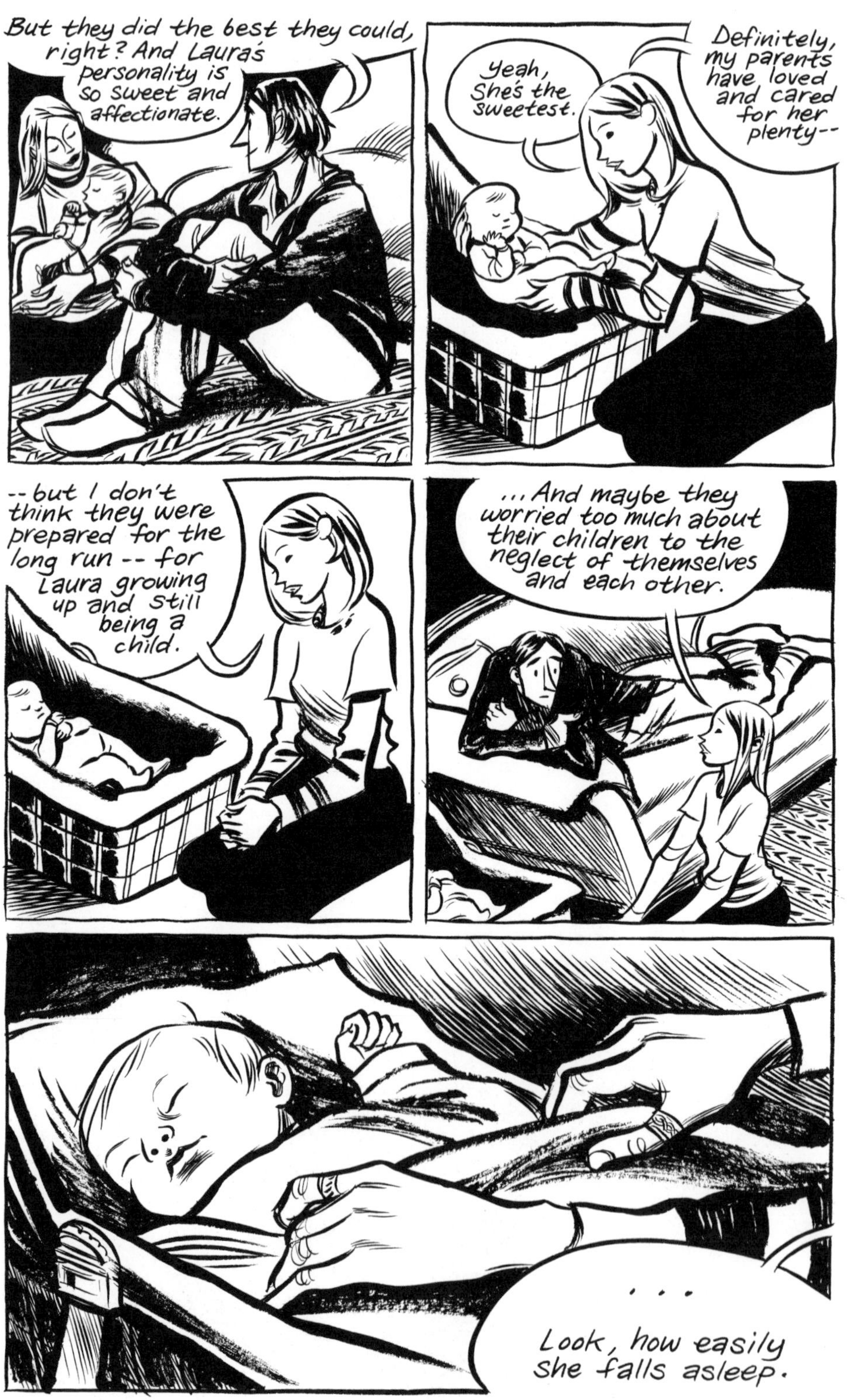
But they did the best they could, right? And Laura's personality is so sweet and affectionate.
Yeah, She's the sweetest.
Definitely, my parents have loved and cared for her plenty--
--but I don't think they were prepared for the long run -- for Laura growing up and still being a child.
...And maybe they worried too much about their children to the neglect of themselves and each other.
. . .
Look, how easily she falls asleep.

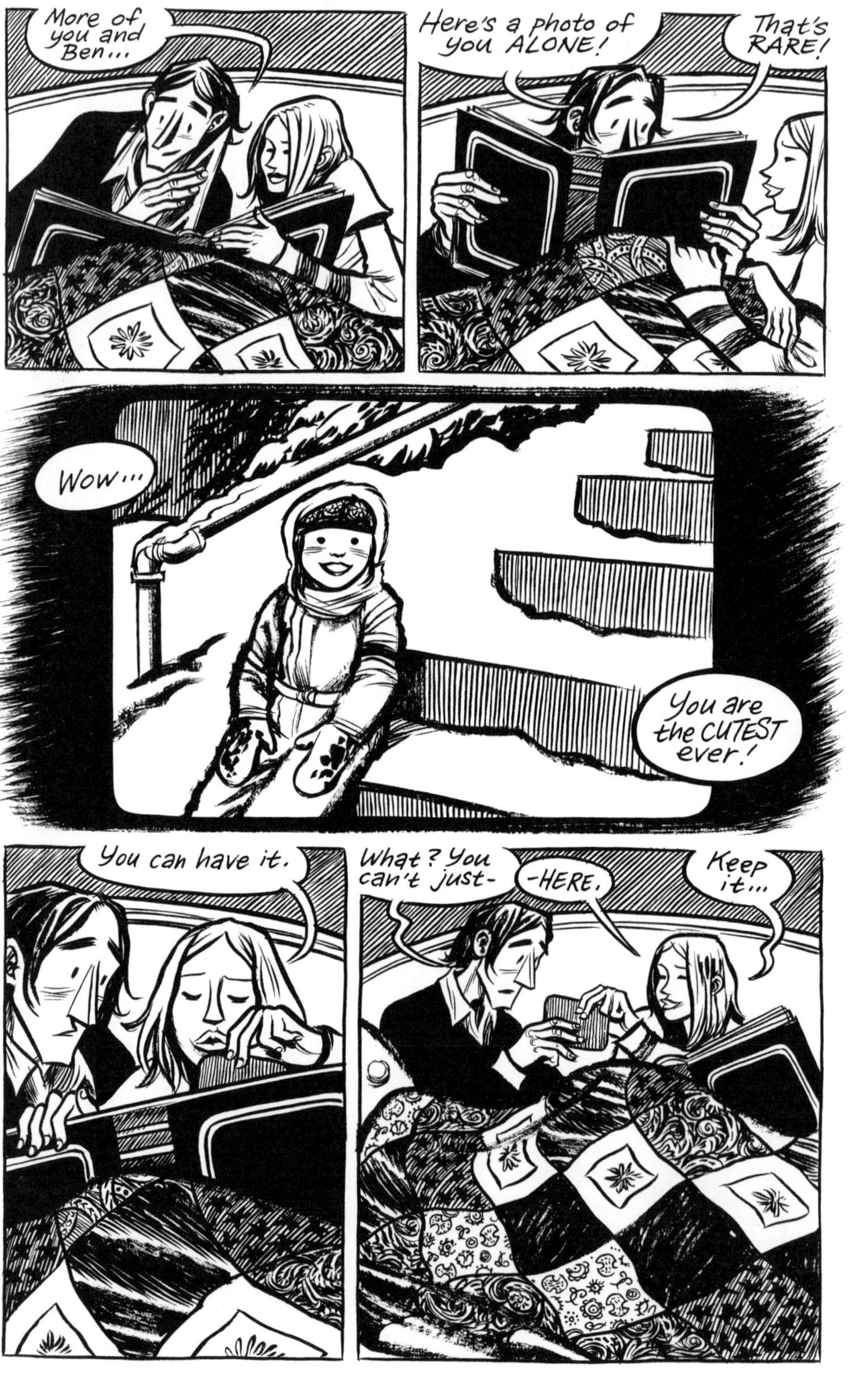
More of you and Ben...
Here's a photo of you ALONE!
That's RARE!
Wow...
You are the CUTEST ever!
You can have it.
What? You can't just-
-HERE.
Keep it...

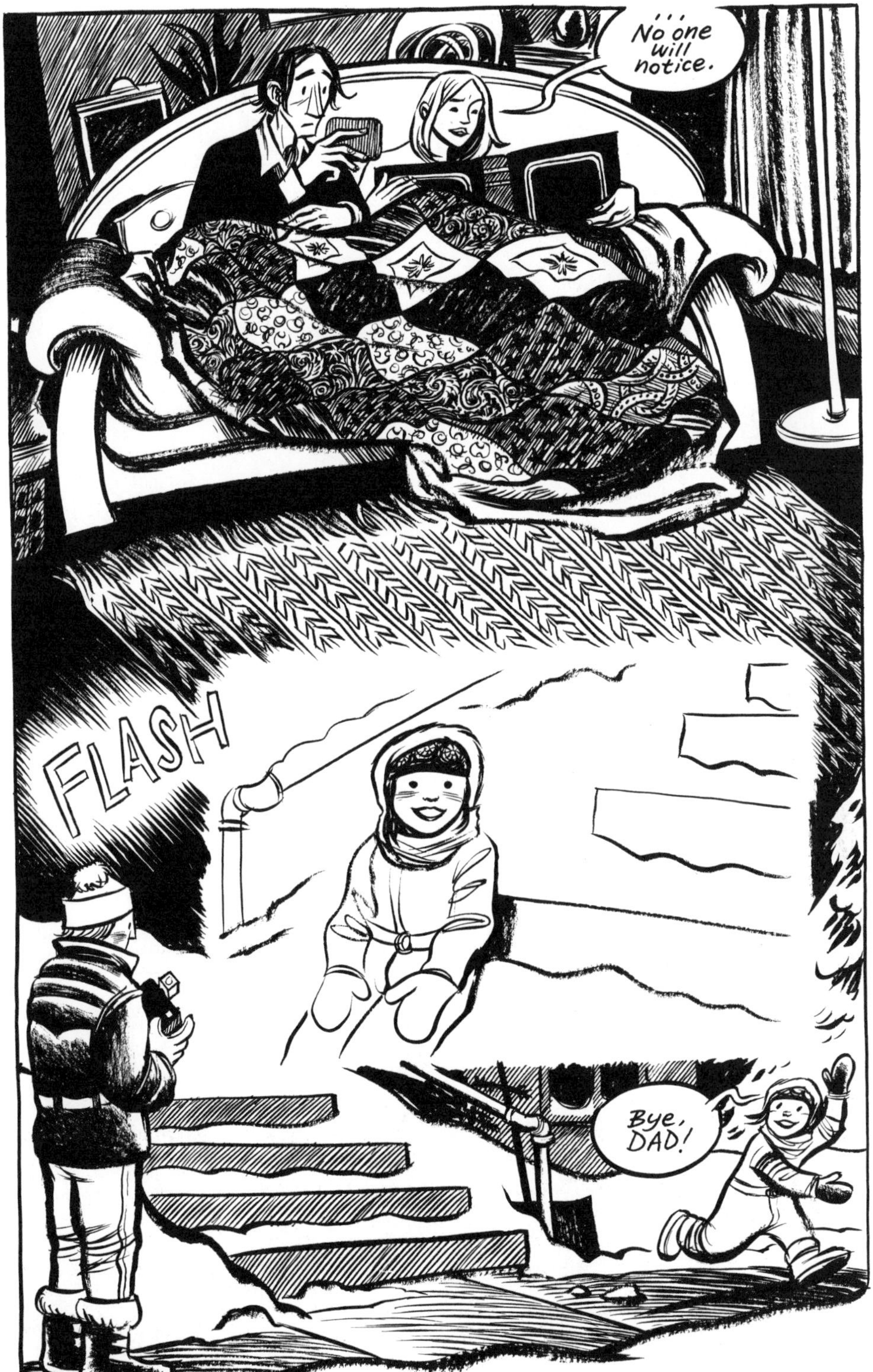
... No one will notice.
FLASH
Bye, DAD!

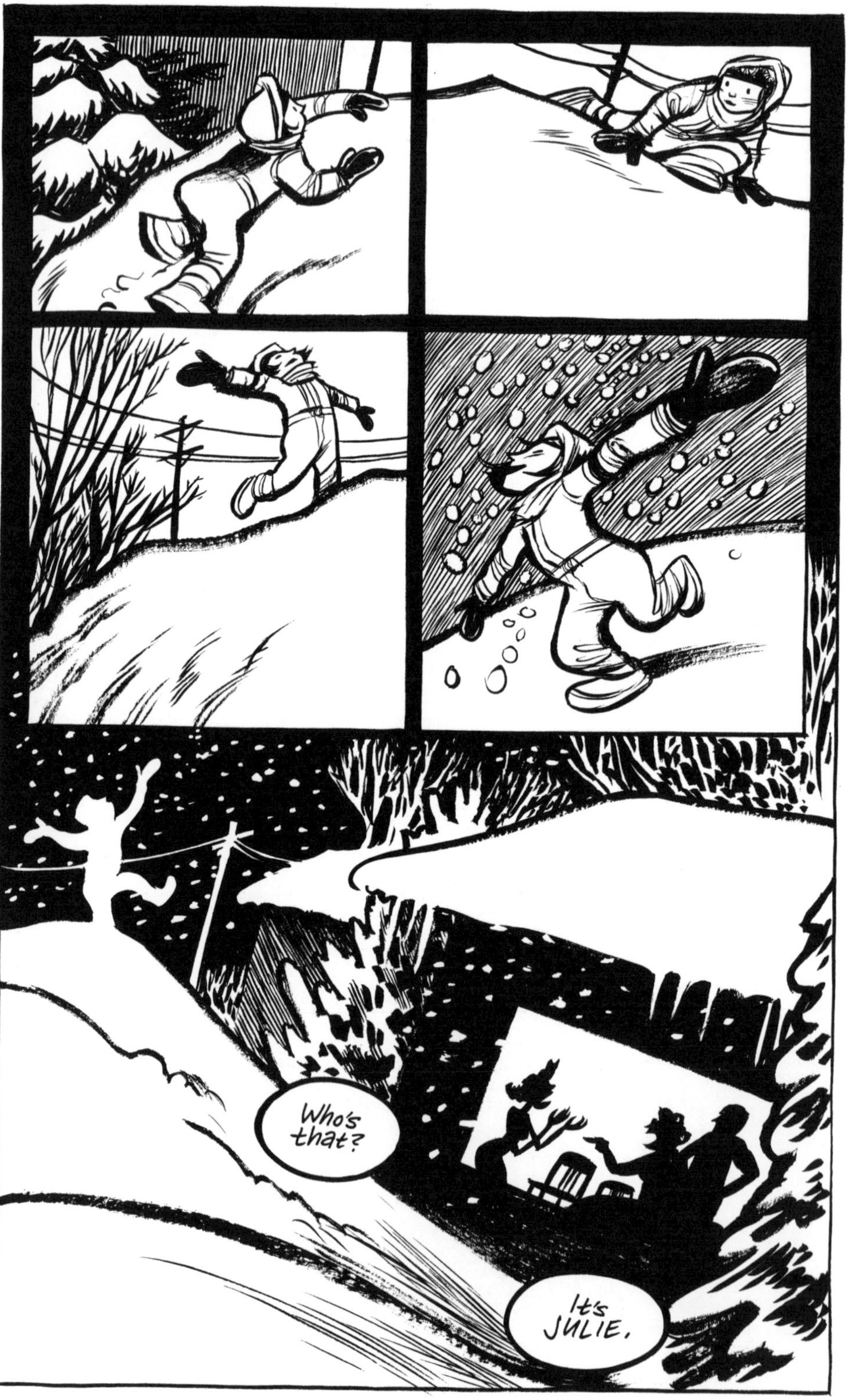
Who's that?
It's JULIE.

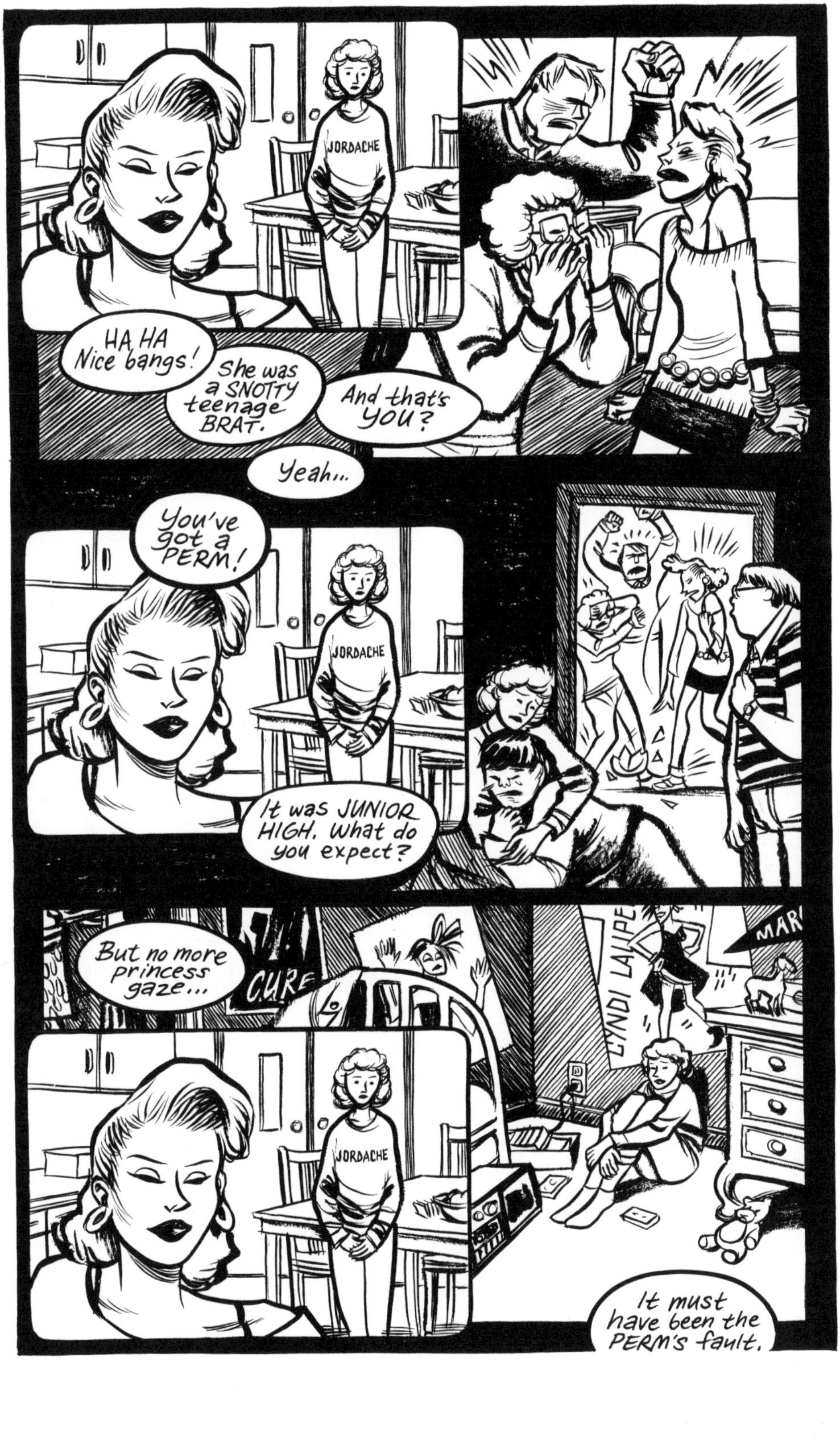
JORDACHE
HA HA Nice bangs!
She was a SNOTTY teenage BRAT.
And that's YOU?
Yeah...
You've got a PERM!
JORDACHE
It was JUNIOR HIGH. What do you expect?
But no more princess gaze...
CURE
JORDACHE
It must have been the PERM's fault.

283

285

287

Soon after, Steve, Laura, and Ben returned, and—nearly simultaneously—Julie and Dave. The kitchen was a jungle of jangling car keys and awkward conversation.

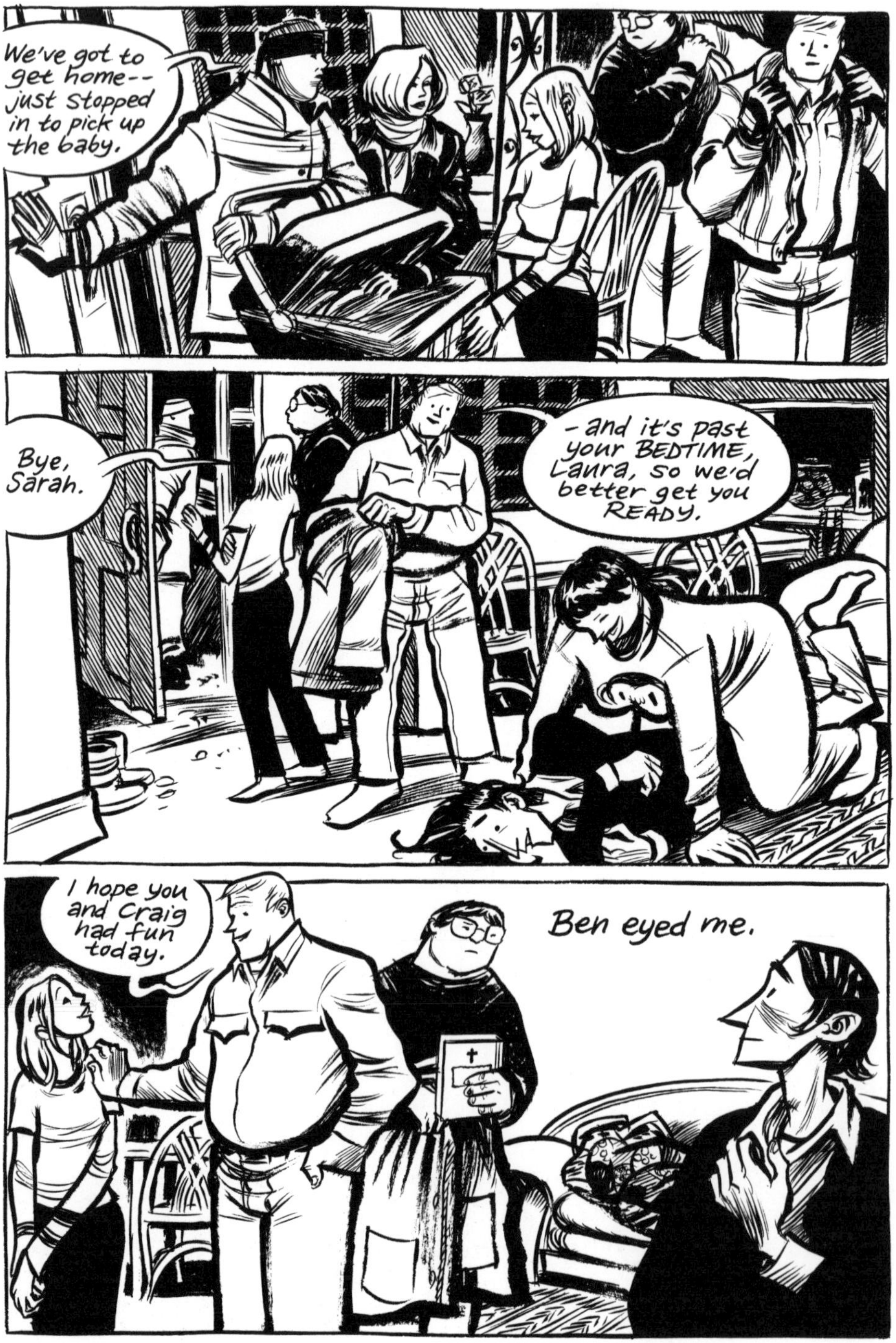
We've got to get home--just stopped in to pick up the baby.
Bye, Sarah.
-and it's past your BEDTIME, Laura, so we'd better get you READY.
I hope you and Craig had fun today.
Ben eyed me.

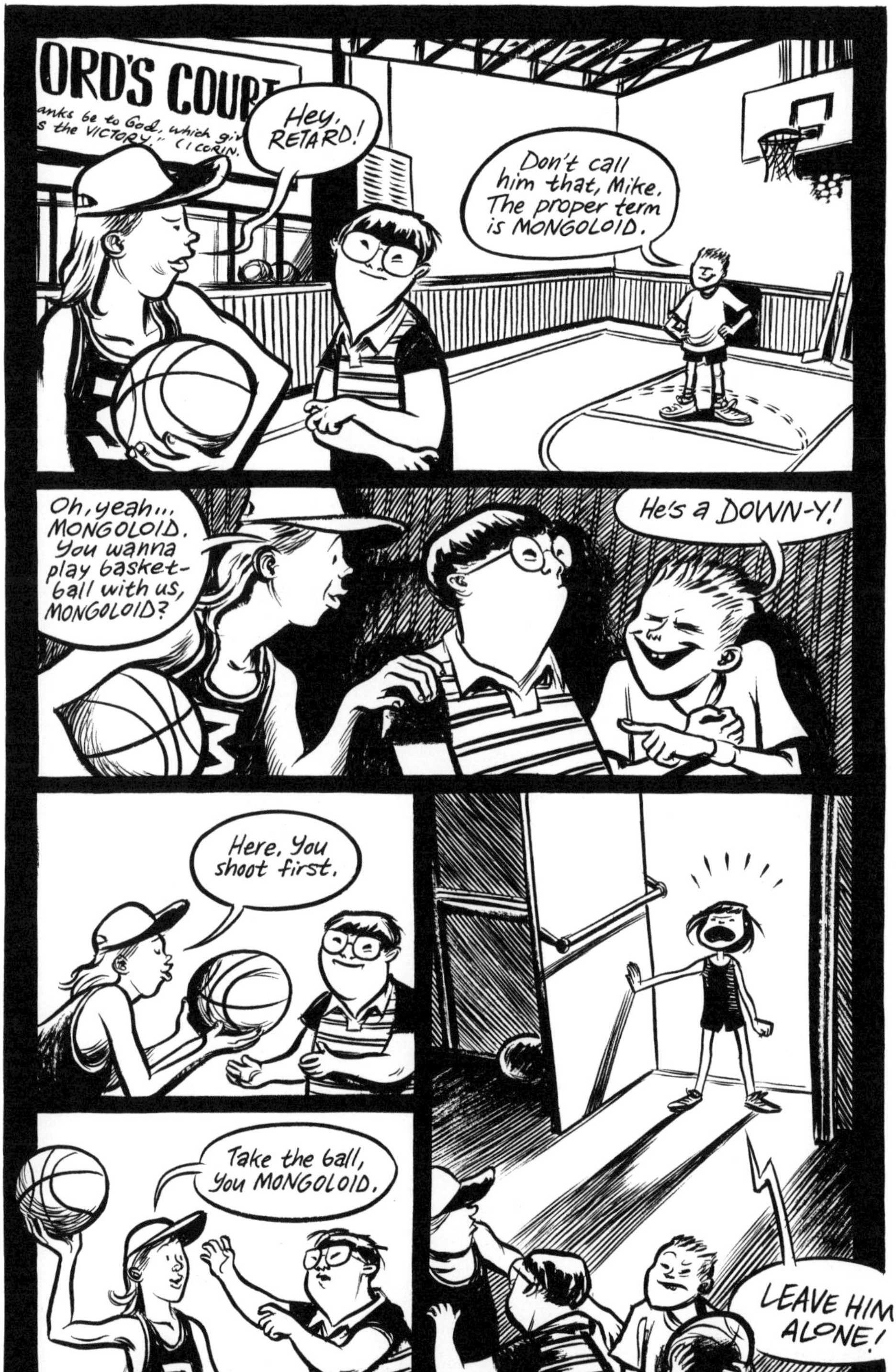
ORD'S COURT
anks be to God, which giv
s the VICTORY." (I CORIN.
Hey, RETARD!
Don't call him that, Mike. The proper term is MONGOLOID.
Oh, yeah... MONGOLOID. You wanna play basket-ball with us, MONGOLOID?
He's a DOWN-Y!
Here. You shoot first.
Take the ball, You MONGOLOID.
LEAVE HIM ALONE!

290

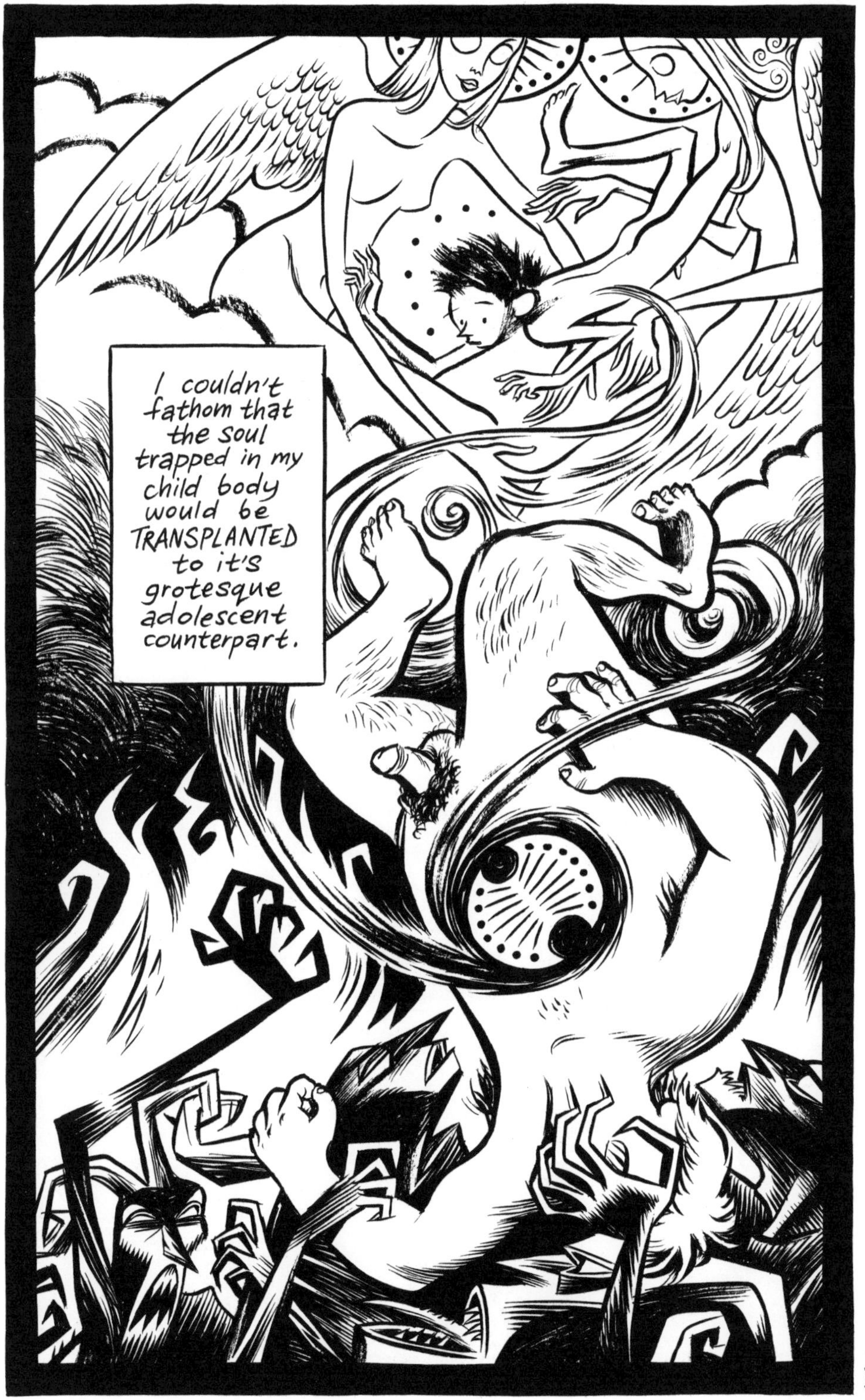
I couldn't fathom that the soul trapped in my child body would be TRANSPLANTED to it's grotesque adolescent counterpart.

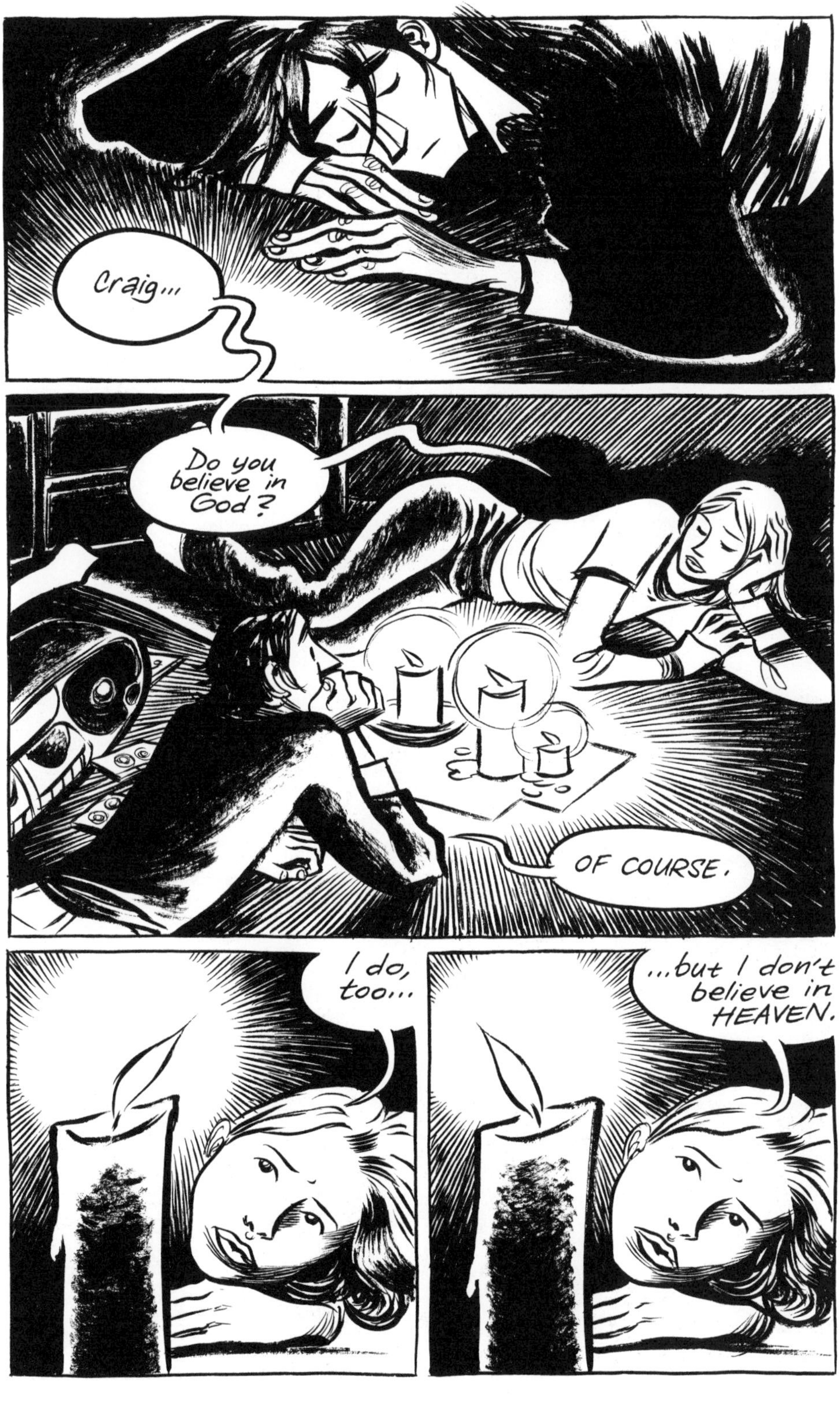
Craig...
Do you believe in God?
OF COURSE.
I do, too...
...but I don't believe in HEAVEN.

297

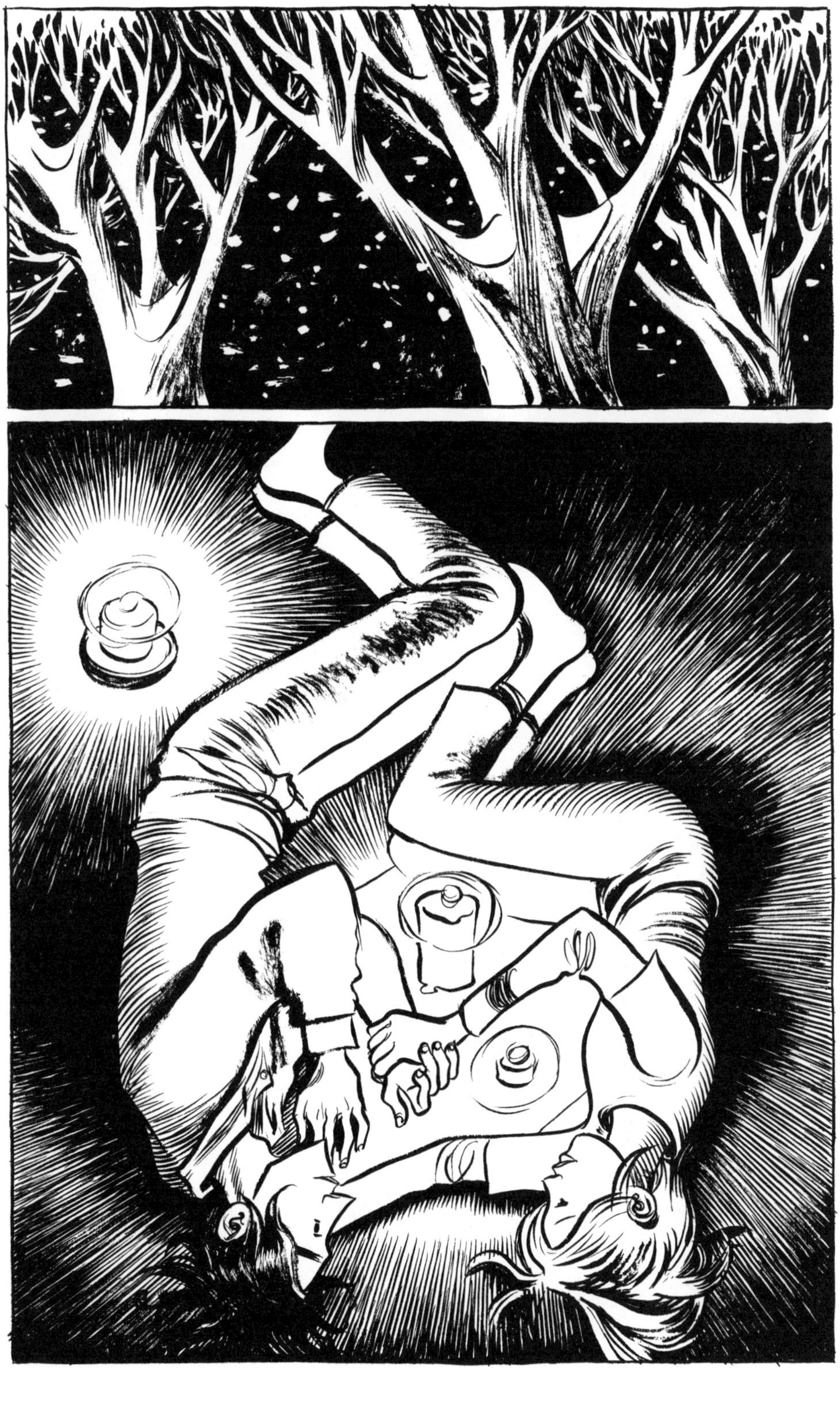

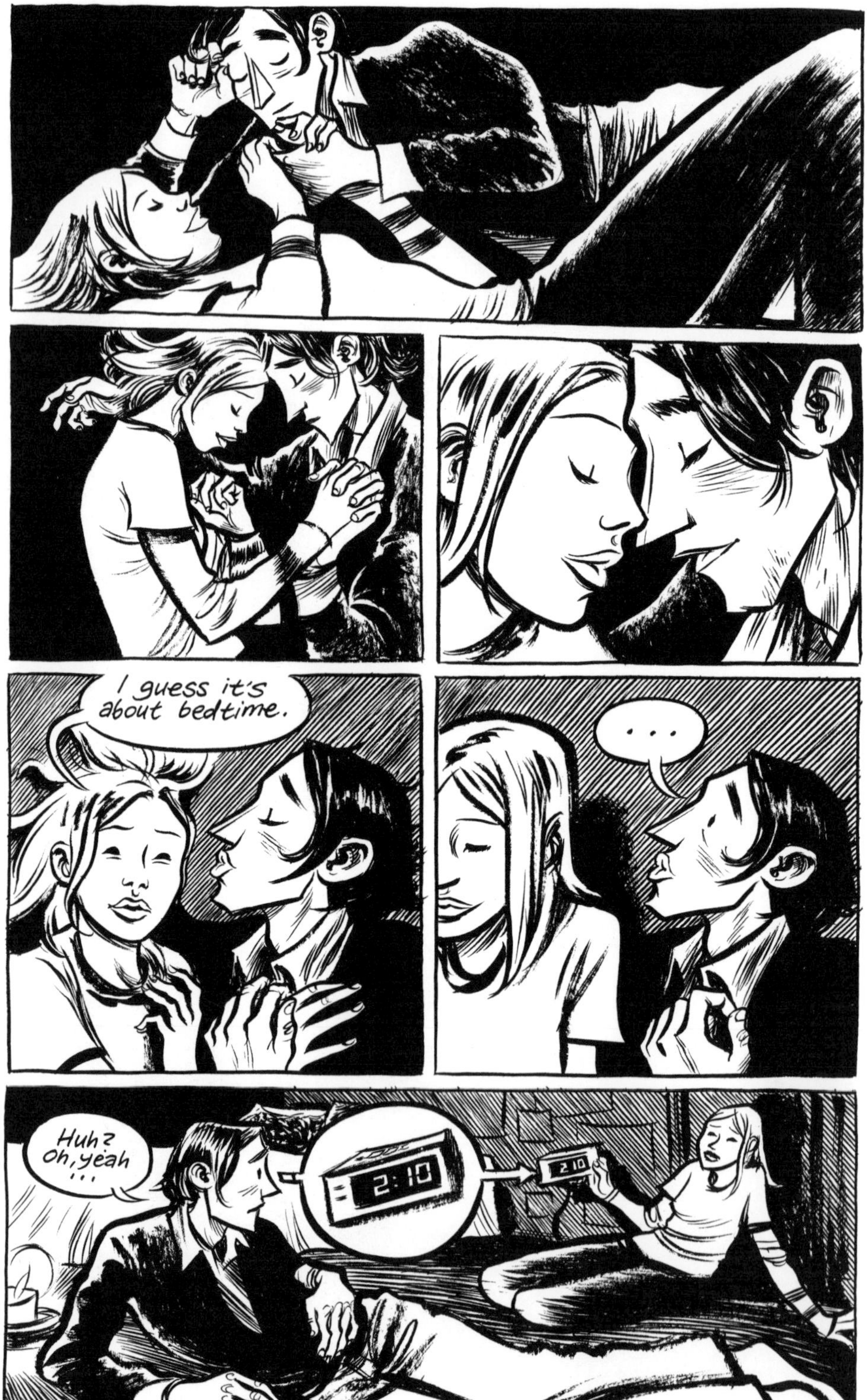
I guess it's about bedtime.
...
Huh? Oh, yeah ...
2:10

303

305

307

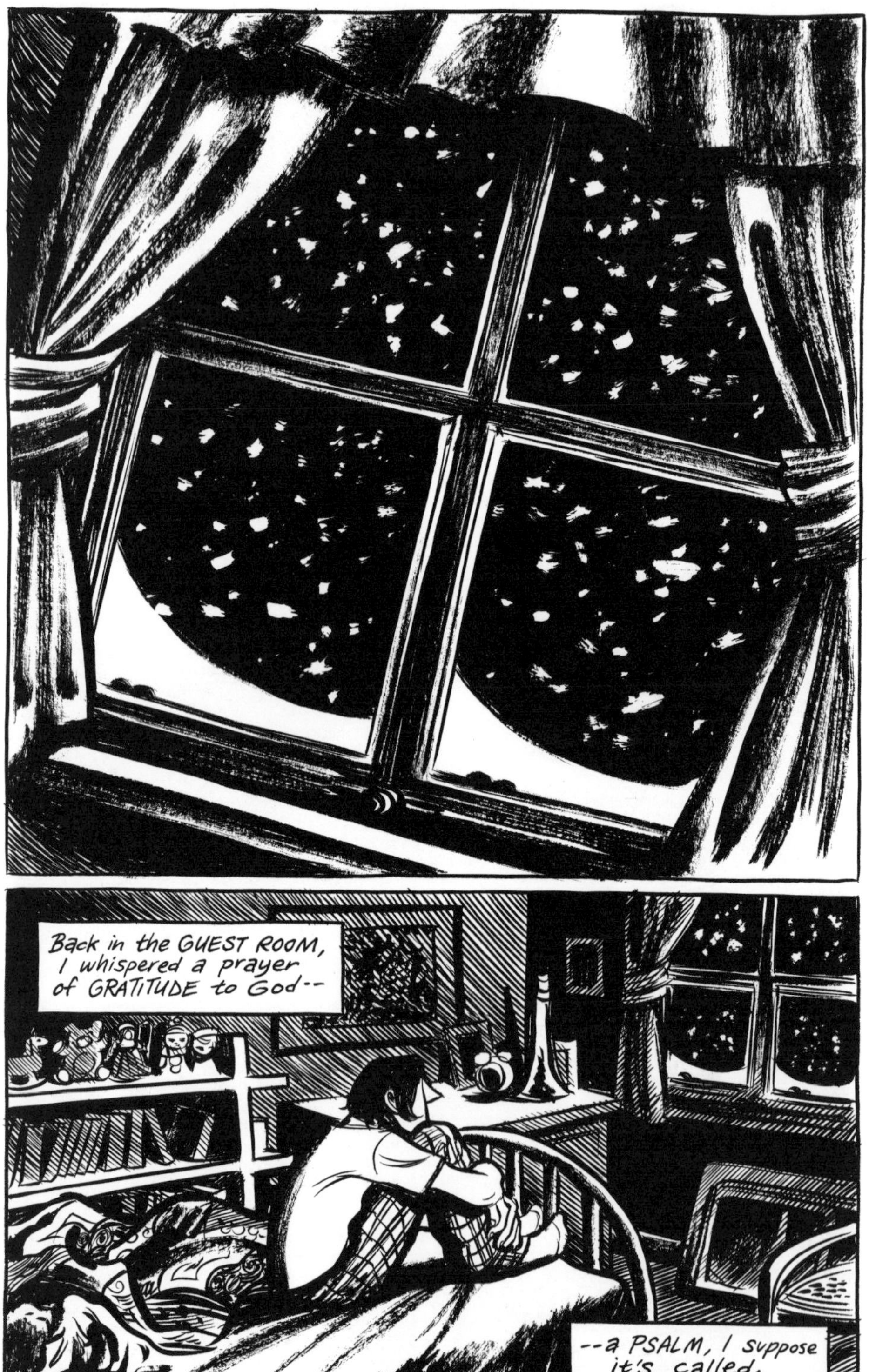
Back in the GUEST ROOM, I whispered a prayer of GRATITUDE to God--
--a PSALM, I suppose it's called.

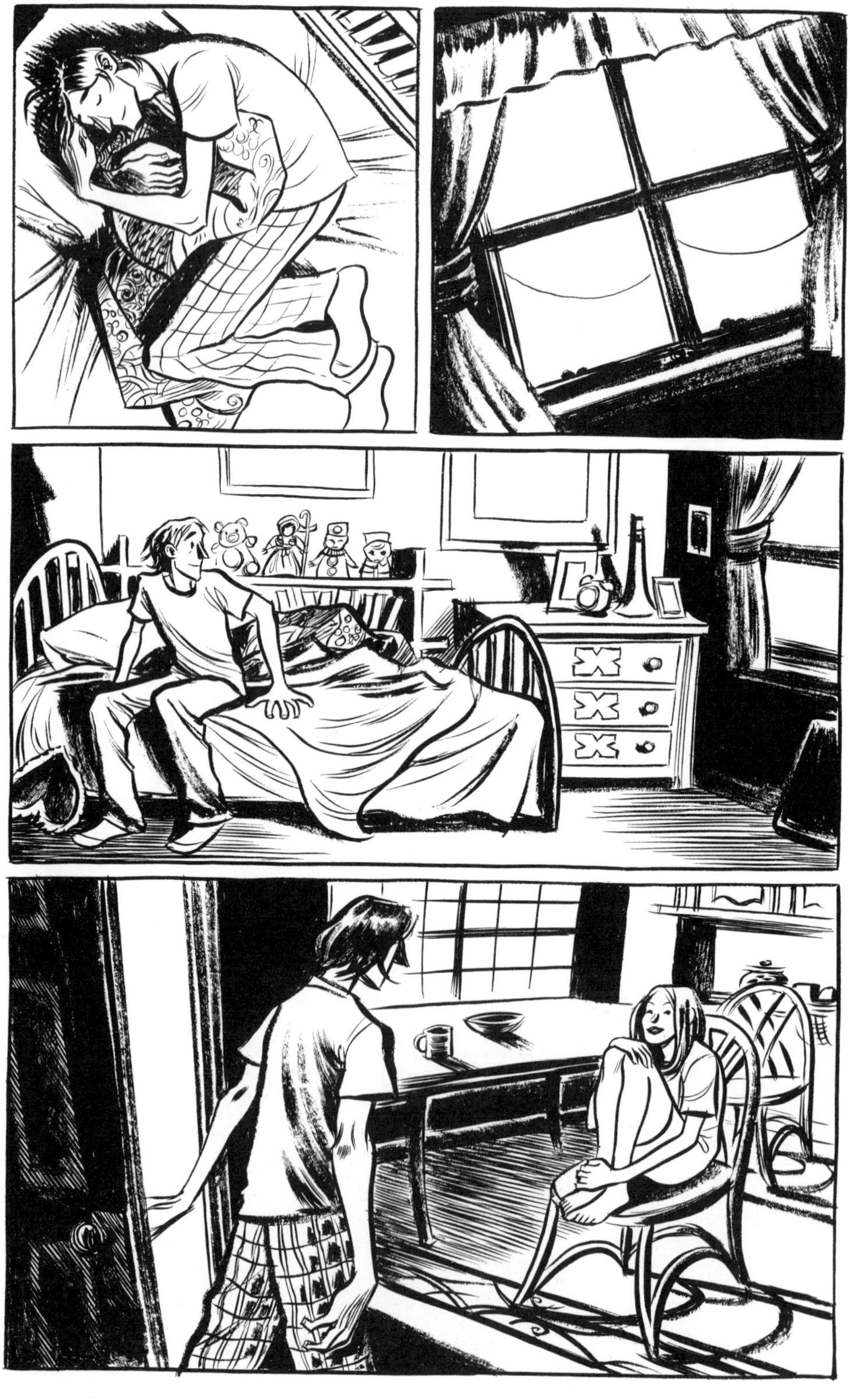

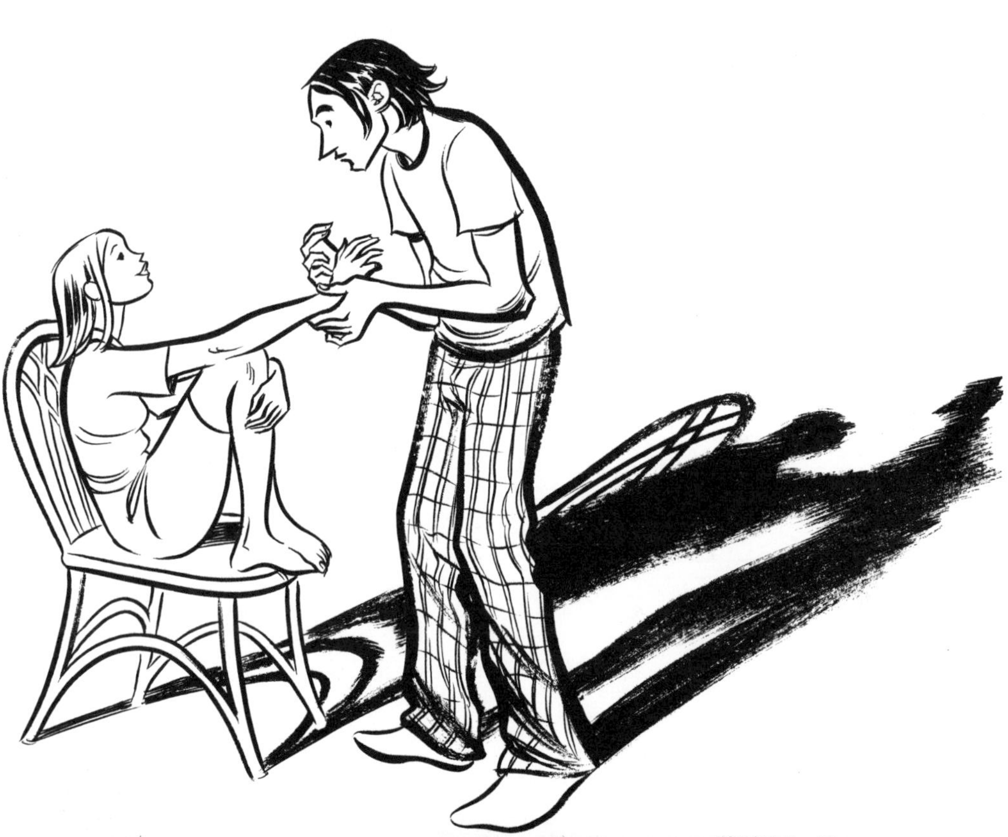

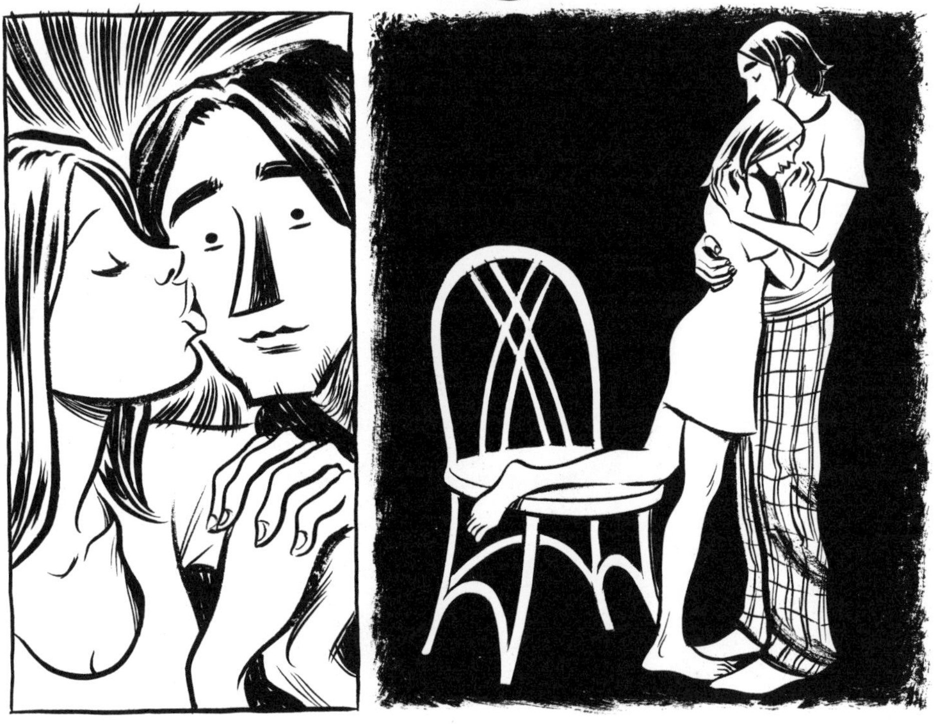

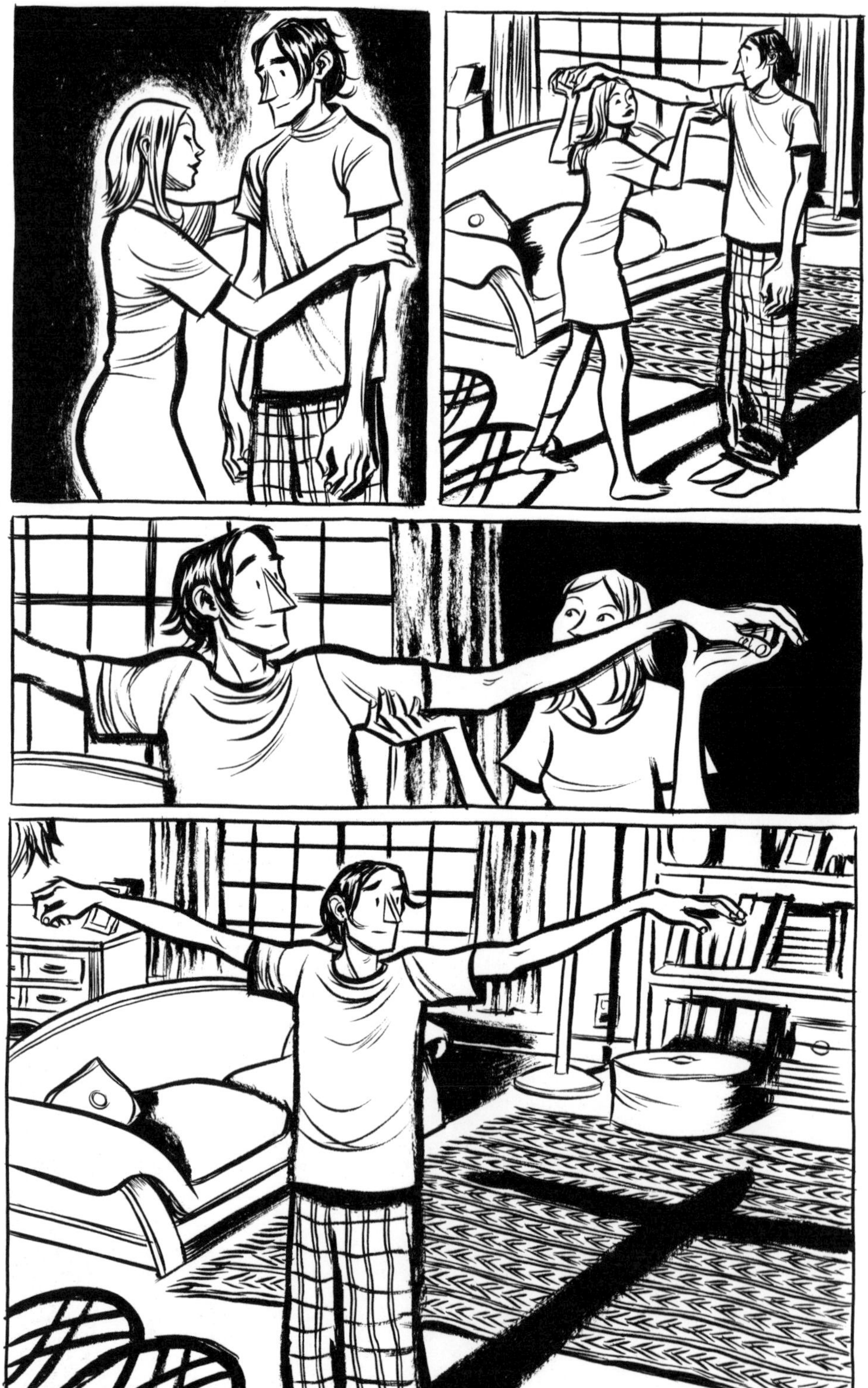

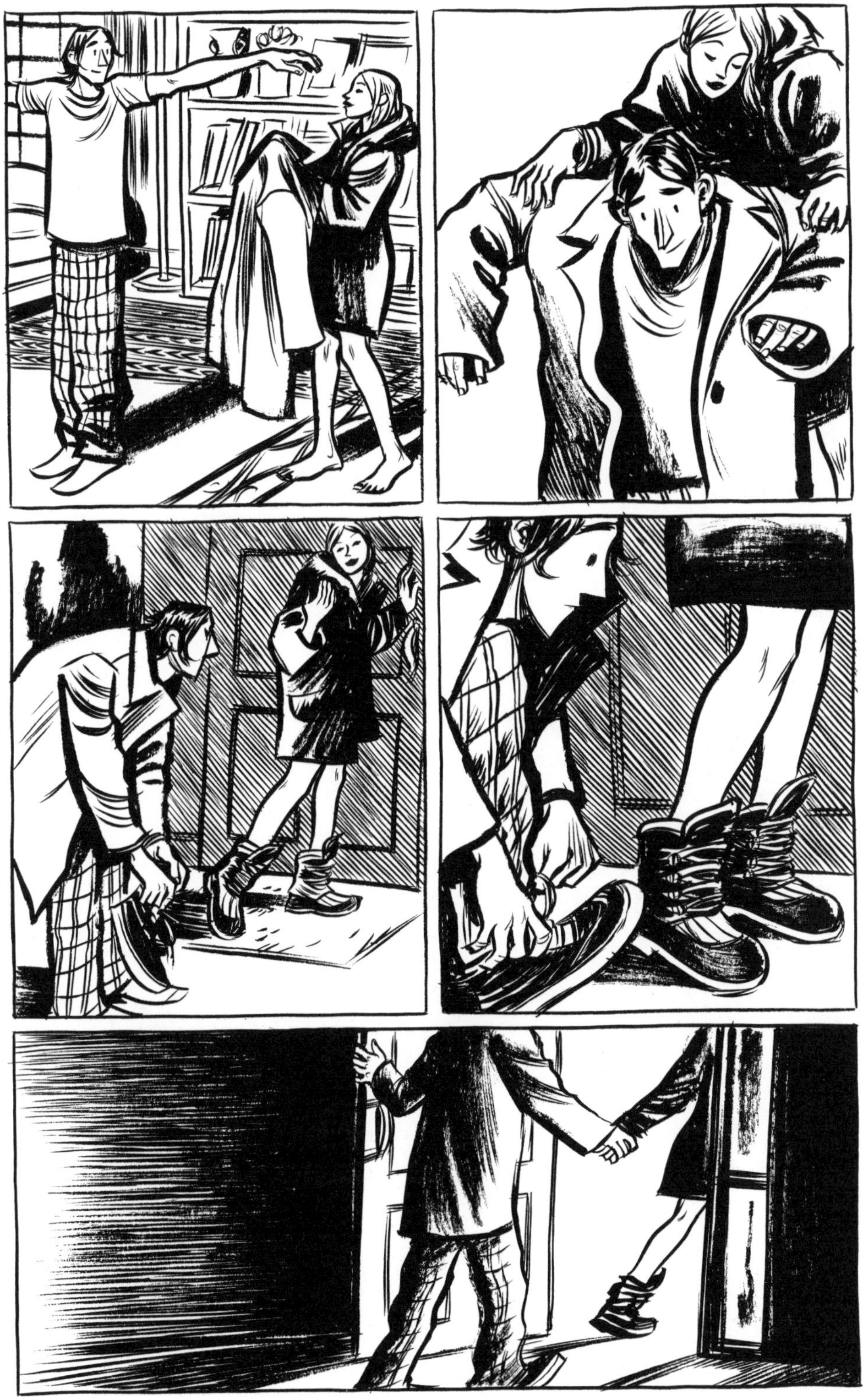

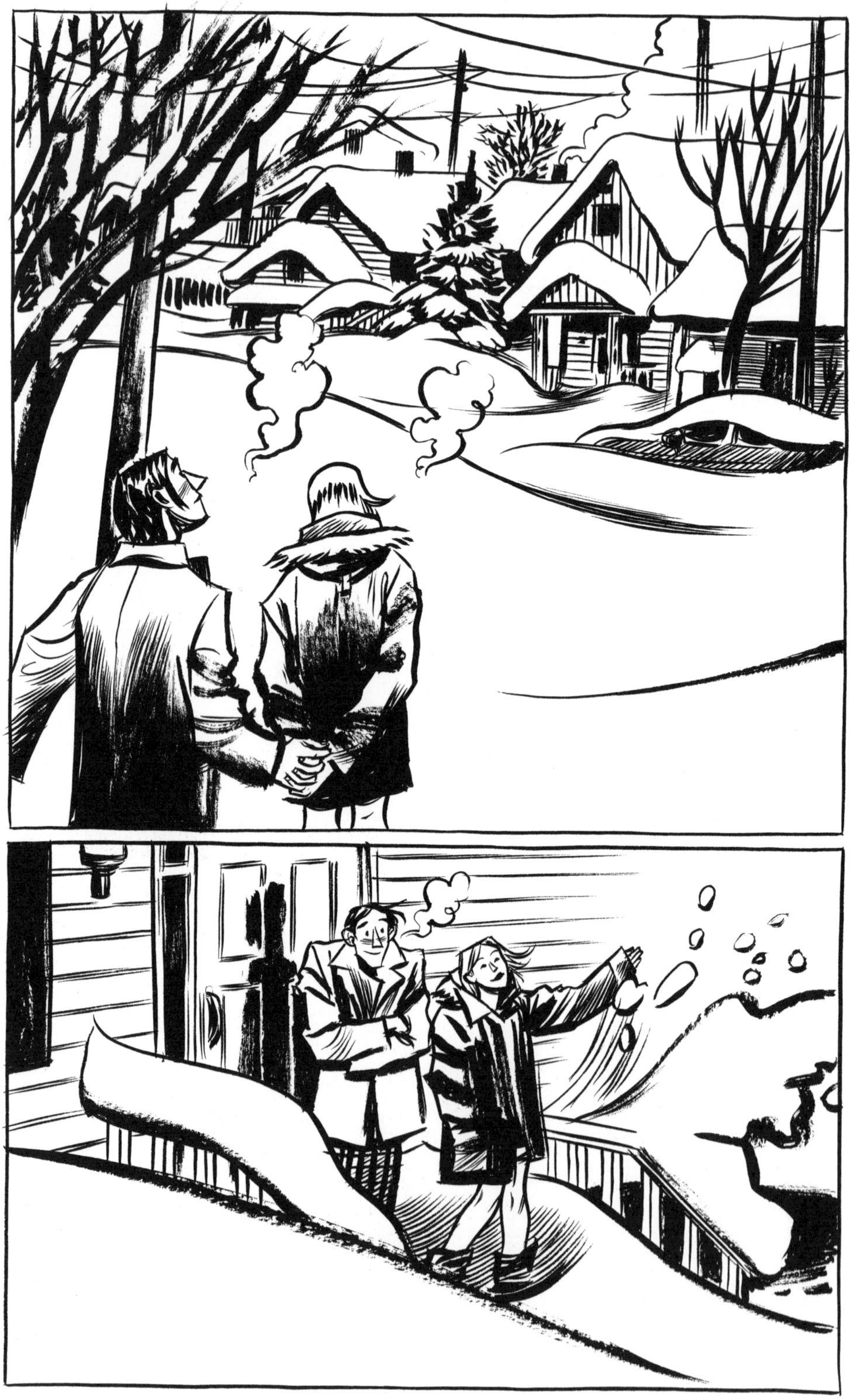

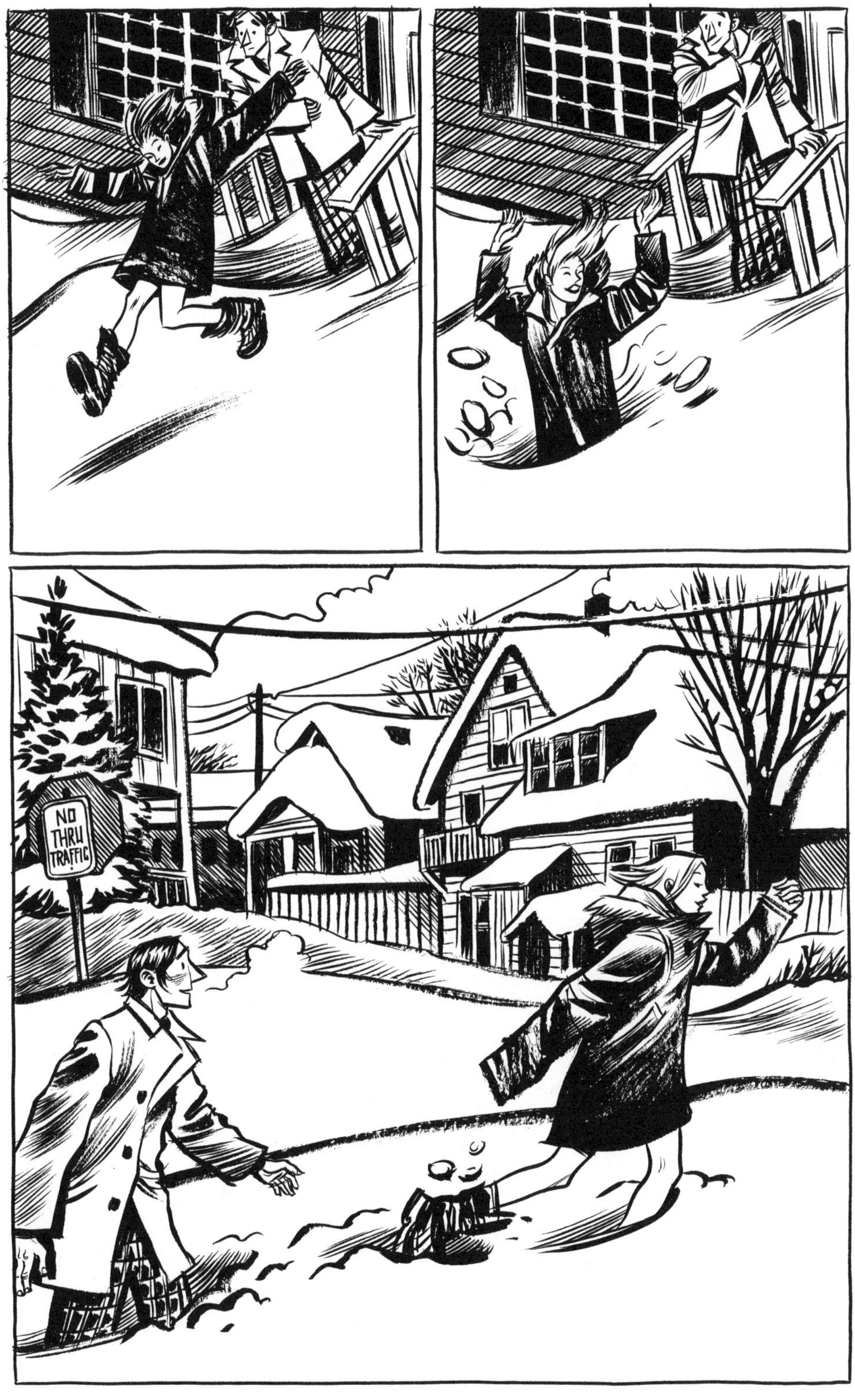
NO THRU TRAFFIC

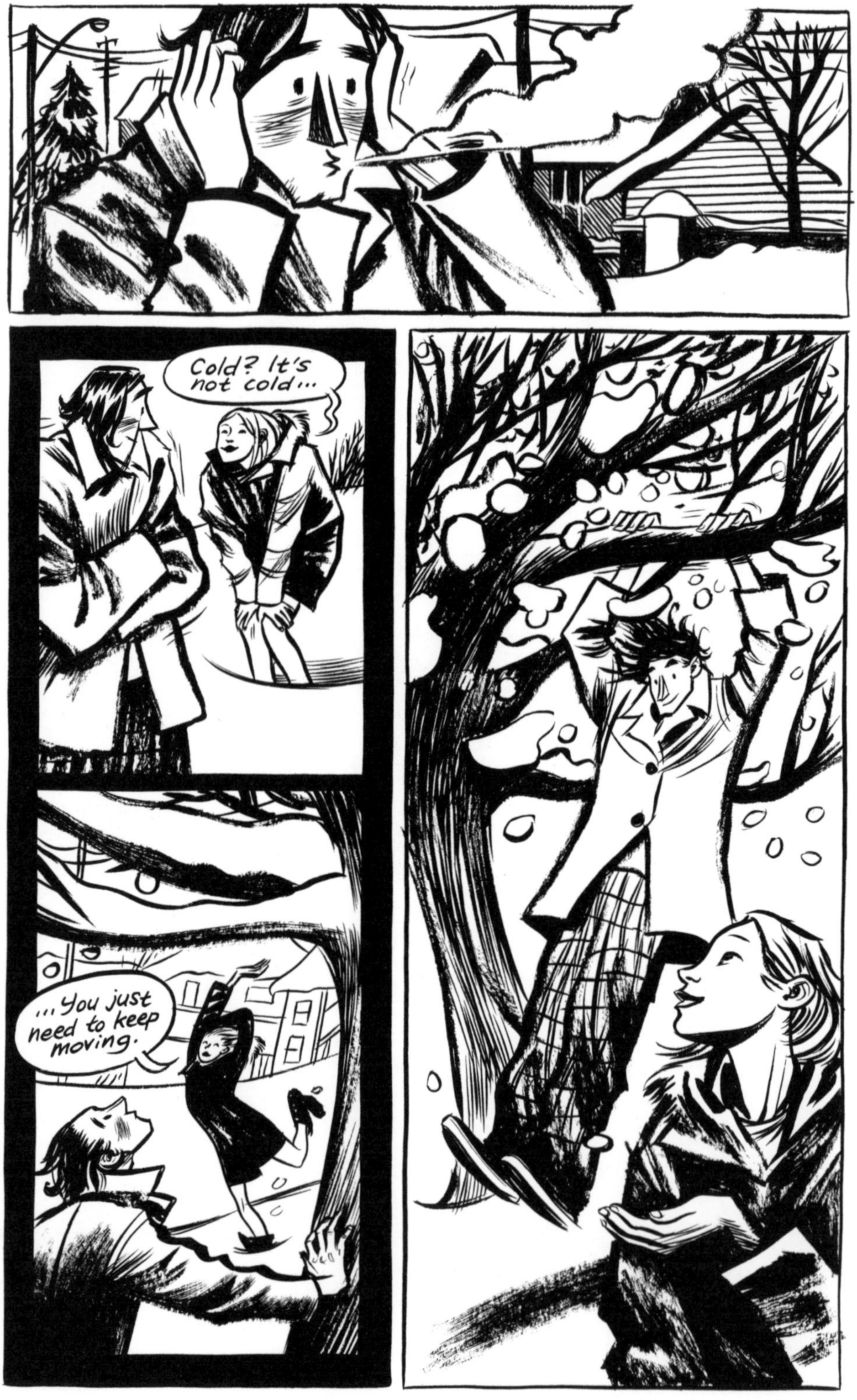
Cold? It's not cold...
...You just need to keep moving.

VI

Teen
Spirit

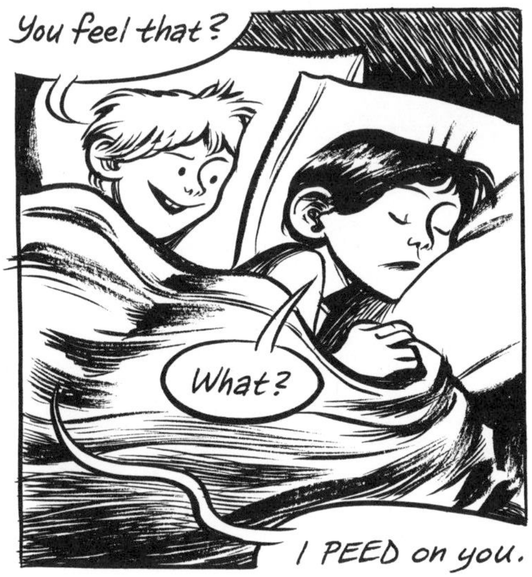
You feel that?
What?
I PEED on you.

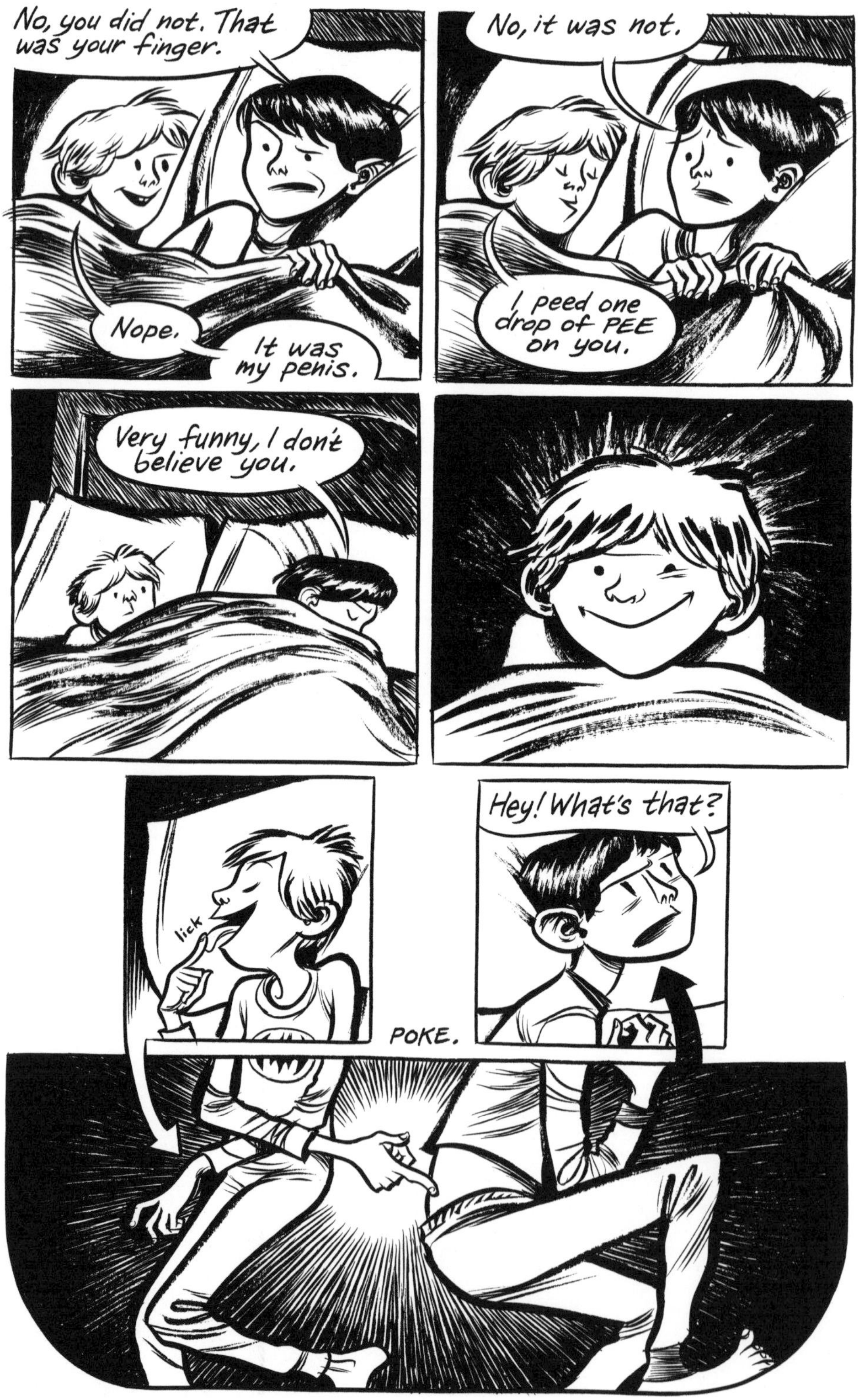
No, you did not. That was your finger.
Nope.
It was my penis.
No, it was not.
I peed one drop of PEE on you.
Very funny, I don't believe you.
lick
Hey! What's that?
POKE.

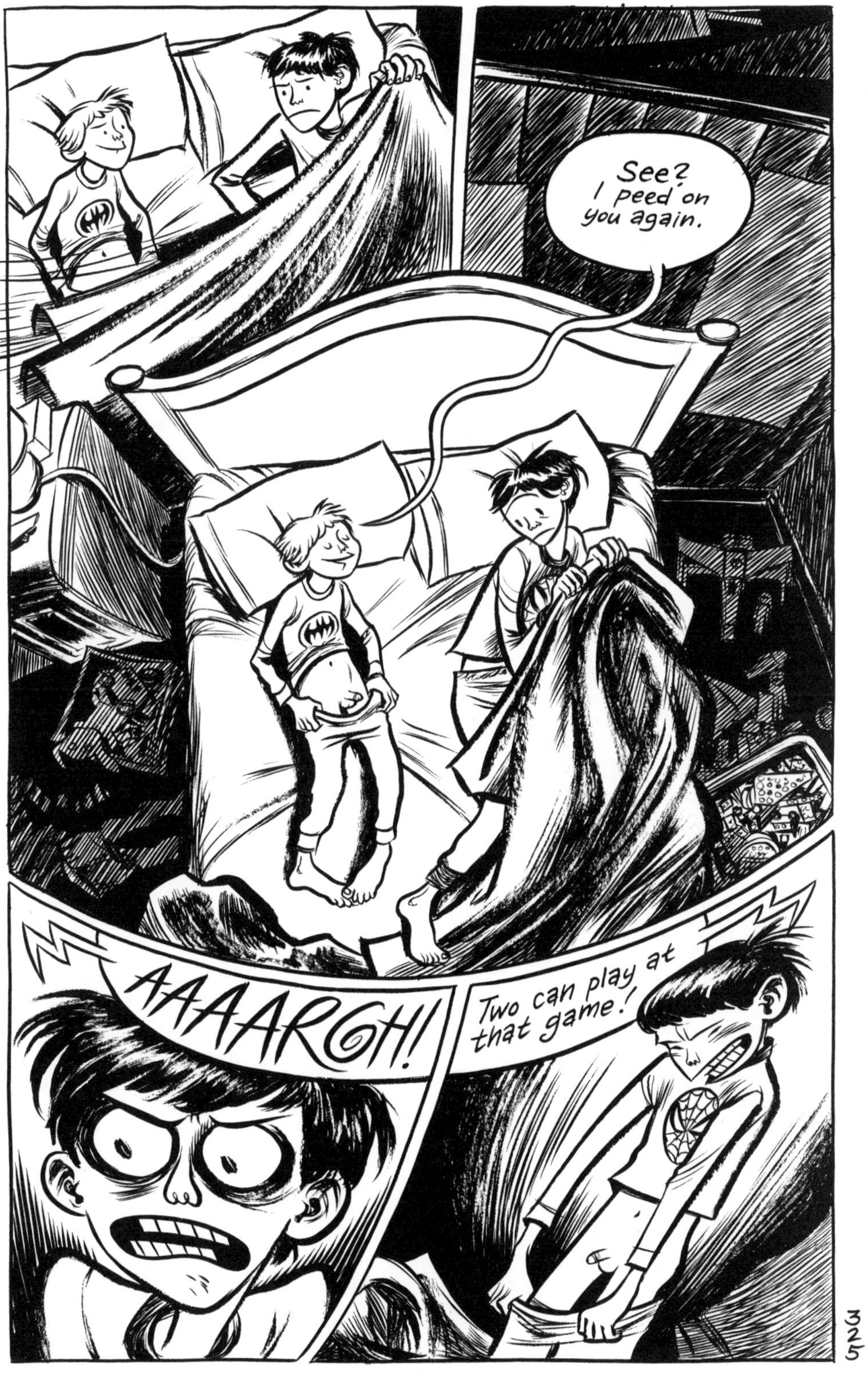
See? I peed on you again.
AAAARGH!
Two can play at that game!

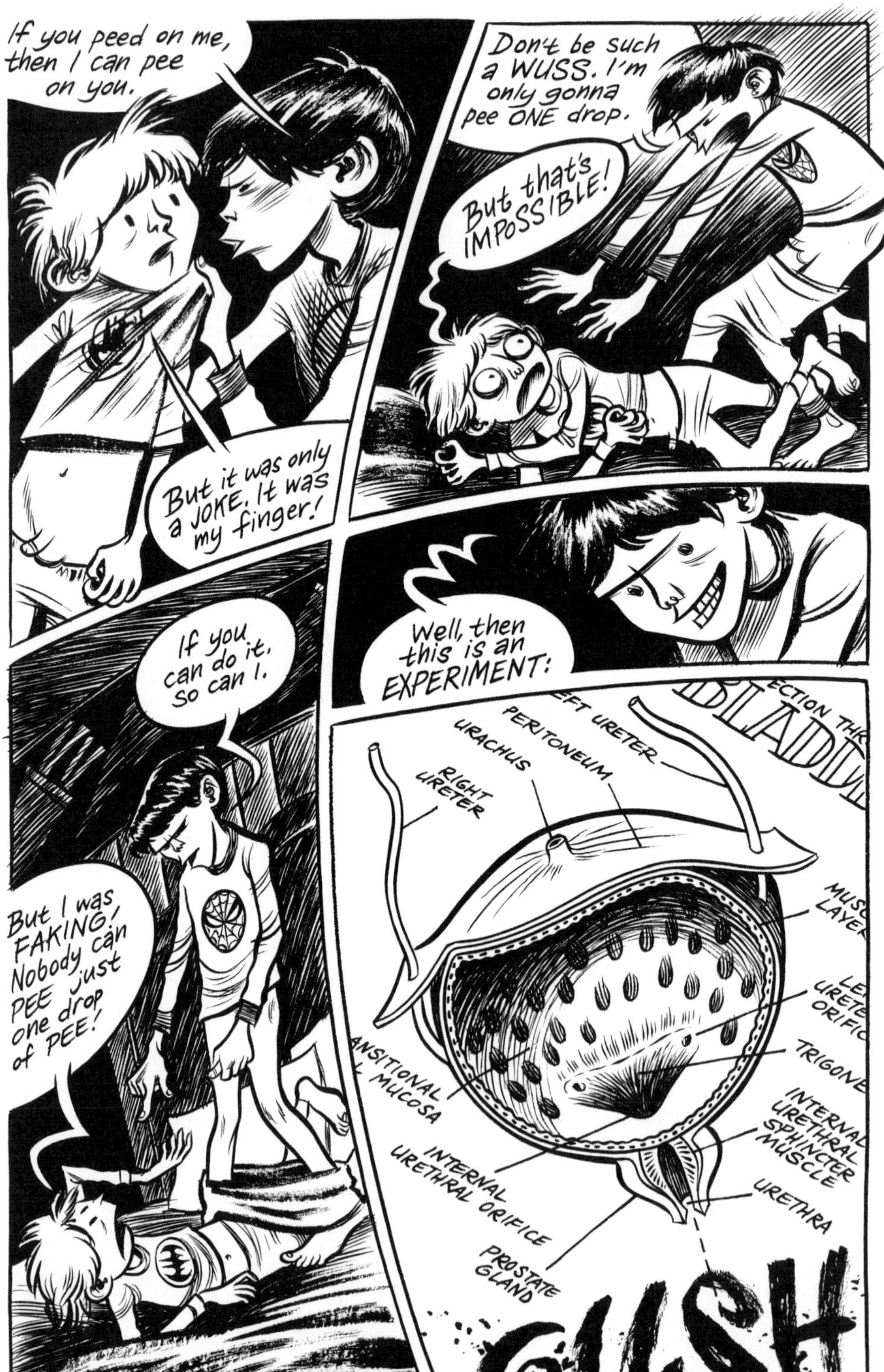
If you peed on me, then I can pee on you.
But it was only a JOKE. It was my finger!
Don't be such a WUSS. I'm only gonna pee ONE drop.
But that's IMPOSSIBLE!
Well, then this is an EXPERIMENT:
If you can do it, so can I.
But I was FAKING! Nobody can PEE just one drop of PEE!
PERITONEUM
URACHUS
RIGHT URETER
TRIGONE
INTERNAL URETHRAL SPHINCTER MUSCLE
URETHRA
INTERNAL URETHRAL ORIFICE
PROSTATE GLAND
GUSH

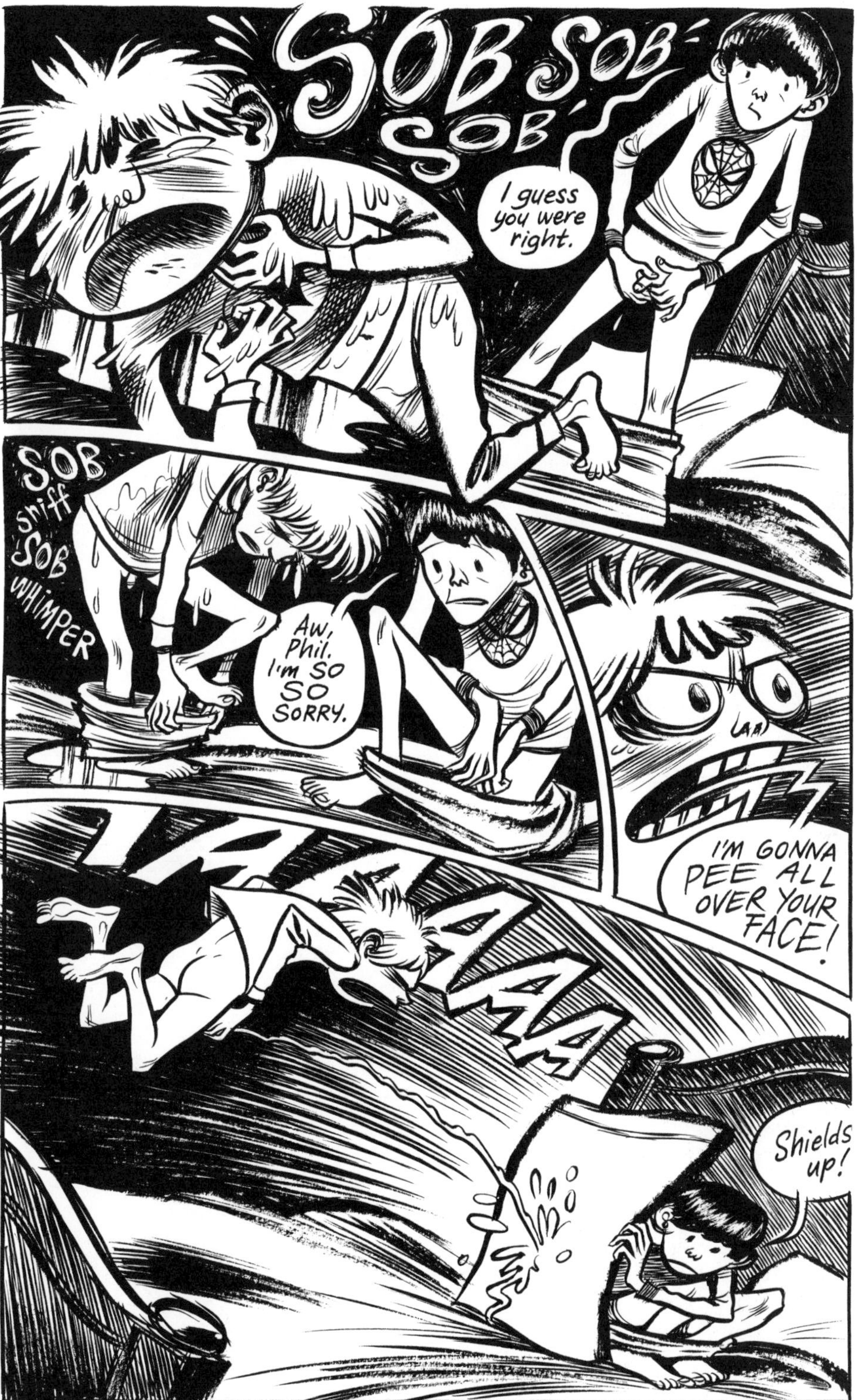
SOB SOB SOB
I guess you were right.
SOB sniff SOB WHIMPER
Aw, Phil. I'm SO SO SORRY.
I'M GONNA PEE ALL OVER YOUR FACE!
YAAAAAAA
Shields up!

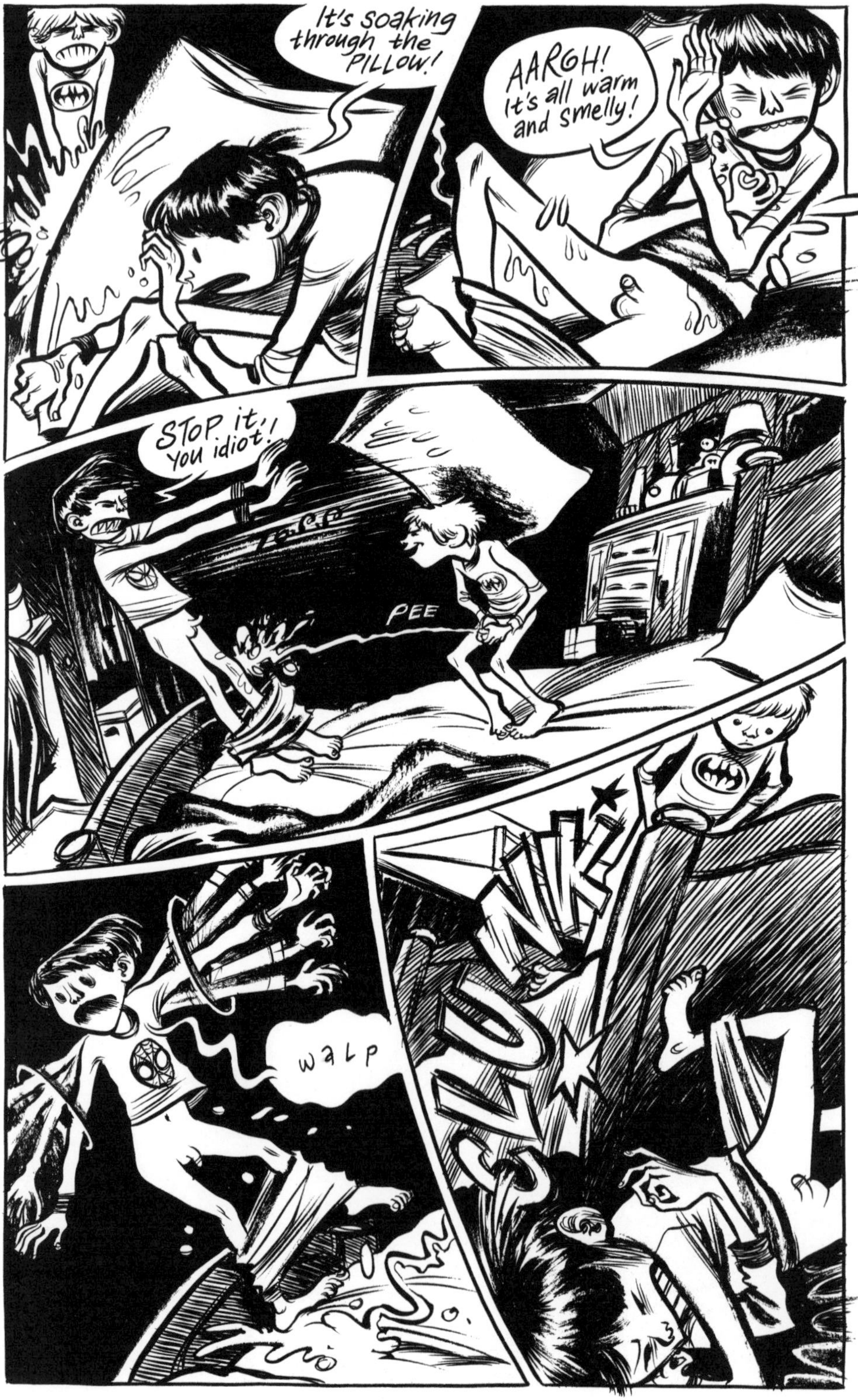
It's soaking through the PILLOW!
AARGH! It's all warm and smelly!
STOP it, you idiot!
PEE
walp
CLUNK!

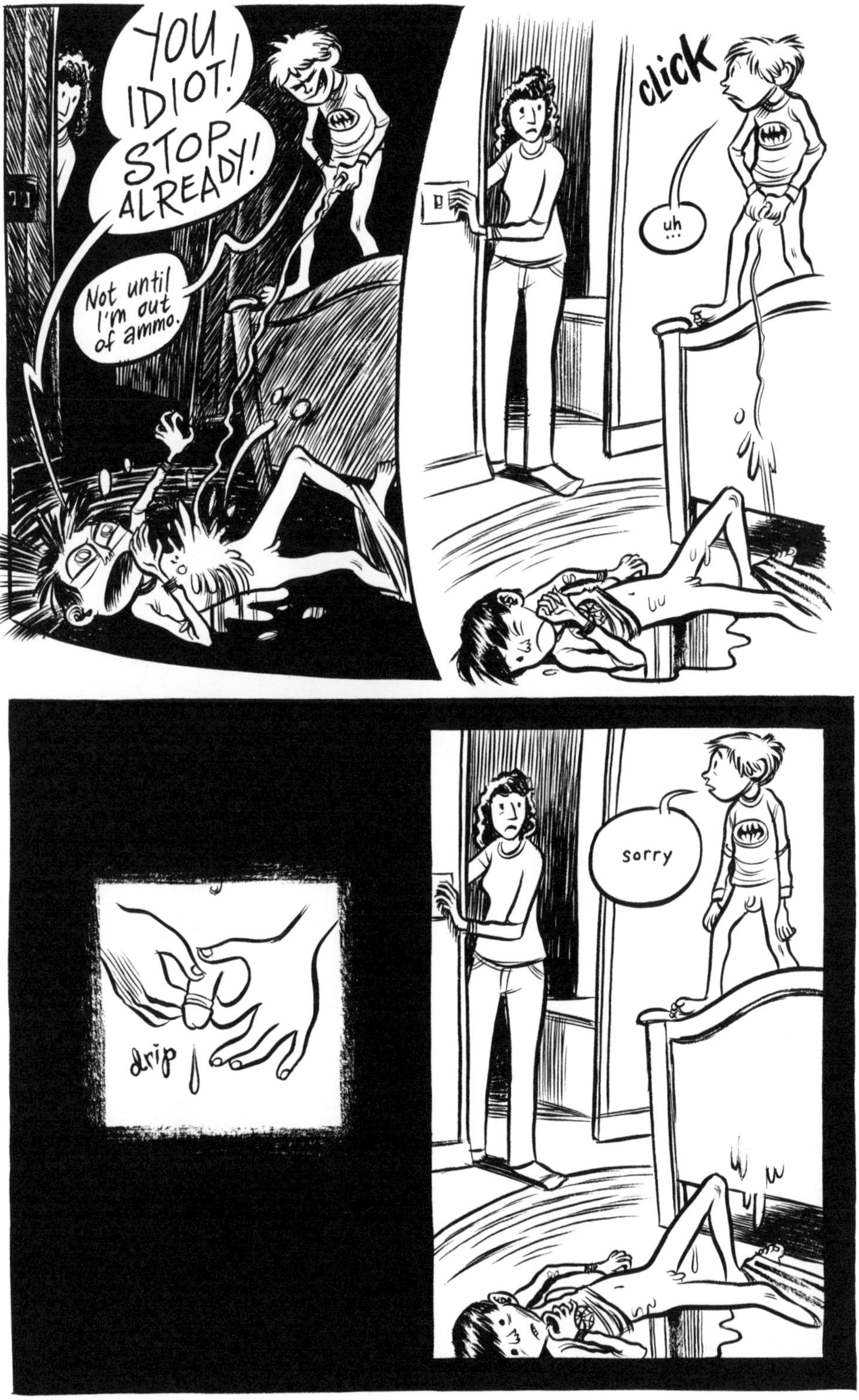
YOU IDIOT!
STOP ALREADY!
Not until I'm out of ammo.
click
uh...
sorry
drip

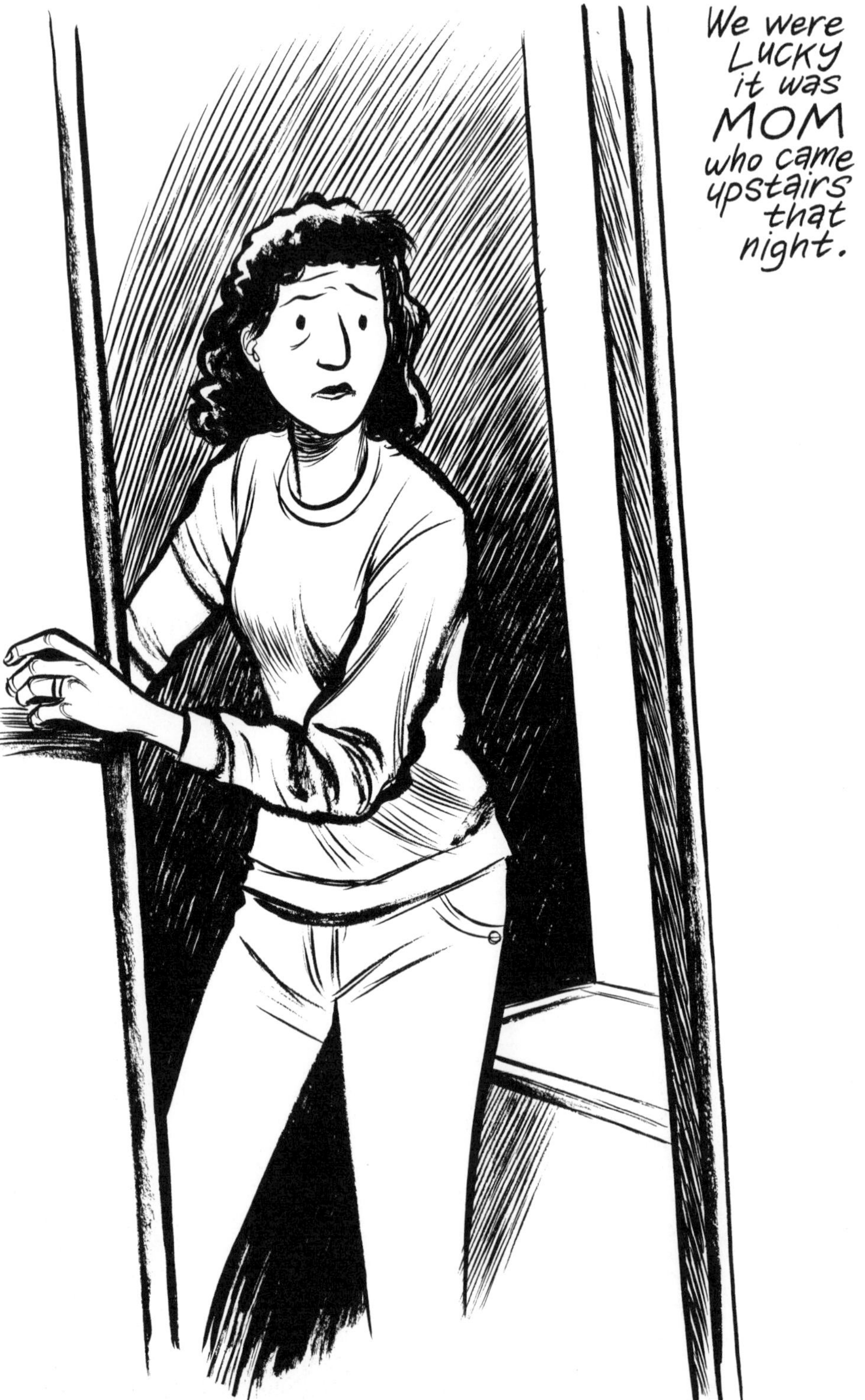
We were LUCKY it was MOM who came upstairs that night.

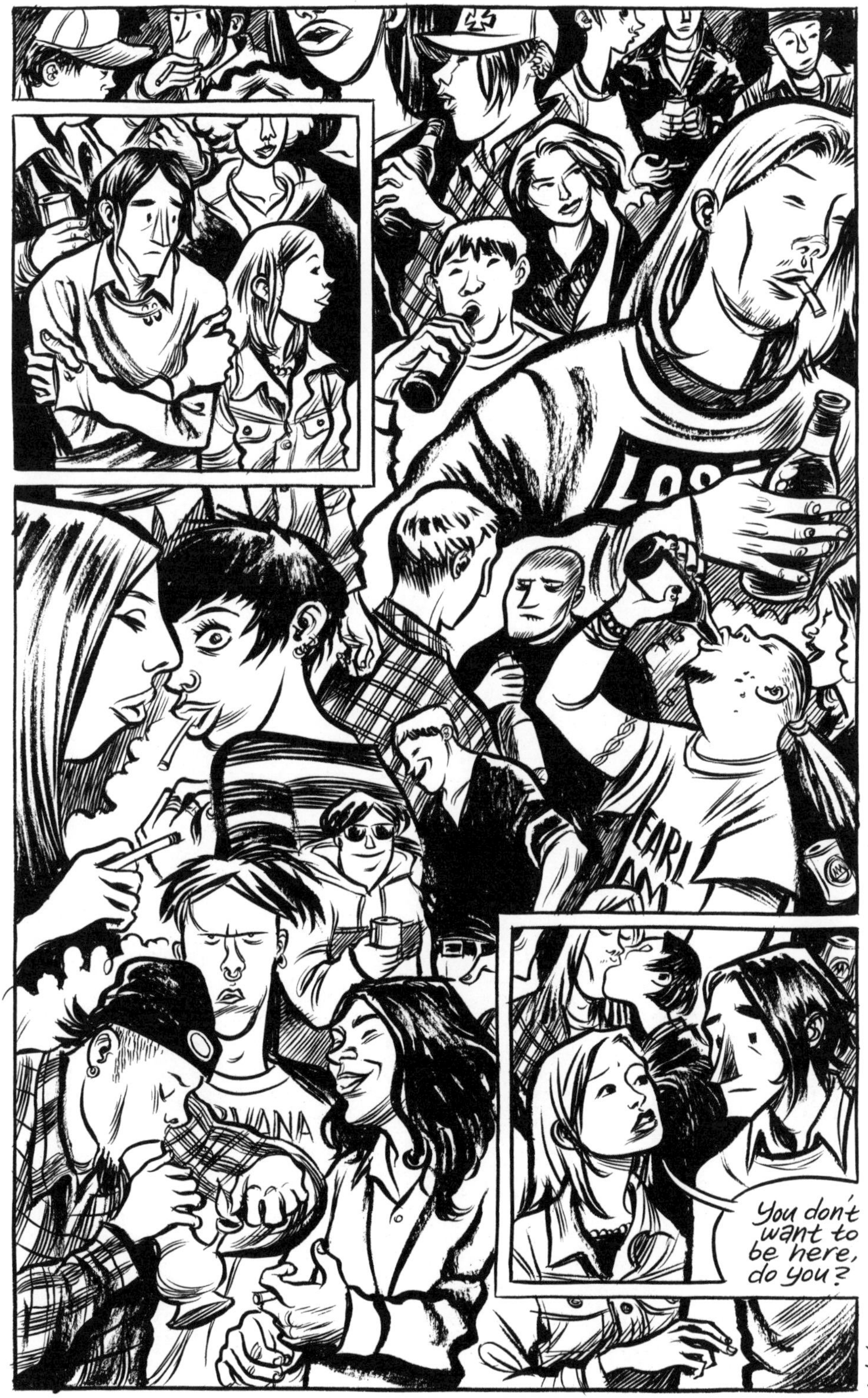
You don't want to be here, do you?

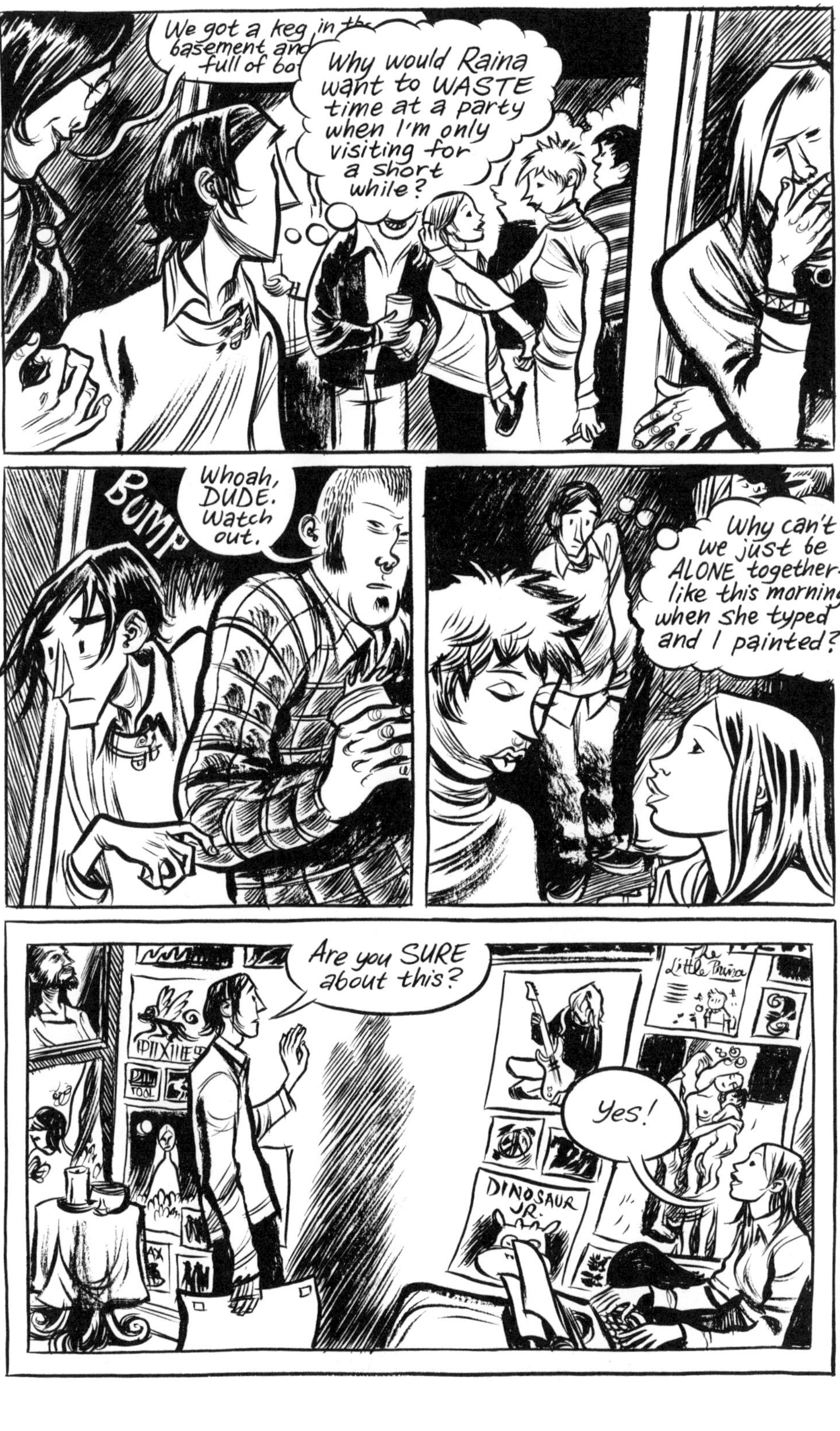
We got a keg in th
basement and
full of bo
Why would Raina want to WASTE time at a party when I'm only visiting for a short while?
BUMP
Whoah, DUDE. Watch out.
Why can't we just be ALONE together- like this morning, when she typed and I painted?
Are you SURE about this?
Yes!
DINOSAUR JR.

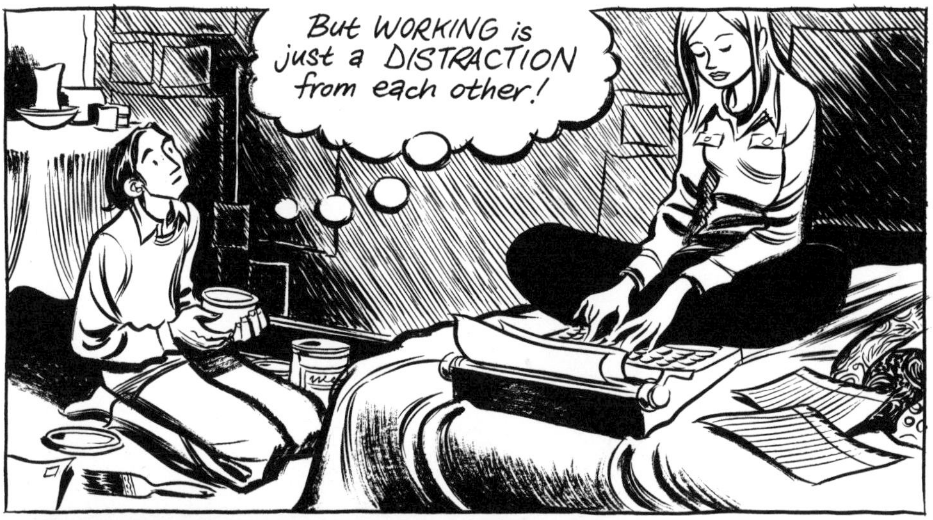
But WORKING is just a DISTRACTION from each other!

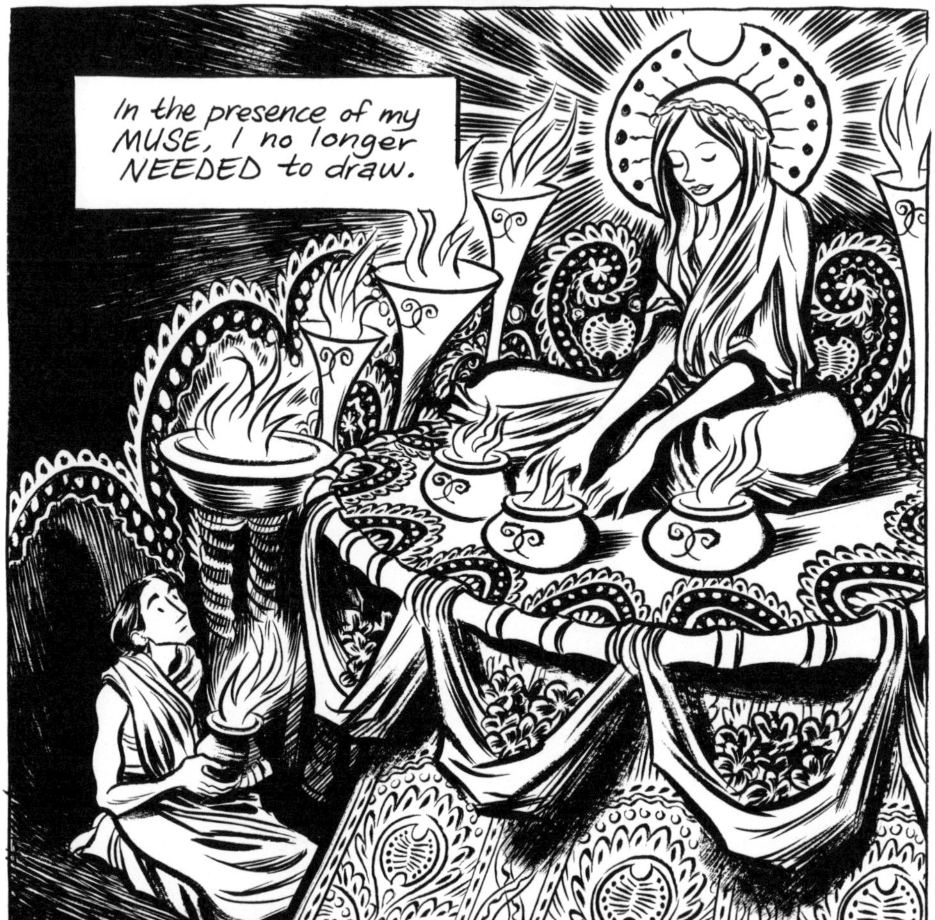
In the presence of my MUSE, I no longer NEEDED to draw.

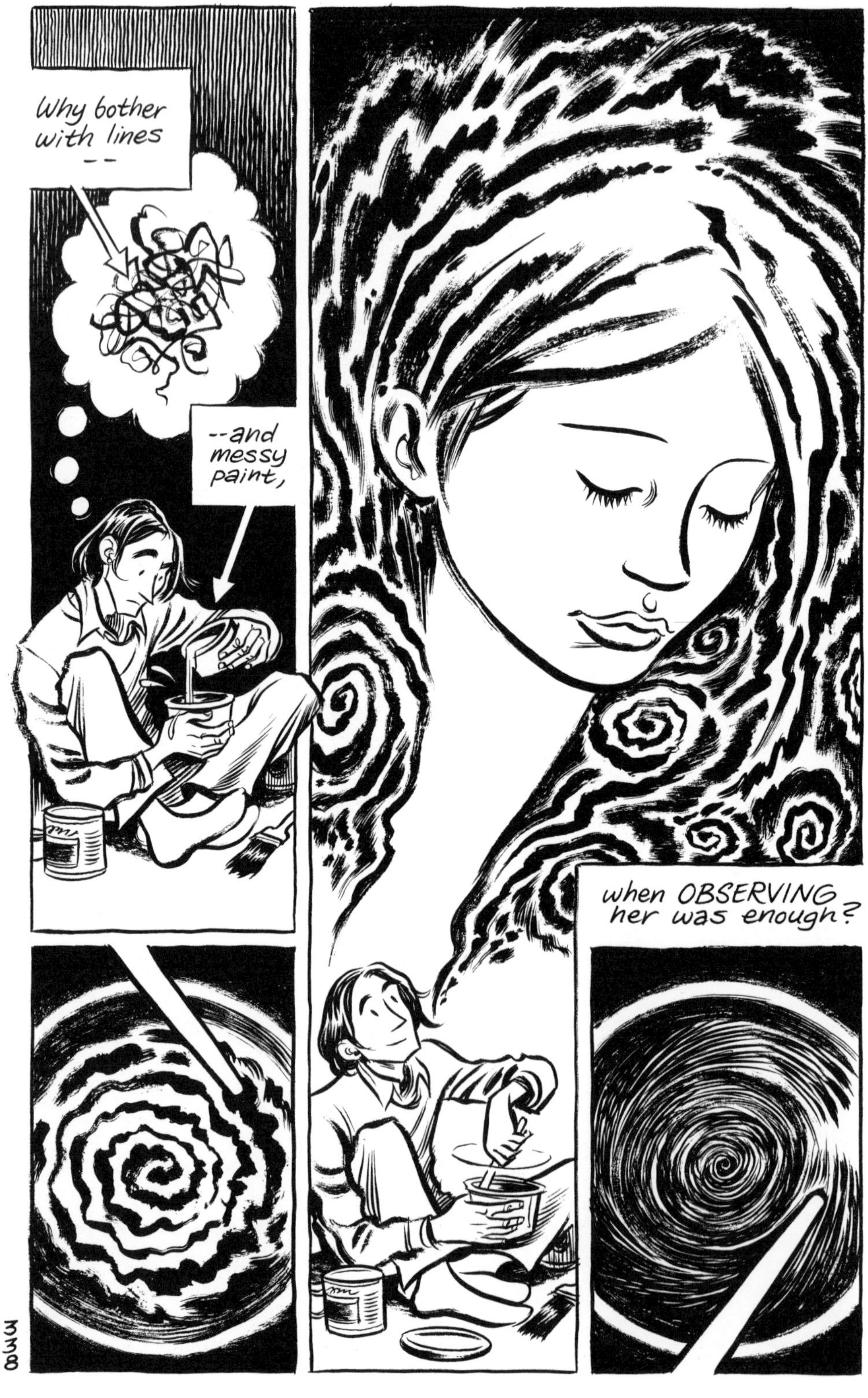
Why bother with lines --
--and messy paint,
when OBSERVING her was enough?

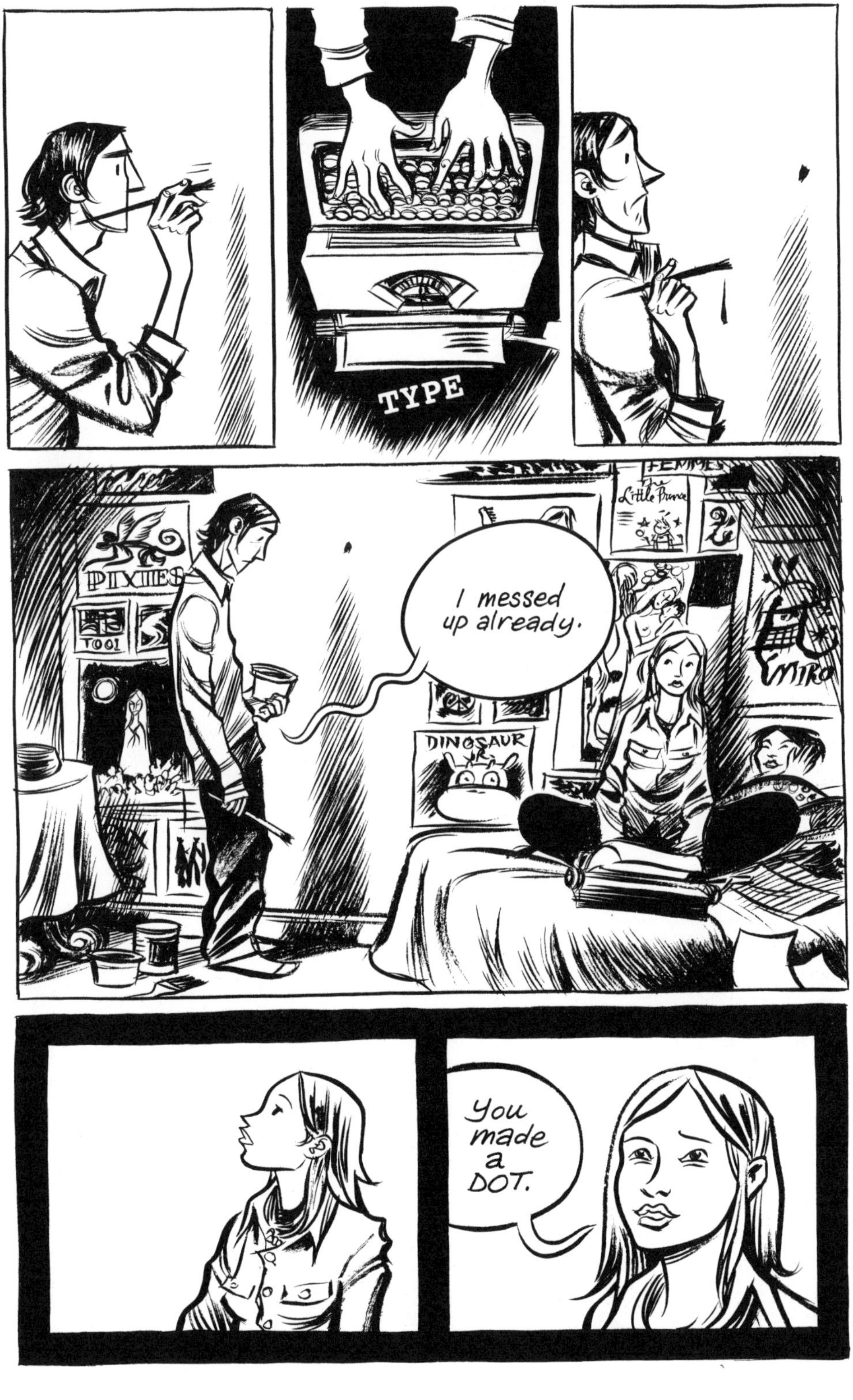
TYPE
PIXIES
DINOSAUR
I messed up already.
You made a DOT.

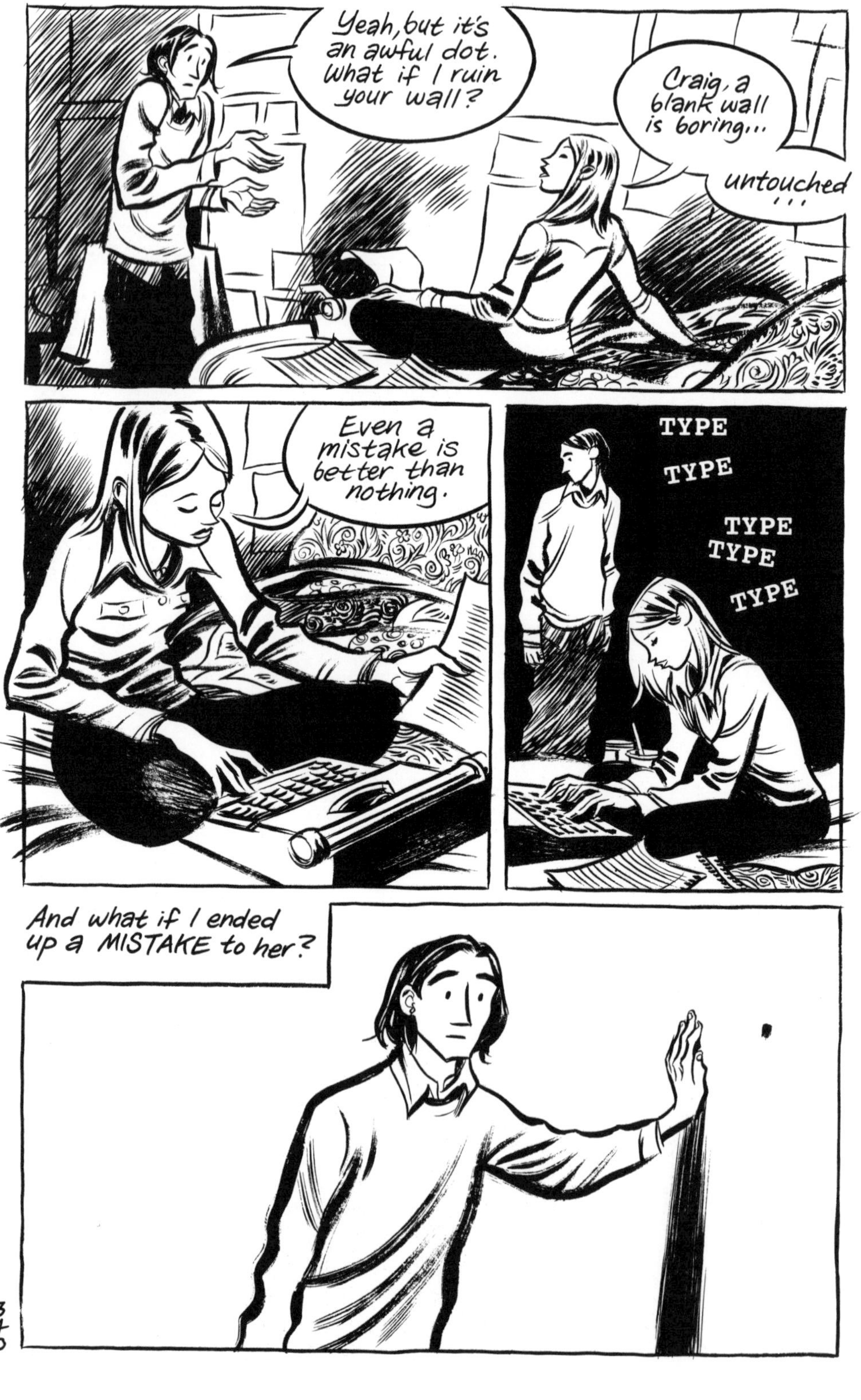

Yeah, but it's an awful dot. What if I ruin your wall?
Craig, a blank wall is boring...
untouched...
Even a mistake is better than nothing.
TYPE
TYPE
TYPE
TYPE
TYPE
And what if I ended up a MISTAKE to her?

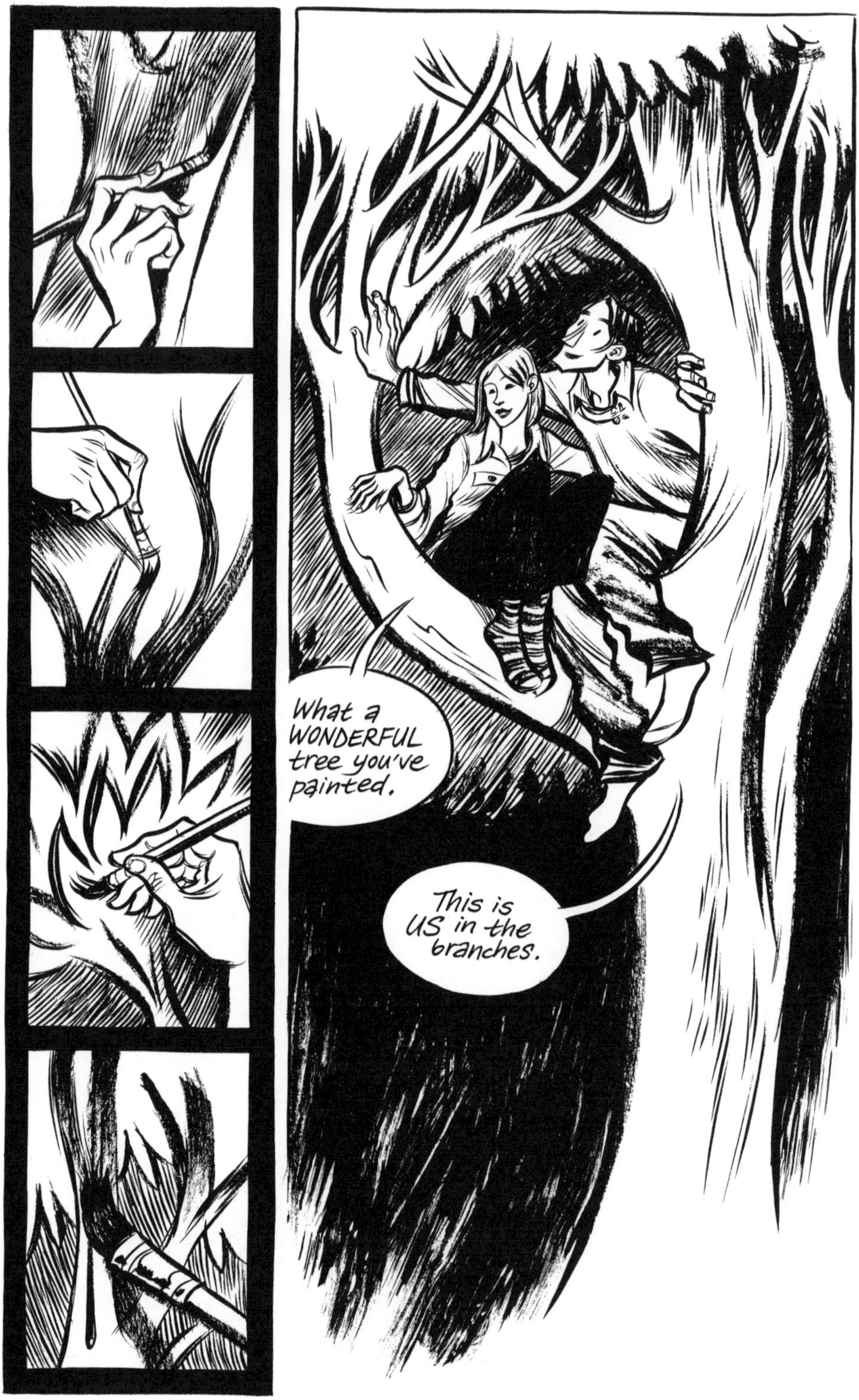
What a WONDERFUL tree you've painted.
This is US in the branches.

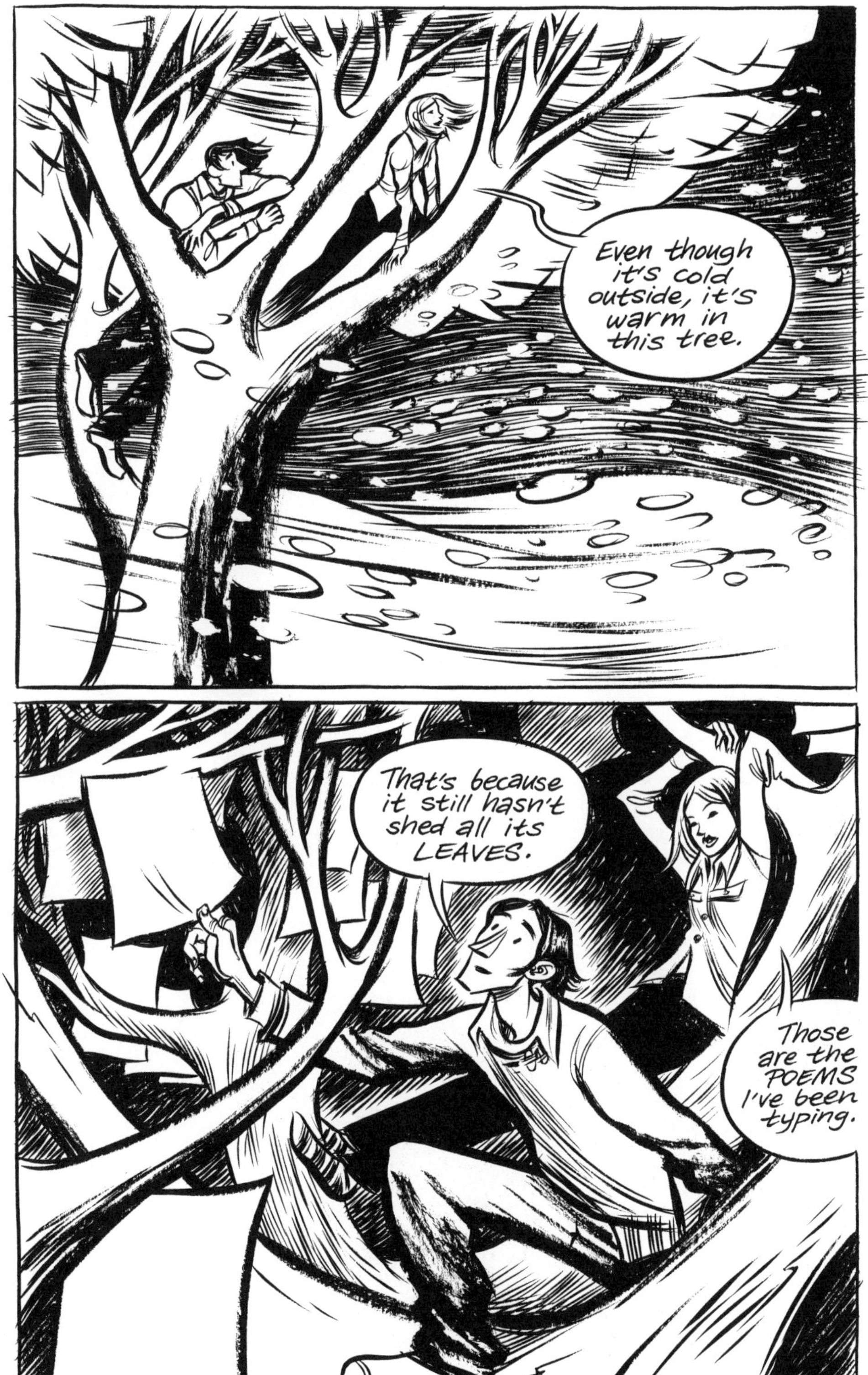
Even though it's cold outside, it's warm in this tree.
That's because it still hasn't shed all its LEAVES.
Those are the POEMS I've been typing.

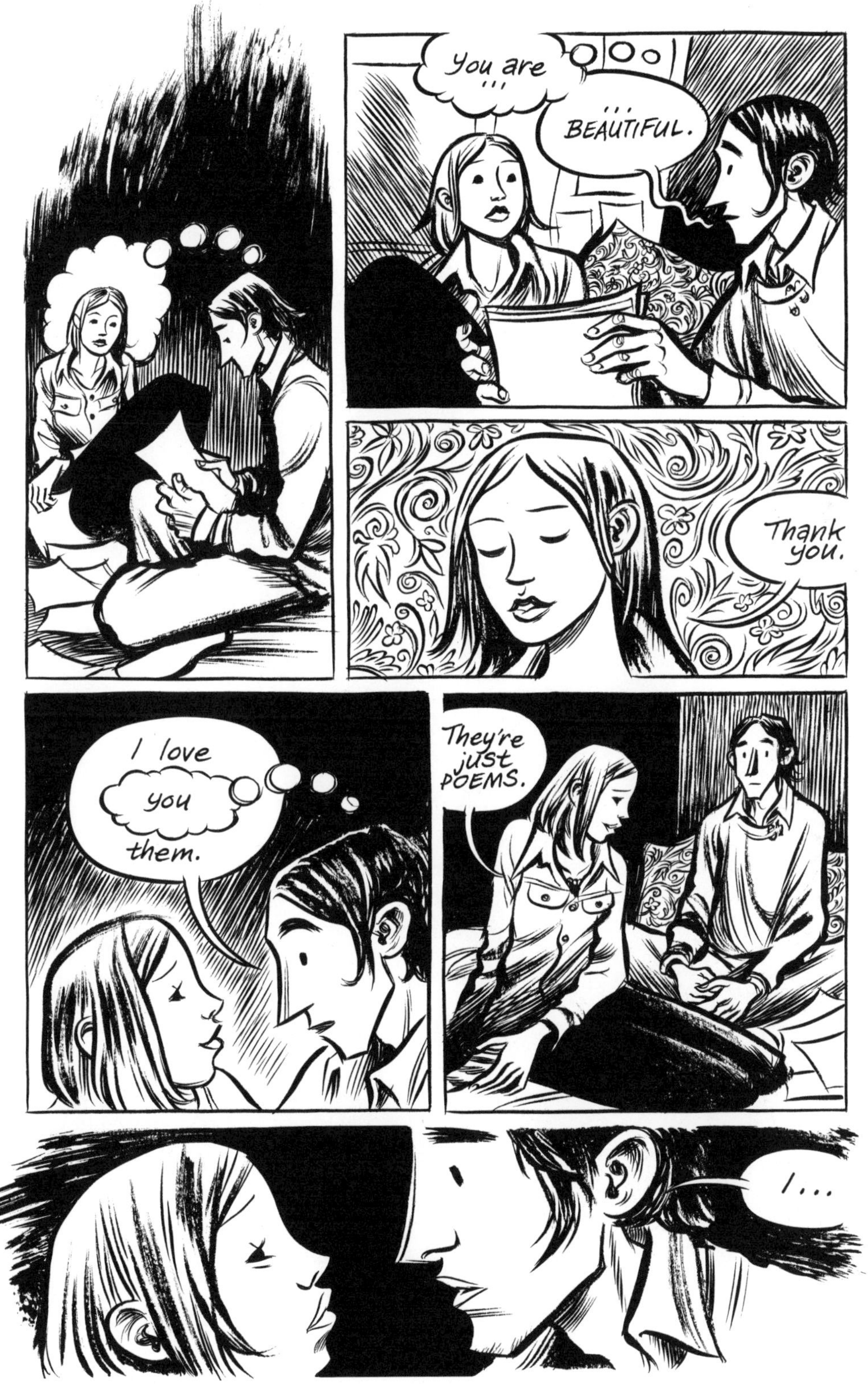
You are ...
... BEAUTIFUL.
Thank you.
I love you them.
They're just POEMS.
I...

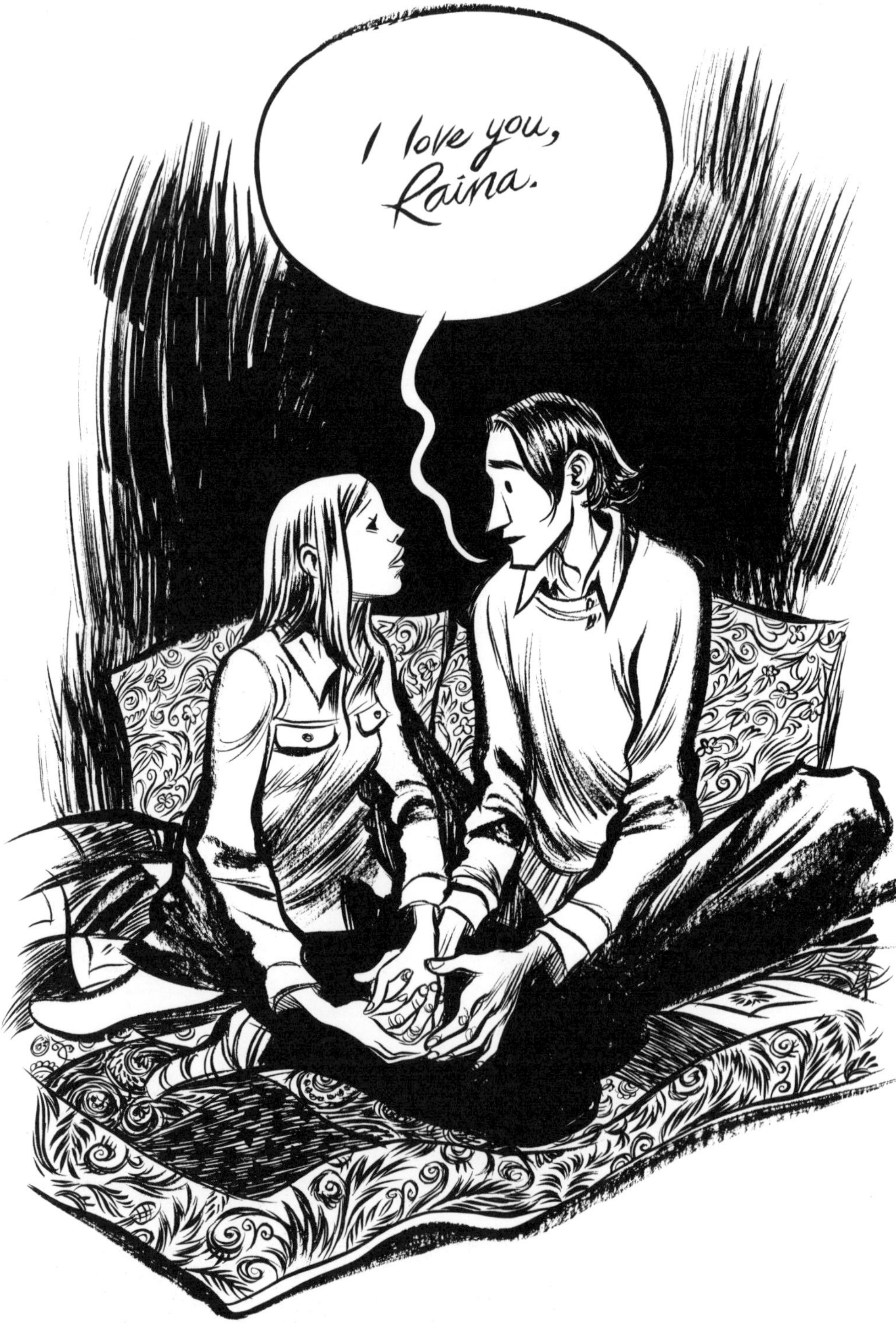
I love you, Raina.

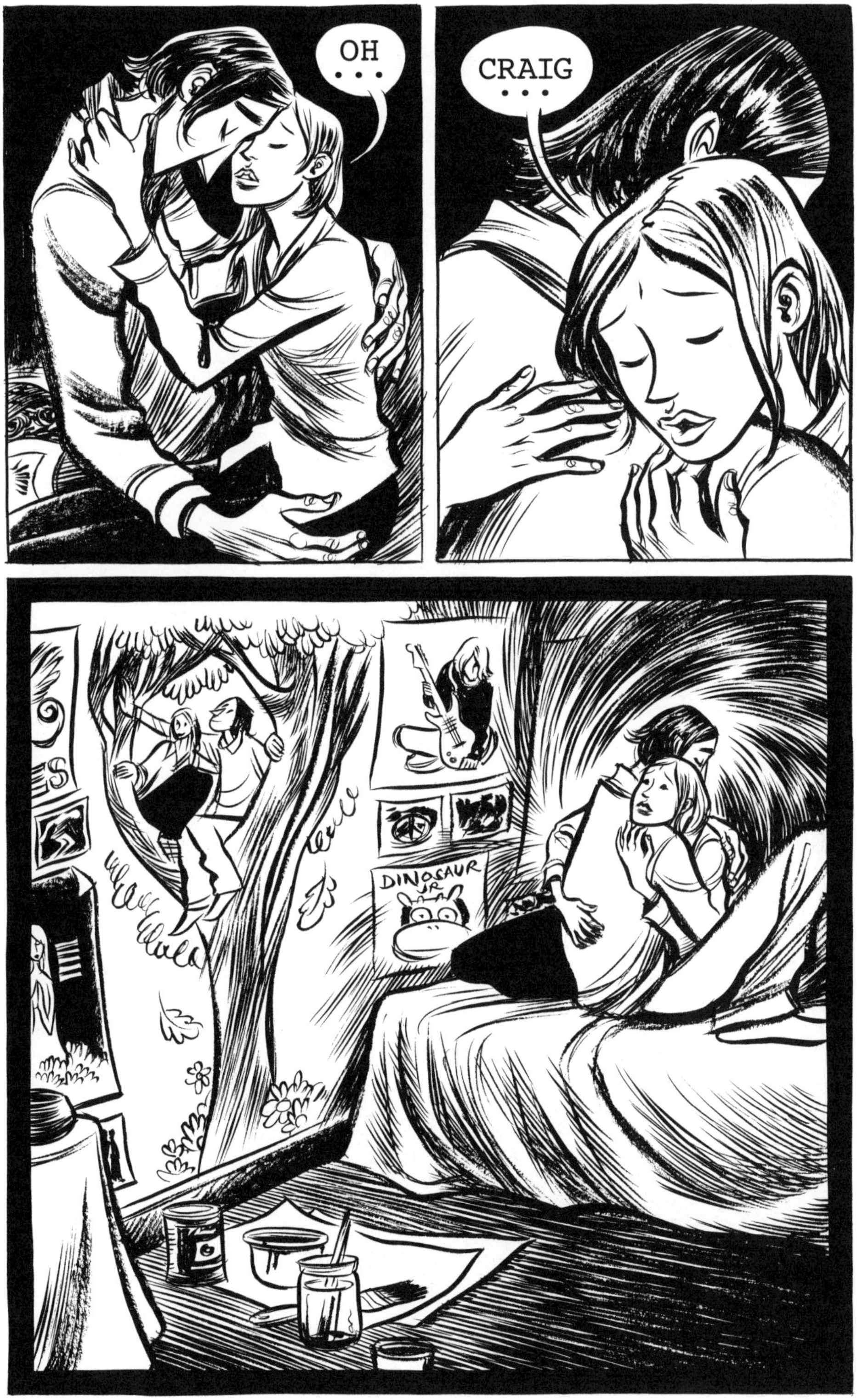
OH . . .
CRAIG . . .
DINOSAUR JR

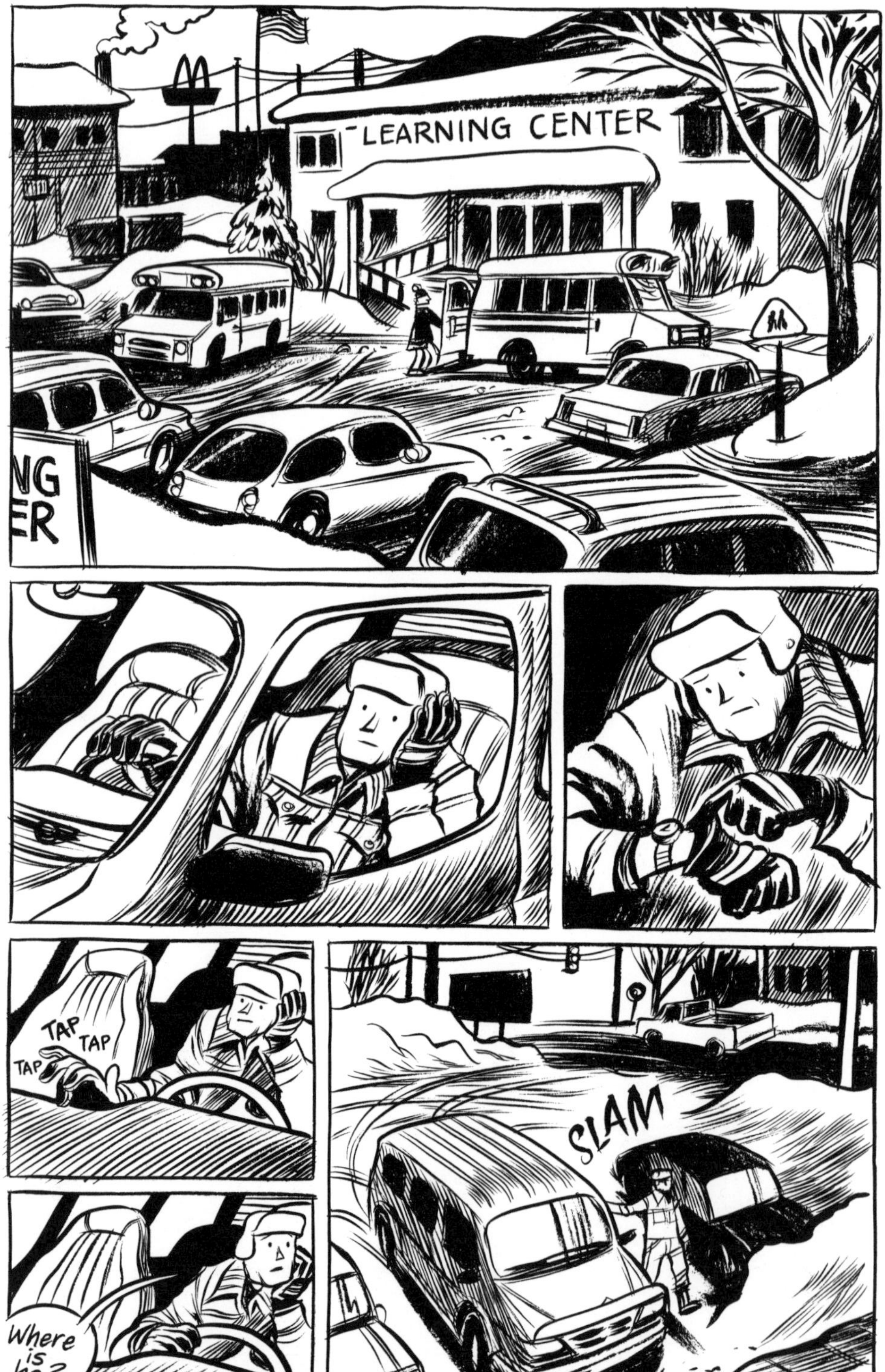
LEARNING CENTER
NG
ER
TAP
TAP
TAP
Where is he?
SLAM

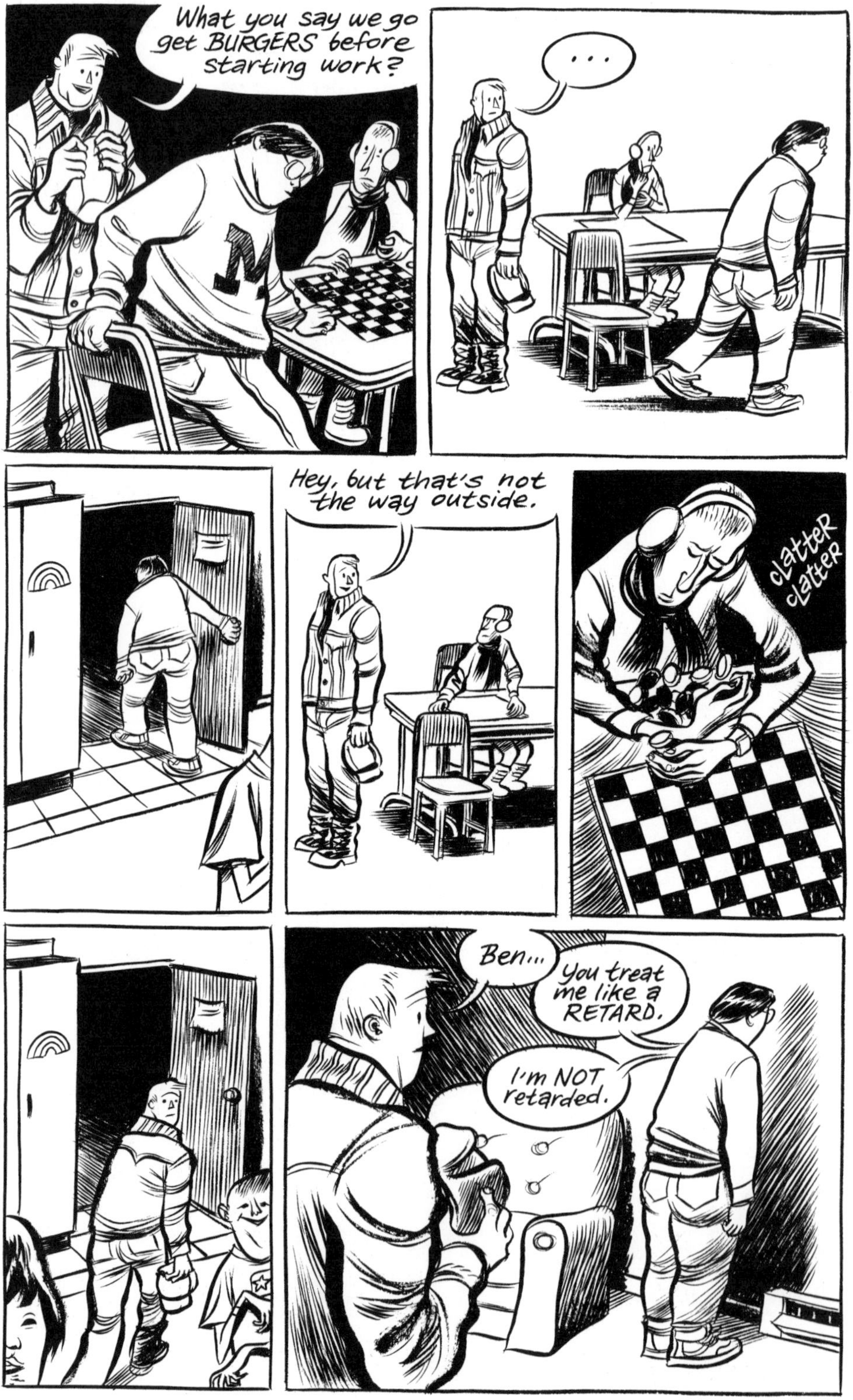

What you say we go get BURGERS before starting work?
. . .
Hey, but that's not the way outside.
clatter clatter
Ben...
You treat me like a RETARD.
I'm NOT retarded.

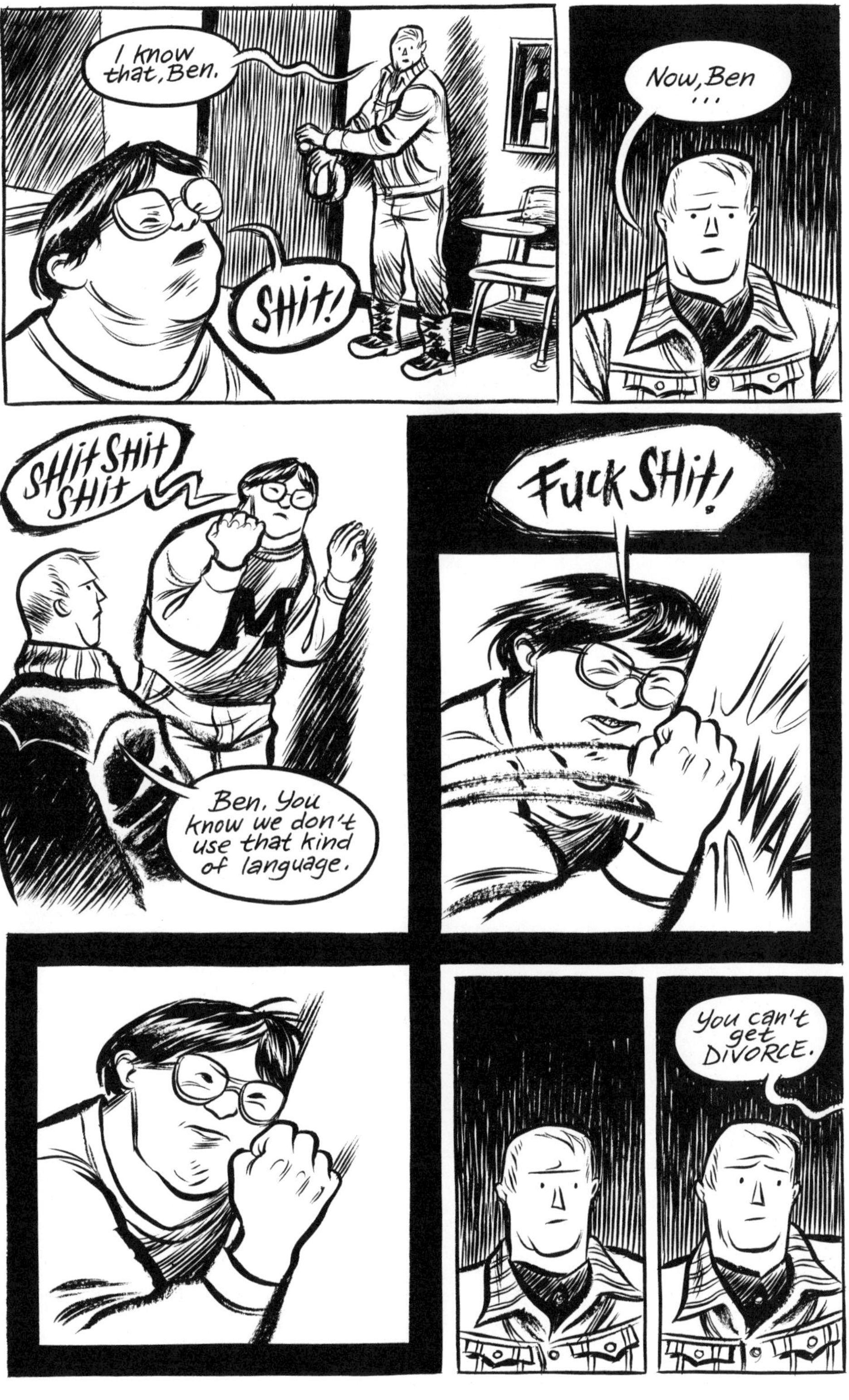
I know that, Ben.
SHIT!
Now, Ben ...
SHIT SHIT SHIT
Ben. You know we don't use that kind of language.
FUCK SHIT!
WAK
You can't get DIVORCE.

352

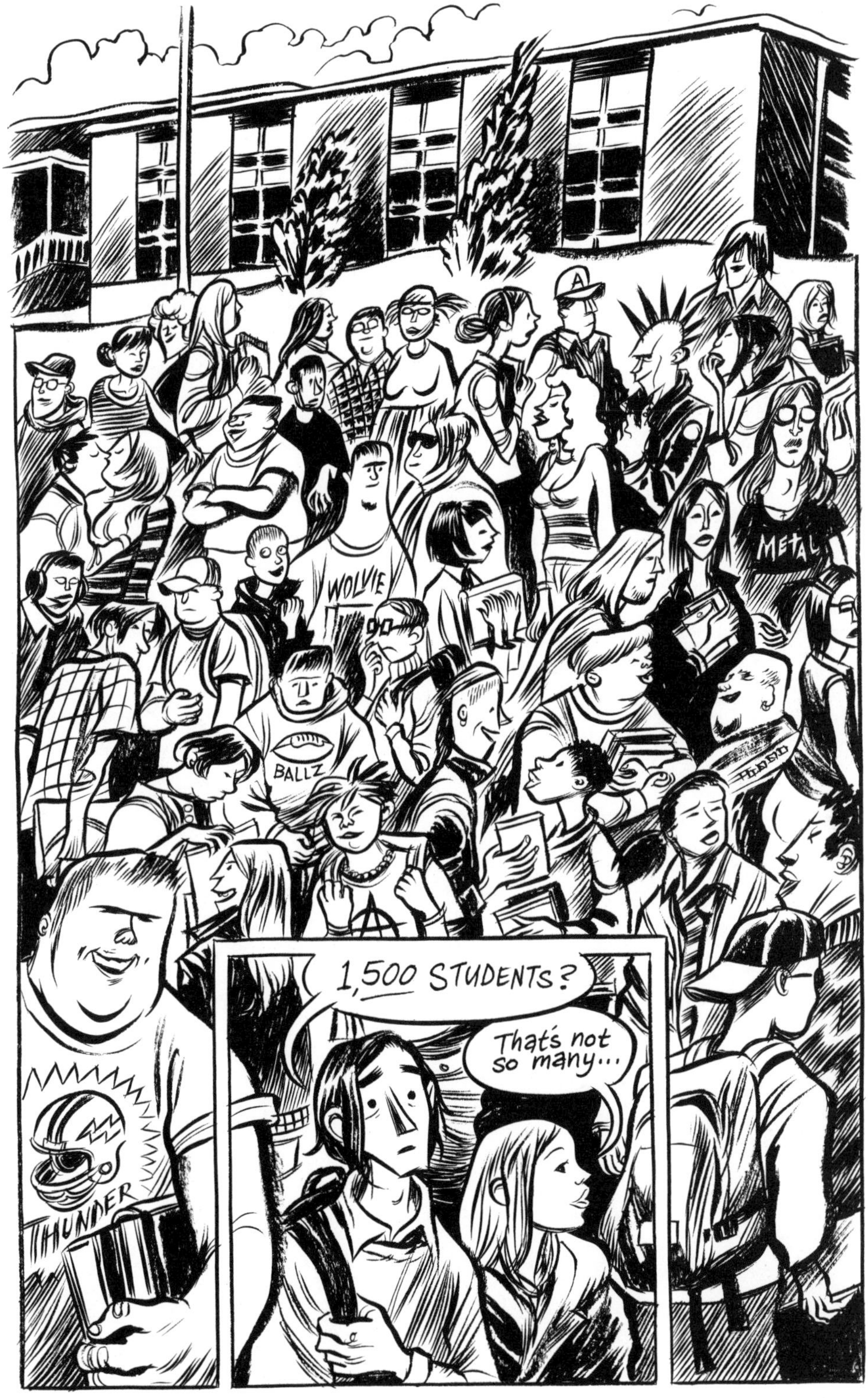
WOLVIE
METAL
BALLZ
THUNDER
1,500 STUDENTS?
That's not so many...

354

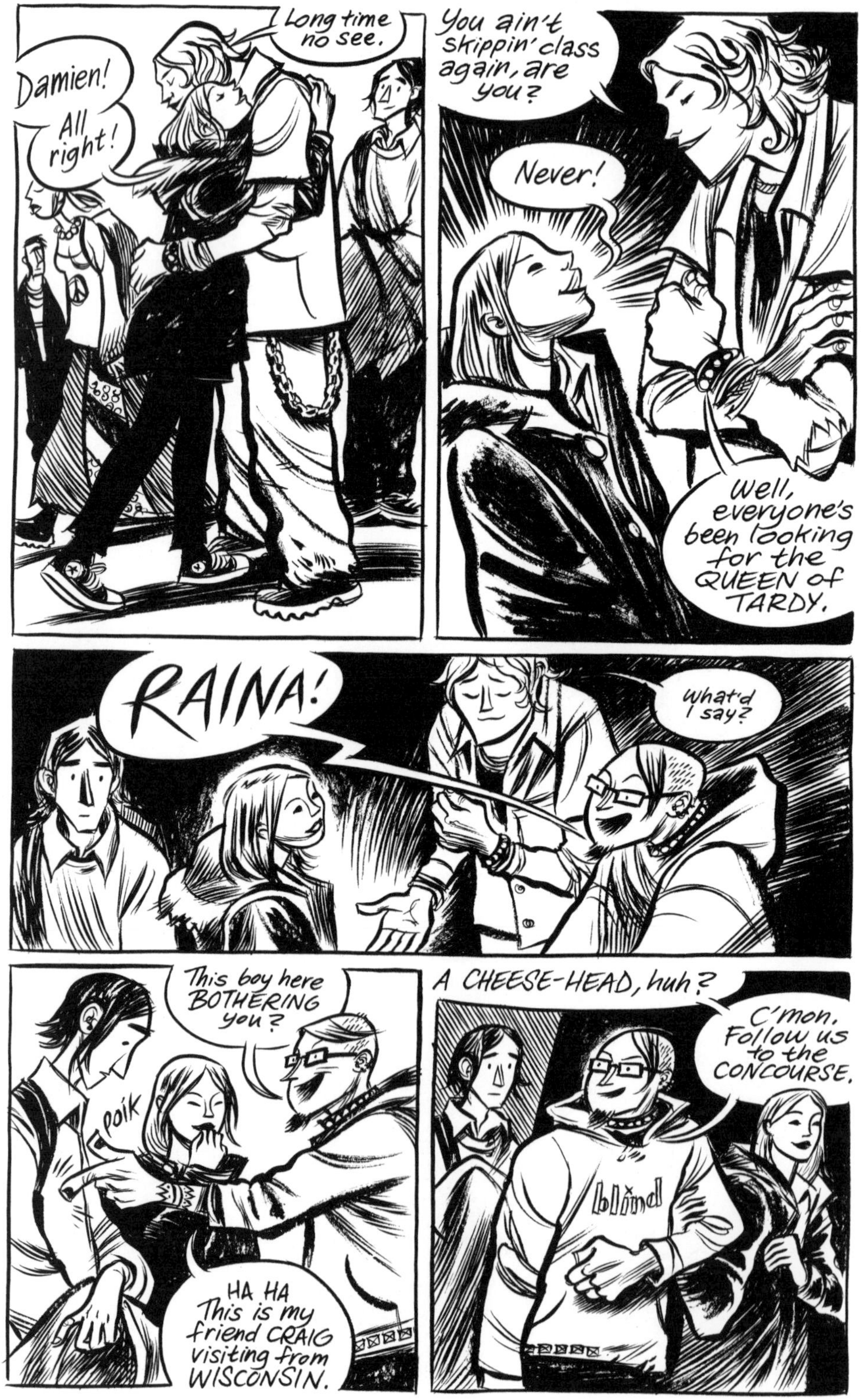
Long time no see.
Damien!
All right!
You ain't skippin' class again, are you?
Never!
Well, everyone's been looking for the QUEEN of TARDY.
RAINA!
What'd I say?
This boy here BOTHERING you?
poik
HA HA This is my friend CRAIG visiting from WISCONSIN.
A CHEESE-HEAD, huh?
C'mon. Follow us to the CONCOURSE.
blind

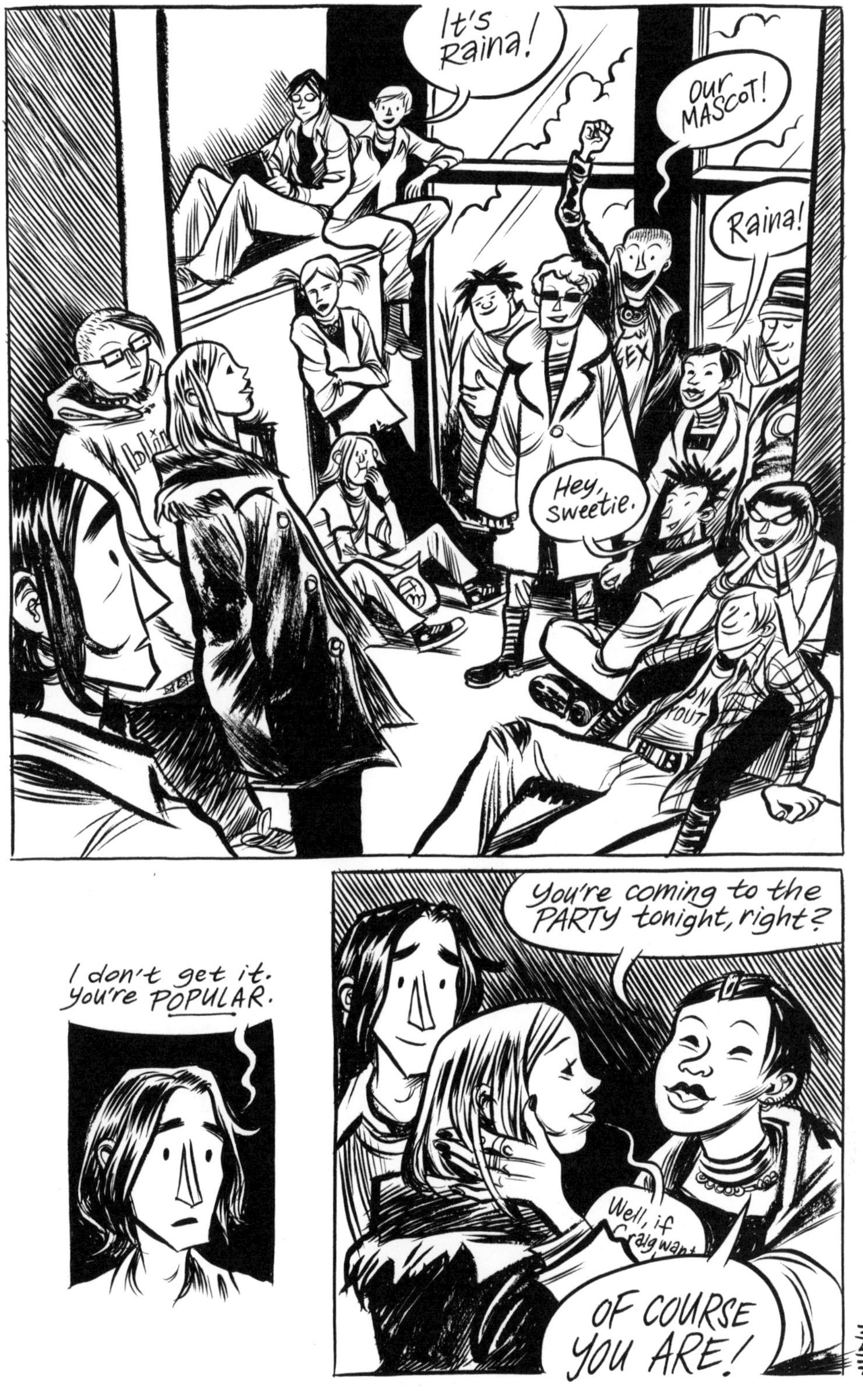
It's Raina!
Our MASCOT!
Raina!
Hey, sweetie.
I don't get it. You're POPULAR.
You're coming to the PARTY tonight, right?
Well, if Craig want
OF COURSE YOU ARE!

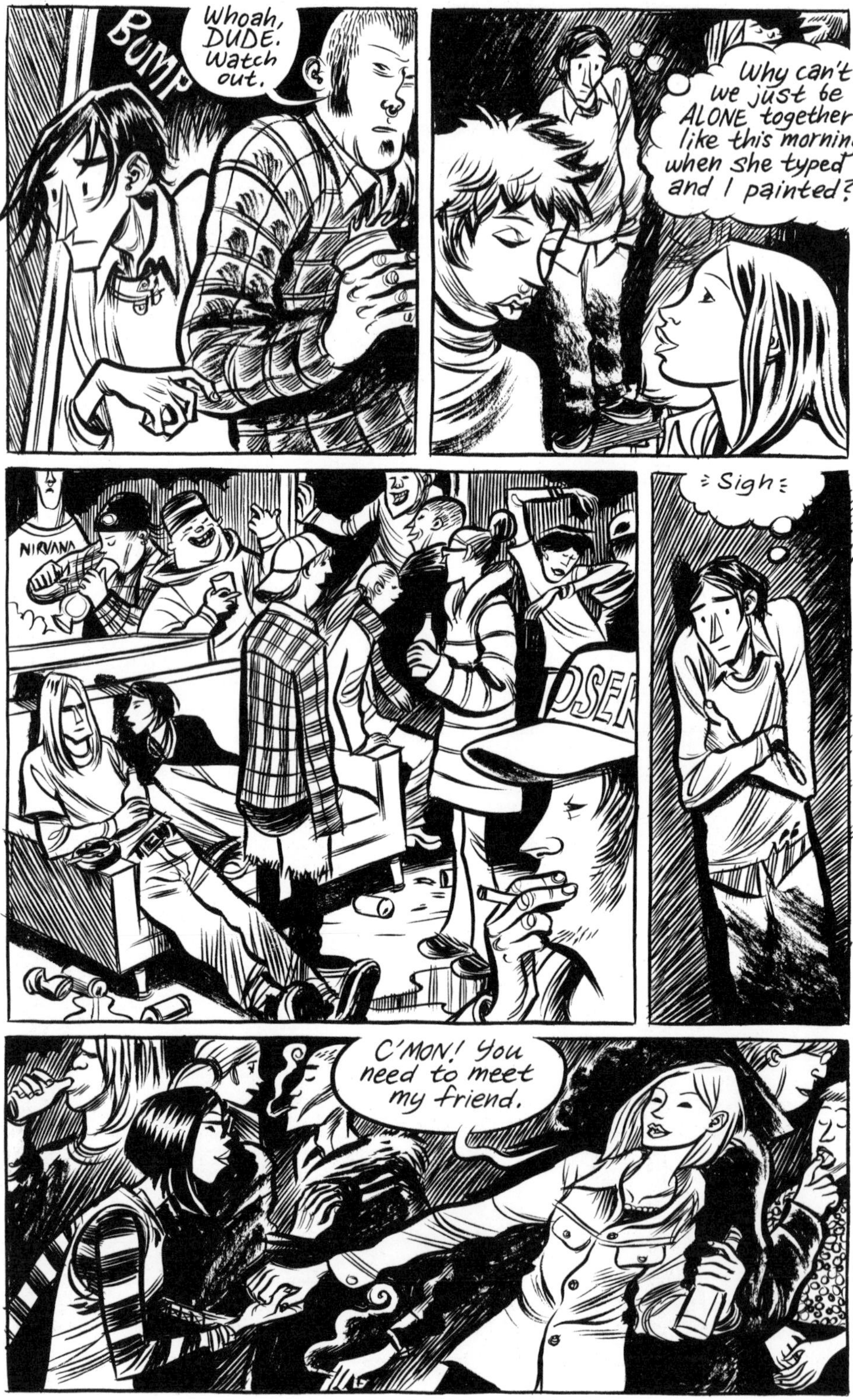
BUMP
Whoah, DUDE. Watch out.
Why can't we just be ALONE together-like this morning, when she typed and I painted?
NIRVANA
Sigh
C'MON! You need to meet my friend.

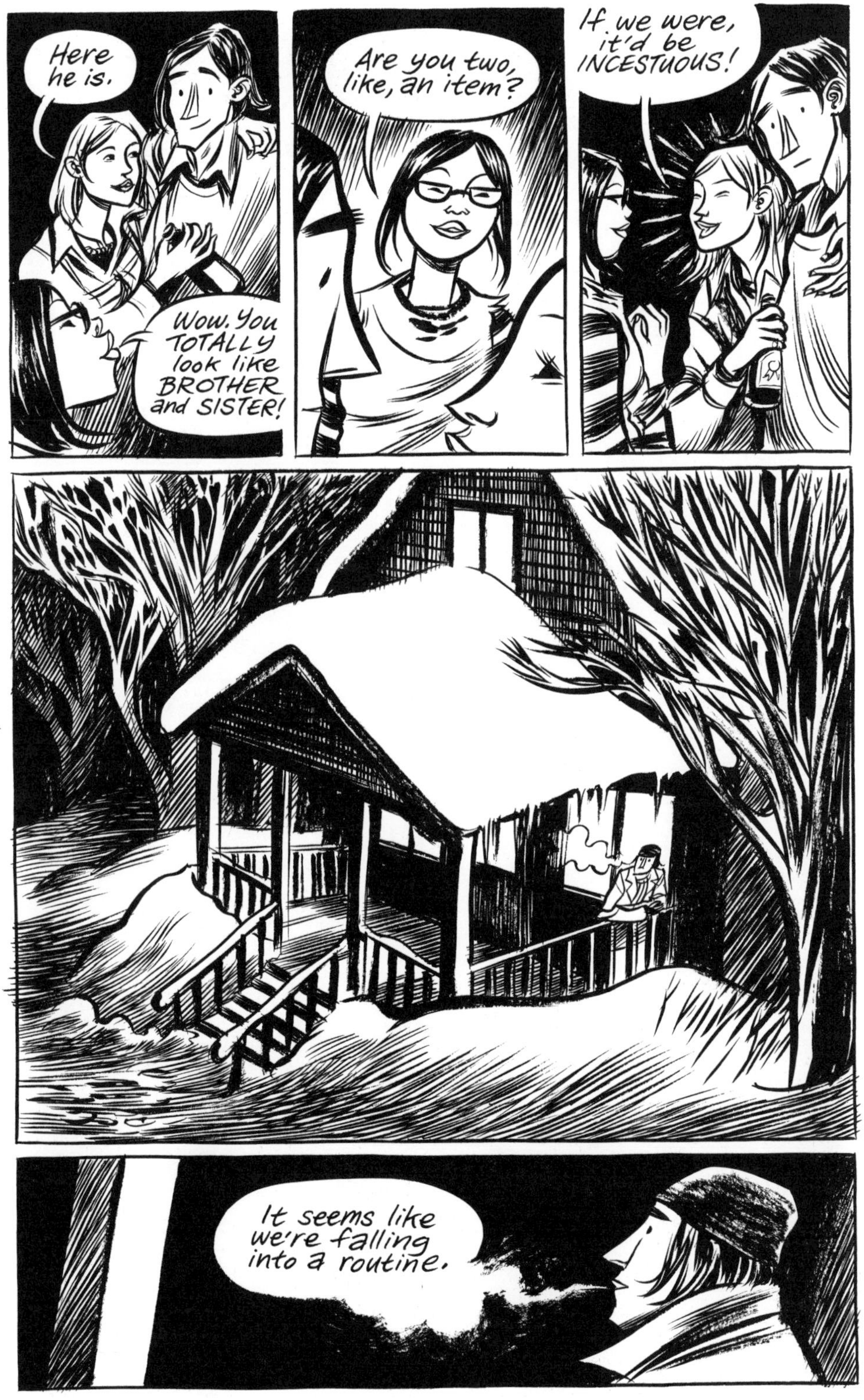
Here he is.
Wow. You TOTALLY look like BROTHER and SISTER!
Are you two, like, an item?
If we were, it'd be INCESTUOUS!
It seems like we're falling into a routine.

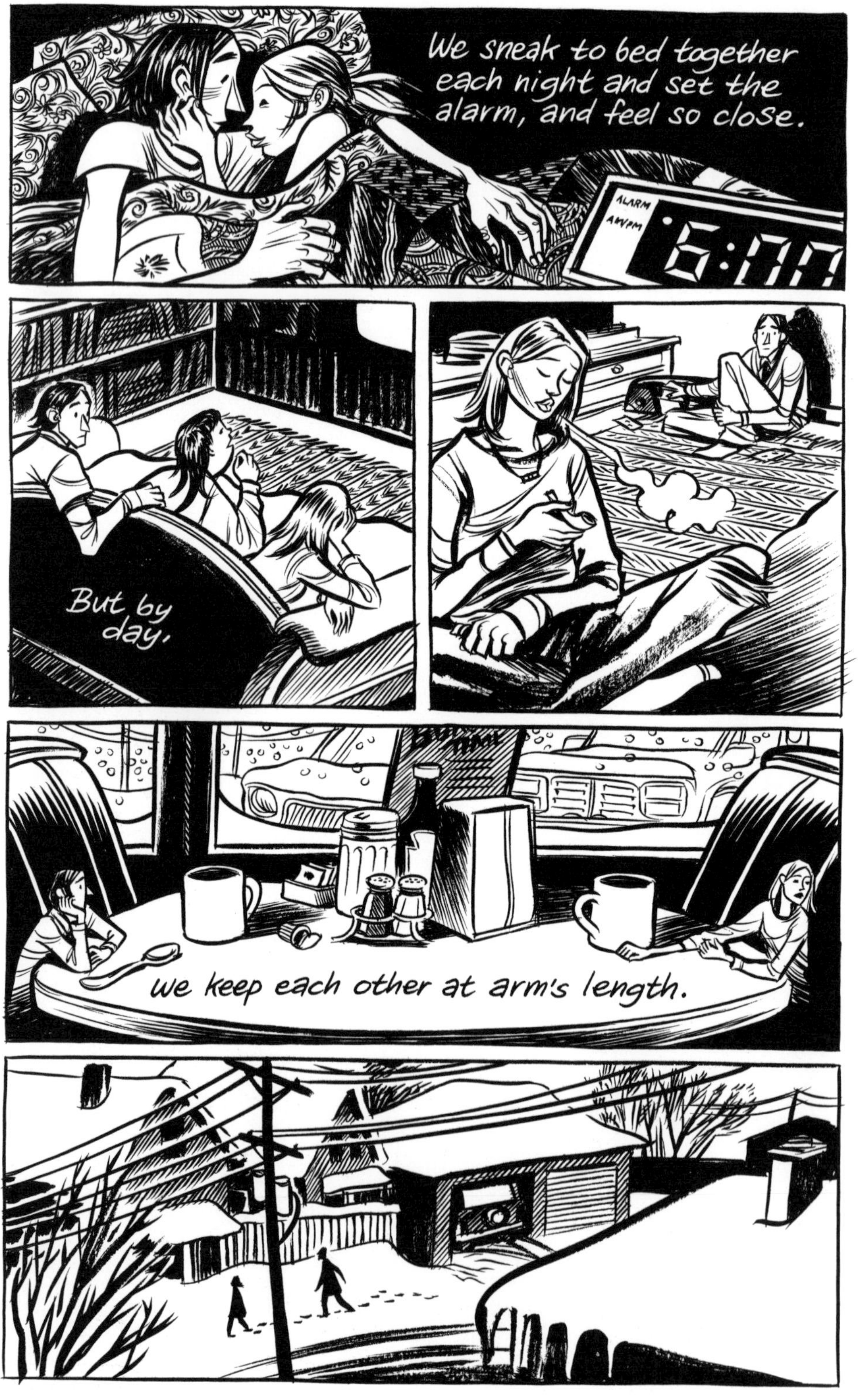
We sneak to bed together each night and set the alarm, and feel so close.
ALARM
But by day,
we keep each other at arm's length.

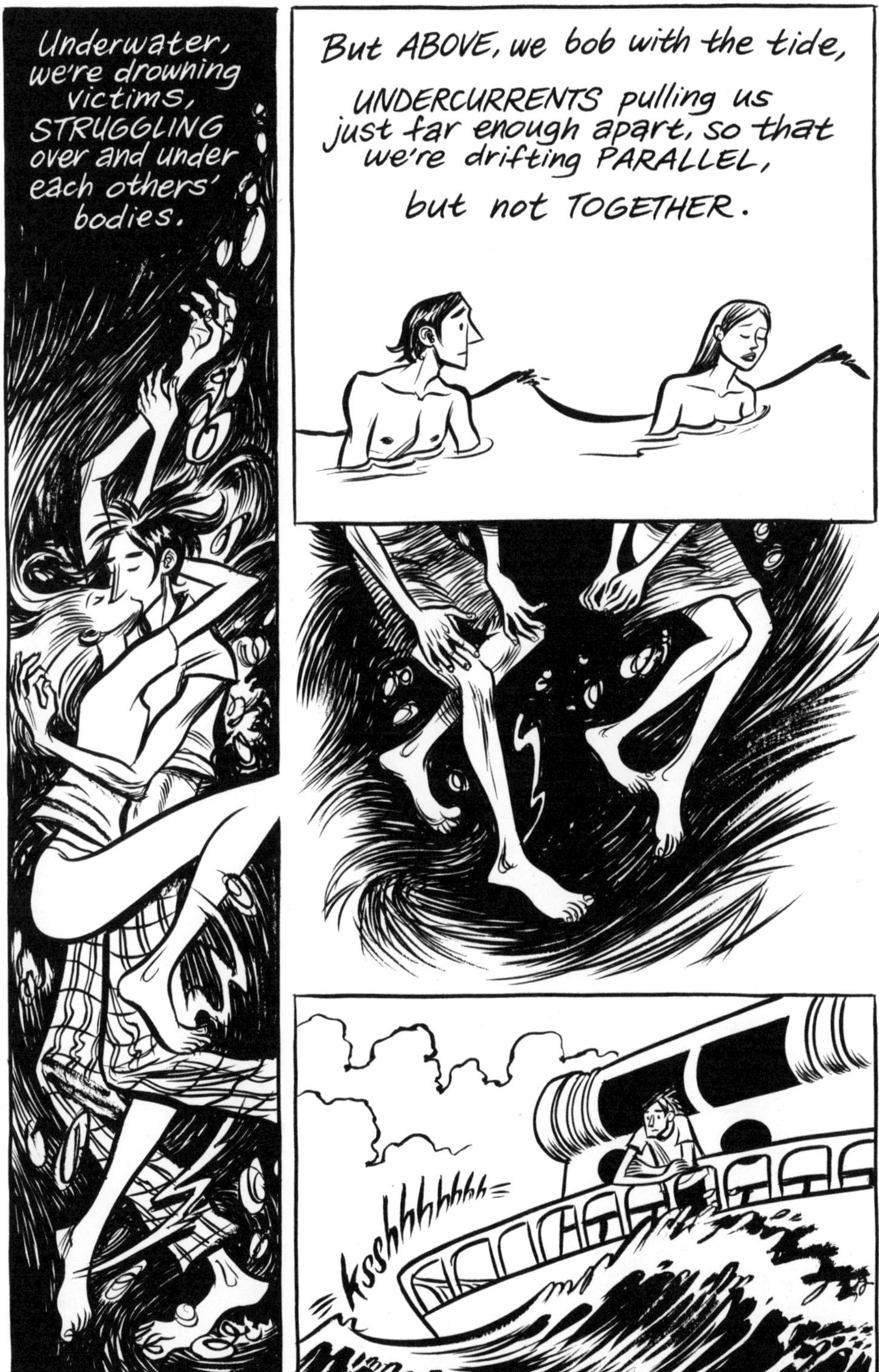
Underwater, we're drowning victims, STRUGGLING over and under each others' bodies.
But ABOVE, we bob with the tide,
UNDERCURRENTS pulling us just far enough apart, so that we're drifting PARALLEL,
but not TOGETHER.
ksshhhhhhhh

362

363

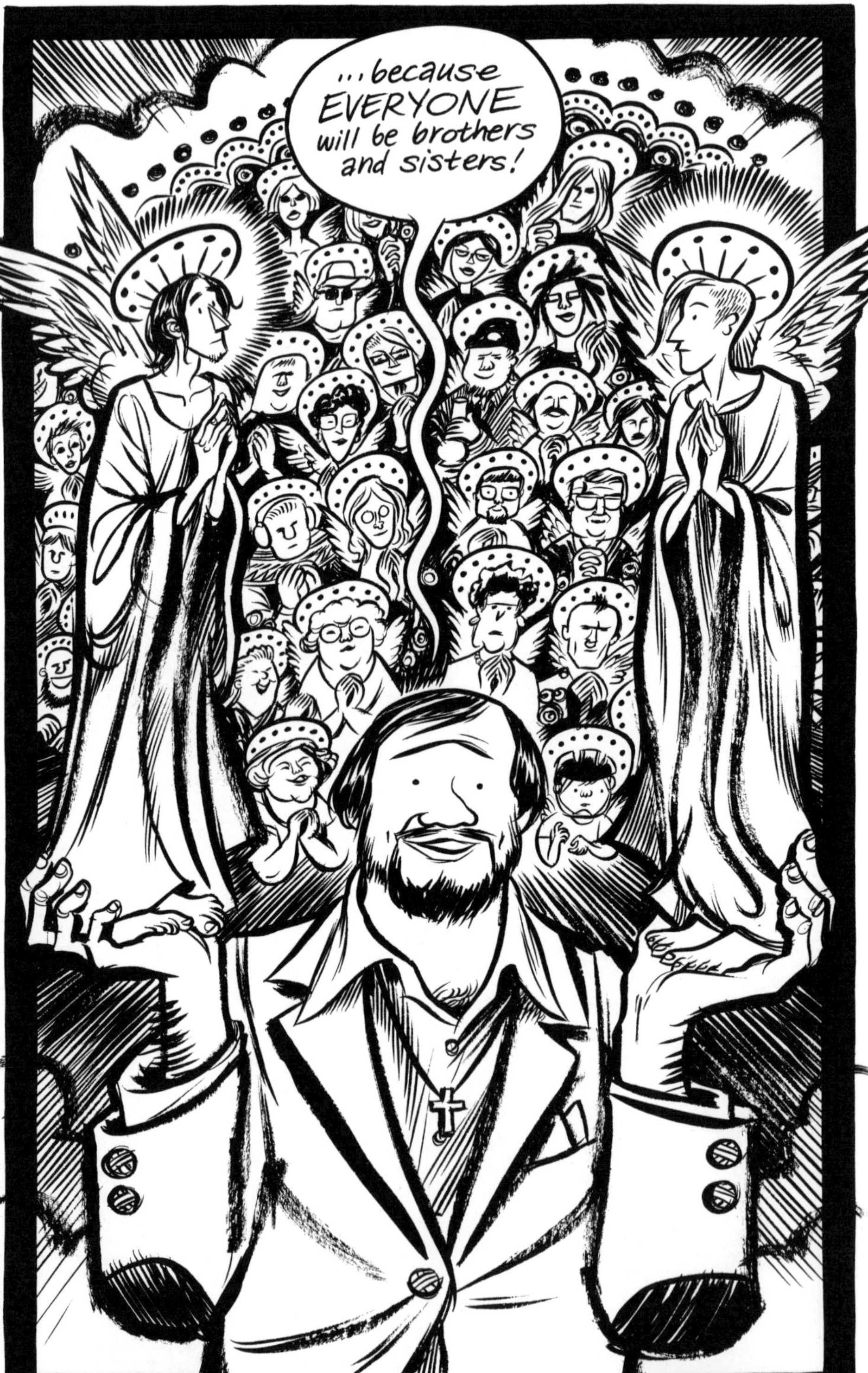
...because EVERYONE will be brothers and sisters!

365

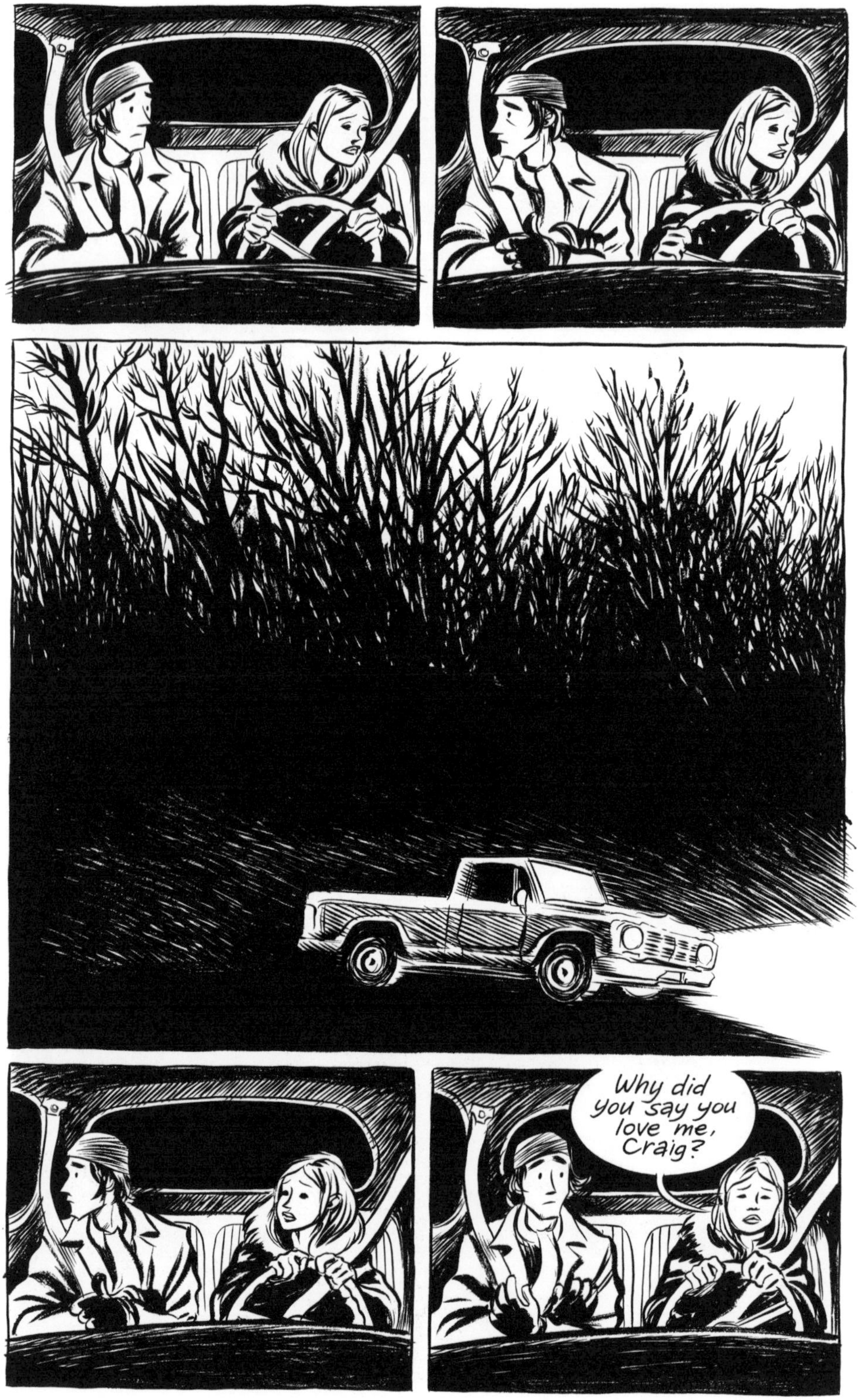
Why did you say you love me, Craig?

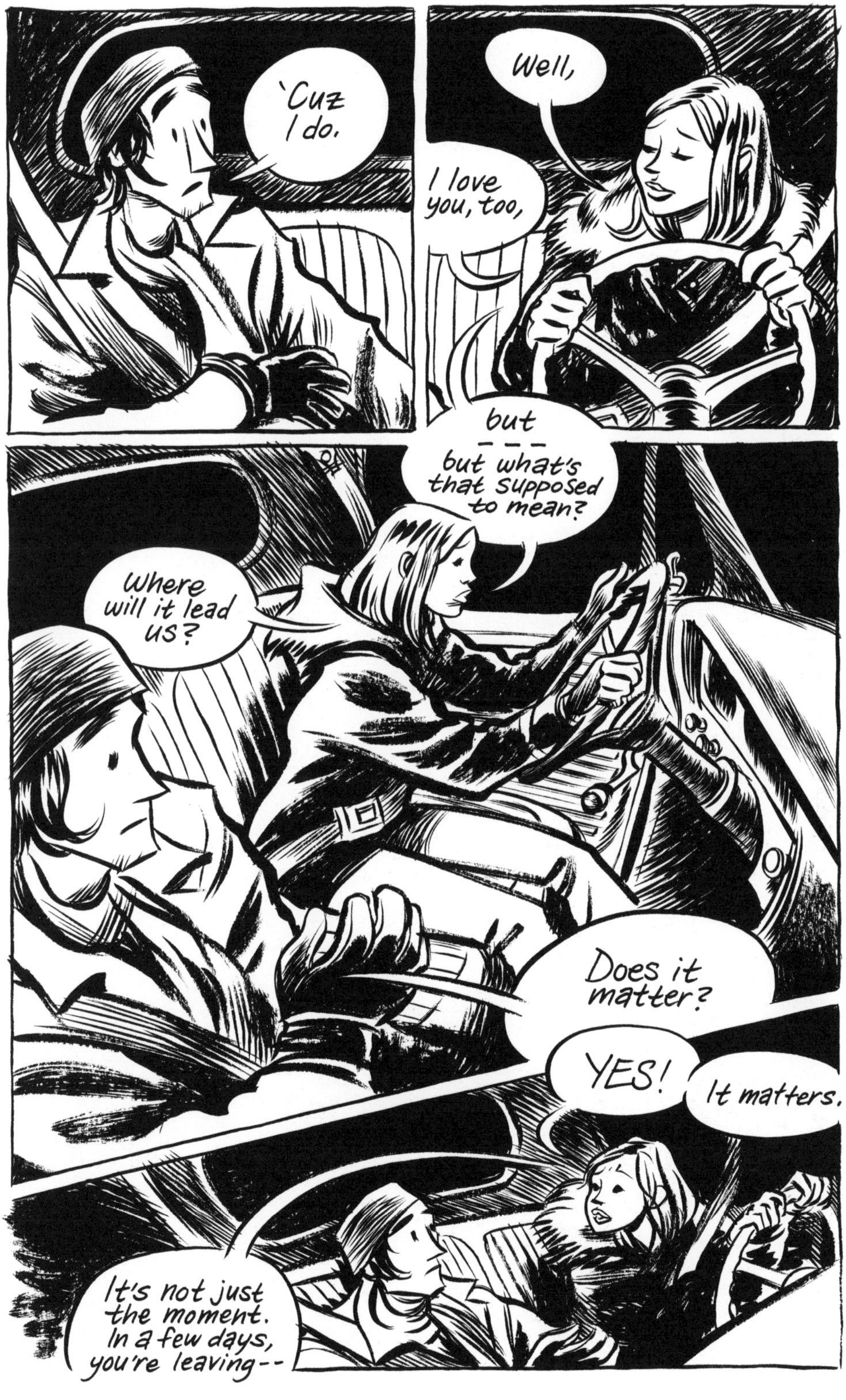
`Cuz I do.
Well,
I love you, too,
but --- but what's that supposed to mean?
Where will it lead us?
Does it matter?
YES!
It matters.
It's not just the moment. In a few days, you're leaving--

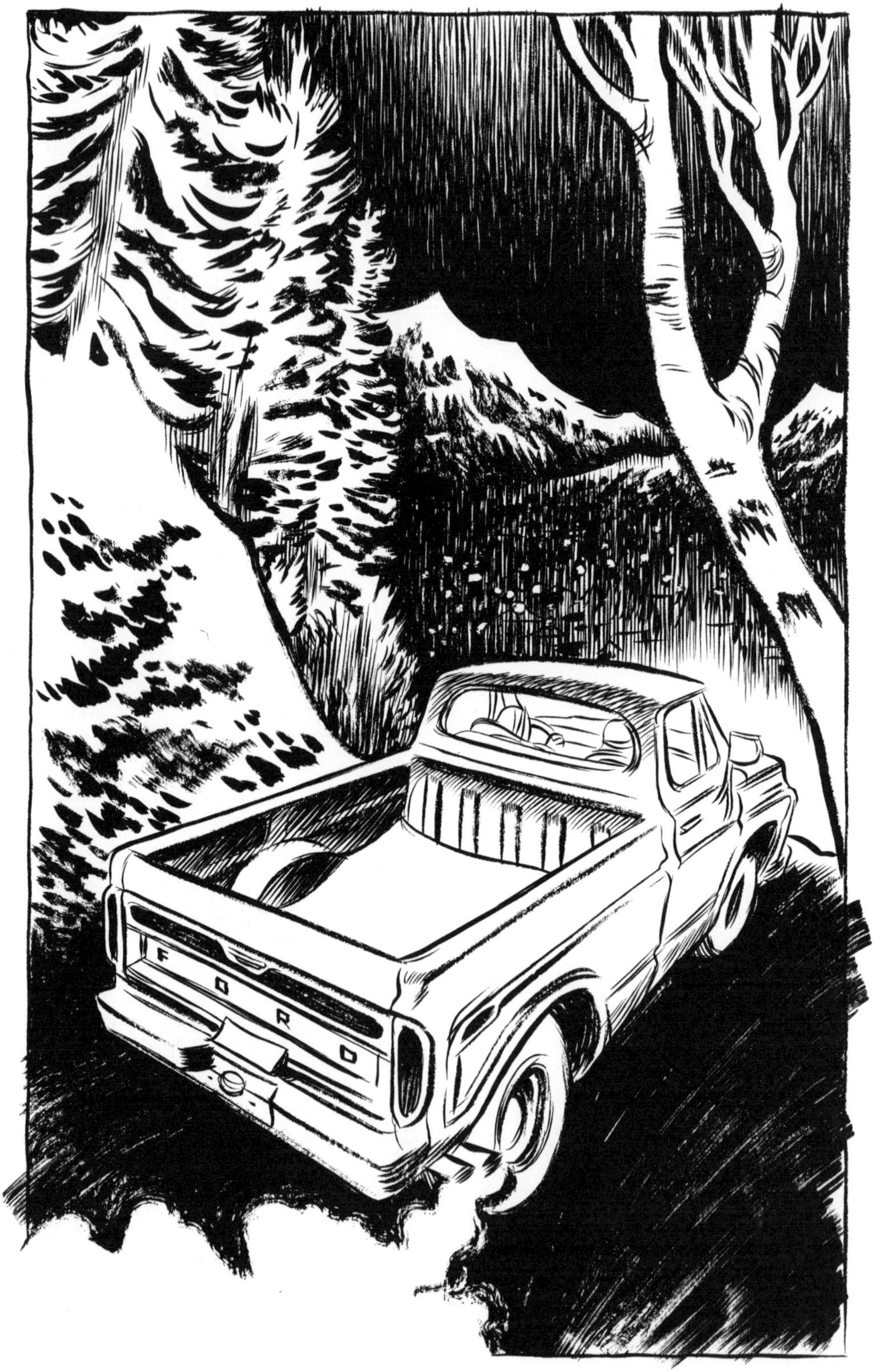
FORD

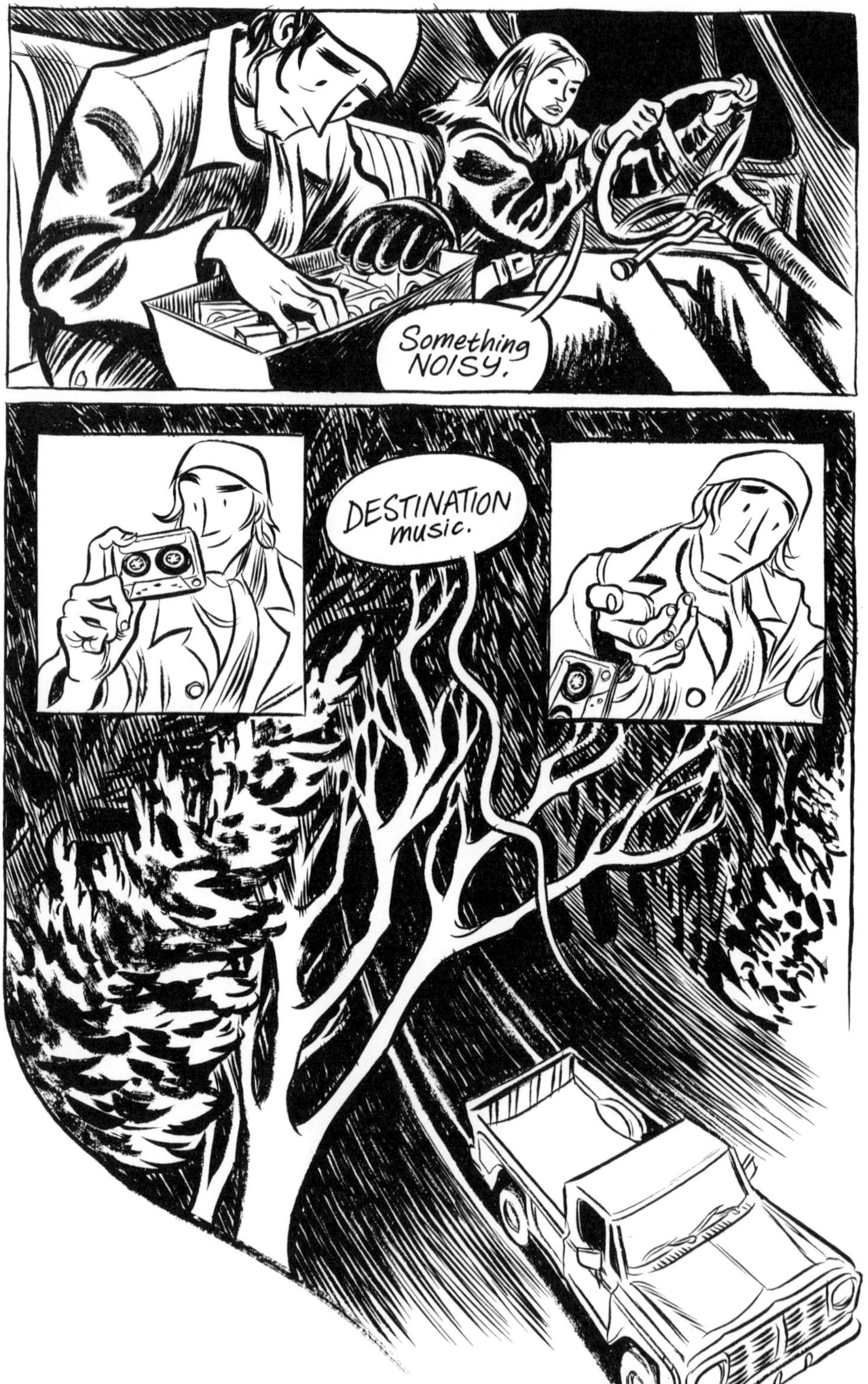
Something NOISY.
DESTINATION music.

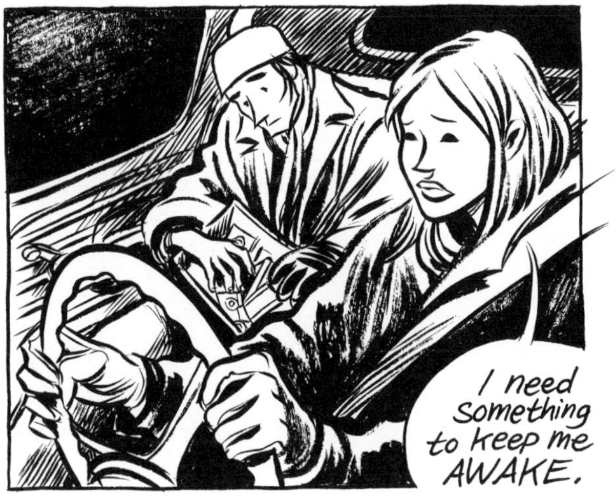
I need something to keep me AWAKE.

VII

Just Like Heaven

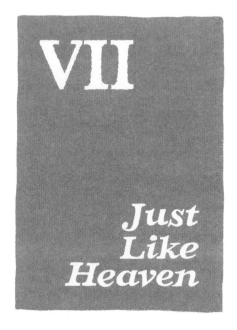

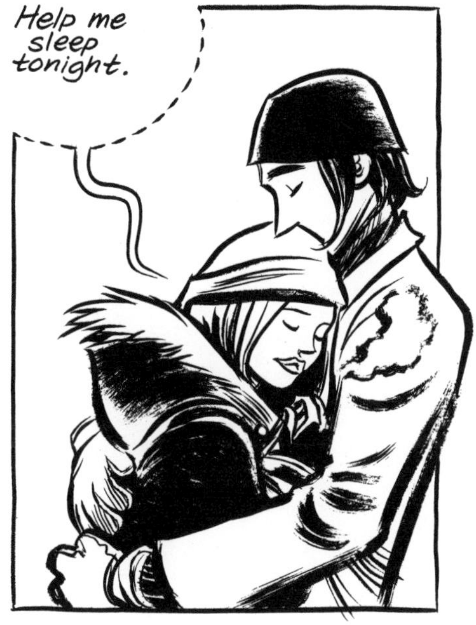
Help me sleep tonight.

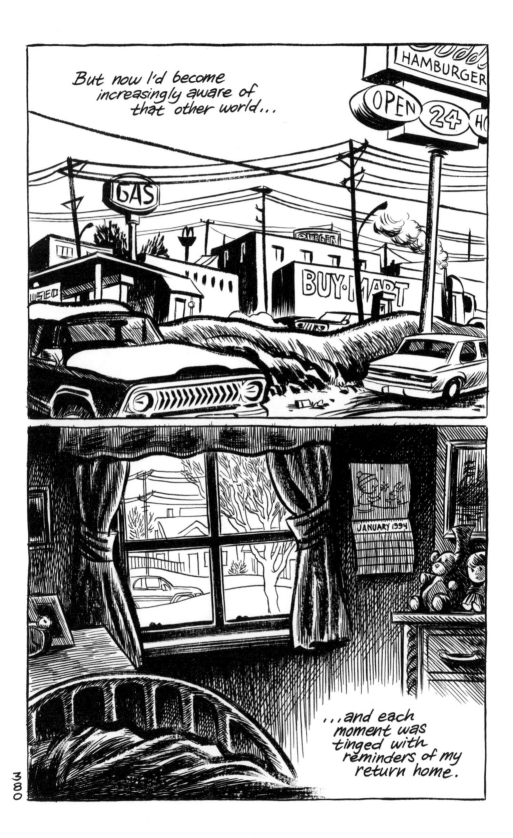

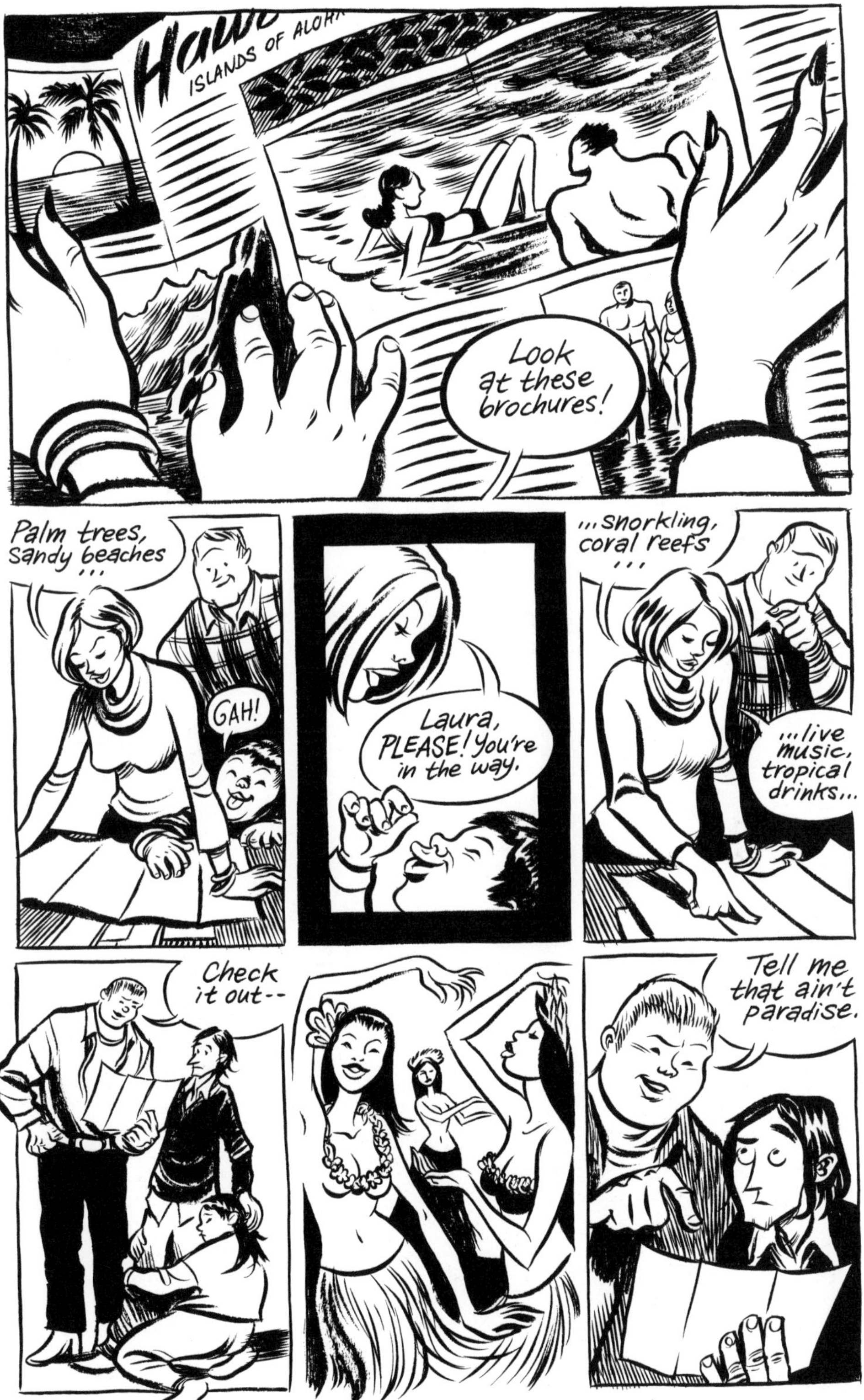
Look at these brochures!
Palm trees, sandy beaches ...
GAH!
Laura, PLEASE! You're in the way.
...snorkling, coral reefs ...
...live music, tropical drinks...
Check it out--
Tell me that ain't paradise.

382

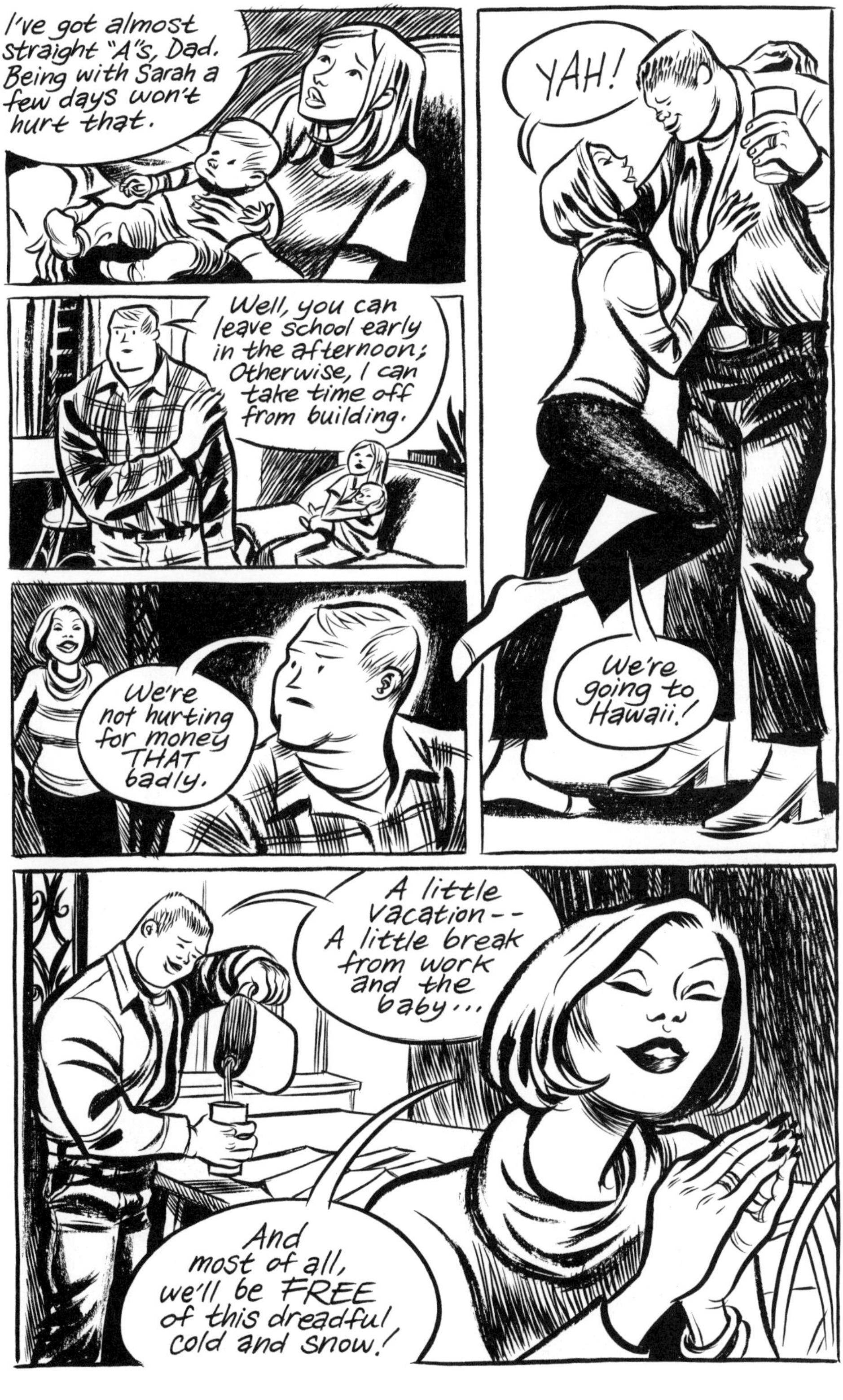
I've got almost straight "A"s, Dad. Being with Sarah a few days won't hurt that.
Well, you can leave school early in the afternoon; Otherwise, I can take time off from building.
We're not hurting for money THAT badly.
YAH!
We're going to Hawaii!
A little vacation-- A little break from work and the baby...
And most of all, we'll be FREE of this dreadful cold and snow!

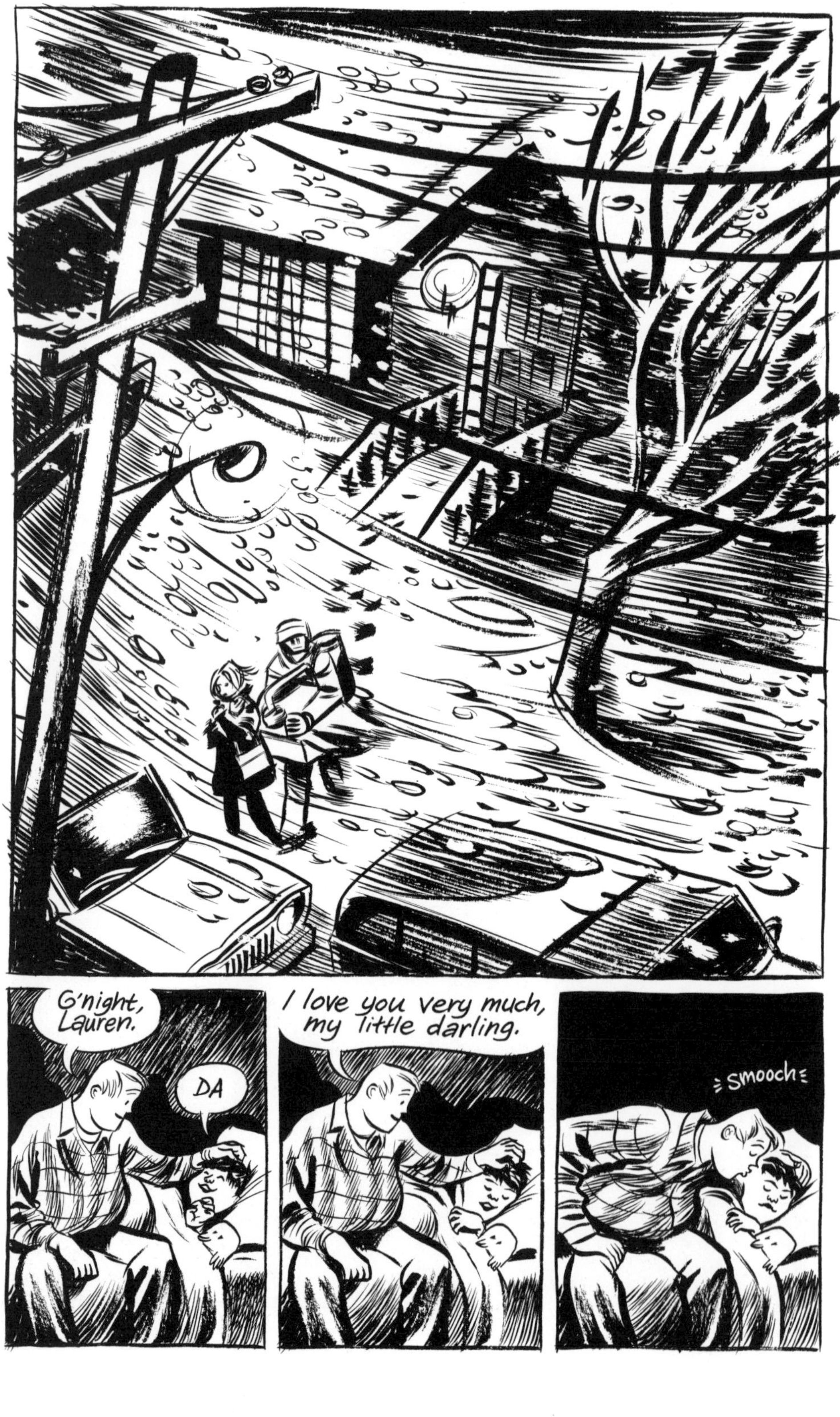

G'night, Lauren.
DA
I love you very much, my little darling.
SMOOCH

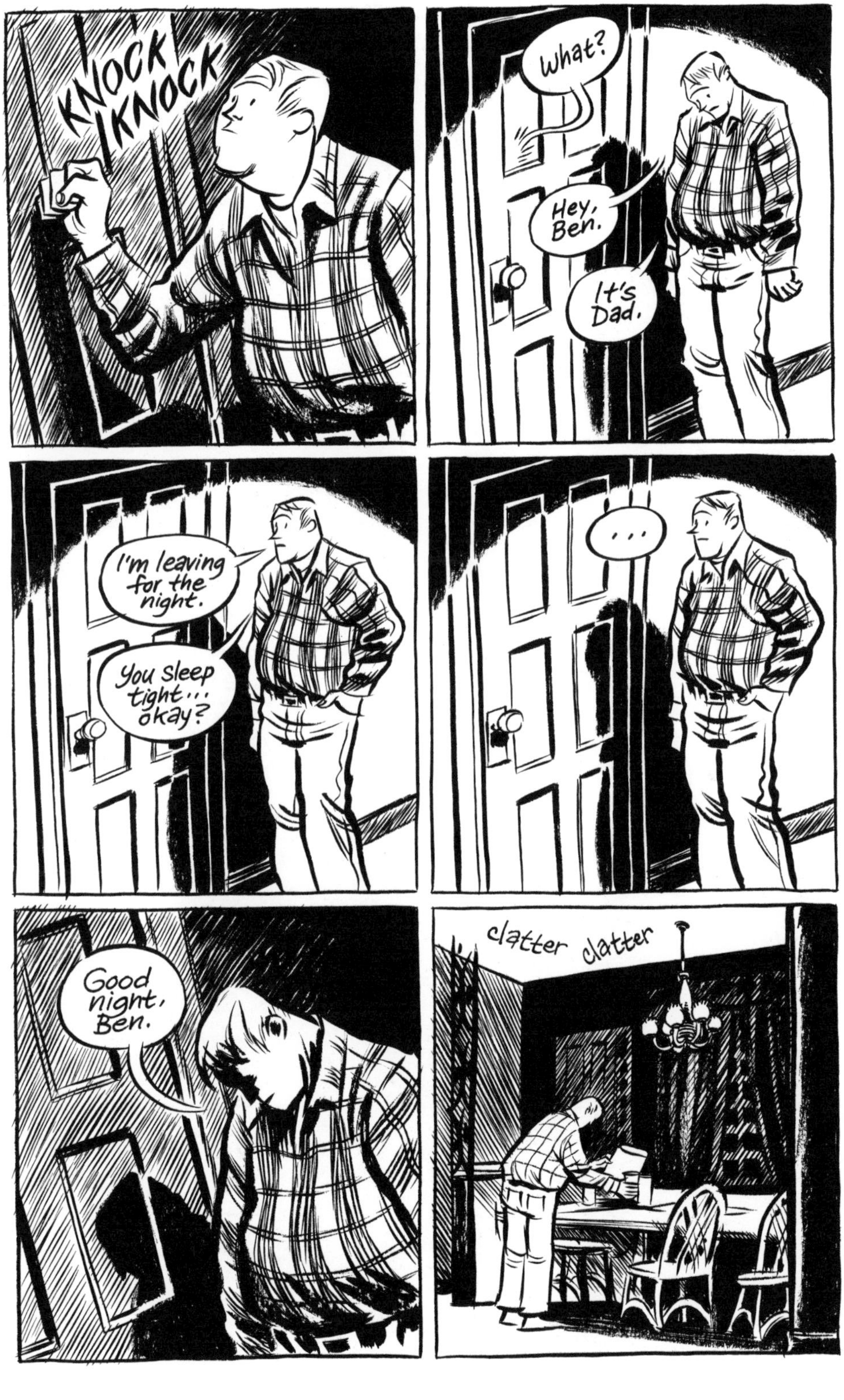
KNOCK KNOCK
What?
Hey, Ben.
It's Dad.
I'm leaving for the night.
You sleep tight... okay?
...
Good night, Ben.
clatter clatter

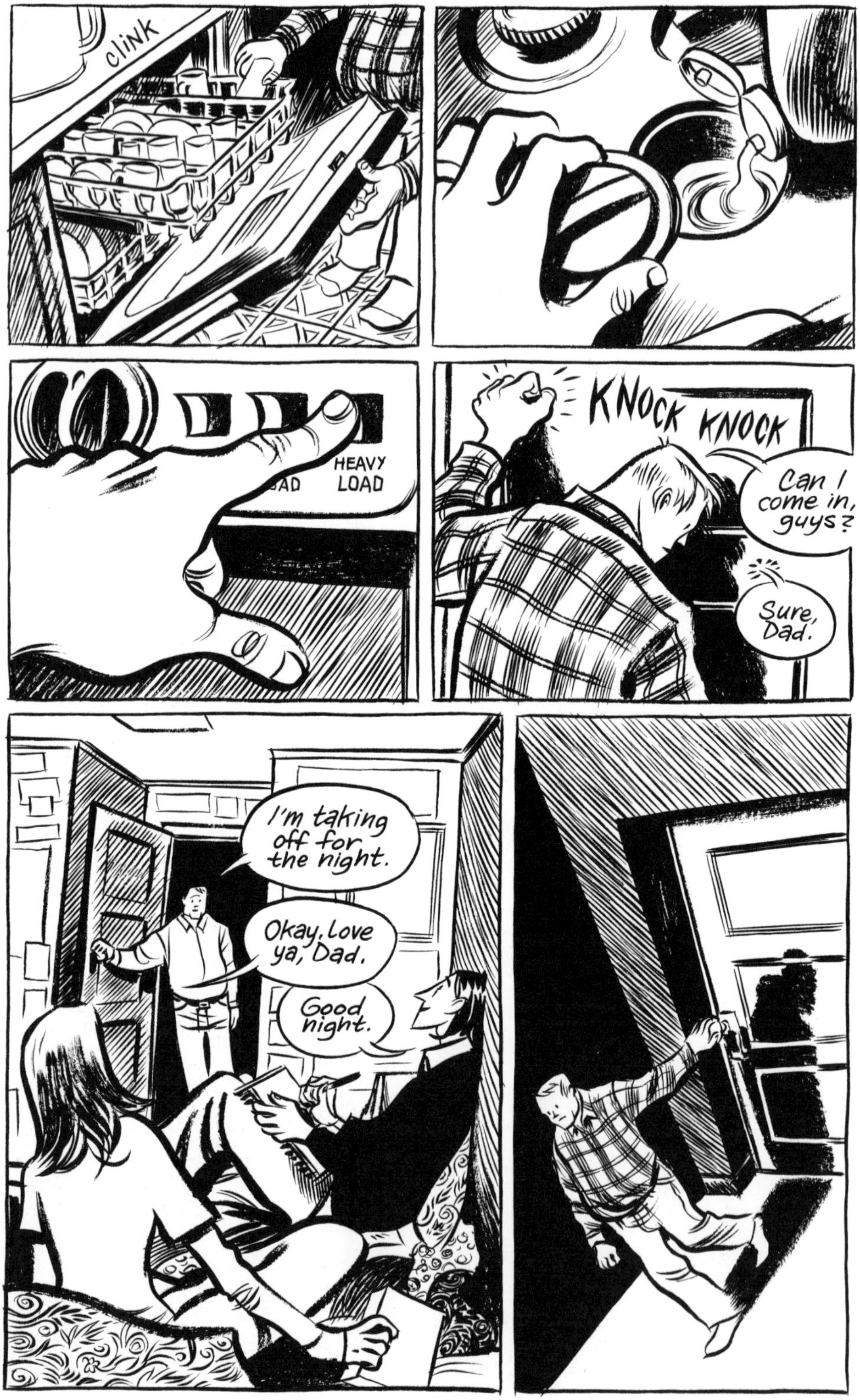
clink
AD
HEAVY LOAD
KNOCK KNOCK
Can I come in, guys?
Sure, Dad.
I'm taking off for the night.
Okay, love ya, Dad.
Good night.

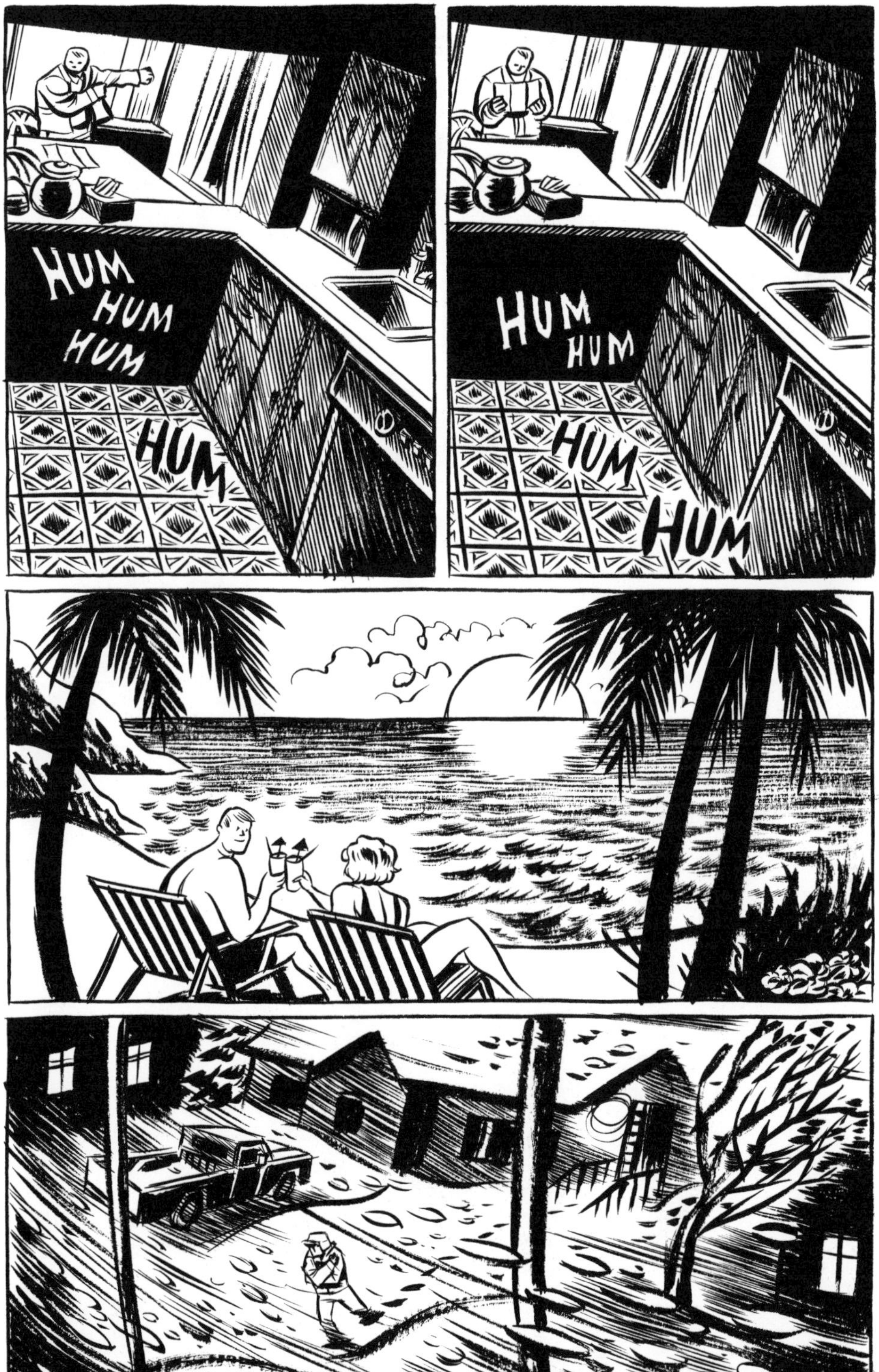
HUM
HUM
HUM
HUM
HUM
HUM
HUM
HUM

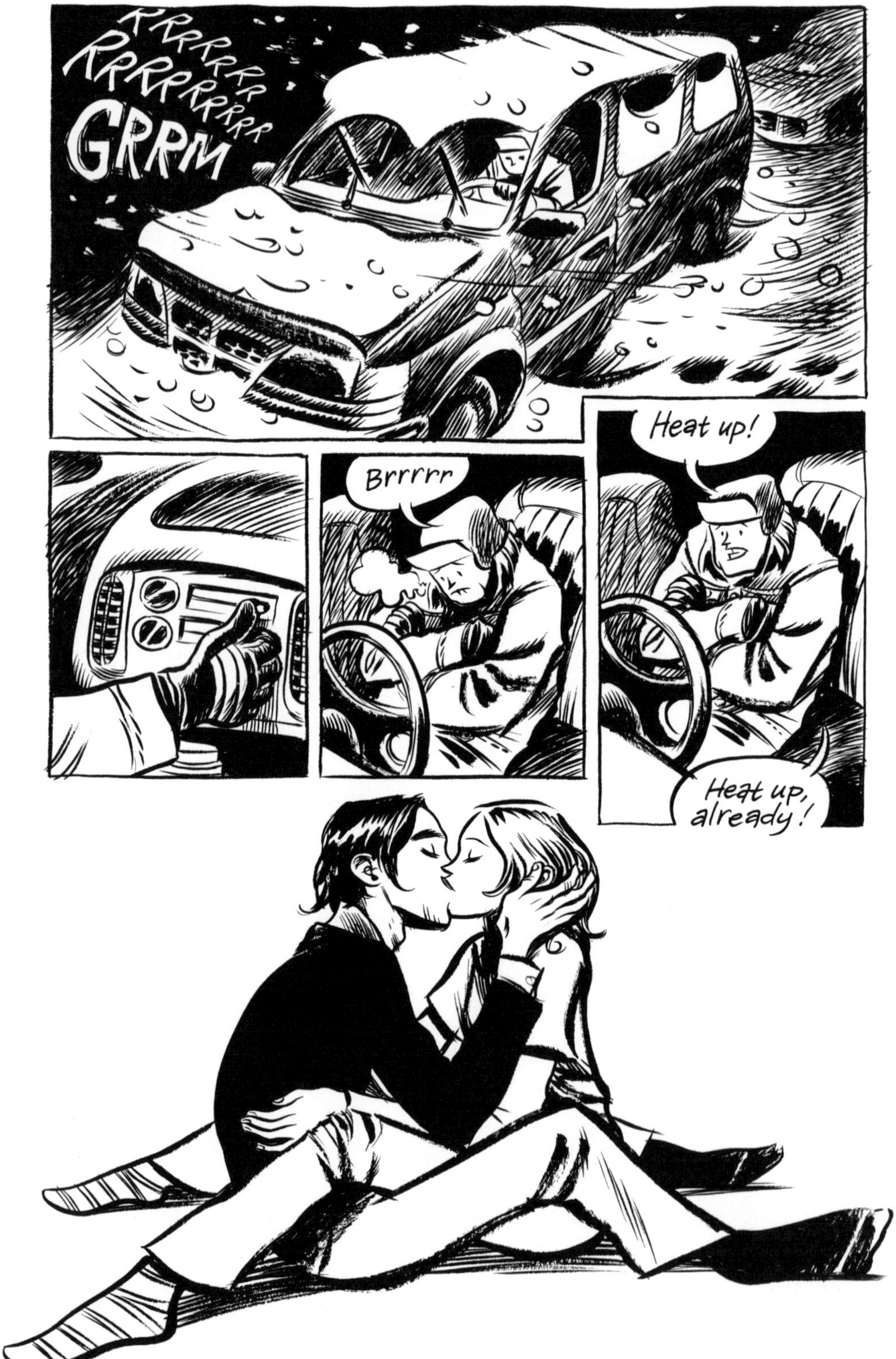
RRRRRRRR
RRRRRRRRRRRR
GRRM
Brrrrr
Heat up!
Heat up, already!

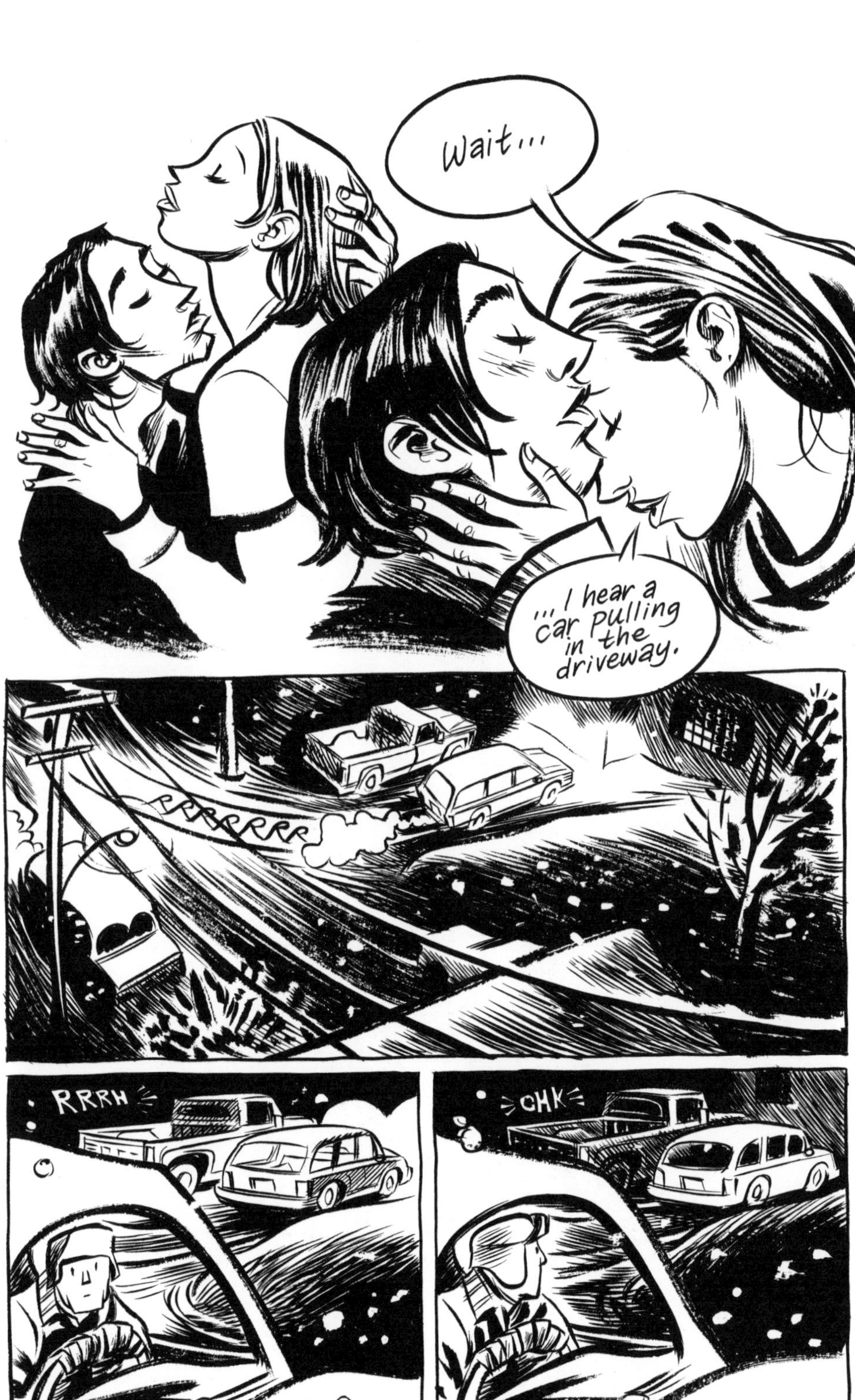
Wait...
...I hear a car pulling in the driveway.
RRRRRRRRR
RRRH
CHK

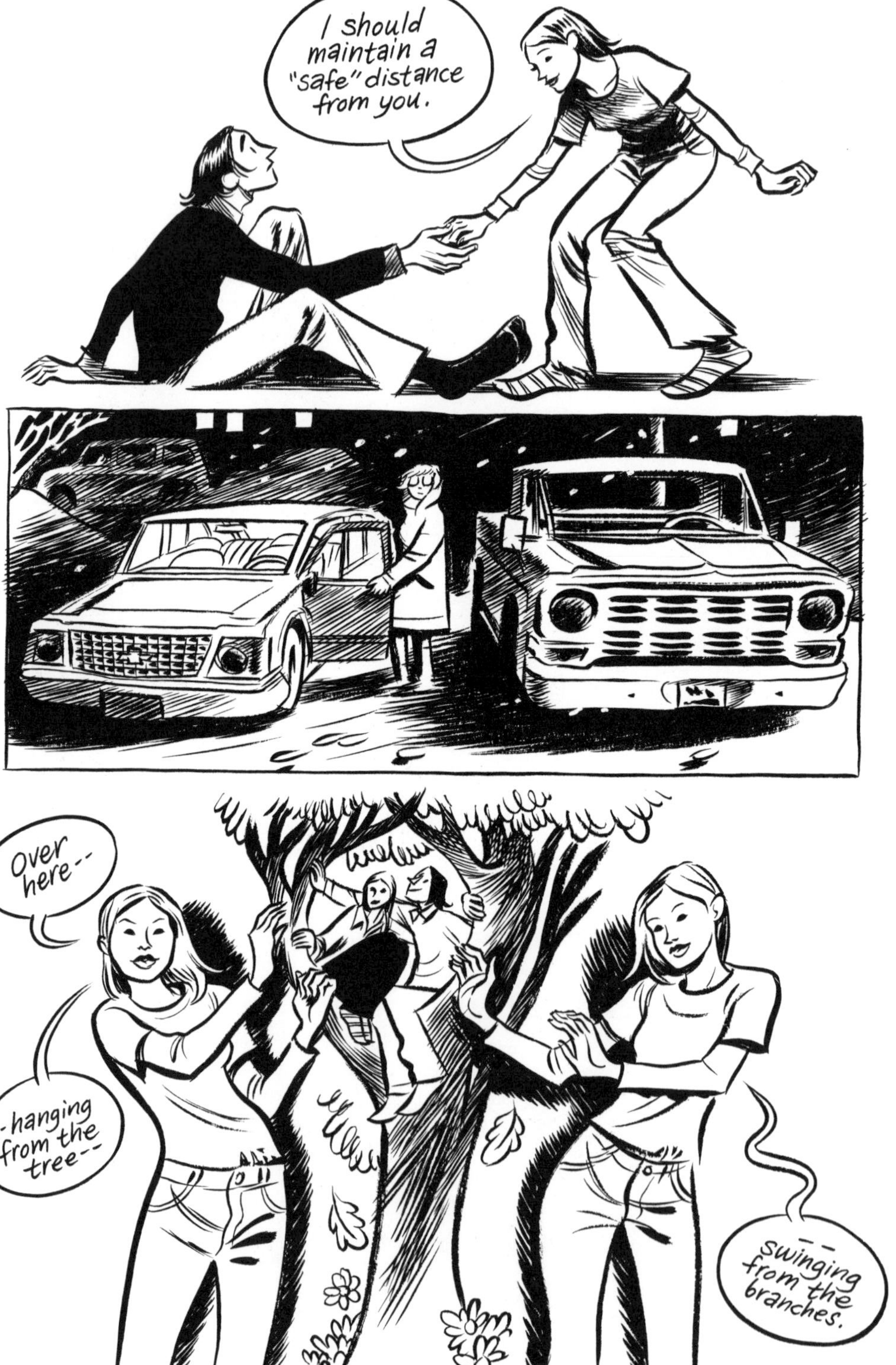

I should maintain a "safe" distance from you.
Over here--
--hanging from the tree--
--swinging from the branches.

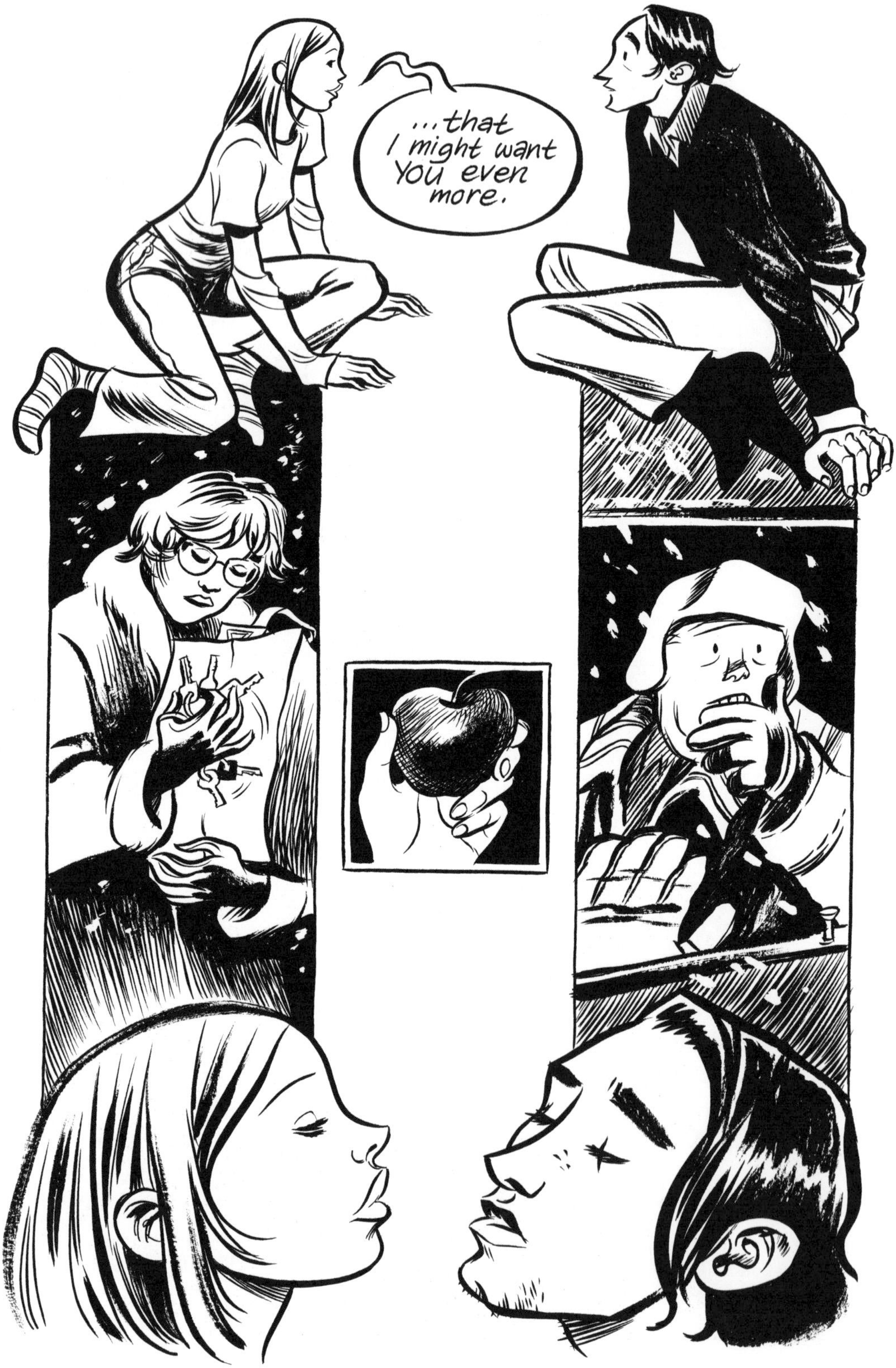
...that I might want you even more.

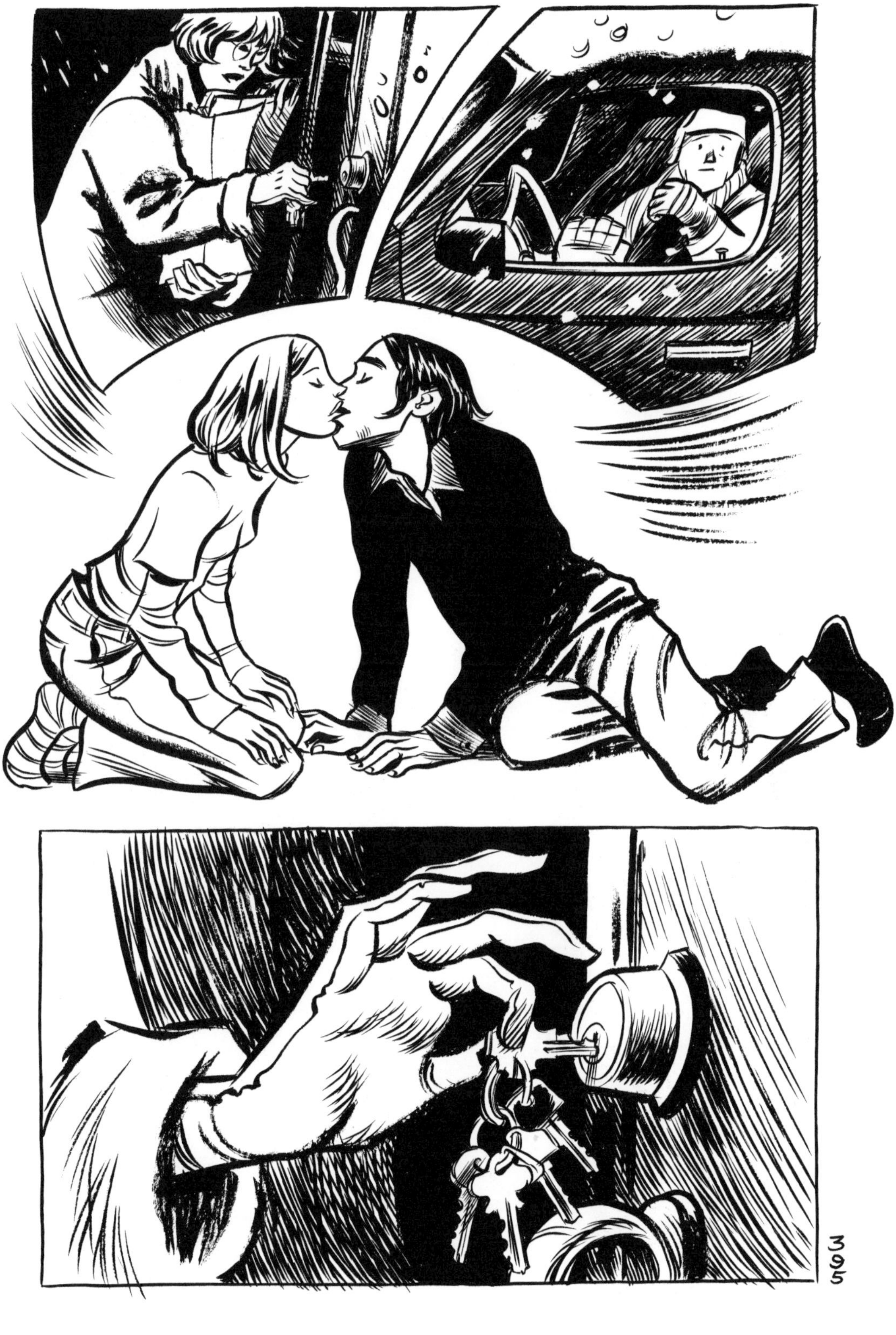

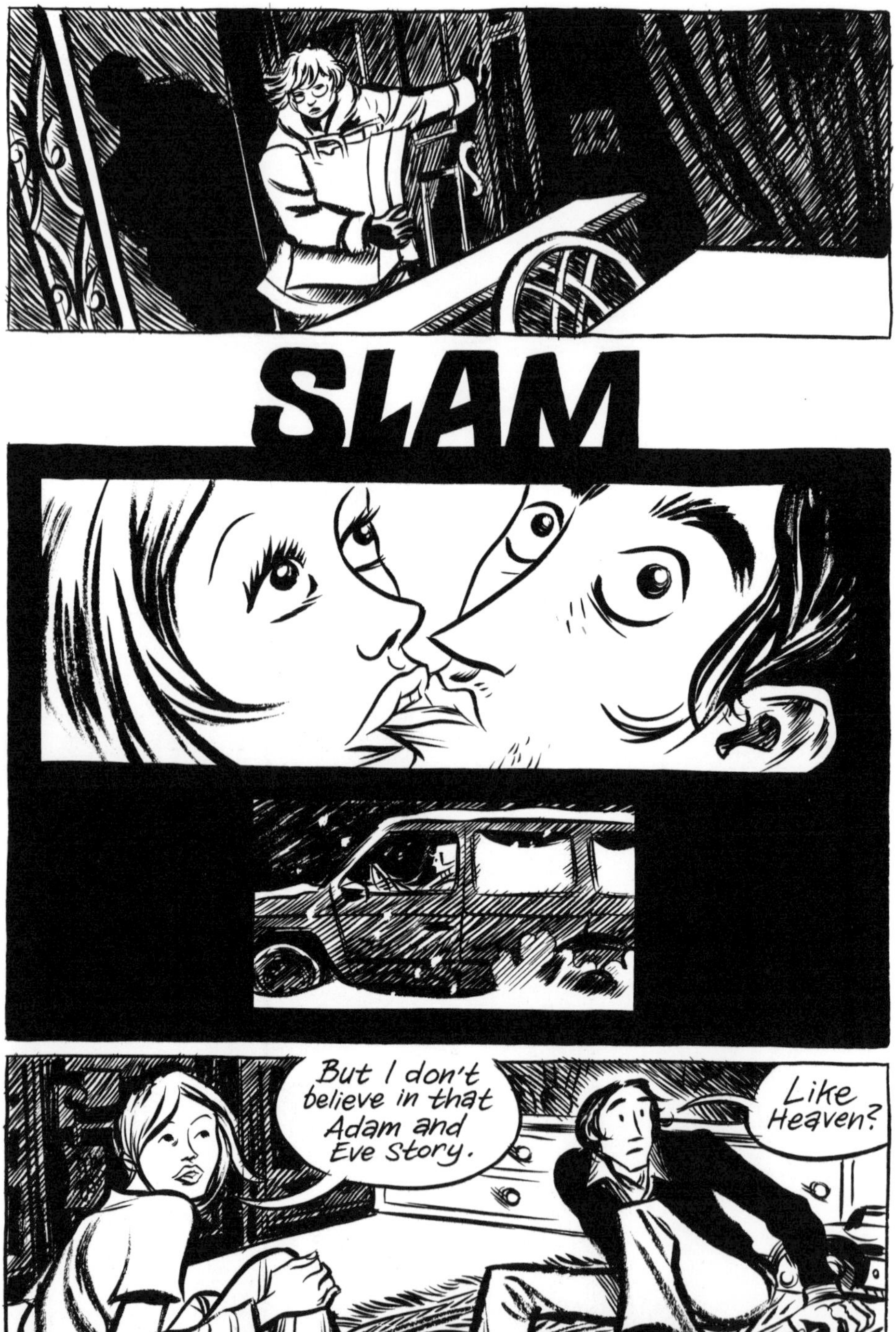
SLAM
But I don't believe in that Adam and Eve story.
Like Heaven?

397

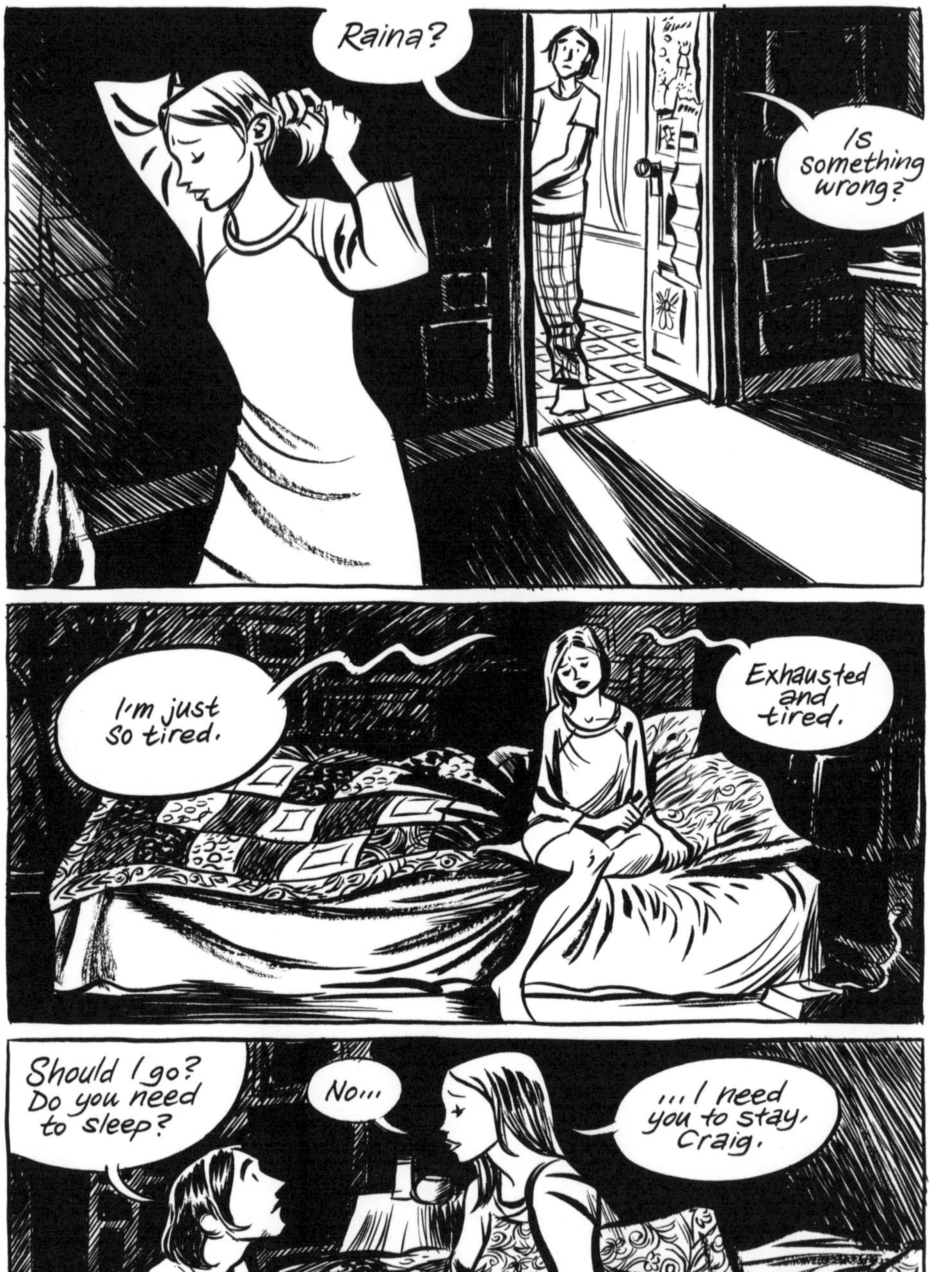
Raina?
Is something wrong?
I'm just so tired.
Exhausted and tired.
Should I go? Do you need to sleep?
No...
...I need you to stay, Craig.
You promised.

401

402

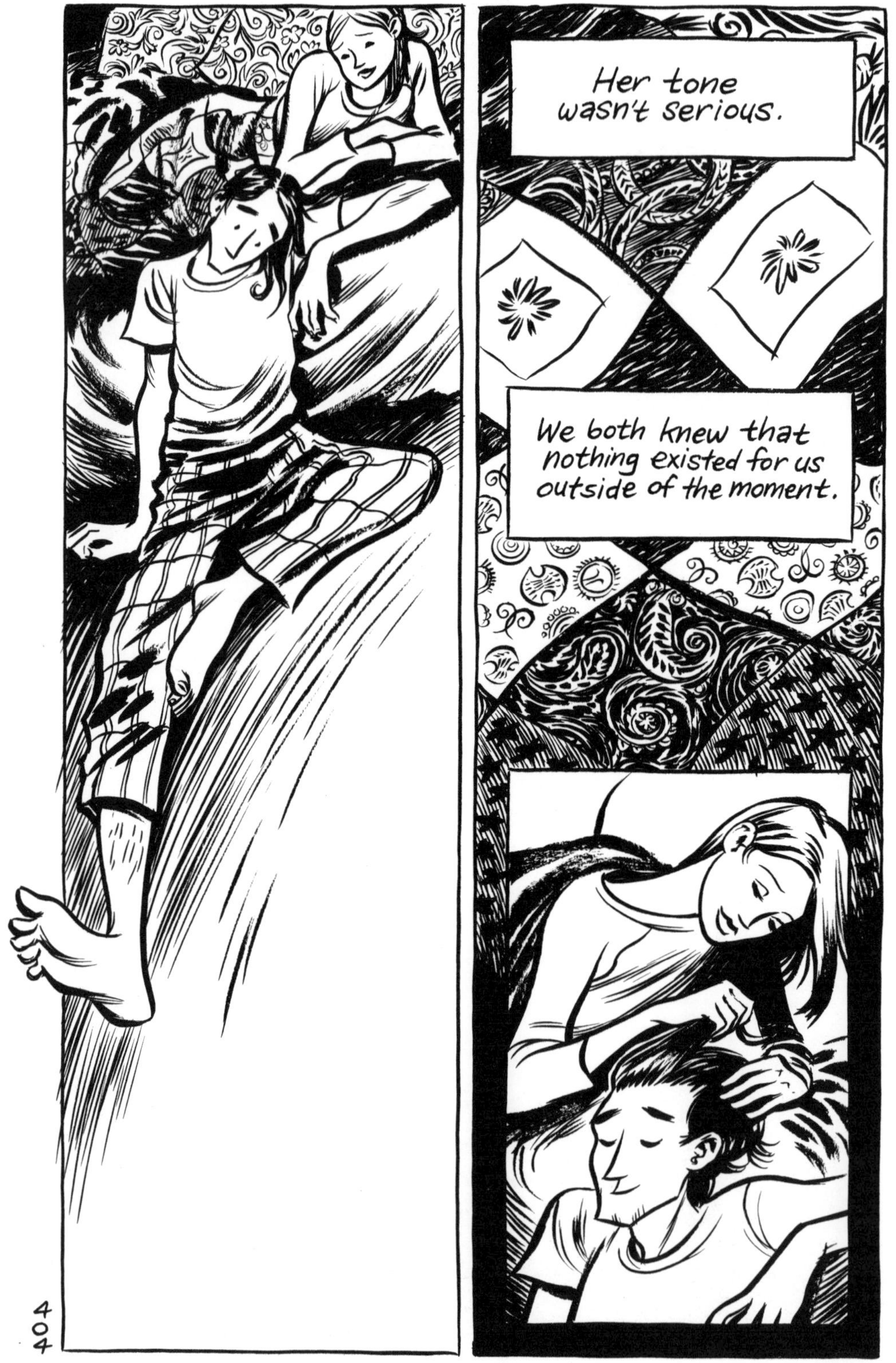
Her tone wasn't serious.
We both knew that nothing existed for us outside of the moment.

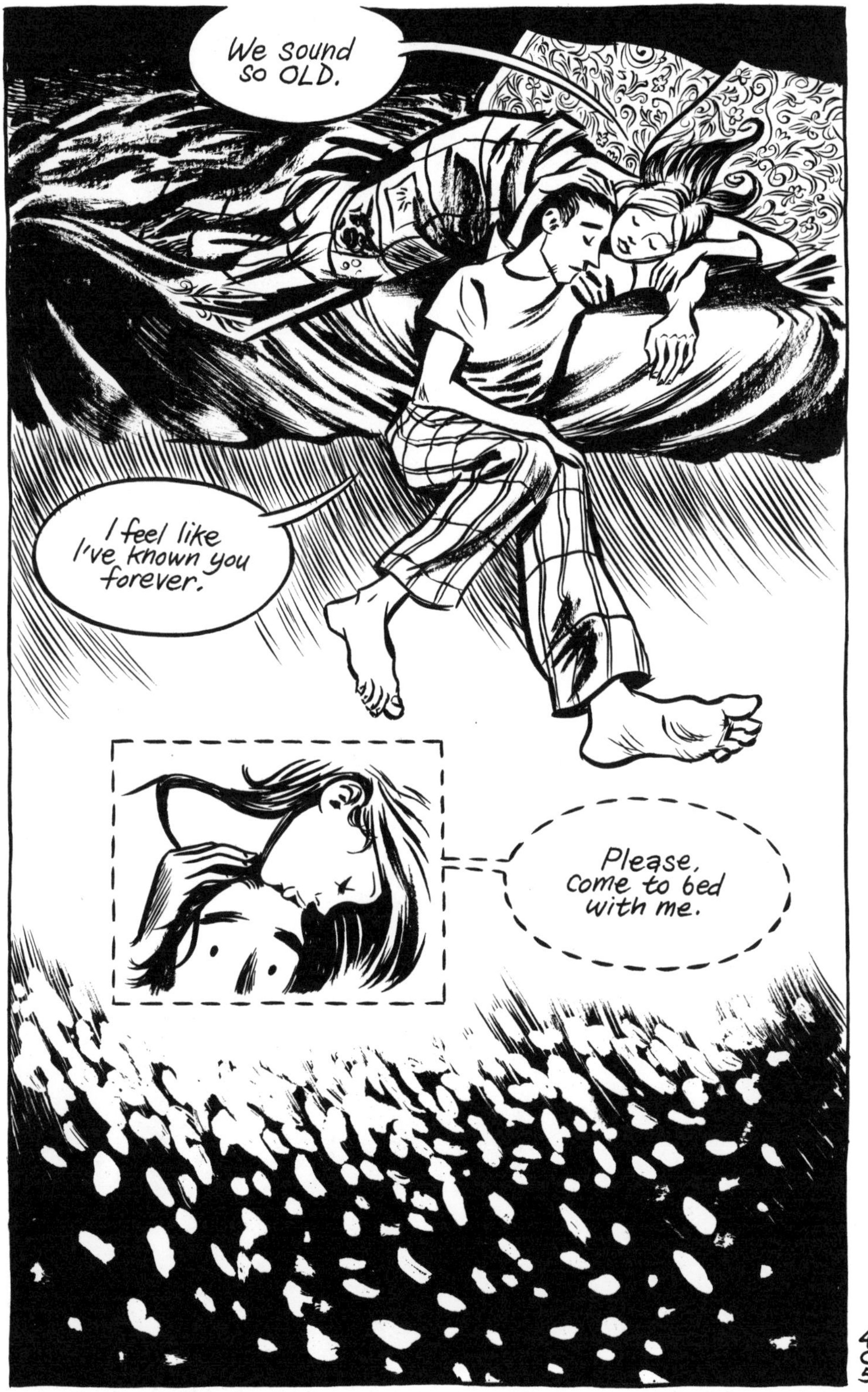
We sound so OLD.
I feel like I've known you forever.
Please, come to bed with me.

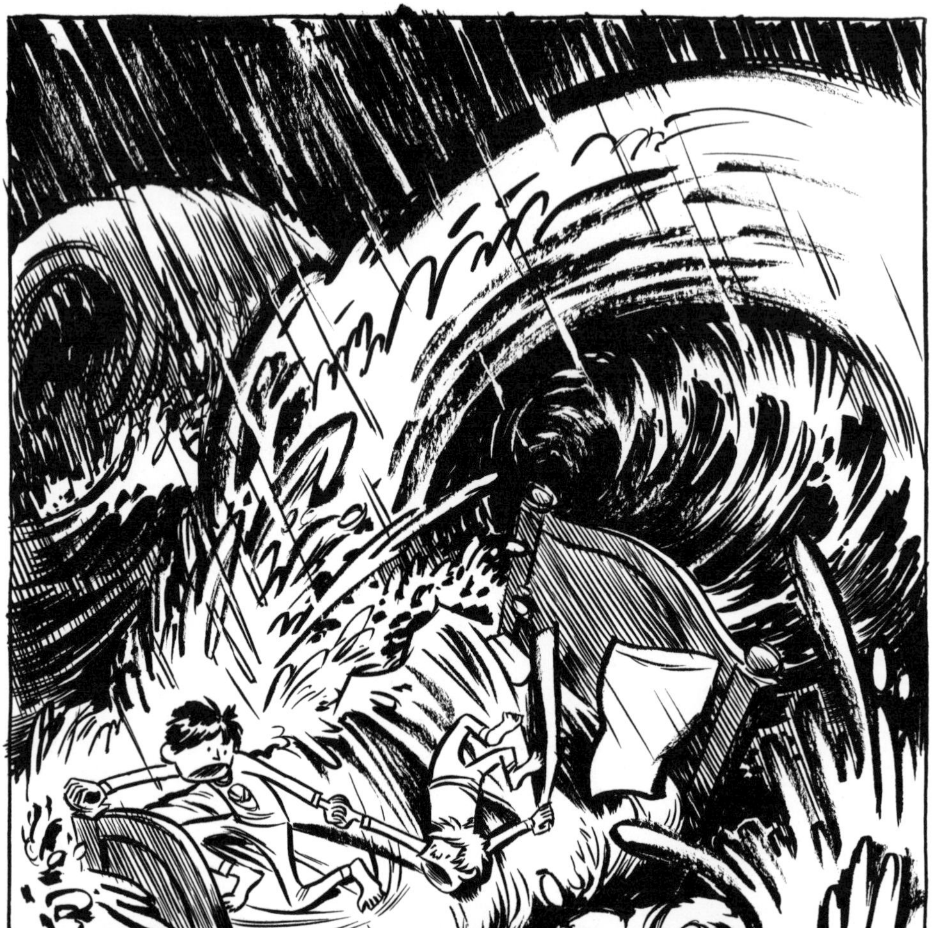
STORM
AT
Sea

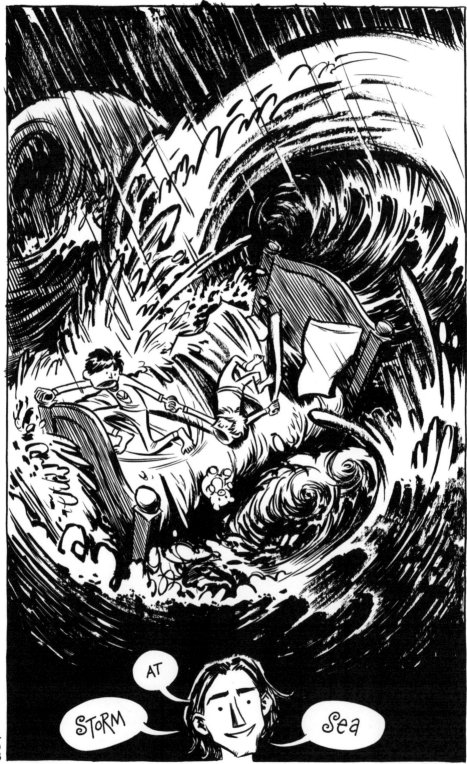

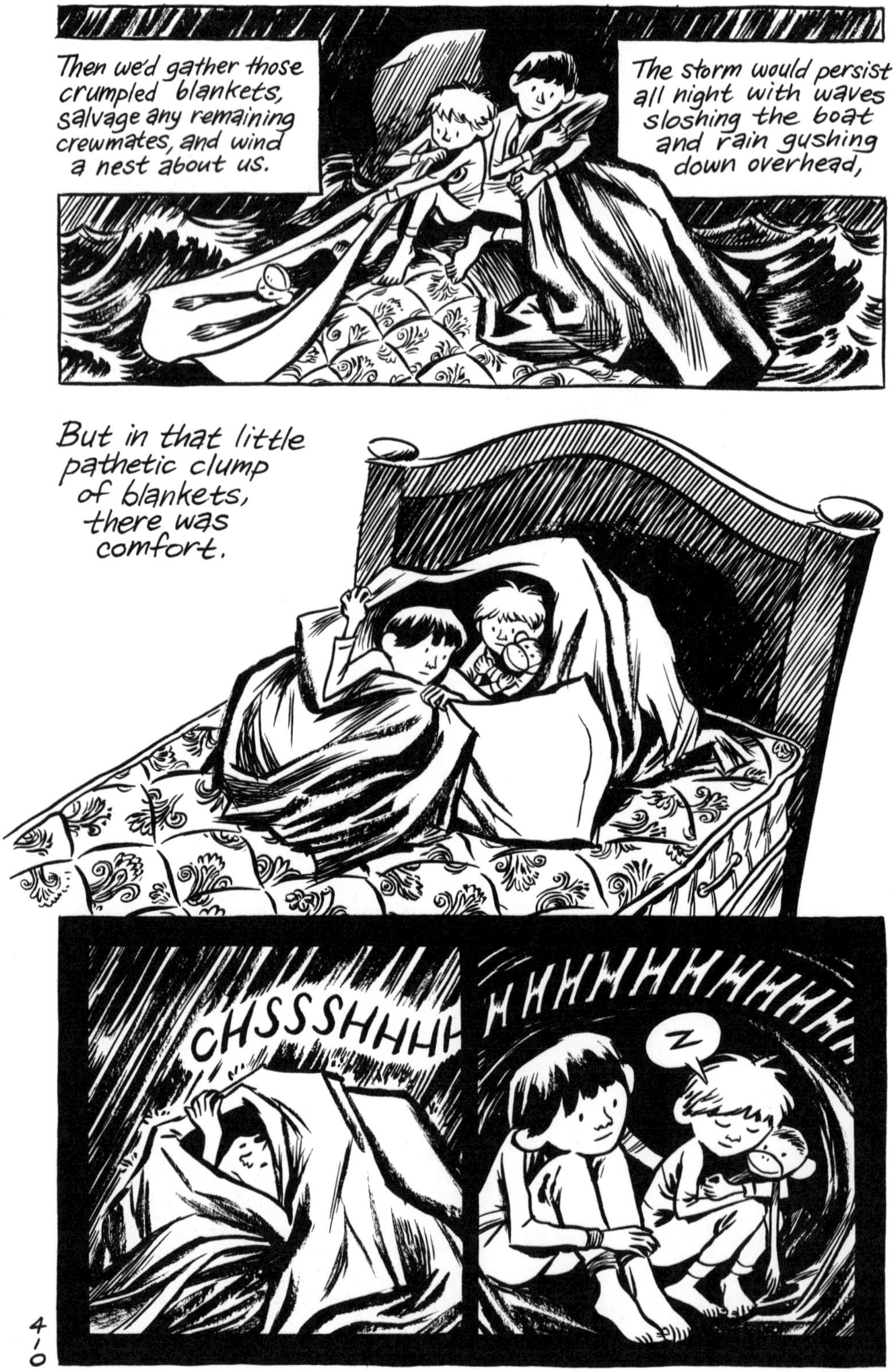
Then we'd gather those crumpled blankets, salvage any remaining crewmates, and wind a nest about us.
The storm would persist all night with waves sloshing the boat and rain gushing down overhead,
But in that little pathetic clump of blankets, there was comfort.
CHSSSHHH
HHHHHHHHHHHH
Z

411

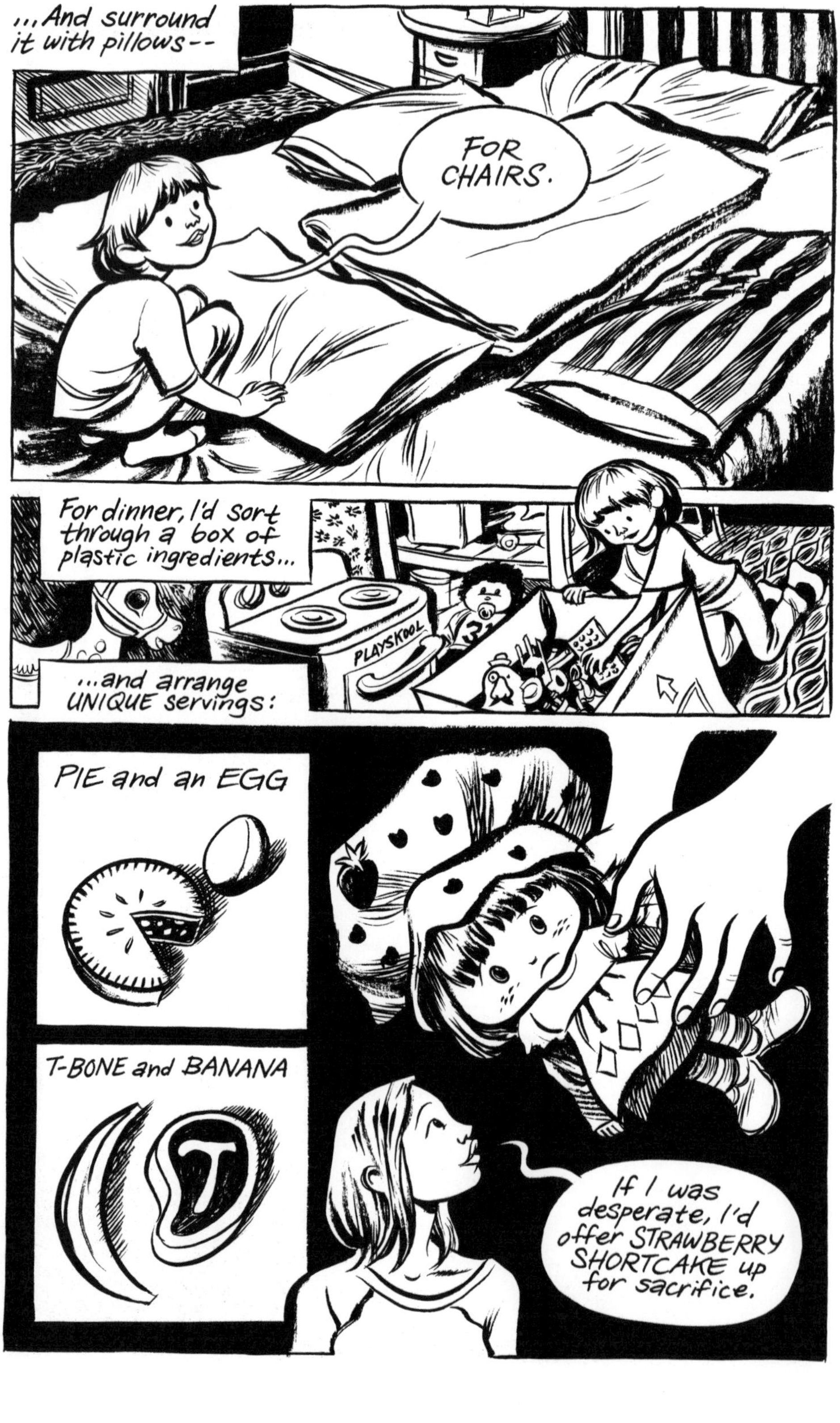
...And surround it with pillows--
FOR CHAIRS.
For dinner, I'd sort through a box of plastic ingredients...
PLAYSKOOL
...and arrange UNIQUE servings:
PIE and an EGG
T-BONE and BANANA
If I was desperate, I'd offer STRAWBERRY SHORTCAKE up for sacrifice.

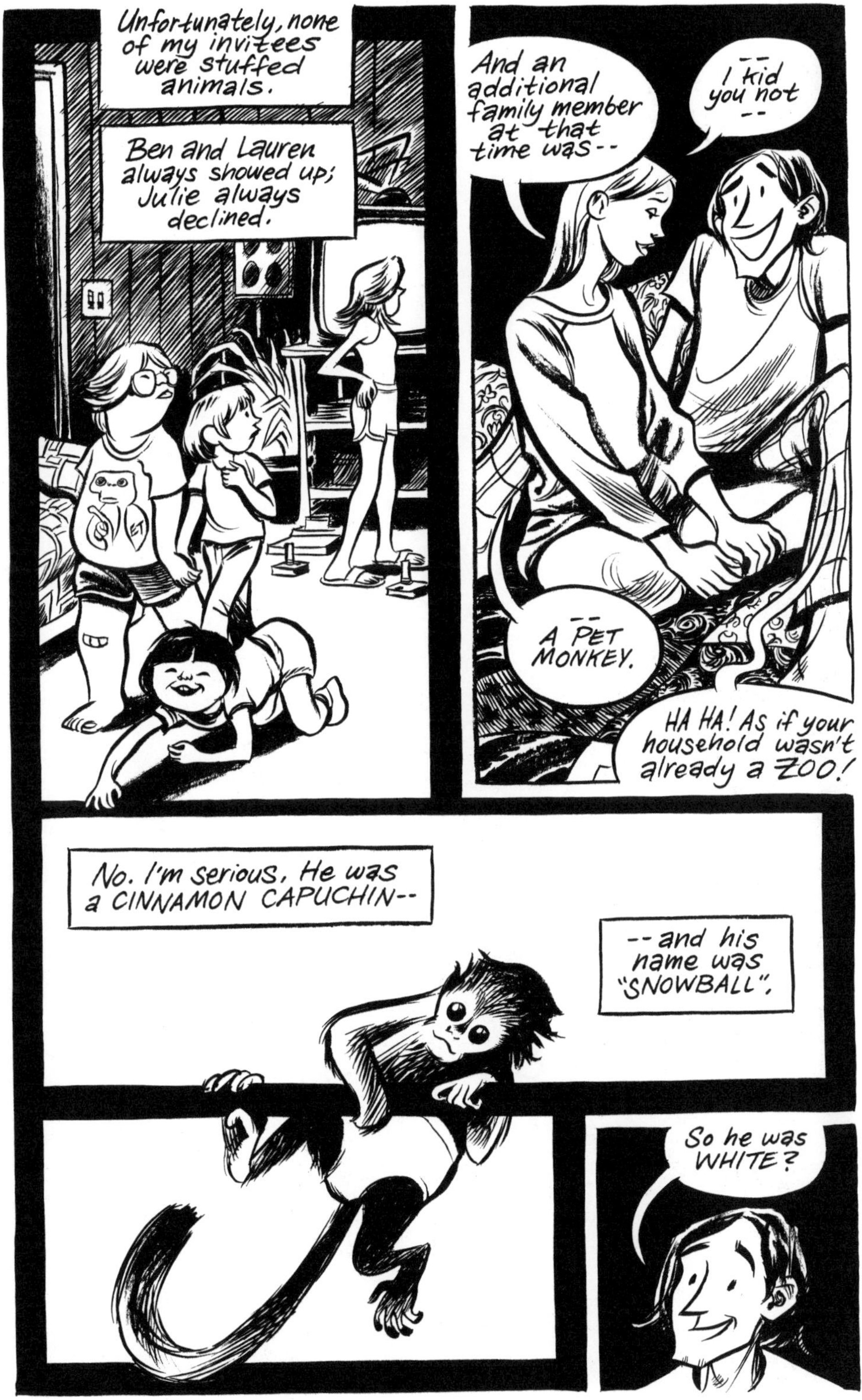

Unfortunately, none of my invitees were stuffed animals.
Ben and Lauren always showed up; Julie always declined.
ET
And an additional family member at that time was--
--I kid you not--
--A PET MONKEY.
HA HA! As if your household wasn't already a ZOO!
No. I'm serious. He was a CINNAMON CAPUCHIN--
--and his name was "SNOWBALL".
So he was WHITE?

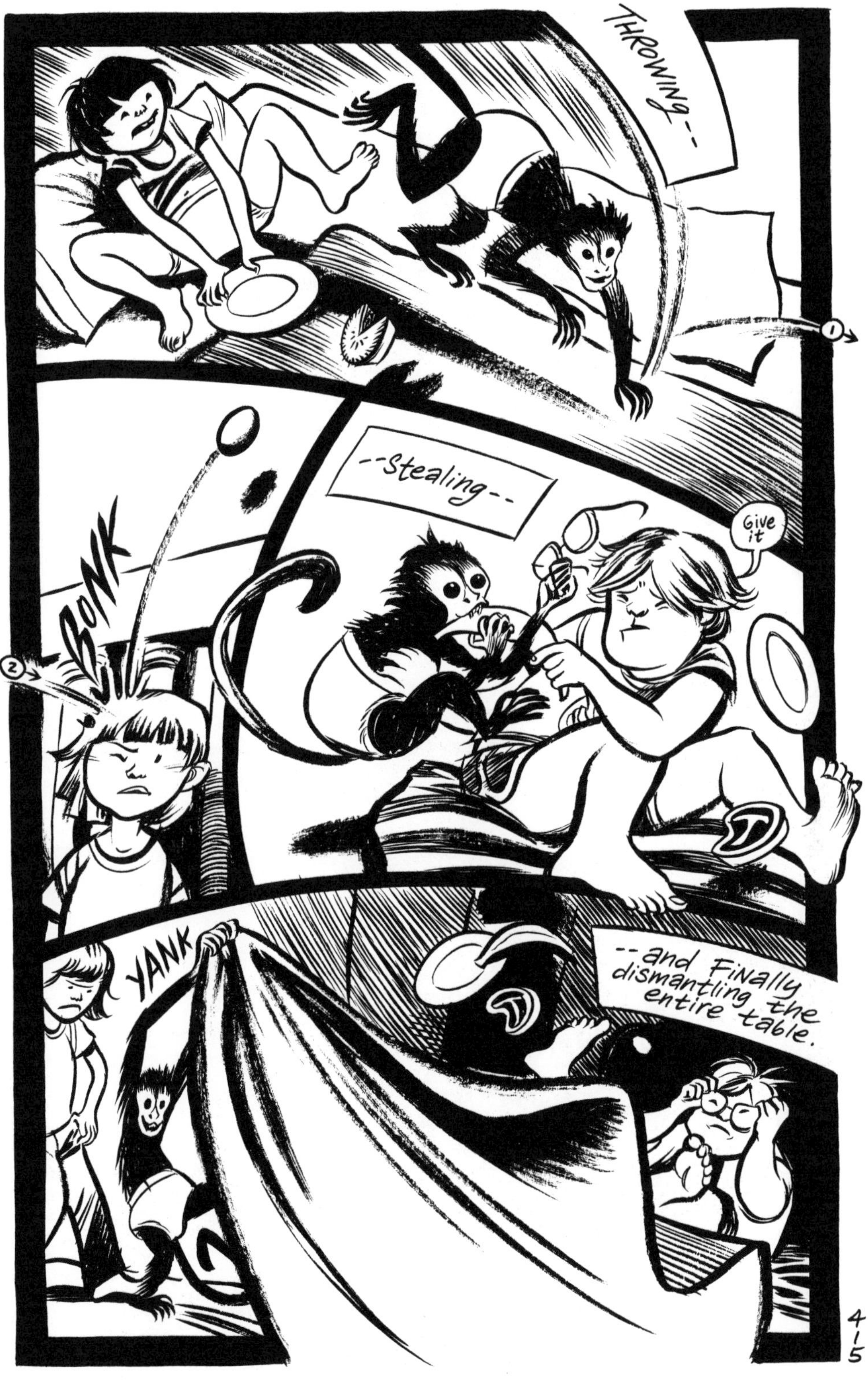

THROWING--
1
--Stealing--
Give it
2
BONK
YANK
--and Finally dismantling the entire table.

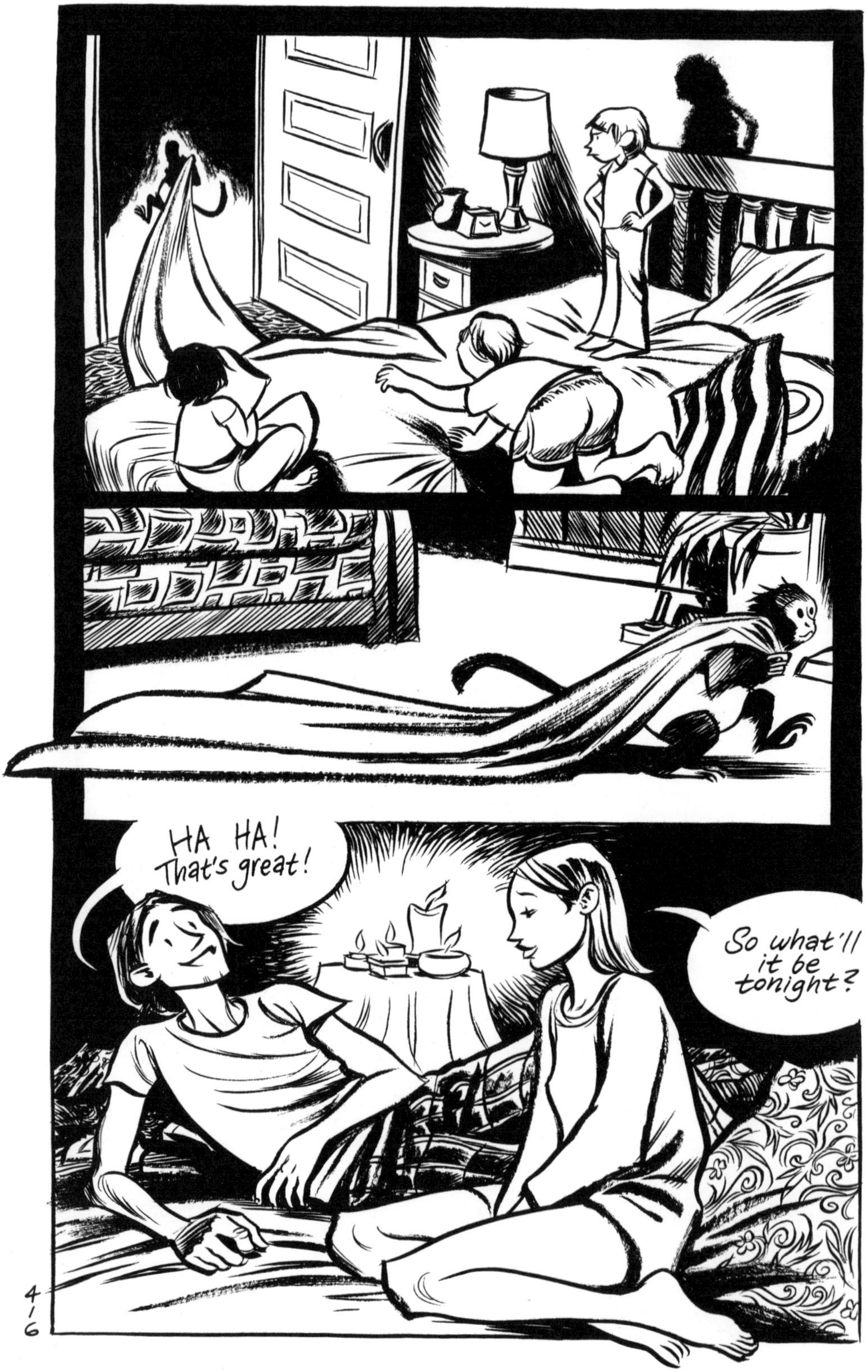
HA HA! That's great!
So what'll it be tonight?

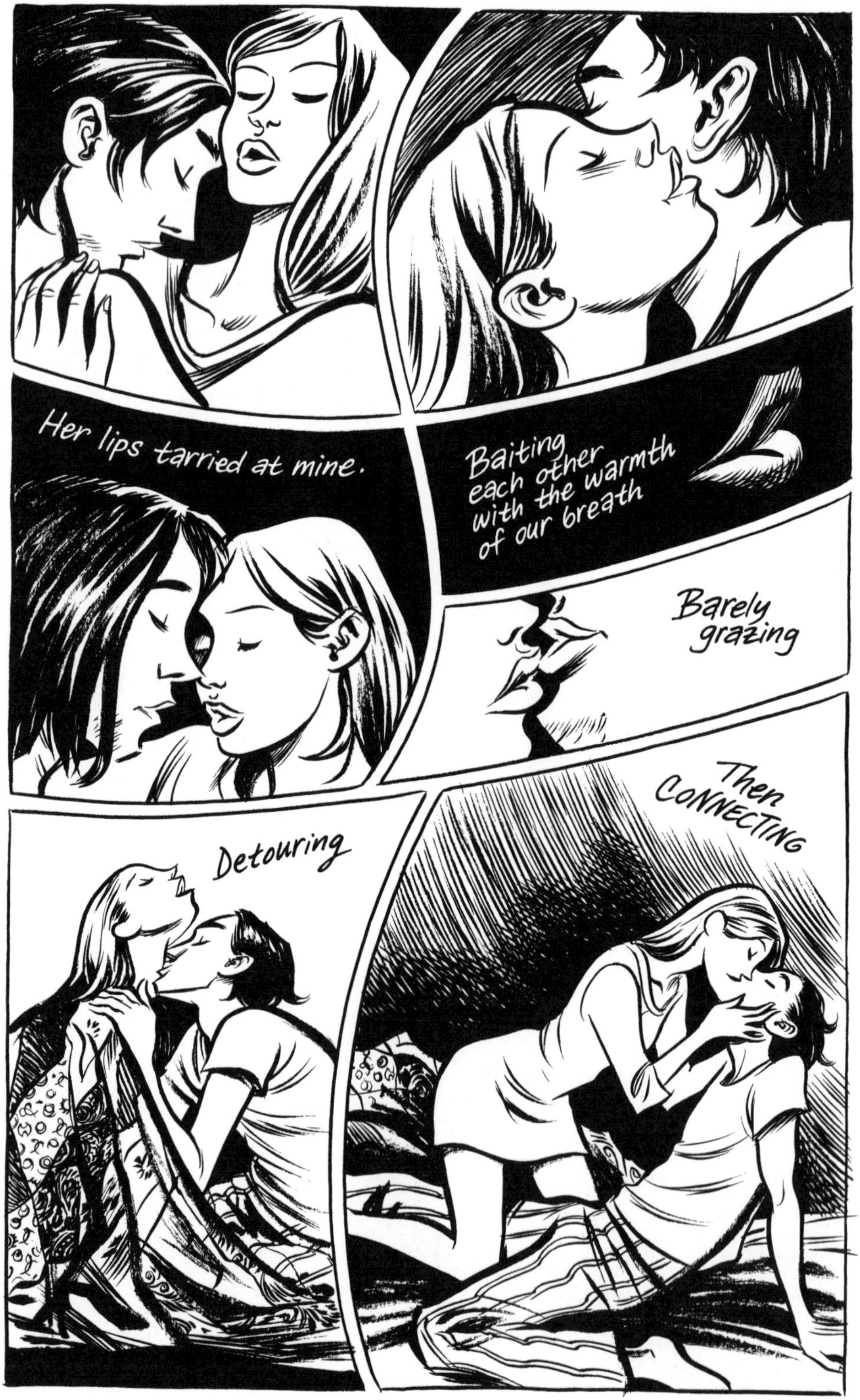

Her lips tarried at mine.
Baiting each other with the warmth of our breath
Barely grazing
Detouring
Then CONNECTING

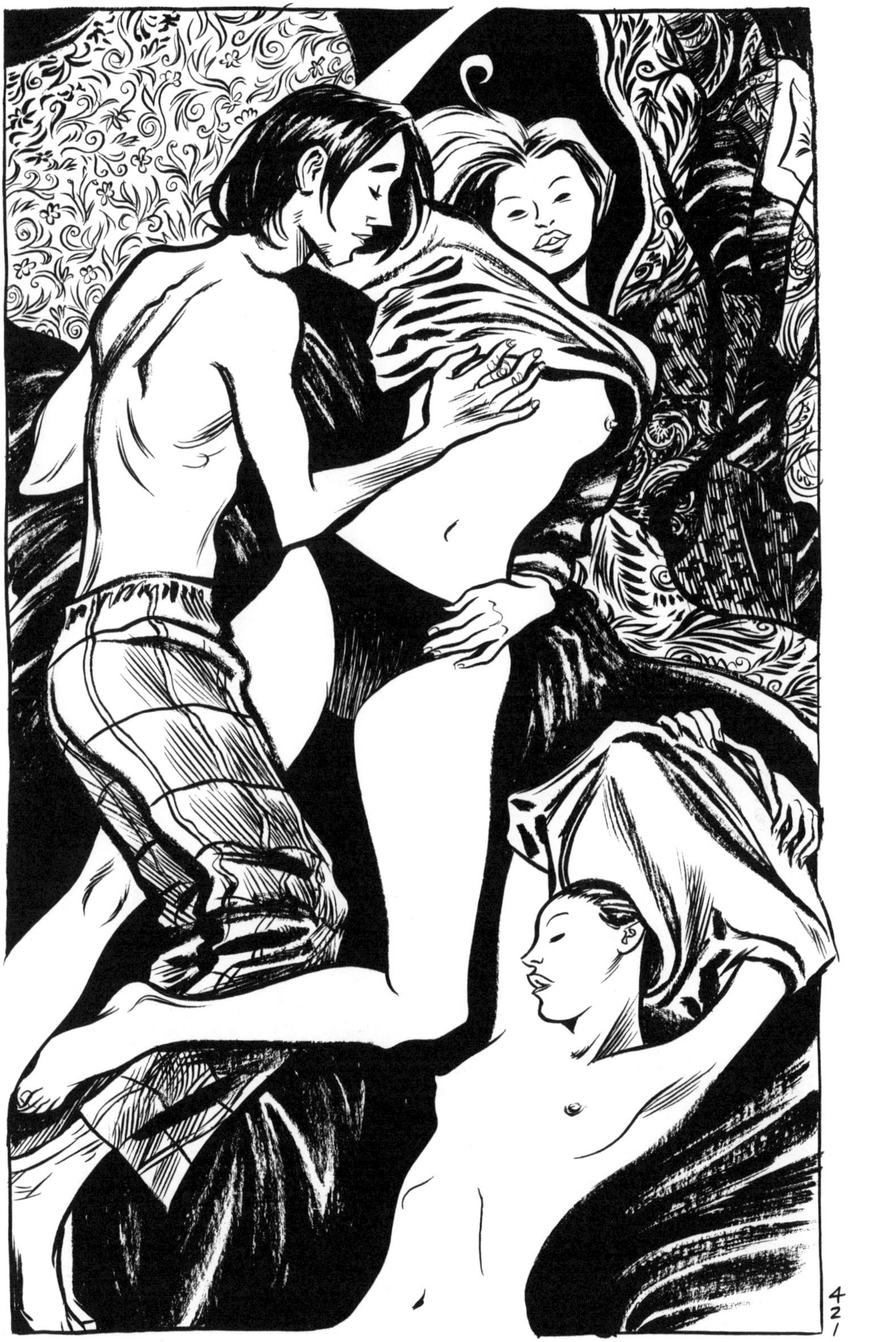

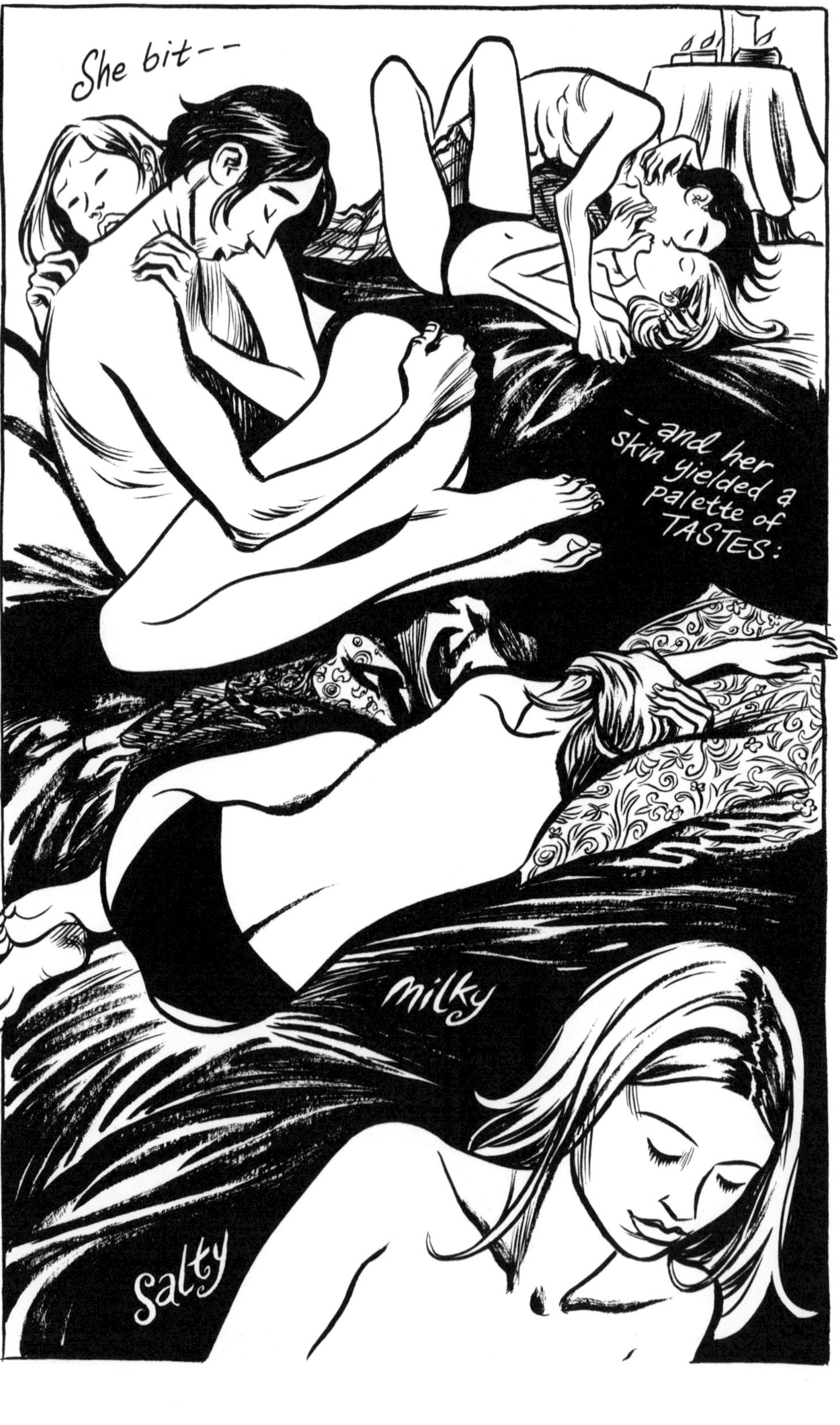
She bit--
--and her skin yielded a palette of TASTES:
milky
salty

... it is never enough.

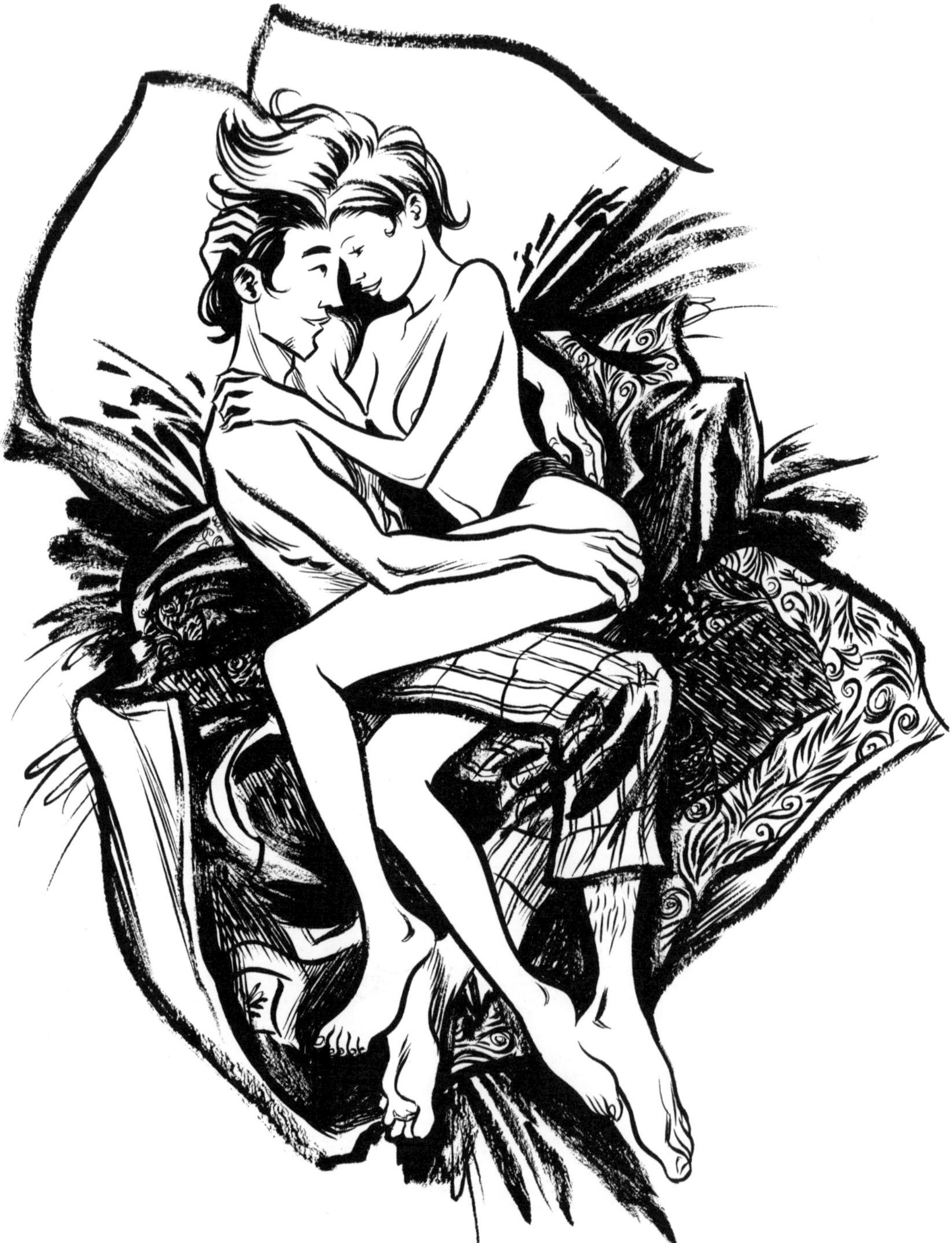

And then she sang to me.

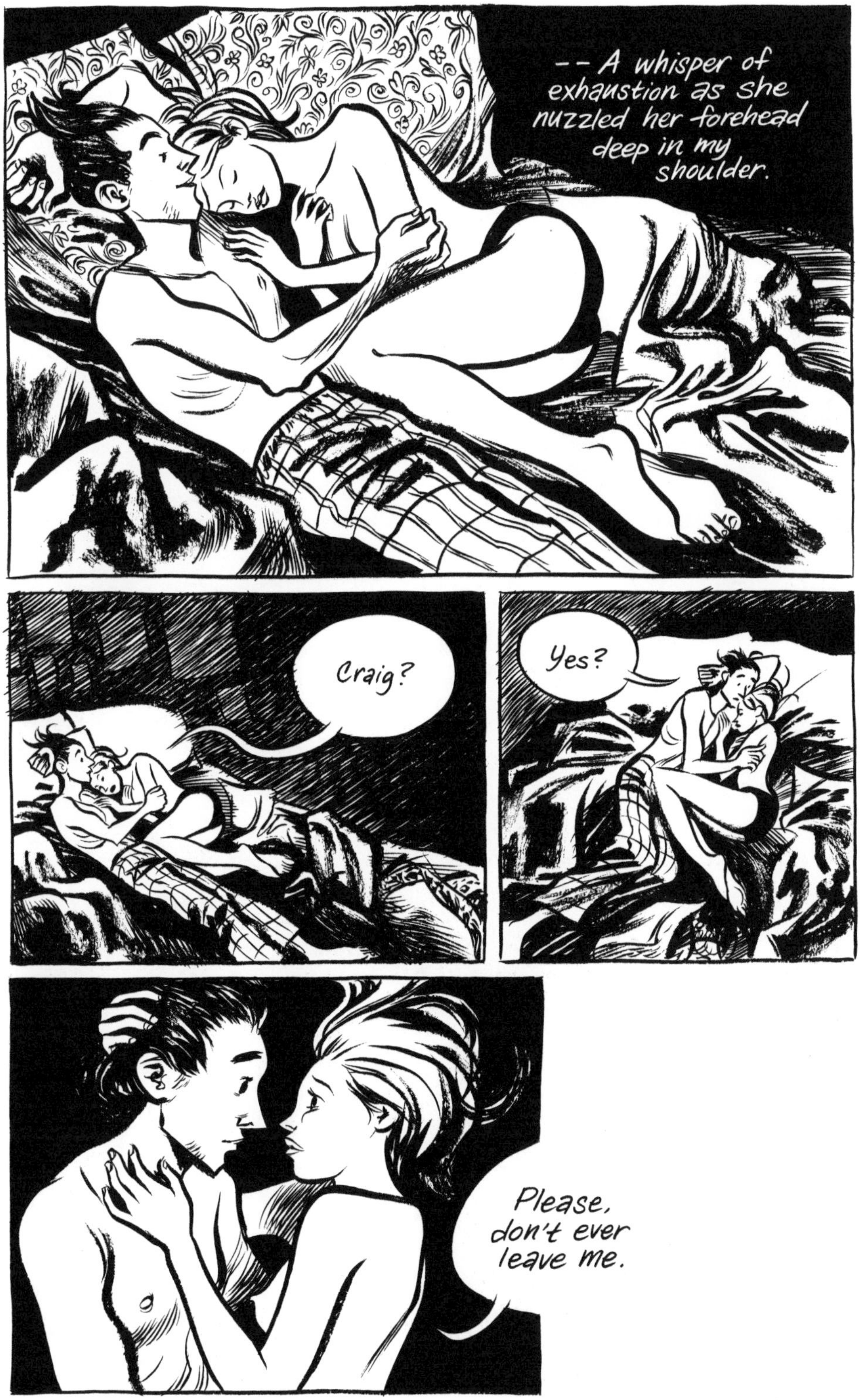
-- A whisper of exhaustion as she nuzzled her forehead deep in my shoulder.
Craig?
Yes?
Please, don't ever leave me.

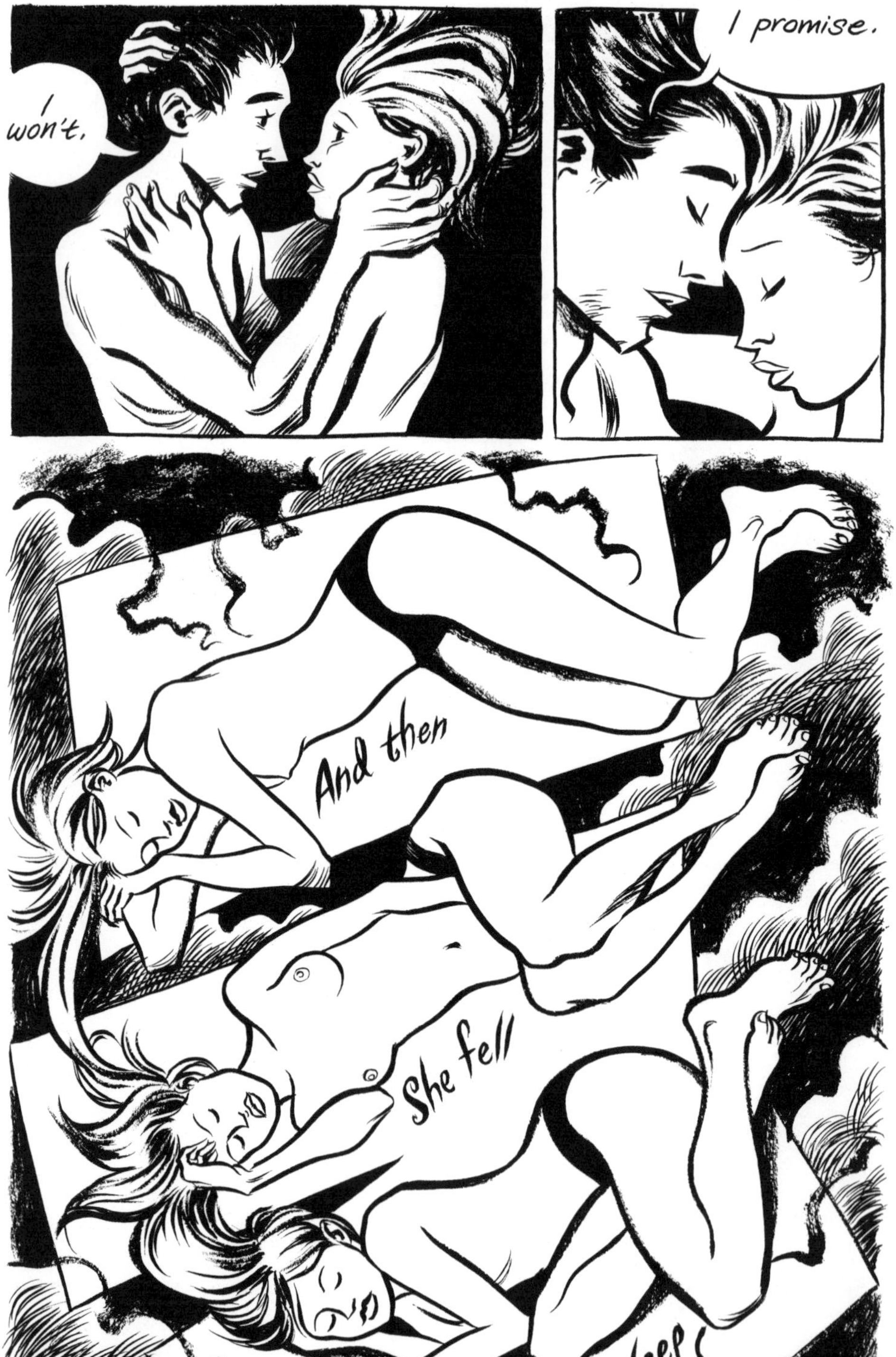
I won't.
I promise.
And then
She fell
asleep

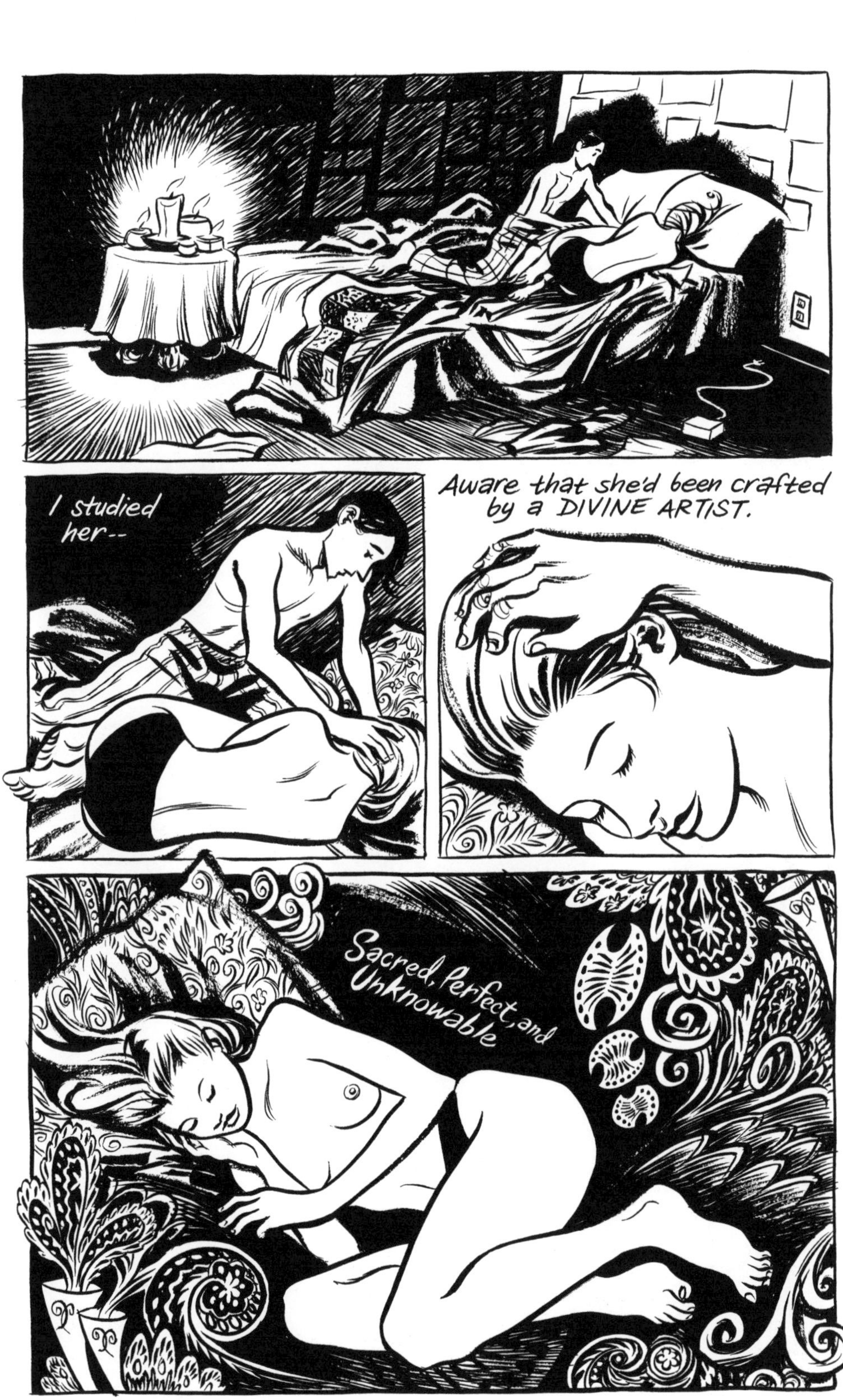
I studied her--
Aware that she'd been crafted by a DIVINE ARTIST.
Sacred, Perfect, and Unknowable

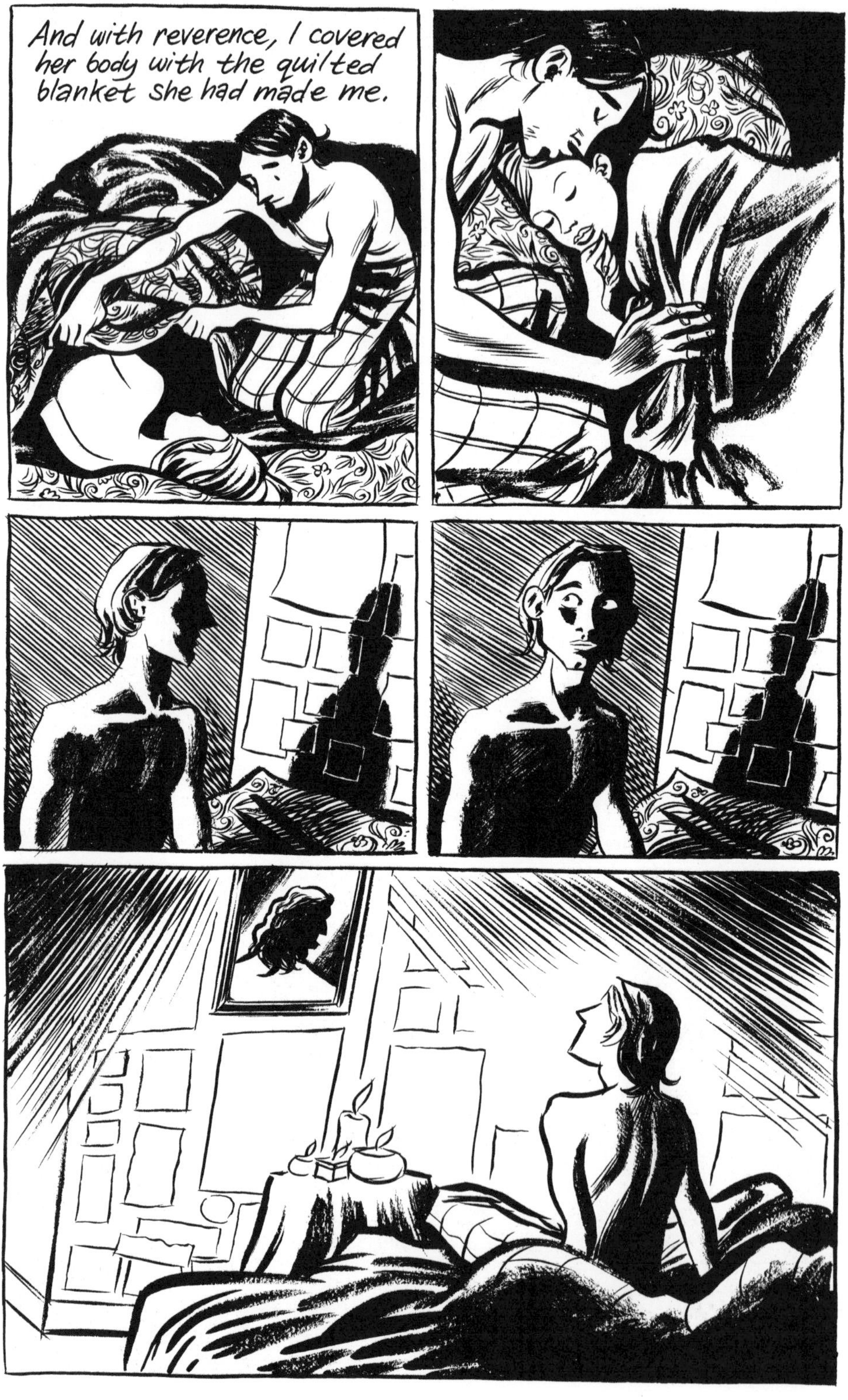
And with reverence, I covered her body with the quilted blanket she had made me.

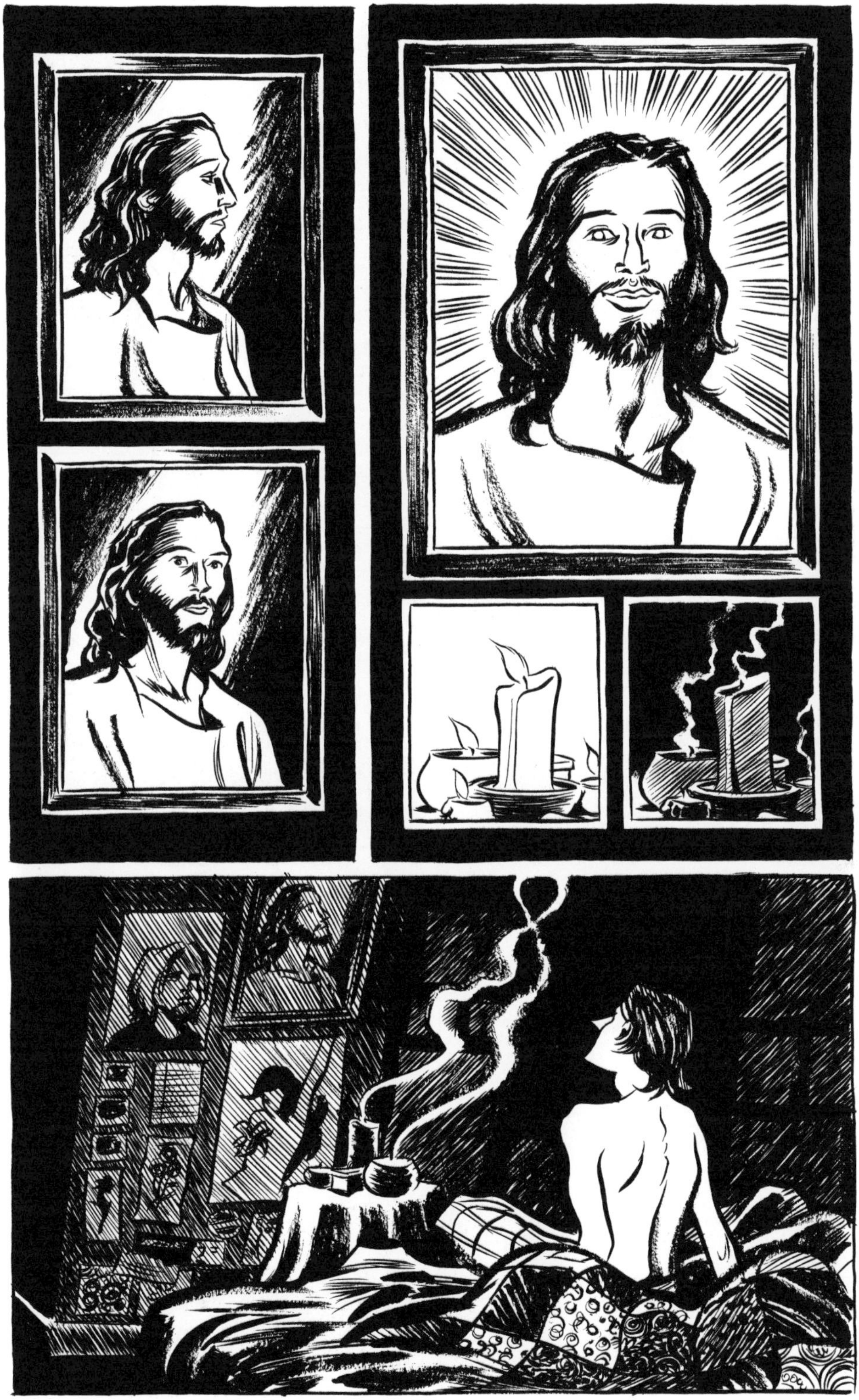

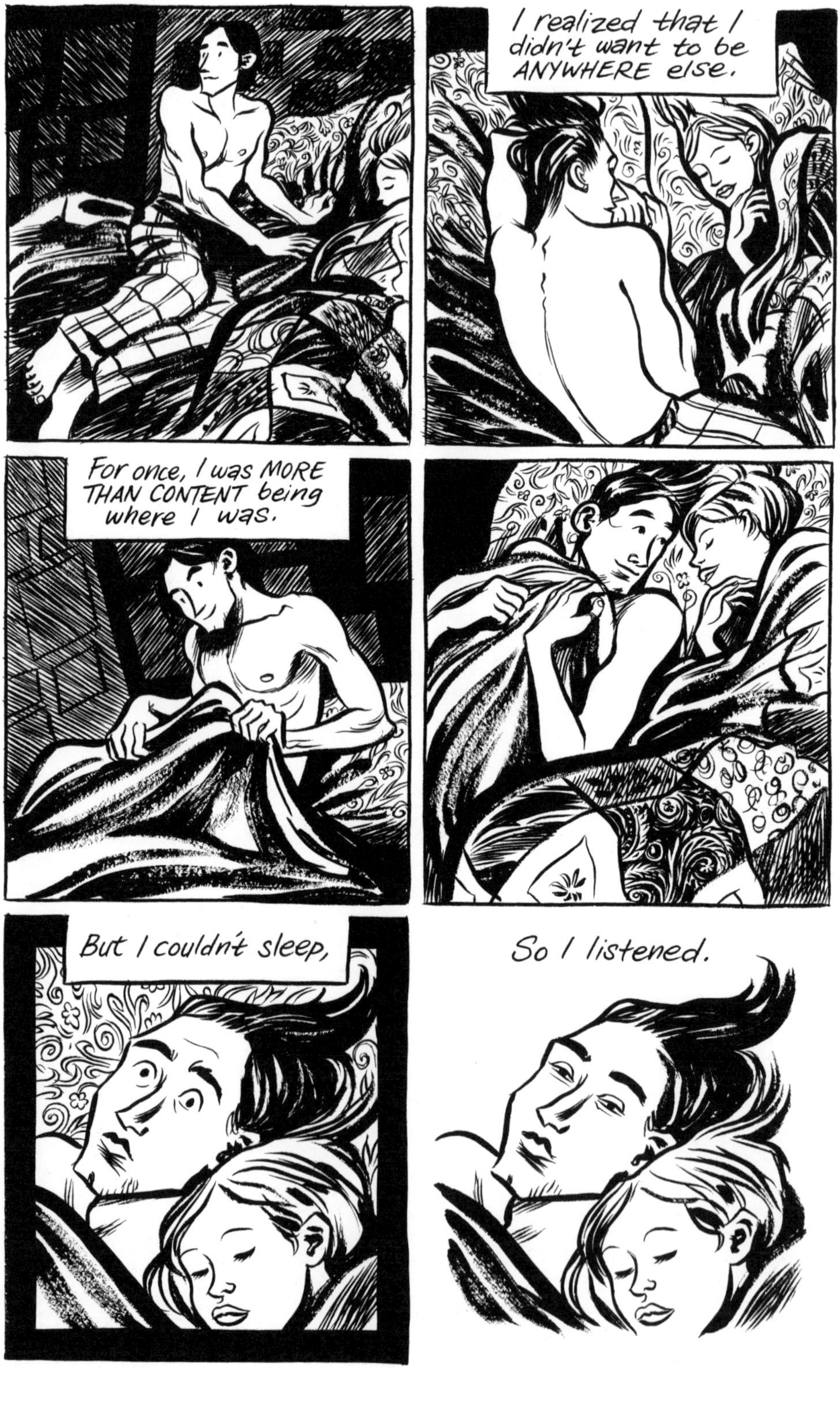
I realized that I didn't want to be ANYWHERE else.
For once, I was MORE THAN CONTENT being where I was.
But I couldn't sleep,
So I listened.

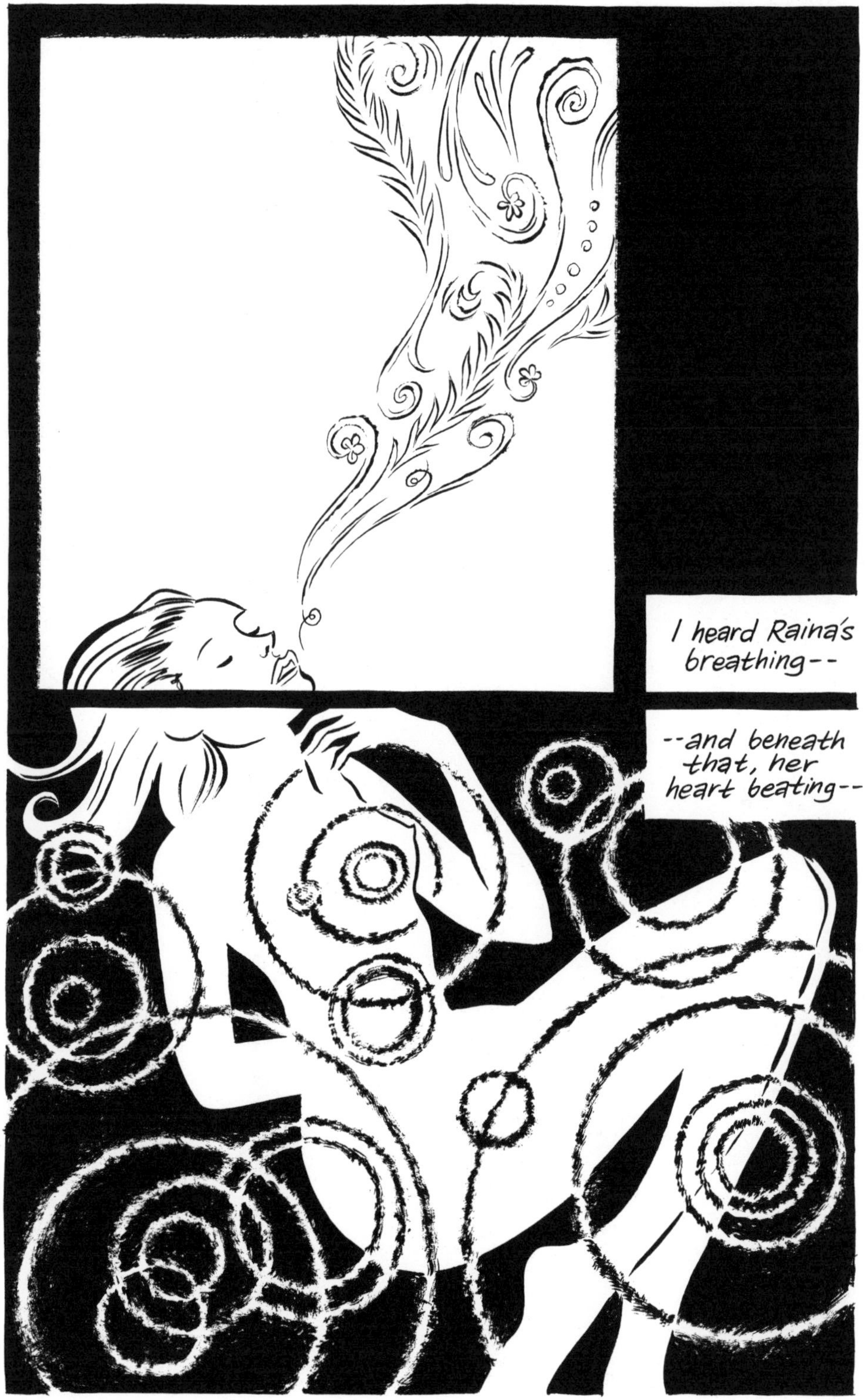
I heard Raina's breathing--
--and beneath that, her heart beating--

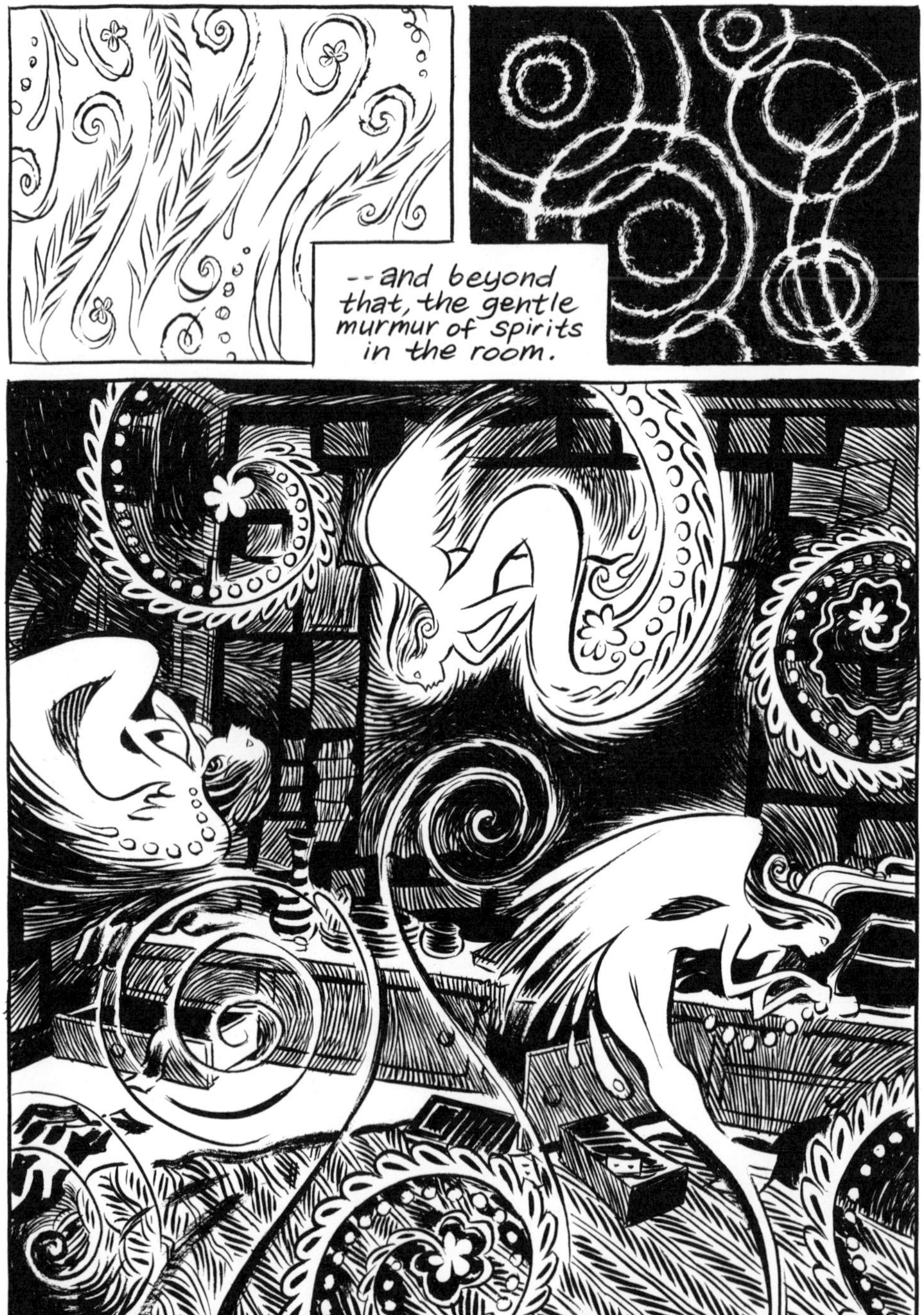
--and beyond that, the gentle murmur of spirits in the room.

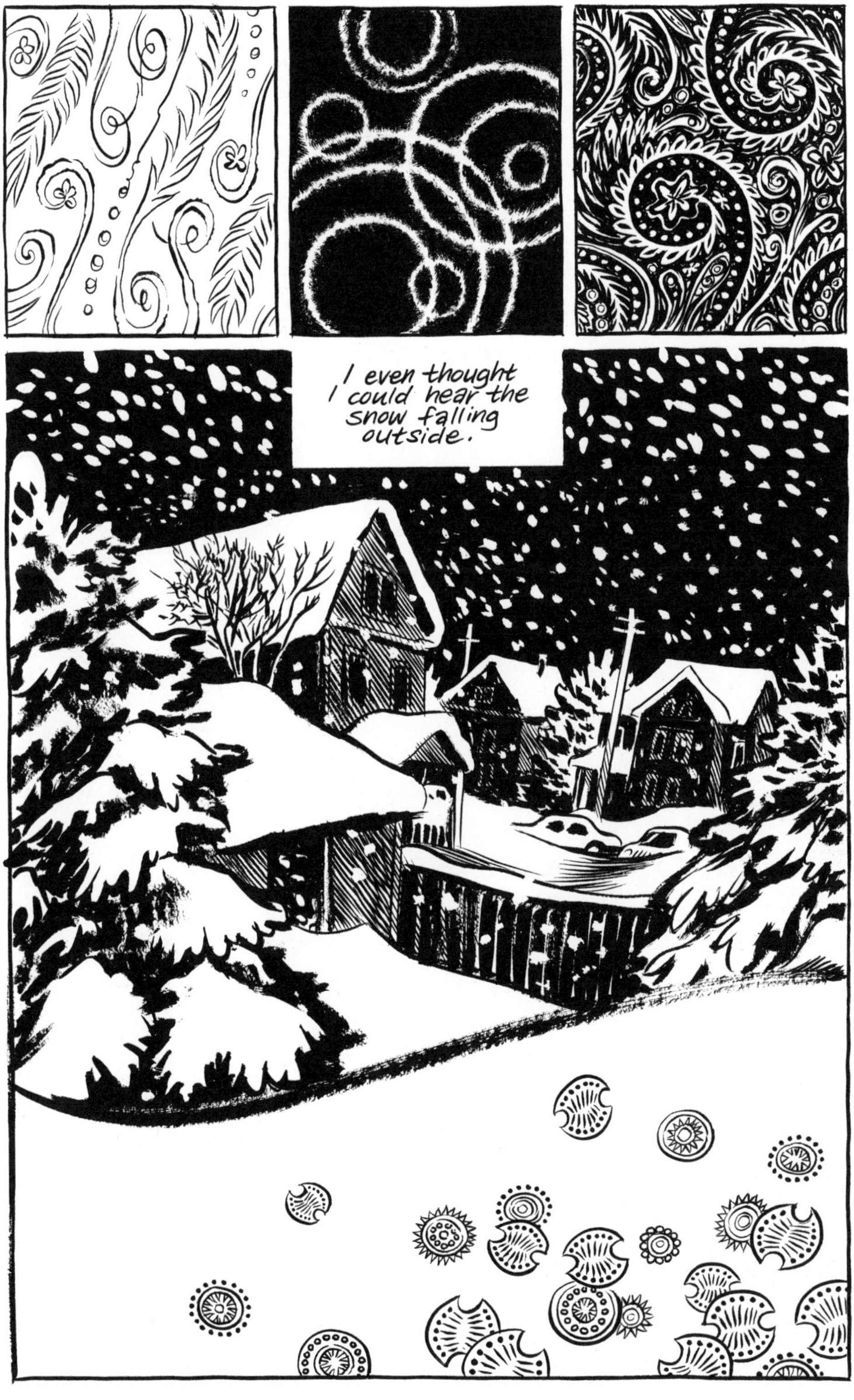
I even thought I could hear the snow falling outside.

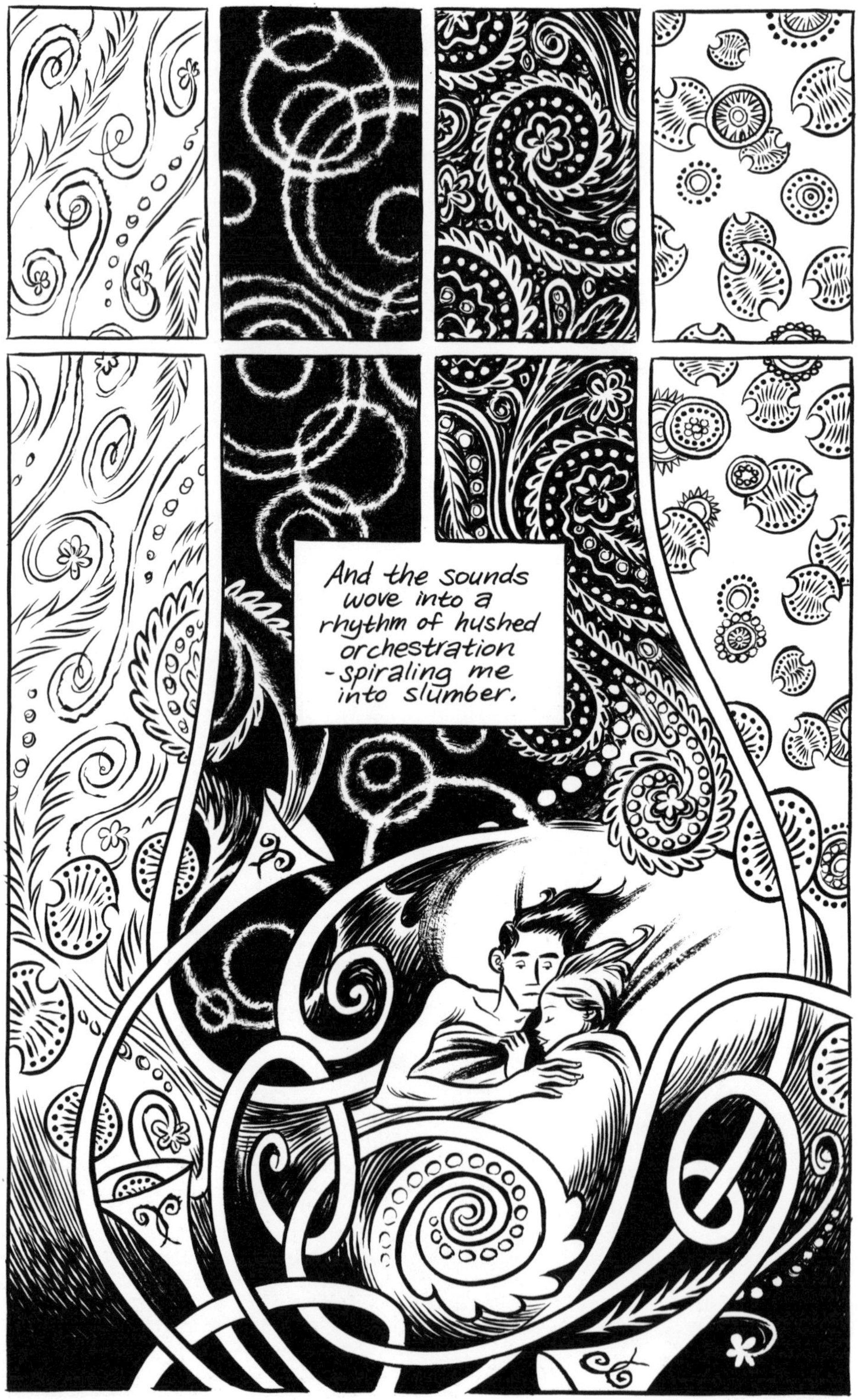
And the sounds wove into a rhythm of hushed orchestration -spiraling me into slumber.

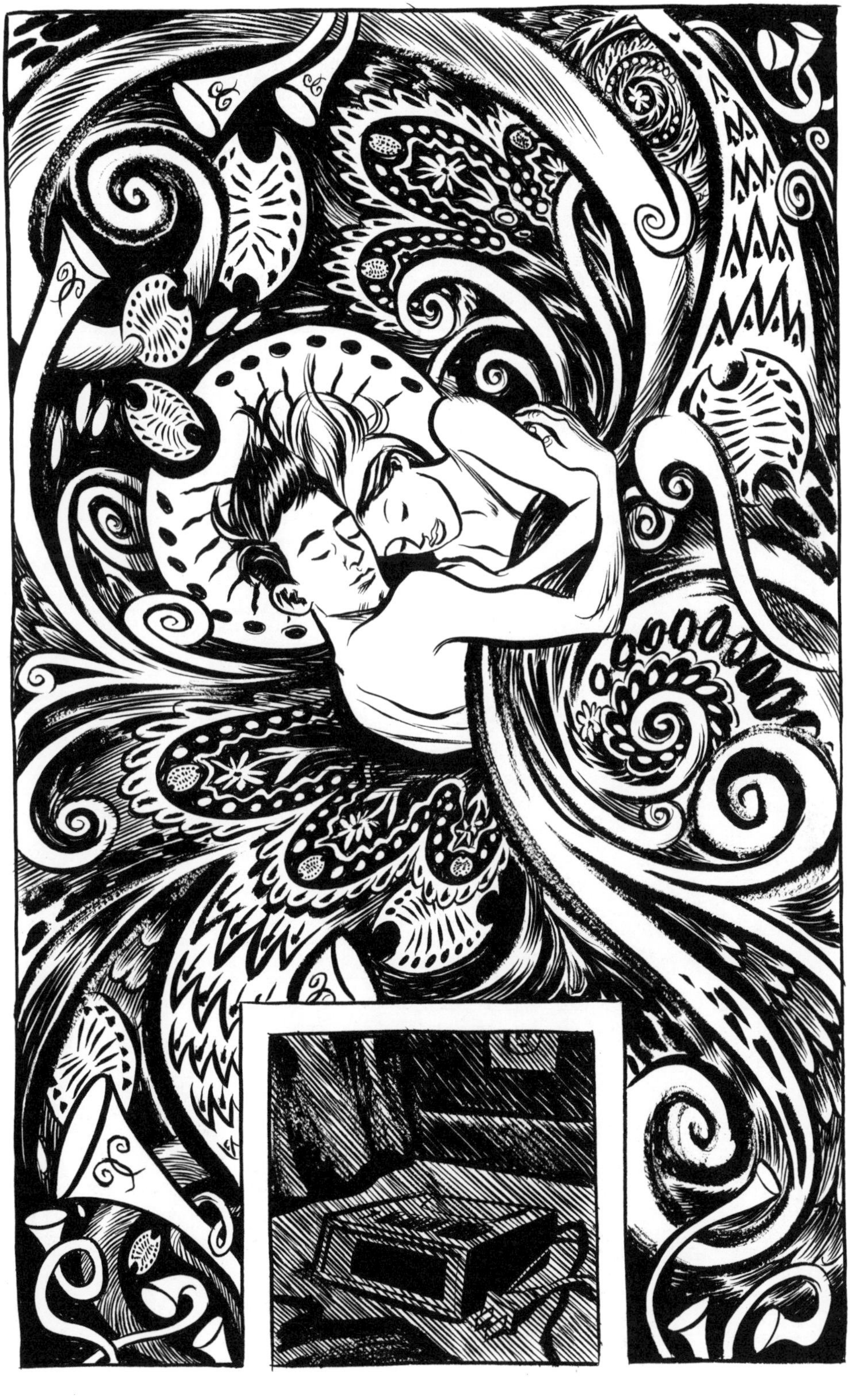

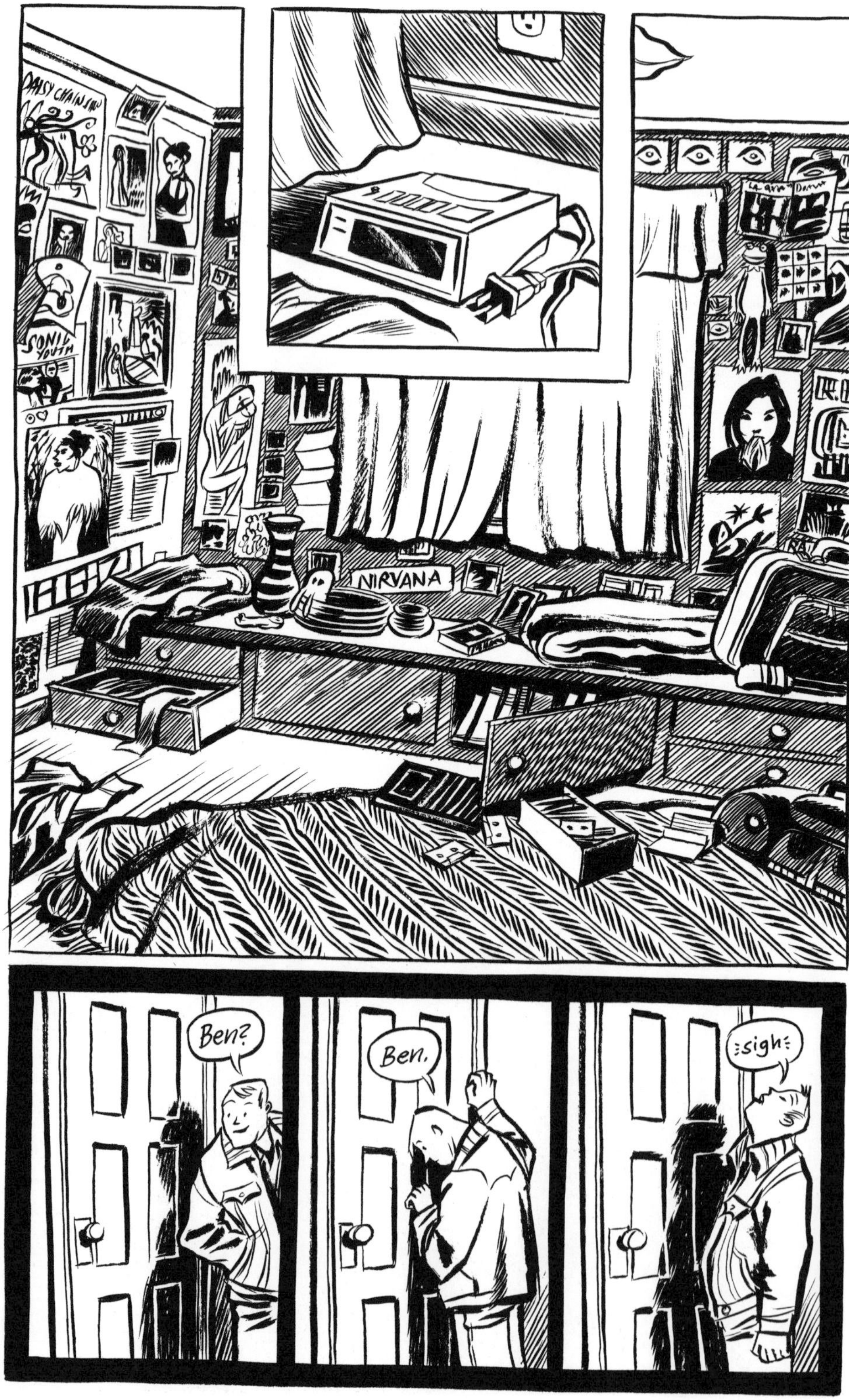
DAISY CHAINSAW
SONIC YOUTH
NIRVANA
Ben?
Ben.
sigh

439

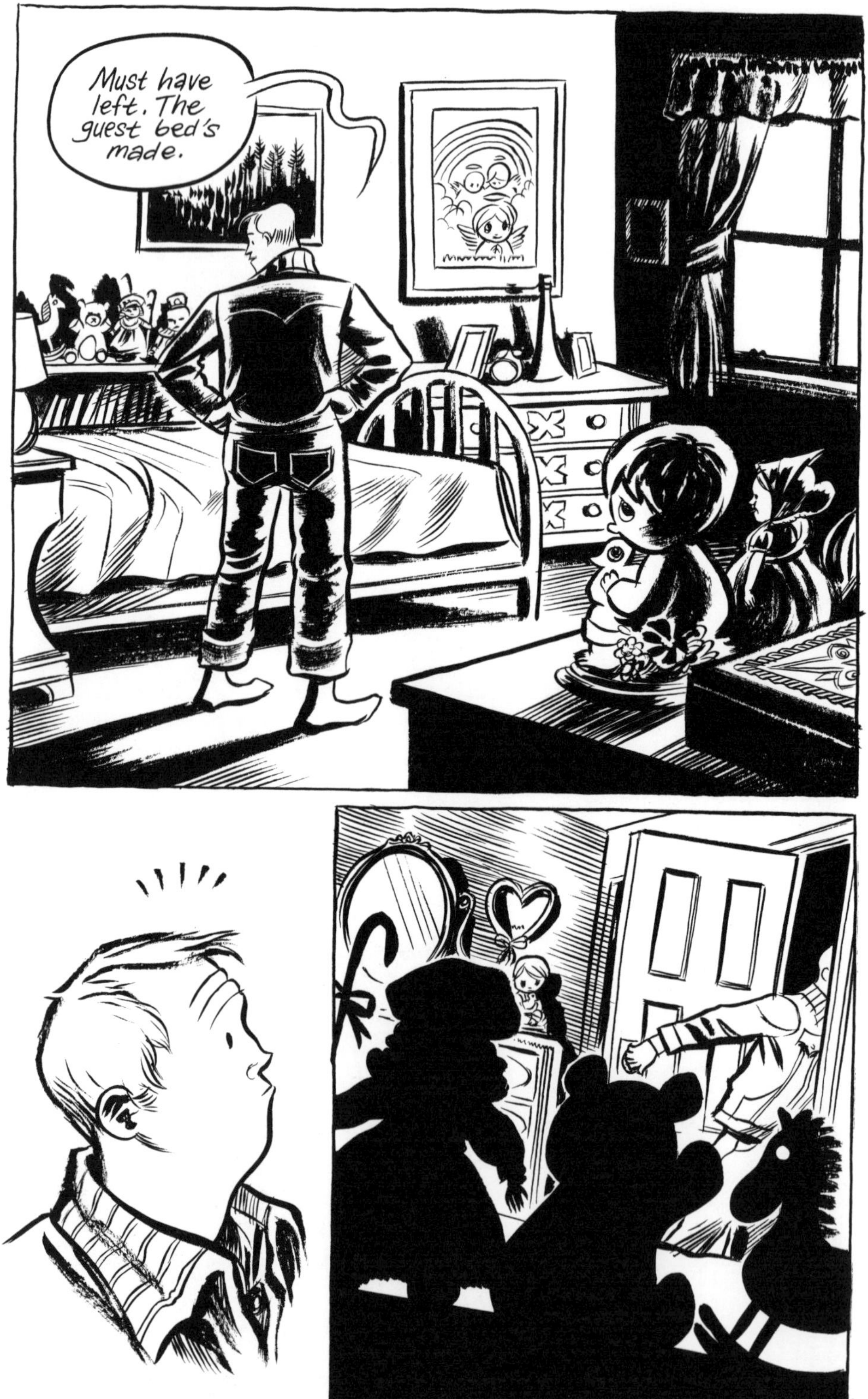
Must have left. The guest bed's made.

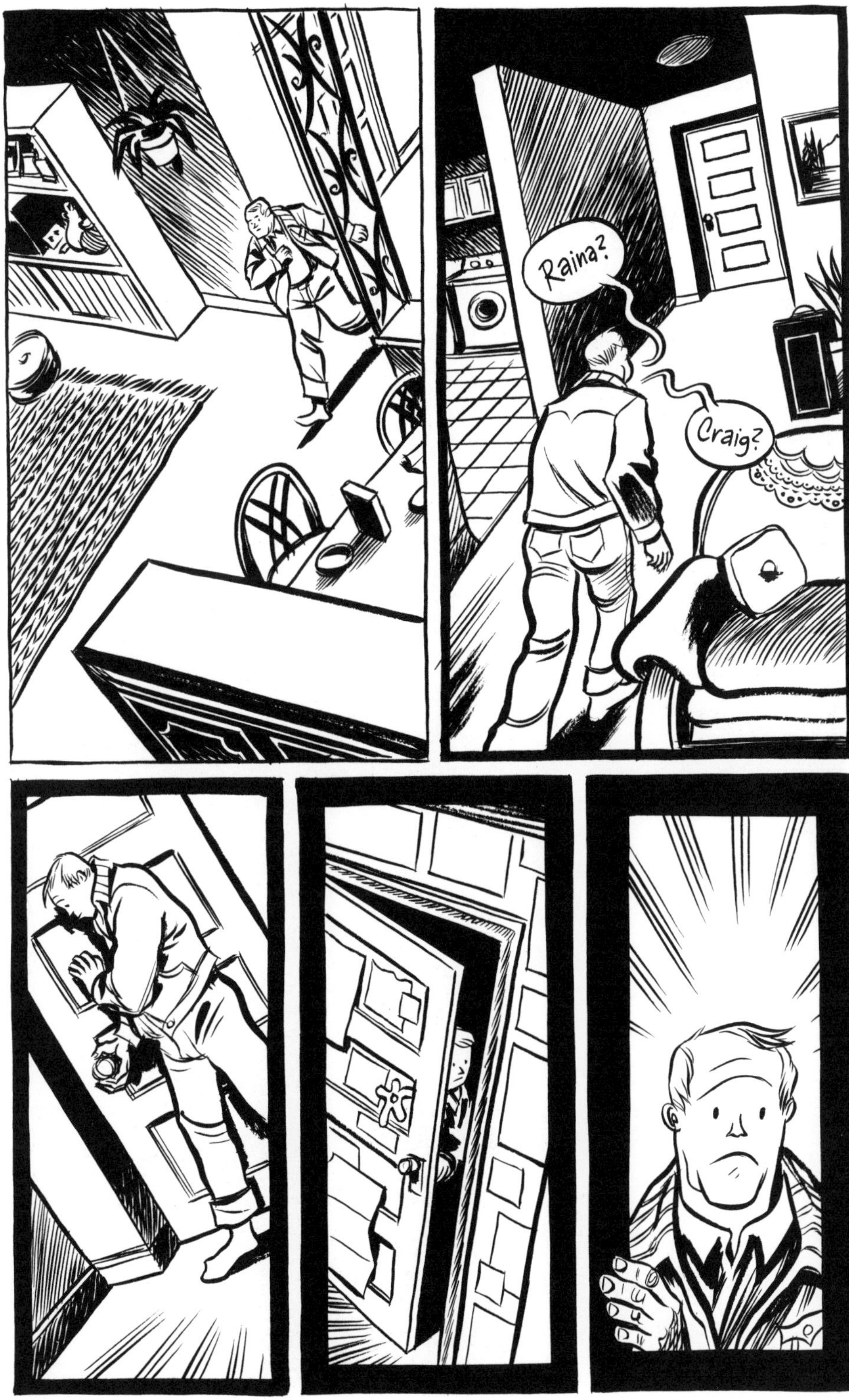
Raina?
Craig?

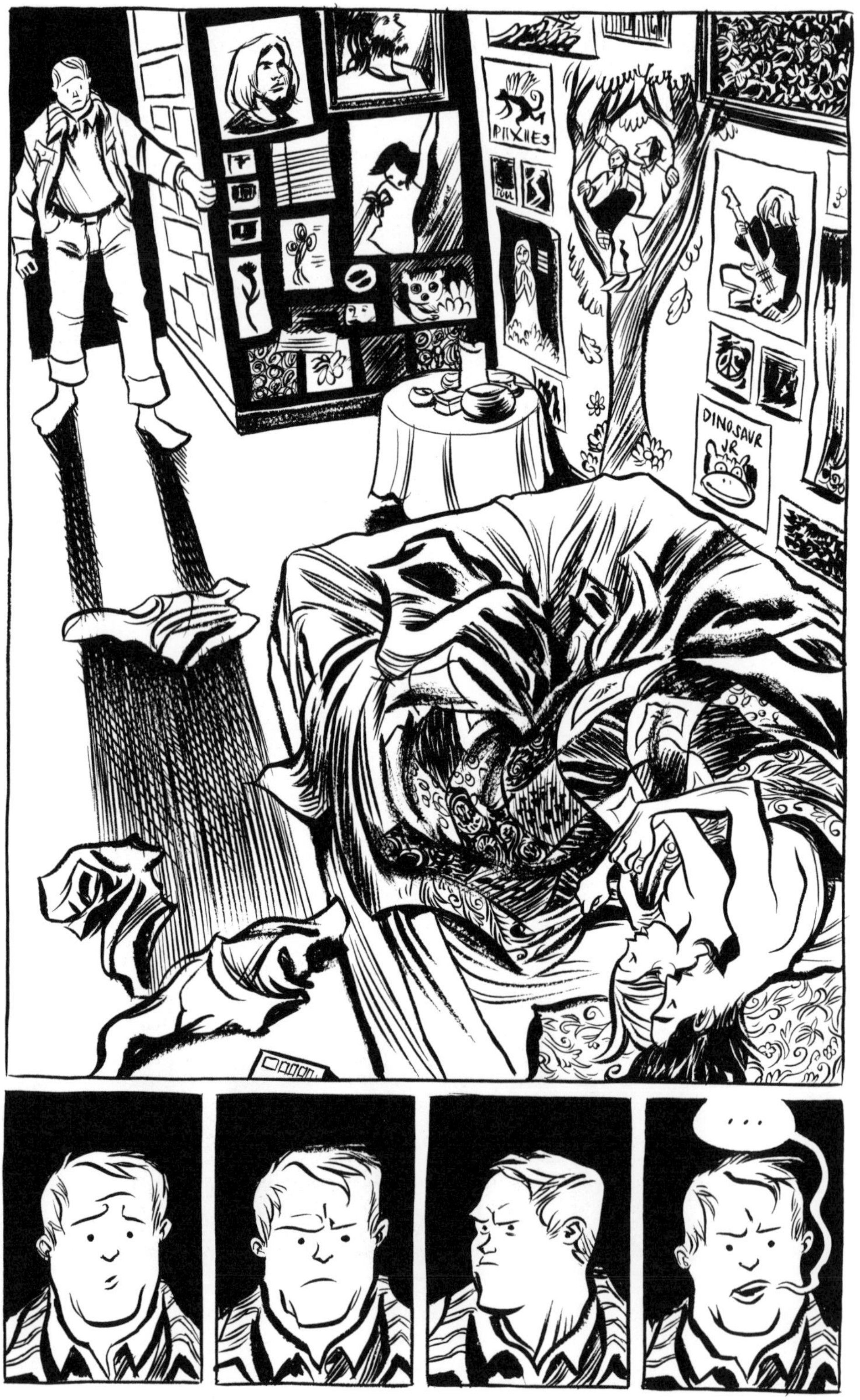
PIXIES
DINOSAUR JR
...

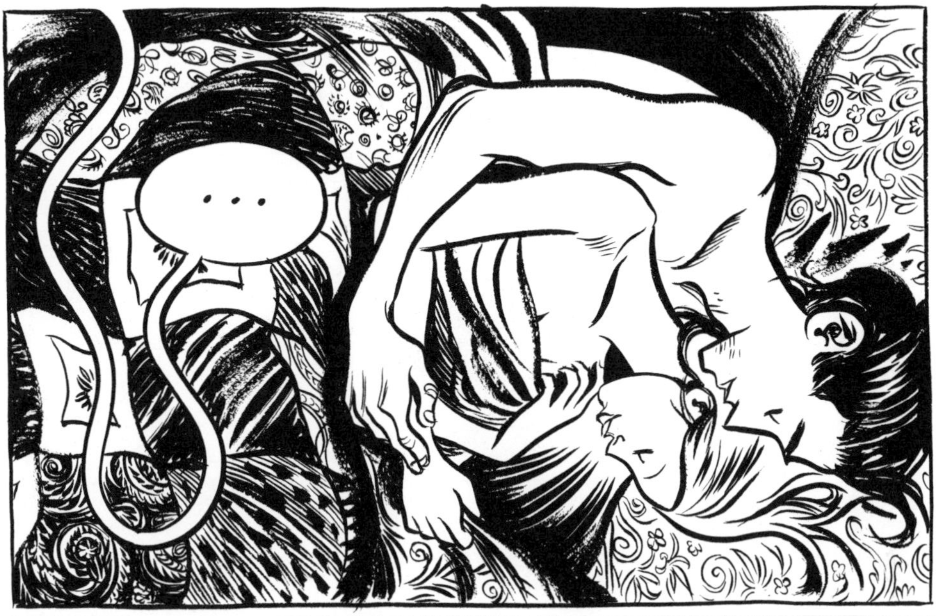
...

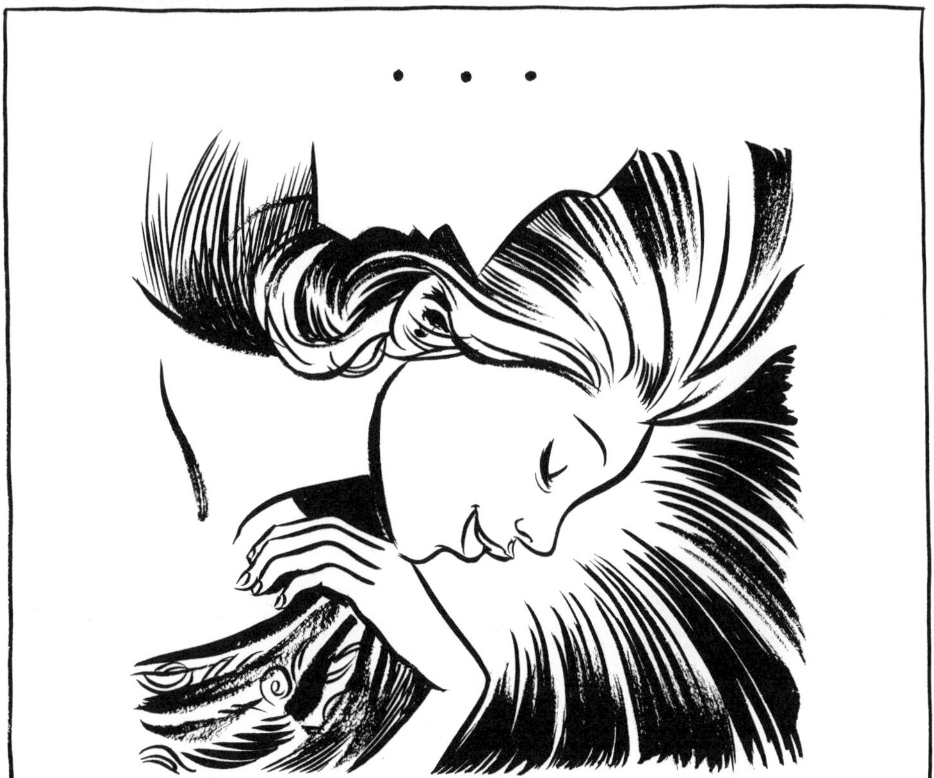
...

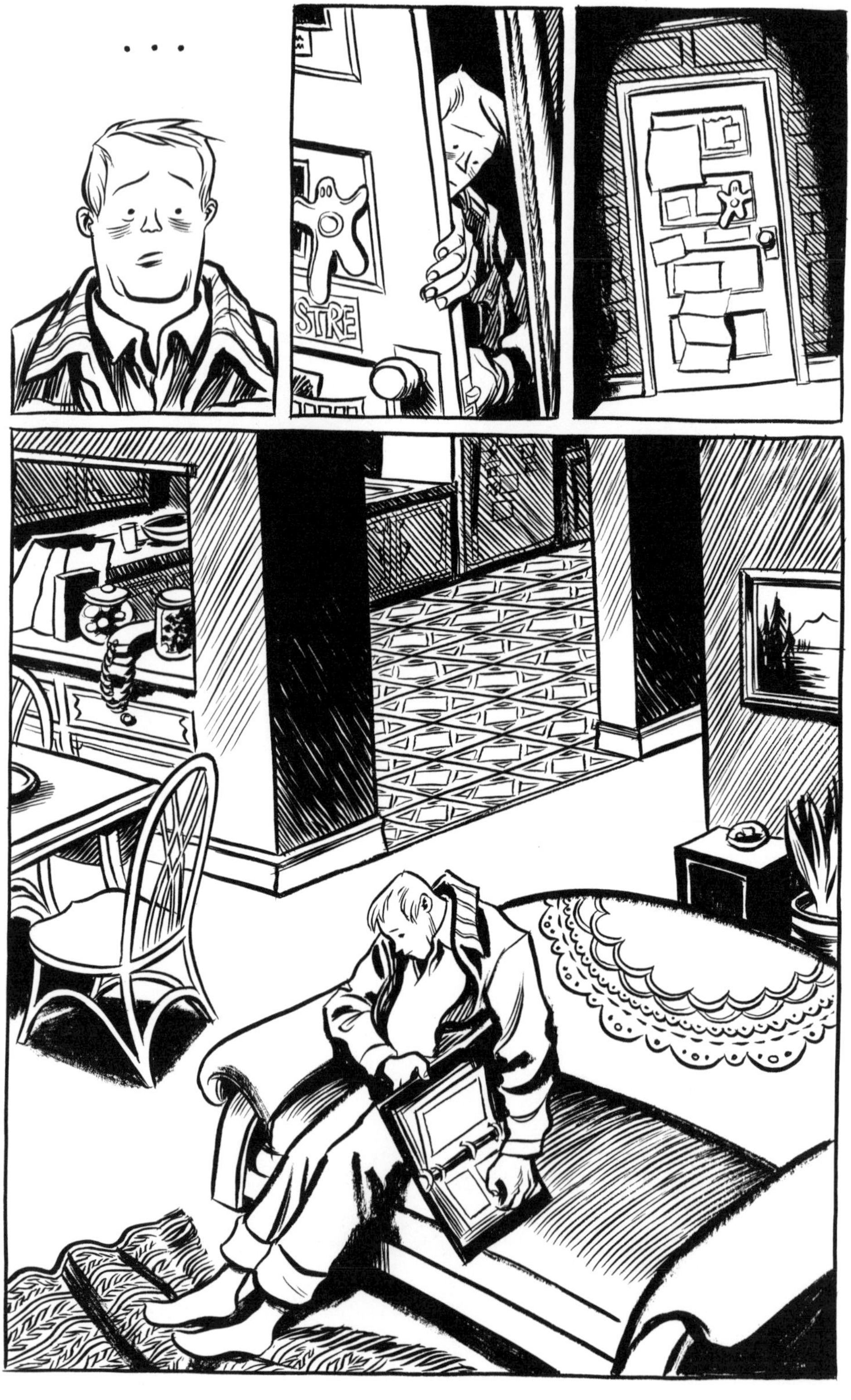
• • •
STIRE

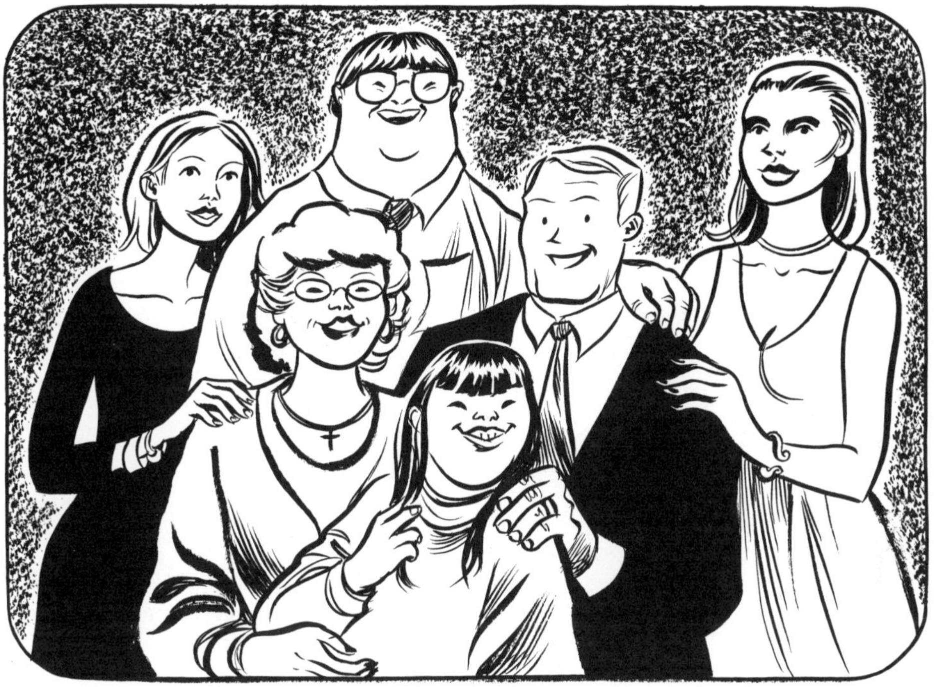

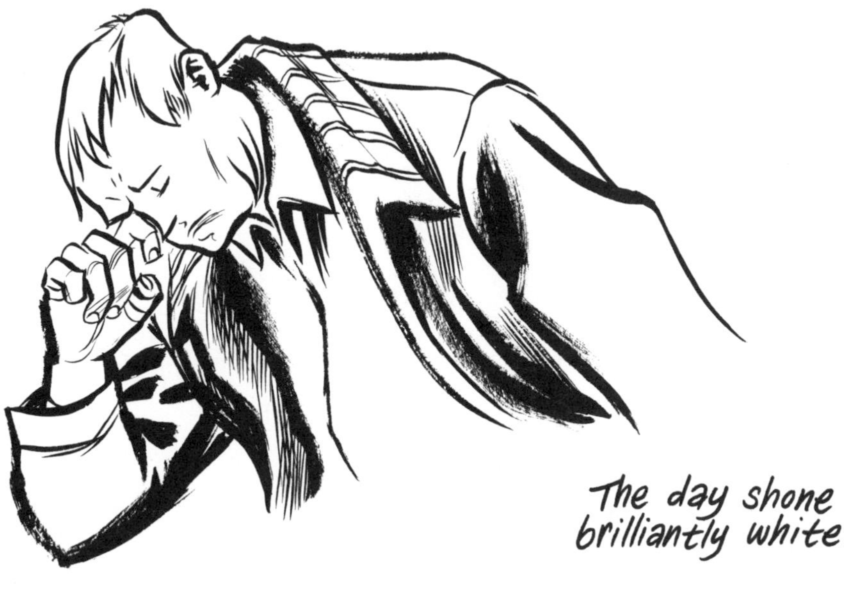
The day shone brilliantly white.

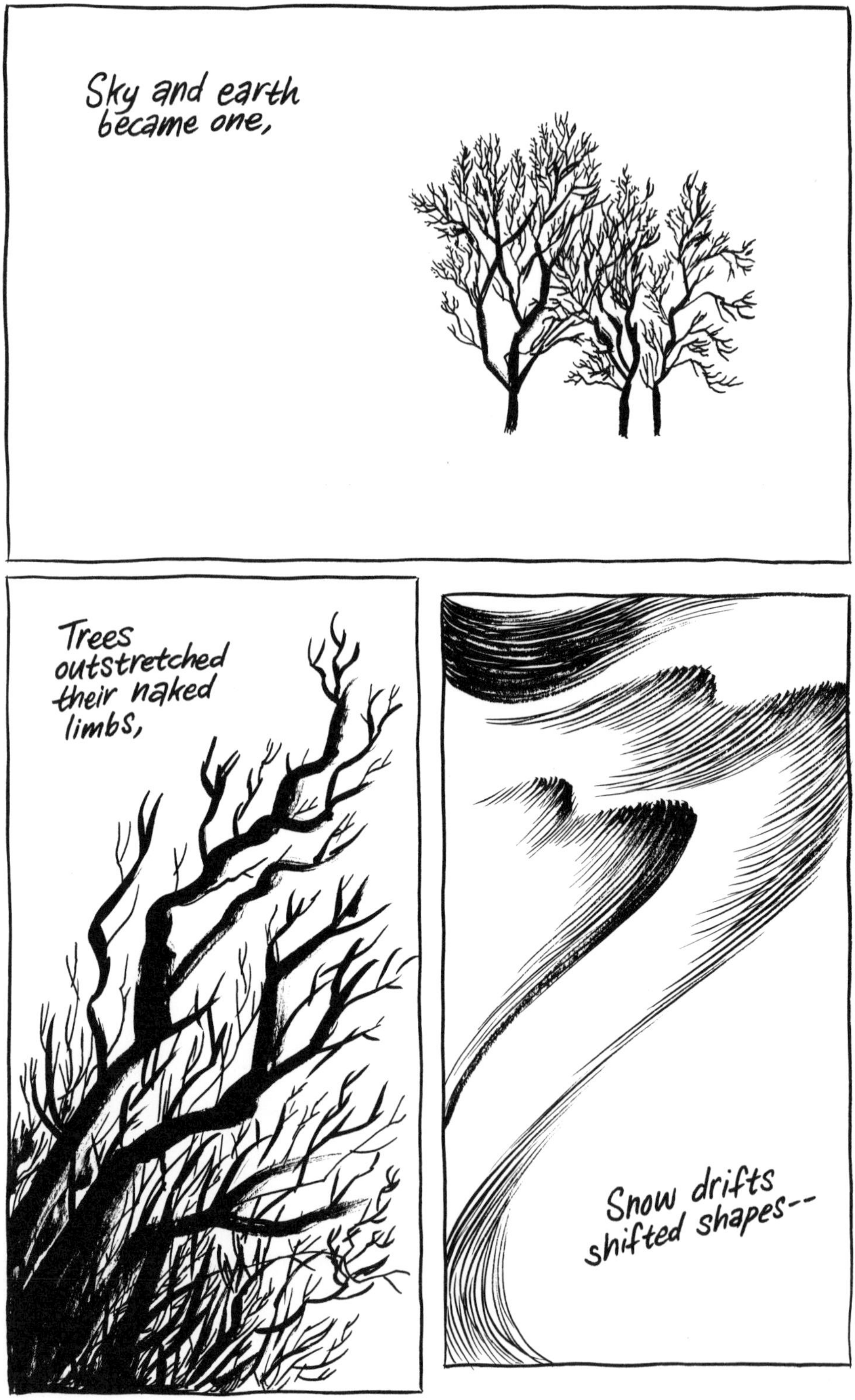
Sky and earth became one,
Trees outstretched their naked limbs,
Snow drifts shifted shapes--

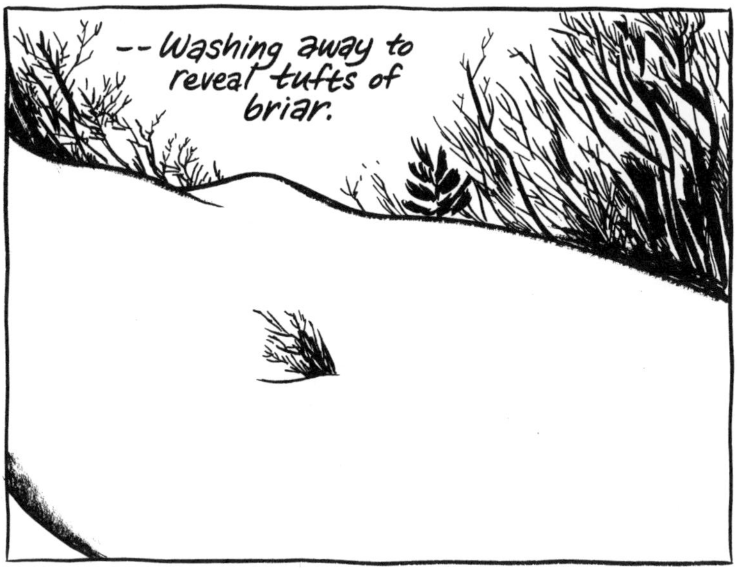
--Washing away to reveal tufts of briar.

VIII

Vanishing Cave

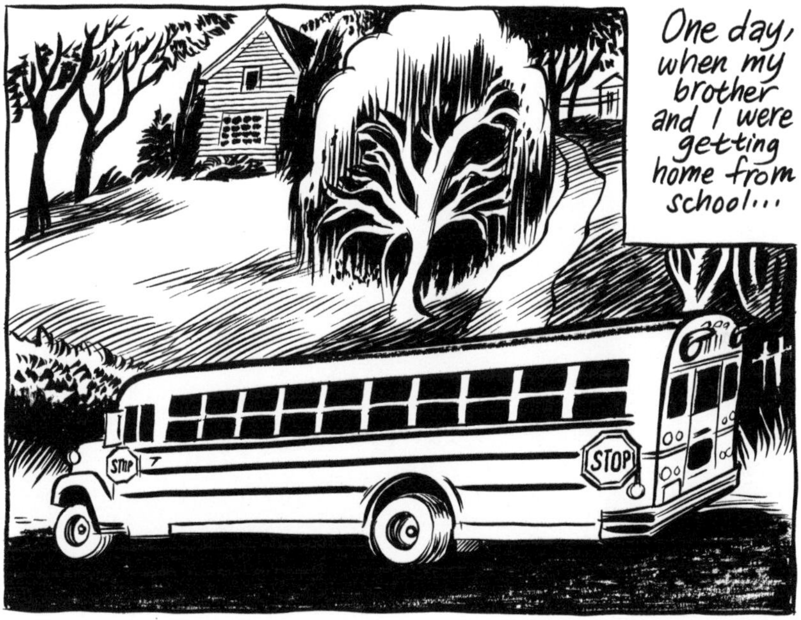
One day, when my brother and I were getting home from school...
STOP
STOP

451

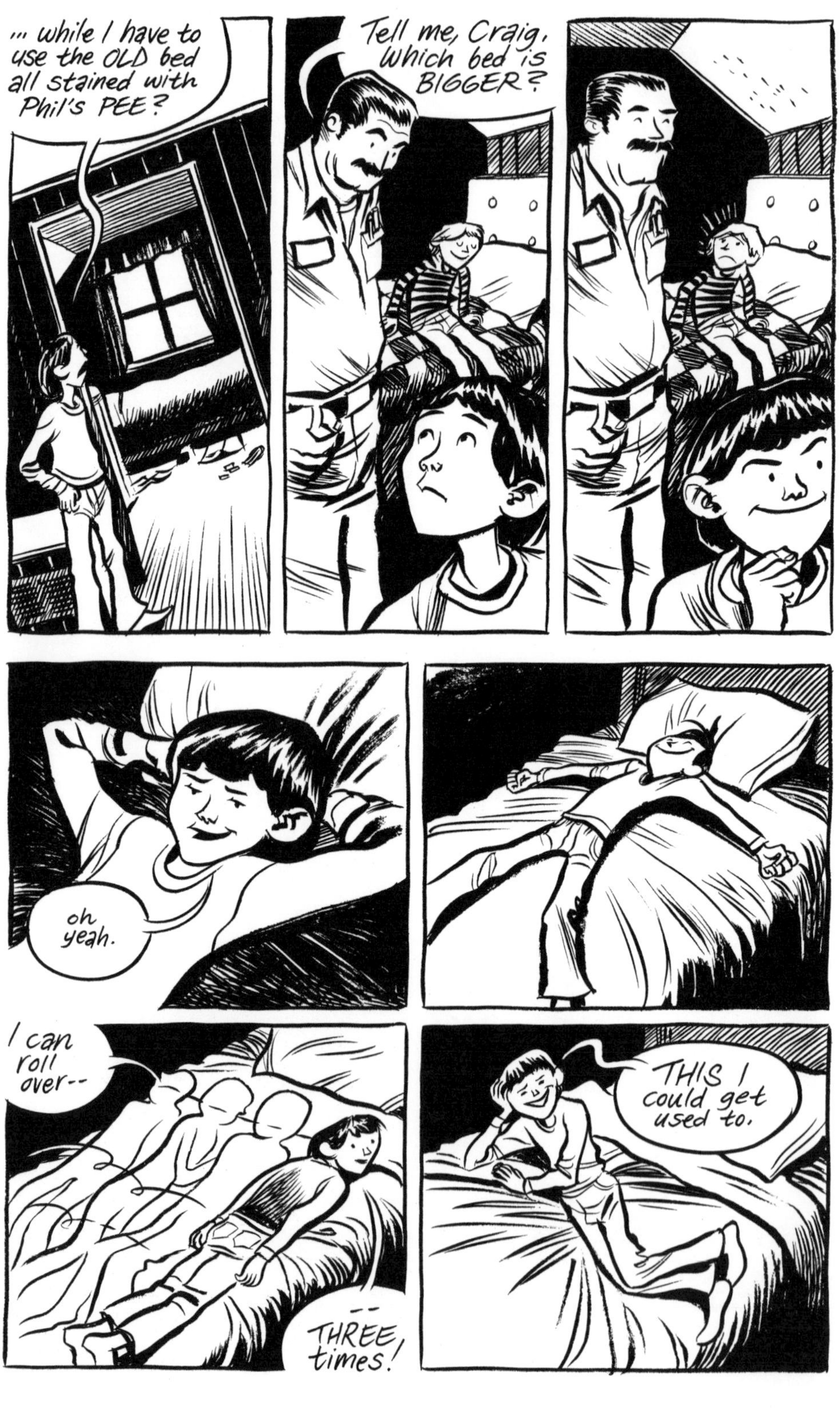
... while I have to use the OLD bed all stained with Phil's PEE?
Tell me, Craig. Which bed is BIGGER?
oh yeah.
I can roll over--
--THREE times!
THIS I could get used to.

That Night

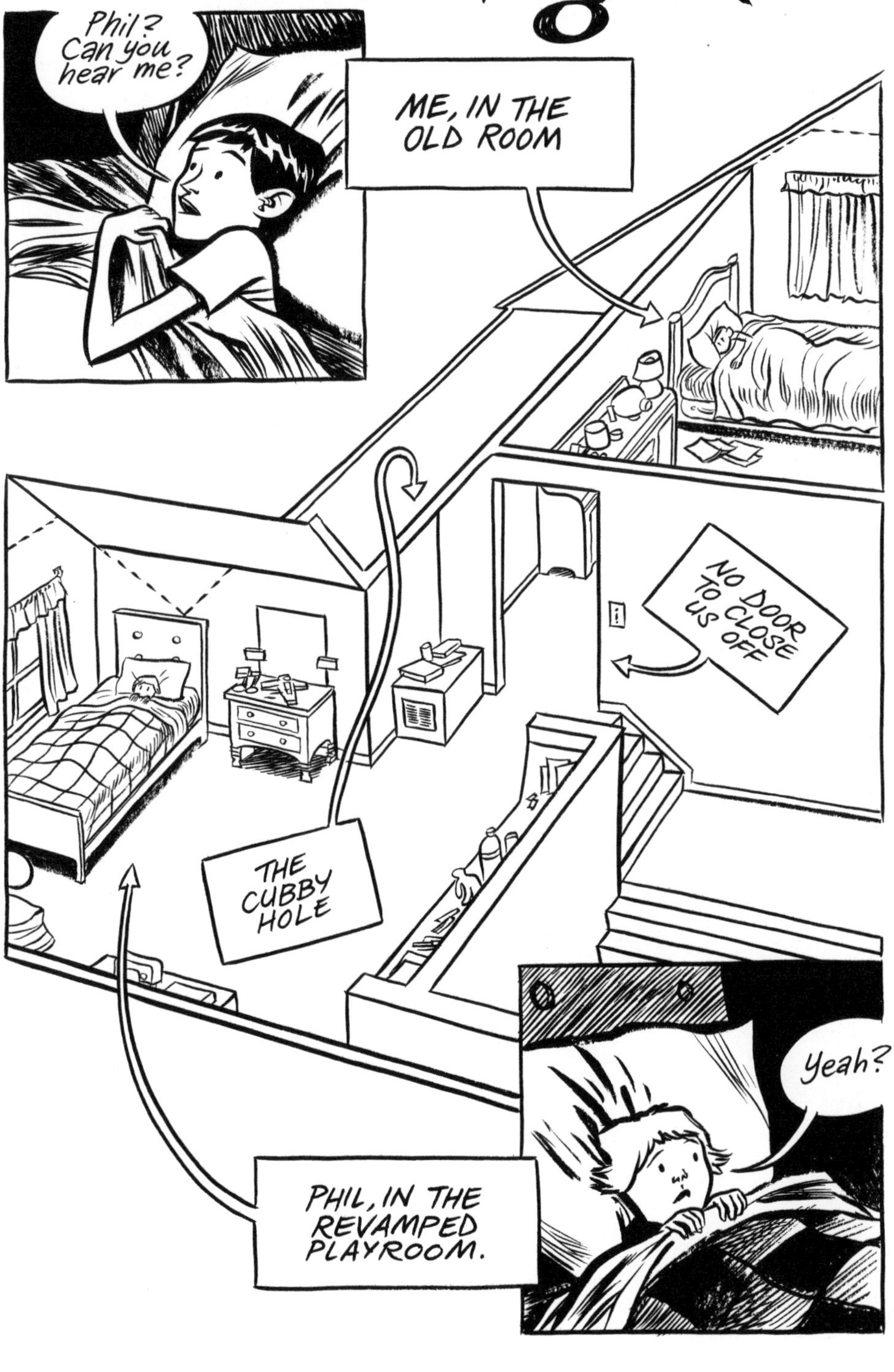
Phil? Can you hear me?
ME, IN THE OLD ROOM
NO DOOR TO CLOSE US OFF
THE CUBBY HOLE
PHIL, IN THE REVAMPED PLAYROOM.
Yeah?

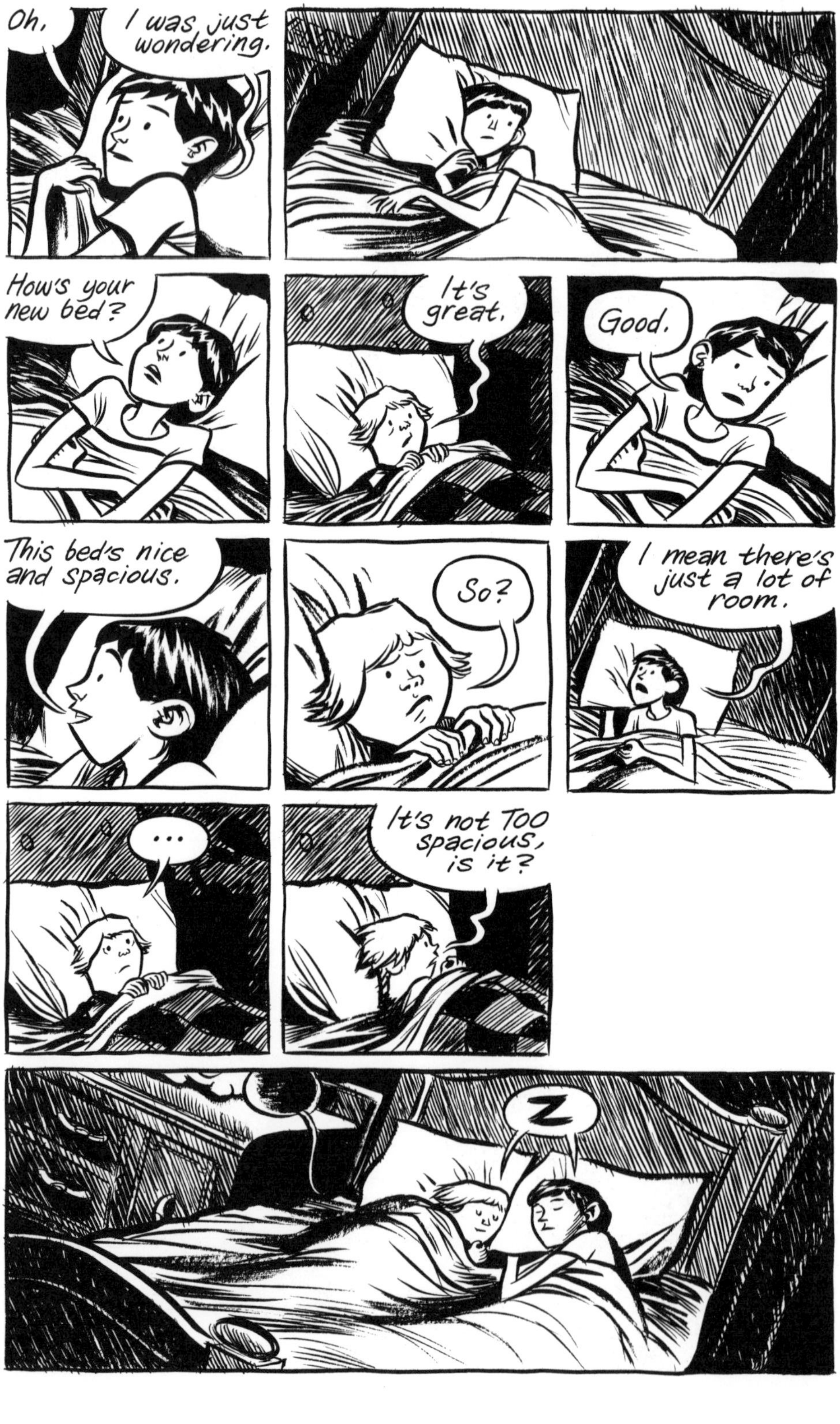

Oh,
I was just wondering.
How's your new bed?
It's great.
Good.
This bed's nice and spacious.
So?
I mean there's just a lot of room.
...
It's not TOO spacious, is it?
Z

and the Night After that

and in Winter

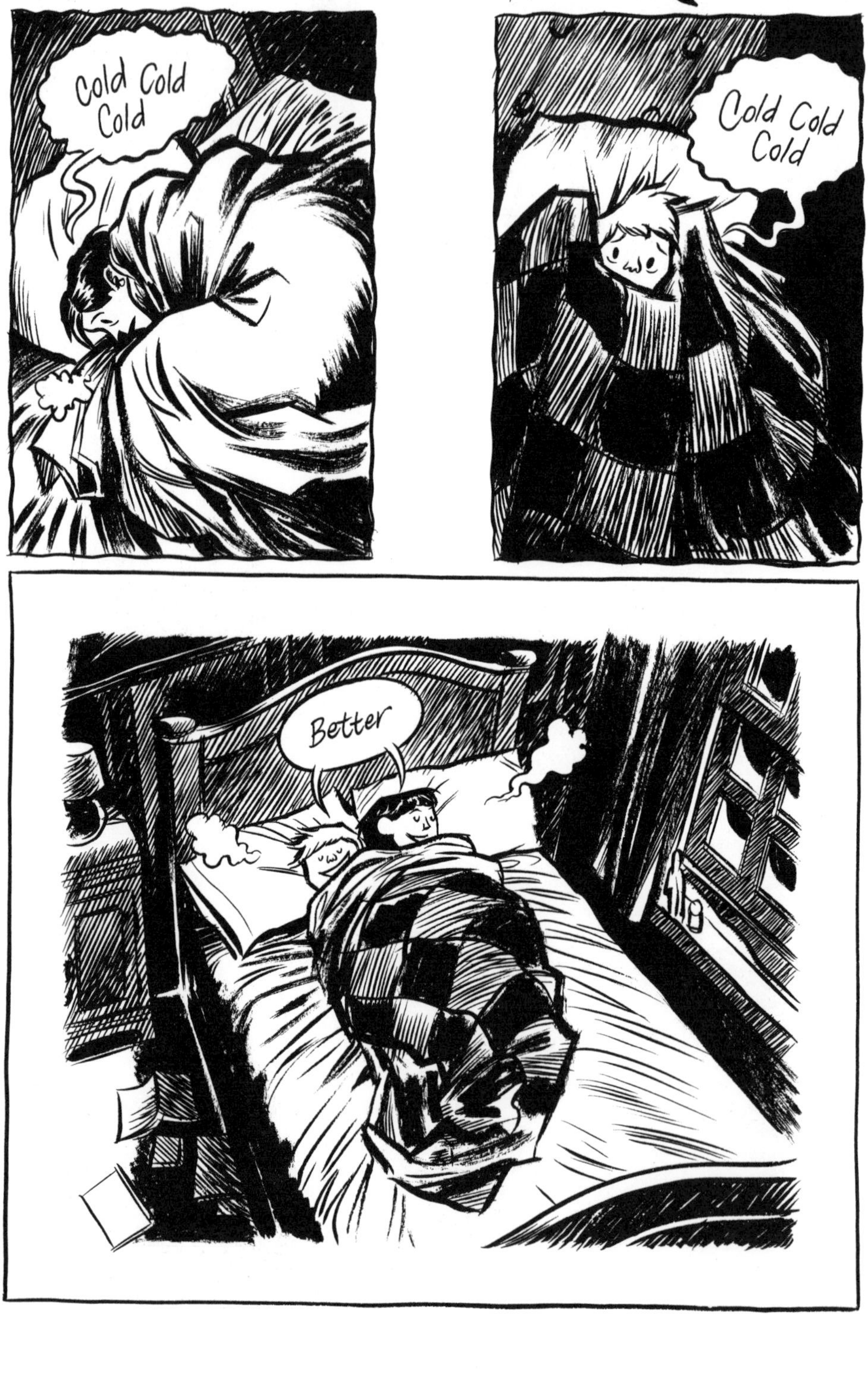
Cold Cold Cold
Cold Cold Cold
Better

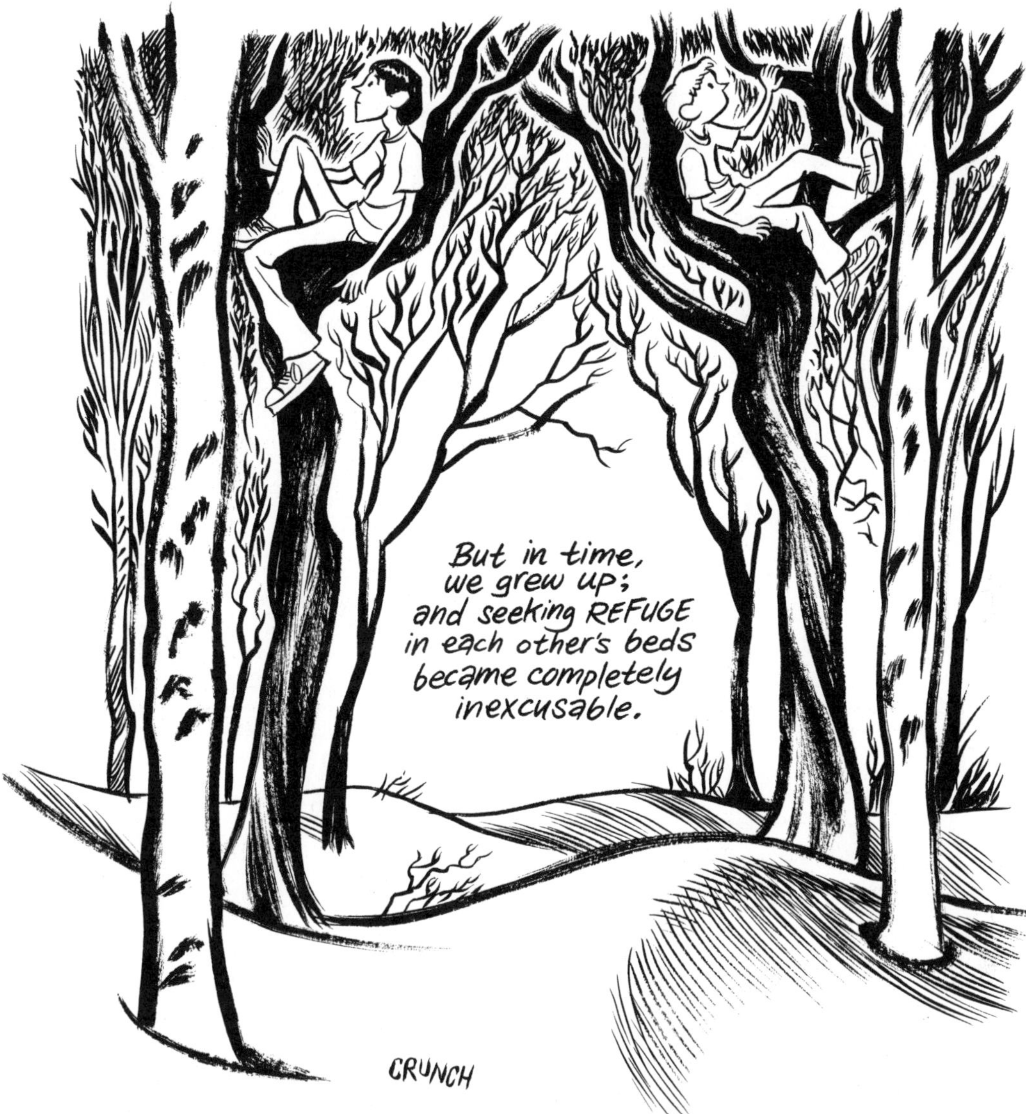
But in time, we grew up; and seeking REFUGE in each other's beds became completely inexcusable.
CRUNCH

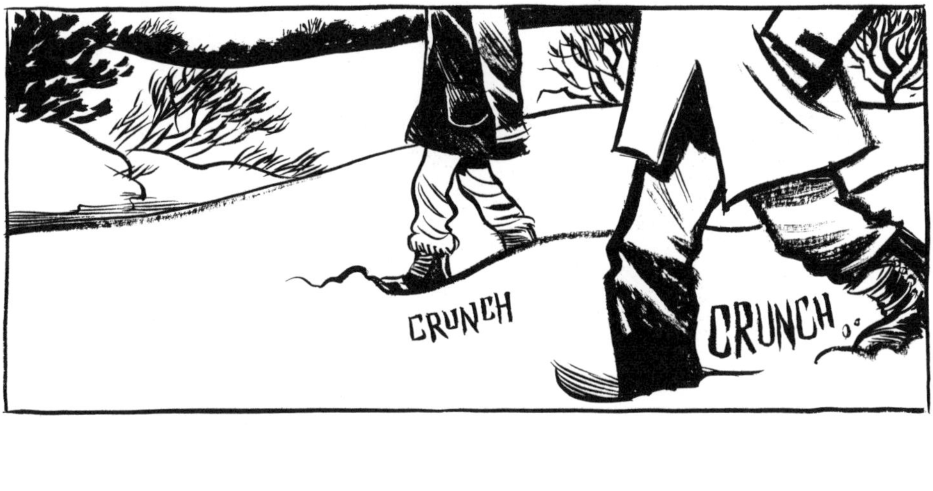
CRUNCH
CRUNCH

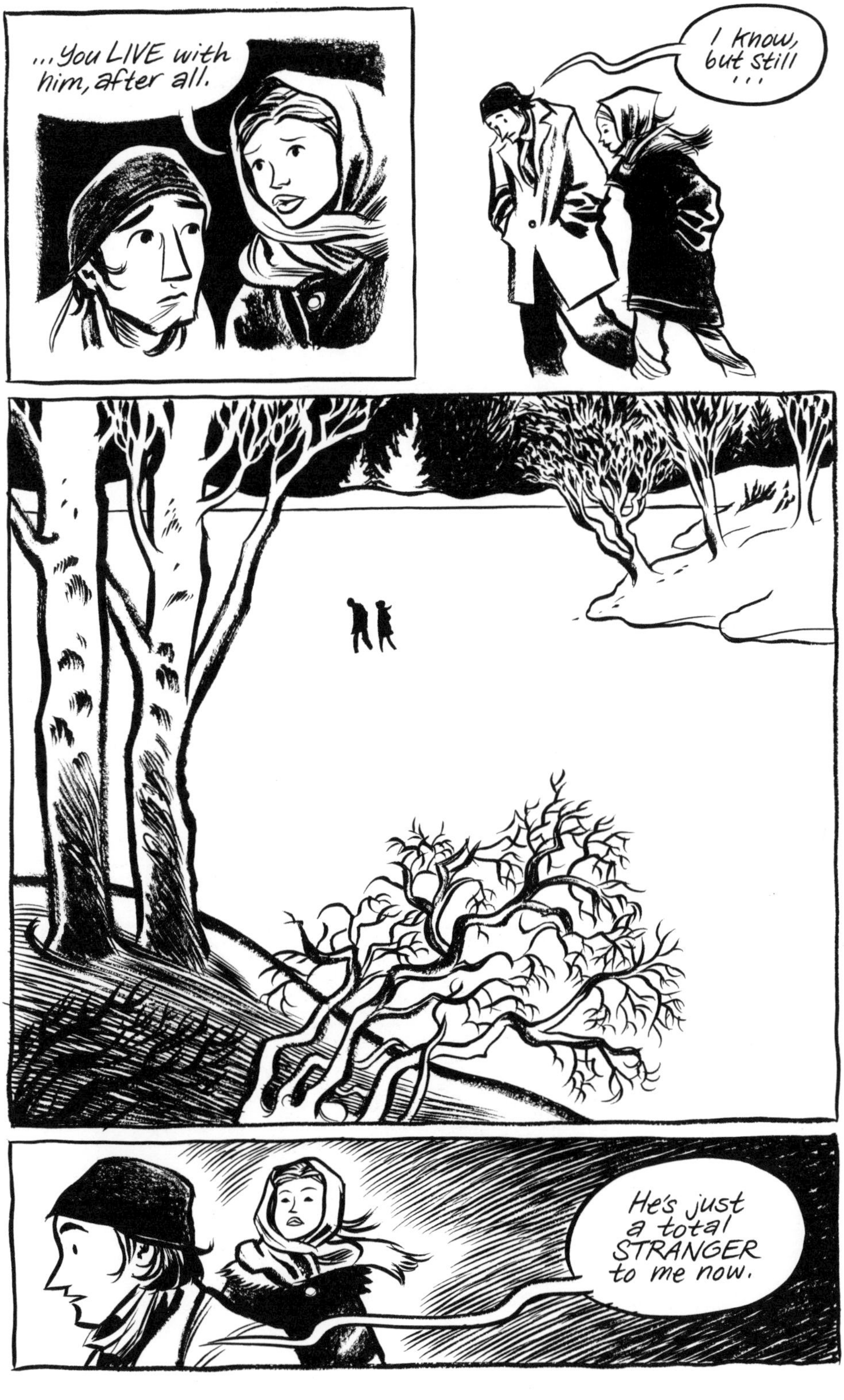
...You LIVE with him, after all.
I know, but still ...
He's just a total STRANGER to me now.

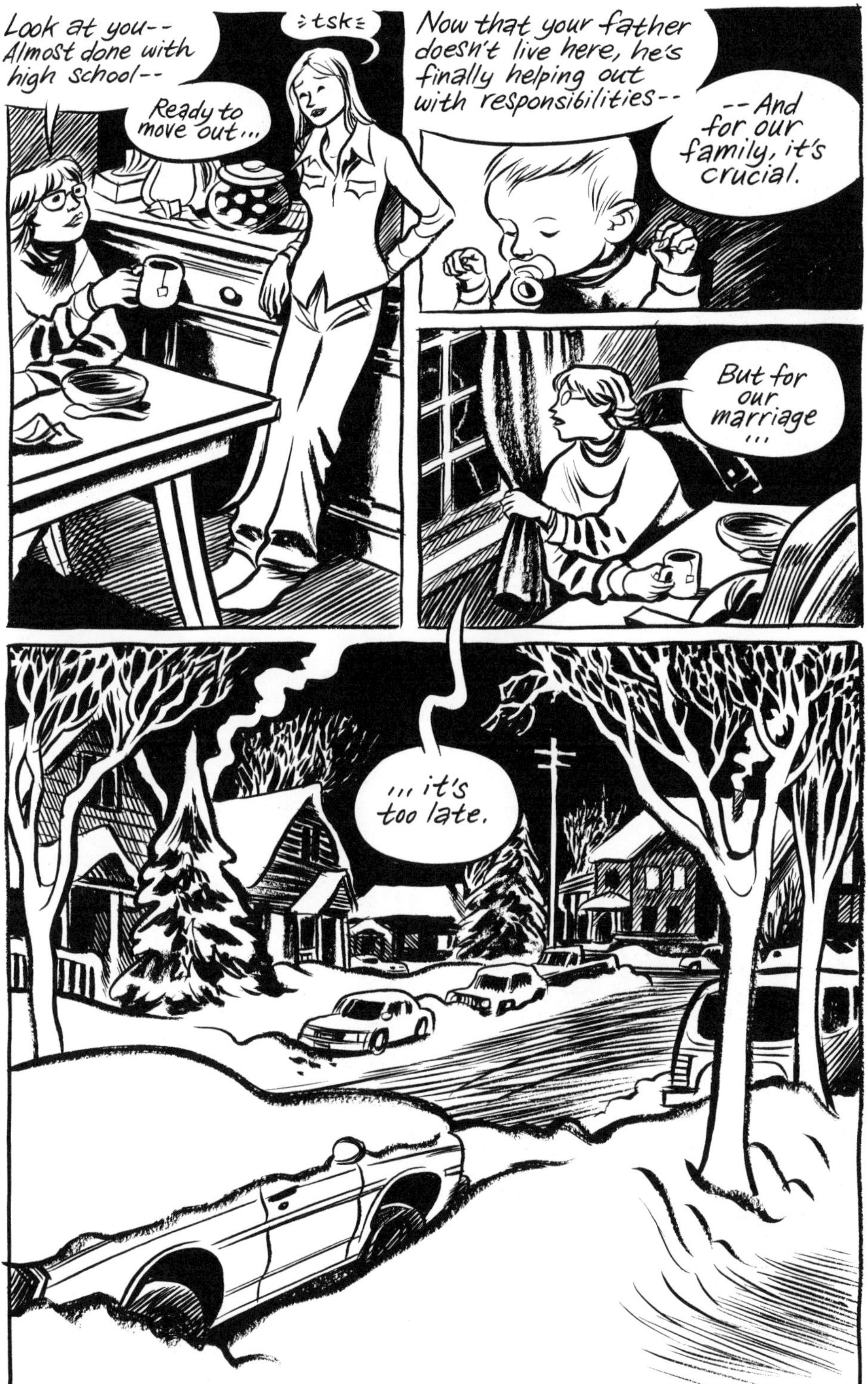
Look at you-- Almost done with high school--
Ready to move out...
:tsk:
Now that your father doesn't live here, he's finally helping out with responsibilities--
--And for our family, it's crucial.
But for our marriage ...
... it's too late.

On our last day
together,
Raina was sick.

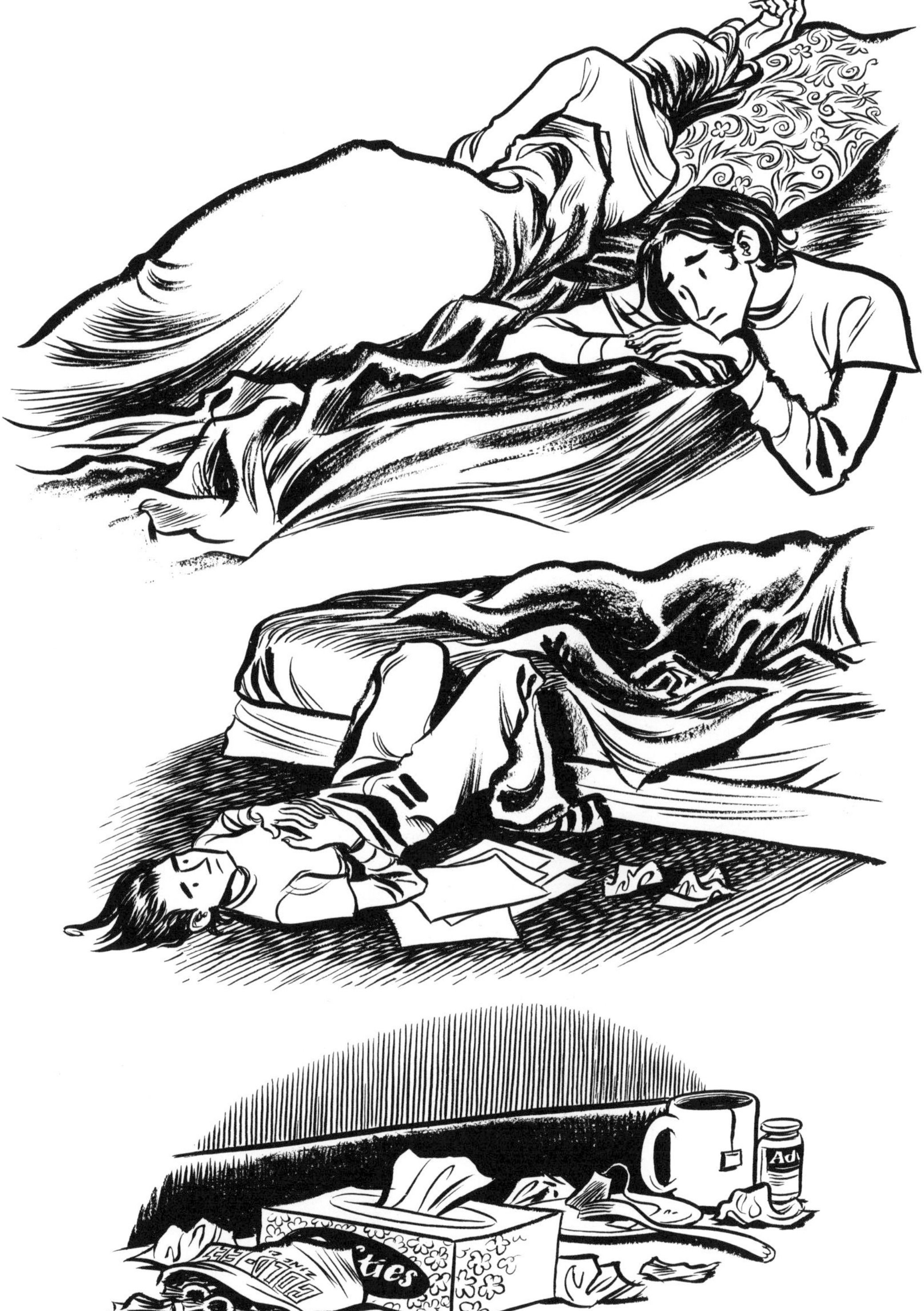
Adv
ties

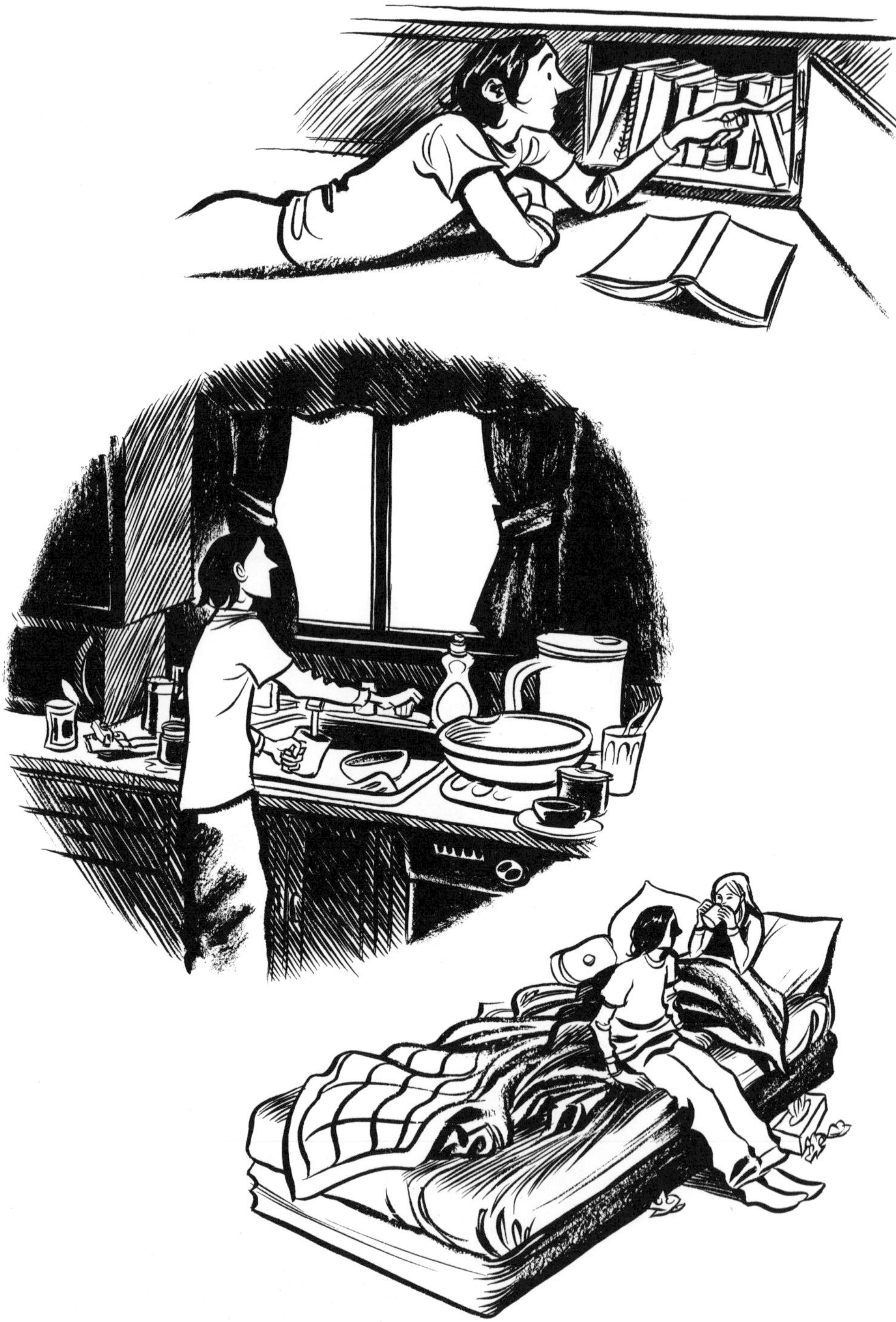

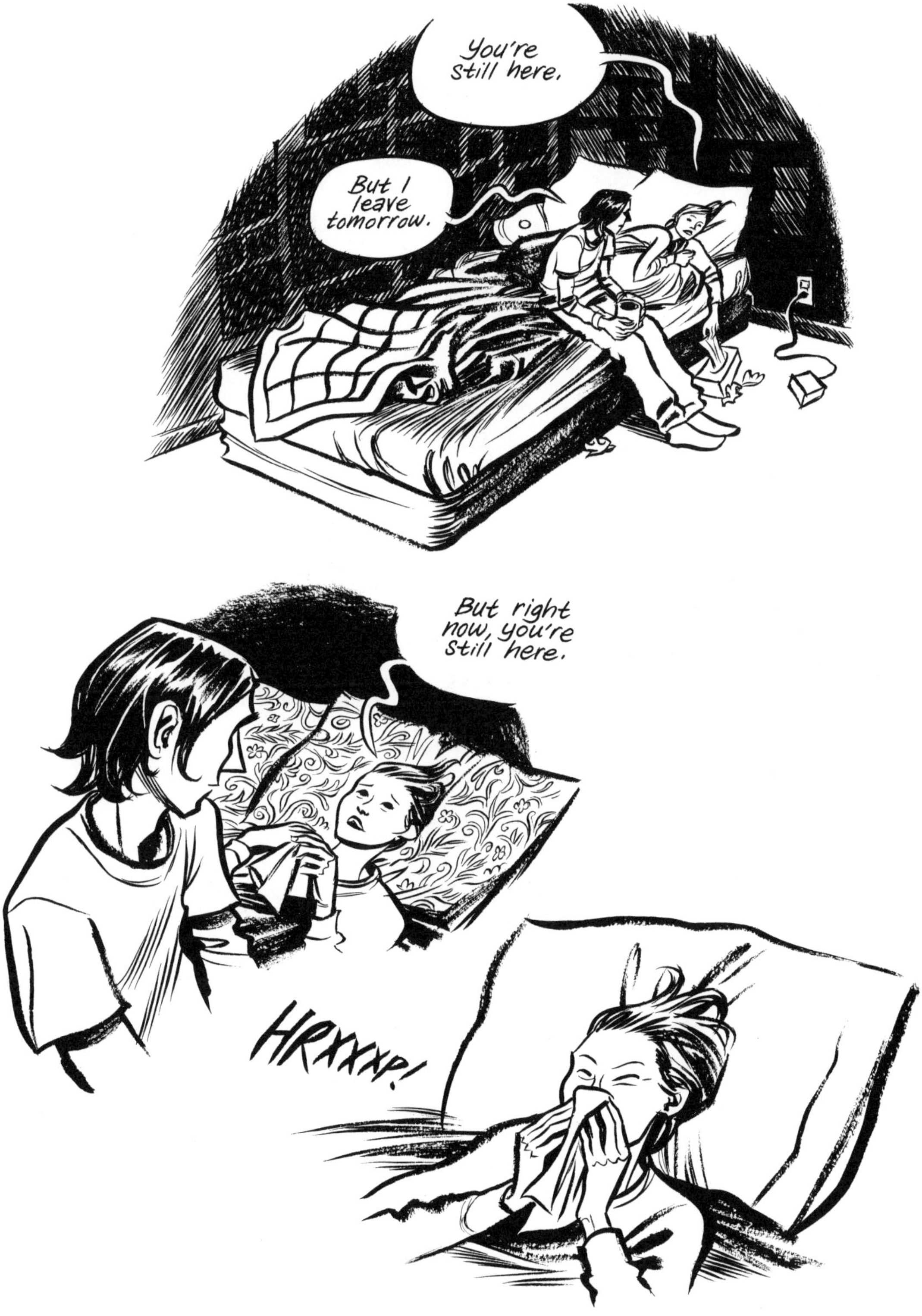
You're still here.
But I leave tomorrow.
But right now, you're still here.
HRXXXP!

469

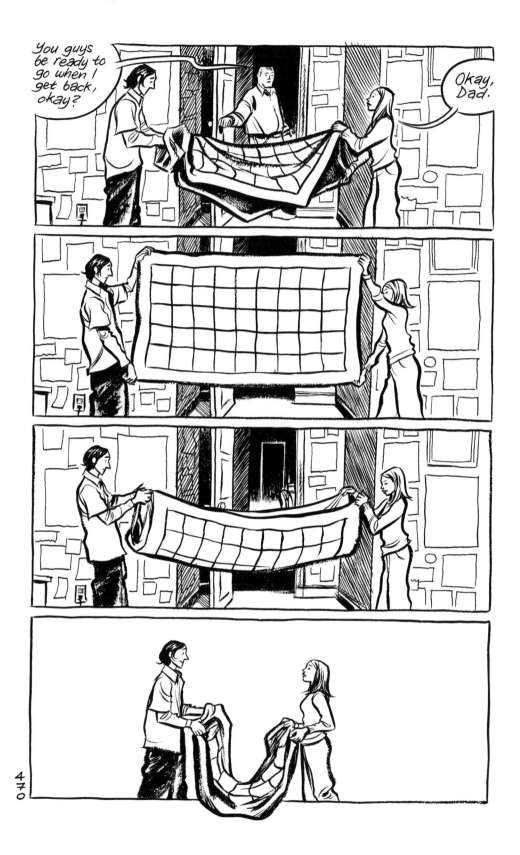

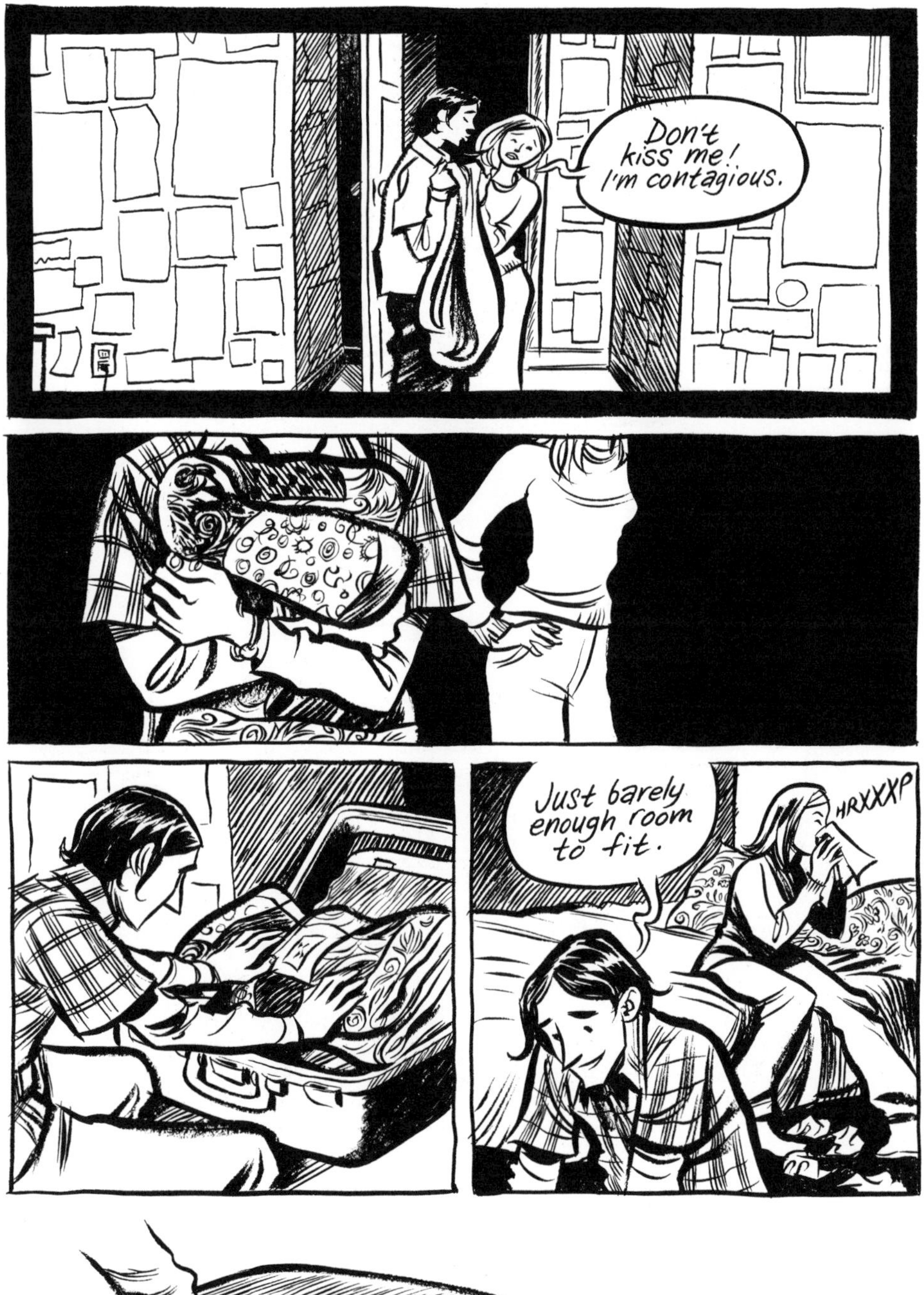
Don't kiss me! I'm contagious.
Just barely enough room to fit.
HRXXXP
click

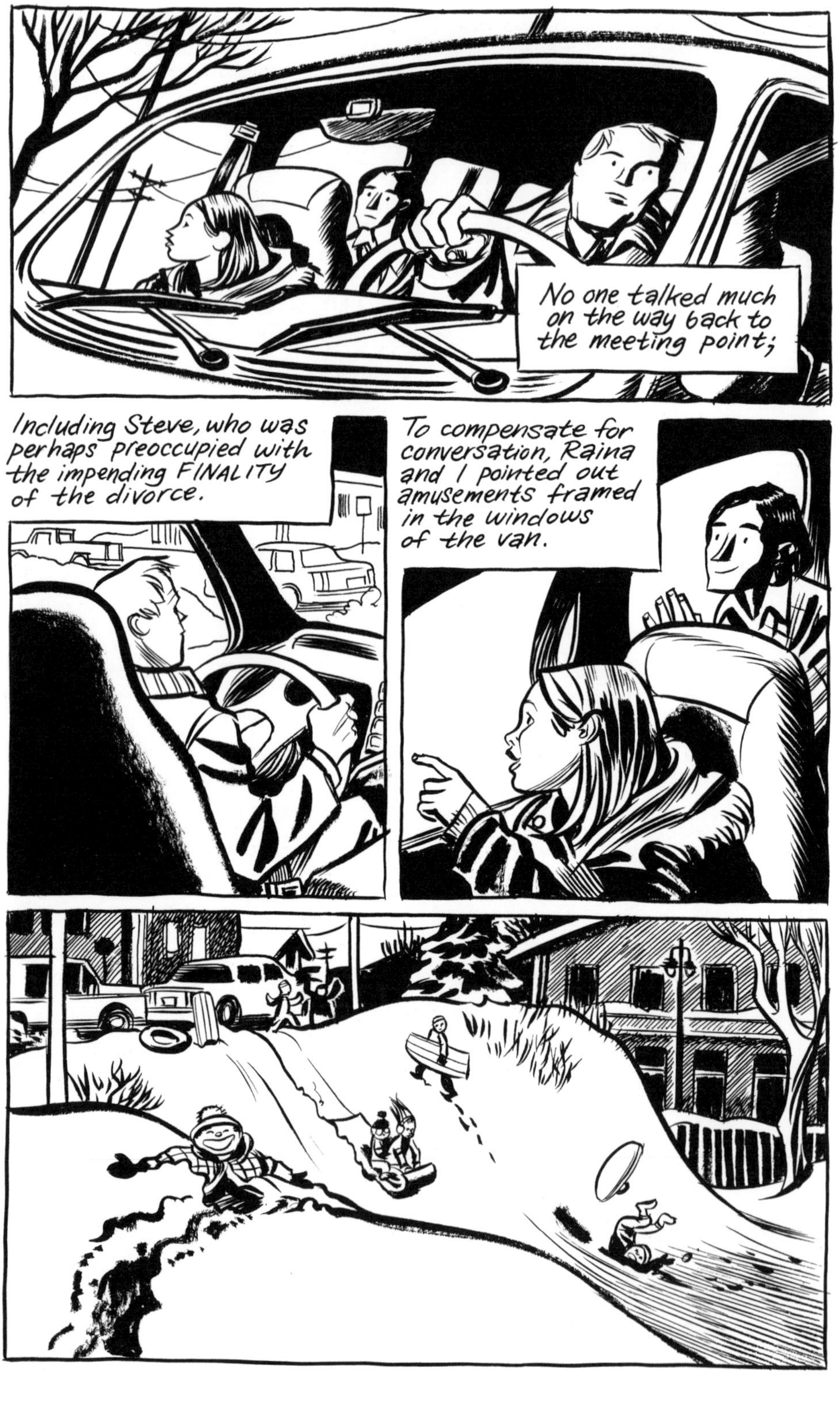
No one talked much on the way back to the meeting point;
Including Steve, who was perhaps preoccupied with the impending FINALITY of the divorce.
To compensate for conversation, Raina and I pointed out amusements framed in the windows of the van.

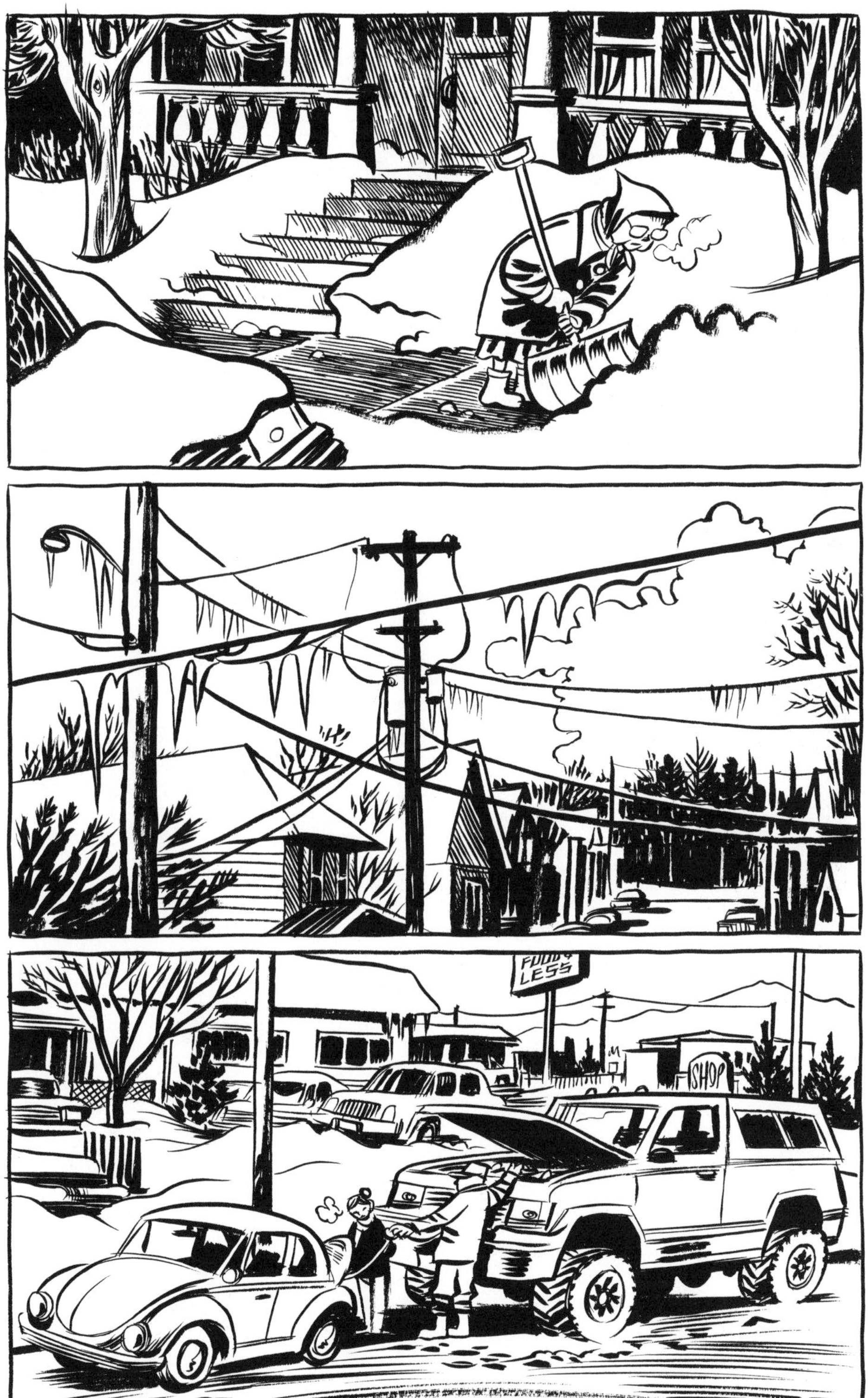
LESS
SHOP

And then for long stretches, nothing captured our interest.

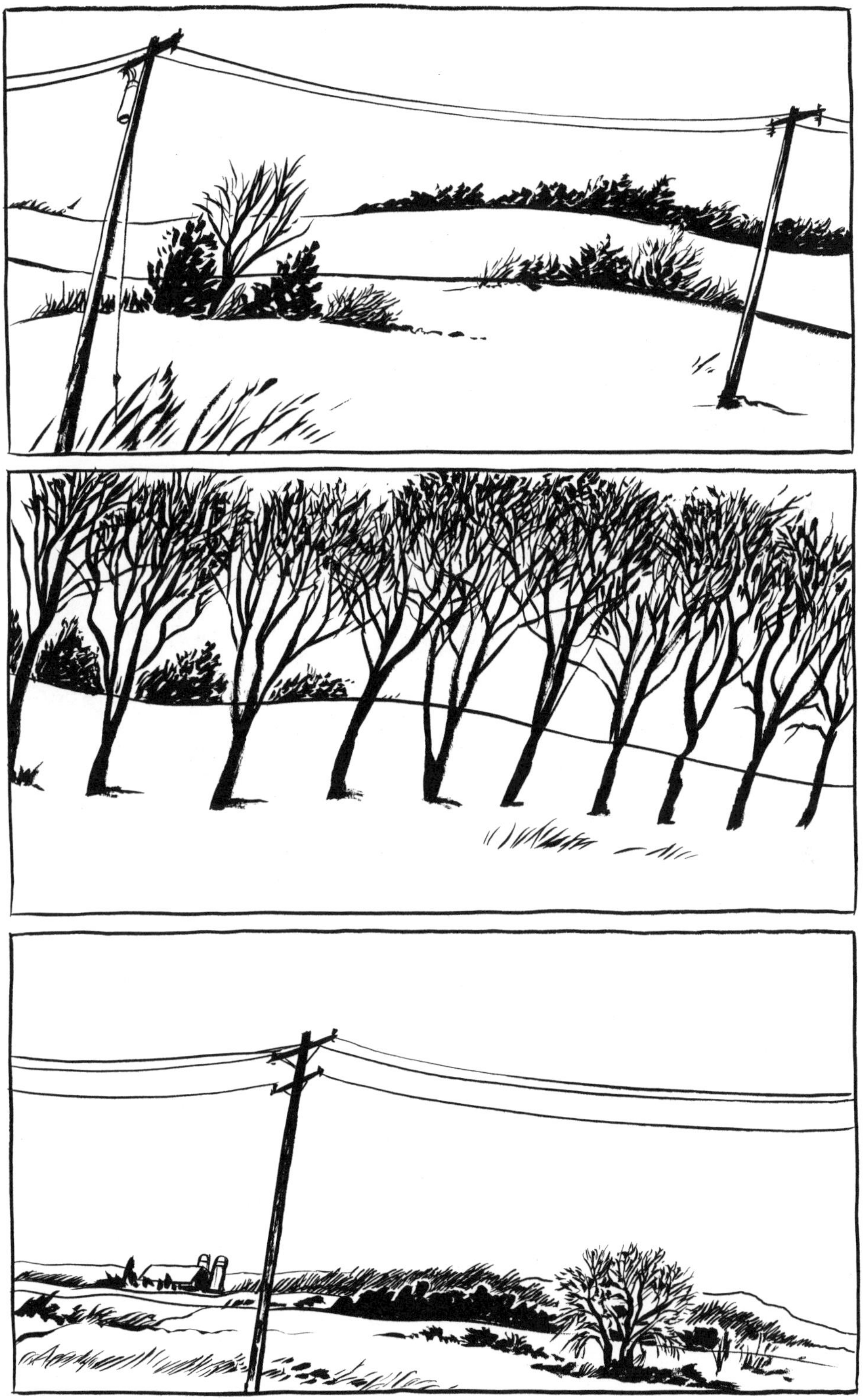

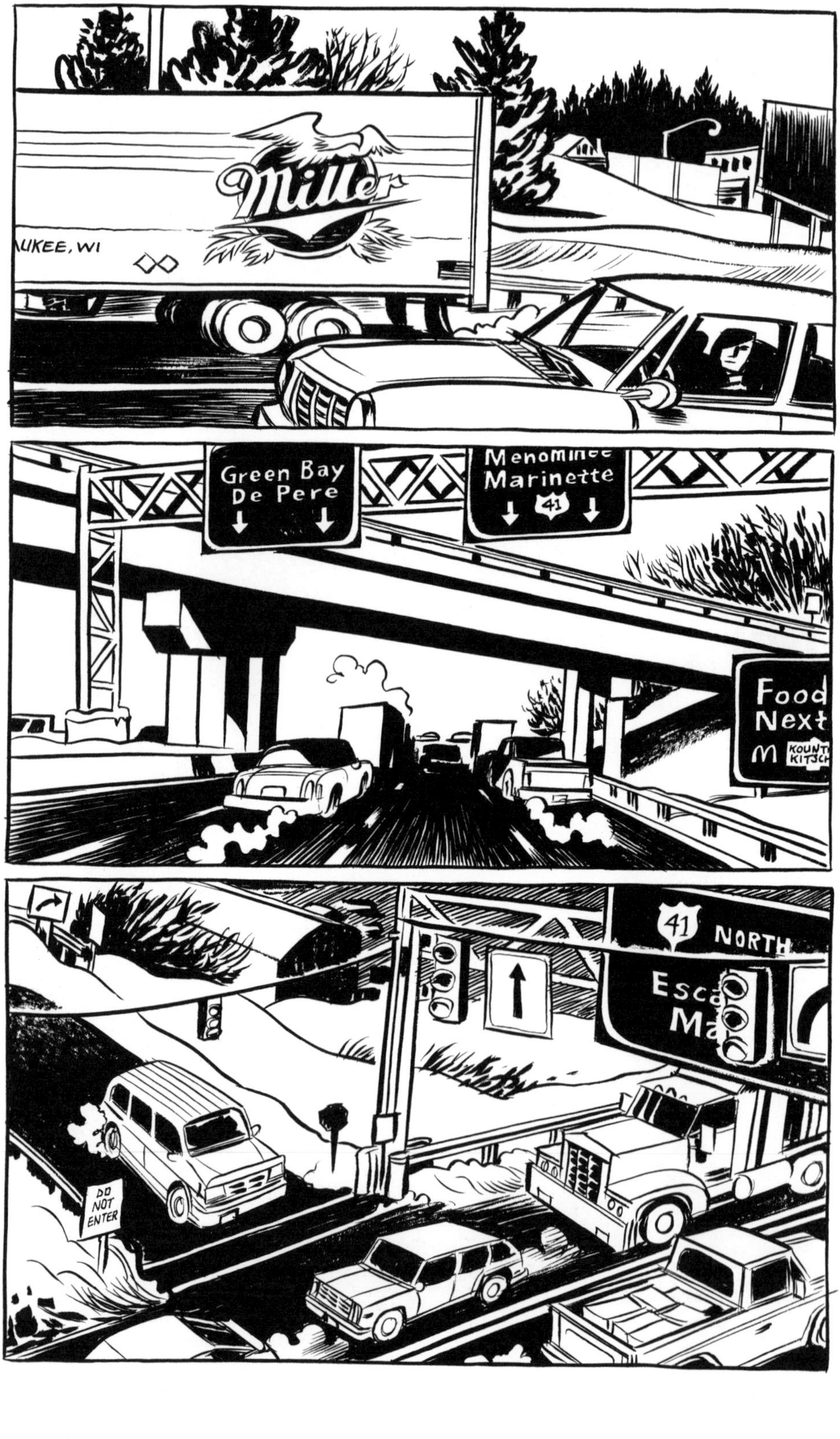
Miller
UKEE, WI
Green Bay
De Pere
Menominee
Marinette
41
Food
Next
41 NORTH
DO NOT ENTER

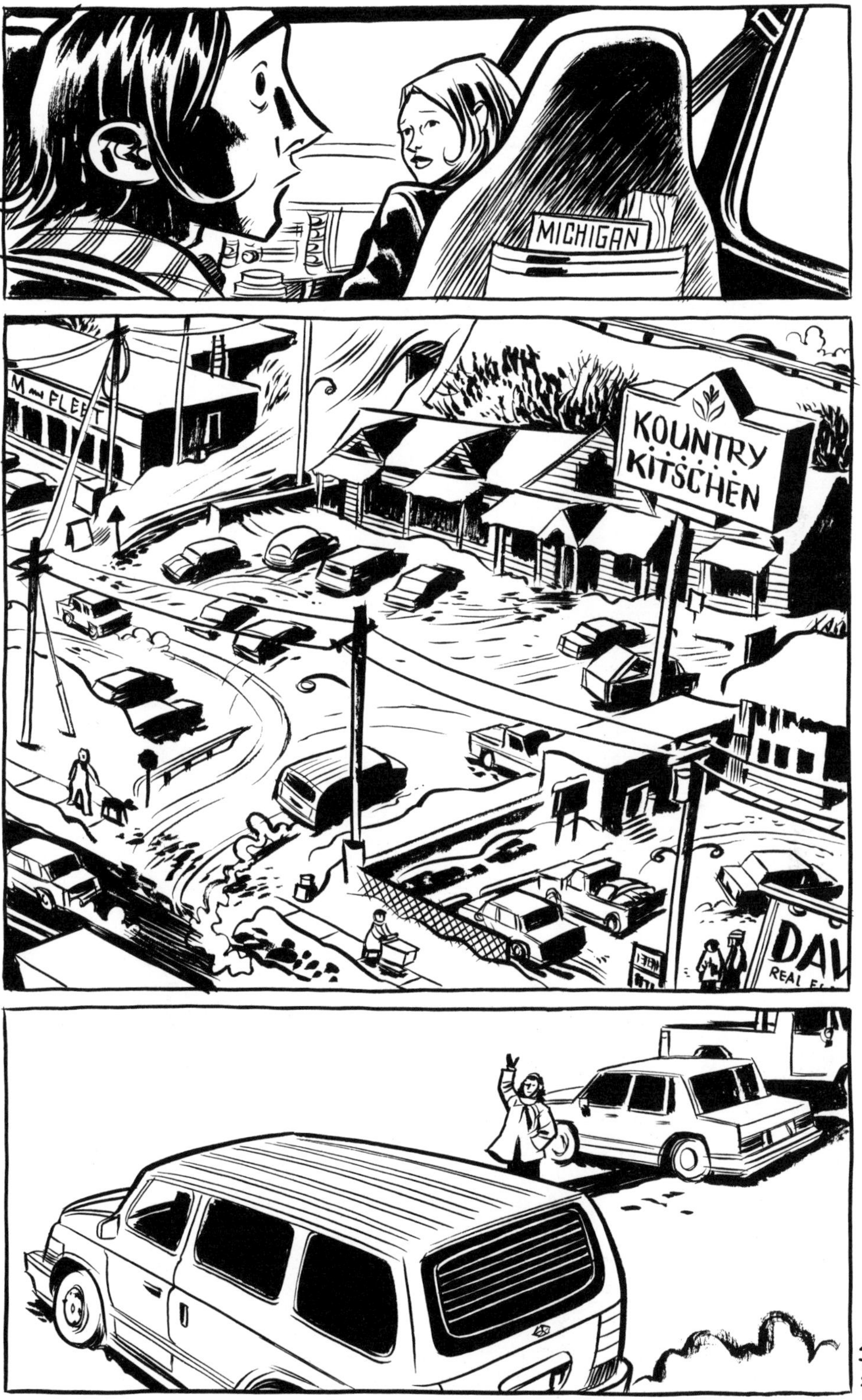
MICHIGAN
KOUNTRY KITSCHEN

At the moment, parental small-talk was practically unbearable --

--except that it constructed a pretense for Raina and I to exchange glances a moment longer.

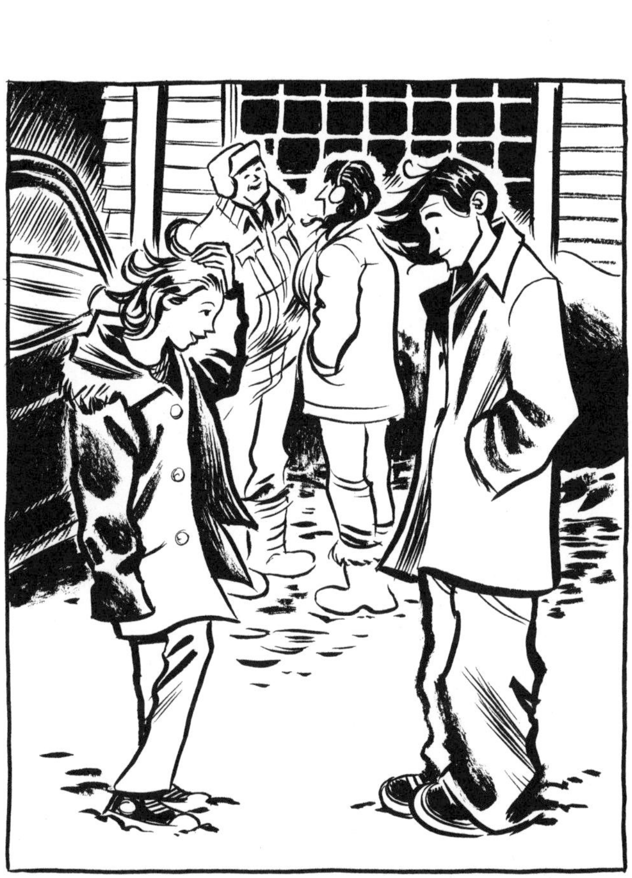

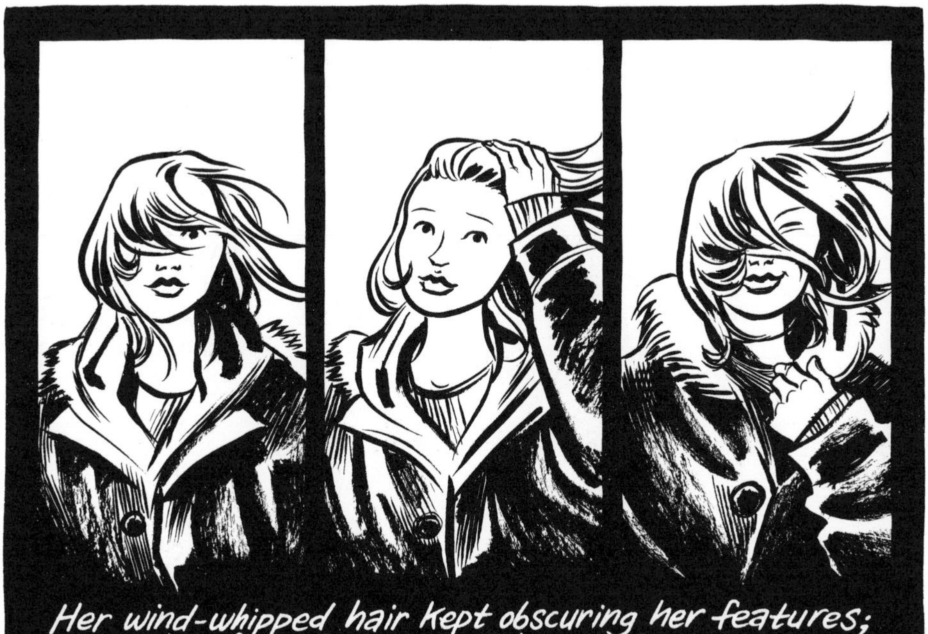
Her wind-whipped hair kept obscuring her features; her face faded in and out of view.

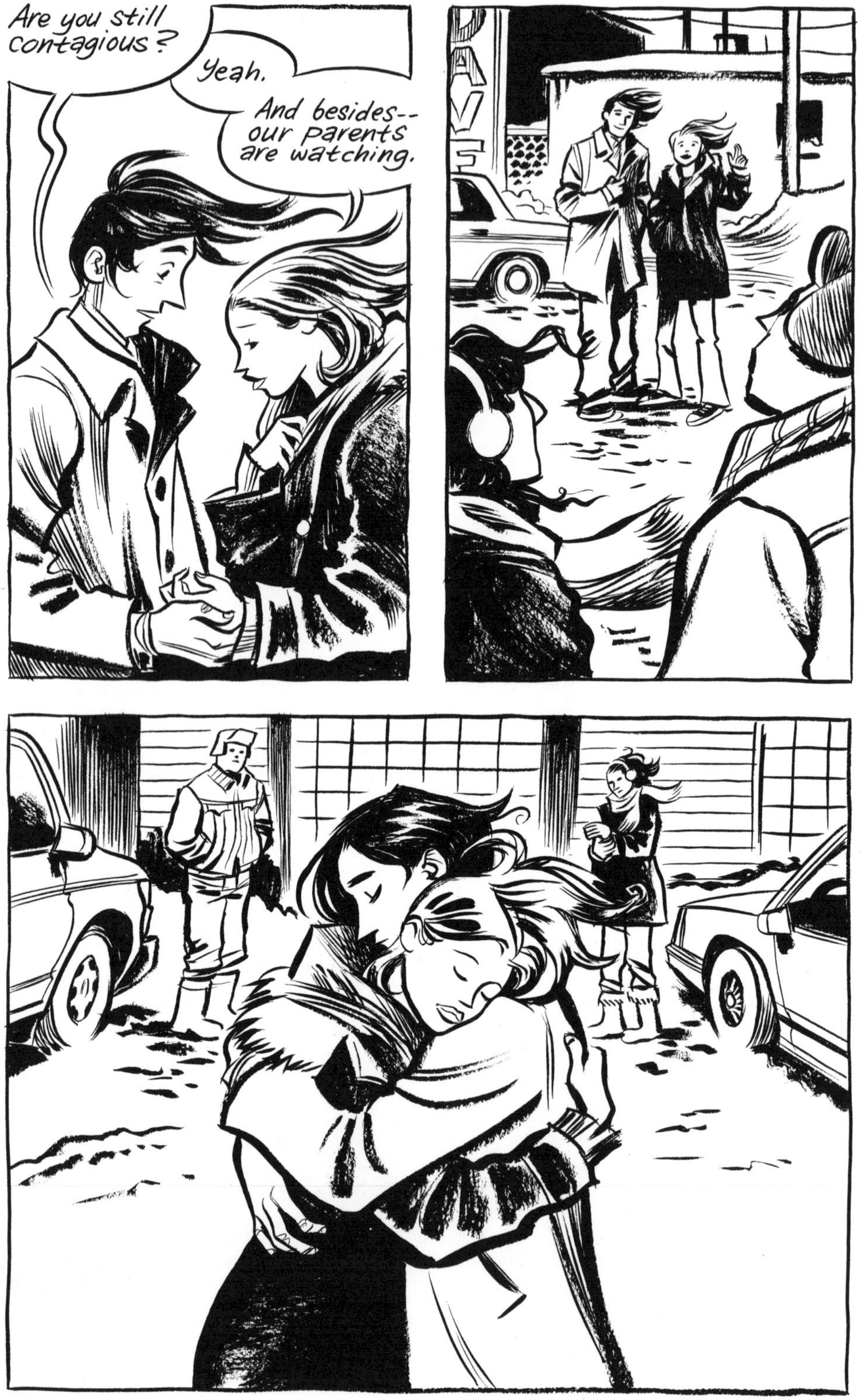
Are you still contagious?
Yeah.
And besides--our parents are watching.

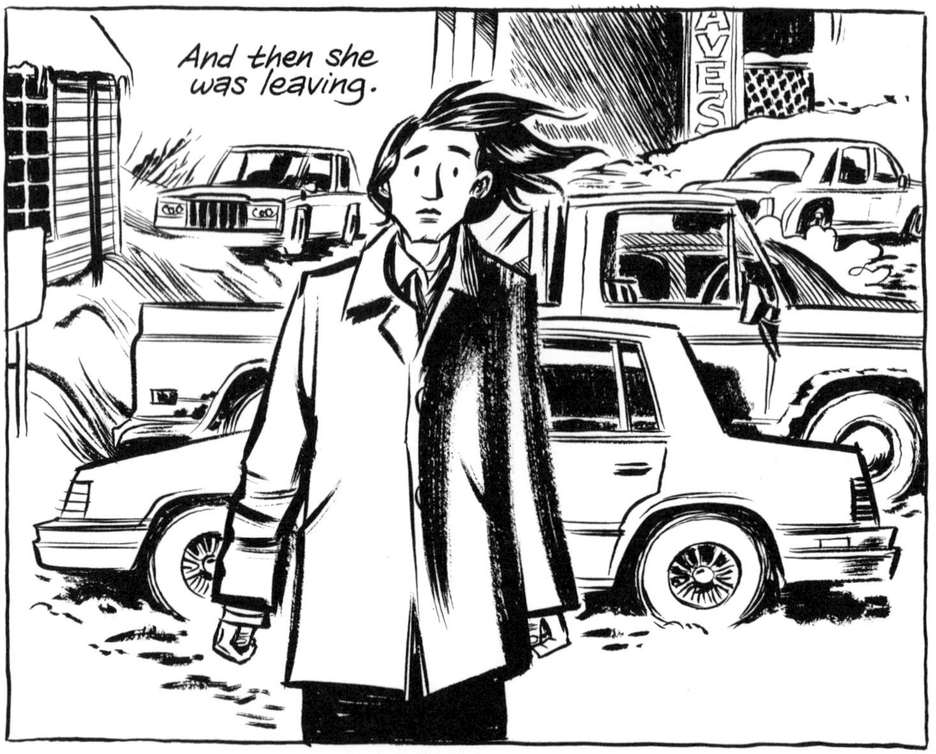
And then she was leaving.

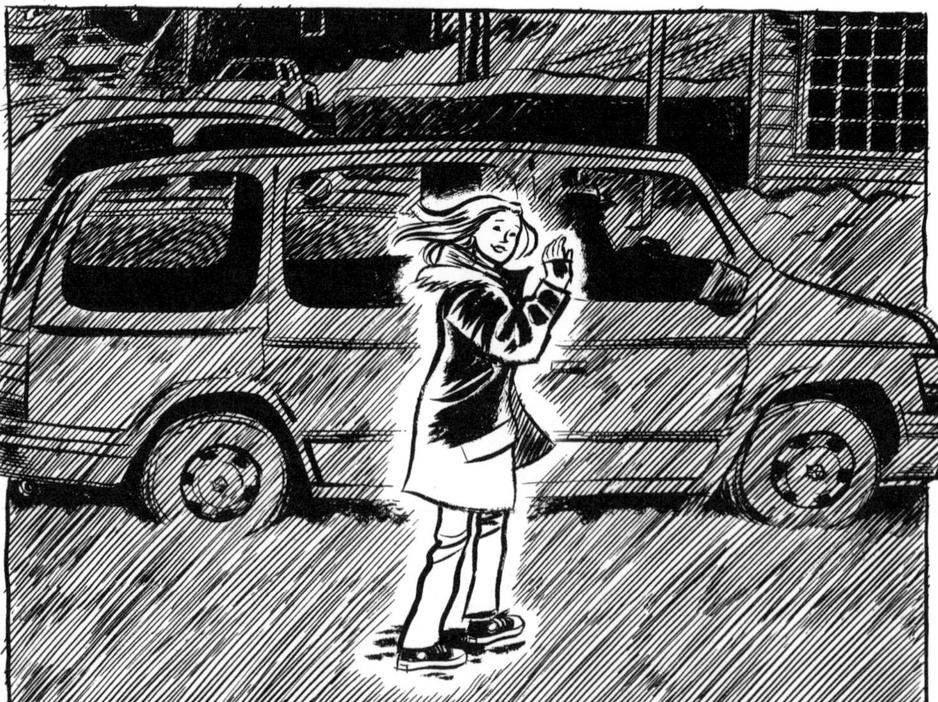

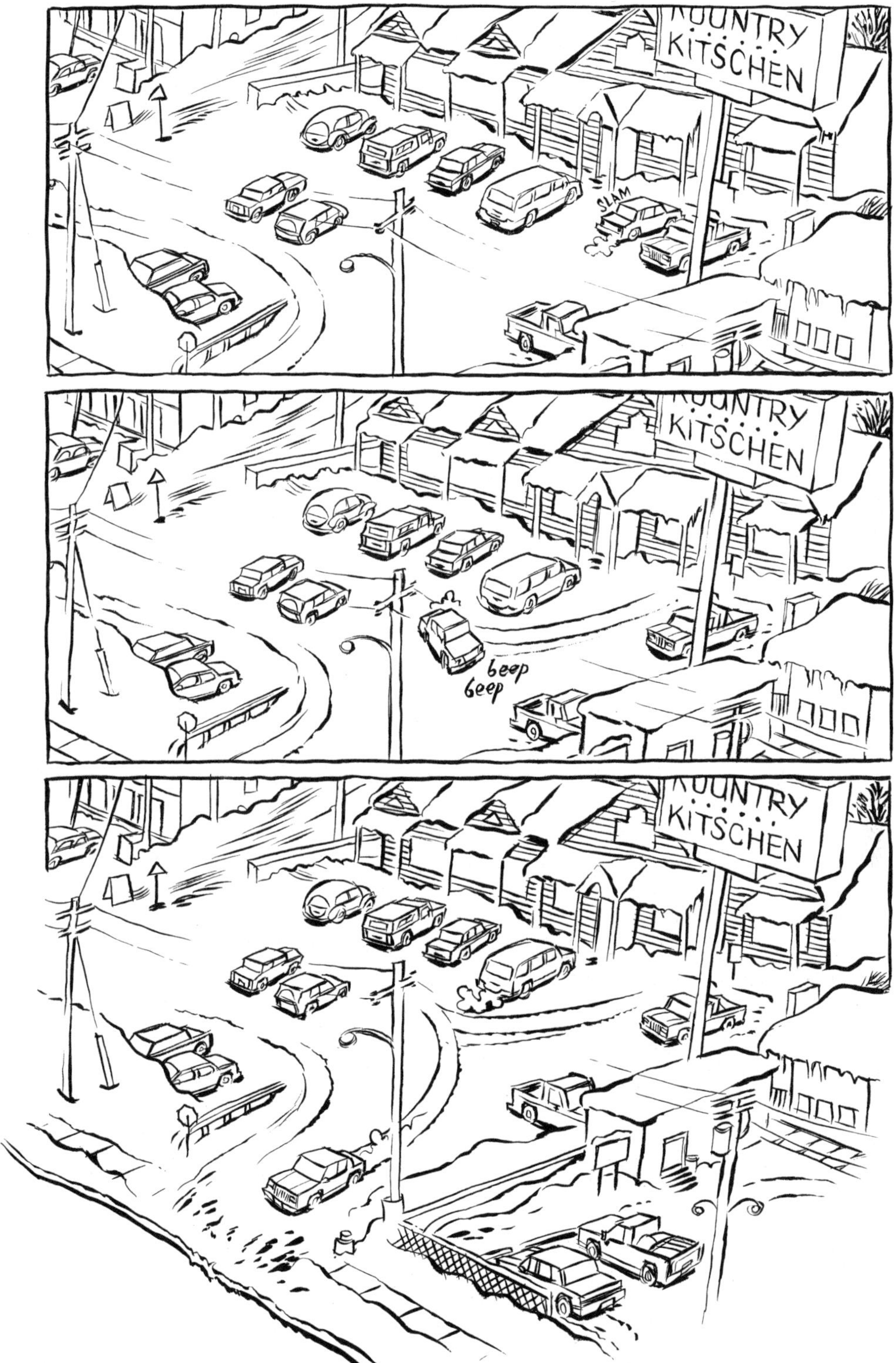
KOUNTRY KITSCHEN
SLAM
KOUNTRY KITSCHEN
beep beep
KOUNTRY KITSCHEN

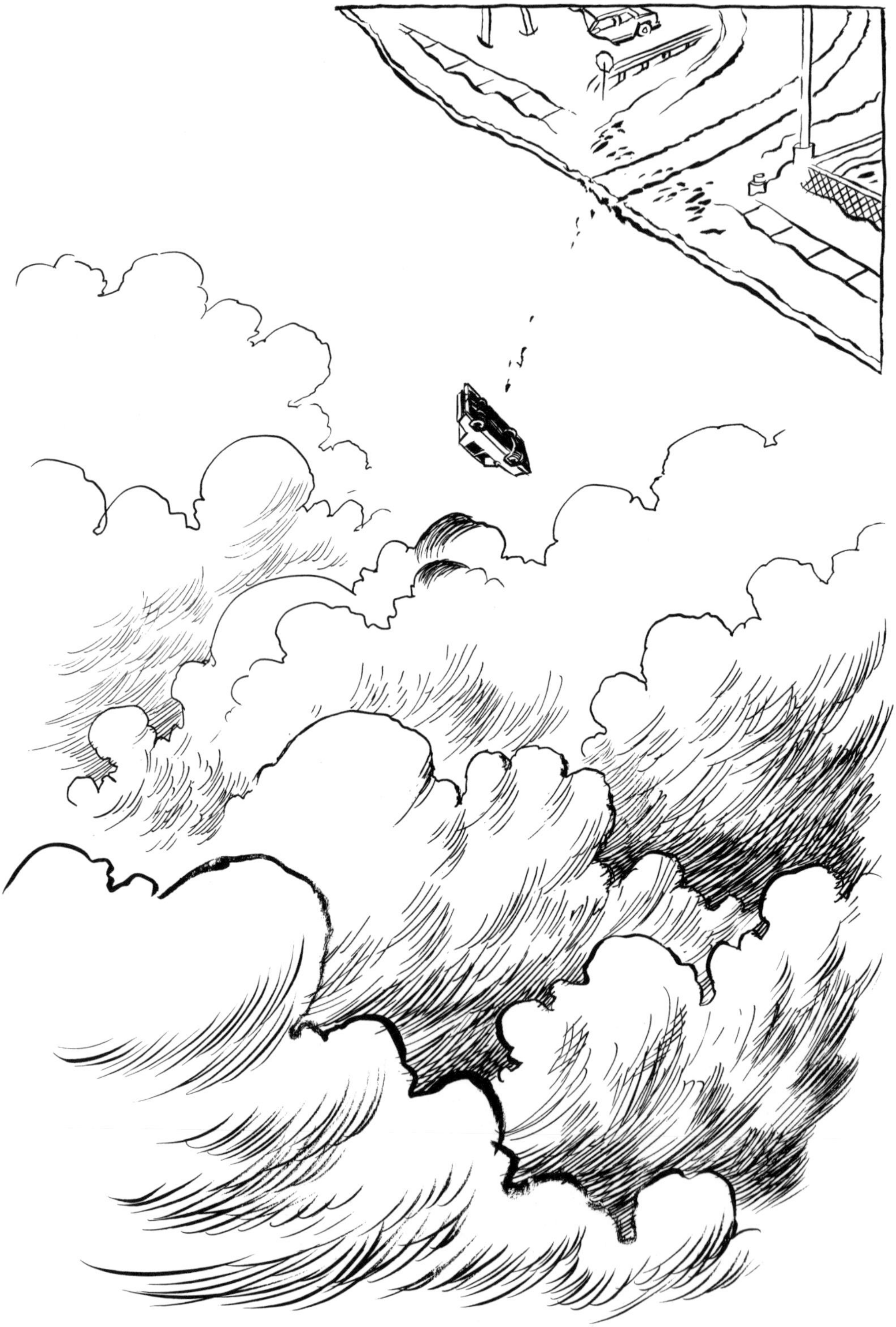

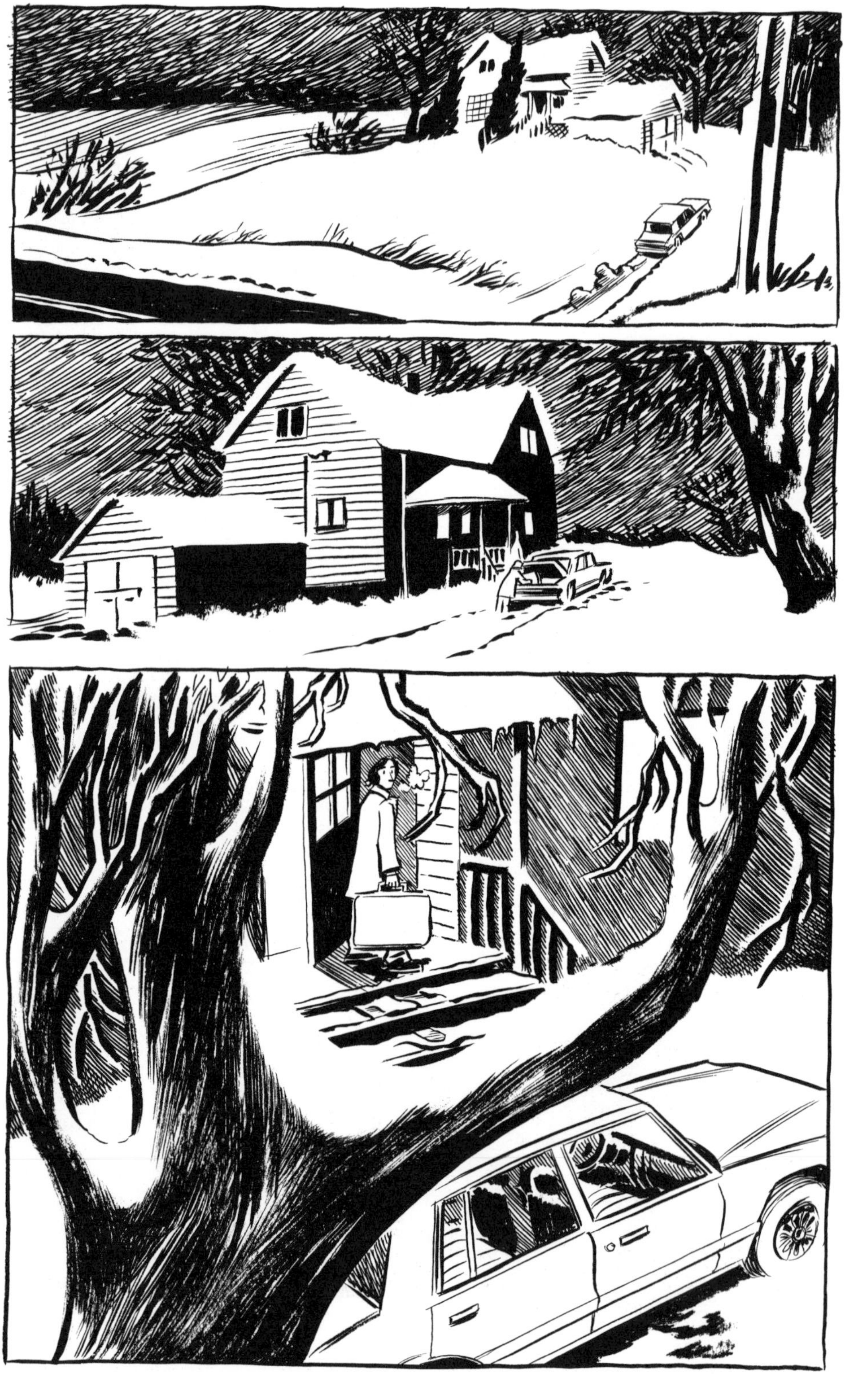

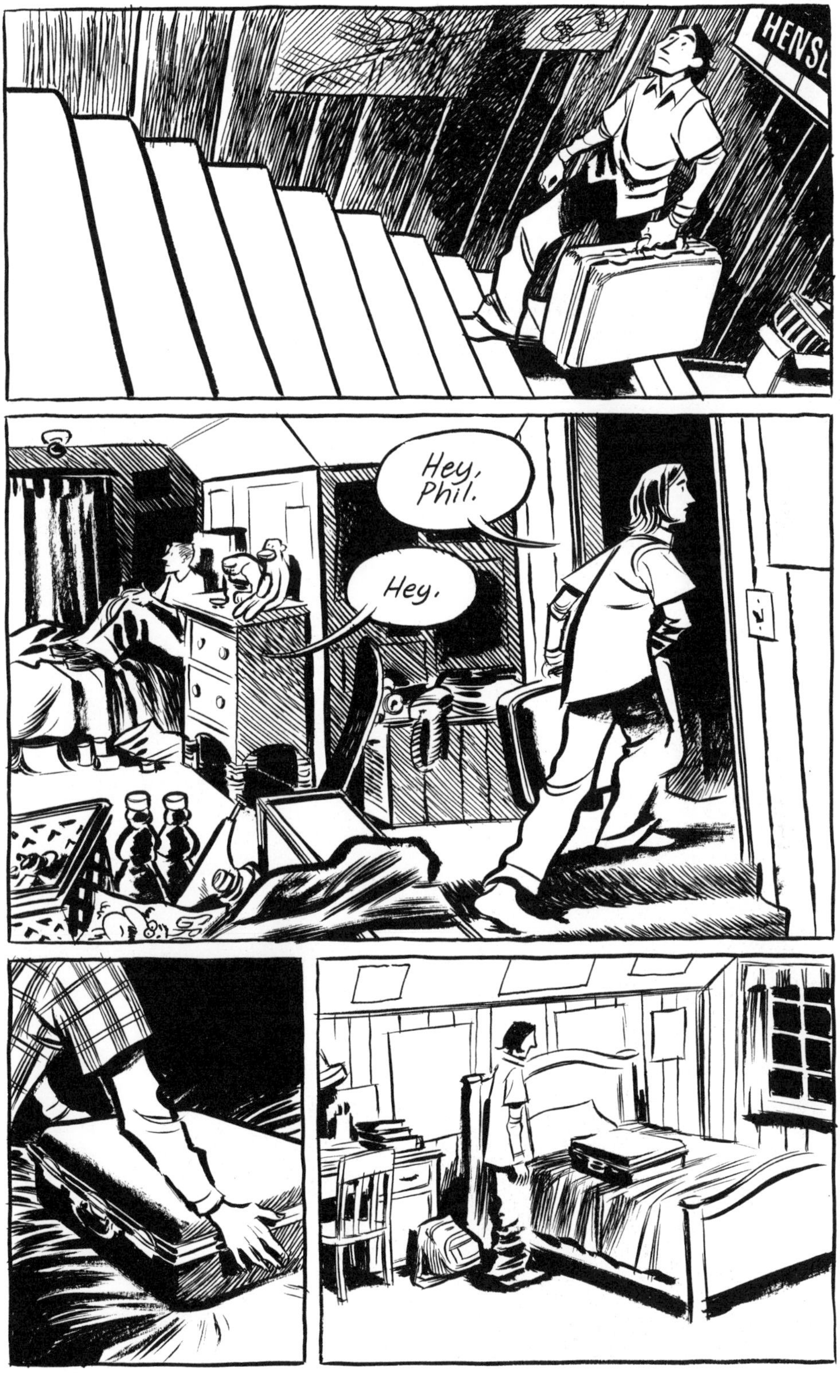
HENSL
Hey, Phil.
Hey.

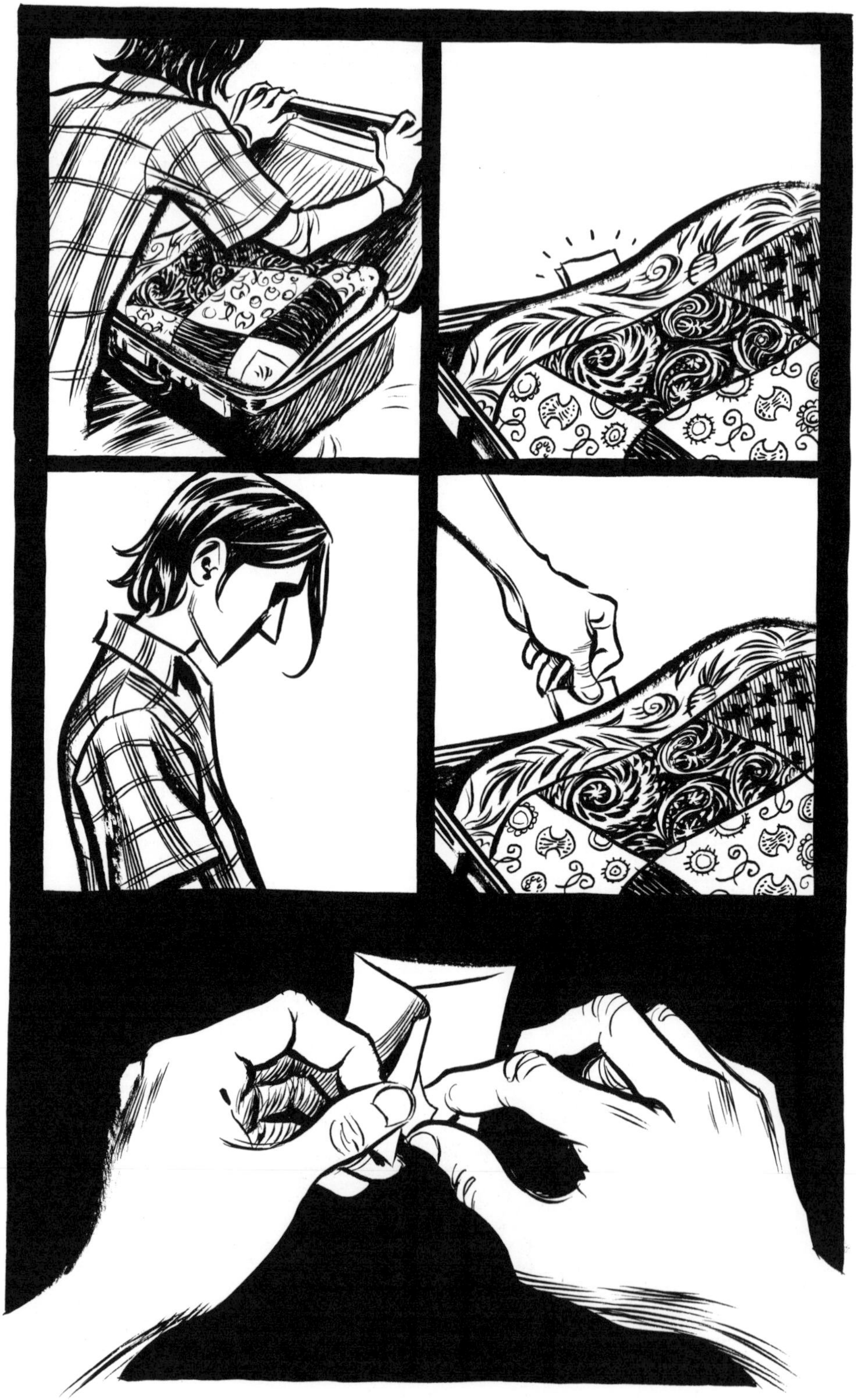

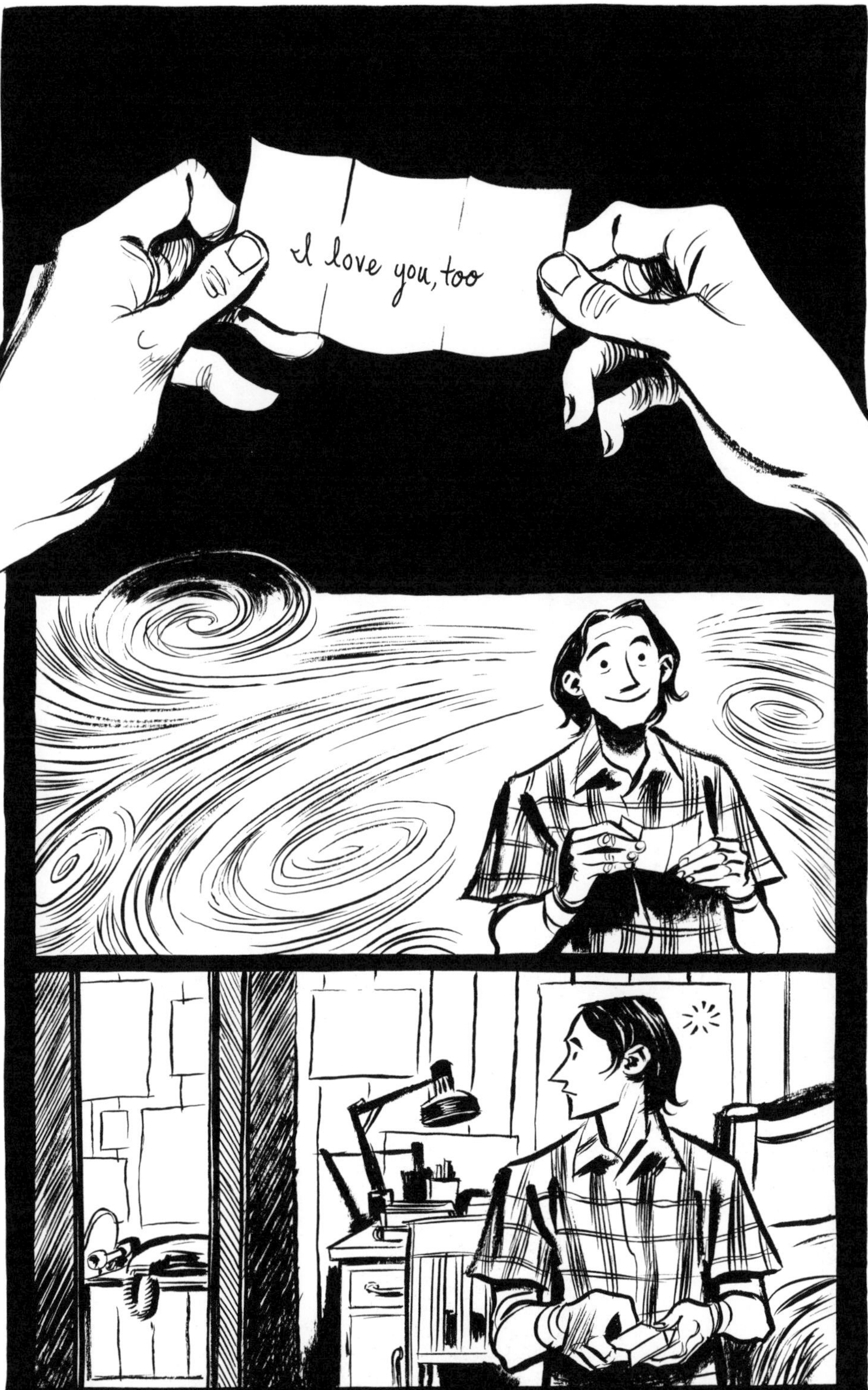
I love you, too

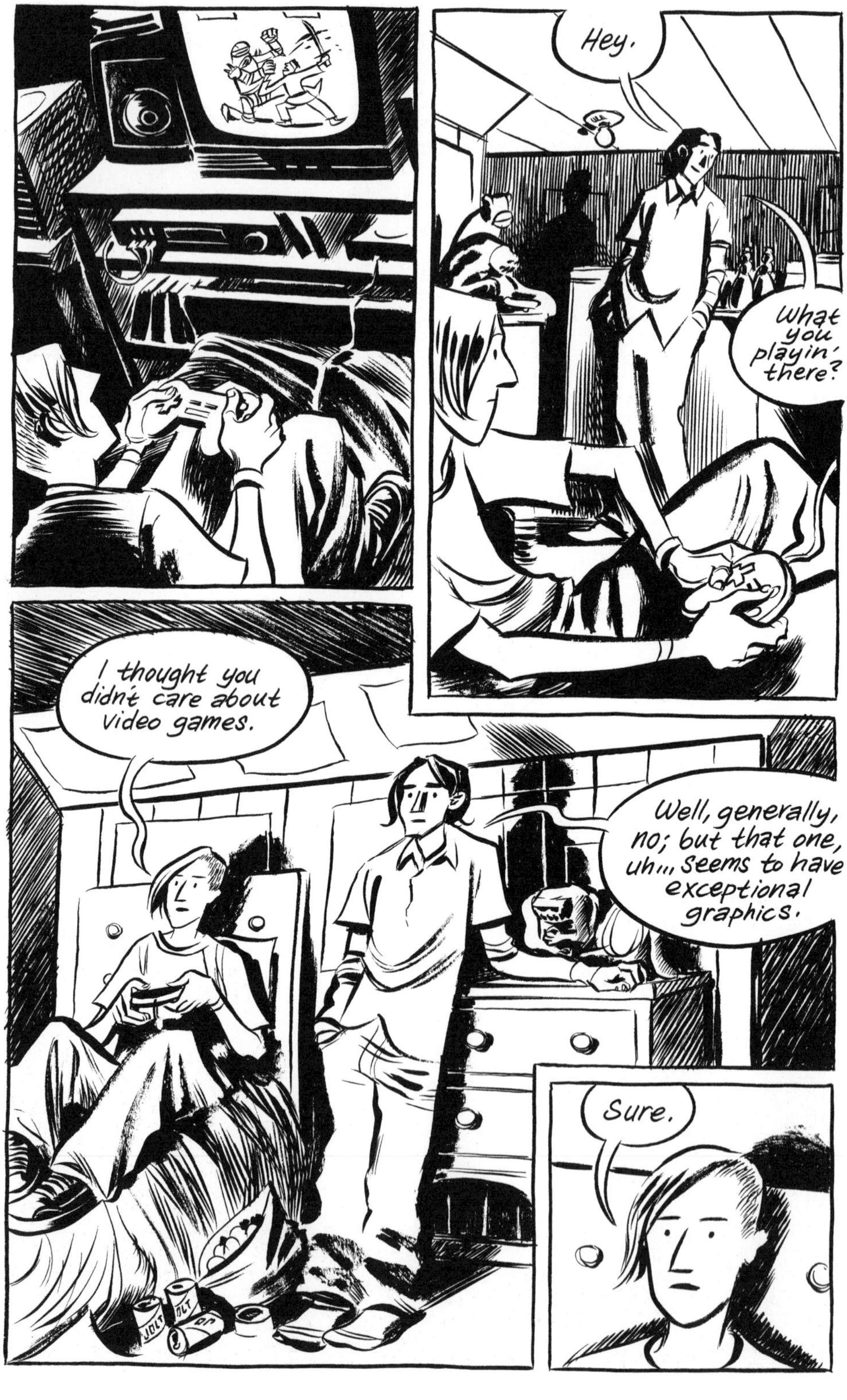

Hey.
What you playin' there?
I thought you didn't care about video games.
Well, generally, no; but that one, uh... seems to have exceptional graphics.
Sure.

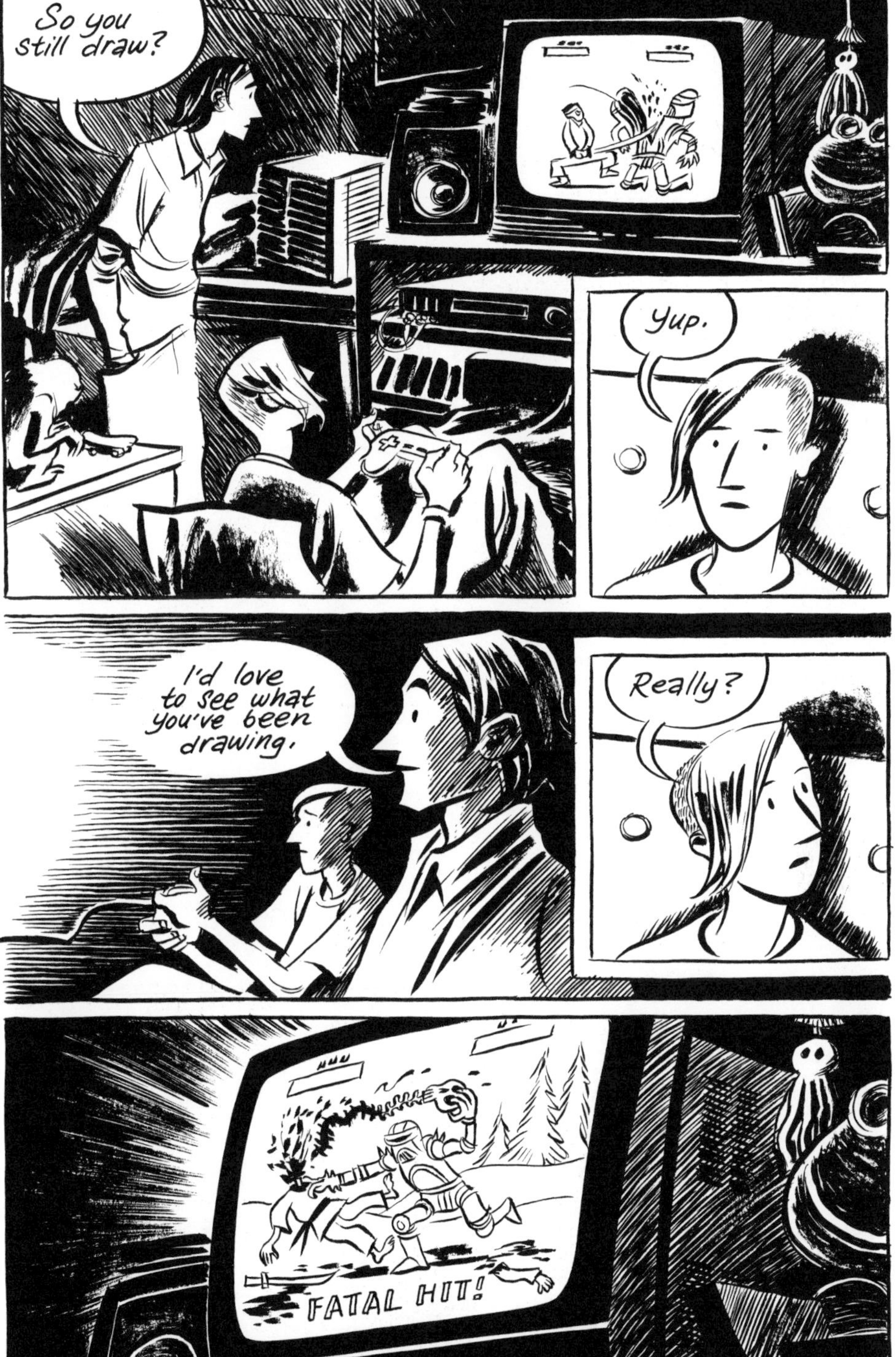
So you still draw?
Yup.
I'd love to see what you've been drawing.
Really?
FATAL HIT!

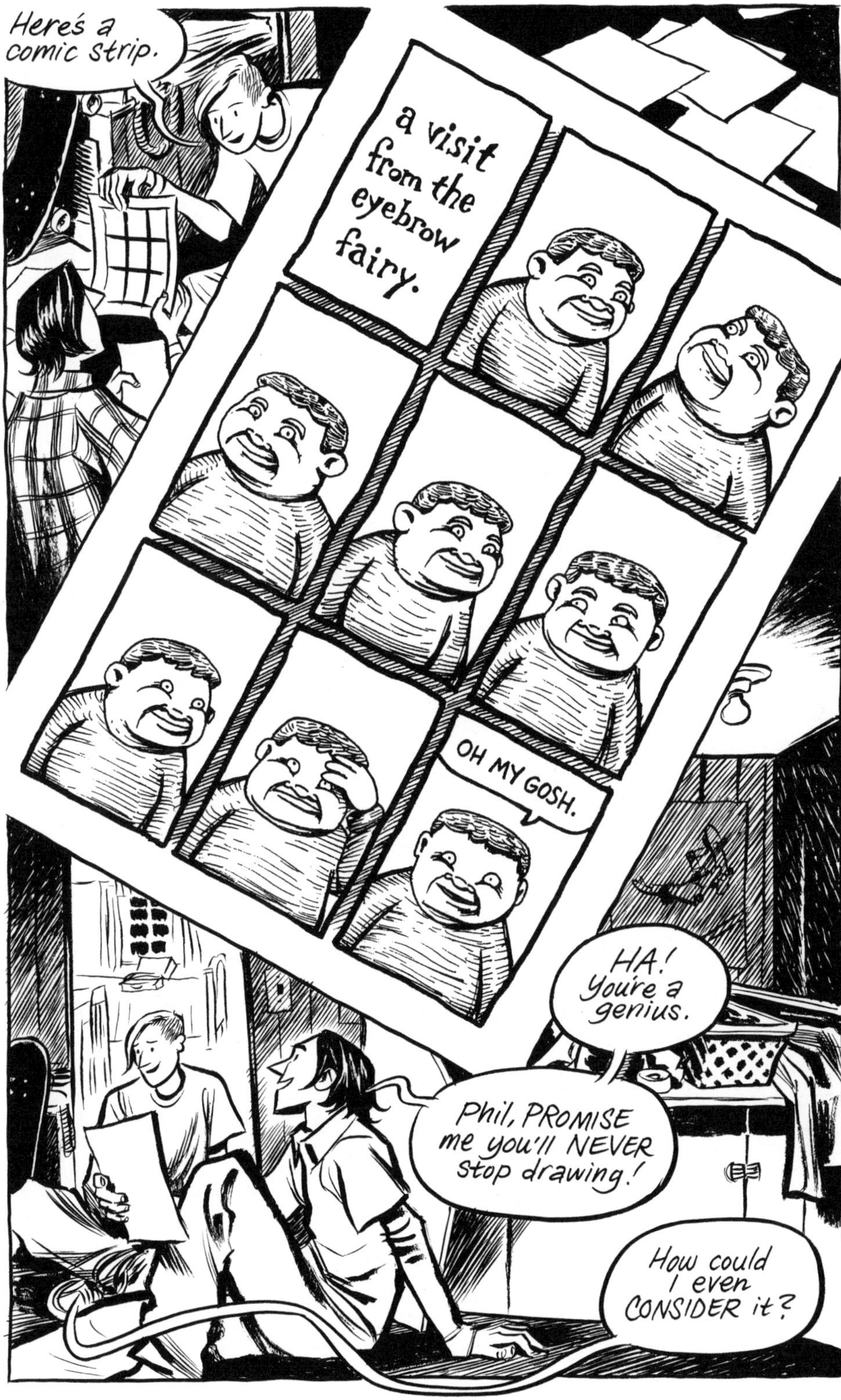

Here's a comic strip.
a visit from the eyebrow fairy.
OH MY GOSH.
HA! You're a genius.
Phil, PROMISE me you'll NEVER stop drawing!
How could I even CONSIDER it?

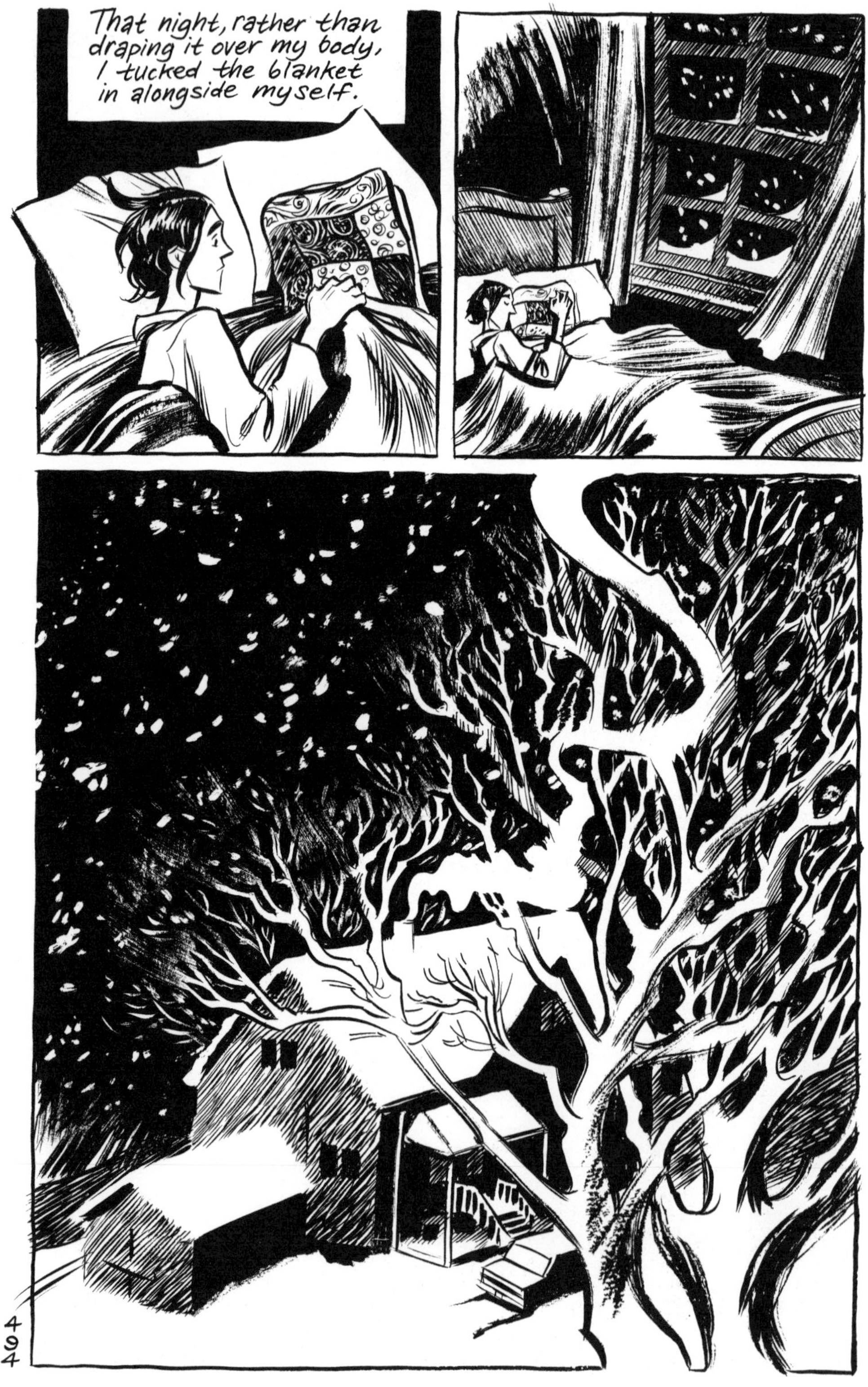
That night, rather than draping it over my body, I tucked the blanket in alongside myself.

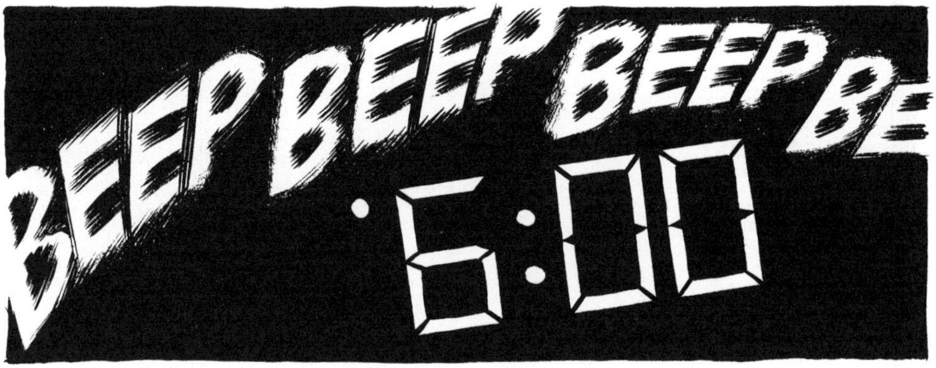
BEEP BEEP BEEP BEEP BE
6:00

SOCRATES ASKS HIS DISCIPLE GLAUCON TO IMAGINE HUMAN BEINGS LIVING WITHIN A DARK CAVERN.

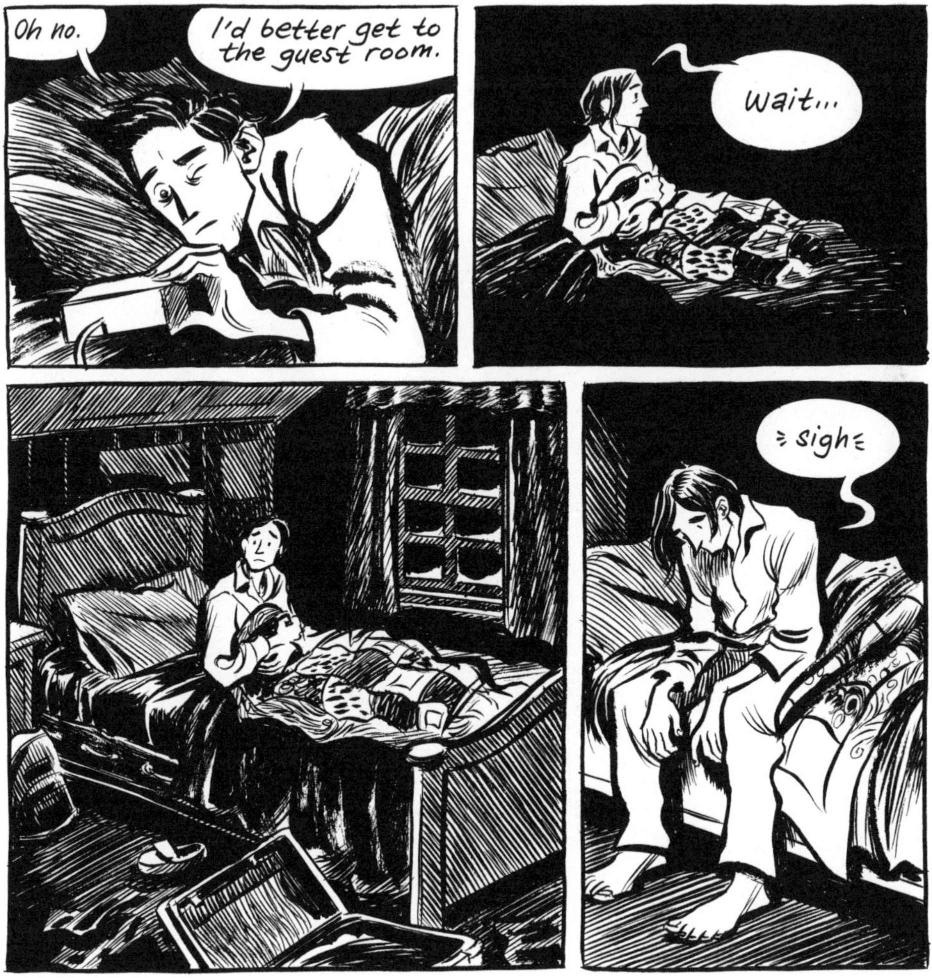
Oh no.
I'd better get to the guest room.
Wait...
sigh

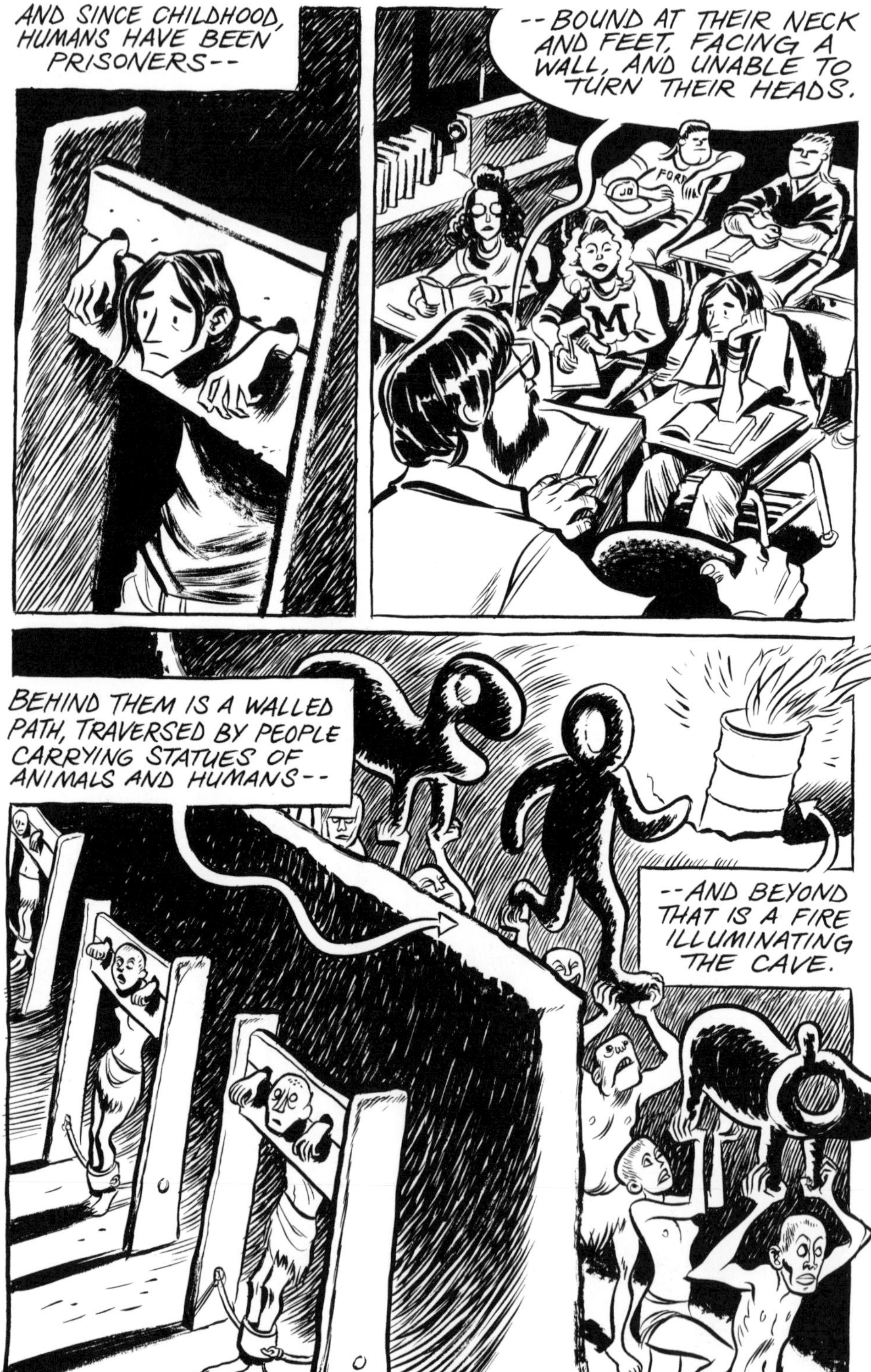
AND SINCE CHILDHOOD, HUMANS HAVE BEEN PRISONERS--
--BOUND AT THEIR NECK AND FEET, FACING A WALL, AND UNABLE TO TURN THEIR HEADS.
FORD
M
BEHIND THEM IS A WALLED PATH, TRAVERSED BY PEOPLE CARRYING STATUES OF ANIMALS AND HUMANS--
--AND BEYOND THAT IS A FIRE ILLUMINATING THE CAVE.

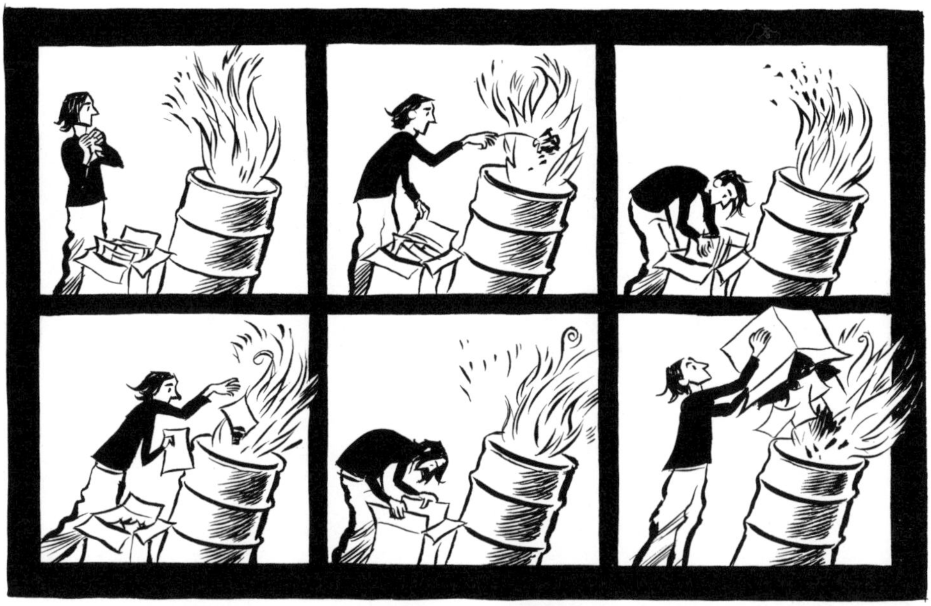

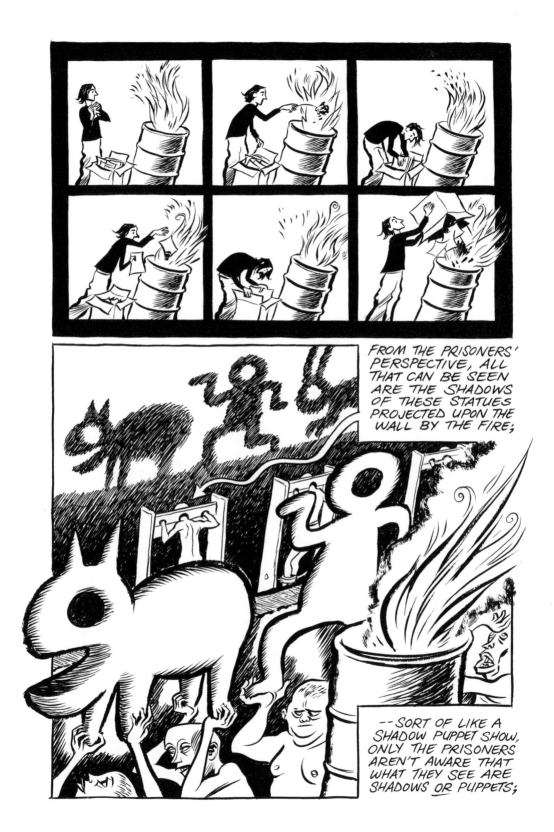

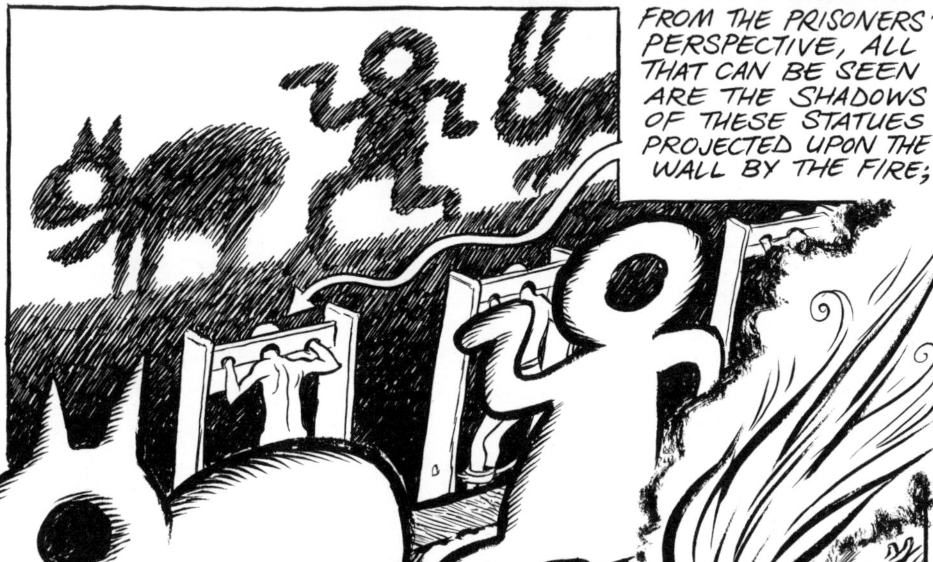
FROM THE PRISONERS' PERSPECTIVE, ALL THAT CAN BE SEEN ARE THE SHADOWS OF THESE STATUES PROJECTED UPON THE WALL BY THE FIRE;
--SORT OF LIKE A SHADOW PUPPET SHOW, ONLY THE PRISONERS AREN'T AWARE THAT WHAT THEY SEE ARE SHADOWS OR PUPPETS;

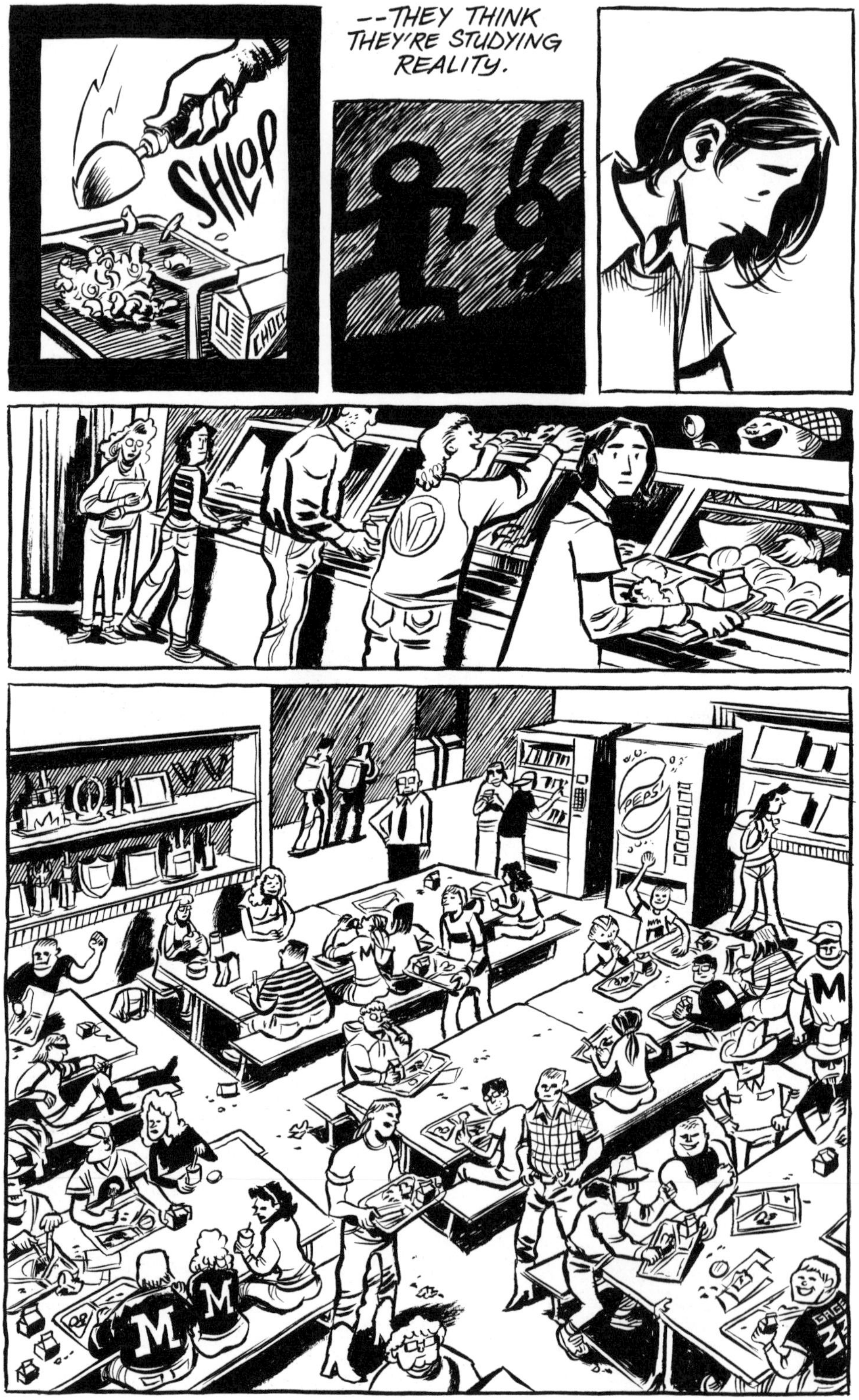
SHLOP
CHOC
--THEY THINK THEY'RE STUDYING REALITY.
PEPSI

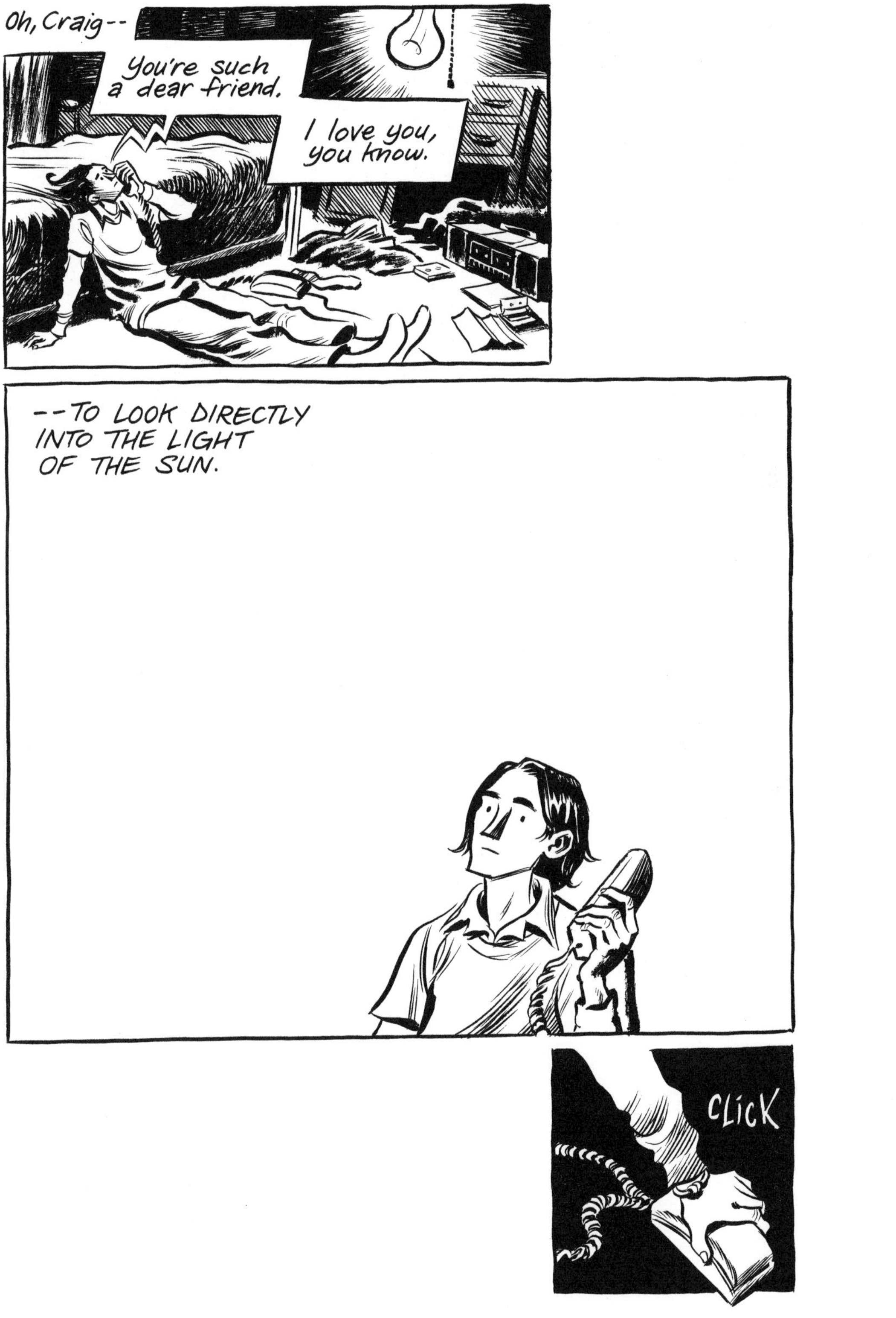
Oh, Craig--
You're such a dear friend.
I love you, you know.
--TO LOOK DIRECTLY INTO THE LIGHT OF THE SUN.
CLICK

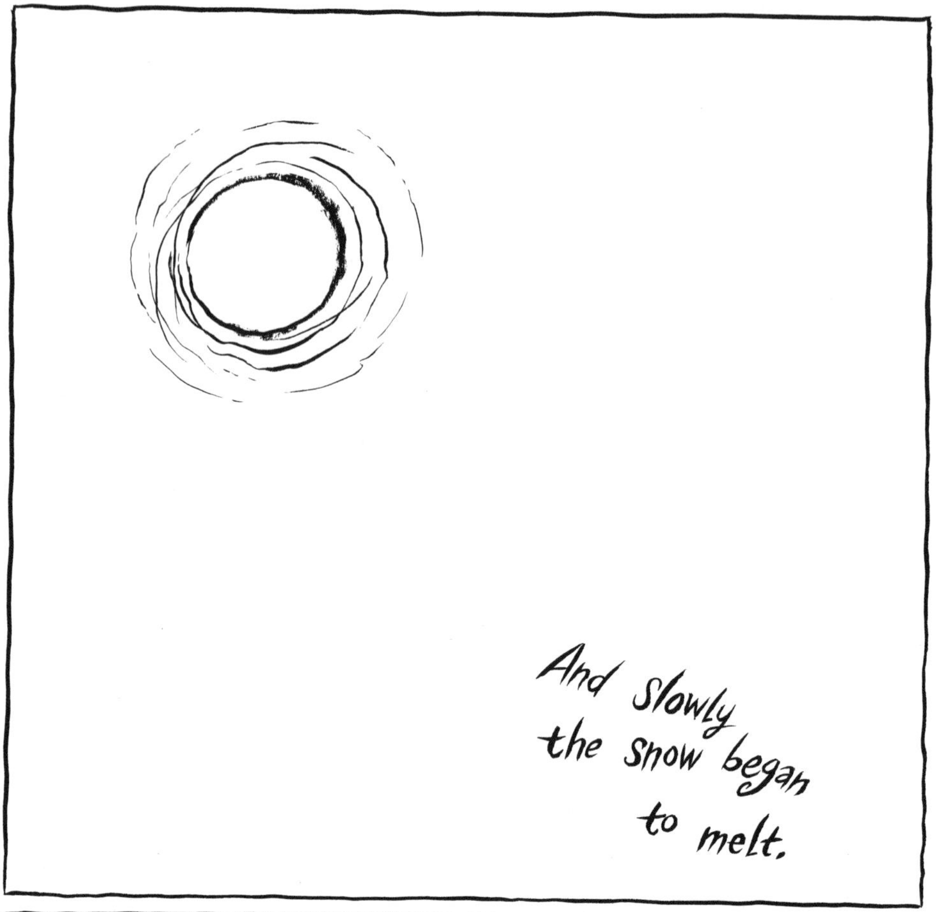
And slowly
the snow began
to melt.

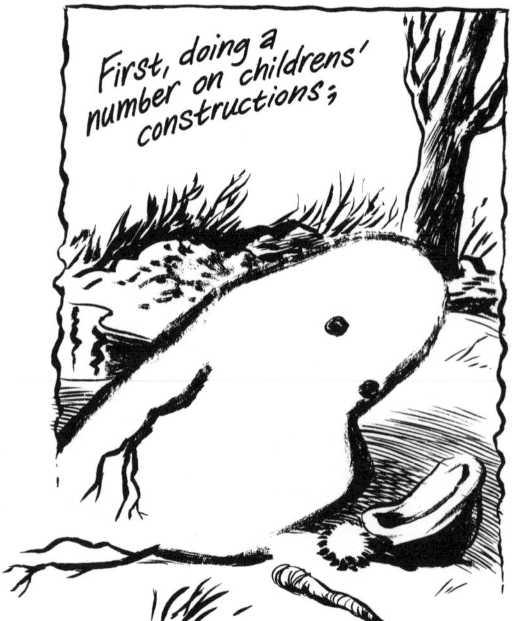
First, doing a
number on childrens'
constructions;

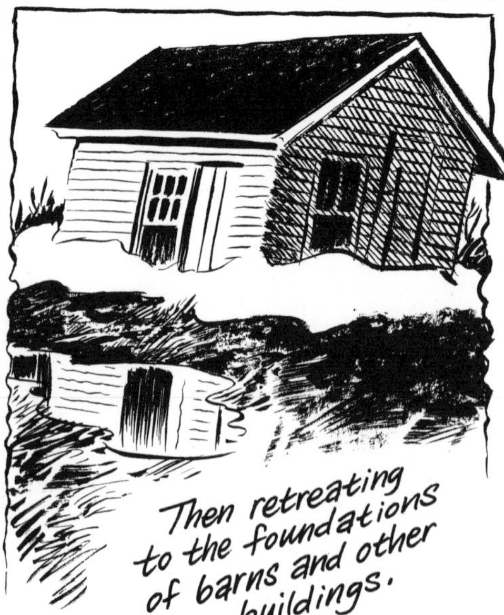
Then retreating
to the foundations
of barns and other
buildings.

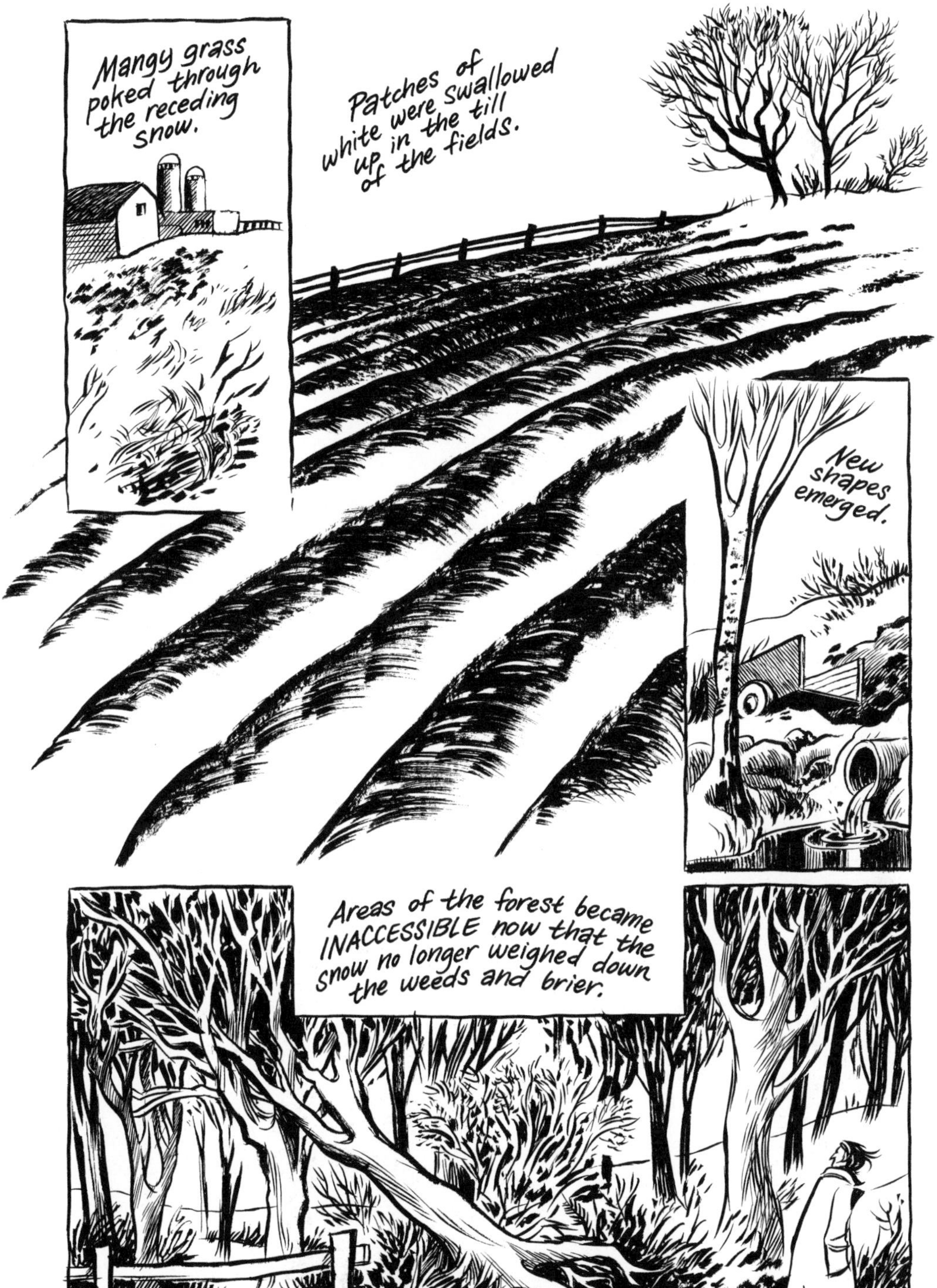
Mangy grass poked through the receding snow.
Patches of white were swallowed up in the till of the fields.
New shapes emerged.
Areas of the forest became INACCESSIBLE now that the snow no longer weighed down the weeds and brier.

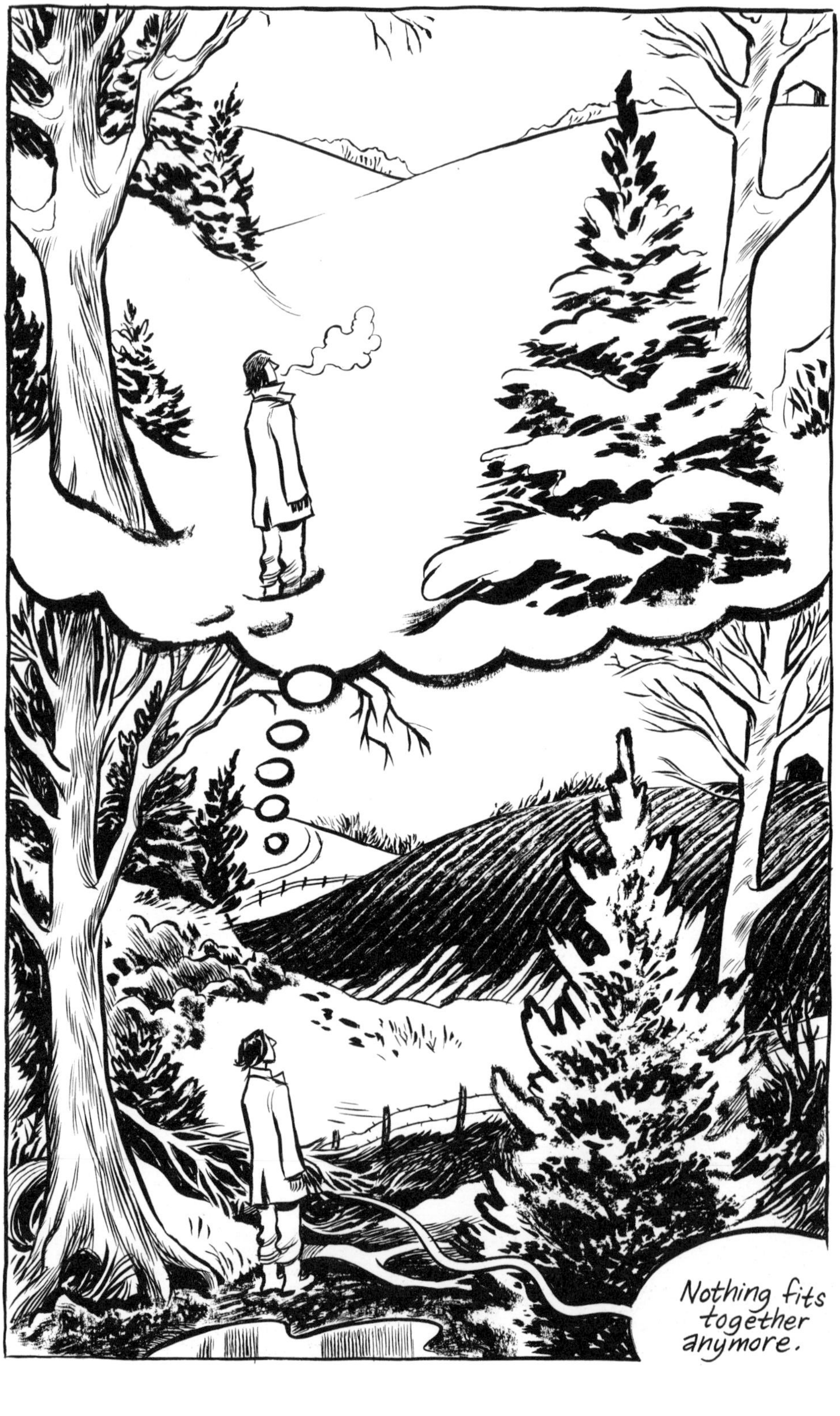
Nothing fits together anymore.

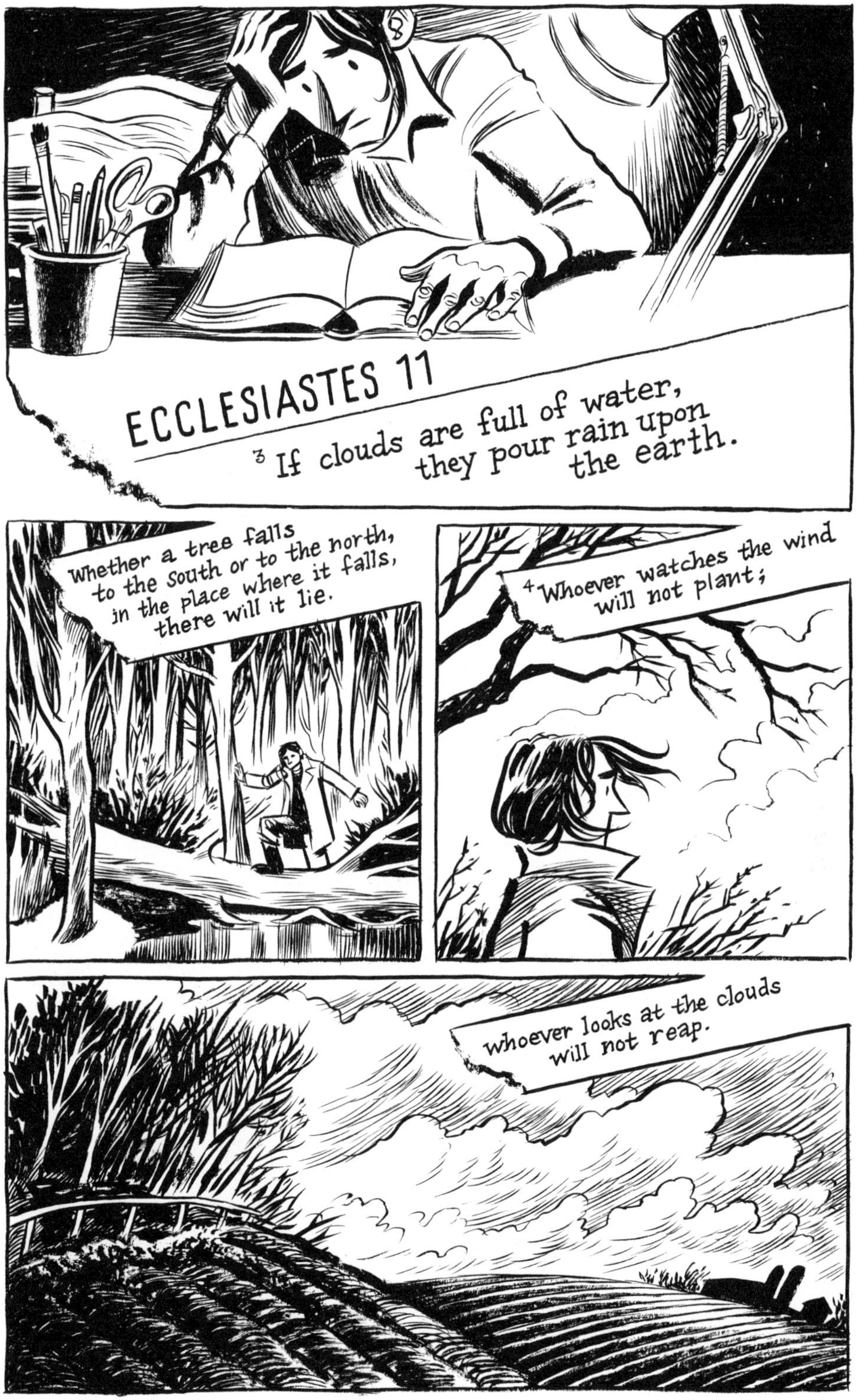
ECCLESIASTES 11
3 If clouds are full of water, they pour rain upon the earth.
Whether a tree falls to the South or to the north, in the place where it falls, there will it lie.
4 Whoever watches the wind will not plant;
whoever looks at the clouds will not reap.

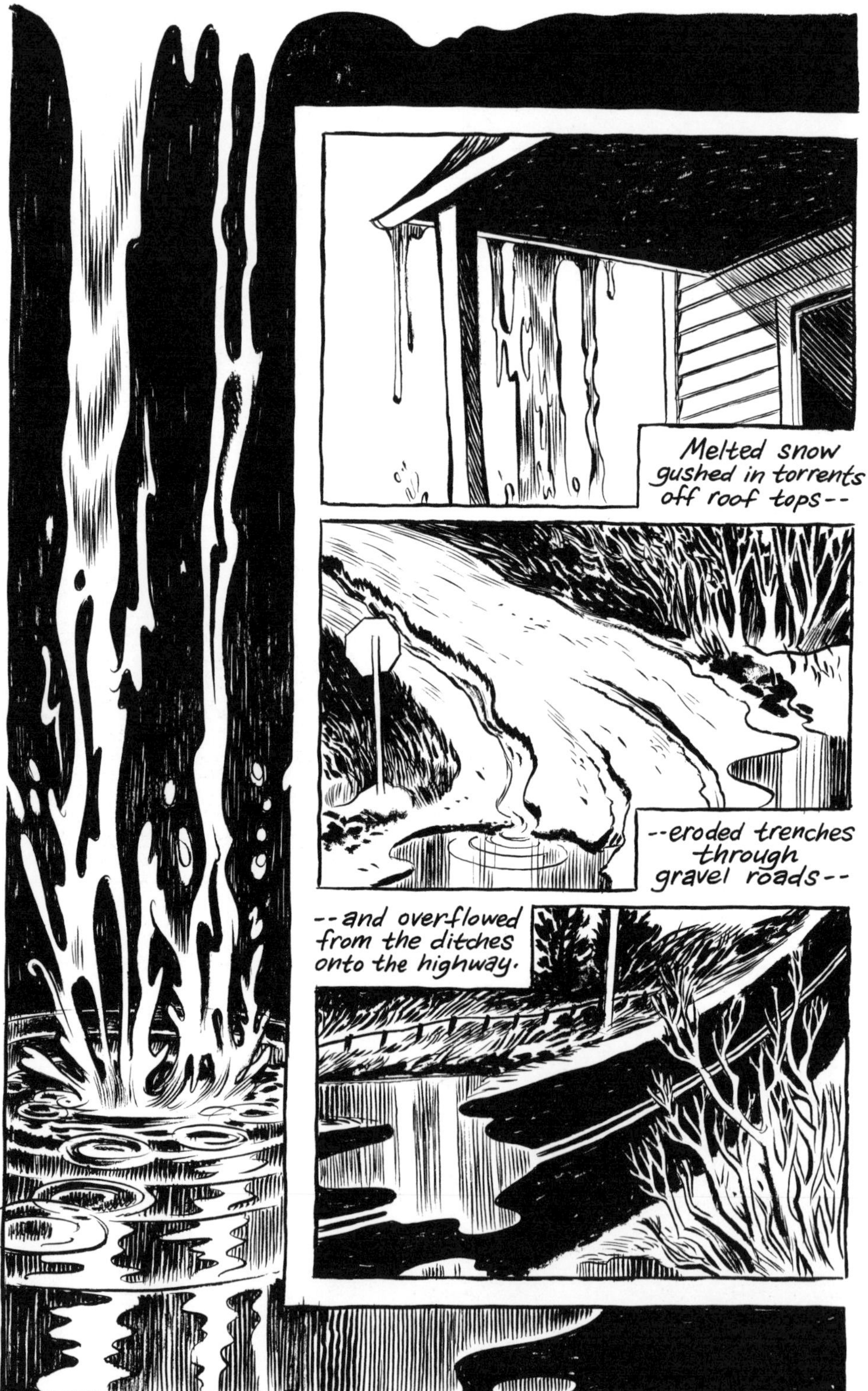
Melted snow gushed in torrents off roof tops--
--eroded trenches through gravel roads--
--and overflowed from the ditches onto the highway.

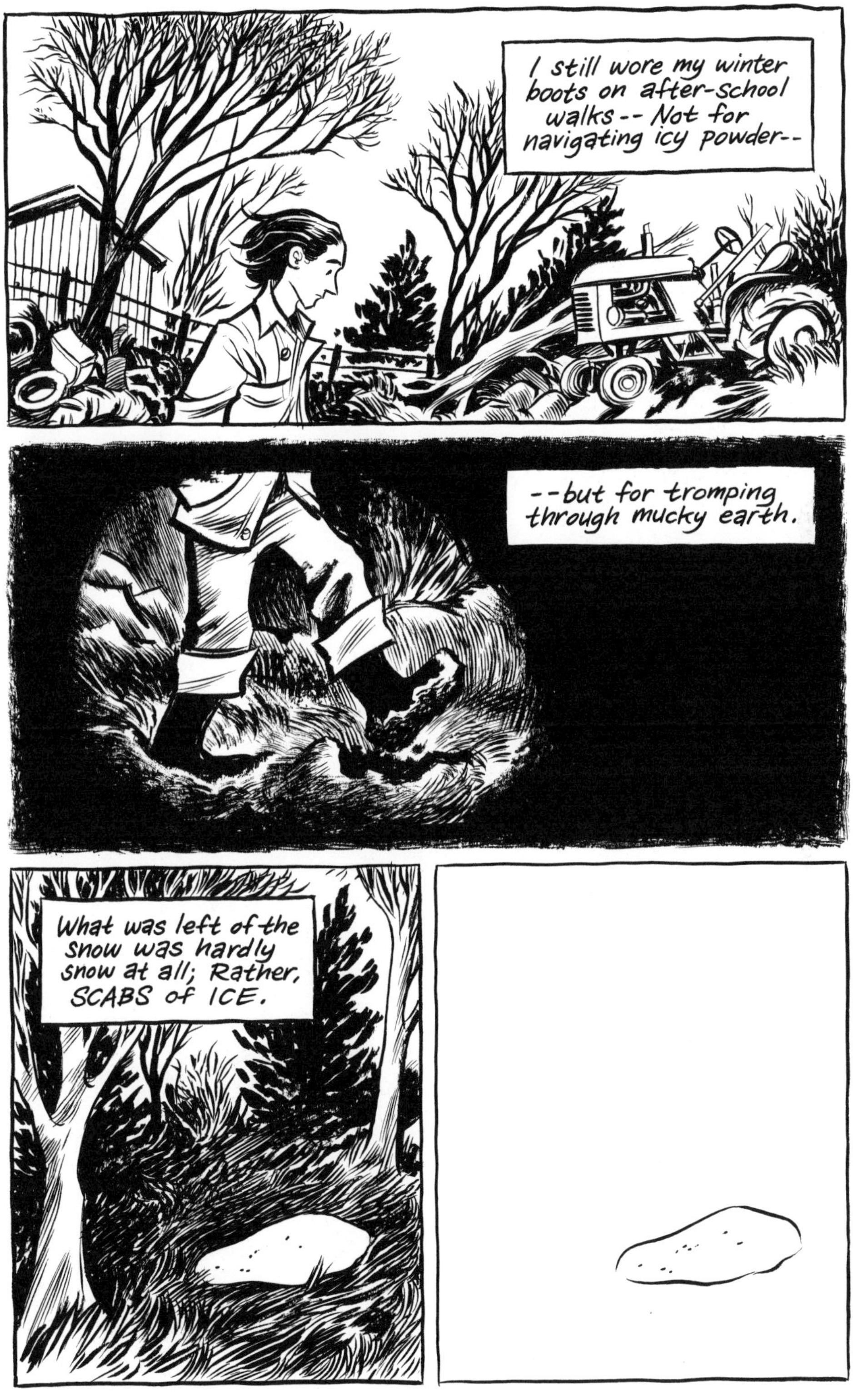
I still wore my winter boots on after-school walks -- Not for navigating icy powder--
--but for tromping through mucky earth.
What was left of the snow was hardly snow at all; Rather, SCABS of ICE.

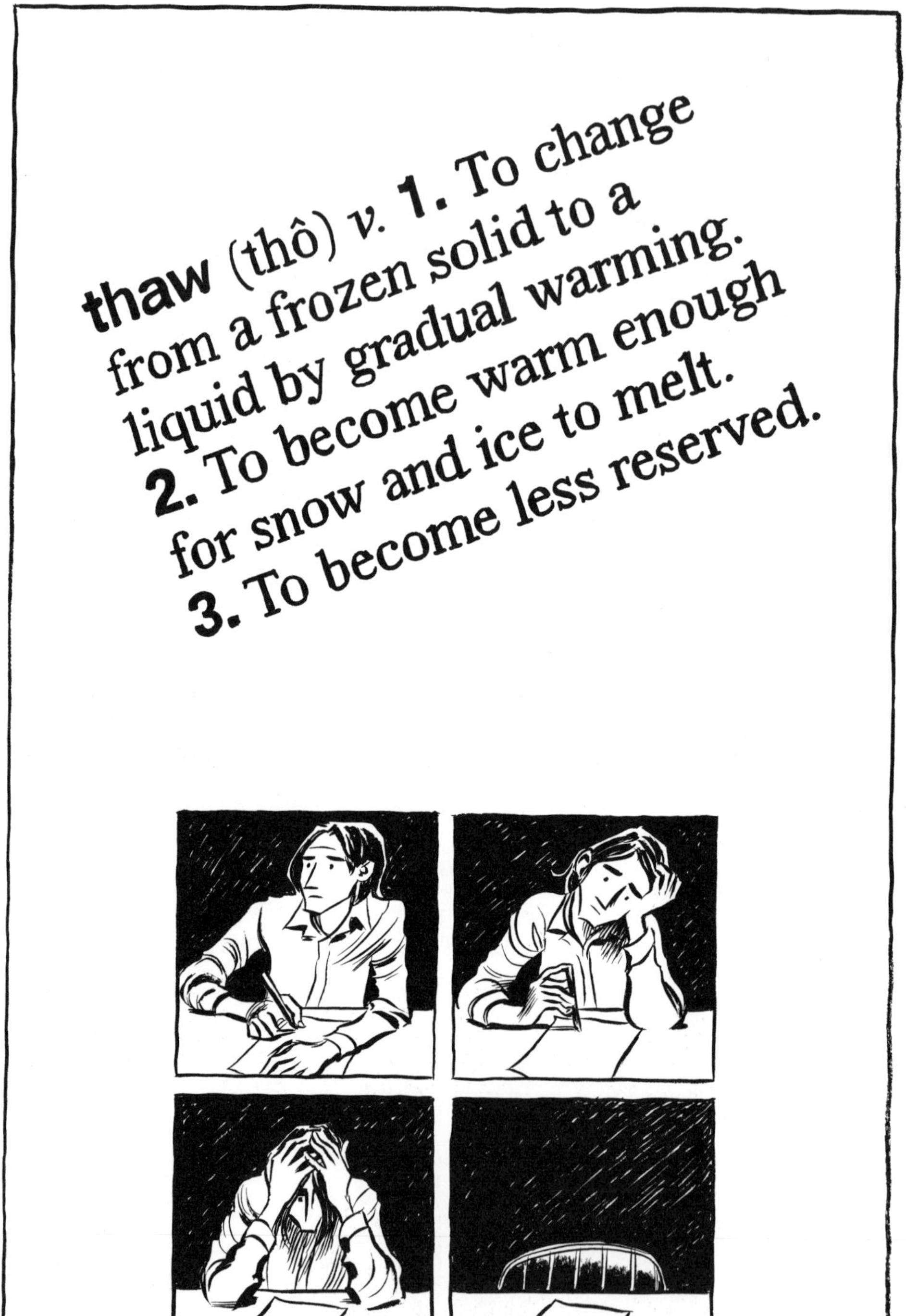
thaw (thô) *v.* **1.** To change from a frozen solid to a liquid by gradual warming.
2. To become warm enough for snow and ice to melt.
3. To become less reserved.

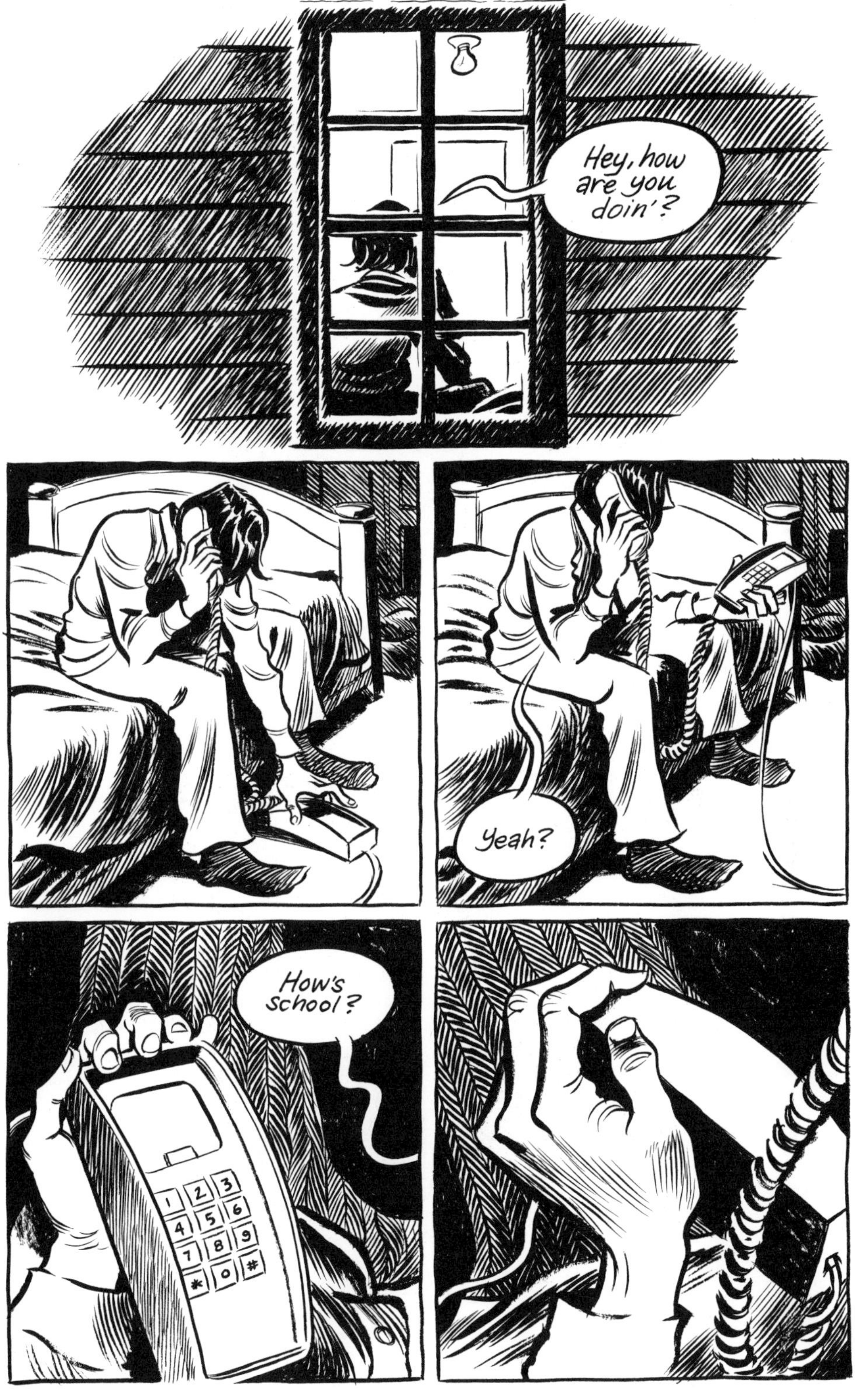
Hey, how are you doin'?
Yeah?
How's school?

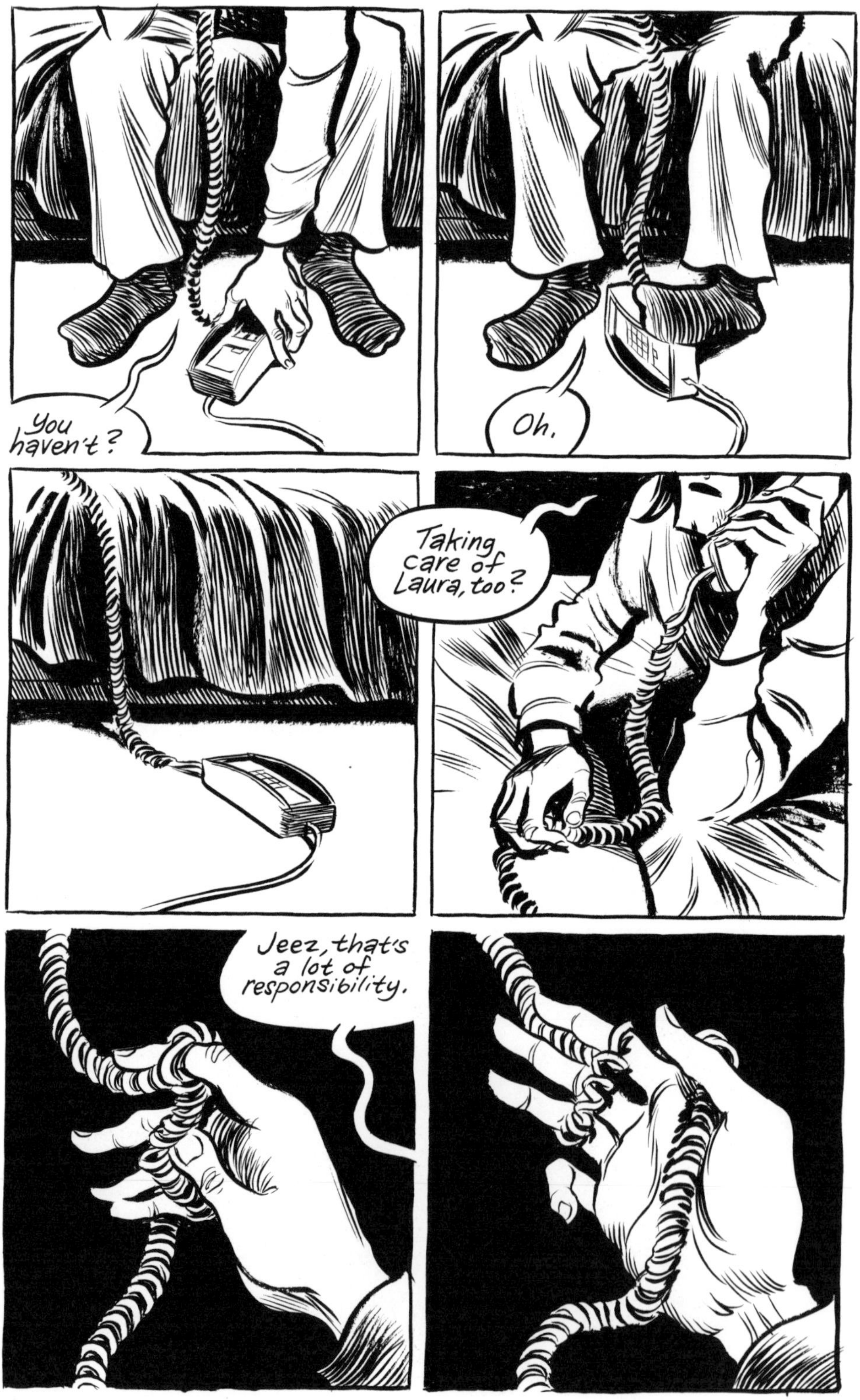
You haven't?
Oh.
Taking care of Laura, too?
Jeez, that's a lot of responsibility.

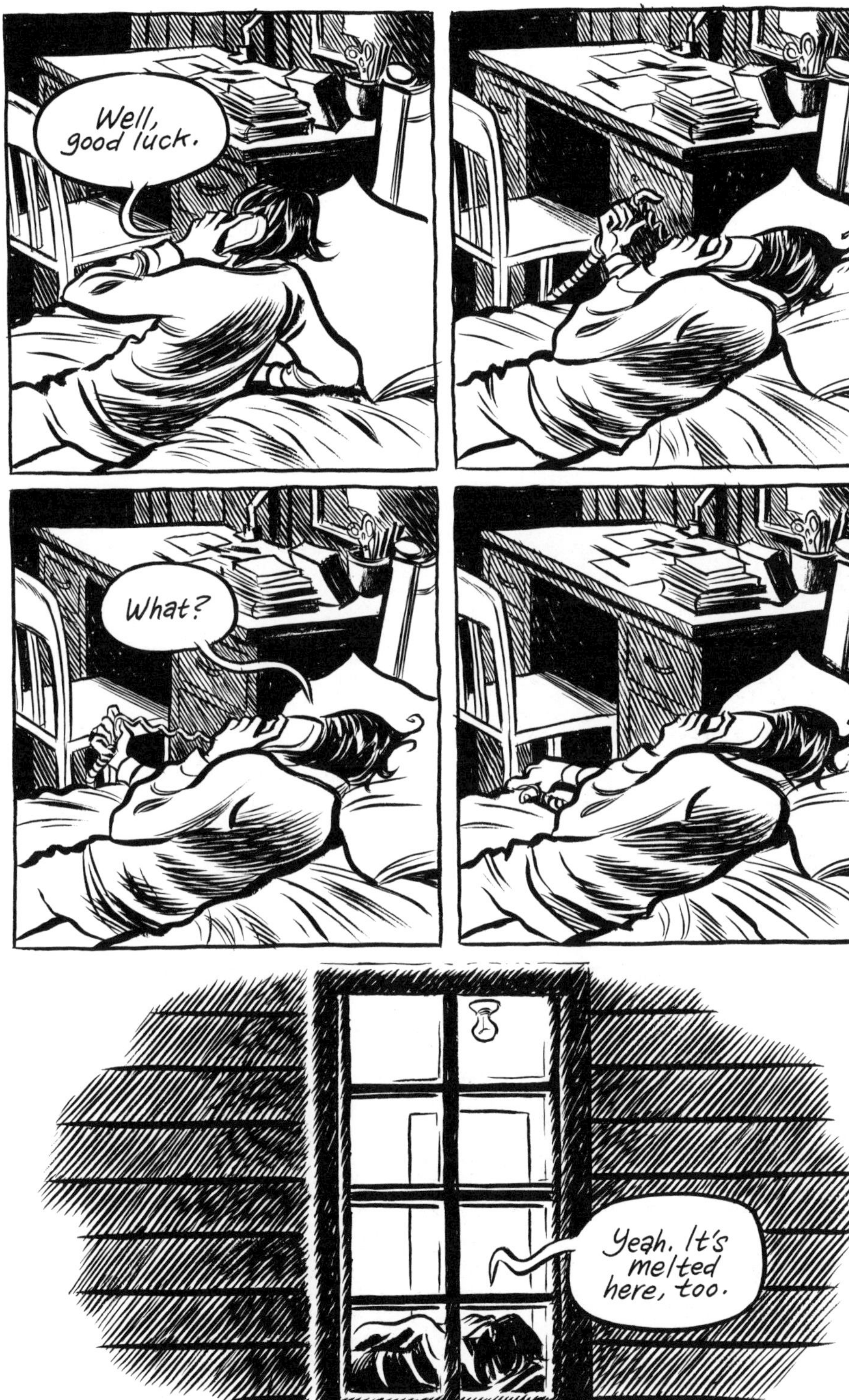
Well, good luck.
What?
Yeah. It's melted here, too.

514

515/5

519

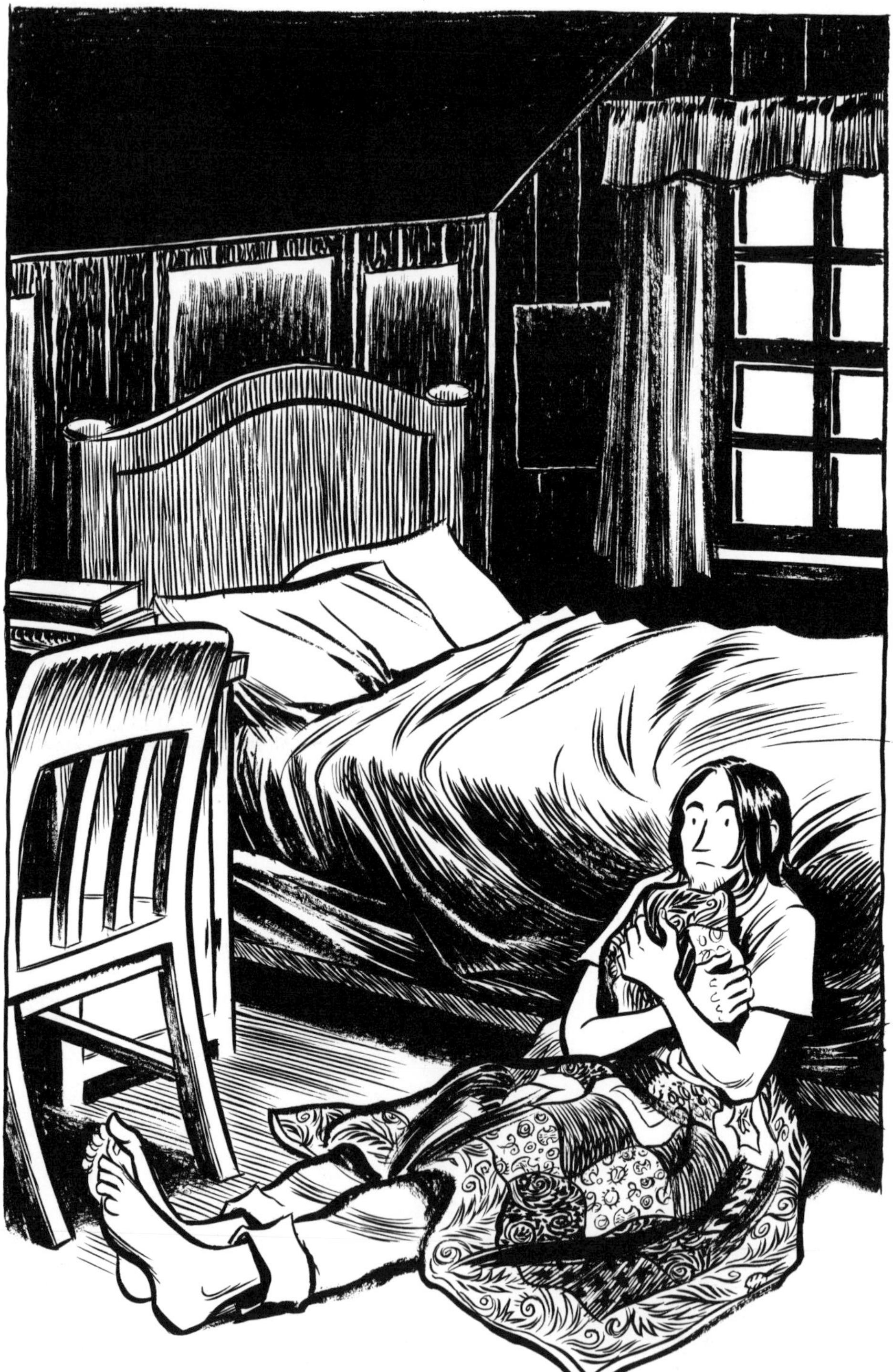

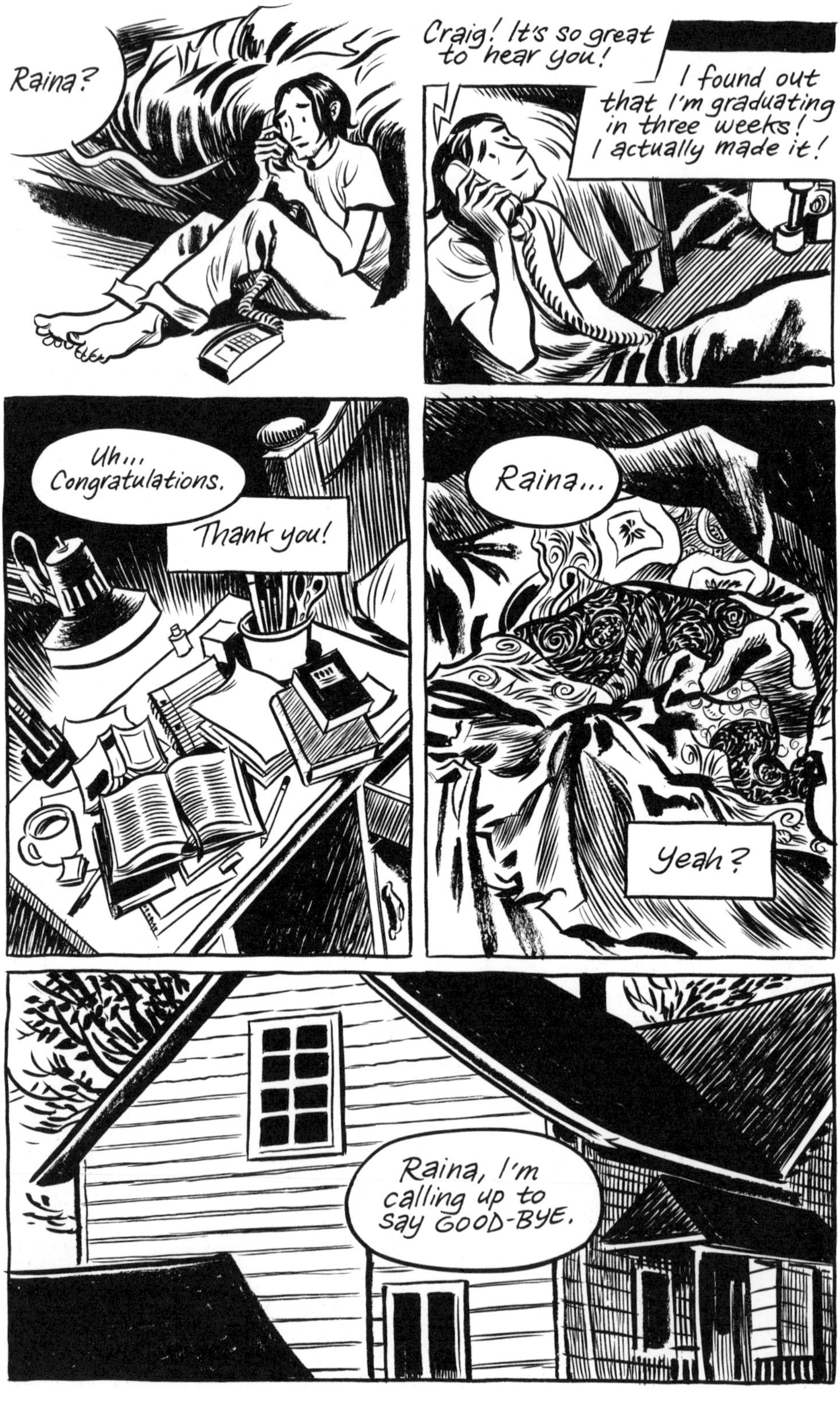
Raina?
Craig! It's so great to hear you!
I found out that I'm graduating in three weeks! I actually made it!
Uh... Congratulations.
Thank you!
Raina...
Yeah?
Raina, I'm calling up to say GOOD-BYE.

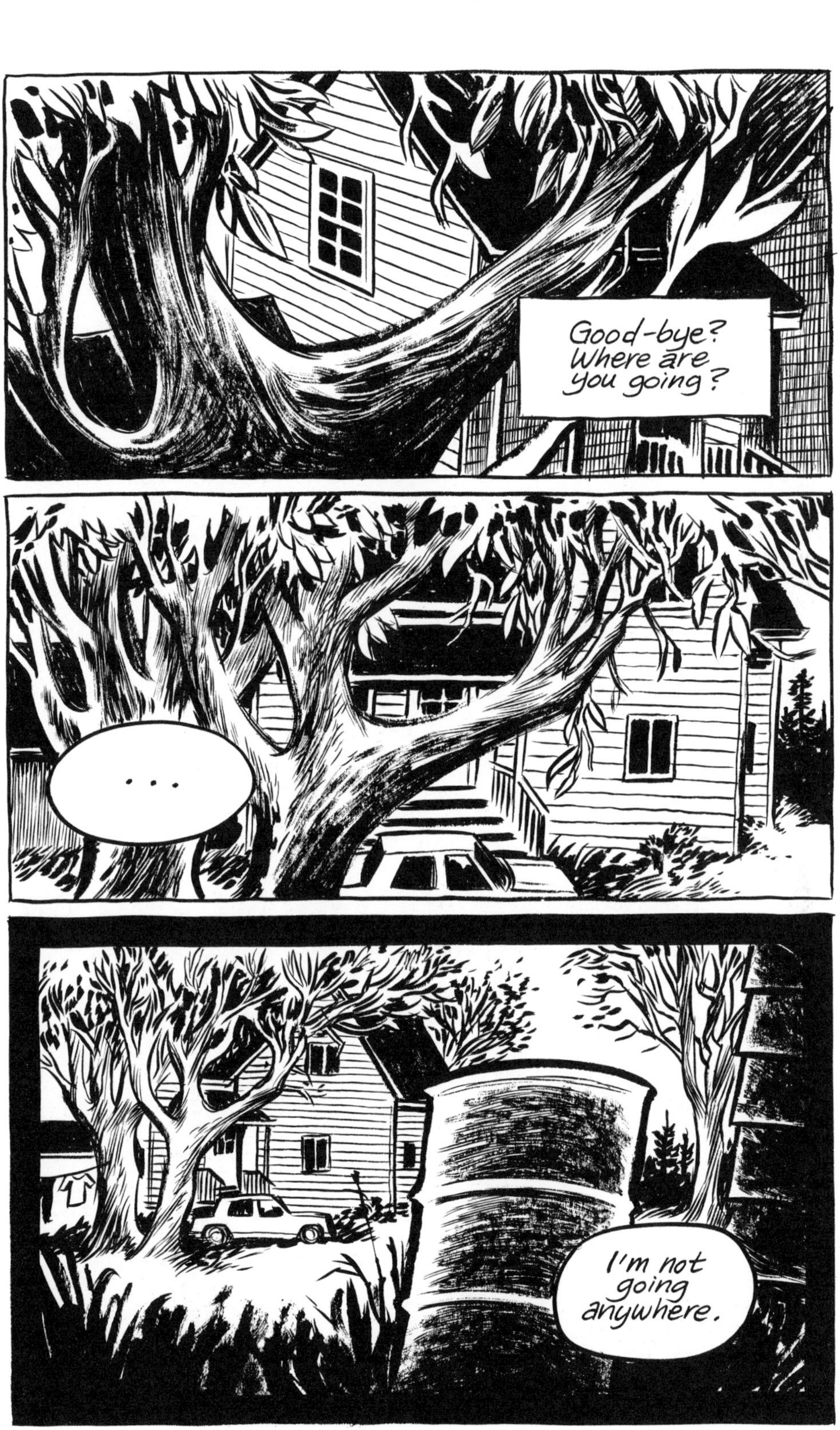
Good-bye? Where are you going?
. . .
I'm not going anywhere.

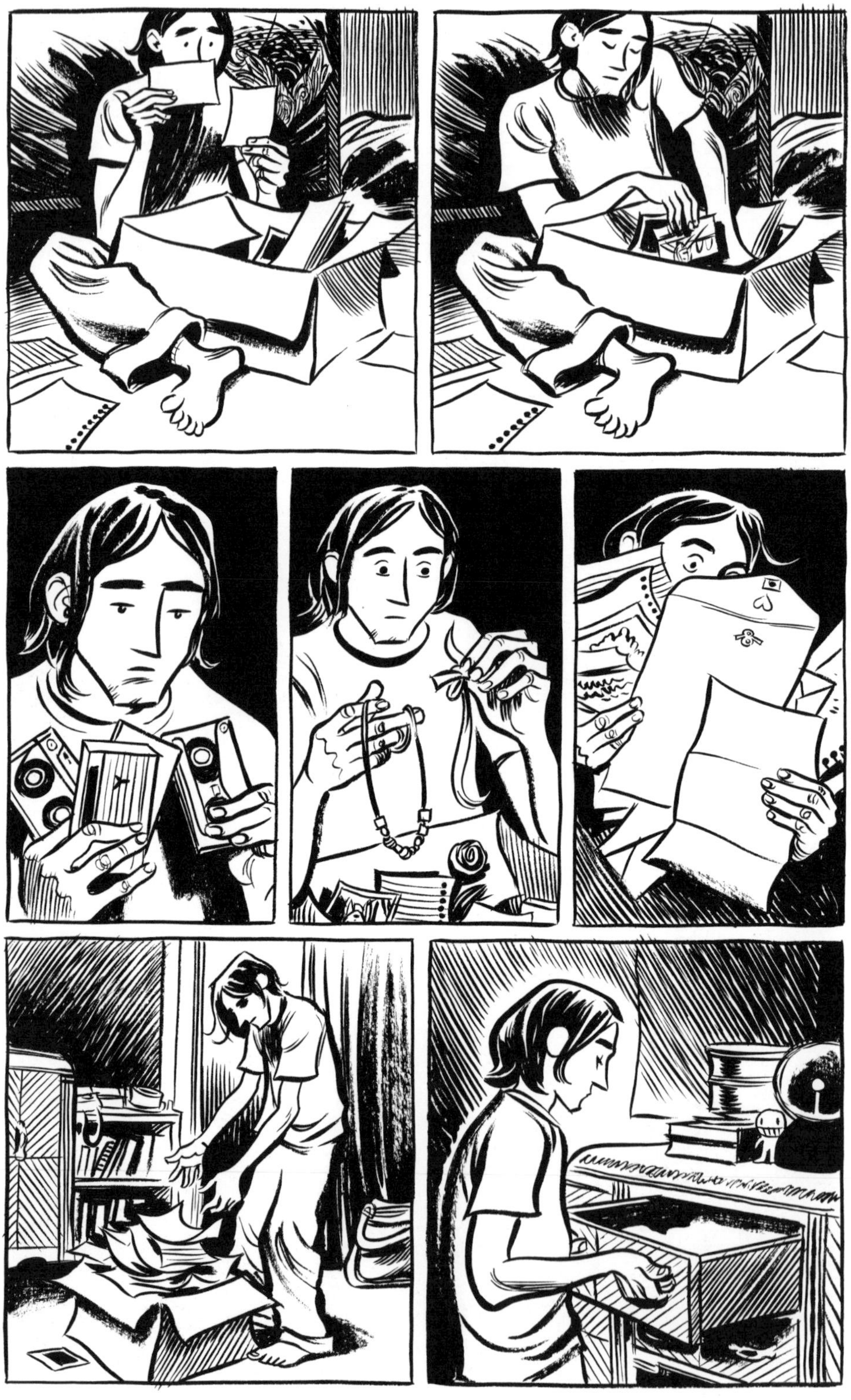

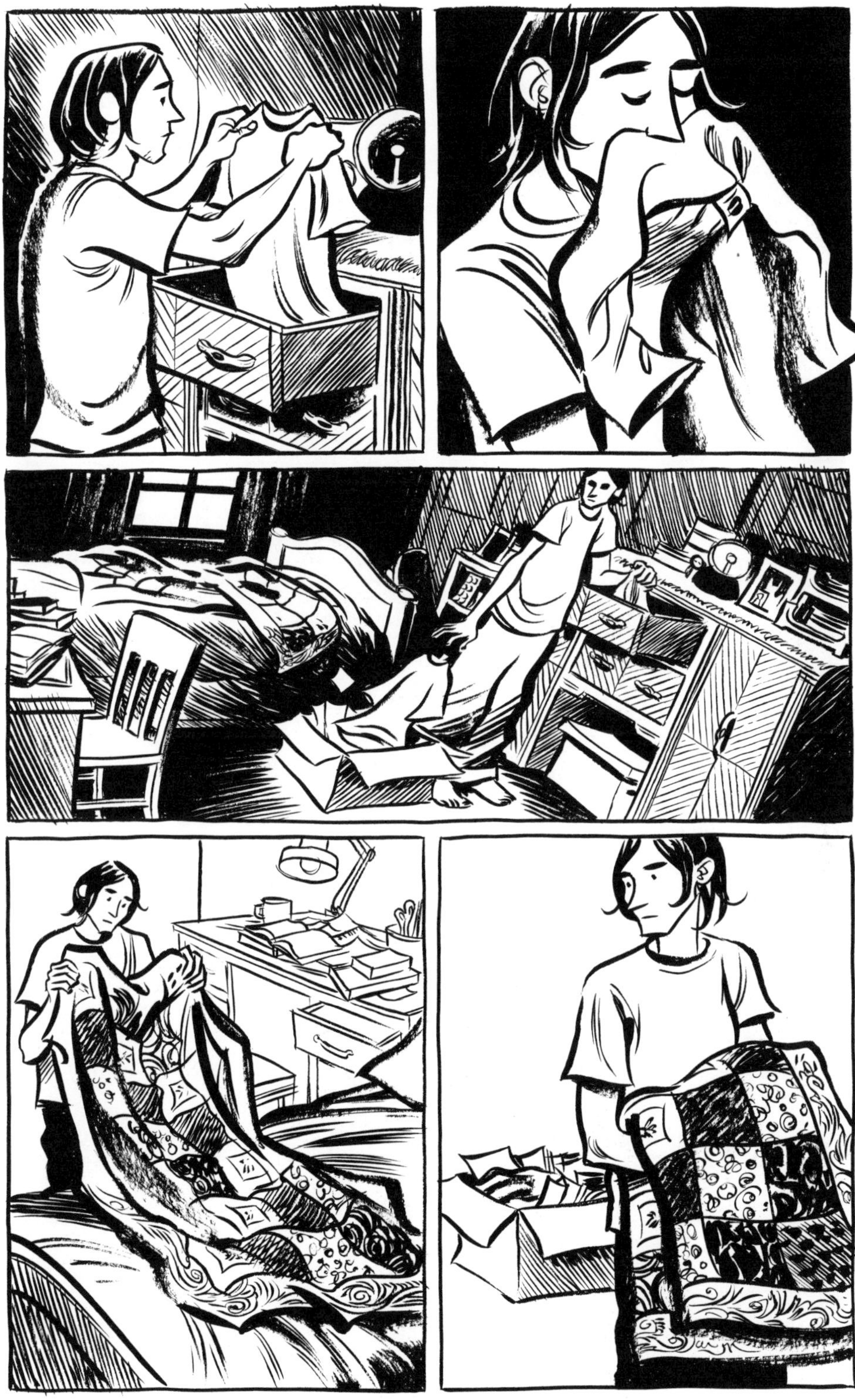

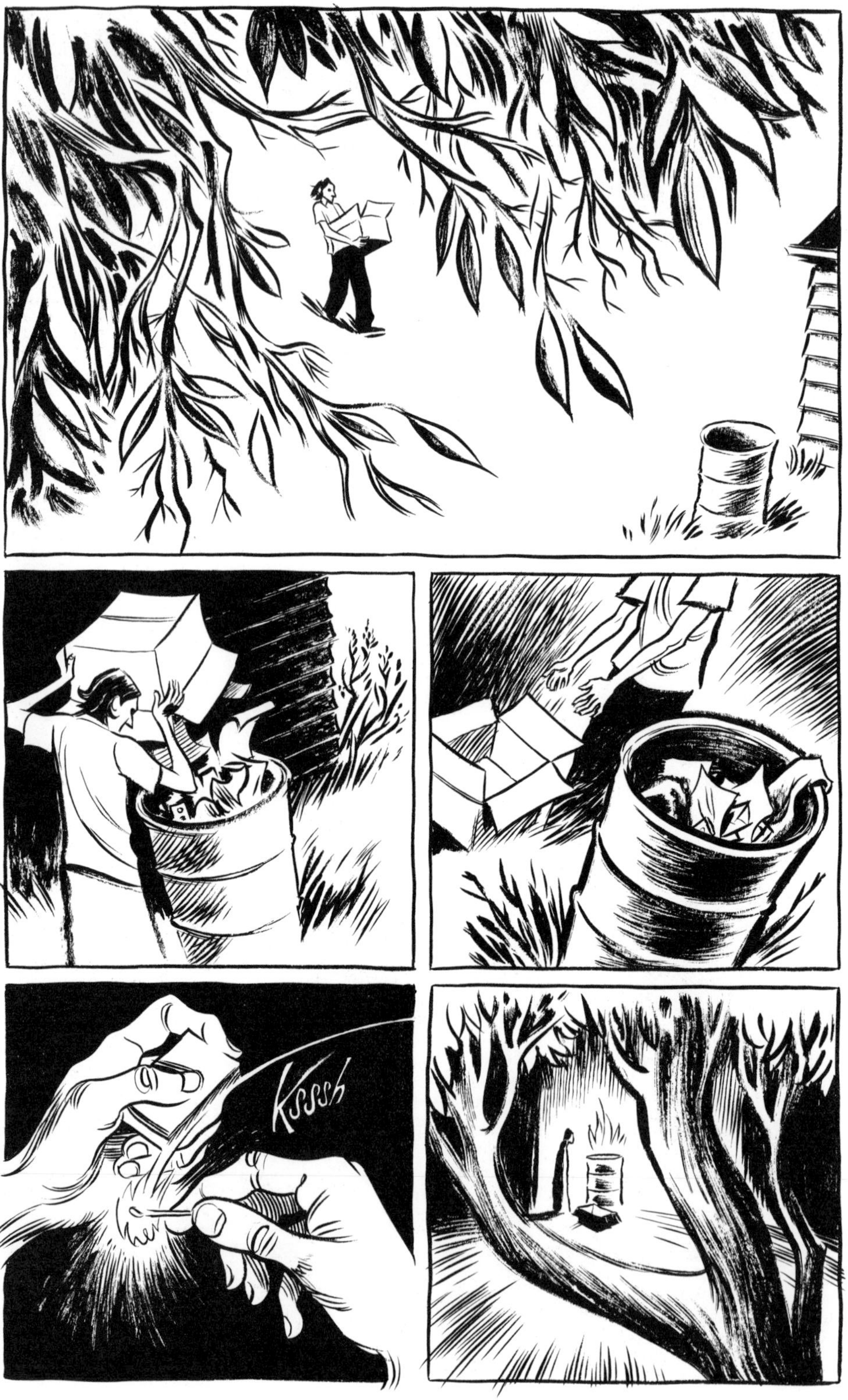
Ksssh

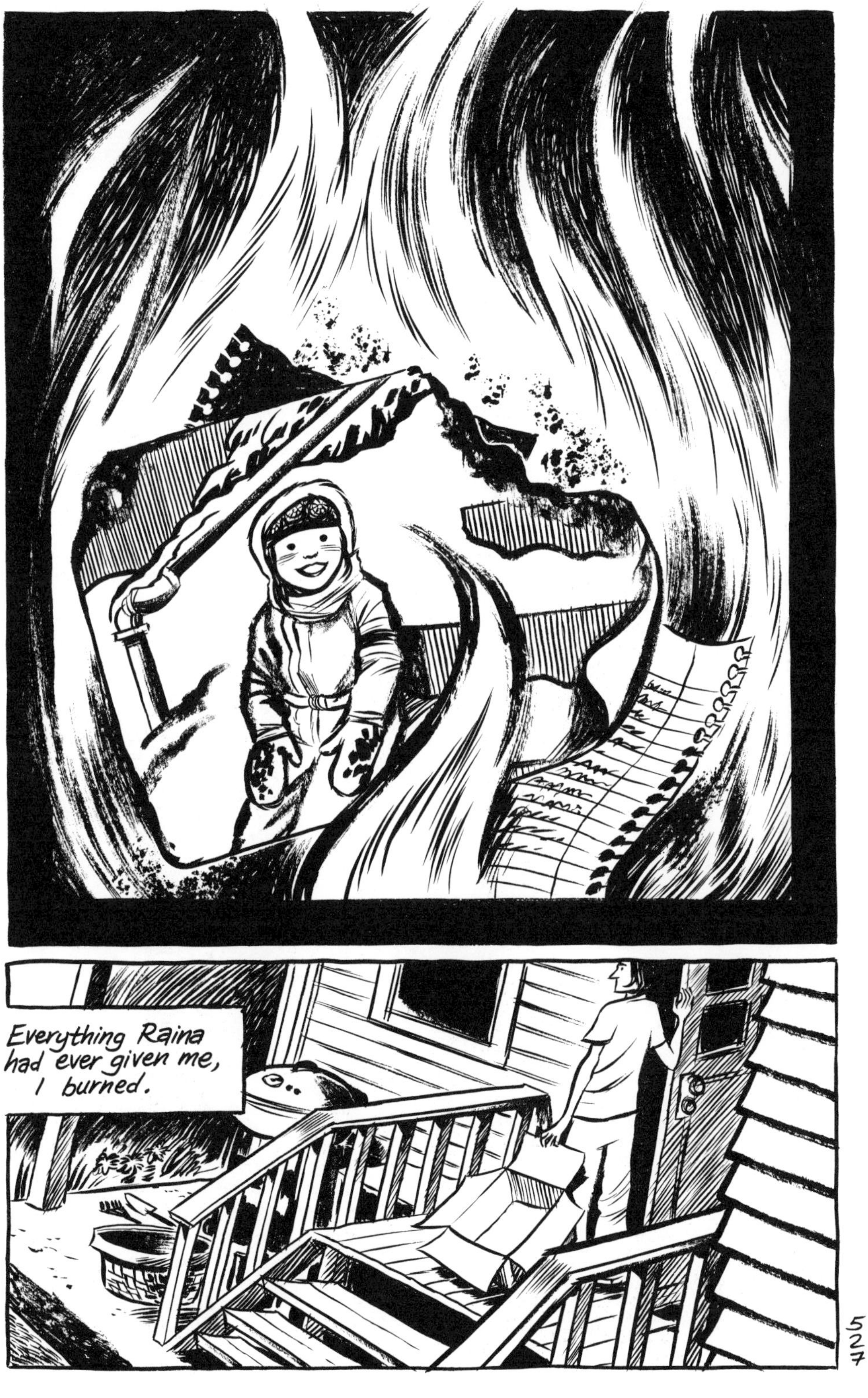
Everything Raina had ever given me, I burned.

I moved out of my
parents' home shortly
after my twentieth birthday.

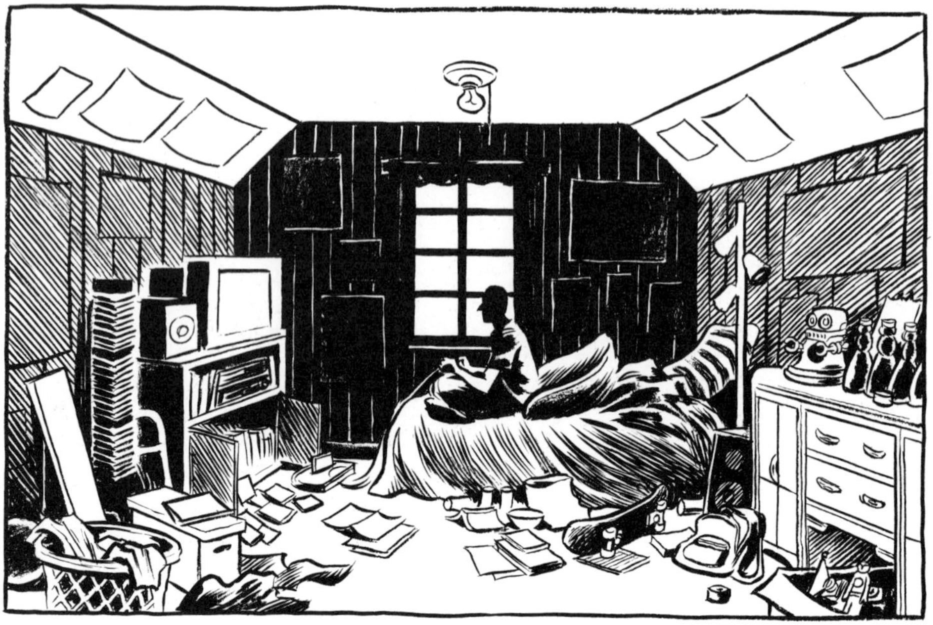

My brother moved into my room,
(because it was bigger).

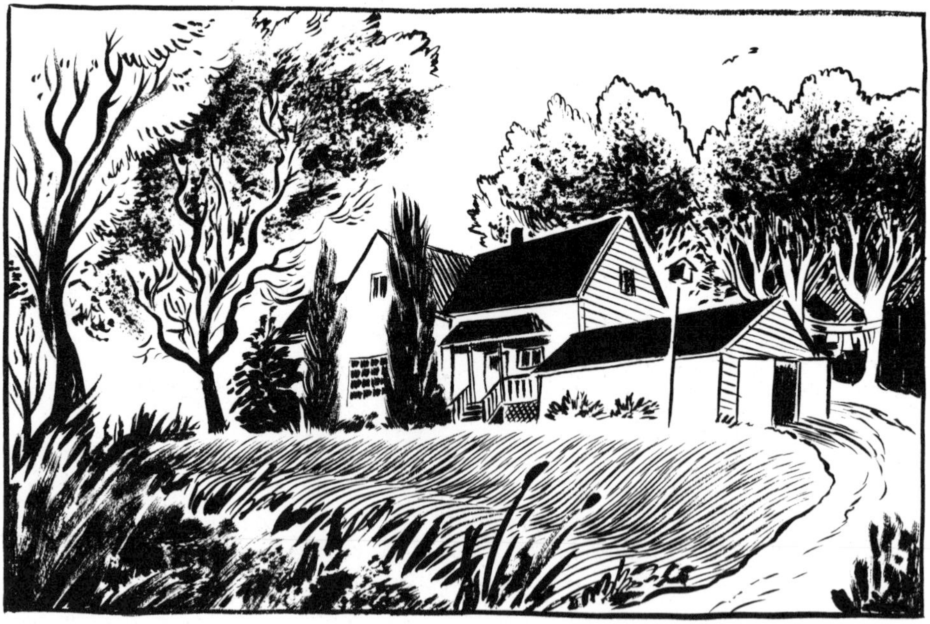

Upon his graduation,
I returned home to visit--

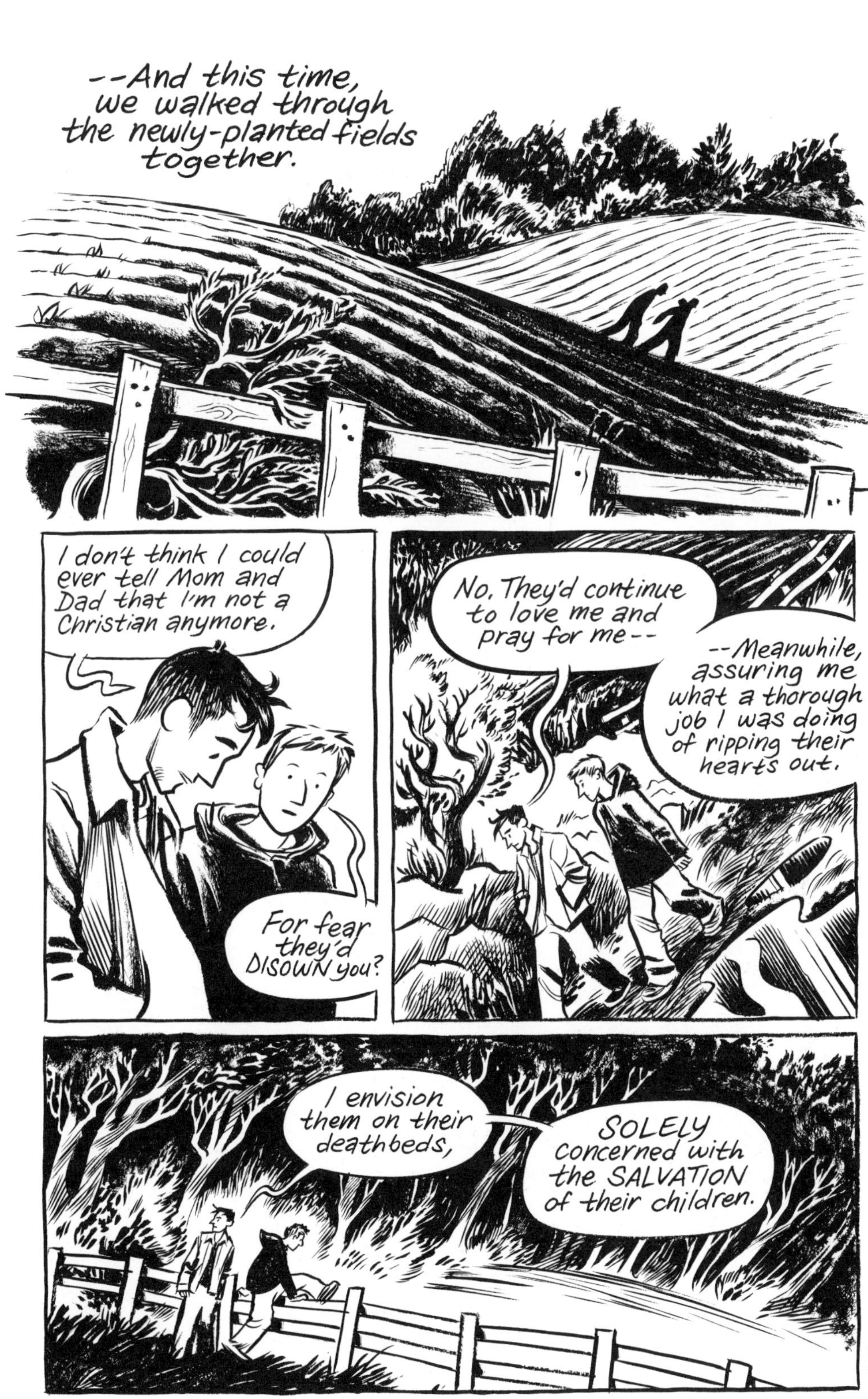
--And this time, we walked through the newly-planted fields together.
I don't think I could ever tell Mom and Dad that I'm not a Christian anymore.
For fear they'd DISOWN you?
No. They'd continue to love me and pray for me--
--Meanwhile, assuring me what a thorough job I was doing of ripping their hearts out.
I envision them on their deathbeds,
SOLELY concerned with the SALVATION of their children.

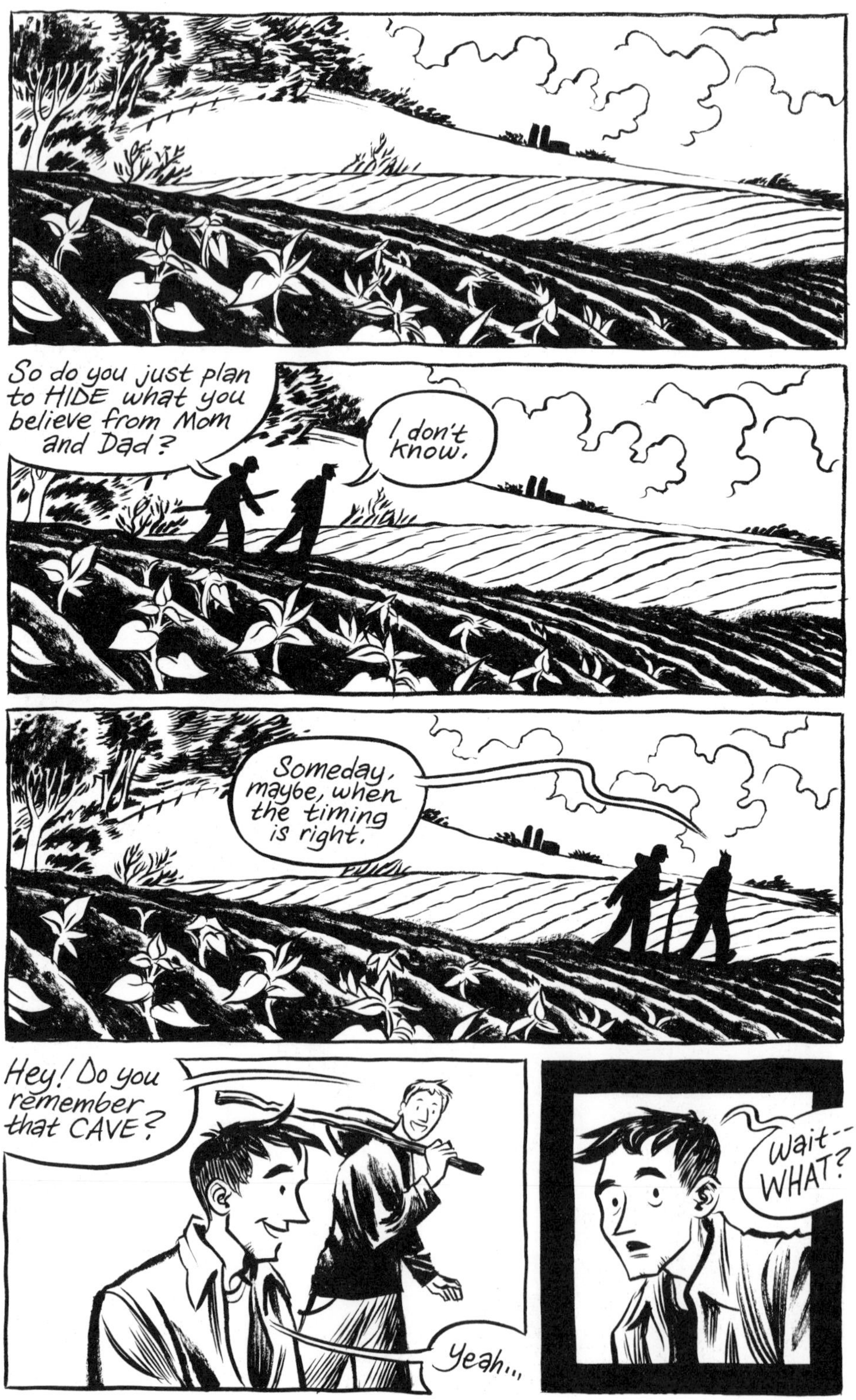

So do you just plan to HIDE what you believe from Mom and Dad?
I don't know.
Someday, maybe, when the timing is right.
Hey! Do you remember that CAVE?
Yeah...
Wait--WHAT?

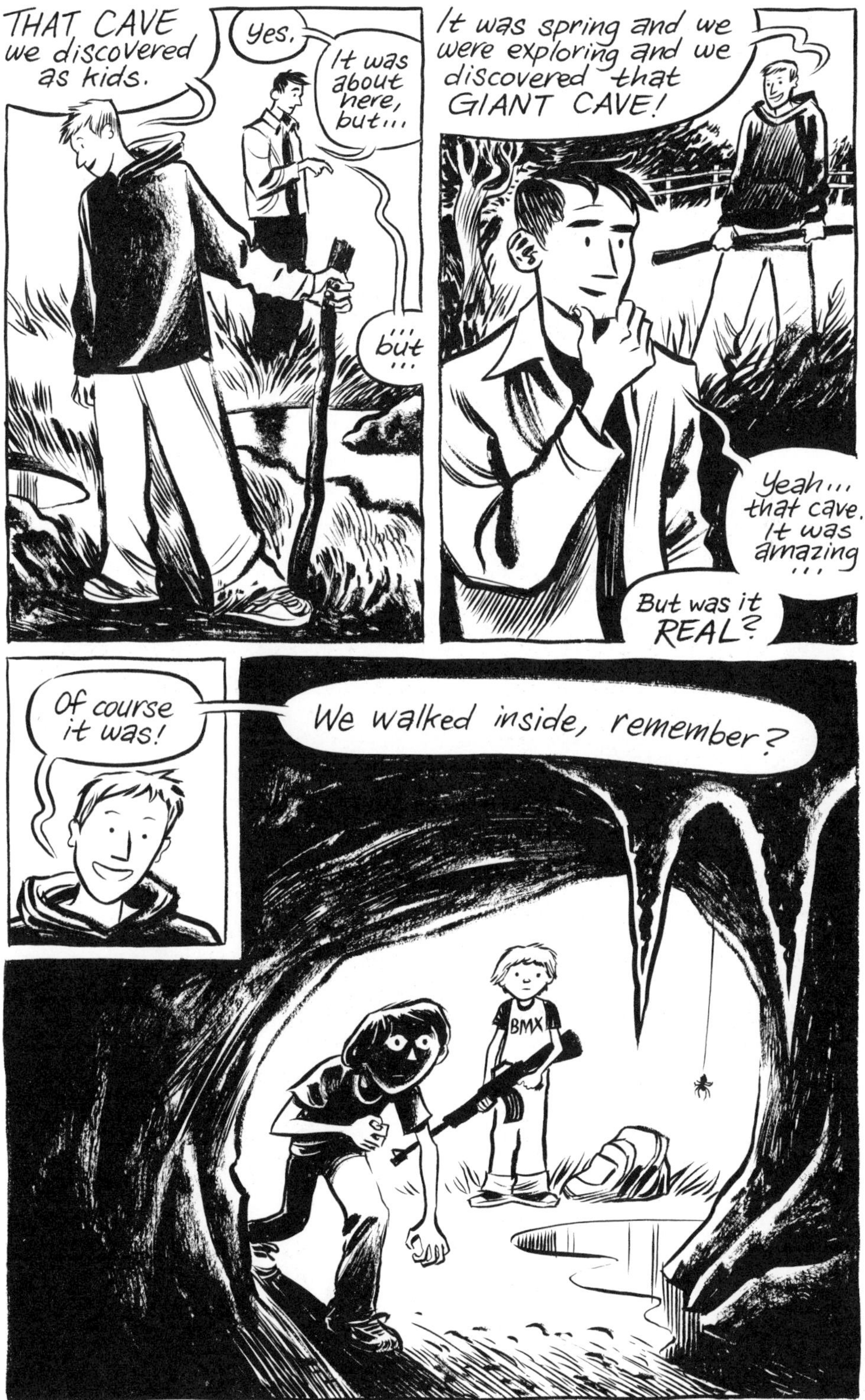
THAT CAVE we discovered as kids.
Yes.
It was about here, but...
...but...
It was spring and we were exploring and we discovered that GIANT CAVE!
Yeah... that cave. It was amazing...
But was it REAL?
Of course it was!
We walked inside, remember?
BMX

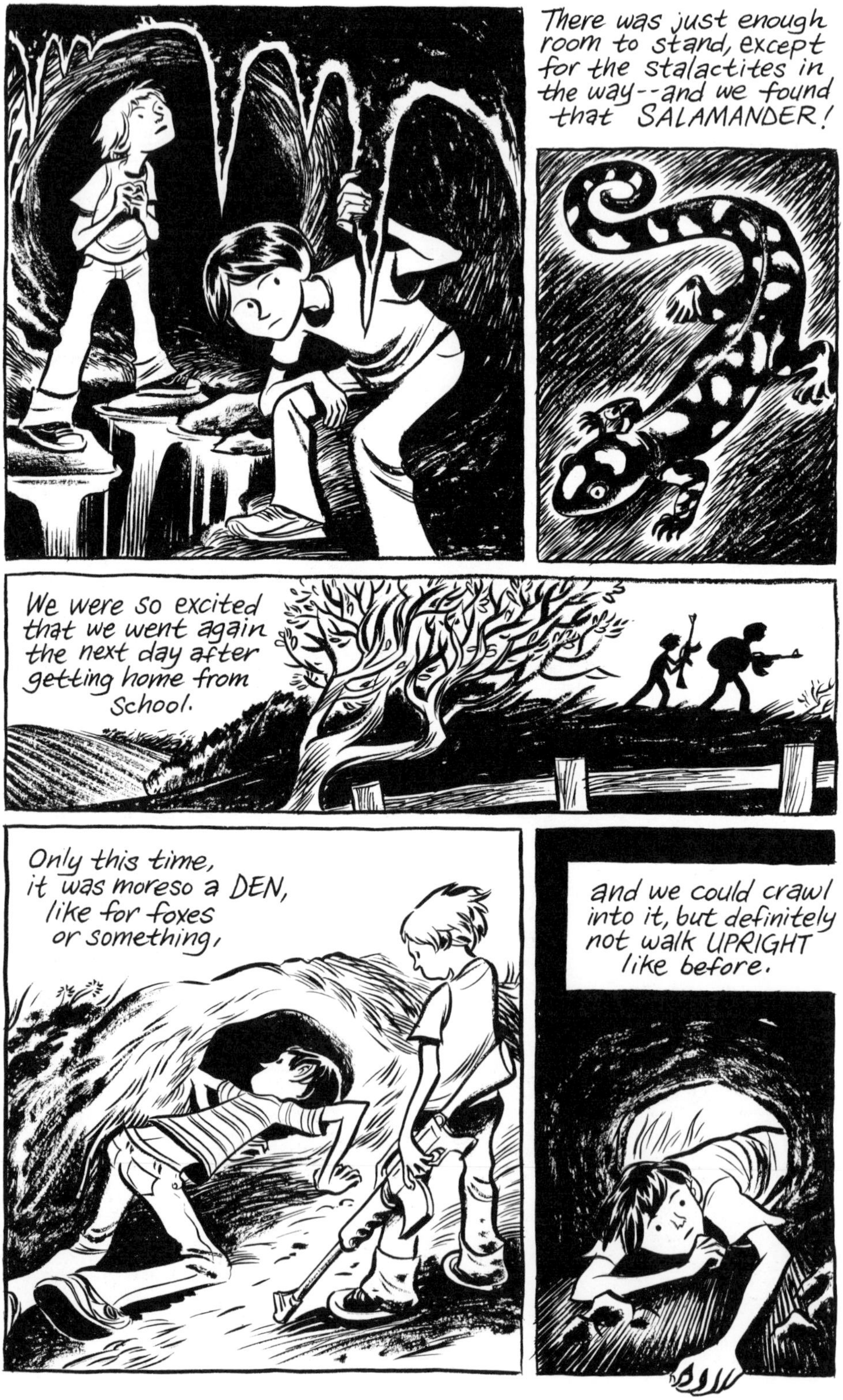
There was just enough room to stand, except for the stalactites in the way--and we found that SALAMANDER!
We were so excited that we went again the next day after getting home from School.
Only this time, it was moreso a DEN, like for foxes or something,
and we could crawl into it, but definitely not walk UPRIGHT like before.

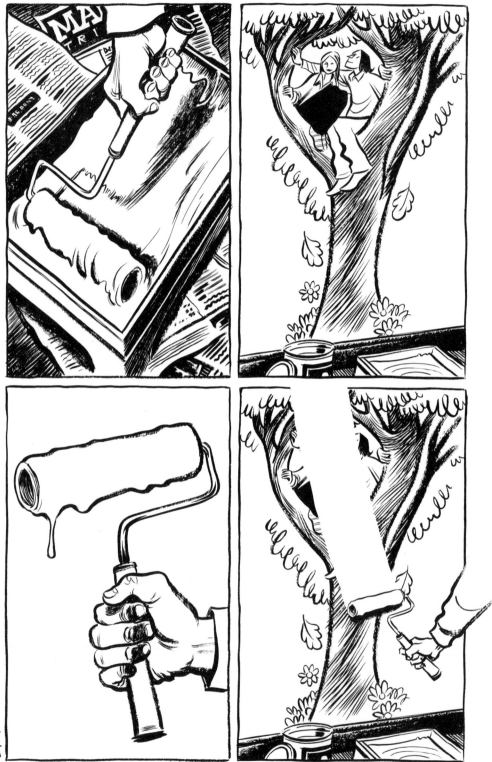

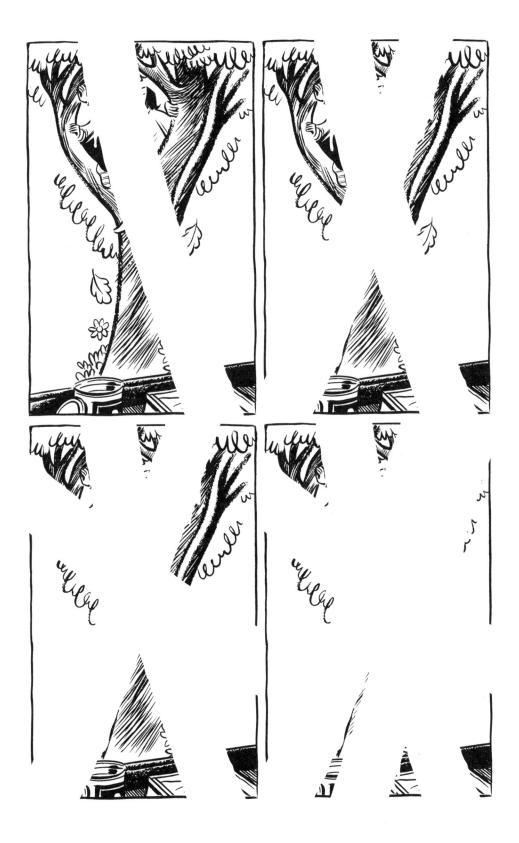

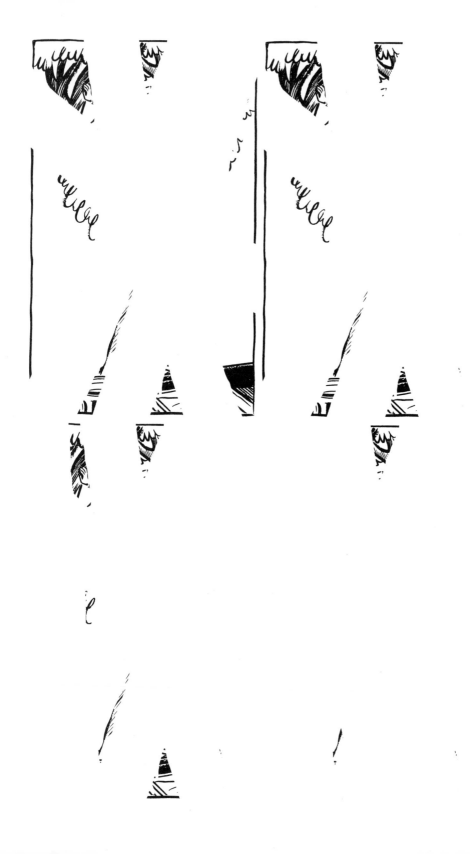

IX

Foot
Notes

Upon moving out of my parents' home, I made a conscious effort to leave my Bible behind.

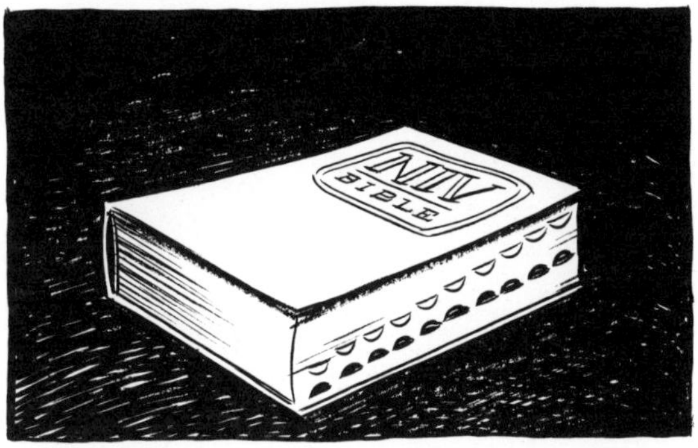
NIV
BIBLE

It was the book of ECCLESIASTES that prompted me to do so.

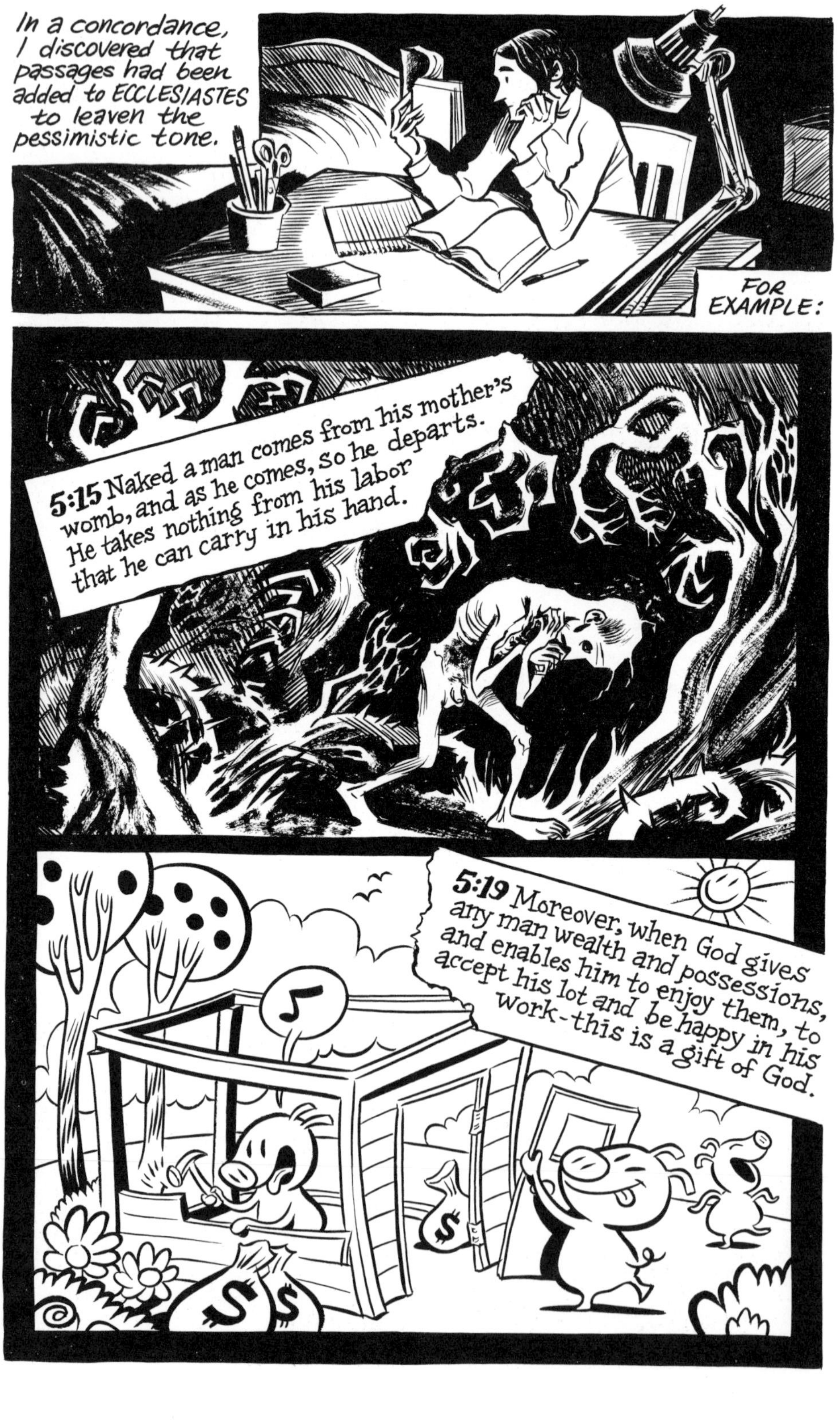
In a concordance, I discovered that passages had been added to ECCLESIASTES to leaven the pessimistic tone.
FOR EXAMPLE:
5:15 Naked a man comes from his mother's womb, and as he comes, so he departs. He takes nothing from his labor that he can carry in his hand.
5:19 Moreover, when God gives any man wealth and possessions, and enables him to enjoy them, to accept his lot and be happy in his work-this is a gift of God.

549

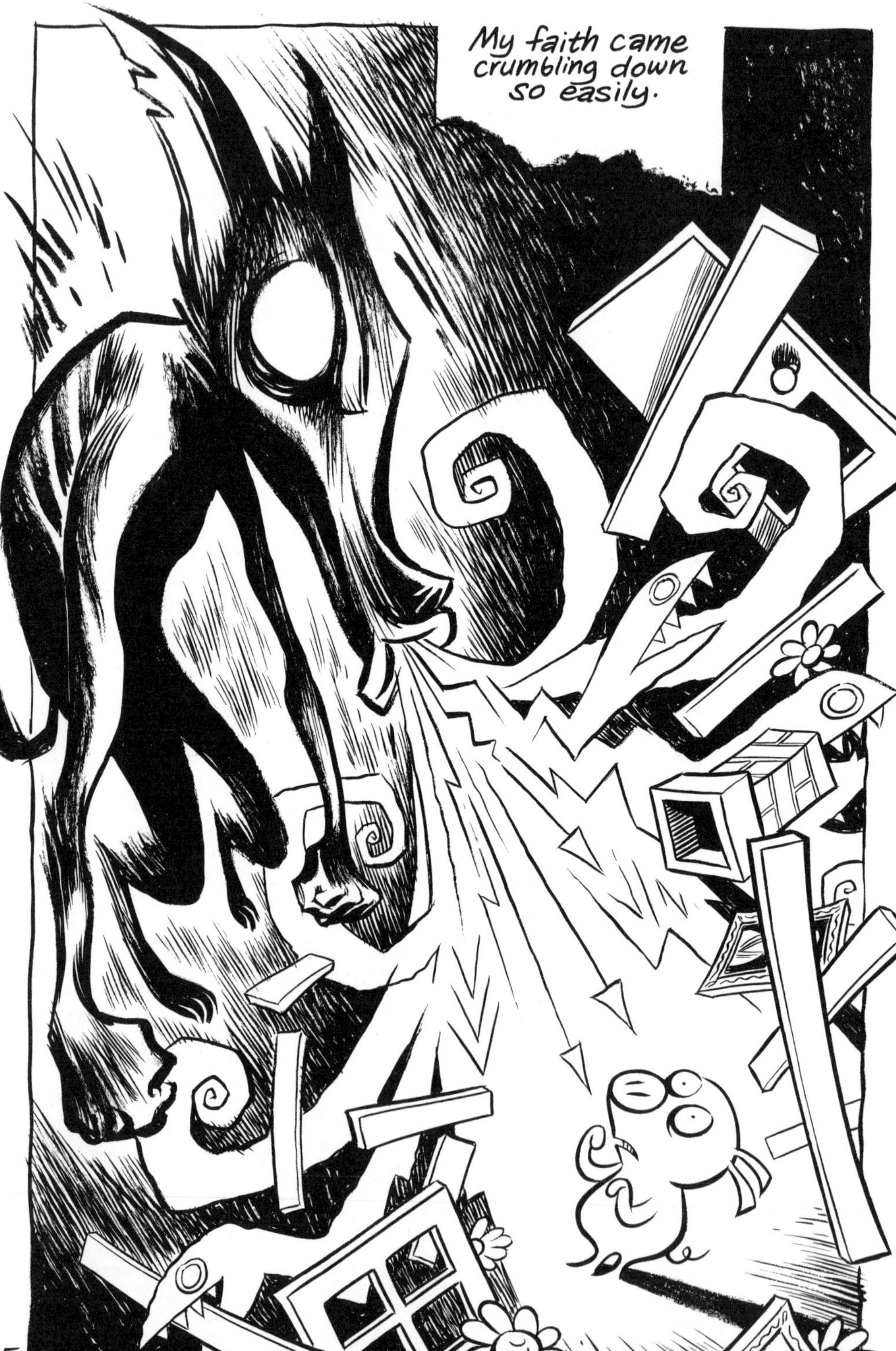
My faith came crumbling down so easily.

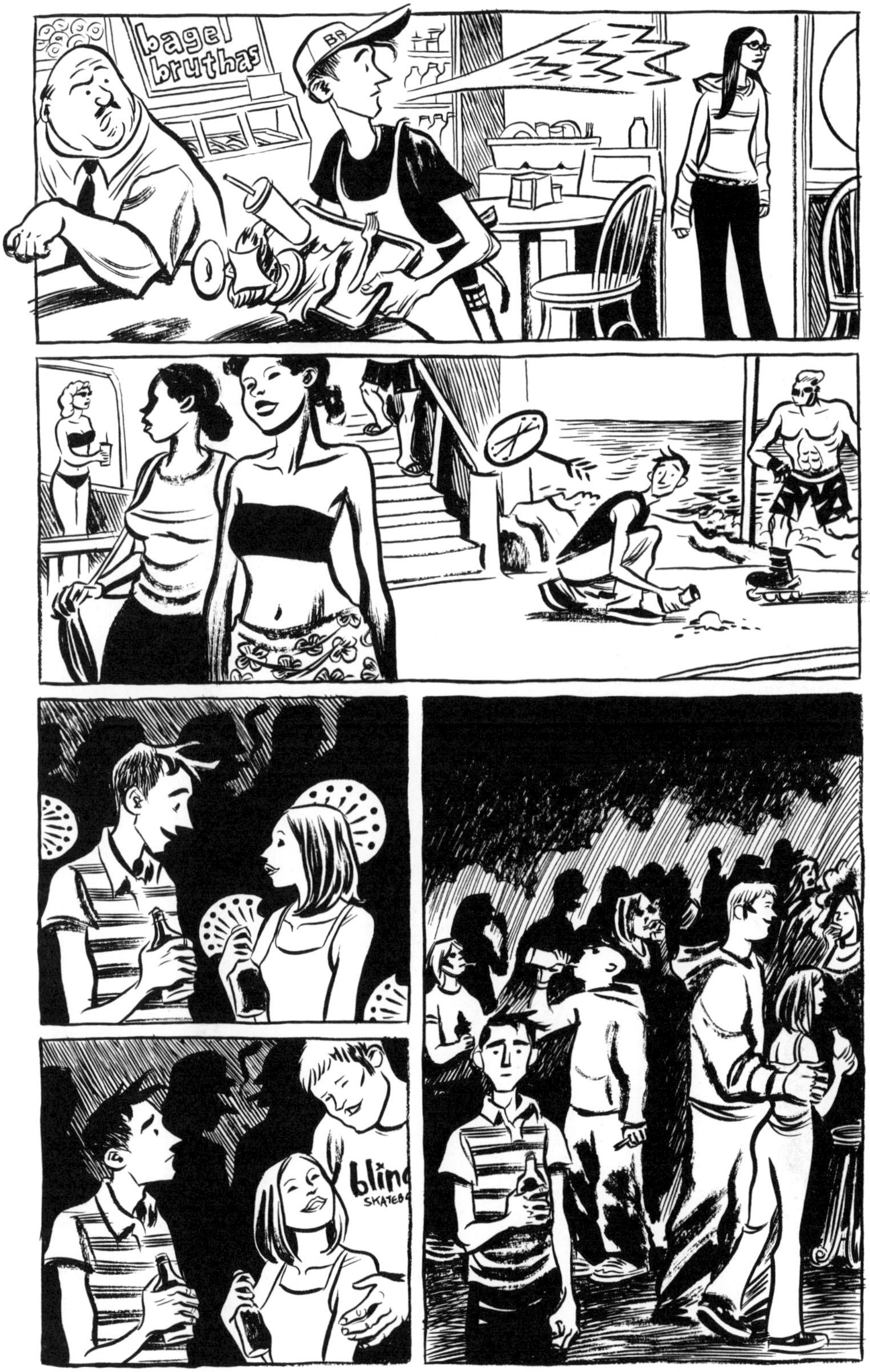
bagel bruthas

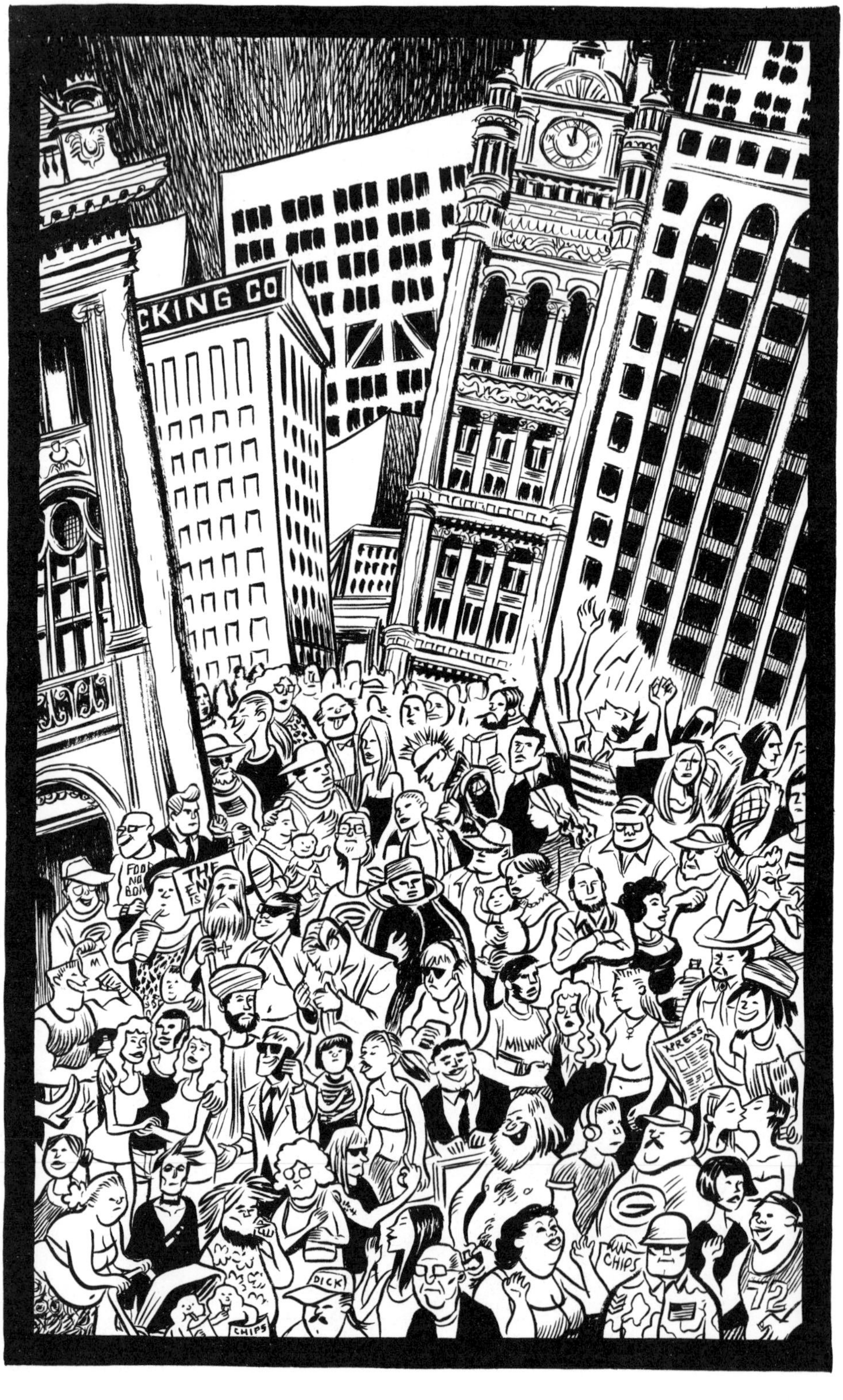
CKING CO
THE
MILWA
XPRESS
CHIPS
DICK
CHIPS
72

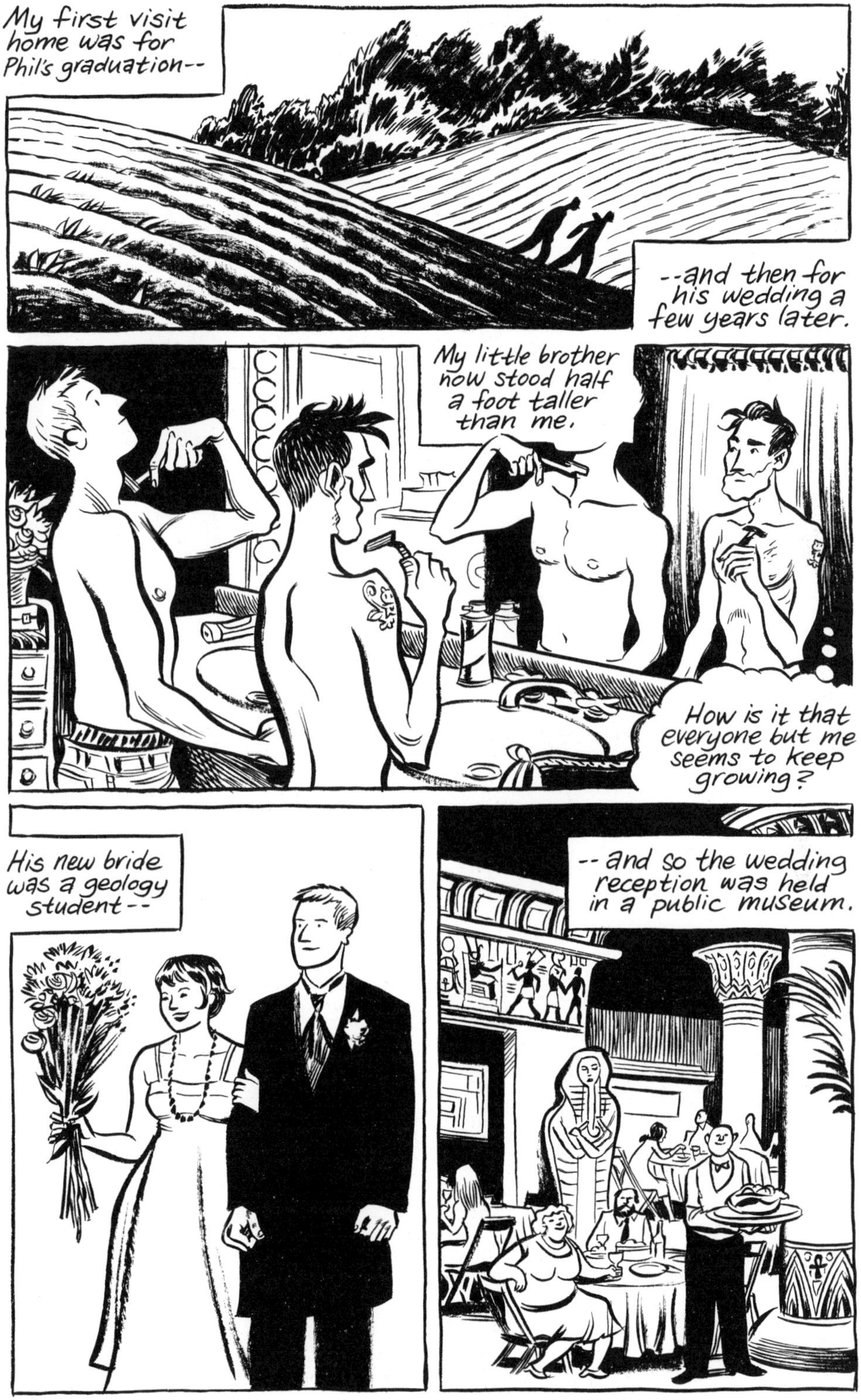
My first visit home was for Phil's graduation--
--and then for his wedding a few years later.
My little brother now stood half a foot taller than me.
How is it that everyone but me seems to keep growing?
His new bride was a geology student--
--and so the wedding reception was held in a public museum.

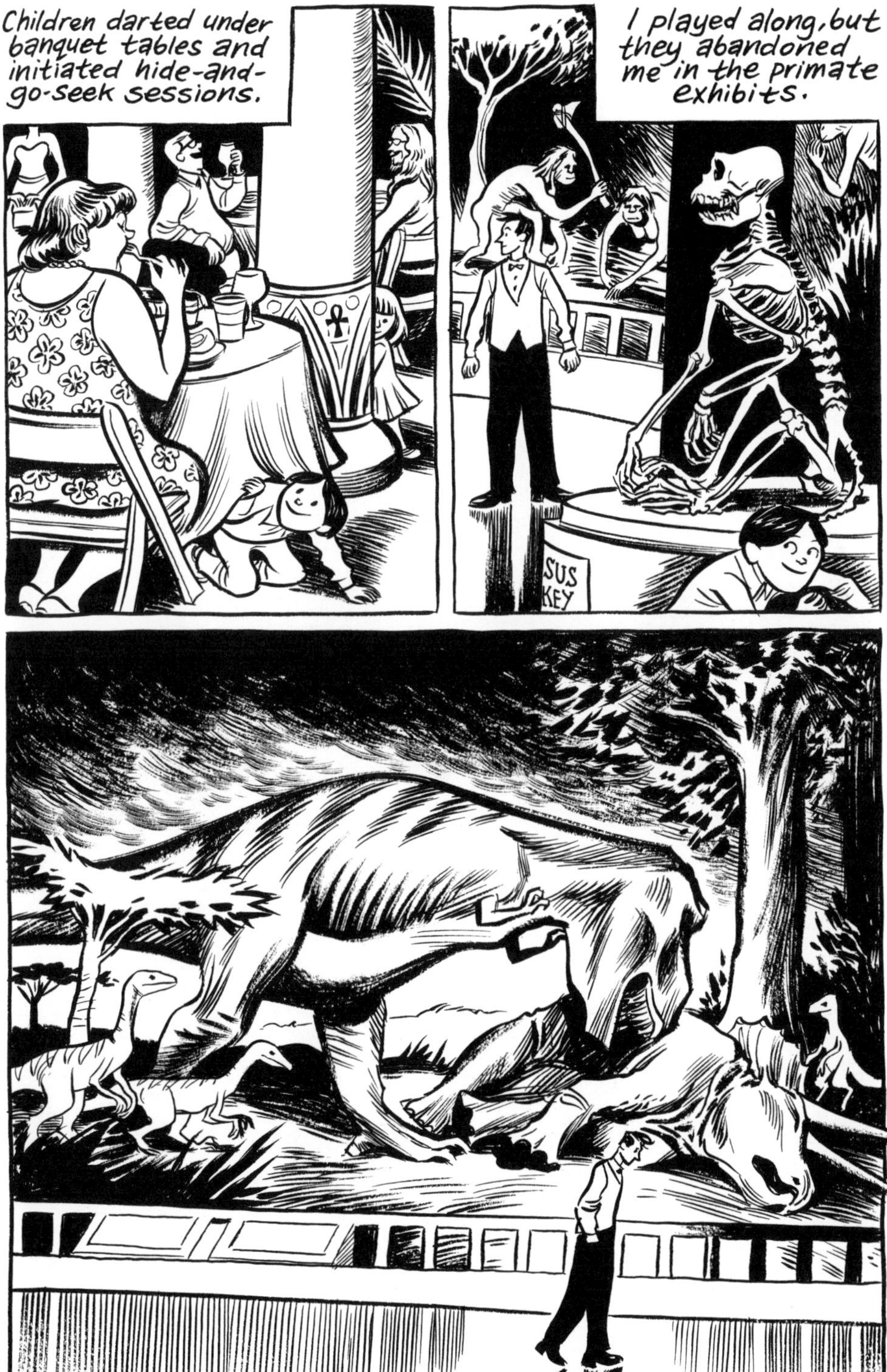
Children darted under banquet tables and initiated hide-and-go-seek sessions.
I played along, but they abandoned me in the primate exhibits.

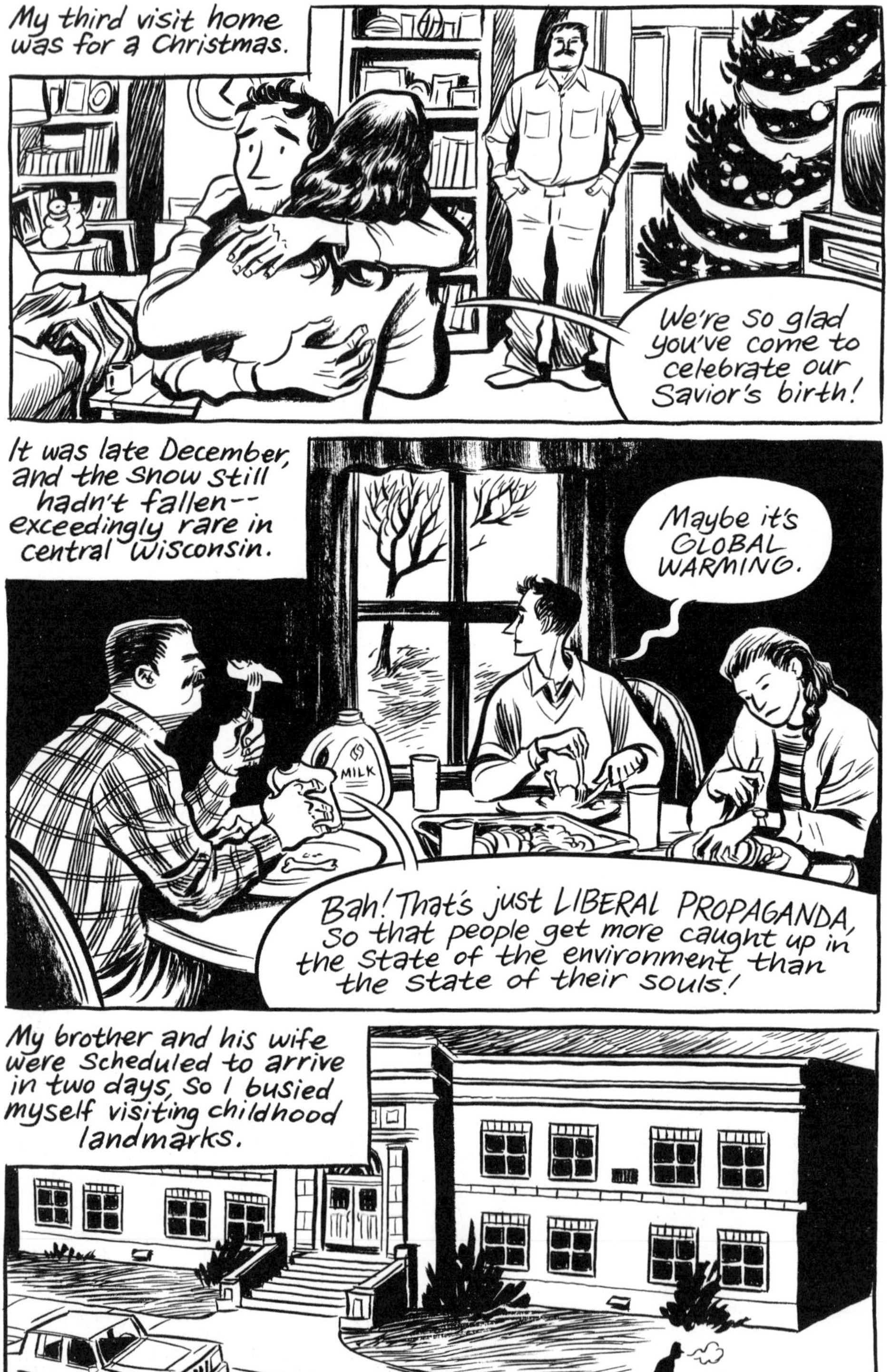
My third visit home was for a Christmas.
We're so glad you've come to celebrate our Savior's birth!
It was late December, and the snow still hadn't fallen-- exceedingly rare in central Wisconsin.
Maybe it's GLOBAL WARMING.
MILK
Bah! That's just LIBERAL PROPAGANDA, so that people get more caught up in the state of the environment than the state of their souls!
My brother and his wife were scheduled to arrive in two days, so I busied myself visiting childhood landmarks.

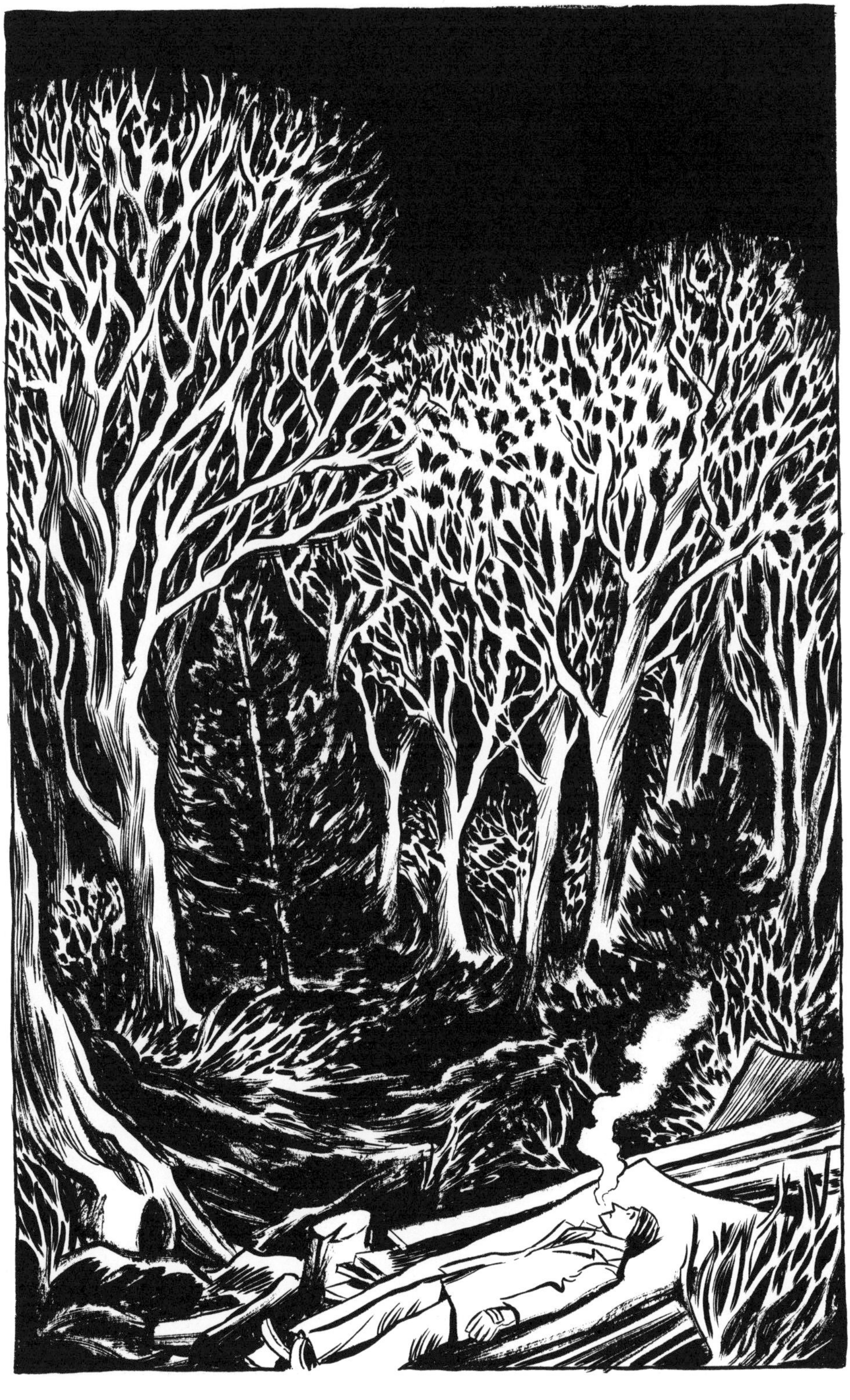

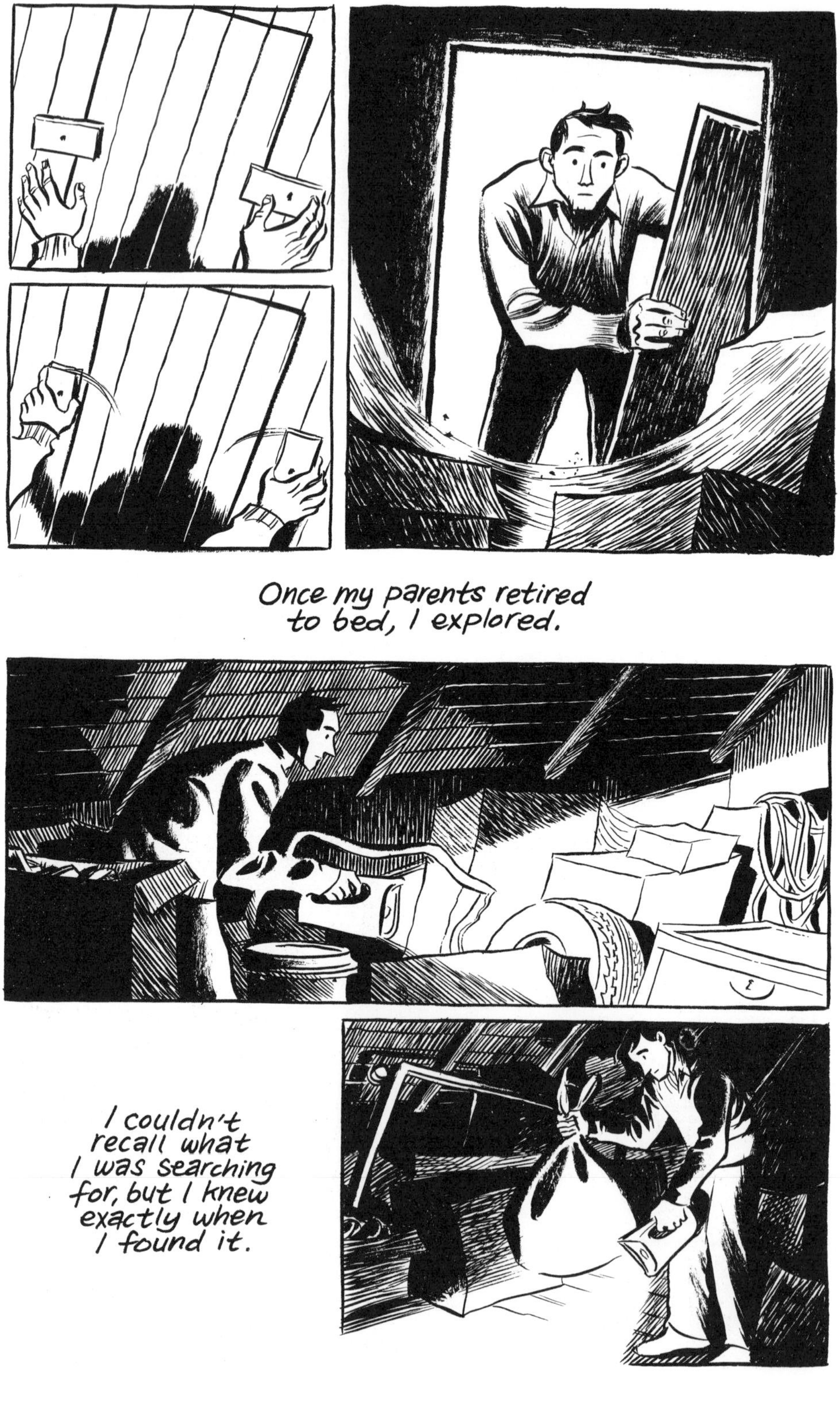
Once my parents retired to bed, I explored.
I couldn't recall what I was searching for, but I knew exactly when I found it.

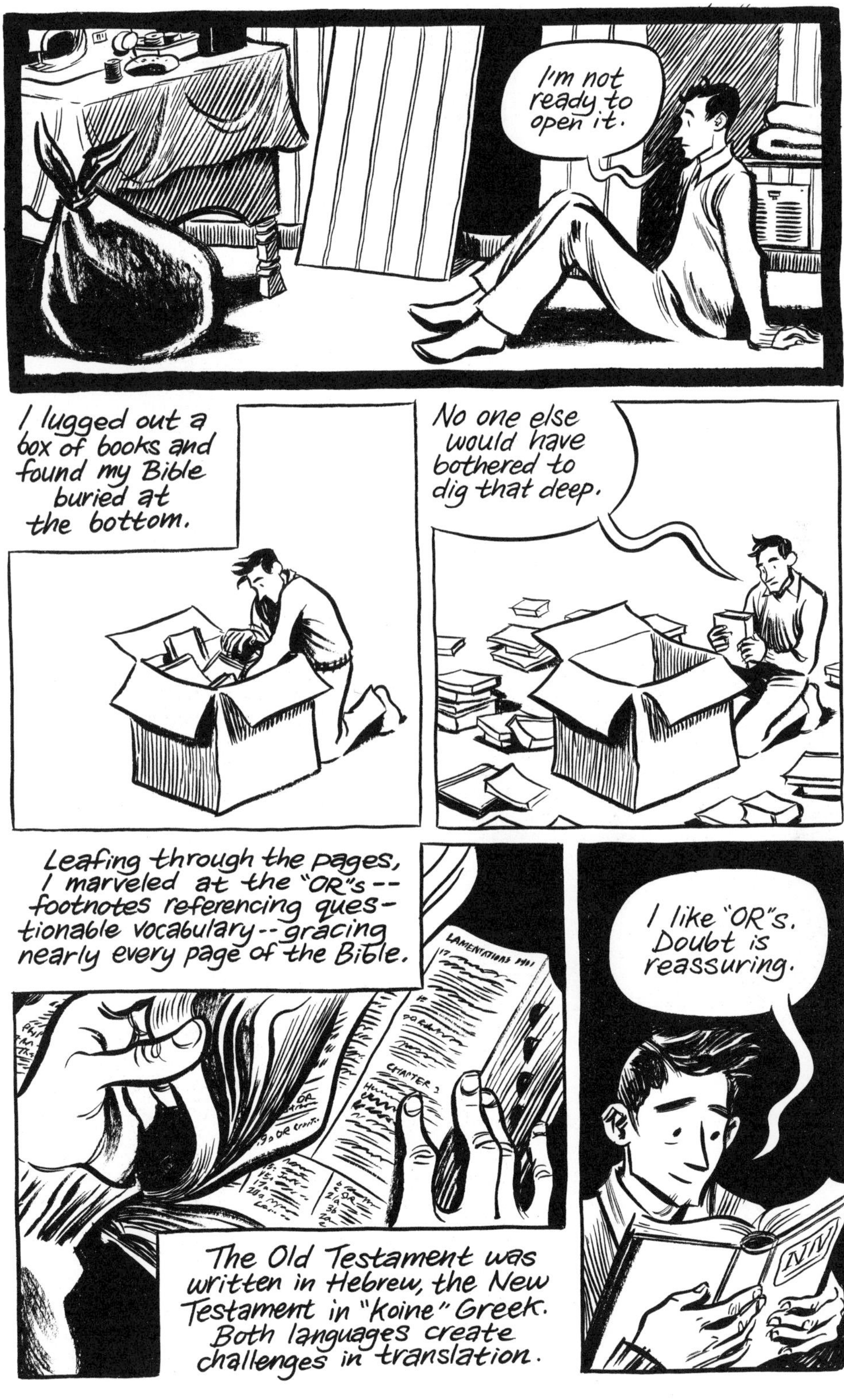
I'm not ready to open it.
I lugged out a box of books and found my Bible buried at the bottom.
No one else would have bothered to dig that deep.
Leafing through the pages, I marveled at the "OR"s -- footnotes referencing questionable vocabulary -- gracing nearly every page of the Bible.
LAMENTATIONS
CHAPTER 3
I like "OR"s. Doubt is reassuring.
The Old Testament was written in Hebrew, the New Testament in "koine" Greek. Both languages create challenges in translation.
NIV

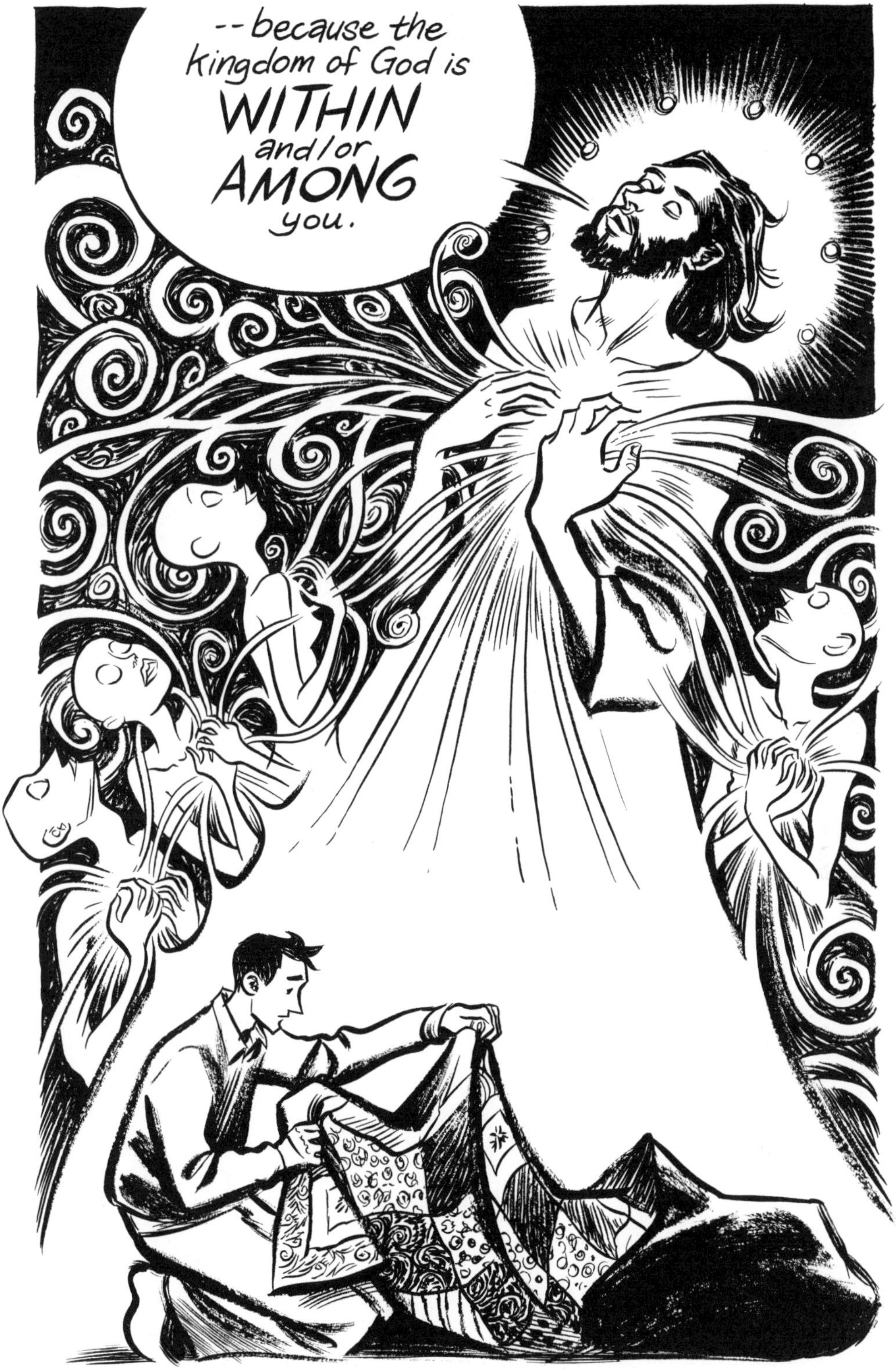
--because the kingdom of God is WITHIN and/or AMONG you.

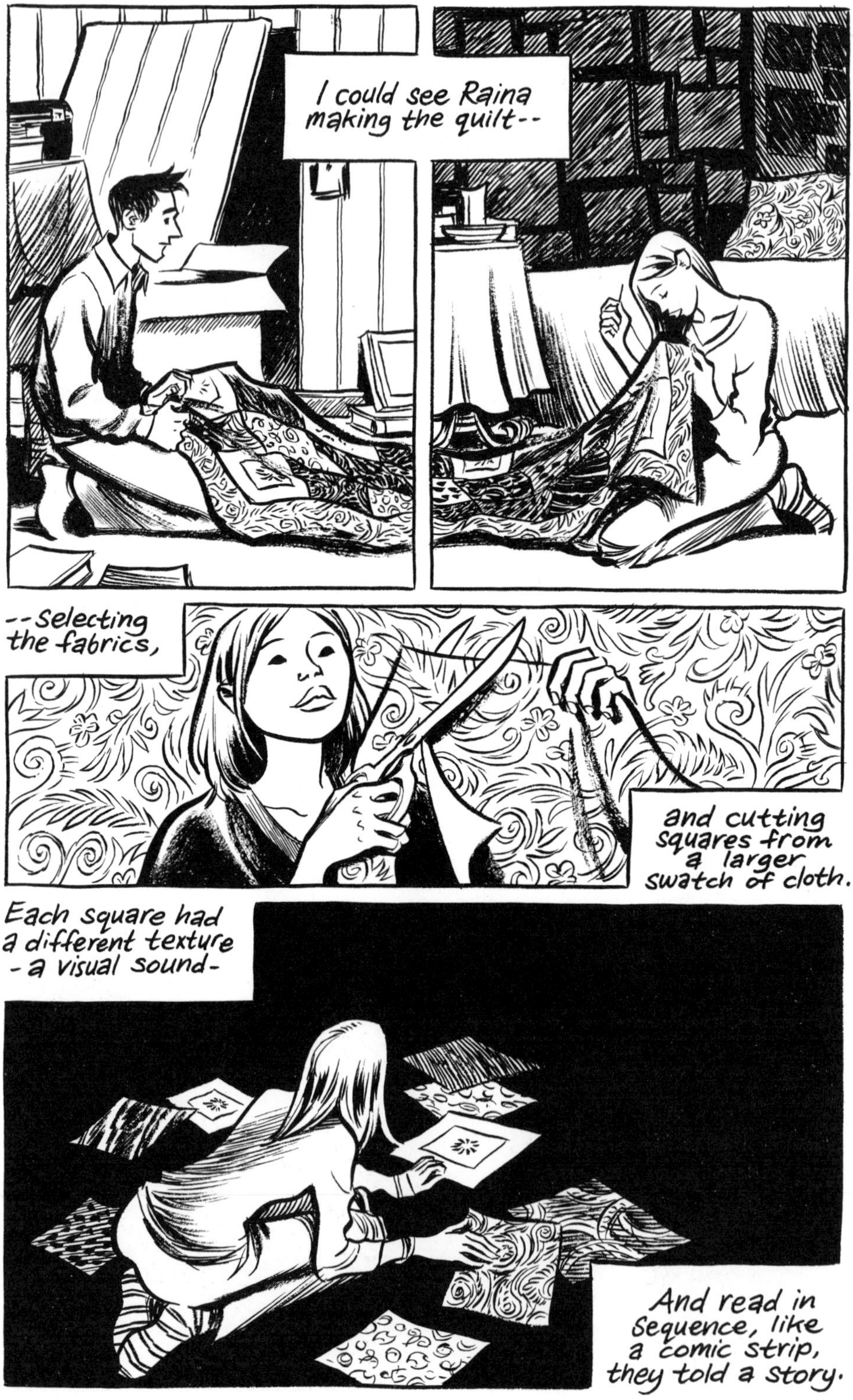
I could see Raina making the quilt--
--Selecting the fabrics,
and cutting squares from a larger swatch of cloth.
Each square had a different texture -a visual sound-
And read in sequence, like a comic strip, they told a story.

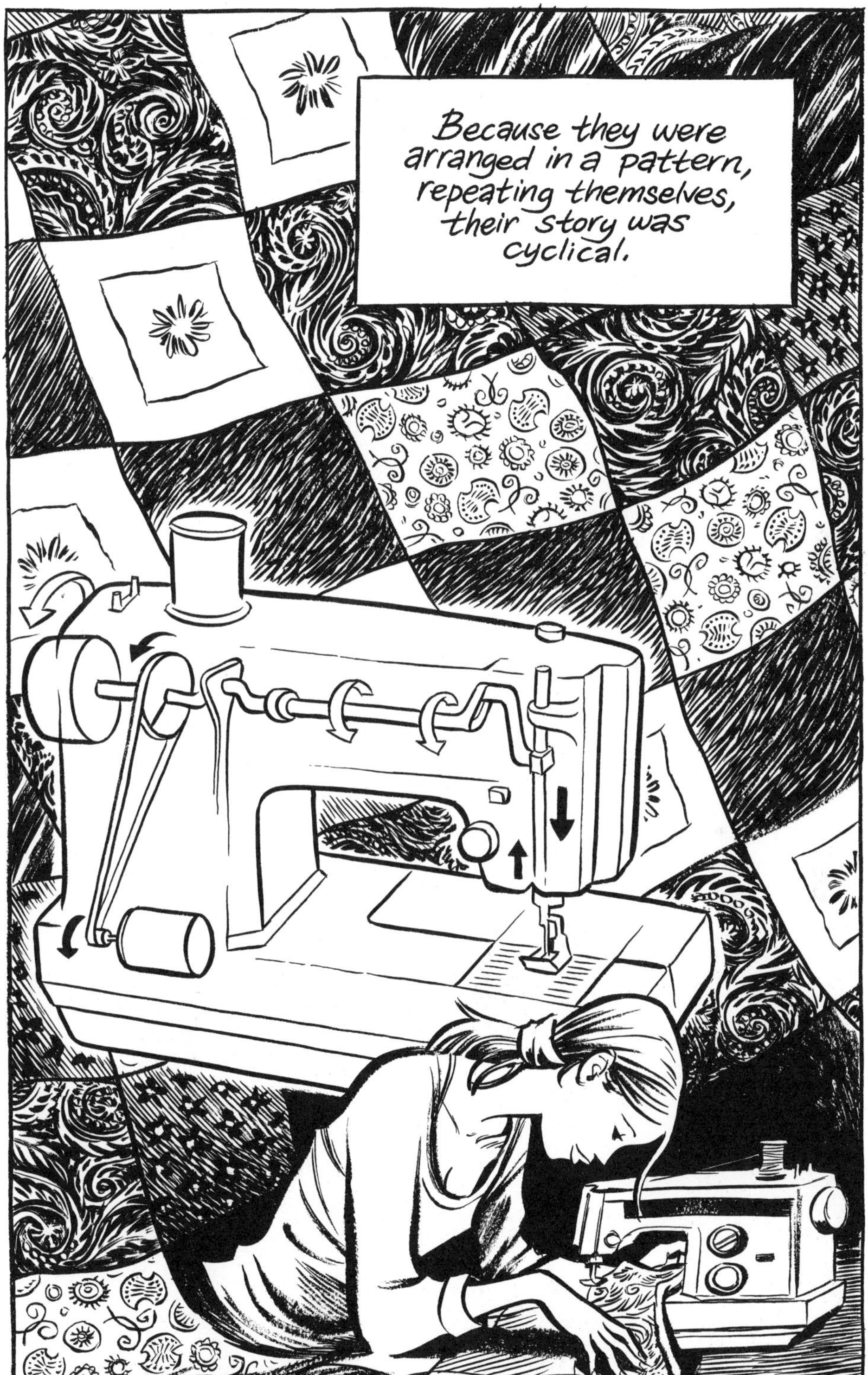
Because they were arranged in a pattern, repeating themselves, their story was cyclical.

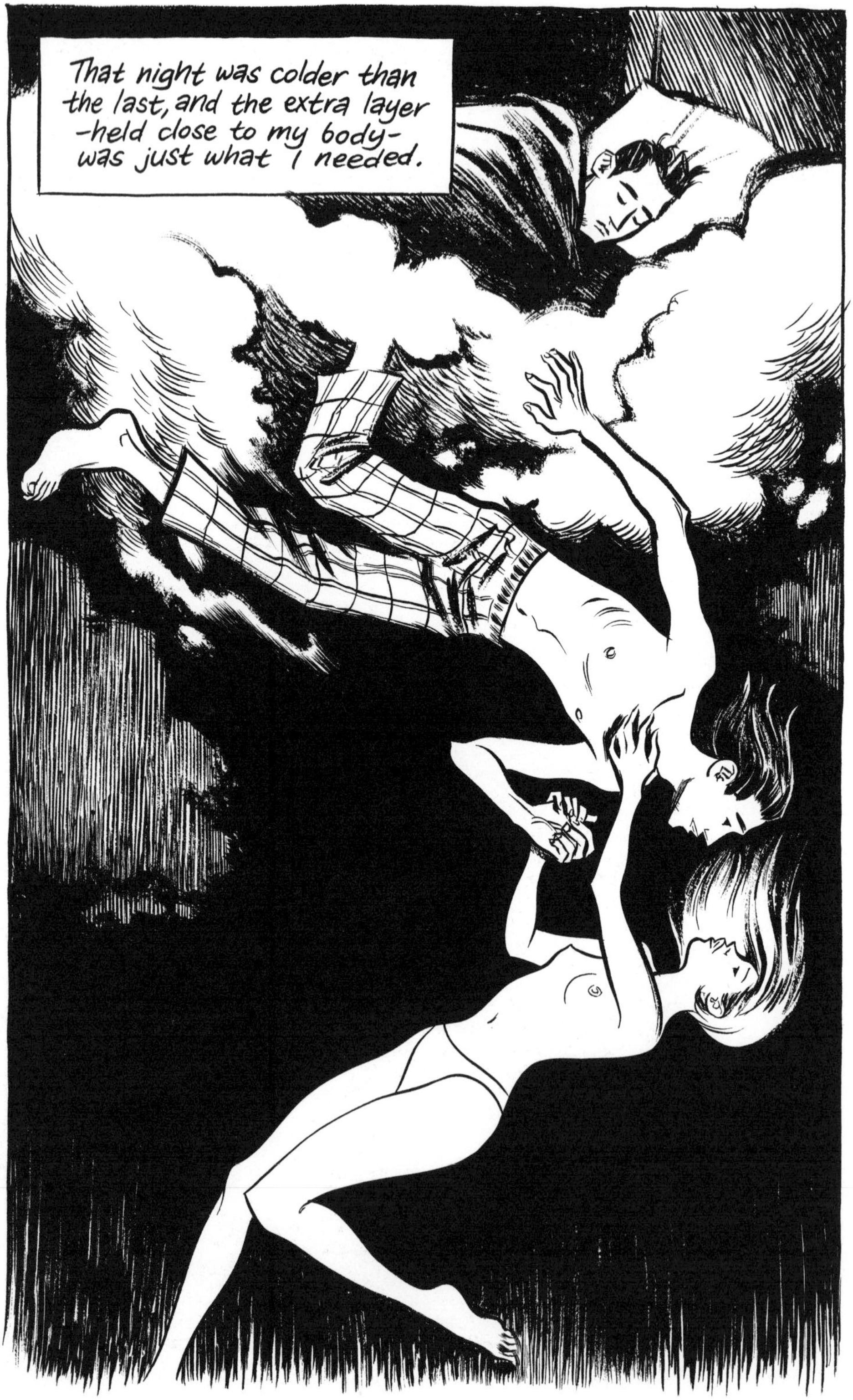
That night was colder than
the last, and the extra layer
-held close to my body-
was just what I needed.

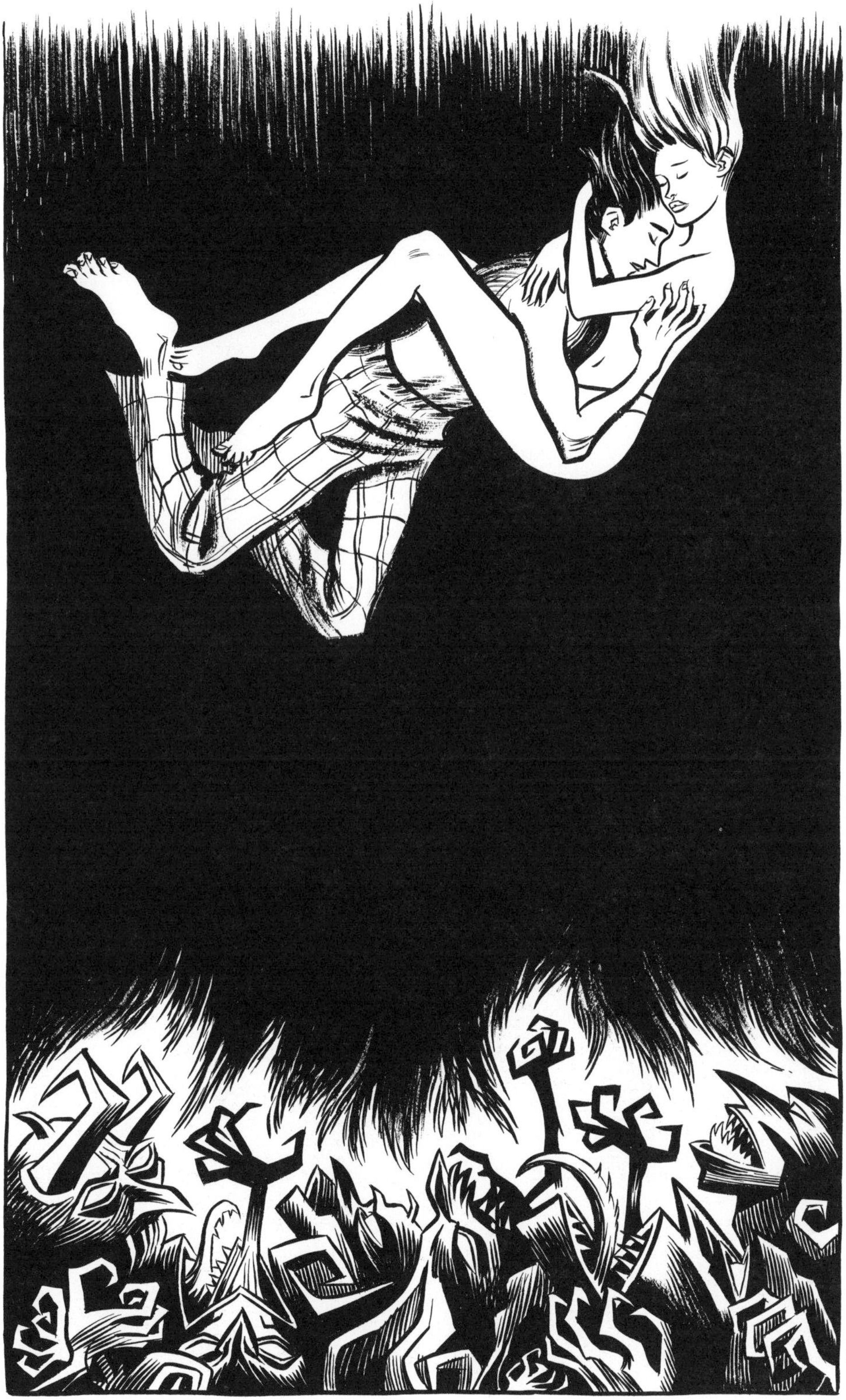

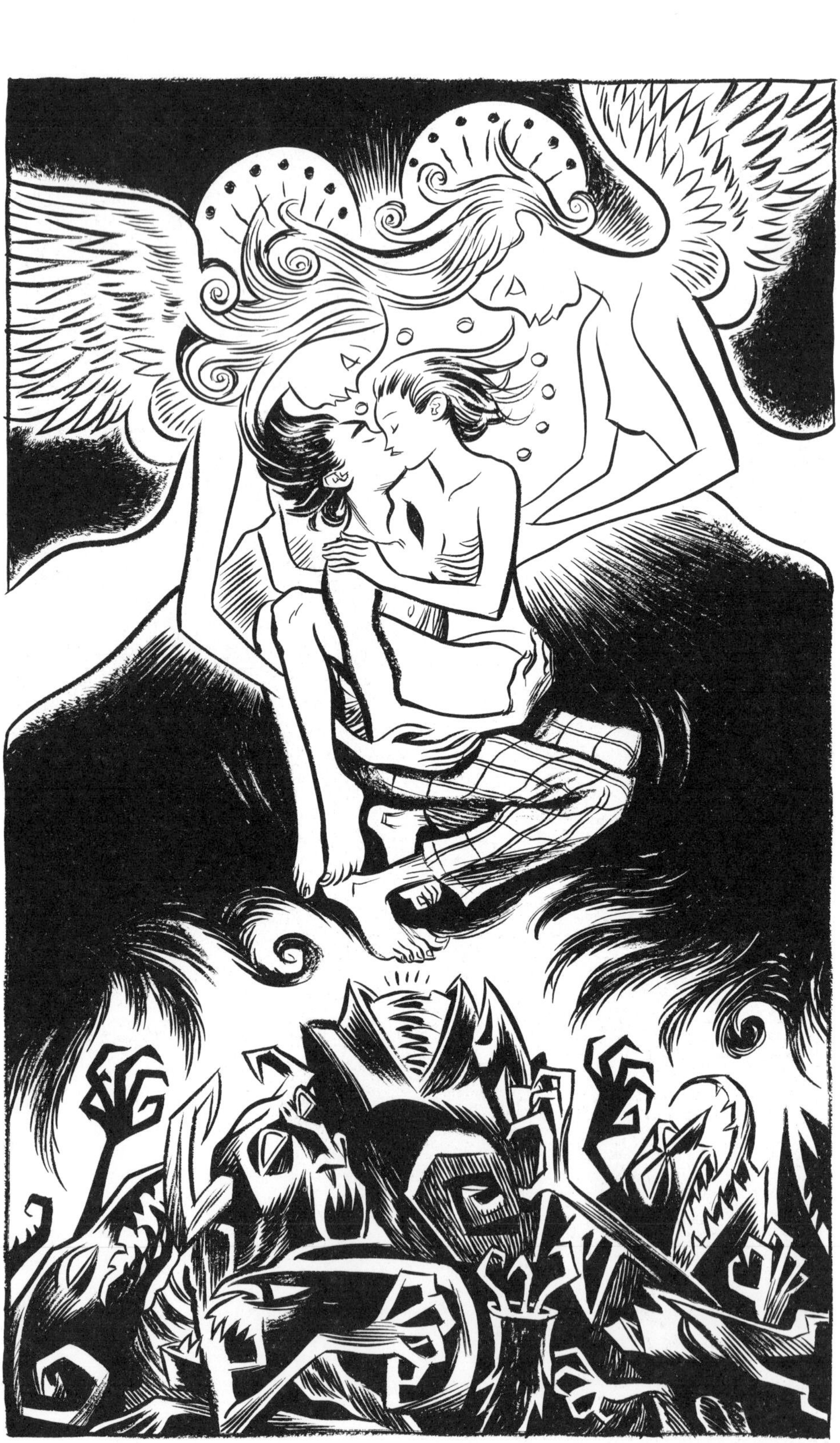

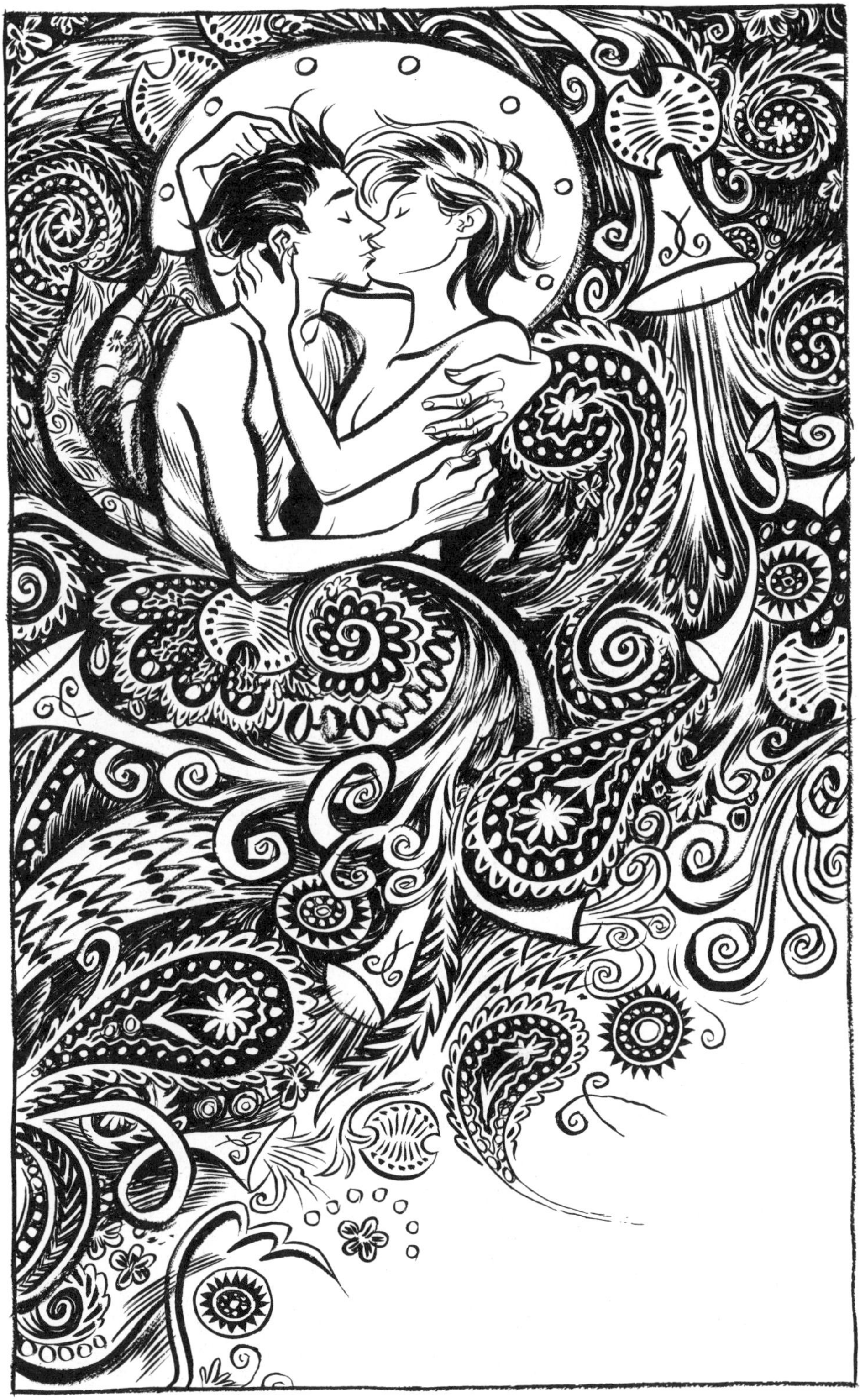

Sometimes, upon waking,

the residual dream can be more appealing than reality,

and one is reluctant to give it up.

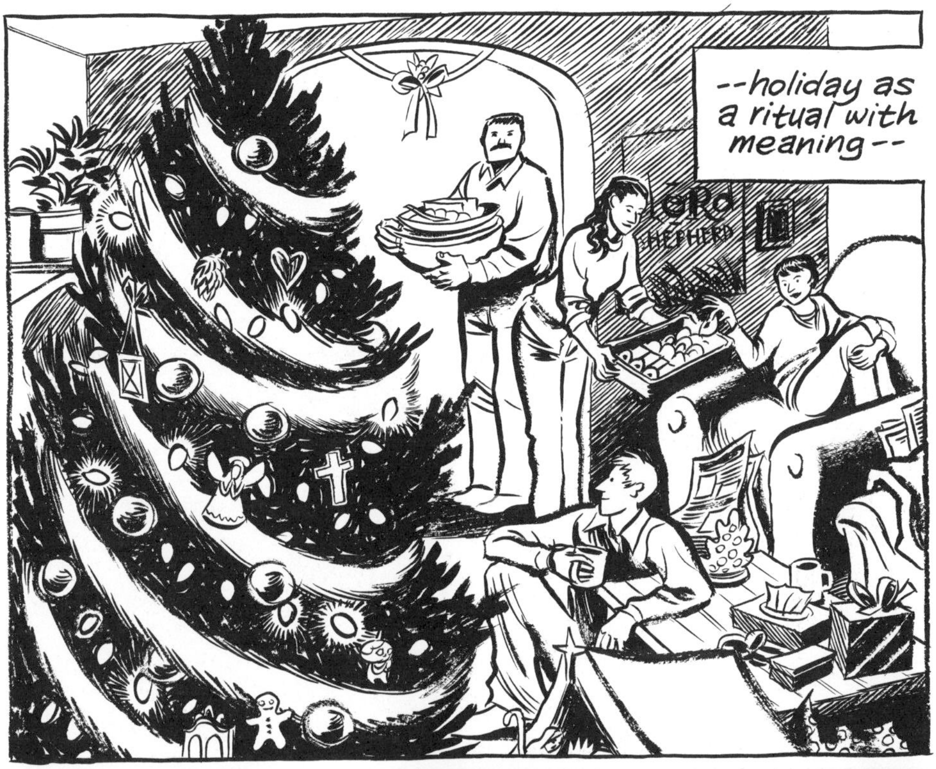
--holiday as a ritual with meaning--

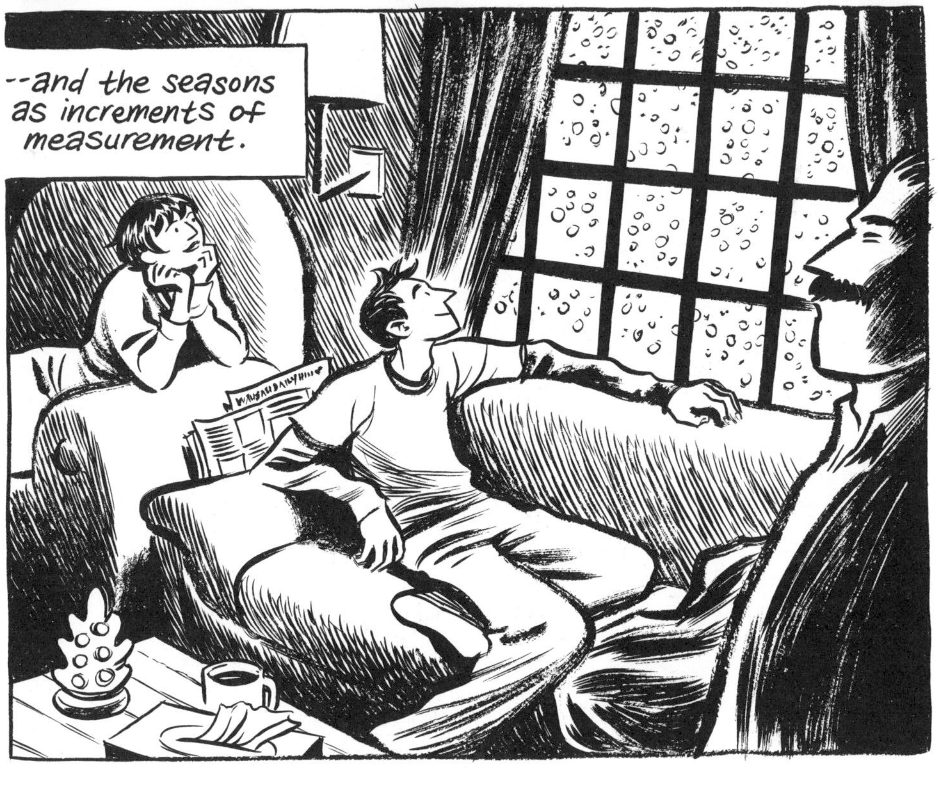
--and the seasons as increments of measurement.

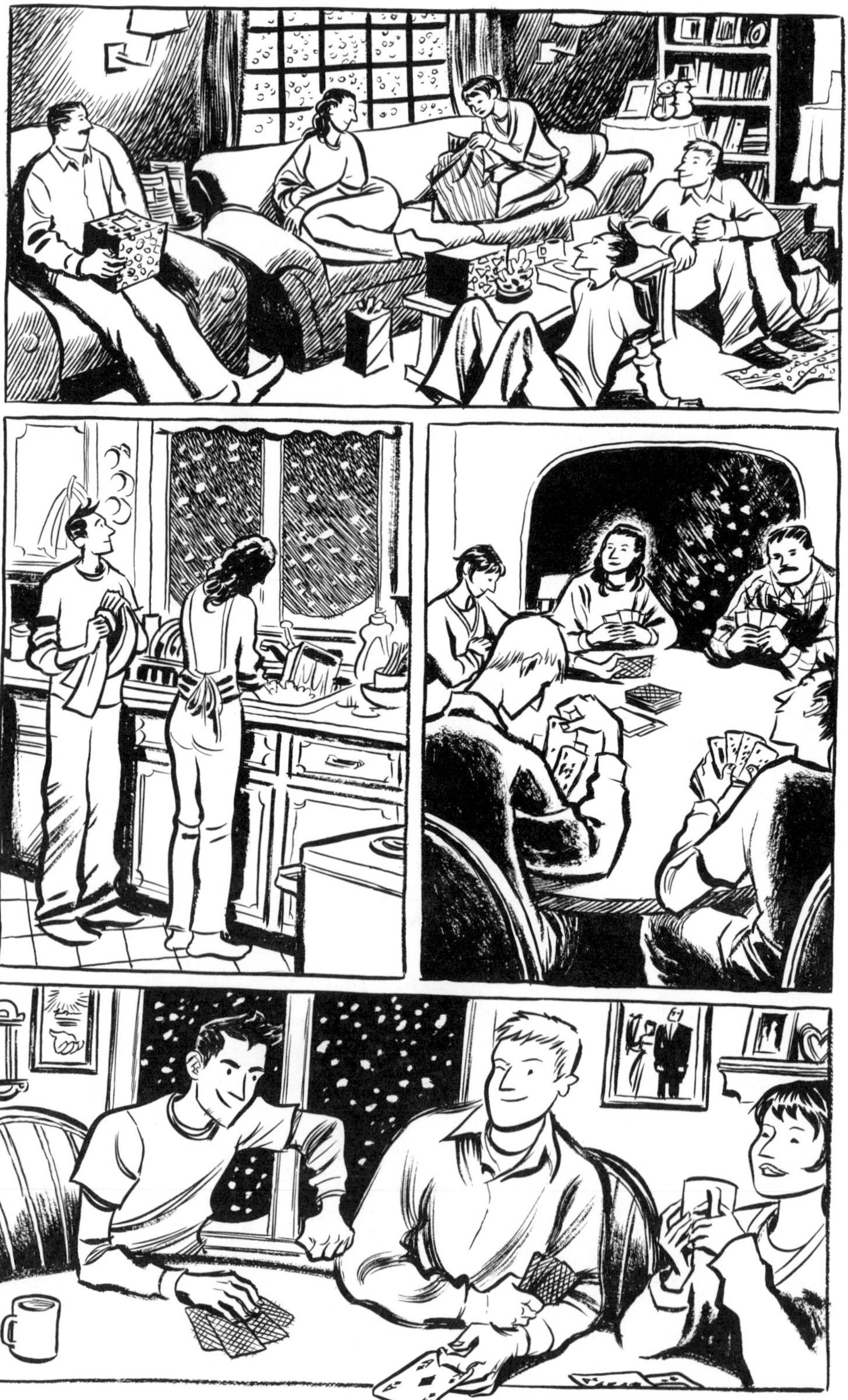

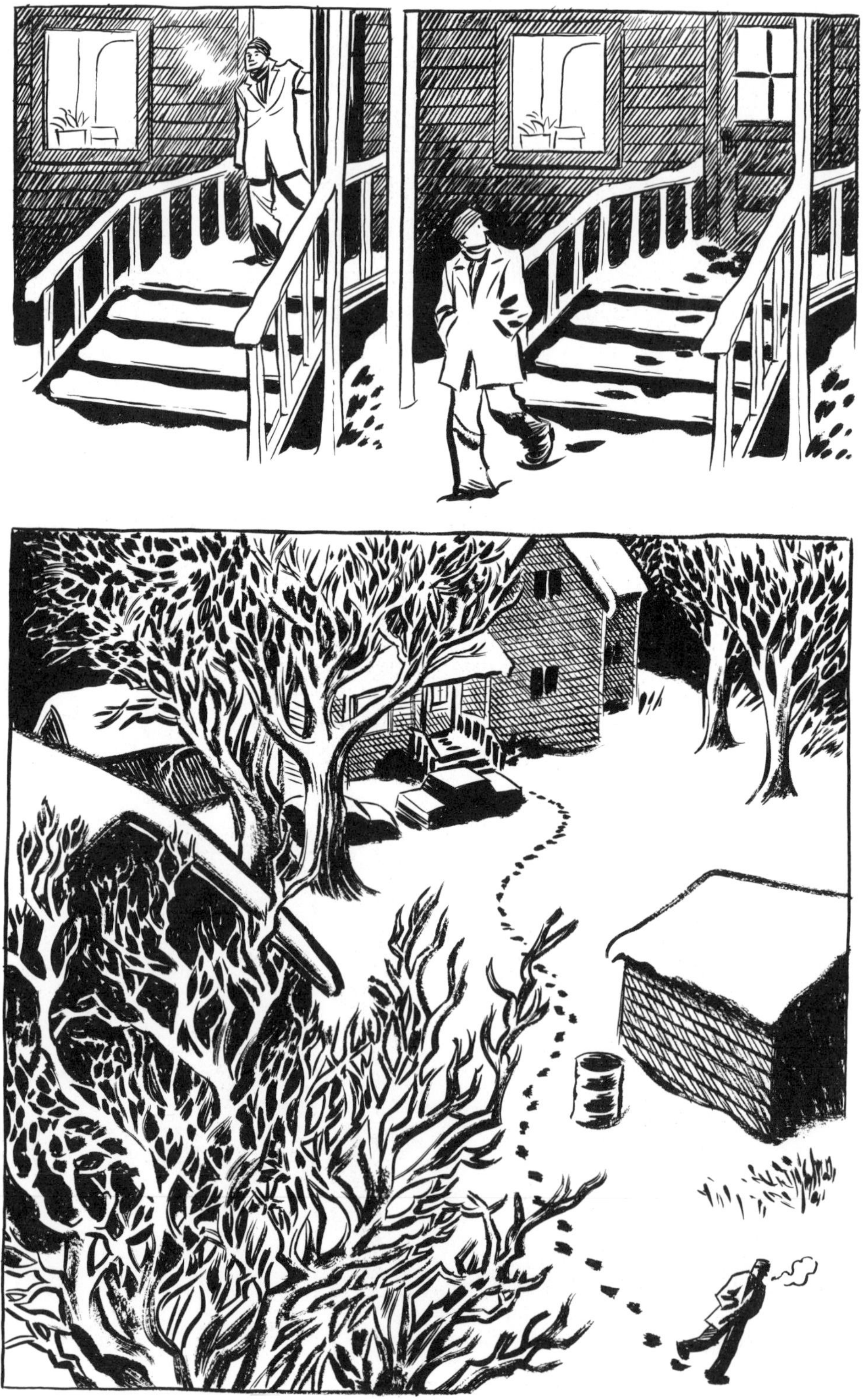

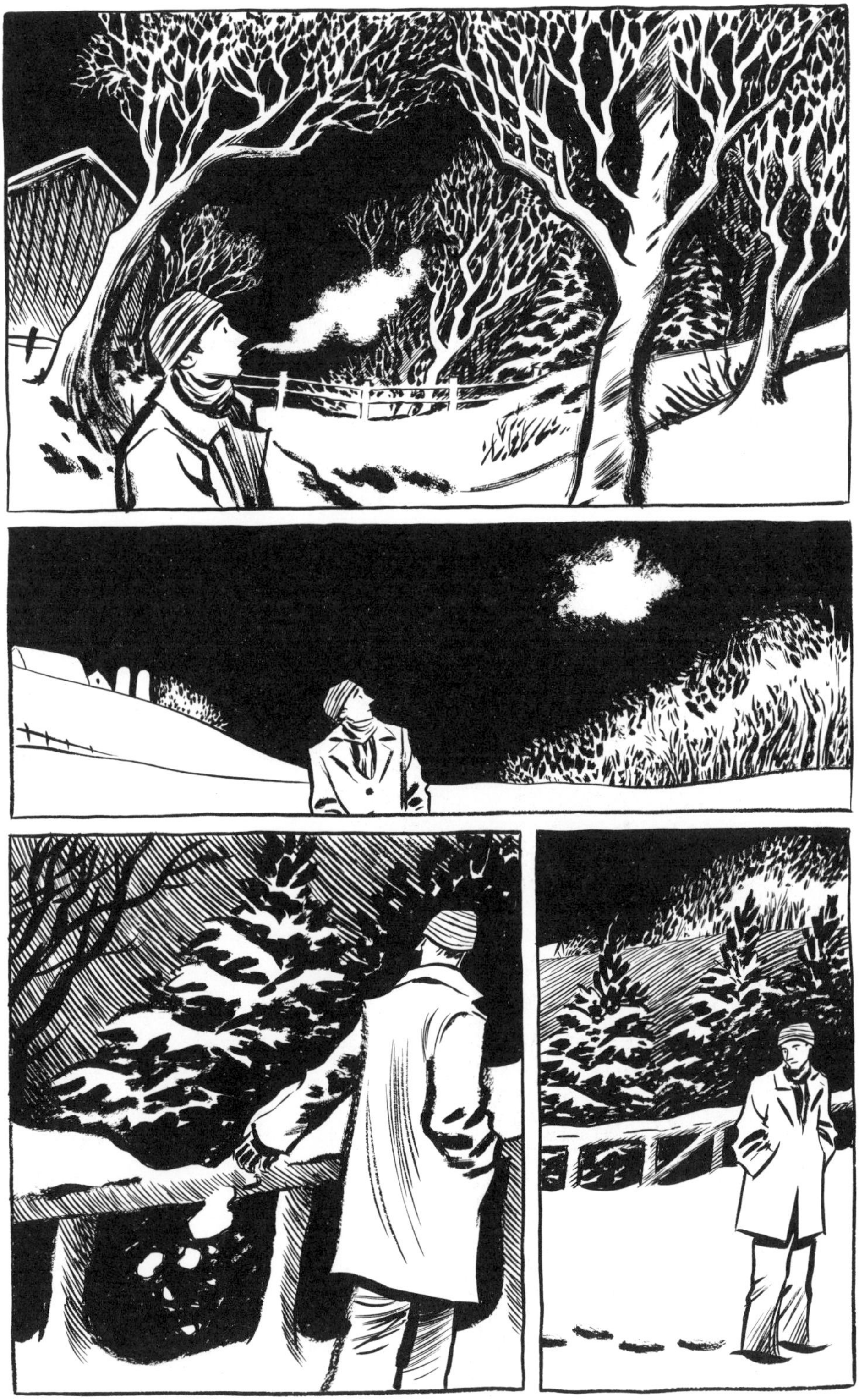

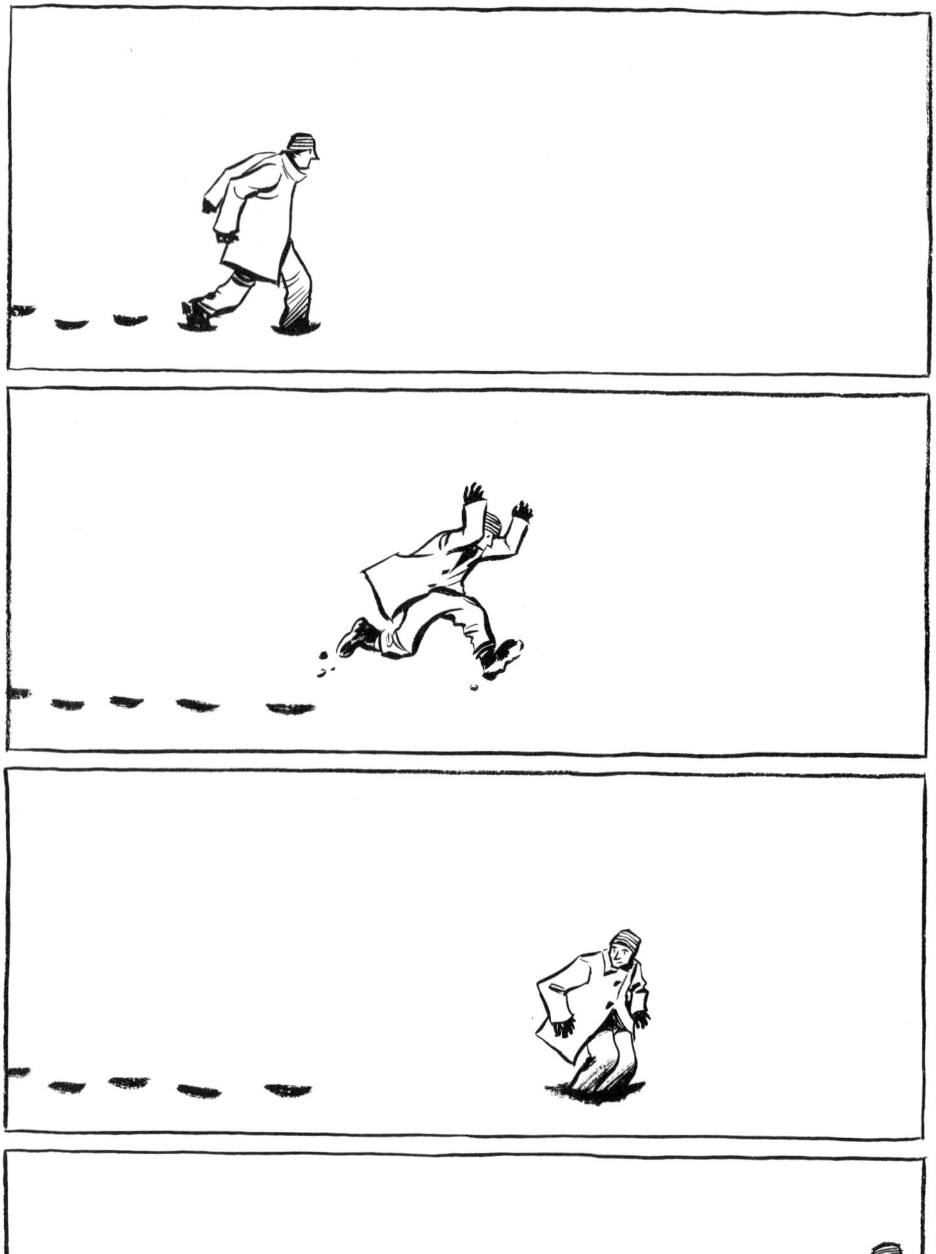

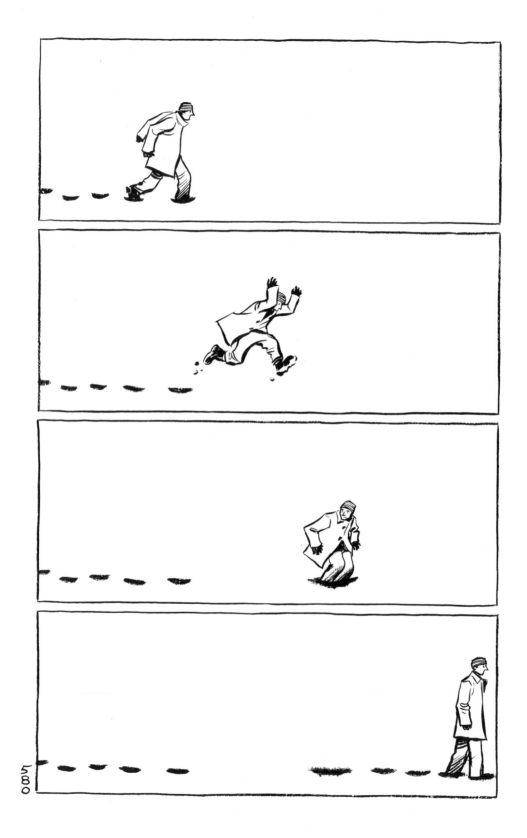

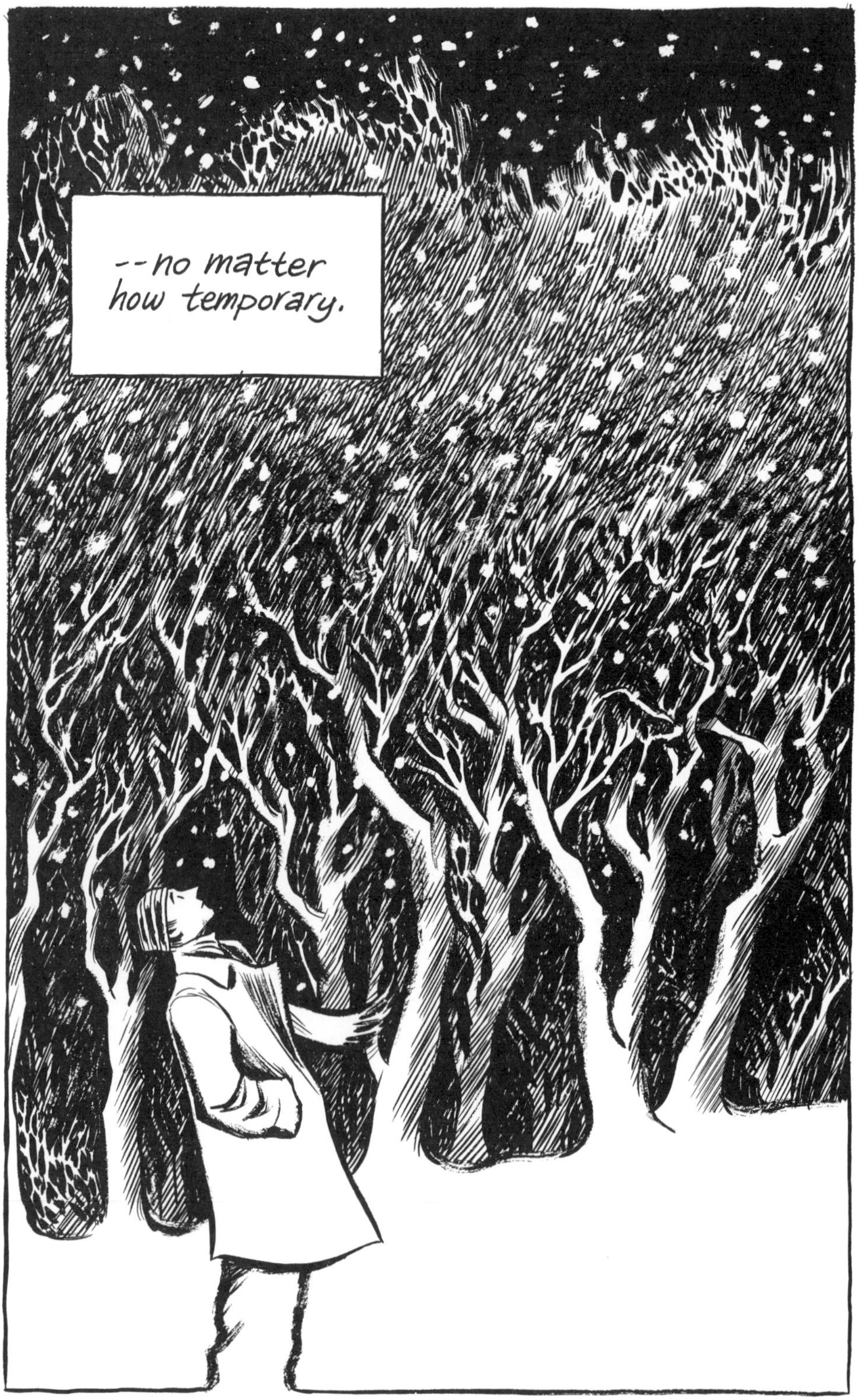
--no matter how temporary.

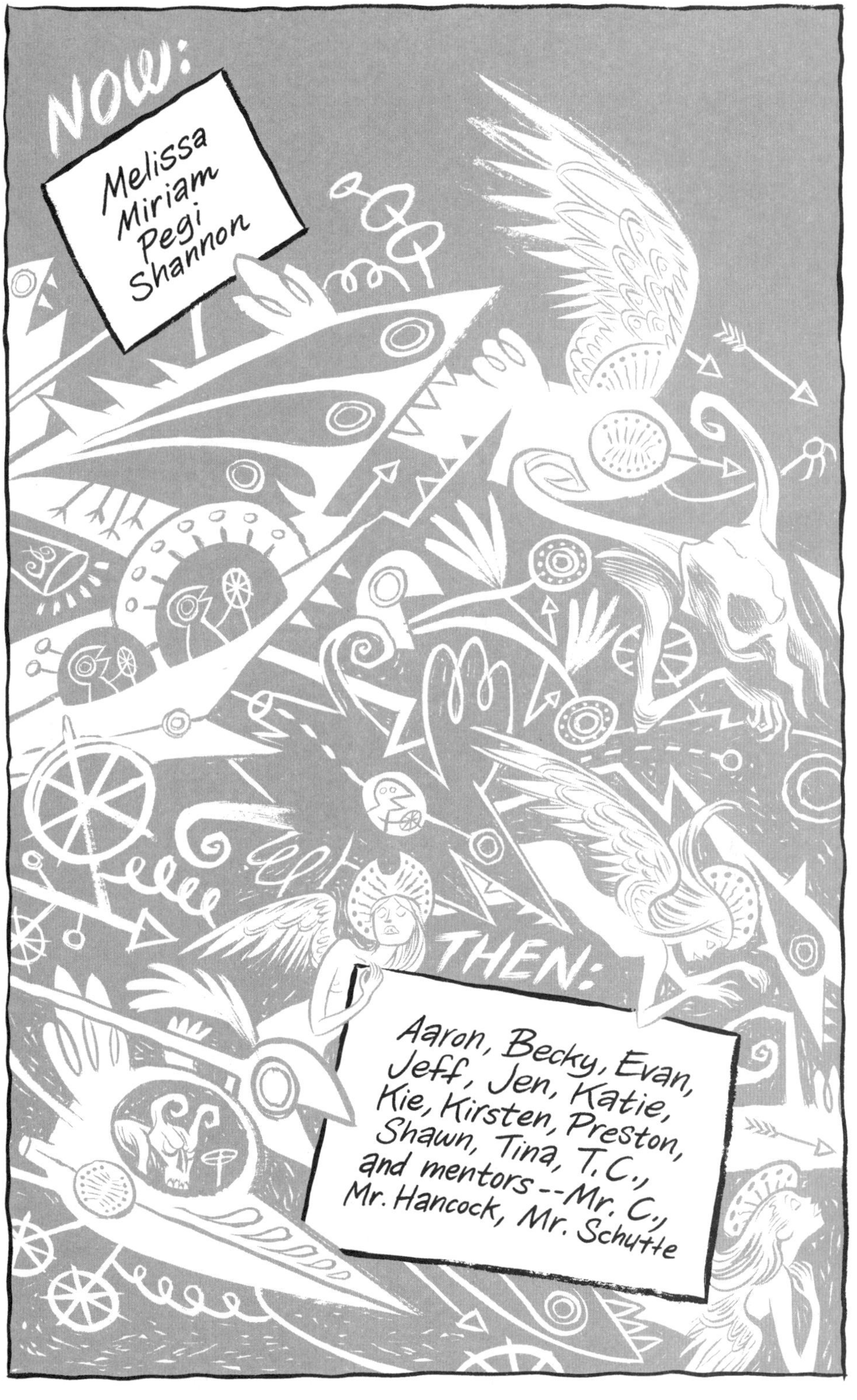
NOW:
Melissa
Miriam
Pegi
Shannon
THEN:
Aaron, Becky, Evan,
Jeff, Jen, Katie,
Kie, Kirsten, Preston,
Shawn, Tina, T.C.,
and mentors--Mr. C.,
Mr. Hancock, Mr. Schutte

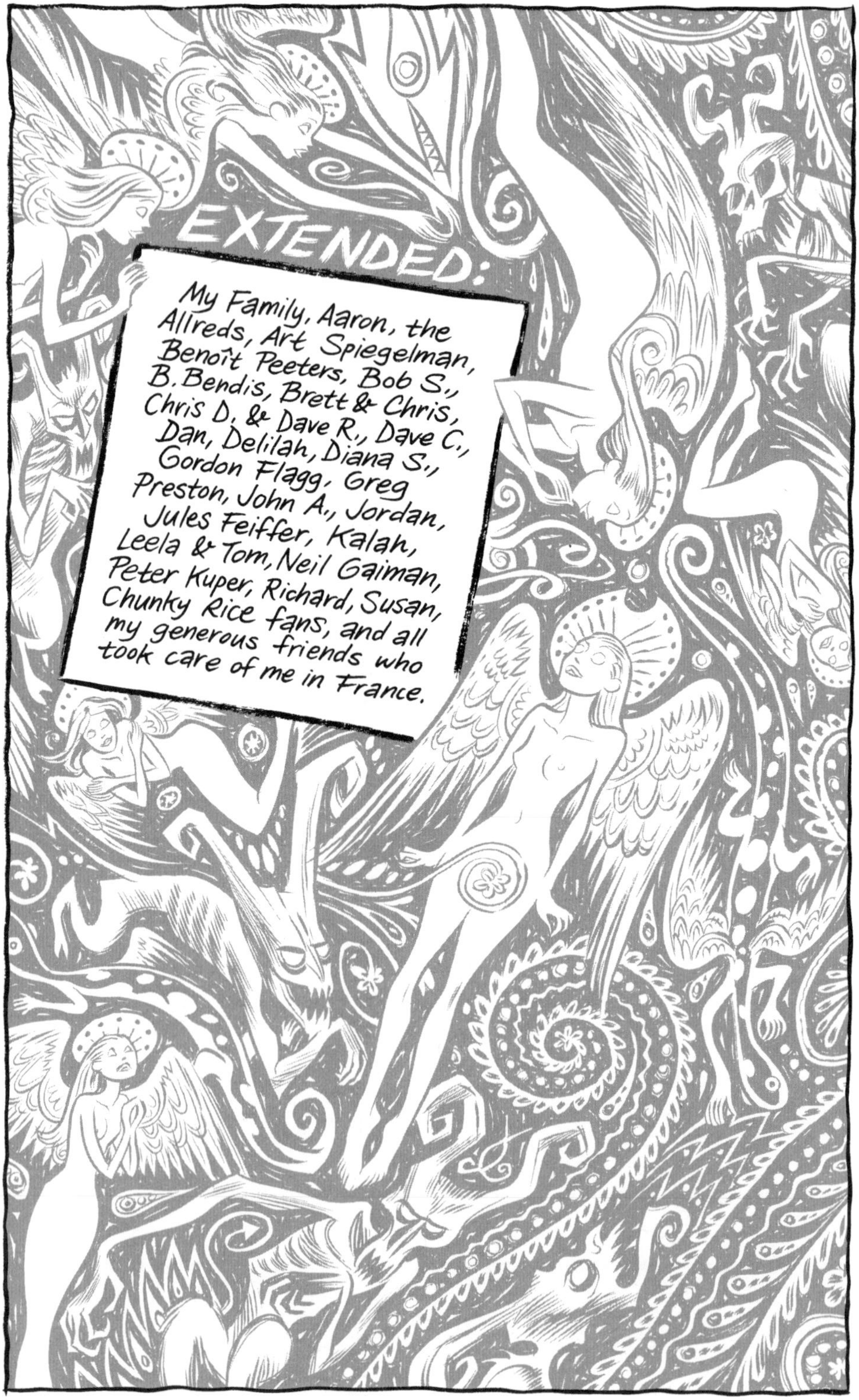
EXTENDED:
My Family, Aaron, the Allreds, Art Spiegelman, Benoît Peeters, Bob S., B. Bendis, Brett & Chris, Chris D. & Dave R., Dave C., Dan, Delilah, Diana S., Gordon Flagg, Greg Preston, John A., Jordan, Jules Feiffer, Kalah, Leela & Tom, Neil Gaiman, Peter Kuper, Richard, Susan, Chunky Rice fans, and all my generous friends who took care of me in France.

EXTRA SPECIAL
ACKNOWLEDGMENTS:

Susan & Colin

Sarah & Joy

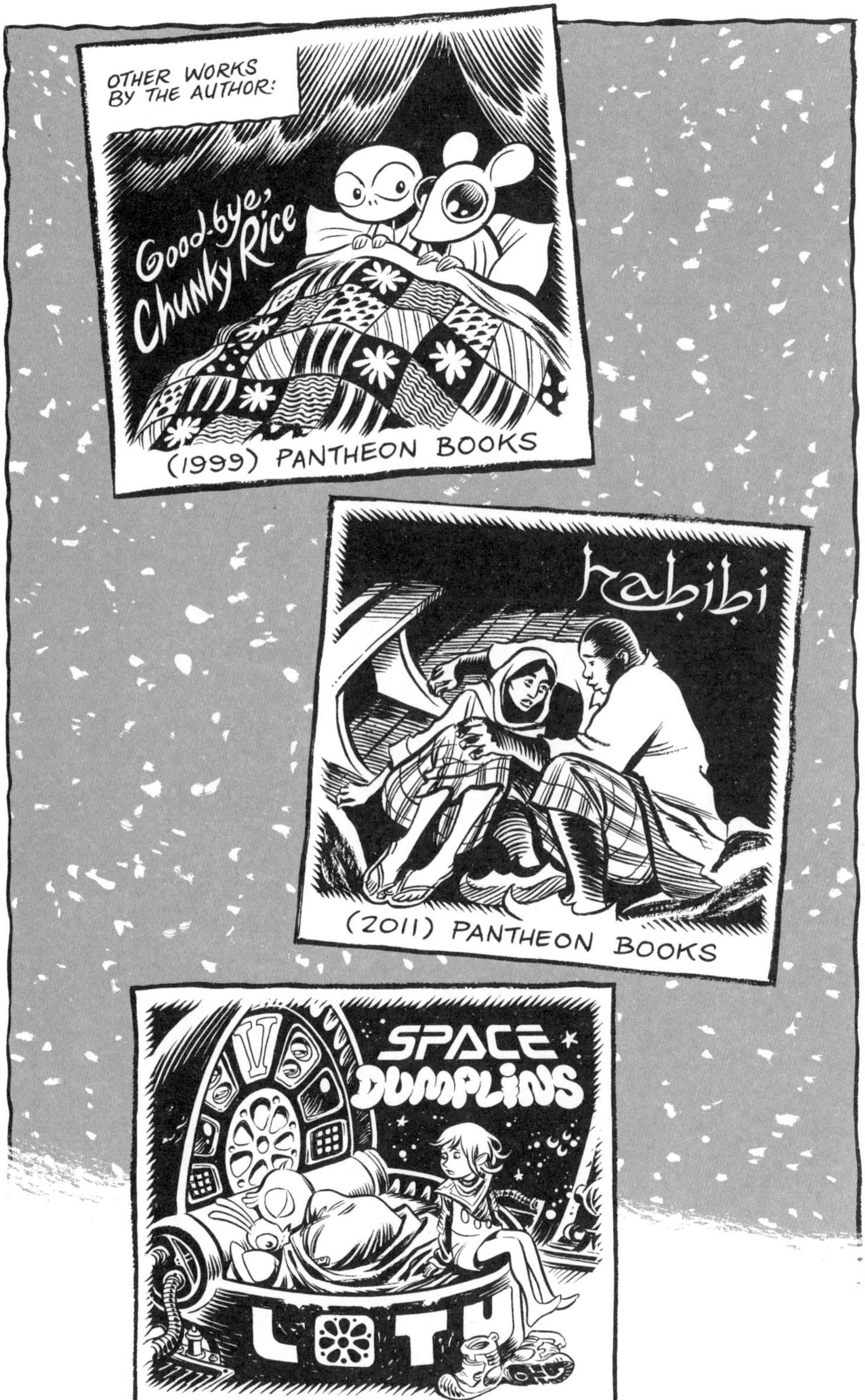
OTHER WORKS BY THE AUTHOR:
Good-bye, Chunky Rice
(1999) PANTHEON BOOKS
Habibi
(2011) PANTHEON BOOKS
SPACE DUMPLINS
(2015) SCHOLASTIC

CRAIG THOMPSON

was born in Traverse City, Michigan,
in 1975, and raised in rural Wisconsin.
His other books include GOOD-BYE,
CHUNKY RICE (1999), CARNET DE
VOYAGE (2004), HABIBI (2011),
and SPACE DUMPLINS (2015).
He lives in Los Angeles, California.

author photo by Greg Preston